Learning to Teach in the Primary School

How can yo... ...to do? What do you need...

To becom... ...rstanding of your pupils... ...nising your classroom, a...

This con... ...h the taught component... ...t provides a sound, acce... ...her needs to acquire in c...

Written ... ...covering an essential co...

- the
- lool
- lool
- app
- mar
- org
- incl
- pro
- resp
- asse

Each ch... ...s a range of learning act... ...are included for those w...

This tex... ...ool teachers, including t... ...CE courses, those on Gr...

James Arthur is Professor of Education at Canterbury Christ Church University, UK. Teresa Grainger is a Professor of Education at Canterbury Christ Church University, UK. David Wray is Professor of Literacy Education at the University of Warwick, UK.

Learning to Teach in the Primary School

Edited by
James Arthur, Teresa Grainger and David Wray

Routledge
Taylor & Francis Group
LONDON AND NEW YORK

First published 2006
by Routledge
2 Park Square, Milton Park, Abingdon, Oxon OX14 4RN

Simultaneously published in the USA and Canada
by Routledge
270 Madison Ave, New York, NY 10016

Reprinted 2007 (three)

Routledge is an imprint of the Taylor & Francis Group, an informa business

Typeset in Bembo by
HWA Text and Data Management, Tunbridge Wells
Printed and bound in Great Britain by
Bell & Bain Ltd, Glasgow

British Library Cataloguing in Publication Data
A catalogue record for this book is available from the British Library

Library of Congress Cataloging in Publication Data
A catalog record for this book has been requested

ISBN10: 0–415–35928–7

ISBN13: 978–0–415–35928–3

Contents

Illustrations

FIGURES

TABLES

TASKS

Contributors

James Arthur is Professor of Education at Canterbury Christ Church University. He has written on the relationship between theory and practice in education, particularly the links between communitarianism, social virtues, citizenship and education. His publications include: *Education with Character: The Moral Economy of Schooling* (Routledge), *Schools and Community: The Communitarian Agenda in Education* (Falmer Press), *Social Literacy, Citizenship, and the National Curriculum* (Routledge), *Teaching Citizenship Education through History* (Routledge), *The Thomist Tradition in Education* and *The Ebbing Tide* (both published by Gracewing), *Teaching Citizenship in the Secondary School* (David Fulton), *Subject Mentoring in the Secondary School* (Routledge) and many articles and chapters in books.

Richard Bailey is Professor of Pedagogy at Roehampton University and was previously Director of the Centre for Physical Education Research, at Canterbury Christ Church University. He is an authority on physical education, and has written widely in the areas of the philosophy of education and child development. He is the author of numerous books and articles, including *Education in the Open Society* (Ashgate, 2000), *Teaching Physical Education 11–18* (Continuum, 2002) and *Teaching Values and Citizenship Across the Curriculum* (Kogan Page, 2001).

Jonathan Barnes is Senior Lecturer in Primary Education at Canterbury Christ Church University and teaches cross-curricular music and geography courses. He has wide experience in further, secondary and primary education both in England and in the developing world. His international work has resulted in a strong inter-cultural and global character to his teaching materials. He has written a wide range of books and articles for teachers on music, citizenship, Kenya, castles, technology, history, geography, cultural connections and creativity. He is particularly interested in promoting cross-curricular and creative thinking in the primary school.

Eve Bearne divides her time at the University of Cambridge Faculty of Education between research and teaching. Her general research interests are concerned with diversity and inclusion, specifically gender, language and literacy. She edited *Differentiation and Diversity* (Routledge) and has written and edited a range of books about language, literacy and inclusion.

Sue Beverton spent many years teaching in mainstream and special schools. While still a school teacher, she led a DfES (then DES) funded project into Family Reading Groups on behalf of the

United Kingdom Literacy Association. This prompted her to develop an interest in school-based research and resulted in moving into higher education. She is a Lecturer and researcher at the School of Education in Durham University, where she is currently Divisional Director of Undergraduate Studies. She also leads the subject team in all Primary English modules contributing to Initial Teacher Training courses. Her research interests include pupil transfer and transition between different key stages and years, and the evolving nature of English as a school subject throughout the compulsory school age range.

Simon Catling is Assistant Dean and Professor of Primary Education at Westminster Institute of Education, Oxford Brookes University. After teaching in primary schools in inner London for 12 years, he has worked since the mid-1980s in Teacher Education and Educational Studies. His teaching and research interests are in curriculum, teaching and learning, with a specific interest in geographical education in primary schools. He has published widely in this area for children, teachers and trainee teachers. He is past President of the Geographical Association and has been a member of the Field Studies Council Executive.

Roland Chaplain is a Chartered Psychologist, working as a Senior Lecturer in Psychology and Education at the University of Cambridge and as a consultant on behaviour management to various schools and LEAs. His current teaching includes advanced courses in applied social psychology, motivation, behaviour management and behaviour difficulties. He has previous experience as a teacher, head teacher and head of psychological services. He has written a number of books on pupil behaviour, effective teaching and school development and is a specialist adviser on teacher stress and children's behaviour for the British Psychological Society.

Hilary Claire has been a primary classroom teacher and deputy head in inner London schools, an educational researcher and an Advisory Teacher for Equal Opportunities. For the past eighteen years she has worked in higher education, mainly on Primary ITE courses, teaching educational studies, history and, more recently, citizenship education. She is the author of many publications in all these fields, with a particular focus on race and gender equality. She is a founder member and on the Steering Group of PENAC – the Primary Educators Network for the Advancement of Citizenship – and a member of the Primary Committee of the Historical Association.

Roy Corden is Professor of language and literacy in Education at Nottingham Trent University. As a teacher, he worked in primary, middle and secondary schools. He was a co-ordinator for the National Oracy project and his book *Literacy and Learning Through Talk* is an NLS/QCA recommended text. Current research interests include the development of dialogic discourse in primary classrooms.

Tricia David has worked in higher education (as a Lecturer, researcher and writer) for the last twenty years. During that time she has been privileged to travel, engaging in research and consultancy projects abroad (for example, for the OECD and the British Council), and to have worked with colleagues in all the countries of the UK. Tricia has over 70 publications to her name. Earlier in her career she was a teacher and head teacher in nursery and primary schools, a researcher and a community educator. Now (officially) retired and an Emeritus Professor of Canterbury Christ Church University, Tricia is enjoying having time to spend with her husband and five grandchildren, and for exciting new interests.

Simon Ellis is a Senior Lecturer in the Centre for Enabling Learning at Canterbury Christ Church University and is actively involved in teacher training at initial and postgraduate levels in the areas of SEN and inclusion. Prior to this he held this post in a part-time capacity and also worked as a KS3 National Strategy Behaviour and Attendance Consultant in an innovative joint programme between Kent LEA and Canterbury Christ Church University. He originally taught as a primary teacher and worked as a SENCO in the primary sector before joining Kent's Behaviour Support Service in 1997 where he initially worked as a specialist teacher and then as a team manager.

Susan Ellis is Senior Lecturer in the Department of Childhood and Primary Studies at Strathclyde University. She teaches language to postgraduate and undergraduate students and also works with classroom teachers on continuing professional development courses. Her current research is on how children's social and emotional development impacts on their imaginative writing and on the management of the literacy curriculum in schools.

Deborah Eyre is the Director of the National Academy for Gifted and Talented Youth at the University of Warwick. She has had a longstanding interest in the education of able/gifted pupils and has worked in this field for over twenty years. Deborah is an active researcher and a leading expert in the education of able pupils in England. She advises the Department for Education and Skills (DfES), the Qualifications and Curriculum Authority (QCA), and the Teacher Training Agency (TTA) and is a specialist advisor to the House of Commons Education Select Committee. Deborah is a respected speaker at international level and is a member of the World Council for Gifted and Talented Children (WCGTC) and also works closely with the European Council for High Ability (ECHA).

Kit Field is the Head of Professional Development in the Faculty of Education at Canterbury Christ Church University. Kit has written several books, chapters and articles in relation to Modern Foreign Languages teaching and learning, Subject Leadership and Continuing Professional Development. Kit is also the vice chair of the UCET CPD committee, chair of the Church Colleges CPD network and is a committee member of the International Professional Development Association.

Robert Fisher is Professor of Education at Brunel University and consultant to many research and professional development projects on thinking skills and creativity, for schools, LEAs and national organisations. He has taught for more than 20 years students of all ages and abilities in schools in the UK and abroad, including Africa and Hong Kong, and was a primary head teacher for five years in Richmond-upon-Thames. He has published more than 20 books on education including *Teaching Thinking*, *Teaching Children to Think*, *Teaching Children to Learn*, *Head Start*, *Unlocking Creativity* and the *Stories for Thinking* series (see website: www.teachingthinking.net).

Caroline Gipps is the Vice Chancellor at the University of Wolverhampton. Previously she was the Deputy Vice Chancellor at Kingston University London, and Dean of Research and Professor of Education at the Institute of Education, London. Trained as a psychologist, test developer, and a qualified teacher, she has carried out research on assessment in the school system for over 20 years. Research projects have included a six year study of the introduction of the national curriculum assessment programme into primary schools; a seminal study of teacher feedback to learners; and the teaching, assessment and feedback strategies used by 'expert' classroom teachers. A current major project is an evaluation of an electronic learning management system in supporting students in their access to, and learning in, higher education. Caroline Gipps has written extensively on assessment and learning, and equity issues.

Teresa Grainger is a Professor of Education at Canterbury Christ Church University, where she leads the Masters programme in Language and Literacy. Teresa has published widely on storytelling, drama, poetry and writing, most recently editing *The RoutledgeFalmer Reader in Language and Literacy* (2004) and writing *Creativity and Writing: Developing Voice and Verve in the Classroom* (2005, Routledge) with Kathy Goouch and Andrew Lambirth. Teresa was President of the United Kingdom Reading Association, now UKLA (2001–2) and Editor of the journal *Reading Literacy and Language* (1998–2003).

Her current research involves exploring drama and writing, teachers as writers, collaborative writing, possibility thinking, the nature of creative teaching and progression in creative learning.

Elizabeth Grugeon is a Senior Lecturer in English in Primary Education at De Montfort University, Bedford. She is co-author (with Lorraine Hubbard, Lyn Dawes and Carol Smith) of *Teaching Speaking and Listening in the Primary School* (3rd edition, 2005, David Fulton Publishers). Elizabeth's special interests are in children's literature and children's oral culture.

Kathy Hall is Professor of Education at the Open University. A former primary and secondary teacher and lecturer in teacher education, she researches literacy pedagogy, and inclusion and assessment. She supervises MPhil/PhD and EdD students working in these areas. She has written extensively for various audiences, recent books being *Making Formative Assessment Work* (with Winifred Burke); *Listening to Stephen Read*, both with Oxford University Press; and *Literacy and Schooling: Towards Renewal in Primary Education Policy* (Ashgate).

Denis Hayes is a Reader in Education at the University of Plymouth. Prior to his appointment he taught in five schools over seventeen years. His publications include *Foundations of Primary Education* (3rd edition, 2004, David Fulton) and *A Student Teacher's Guide to Primary School Placement* (2003, Routledge). Dr Hayes' research interests focus on the experiences and emotions of student (trainee) primary teachers on school placement, the role of the teacher and the effective use of interactive teaching skills.

Cathie Holden is Reader in Education at the University of Exeter, UK, where she teaches citizenship on both the primary and secondary PGCE. Prior to this she taught in middle schools for 15 years. Her research interests are around student teachers' and children's understanding of global issues and the implications of this for the classroom. Books include: *Visions of the Future: Why We Need to Teach for Tomorrow* (with David Hicks), *Children as Citizens: Education for Participation* and *Education for Citizenship: Ideas Into Action* (both with Nick Clough).

Lorraine Hubbard is a Senior Lecturer in English in Primary Education at De Montfort University, Bedford. She is co-author (with Elizabeth Grugeon, Lyn Dawes and Carol Smith) of *Teaching Speaking and Listening in the Primary School* (3rd edition, 2005, David Fulton Publishers). Lorraine has special interests in literacy in the European Context.

Peter Kelly teaches on the Masters degree programme at the Faculty of Education, University of Plymouth, where he is a Senior Lecturer. Until 2002 he was a primary head teacher. His current research explores the relation between discourse, learning and identity in primary classrooms.

Maureen Lewis has been involved in primary education for many years – as a teacher, researcher, consultant and author. In the last few years she was a regional director for the National Literacy Strategy and the Primary National Strategy – a role which enabled her to reflect on the complex interplay of factors through which national curriculum policy is developed and implemented.

Jane Medwell taught in primary schools in Cardiff and Devon and has lectured in a number of universities including Cardiff, Plymouth and, currently, Warwick. She has researched and published widely especially in the areas of computers and literacy and the effective teaching of literacy.

Elaine Millard worked as an English teacher from 1968–88, in a variety of 11–18 comprehensive schools in Sheffield, and from 1989–90 as an advisory teacher for Nottingham LEA, where she helped both primary and secondary schools prepare for the introduction of the National Curriculum in English. She joined Sheffield University's School of Education in 1990 and was one of the creators of the university's Masters Degree in Literacy. She now supervises MPhil/PhD students working on literacy research. Her own research interests span issues in the development of literacy at all levels, from early reading to critical theory. Her current research focuses on gender, race and class differences in the development of home and school-based literacies.

Helen Moylett works for the Primary National Strategy as a senior regional adviser for the Foundation Stage. Prior to that she was the head of an early years centre providing integrated care and education for young children and support for their families. Earlier in her career she worked at Manchester Metropolitan University as a Senior Lecturer in early years and education studies and before that as a senior advisory teacher in Manchester. Helen has also been a home school teacher in what would now be known as an extended primary school, and a junior, infant and nursery class teacher in inner city Manchester. She has co-edited three early years books with Professor Lesley Abbott; her research interests include working with parents and listening to young children. She is currently working on the national birth to five quality framework.

Anny Northcote is currently Senior Lecturer in primary English at Bath Spa University College. She previously spent many years working in London as a classroom teacher and as an advisor for supporting bilingual learners, followed by nine years as Senior Lecturer of primary language and literacy on primary ITE courses at London Metropolitan University. Her main interests are in the areas of linguistic diversity and children's literature and she has researched into bilingual children's reading preferences.

Alison Pickering taught in primary schools in inner London and Sydney, Australia prior to her appointment as deputy head teacher of a primary school in Richmond-upon-Thames. She is currently Course Director for undergraduate routes into teaching in the School of Education at Kingston University. Her main areas of interest are primary science, cross-curricular approaches to learning, and creative approaches to assessment.

Colin Richards is Professor of Education at St Martin's College and Visiting Professor at the Universities of Leicester, Warwick and Newcastle and at the National Institute of Education in Singapore. He was a primary class teacher, deputy head teacher and Lecturer in education before becoming an HMI in 1983. After inspecting schools in the North East of England he became Staff Inspector (Curriculum) in 1987. From 1994 to 1996 he was Ofsted's Specialist Adviser in Primary Education. Since leaving the Inspectorate he has maintained a keen interest in the issues of standards, the primary curriculum and school inspection. He has published widely and is a frequent contributor to the national press, particularly the *Times Educational Supplement* and *Education Journal*. As well as being a small school enthusiast he is chair of governors of a Cumbrian secondary school and a fervent lover of the Lake District in which he lives. He greatly treasures the epithet 'an old-fashioned HMI', bestowed on him by a former chief inspector of schools.

Kieron Sheehy is Lecturer in Developmental Psychology at the Open University. He researches and publishes in the areas of inclusive education and technology, and child development.

Janet Tod is Professor of Education at Canterbury Christ Church University. She is a chartered educational and clinical psychologist and qualified speech therapist. Her work involves teaching, research and publication at undergraduate and postgraduate levels in the area of Special Educational Needs and Inclusion. She is best known for her research and publication in the area of IEPs (Individual Education Plans) and dyslexia. She is currently research co-ordinator for a TTA funded initial teacher education professional resource network (IPRN) for behaviour and is co-author of a recently published TTA funded EPPI review in the area of behaviour management.

Samantha Twiselton is the Programme Leader for the Primary PGCE at St Martin's College and the co-ordinator of Initial Teacher Education for ESCalate, the education subject centre for the promotion of learning and teaching in Higher Education. She lectures in primary English and education studies, having been a primary classroom teacher for a number of years. Her PhD was in the development of teacher knowledge and expertise in Initial Teacher Education. She lives in the Lake District with her husband and two children and will one day find enough time to actually get out there and walk in it.

Ben Whitney is Team Leader (Pupil Attendance and Child Welfare) at Wolverhampton City Council Lifelong Learning. He manages the team of Education Welfare Officers and is LEA lead officer for child protection. He previously worked in similar roles for Staffordshire LEA for over 14 years and has written widely on education welfare issues including *Protecting Children* (RoutledgeFalmer, 2004). He was a member of the group responsible for producing *Learning to Protect*, a resource pack published by the NSPCC for use in Initial Teacher Training.

Elizabeth Wood is Reader in Early Childhood Education at the University of Exeter. Her research interests include the role of play in learning; teachers' professional knowledge and practice; curriculum, pedagogy and assessment in early childhood; and gender and under-achievement. She has co-authored two books on play, including a new edition of *Play, Learning and the Early Childhood Curriculum* (Sage, 2005 with Jane Attfield), and *Teaching Through Play* (Open University Press, 1997 with Neville Bennett). Elizabeth contributes regularly to in-service courses and conferences both nationally and internationally, and publishes widely in research and professional journals.

David Wray taught in primary schools for 10 years and is currently Professor of Literacy Education at the University of Warwick. He has published over 30 books on aspects of literacy teaching and is best known for his work on developing teaching strategies to help pupils access the curriculum through literacy. This has resulted in such innovations as the Extending Interactions with Texts (EXIT) model to guide the teaching of reading to learn, and writing frames to help with the writing of factual text types. His work has been made an integral part of the National Literacy Strategy at both primary and secondary levels. His major publications include: *Extending Literacy* (Routledge); *English 7–11* (Routledge); *Developing Children's Non-Fiction Writing* (Scholastic); *Writing Frames* and *Writing across the Curriculum* (University of Reading Reading and Language Information Centre); *Literacy in the Secondary School* (Fulton); and *Teaching Literacy Effectively* (RoutledgeFalmer).

Dominic Wyse is a Lecturer in Primary and Early Years Education at the University of Cambridge. His main research interests include primary education, creativity and the study of childhood. His publications have included books and research papers critically analysing government policy on the teaching of English. His most recent paper reports some empirical work on children's conceptions of grammar. His most recent books are *Creativity in the Primary Curriculum* (David Fulton Publishers) edited with Russell Jones and *An Introduction to Childhood Studies* (Blackwell Publishers) edited by Dominic Wyse. He is currently working with David Spendlove from Manchester University on externally funded research addressing creativity in Merseyside and Manchester/Salford schools as part of the Creative Partnerships initiative.

Acknowledgements

The authors would like to thank Anna Clarkson at Routledge for all her support. We would especially like to warmly thank Kerry Riches who has helped us manage this project through all the key stages of production. Her assistance and expertise has been invaluable and we are most appreciative and grateful for her significant contribution. We would like also to thank Sunita Mayes for her early secretarial help on this book.

Introduction

WHAT IS PRIMARY TEACHING?

Teaching in primary schools has often been thought of as having a somewhat lower status than 'real' teaching – that is, teaching a proper subject in a proper school, which means a secondary school. Primary teaching, so the folklore tells us, is just looking after young children until they get to the 'proper' school – showing them how to hold a pencil, wiping their noses, telling them a story or two, but not actually teaching them too much of real importance. Those (fairly rare) teachers who have made the change from teaching in secondary schools to primary schools often find that parents, even pupils, ask them why they have 'come down here', the idea that someone might voluntarily choose primary teaching over secondary being a hard one to grasp.

Thankfully, at least in official quarters, the image of primary teaching has changed and we now recognise that primary school is a crucial period, perhaps the most crucial, in children's learning during which children have to be taught those complex skills which are the foundation of all the learning they will do in the rest of their lives. It is primary teachers that teach children to read, to write, to manipulate numbers, to observe and record their experiences of the world, and provide them with experiences which stimulate their imaginations and expand their worlds. Primary teachers now, far from being seen as child-minders with little expertise, are viewed as professional learning enablers, possessing an incredibly complex range of skills which must be employed in collaboration with vision and imagination.

Even when the complexity of the primary teacher's job is recognised, there are still a number of different ways of conceptualising what makes a good primary teacher. A description which is often used is that primary teaching is a vocation – rather like the priesthood, you have to have a calling in order to be a good primary teacher. This view produces such ideas as the belief that good teachers are born, not made, and that to become a teacher all you really need to do is to work for a while alongside another experienced teacher and copy what he or she does. This used to be referred to as a 'sitting with Nellie' approach to becoming a teacher. It does have the merit that, if Nellie *is* a good teacher, then watching and copying what she does will almost certainly pass on some pretty good habits of classroom action. But what if Nellie's classroom changes, as classrooms have changed, radically, over the past 20 years? Those good habits will need to be changed as well, if Nellie is to remain effective as a teacher. And the trouble with habits, as all those nail-biters and chocoholics among you will know, is that they can be extraordinarily resistant to change. Nellie will need to have an understanding about why she does what she does, why it works now but might not work in the future, and how she will go about changing her practices. Having a vocation will only get her so far. This does not mean, of course, that feeling that primary teaching is your vocation is wrong. It is just that successful teaching needs more than this feeling of being 'born to teach'. It is also true that many teachers can develop into highly effective practitioners without ever feeling such an inner calling.

Another popular way of conceptualising teaching is to describe it as a craft, with the implication that it consists of an integrated collection of skilful activities. Other crafts are such activities as plumbing and wood-turning, all very skilful in their own rights (and in some cases more lucrative as careers than primary teaching!). A craft view of teaching does allow for changes in practice to a much greater extent than might a vocation view. In the same way that plumbers have to change their practices to accommodate innovations such as plastic rather than copper piping, so teachers have to adapt their skills to deal with changing classroom situations such as the use of ICT to provide stimulus and information to pupils. Naturally, there is a large element of craft involved in the role of the primary teacher. For most beginning teachers, learning these craft elements looms pretty large in their early experiences of teaching. Learning to talk to large groups of pupils in an authoritative yet approachable way, learning to ask questions and respond to answers, learning to plan appropriate activities for all the pupils in a class, learning how to write informative reports to parents about the progress of their offspring – all these have a significant craft element to them, and many beginning teachers see their principal aim in their first few years of teaching as mastering these skills and becoming craftsmen/women of the classroom. Yet this is not all there is to successful primary teaching, nor to the process of becoming a successful teacher. The two simple facts that set teaching apart from other crafts are the two Cs – consequence and complexity.

Let us take consequence first. What is the consequence of a plumber failing to do a job properly? Well, the worst-case scenario is a flooded house, which may be costly to put right but, in the end, is usually repairable. But the consequence of a teacher failing a pupil or group of pupils can be much, much more serious. Teachers who fail produce pupils who fail and if, as in the old adage, 'nothing succeeds like success', then nothing fails like failure. Failing children can easily develop a self image which incorporates failure – a view of themselves which can persist throughout their lives and severely limit their achievement of their potential. Teachers who fail to teach their pupils to read or write do far more damage than any plumber who fails to connect two pipes properly. The consequences of teaching are greater and longer lasting than most other crafts.

In terms of complexity also, the craft of teaching outdoes most others. Indeed, teaching is so complex an activity that it is sometimes almost impossible to predict what will happen when you engage in it. A plumber might weld together two pipes and 99 times out of 100, if the job is done carefully, the result will be the same. A teacher, on the other hand, can teach the same lesson twice to different groups of pupils, and with one achieve success but with the other have a disaster. Why? Well, it is pretty obvious that a number of variables in each case were not the same. The groups were different, with different personalities, abilities, interests, aptitudes, moods etc. The performance of the teacher may have been different, no teacher being a robot who can repeat exactly the same sequence of actions. The teacher may have been in a different mood, the physical environment of the teaching room slightly different, the time of day different, and so on virtually ad infinitum. The point here is that any act of teaching is an incredibly complicated affair: there are so many things that can influence it. One of the key characteristics of really effective teachers is the ability to hold a lot of this complexity in their minds as they plan for, implement and evaluate their teaching. Although not even the most skilful teacher can deal with the entire complexity of the teaching process, teaching is a process immensely more complex in its nature than crafts such as plumbing.

It also, in essence, involves dealing with quite different 'matter' than crafts such as plumbing. Although some plumbers will swear that they do, in general pipes and the other 'matter' of this craft do not react back when the plumber operates upon them. Pipes are inert, without personalities of their own. Children, however, are not inert: they do react back to teaching and such reactions can make or break the success of the teaching enterprise. Good teachers are able to predict, work with, and influence the personalities of those they are working with. They are not, therefore, simply concerned with pupils' knowledge but also with their feelings. Producing children who knew a lot but valued nothing of what they knew would be an odd state of affairs in teaching. So attitude development is at least as important an aspect of teaching as knowledge transmission.

By concentrating on practical teaching skills and methods – the mechanics of teaching – it is possible to produce a mechanistic 'teacher' who is able to manage a class and instruct pupils with a fair show of competence. The emphasis here is on what the teacher can do (a trade), rather than what the teacher is and can become (an educator). You need to be aware of the larger social setting, have the flexibility to anticipate change, and to adapt your teaching methods to new demands.

Teaching in a primary school is, above all, a 'self-giving' enterprise concerned with the betterment or good of pupils. Pupils spend the greatest amount of their daily time with teachers, and so you will have significant opportunities to influence them. The time spent by pupils in the company of teachers is, therefore, inevitably personal and formative. Good teachers are connected to their pupils, for at the heart of the practice of education is the relationship between teacher and pupil. It is this relationship that sets the tone for all else in the classroom.

For all these reasons, when we talk about teaching we use the notion of professional decision-making to represent it.

So our third way of conceptualising primary teaching, and the approach we use in this book, is as a professional activity. This term implies a number of attributes within the teacher, including:

- high levels of relevant knowledge about what is being taught and the pupils to whom it is being taught;
- knowledge of, and skill in using, a range of strategies for presenting, explaining and illustrating ideas to learners;
- the capacity to engage in thoughtful, considered action in implementing such strategies, taking into account the needs and responses of the learners as they develop and manifest themselves;
- an understanding of the importance of learners' attitudes towards what they are learning and an ability to influence and develop these attitudes;
- the ability and willingness to learn from a variety of sources about effective teaching and to adapt practices to fit this on-going learning.

It is one of the aims of this book to help you begin to develop such professional attributes.

HOW CAN THIS BOOK HELP ME?

From what we have just said, you may already have realised that the book you are holding is not simply a collection of 'tips for the beginning teacher'. You *will* find within its pages a great deal of very practical advice about primary teaching but our aims in the book go beyond this. We are aiming to give you practical advice but always to give you our rationale for why such advice might be useful, where it comes from, on what basis it has been formulated and how you might evaluate its usefulness. In short, this book is intended to be both practical and theoretical, an intention which reflects a view of teaching as a highly skilled and knowledgeable professional activity.

The book, therefore, will help move you on in your development as a skilful, professional primary teacher by providing you with background insights into a range of issues which affect the decisions you make in the classroom, and illustrating how such insights affect your classroom practice. Of course, you cannot learn to teach simply by reading a book, and our intention is that this book will work alongside the other experiences which make up your initial teacher training/education course, especially those experiences that involve you working directly in classrooms.

WHAT'S IN THE BOOK?

The aim of this book is to provide vital support to student teachers and their tutors, particularly during the school placement element of their initial teacher education courses. It provides a sound and practical introduction to the teaching skills that a student teacher will need to acquire and to the theory underpinning them.

The book is divided into units, each covering an essential issue/concept or skill. Each unit contains an introduction to the key concepts/issues and several learning activities for student teachers presented in the form of tasks. There are also annotated lists of suggested reading for students and tutors who want to explore topics in more detail.

The book is structured into nine sections, each focusing upon a discrete aspect of becoming a professional primary teacher.

Section 1: Becoming a teacher

This section includes units:

- examining the nature of teaching, both formal and informal;
- exploring the standards required for qualified teacher status with particular emphasis on the professional values and practices of teaching.

Section 2: Exploring the nature of learning and teaching

This section includes units:

- outlining aspects of child development theory and research which you need to understand in order to provide appropriate learning opportunities for children;
- examining a number of conceptualisations of learning, from behaviourist accounts to more recent socio-cultural accounts, and the implications of these for teaching;
- discussing a range of insights into learning and appropriate teaching strategies that respond to these;
- introducing a range of different teaching skills which you need to develop to be successful in the classroom.

Section 3: Planning and managing learning

Here you will find units examining such issues as:

- planning classroom work, for medium and long-term periods;
- planning for the short term, including lesson planning and evaluation;
- managing learning, in particular issues of behaviour management;
- managing group work in classrooms;
- planning for a variety of classroom organisational systems;
- planning educational visits and other out-of-school learning experiences.

Section 4: Approaches to the curriculum

This section includes units focusing on:

- the aims of primary education;
- conceptions of the school curriculum and its formal, informal and hidden aims;
- the rationale for and emergence of the National Curriculum and its related documentation;
- the implications of the current Scottish Curriculum 5–14 guidelines, and their impact upon primary school teaching.

Section 5: Recent developments in primary education

In this section you will find units exploring currently important issues such as:

- creative teaching and teaching for creativity across the curriculum;
- thinking skills and the concept of multiple intelligences;
- learning through dialogue and the implications for group work;
- citizenship and moral education;
- the provision which might be made for children who are gifted and talented.

Section 6: Diversity and inclusion

Here you will find units introducing the following issues:

- inclusion and barriers to learning and participation;
- difference, diversity and differentiation;
- classroom strategies for maximising the opportunities presented by classes of diverse ethnic characters;
- current thinking about gender differences and their impact upon school achievement;
- making the most of linguistic diversity.

Section 7: Assessment

Units here examine:

- the nature of on-going, formative assessment of pupil's progress and a range of approaches to this;
- current national approaches to summative assessment, including the development and use of SATs.

Section 8: Partnership in practice

This section includes units on:

- managing learning support assistants, parent helpers and others in the classroom;
- developing relationships with parents, governors and making partnerships in the community;
- working with other agencies, such as social workers, special needs support teachers, and educational psychologists;
- child protection issues and the guidelines surrounding suspected child abuse.

Section 9: Your professional development

The final section of the book includes units on:

- applying for a job and what to expect in induction;
- the professional duties and legal responsibilities of the primary teacher;
- professional development, career opportunities and further qualifications.

HOW CAN I USE THE BOOK?

There are a number of ways in which you might use this book. You might, of course, want to sit yourself comfortably and just read it from cover to cover. We anticipate, however, that, as gripping a read as this book is, you will probably not want to approach it in quite that way!

It is more likely that you will want to read units from the book separately. The book has been designed so that each unit, while written to be part of a coherent whole, is also free-standing. The book can, therefore, be used in a very flexible way. You might use a number of approaches:

- You might read a particular unit after you have touched upon similar material in a college or university session. The unit will then serve as a revision of material you may have covered in the session, or extend your understanding of this material.
- You might prepare for a particular college or university session by reading the relevant unit in advance. You are likely to find the session much more rewarding and useful if you have prepared in this way by developing your background knowledge of the topics to be covered.
- You might find that, because of the pressure on time in a course of teacher training (as in the case of most PGCE courses, for example), there simply is not enough college or university time available to cover some issues in any more than a cursory way. In this case, this book will help you ensure that you do not miss anything really important and you can read units to 'fill in the gaps' in your course coverage.

However you use this book, we hope it will help inspire in you the same passionate interest in education, and primary education in particular, that is felt by every one of the contributors to the book. Education is endlessly fascinating as a subject, and, of course, teaching children is one of the most important activities we can engage in. Enjoy the experience – and enjoy the book. We hope you find it useful.

James Arthur, Teresa Grainger and David Wray

1 Becoming a Teacher

Unit 1.1

Primary Teaching

A personal perspective

Colin Richards

INTRODUCTION

Primary teaching is an immensely complicated business. It involves the interplay of so many elements including interpersonal, intellectual, physical, spiritual, even aesthetic dimensions. Neither is it one thing, but it changes in form and substance from hour to hour, lesson to lesson, class to class and year to year. Some people see it as scientific in orientation, involving the selection of the best ways to 'deliver' material to young minds; others stress its artistic side and place emphasis on the 'feel' or style of teaching. So what is this thing called primary teaching? It is the purpose of this unit to open this up for discussion.

OBJECTIVES

By the end of this unit you should be beginning to:

- form a view of the nature of primary teaching;
- develop an awareness of the personal qualities and skills you require as a primary teacher;
- form views as to the purposes of primary teaching;
- be overawed at the responsibility of being a primary school teacher.

'ACROSTIC' TEACHING

When you begin teaching you will be surprised at the range of different types of writing which the children are expected to engage in. Children have to learn to write narrative accounts, imaginative stories, descriptions of their 'experiments', diaries, letters, poems etc. Many are introduced to acrostics and enjoy the challenge these present. What are acrostics? ... They are poems or other compositions in which certain letters in each line form a word or words.

I use an acrostic when giving an introductory talk to students at the beginning of their course of teacher education. You will notice that I don't call them 'trainees' and I don't talk of 'teacher training'. Like you they are not being introduced to a simple straightforward activity where they can be trained to perform like machine operators on a production line or like circus animals. They are being inducted into a very complex professional activity – illustrated, for example, by the fact that this introductory text you are reading contains over thirty units and it is just an introduction!

I present the following:

T.........
E.........
A.........
C.........
H.........
I.........
N.........
G.........

and ask the students to characterise primary teaching using eight adjectives corresponding to the eight letters.

Task 1.1.1
The nature of primary teaching

What do you think primary teaching is like? What does it feel like? What kind of activity is it? Make your list and share it with fellow students.

Of course there are no right or wrong answers and an activity as complex as primary teaching cannot be captured in eight words.

As 'a starter for eight' I offer you (as I do my students) the following:

Tiring: primary teaching is very demanding work – demanding physically as you have to cope with a class of very active, growing human beings; demanding interpersonally as you have to deal with the myriad of social interactions occurring in a crowded classroom; demanding intellectually as you have to translate complex ideas in your head into terms that children of a particular age can understand.

Exhilarating: primary teaching is equally (but paradoxically) invigorating work – when both you and the children get 'fired' up with enthusiasm for a particular activity, project or piece of work.

Amusing: primary teaching is enlivened by countless amusing incidents during the course of a day. Some children are natural and conscious comedians; others are unintentionally so; primary classrooms provide endless scope for amusement. 'Never a dull moment' captures this characteristic.

Chaotic: primary teaching can appear (and sometimes is) chaotic as unforeseen circumstances arise and have to be coped with, as parents, the head teacher and children make conflicting demands which have somehow to be met, and as the daily business of managing the learning of twenty or thirty lively youngsters has to be conducted.

Hectic: primary teaching occurs in an extremely busy place called a classroom where a multitude of activities (some intended by the teachers, others unintended!) take place and where nothing or nobody stands still for long. Stamina, patience and ability to cope with the unexpected are at a premium.

Inspiring: primary teaching can be inspiring. You can be inspired by the amazing abilities children can reveal, for example, in the creative arts; you can be inspired by the personal qualities of kindness and consideration children can show one another; you can be inspired by the fact that children with unbelievably difficult home circumstances come to school and manage to learn at all; you can be inspired by the work of your colleagues in school from whom you can learn so much.

Never-ending: primary teaching is not a 'nine till three-thirty' occupation. In fact it's not so much an occupation as a way of life. It is never complete, never mastered, never perfected. There is always more to learn and more to do for the children in your class. Teaching can take over your whole life with its never-ending demands but you have to learn to temper these demands with your own personal needs. Doing this can be conscience-wracking but is absolutely essential – to your own and, indirectly, your children's well-being.

Gratifying: primary teaching can be intensely gratifying (despite some inevitable frustrations). Teaching a child to read, seeing another child's delight on mastering a skill, telling a story which captivates the whole class, having a lesson which goes really well – such activities can and will give you tremendous satisfaction.

A SENSE OF STYLE

You can see from my acrostic that I believe that primary teaching is an extremely complex activity, whether considered in theoretical or practical terms. It's an amalgam of so many elements – interpersonal, intellectual, physical, spiritual, even aesthetic. It changes subtly in form, substance and 'feel' hour to hour, lesson to lesson, class to class, year to year. It involves notions such as 'respect', 'concern', 'care' and 'intellectual integrity' that are impossible to define but which are deeply influential in determining the nature of life in classrooms. The ends and means, aims and methods, of teaching are inextricably interwoven. It is a moral enterprise as well as a practical activity. The word 'style' captures something of what I am trying to convey – a sense of considered professional judgement, of personal response, of quality, of distinctive style – which each practitioner, including you, needs to foster. Primary teaching involves far more than the routine reproduction of established procedures; it goes well beyond establishing and maintaining patterns of classroom organisation. It cannot be pinned down in a few straightforward sentences (or in a simple acrostic!).

TEACHING: SCIENCE? ART? OR CRAFT?

Some educational researchers such as Muijs and Reynolds (2001) argue that it is possible to create a science of teaching. They believe that it is possible to study teaching by comparing the results of different methods in terms of the outcomes they produce in children and thereby arrive at objective findings as to which teaching methods are effective in which contexts. You will come across books with titles like *Effective Teaching* which claim to provide scientifically defensible evidence on which to base decisions about how to teach.

Some educationists such as Marland (1975) regard teaching as essentially a craft – a set of difficult and complex techniques which can be picked up from, or taught by, skilled practitioners and which can be honed and perfected over the years. You will come across books with titles like *The Craft of the Classroom* which embody this approach.

Still others such as Eisner (1979) regard teaching as essentially an art – a complex creative activity concerned with the promotion of human learning and involving imagination, sensitivity and personal response and an indefinable element of professional judgement, none of which can be taught directly by another person (though they can be learnt indirectly). He talks of the need to 'recognise the contingent nature of educational practice, to savour its complexity, and to be not afraid to use whatever artistry we can master to deal with its problems' and he warns against 'pseudo-science' (p. 33).

Task 1.1.2
Teaching: science, art or craft?

Based on your experience of teaching at school, at university or on this course, how would you characterise teaching – as science, art or craft? Try to justify your answer to fellow students.

Again, as in response to Task 1.1.1, there are no absolutely right or wrong answers.

From what I have written already you will see that I characterise teaching as an art, although an art which also involves some craft skills which can be taught and even trained for. I do not see that there can ever be an objective science of teaching involving the rigorous definition of methods and the clear measurement of outcomes. I believe that such a science is logically impossible since 'the power to teach' is a highly complex amalgam of judgement, technique and personal qualities whose assessment is inevitably subjective and can never be susceptible to quantification or measurement. But that perspective is my own personal one. Other educationists have different ideas of the nature of teaching including some who subscribe to the notion of 'the science of the art of teaching'!

ENACTIVE, PRE-ACTIVE AND POST-ACTIVE PRIMARY TEACHING

What activities are involved in being a primary teacher? What should the balance be between the different kinds of activity?

To outsiders and perhaps to most primary age children (although we don't know because we haven't asked them), 'teaching' conjures up an image of a teacher in front of a class describing, explaining, instructing or demonstrating something to her pupils. This is enactive teaching – teaching in action, the full frontal interaction of teacher and children. Of course enactive teaching doesn't only take place in classrooms – it occurs in the hall, in the school grounds and on school trips. Nor does it always involve direct interaction with a class of children – the teacher may be teaching individuals or groups or may be setting up activities where children learn for themselves, for example. There has been a considerable amount of research into enactive teaching in English primary schools – referred to in other parts of this book. However, there is far more to teaching than enactive teaching, even though this is the core activity.

There is pre-active teaching involving the preparation and planning for children's learning, the organisation of the classroom, the collection and organisation of teaching resources, the management of visits or activities outside the classroom and the briefing of other adults who work with children. Interestingly, there has been little research into how primary teachers actually plan, prepare and organise their work. Pre-active teaching is essential to the success of enactive teaching – hence the emphasis on planning and managing learning in Section 3 of this book.

There is also post-active teaching which involves considered reflection on practice, writing up evaluations, marking children's work, making assessments of children's progress and keeping records. At its best this feeds into pre-active teaching as reflection and assessment inform planning and preparation. There is plenty of advice available on assessment and record-keeping (see Section 7) but again a dearth of research into how teachers actually engage in post-active teaching – you might consider undertaking some research of your own later in your career.

But there is still more to primary teaching as a professional activity. Teachers have to engage in a variety of extra-class activities – administrative tasks, staff meetings, clubs, consultations with parents and attendance at professional development courses – which relate indirectly to teaching but can't be fitted into my neat (too neat?) threefold classification.

There was some interesting work carried out a decade or more ago by Campbell and Neill (1994) into the nature of primary teachers' work, especially the amount of time devoted to a variety of activities. The research makes interesting reading, though the categories the researchers used are rather different from my classification and the findings are dated. Campbell found that on average the 374 infant and junior teachers in his study spent 52.6 hours a week on professional activity – subdivided into 18.3 hours for teaching (i.e. enactive teaching), 15.7 hours for preparation/marking (i.e. an amalgam of pre-active and post-active teaching), 14.1 hours on administration, 7.2 hours on professional development (including staff meetings and reading), and 4.5 hours on a rag-bag of other activities which didn't fit into any of their other categories. Clearly this research gave the lie to the idea of primary teaching as a 'nine to three-thirty' occupation!

To many, including the researchers, one of the most surprising findings was the relatively small proportion of the teachers' total work time devoted to what I have called enactive teaching, i.e. about a third. It is interesting to speculate whether the figures would be any different were the research to be conducted today. I doubt if there would be any substantial changes despite recent government initiatives in reforming the school workforce. I believe that this is how it should be. Enactive teaching requires a large input of pre-active teaching if it is to be successful and it needs to be followed up by considerable, though somewhat less, post-active activity to ensure a professional cycle of planning – teaching – assessment – reflection – planning – teaching – assessment … ad infinitum. Remember primary teaching is 'never-ending'.

Task 1.1.3
The characteristics of a good teacher

In a small group consider what makes a good teacher and what knowledge and personal qualities are needed.

Would children come up with the same answers? Discuss the issue with a small group of primary-aged children.

THE PERSONAL QUALITIES AND KNOWLEDGE REQUIRED OF PRIMARY TEACHERS

There has been very little research into how children view good teachers. Over thirty years ago Philip Taylor asked both primary and secondary-aged children and got very similar results from both. In his words:

> Pupils expect teachers to teach. They value lucid exposition, the clear statement of problems and guidance in their solution. Personal qualities of kindness, sympathy and patience are secondary, appreciated by pupils if they make the teacher more effective in carrying out his primary, intellectual task … there appears to be little demand by pupils that teachers shall be friends or temporary mothers and fathers.
>
> (Musgrove and Taylor 1969: 17)

How do these findings compare with the results of your small group discussions?

The knowledge required to be a primary teacher has changed since the introduction of what was then teacher training in the nineteenth century but the personal qualities needed have remained the same. The following paragraph in the introduction to the professional standards you are required to meet by the government (DfES/TTA 2002: 4) captures something of this demanding professional amalgam:

> teaching involves a lot more than care, mutual respect and well-placed optimism. It demands knowledge and practical skills; the ability to make informed judgements, and to balance pressures and challenges; practice and creativity; interest and effort; as well as an understanding of how children learn and develop.

In a letter published a few years ago in the *Times Educational Supplement* I characterised the expectations of teachers held by the government and the wider society as representing

> a set of demands which properly exemplified would need the omni-competence of Leonardo da Vinci, the diplomatic expertise of Kofi Annan, the histrionic skills of Julie Walters, the grim determination of Alex Ferguson and the saintliness of Mother Teresa, coupled with the omniscience of God.

Admittedly over-the-top (and with a very large tongue in cheek), this does represent the inflated expectations of us as teachers. None of us are perfect human beings (nor for that matter are the children in our classes, their parents or our politicians) but those expectations are a powerful influence on how many teachers view themselves and on causing so many to feel guilty about falling short. We can aspire to educational sainthood but hardly hope to achieve it. However, in its pursuit we can at least aspire to show such qualities as 'care', 'respect', 'optimism', 'interest' and 'effort' – required of us, quite properly in my view, by officialdom.

The knowledge required of you as primary teachers is of seven kinds – each important, though one (the second) is, in my view, more important than the others. You certainly need subject content knowledge – an understanding of the main concepts, principles, skills and content of the areas which you will have to teach. That's a tall order given that the curriculum you are required to teach in key stages 1 and 2 comprises eleven subjects as well as cross-curricular areas such as personal and social education and citizenship and given that the curriculum required in the Foundation Stage comprises six broad areas of learning. You can't assume that you have the required subject knowledge as a result of your own education, whether at college or university. You will need to audit, and where necessary, top up your subject knowledge by reading or attending courses. Begin now if you haven't done this already.

The second kind of knowledge involves the application of subject knowledge in teaching your children – sometimes termed, rather grandly, 'pedagogical subject knowledge'. This crucially important area involves knowing how to make the knowledge, skills and understandings of subjects accessible and meaningful to children – how best to represent particular ideas; what illustrations to use; what demonstrations or experiments to employ; what stories to tell; what examples to draw on; what kind of explanations to offer; how to relate what needs to be taught to children's experiences or interests, and so on. You will begin to develop this applied expertise in your course of initial teacher education, you will need to add to it through continuing professional development and over time you will add to it from 'the wisdom of practice' – your colleagues' and hopefully your own. Application of subject knowledge also draws on knowledge of children's development, including aspects of how children learn and what motivates them; of developmental sequences (in as far as we can identify them); and of learning difficulties and other special needs (see Sections 2 and 6 of this book).

You also need to develop curriculum knowledge, i.e. knowledge of National Curriculum requirements; of national strategies and project materials; of policies, guidelines and schemes of work; and of the range of published materials and sources available as 'tools of the trade' to help you teach your class. You cannot be expected to keep abreast of developments in every area but you can be expected to know to whom to turn for advice and to give advice in turn in any area of the curriculum where you act as a co-ordinator.

There are still others areas of professional knowledge you need to acquire. According to Shulman (1987) these include general pedagogical knowledge (including teaching strategies, techniques, classroom management and organisation), knowledge of educational contexts (ranging from the workings of small groups, the ways in which schools are organised, run, financed and governed, to the characteristics of communities and cultures) and knowledge of educational ends, purposes and values.

You can see that primary teaching involves much more than a knowledge of how to teach 'reading, writing and number' – a view too many politicians, local and national, seem to hold!

THE PURPOSES OF PRIMARY TEACHING

The state first provided elementary education for children of primary-school age in the latter half of the nineteenth century. The state system complemented a rather chaotic and ad hoc collection of schools established earlier by the churches. Now over 95 per cent of children aged four to eleven attend state primary schools and are taught by teachers employed by local education authorities but working to national requirements and guidelines such as the National Curriculum and the Code of Practice for Children with Special Educational Needs.

Over that period of time primary teaching has served a variety of purposes, though the relative importance of these has changed from time to time. As a primary teacher you will play a part in fulfilling these purposes. You will need to form your own view of their relative importance and decide how best to fulfil them or possibly subvert aspects of them.

One major purpose of primary teaching has been, and is, *instruction* – here broadly conceived to include the fostering of:

- procedural knowledge
  - helping children to acquire and use information, e.g. learning and applying the four rules of number, learning how to spell, learning facts in science or history
- conceptual knowledge
  - helping children to understand ideas
  - helping children to understand principles, e.g. learning how to conduct fair tests in science, learning the importance of chronology in history
- skills acquisition
  - helping children to acquire manipulative and other physical skills such as cutting, handwriting or gymnastics
  - helping children to acquire complex skills such as reading
- metacognitive knowledge
  - helping children to be more knowledgeable about how they learn and how they can improve their learning.

Over time the relative importance of these components has changed. In the nineteenth century most emphasis was placed on *procedural knowledge* and *skills acquisition*, often of an elementary kind. The latter half of the twentieth century saw an increasing emphasis on *conceptual knowledge* and more advanced *skills acquisition*. Currently there is a growing interest in fostering *metacognitive knowledge* (see Section 2). As a primary teacher in the early part of the twenty-first century you will need to foster all four components – not an easy task.

A second major purpose of primary teaching has been, and is, *socialisation*. Children need to be introduced into a wider society than the home; they need to be able to relate to their peers and to work with them. They need to be inducted into the norms and values of British society. They need to be socialised into the 'strange' world of school which operates very differently from most homes and involves a great deal of fundamental but often unacknowledged learning – graphically captured (for all time?) in Philip Jackson's brilliant first chapter in his book *Life in Classrooms* (1968). As a teacher, especially if you are an early years teacher, you will be a most significant agent in children's socialisation. This process has always been a major purpose of primary teaching, especially in the nineteenth century when large numbers of children entered formal education for the first time and had to be compelled to 'accept their place in society', as the Victorians might have put it. But it is still very significant today – partly as a result of our increasingly complex, rich multi-cultural society where the values of tolerance and respect for others are so much needed and where they can be fostered and reinforced from the minute children enter school. Contemporary children need to find a place – a comfortable, affirming place – in our society. Primary teaching needs to help them find it and make it their own.

Linked to socialisation is another function of primary teaching. Teachers are concerned with children's *welfare* – physical, mental, emotional and social. Primary schools are the most accessible 'outposts' of the welfare state as far as most parents and children are concerned. They are crucially important points of contact, especially for economically disadvantaged families. In the late nineteenth and early twentieth centuries primary teachers were particularly concerned for children's physical welfare – as illustrated by the introduction of school meals and medical inspections and the emphasis placed on physical training. In very recent years there has been a resurgence of concern about children's welfare. Now under the 'Every Child Matters' legislation, every primary teacher, including you, will have to work with other agents and agencies to promote children's well-being (see Section 8). Especially in the area of welfare it is not easy to decide on the limits of a teacher's care for their children (Nias 1997). This is yet another dimension to primary teaching – no wonder your course of teacher education is so crowded and this book so long!

There is a fourth function of primary teaching – and one with which you may feel uncomfortable. Traditionally primary teaching has also involved the *classification* of children in order to 'sort' them out for their secondary education. Classification wasn't a major purpose in Victorian times: the working-class children who were taught in the state elementary schools were not expected to go on to any form of secondary education. However, in the first three-quarters of the twentieth century primary teachers played a major part in identifying children of different abilities and preparing them for different forms of secondary education – grammar, secondary modern and, to a far lesser extent, technical education. That classification function still applies in those parts of the country that retain selective schools. However, I would argue that currently a different form of classification influences the practice of many primary teachers as a result of the introduction of national testing and the classification of children into levels. Too often children are described as 'level twos', 'level fours' etc., are classified as such, and given a subtly different curriculum so that these levels begin to define them in ways which narrow their views of themselves and their ability to learn. As a primary teacher you will need to work within the system as it is but you also have a professional duty to work to change it if, like me, you feel it works against the interests of children in your care.

Task 1.1.4
The purposes of primary teaching

In pairs consider the relative importance of the four purposes of primary teaching. Make a list of the kinds of activities teachers engage in related to each of the four purposes. Primary teachers in other countries do not necessarily see their role in these terms (see Alexander 2000). Should any of these purposes *not* apply to primary teaching in the United Kingdon? Why not?

SUMMARY: THE IMPORTANCE OF PRIMARY TEACHING

I hope that by now you have realised how demanding primary teaching is and how important it is, especially to the children themselves. Philip Jackson reminds us that children spend around 7,000 hours in primary school spread over six or seven years of their young lives. There is no other activity that occupies as much of the child's time as attending school.

> Apart from the bedroom there is no single enclosure in which he spends a longer time than he does in the classroom. During his primary school years he is a more familiar sight to his teacher than to his father, and possibly even his mother.
>
> (Jackson 1968: 5)

As his or her teacher you are an incredibly (and frighteningly) significant person; your teaching will help shape attitudes to learning at a most sensitive period in children's development. After all:

> These seven years are among the most vivid of our existence. Everyday is full of new experiences; the relatively static seems permanent; time seems to last much longer; *events and individuals leave deeper impressions and more lasting memories than later in life.* Without discussing what are the happiest years, we may at least agree that every stage of life should be lived for its own sake as happily and fully as possible. *We must above all respect this right on behalf of children, whose happiness is a good deal at the mercy of circumstances and people beyond their control.*
>
> (Scottish Education Department 1946: 5, my italics)

To return to my acrostic, becoming a primary school teacher is demanding, difficult and exhausting and at times can be a fazing experience. But it is also immensely rewarding, incredibly fascinating, never-for-a-moment boring (unless you make it so!), often very humorous and, because never-ending, always unfini….

Hopefully you are up for it?

ANNOTATED FURTHER READING

Alexander, R. (2000) *Culture and Pedagogy: International Comparisons in Primary Education*, Oxford: Blackwell. A fascinating analysis of primary teaching as practised in France, Russia, India, the United States and England.

Campbell, R.J. and Neill, S. (1995) *Primary Teachers at Work*, London: Routledge. Though over a decade old, its findings provide plenty of food for thought as to the nature of the demands, responsibilities and work of English infant and junior teachers.

Jackson, P. (1968) *Life in Classrooms*, New York: Holt, Rinehart and Winston. This offers a complementary but rather different characterisation of teaching primary-aged children to that offered in this unit. Nearly forty years on it is still the most evocative description of life as lived in classrooms.

Nias, J. (1989) *Primary Teachers Talking: A Study of Teaching at Work*, London: Routledge. This gets 'under the skin' of being a primary teacher based on in-depth interviews carried out over a number of years.

Nias, J. (1997) 'Would schools improve if teachers cared less?', *Education 3–13*, 25(3): 11–22. A thought-provoking essay on the place of care in primary teaching.

REFERENCES

Alexander, R. (2000) *Culture and Pedagogy: International Comparisons in Primary Education*, Oxford: Blackwell.

Campbell, R.J. and Neill, S. (1994) *Primary Teachers at Work*, London: Routledge.

Department for Education and Skills (DfES) and Teacher Training Agency (TTA) (2002) *Qualifying to Teach: Professional Standards for Qualified Teacher Status and Requirements for Initial Teacher Training*, London: Department for Education and Skills/Teacher Training Agency.

Eisner, E. (1979) *The Educational Imagination*, New York: Collier-Macmillan.

Jackson, P. (1968) *Life in Classrooms*, New York: Holt, Rinehart and Winston.

Marland, M. (1975) *The Craft of the Classroom*, London: Heinemann Educational.

Muijs, D. and Reynolds, D. (2001) *Effective Teaching: Evidence and Practice*, London: Paul Chapman.

Musgrove, F. and Taylor, P. (1969) *Society and the Teacher's Role*, London: Routledge and Kegan Paul.

Nias, J. (1997) 'Would schools improve if teachers cared less?', *Education 3–13*, 25(3): 11–22.

Scottish Education Department (1946) *Primary Education*, Edinburgh: His Majesty's Stationery Office.

Shulman, L. (1987) 'Knowledge and teaching: foundations of the new reforms', *Harvard Educational Review*, 57: 1–22.

Unit 1.2

Professionalism and Trainee Teachers

Denis Hayes

INTRODUCTION

To help ensure continued professional competence, national standards for qualified teacher status were established in the UK through what amounts to a national curriculum for pre-service education and training. To gain qualified teacher status (QTS), training providers (e.g. faculties of education) have to confirm that you have met all the required standards. In addition, an *induction year* has been established (DfEE 1999) to monitor your progress during the first year as a newly qualified teacher.

The quality of your relationships with pupils, parents and colleagues lie at the heart of your professionalism. Children look to you for example, guidance and inspiration to learn. Parents trust you to keep them informed about their children's progress. Colleagues rely on you for support, cooperation and making a positive contribution to the team effort. Above all else, your professional behaviour is evaluated in the way that you provide opportunities for children to succeed in learning.

OBJECTIVES

- to examine the content of the standards document regarding professional values and practice (DfES/ TTA 2002);
- to explore the practical implementation of each standard;
- to identify sources of evidence for meeting each standard;
- to offer case studies that illuminate key issues.

The information provided in the unit will refer specifically to the following aspects of teacher behaviour:

- promoting high expectations of pupils (Standard 1.1);
- treating children fairly and consistently (1.2);
- demonstrating positive values (1.3);
- communicating sensitively with parents (1.4);
- contributing to wider aspects of school life (1.5);
- involving support staff (1.6);
- evaluating the quality of teaching (1.7);
- demonstrating a responsible professional attitude (1.8).

STANDARDS FOR TRAINEE TEACHERS

You meet the standards relating to professional values and practice by convincing tutors and host teachers in school that you are able to apply them on a consistent basis. Meeting a professional standard is not simply a case of 'doing it once' to prove that you possess the ability, but learning to conduct yourself in such a way that these qualities are a recognisable part of your regular behaviour as a teacher. Consistency is a particularly important quality to possess in maintaining professional values and practice because colleagues and pupils in school must be confident that you will respond predictably and reasonably, even when under duress. Professional behaviour is the cornerstone of your work as a teacher, so must assume a high priority.

The following summaries relate specifically to each of the key standards for professional values and practice; however, this sub-division is purely for organisational reasons, as many of the standards are interdependent.

Promoting high expectations of pupils

The principle that every pupil deserves to receive a good education is reflected in the National Curriculum 2000 for England and Wales (DfEE/QCA 1999: 31):

> When planning, teachers should set high expectations and provide opportunities for all pupils to achieve, including boys and girls, pupils with special educational needs, pupils with disabilities, pupils from all social and cultural backgrounds, pupils of different ethnic groups including travellers, refugees and asylum seekers, and those from diverse linguistic backgrounds.

Qualifying to Teach (DfEE/TTA 2002) also stresses that your professional values and practice should be based on having high expectations of all pupils and being committed to raising their educational achievement. It is therefore essential for you to treat pupils with courtesy and consideration and show concern for their development as learners. This approach involves giving all children full opportunity to learn without hindrance and providing them with benchmarks for success.

You should not confuse high expectations with unreasonable ones. For instance, setting tasks that are too demanding can quickly lead to pupil demoralisation and a lowering of self-esteem. The success with which you establish and maintain expectations will depend to a considerable extent on your ability to assess each pupil's knowledge and grasp of concepts. The greater your skill in assessment, the more precise you can be in setting work that suits a child's capability.

Your expectations should not only relate to academic success but extend to standards of behaviour. A small number of children choose to misbehave rather than to apply themselves to their work. Others do not apply themselves to the work because they are confused about where the boundaries lie. Yet others may come from a home background in which success in school is not regarded as a priority. As the teacher you have to establish and maintain high expectations while taking account of the different factors that impinge upon achievement; namely, pupil motivation, confidence, natural ability, willingness to persevere, personality and even state of health. Your decisions about what is and what is not acceptable from each child will depend in part on these factors but also on your own skill in putting across the lesson, maintaining interest and managing learning.

Over time your judgements will become better informed and more perceptive. In turn, pupils will feel comfortable with the demands that you ask of them and be more likely to apply themselves enthusiastically to the tasks. This confidence will translate into more assured classroom practice and help with your acceptance as a teacher.

Treating children fairly and consistently

Discrimination is not allowed in schools on any basis whatsoever (e.g. see DfES 2003). Furthermore, all qualified teachers must recognise and respond effectively to equal opportunities issues and challenge incidents of bullying and harassment. Showing deliberate or unintentional bias towards pupils which can be construed as discriminatory leaves you open to charges of unprofessional conduct, so it is important to be as impartial as possible at all times.

Not only must all children be granted the same curriculum opportunities, support and encouragement, but it is not appropriate to label children due to circumstances beyond their control such as home background or physical appearance. A teasing pleasantry about a child's looks or domestic circumstances may be more hurtful and do greater damage than you imagine. A useful antidote to discriminatory attitudes is to develop a positive attitude towards achievement and to adopt an 'all things are possible' working atmosphere in which children are resolute in facing challenges without fear of recrimination. One way and another, it is part of your responsibility to treat children respectfully, even when their behaviour does not warrant it.

Particular care needs to be paid to communicating effectively with children for whom English is an additional language. In such cases, strategies include the use of steady, well articulated speech, the availability of learning aids and making a special effort to involve all the children in creative activities where spoken English is not essential to complete the work and gain fulfilment. As some children may become frustrated by their inability to conform and contribute to classroom discussion, enlisting the help of a sympathetic child (a 'buddy') to help them to adjust, and the close involvement of teaching assistants who possess appropriate language skills are important strategies. It is important for you to remember that EAL children may be bright and articulate in their first tongue, so they should not be given a surfeit of trivial or repetitive tasks to keep them occupied on the assumption they are unable to cope with the more demanding work.

Task 1.2.1
Relating to pupils

In your mind divide your class list into three groups: (1) children that I enjoy teaching; (2) children that I don't relate to particularly well; (3) children that I wish were in someone else's class. Over the next few days make a determined effort to view all children as (1) and resist the temptation to blame them for problems that arise. Monitor how adopting such a positive attitude transforms the way that you approach your teaching.

Demonstrating positive values through your attitude

In recent years the emphasis has moved away from arguing the case for teaching as a profession to an examination of what it means to be *professional*. In other words, the focus has shifted from a consideration of whether teaching fulfils the necessary criteria (properly qualified and remunerated, a defined career structure, etc.) to the application of the positive values deemed to characterise a professional person in a variety of contexts. There are a number of aspects of professionalism that you must come to terms with in addition to teaching, such as caring for children, working with colleagues, dealing with parents, evaluating your progress as a teacher and contributing your expertise and knowledge to the team effort.

Although there are subtle variations in different schools about indicators of appropriate professional behaviour, it is taken for granted that you will set a good example through your appearance, speech and response to situations. This assumption does not, of course, necessitate that you should suppress your personality and become stilted, but that immature behaviour is strictly off-limits! Furthermore, you have to take some responsibility for your own professional development by keeping up-to-date with research and theories in teaching and possessing an understanding of school policies and practices in pastoral areas, personal safety matters and bullying.

As a new teacher and a guest in school you need to adjust quickly to the existing school culture; balance your enthusiasm with watchfulness; listen, respond and accommodate fresh thinking; and learn how to 'stand outside' yourself and evaluate your progress in terms of the way in which you project positive values through what you say and do.

Paul had been a successful manager before deciding to train as a teacher. He was used to being the person in charge and, despite his sparkling personality, found it hard to accept advice when he had relied on his own wits and instincts so much in the past. Paul had strong interpersonal skills and related well to other adults, especially parents and non-teaching staff, which occasionally distracted him from other classroom duties. The inexperienced class teacher in whose classroom Paul was placed was unsure about how to approach the situation, but the more experienced school mentor had no such qualms and spoke to Paul at length and unequivocally about the situation. Paul accepted the criticisms with grace and made a strenuous effort to conform. During his next and final school placement Paul was so well regarded that he was short-listed for a vacancy and appointed at the school as an NQT.

Communicating sensitively with parents

Parents are the first educators of their children. A report for the DfES about the impact of parental involvement on pupils' education found that what parents do with their children at home is the single most significant factor in fostering academic success (Desforges and Abouchaar 2003). Parents teach their children particular sets of values, set boundaries for their behaviour and show them the consequences of disobedience. They talk to their children and answer their questions. They show them books, introduce them to games and offer them opportunities to play alone and with friends. Once formal schooling begins, teachers assume some of the responsibility, but the closer your partnership with parents, the more likely that the children will benefit from the combined efforts of both parties. Some schools provide training evenings for parents who are interested in knowing more about how they can help their children directly.

Parents who are struggling with life will sometimes come into school to seek comfort or reassurance from you, but it pays to be cautious about being drawn into delicate discussions. If you find that a parent is keeping you from your duties it is quite in order to say something to the effect that you are sorry to have to interrupt them, but you will be in trouble if you don't get back to work. A cheery goodbye as you walk away may provide the spark of encouragement that the parent requires. It is important that you never release information about another child or discuss his or her progress with anyone other than the parent or legal guardian.

Legislation has established the rights of parents to be well-informed about the curriculum offered by each school and to know about their child's progress through reports and informal access to teachers (see, for example, Beveridge 2004). With each school's budget depending in large measure upon the number of pupils on roll, there is extra incentive for head teachers and governors to ensure that parents are welcomed and made to feel part of the school community. Parent areas are a common feature of primary schools and almost every school has regular meetings with groups of parents in a parent-teacher forum. This often provides the impetus for fund-raising, school events, and (sometimes) policy decisions.

Formal contact with parents takes many forms but is usually based on a set of appointments drawn up for them to come in to the school during the late afternoon or evening. You will not normally have to undertake anything more than a practice event with the teacher playing the part of a parent but you should take any opportunity to sit alongside the teacher during a formal event if given the opportunity, both to learn strategies and to experience some of the strong emotions attached to the occasion. Very few parents want to trick teachers or intimidate them, so it is worth viewing contact with parents as a wonderful opportunity to celebrate achievement and share information, ideas and concerns, in addition to giving them facts and figures about academic attainment.

Contributing to wider aspects of school life

While on school placement, you become temporary, full-time members of the staff but the transition from being an outsider to an accepted member of the team (the 'rite of passage') is never smooth (Eisenhart *et al.* 1991). The rite of passage model describes how you pass through three principal stages as you are assimilated into the life of the school: separation, transition and incorporation. Thus, you first have to psychologically separate yourself from the procedures and priorities gained from the previous school experience. You then absorb the different expectations of the new school situation, eventually becoming incorporated into its ways and expectations. Although you may be given advice about how to behave in appropriate ways in school (enthusiastic, courteous and dependable) and general teaching skills (planning, motivating pupils, managing the class, assessing progress) the process of enculturation into the new school setting relies heavily on advice from the host teachers. As a result, negotiating the rite of passage depends on your ability to 'read' the situation with guidance from staff and respond appropriately. You may fit in to one school placement setting with ease and yet struggle in the next, depending on your skill in accommodating the way things are done there and responding appropriately (Nias 1989).

No school placement runs smoothly all the time and there are bound to be occasions when you experience self-doubt. However, an important part of your rite of passage is to learn to work under pressure without becoming overwhelmed, and demonstrating wholehearted commitment to the work. Paying attention to small points of your behaviour makes a considerable difference to the way in which you contribute to school life:

- acknowledging the presence of teachers and ancillary staff by a pleasant word and smile;
- expressing your gratitude for advice, assistance and guidance from teachers and assistants;
- volunteering to help with practical tasks and providing some resources for lessons;
- showing that you are serious about the job by maintaining your teaching file, keeping up-to-date with planning and responding to advice.

There are numerous ways of contributing practically to school life, including assisting with clubs, helping teachers with supervisory duties and volunteering to help with outings. Whatever way you choose to demonstrate that you are wholeheartedly committed, it is nevertheless essential to remember that the first call on your energy and expertise relates to lesson preparation and teaching.

> Trudy, a mature trainee, determined that she was going to throw herself wholeheartedly into school life. She was highly conscientious and worked late every evening. Her file was immaculate and the tutor commended the quality of her teaching. In addition, Trudy volunteered to help with a lunchtime club and an after-school homework club. She was a bright presence around the school and interacted breezily with staff and parents. Initially the class teacher was delighted to have such an exceptional student, but after a few weeks Trudy began to find difficulty with her teaching, became quite reclusive and looked permanently tired. The second half of the placement was much less successful than the first half and Trudy only just struggled through to the end. Instead of pacing herself she had expended too much effort early on and simply ran out of steam.

Task 1.2.2
Contributing to the corporate life of the school

Consider how your colleagues in school would respond if asked the following questions about you.

- What is your prevailing countenance: gloomy, cheerful, unpredictable?
- Do you seem pleased to be in the school?
- Do you like the children?
- What attempt do you make to be friendly to ancillary staff?

On the basis of these predicted responses make a conscious effort to improve in all four areas by

- Trying to be cheerful.
- Making positive comments about the work situation.
- Speaking warmly about the children and *to* the children.
- Determining to treat everyone in a friendly, non-patronising way.

Involving other adults

The use of assistants to support children's learning and help the teacher to organise and manage the classroom is common in primary schools. Voluntary help from parents and young people on work experience can also make a significant contribution to the learning programme. If the assistant is paid, she or he is usually referred to as a Teaching Assistant (TA) and will have a job description to which she or he is required to conform. A TA who works on a one-to-one basis with a child identified as having special learning needs is sometimes known as a Learning Support Assistant (LSA). TAs are gradually assuming more responsibility for pupils' learning and there has been a large increase in their numbers to support the work of class teachers. The development of Higher Level Teaching Assistants (HLTA) to take a more active and direct role in pupils' learning is a key initiative in England, though their precise role is still being worked through (TTA 2004).

Involvement of large numbers of TAs to support children's learning means that you must develop new management skills, both in knowing how to relate to TAs and how to use their knowledge and skills profitably. Many teachers try to set aside a time each week to discuss matters of mutual concern, thank assistants for their efforts and acknowledge their contribution. If the assistant has been at the school for a long time and has become attached to a particular way of working, it may be difficult for you to implement changes. Under such circumstances, you need diplomacy and patience to make adjustments.

All assistants, whether paid TAs or parent helpers, benefit from being clear about your expectations and being involved in tasks that require more than 'babysitting' a group of children. Rather than letting the TA be a passive onlooker during the time that you interact with the children, it may be appropriate to ask her/him to pay special attention to the responses and involvement of individual pupils that you have identified. Subsequently, the TA is able to provide illuminative feedback that will provide detailed insights into the children's learning that you could not possibly accrue on your own. If the assistant is a parent, your reputation can hinge on the informal conversations that the assistant has with neighbours and friends about you!

> Although Meena loved children she had always been shy with adults. The class teacher was impressed by Meena's diligence and natural manner when teaching but anxious about her inhibitions. Entering the staffroom caused Meena particular anguish and so she avoided doing so whenever possible. The situation became so serious that the faculty tutor was asked to mediate, as on the one hand Meena was a very capable classroom teacher but on the other hand her impact on the corporate life of the school was negligible. There were also concerns about how she would relate to parents, but inexplicably Meena proved to be skilled in this area and was not at all fazed. It was decided that Meena should be nurtured rather than criticised. As a result of the careful and sensitive treatment she received, Meena became much more confident and was eventually appointed as a reception teacher in a local school.

Task 1.2.3
Relating to adults in school

Keep a mental record of how many adults you communicate with in school in the following ways:

1   A nodding encounter.
2   Exchanging a few words.
3   An extended conversation.

Over the following week, make an effort to improve the level of communication by moving more of (1) into (2) and (2) into (3). Monitor how participants' attitudes towards you alter and the impacts upon your confidence and sense of belonging.

Evaluating the quality of teaching

An important element of professional responsibility is the need to interrogate your own practice, evaluate its quality and see how you can improve your effectiveness as a practitioner. Broadly speaking there are two ways to approach the evaluation: (1) by reflecting *during* your teaching and (2) by reflecting *retrospectively*. Carrying out an evaluation *during* teaching requires you to be alert to what is happening around you in the classroom and how successful you are being in accomplishing what you set out to do. Although you are bound to make subtle changes instinctively as children respond to you and apply themselves to the tasks, it is also important to 'talk inwardly' to yourself as the lesson proceeds. This internal conversation requires determination and self-discipline as you re-conceptualise ideas and re-formulate your actions. Effective teachers carry out this internal dialogue so spontaneously that they make everything seem effortless, but don't be fooled by the apparent ease with which they negotiate classroom life.

The same principles of determination and self-discipline also apply to your *retrospective* evaluations, which usually involve a written element. If your lesson has been observed, it is normal to receive feedback (written, spoken or both) from the tutor or mentor, and spend time discussing its strengths and shortcomings. In addition, most trainees are expected to keep a reflective journal in which they identify key points and, in the case of weaker aspects, indicate the action they intend to take. A simple way to approach your reflective writing is to adopt a threefold perspective. The first perspective focuses on the adequacy of your planning and resources, the second on your own role and the third on the children's responses. Thus, under *planning and resources* you may want to comment on:

- thoroughness of planning (amount of detail, consideration of practicalities);
- appropriateness of planning (specified learning intentions, adequacy of differentiation);
- employment of resources (consumables and equipment, availability, distribution and organisation);
- equal opportunity issues (consideration for the needs of gifted and slow learners, pupils for whom English is an additional language);
- health and safety issues (training the children, clarity about use of equipment, awareness of hazards).

When considering your *own role* you may want to comment on:

- the efficiency of your pre-lesson organisation;
- your success in engaging children and holding their attention;

- the clarity with which you presented and explained ideas;
- the way that you managed pupils' learning.

A written evaluation of the *children's responses* might include:

- their willingness to answer and ask questions;
- the enthusiasm with which they attended to their work;
- their general behaviour and purposefulness.

It is not necessary to comment on all three dimensions referred to above on every occasion. You may, in discussion with the tutor, wish to concentrate on a specific aspect that was identified as a priority in a previous discussion (a 'target'). In doing so it is important to remind yourself that children need warm human beings, not depersonalised evaluators, to correct their misdemeanours and celebrate their successes. In short, when judging the extent of your teaching success you should not only view it in terms of a list of stated requirements (adequate planning, organisation, management and assessment) but in terms of the extent to which you evoke children's enthusiasm for learning and thirst for knowledge.

Demonstrating a responsible professional attitude

Acceptance in school is not a simple case of whether you are welcomed or whether you are not. Some trainees get disgruntled if they don't immediately feel welcomed by all staff, but they fail to recognise the subtleties of interpersonal and professional relationships existing in a school. It is an evolving process, untidy and difficult to define precisely. In developing a professional approach to teaching, it is essential for you to be positive about life in general, avoid the temptation to moan and give due consideration to other people's ideas. Other attributes include 'active' listening, speaking openly yet courteously and being willing to learn from colleagues. Practical considerations include arriving well before school, using time productively and gaining a solid reputation as an effective practitioner or, at least, someone with the potential to become one. Professionalism entails that you are open with every member of staff and empathise with individual concerns and predicaments. Trainees who make an effort to be pleasant, show an interest in the children and establish a harmonious relationship with parents and carers not only endear themselves to all concerned but also elicit a great deal of valuable information about pupils' lives out of school. Your personality, attitude to children in the classroom, pleasantness during informal contacts, willingness to take time finding out something of a child's interests and approach to learning will make their mark. Remember that you are talked about regularly at home and at the school gate; your reputation goes before you and influences parents' reactions and pupils' attitudes towards school.

EVIDENCE OF SUCCESS

Providing *evidence* that you have met the standards in values and practice is not as straightforward as with other areas of professional competence. For instance, whereas it is relatively simple to show that you have carried out an assessment of a child's work or differentiated activities in plans, it is far harder to demonstrate, say, that you have treated pupils consistently or shown sensitivity towards parents and carers. Nevertheless, an ethic of care and concern for others and open, sincere relationships with adults and children should underpin all that you do and say as an emerging professional.

Evidence checklist for professional values and practice

1.1   Your lesson plans, introductions, level of activities, encouragement to achieve and feedback to children clearly indicate your expectations of them.

1.2   You make every effort to ensure that each child has a fair share of your time and opportunity to access resources and ask questions.

1.3   You speak and react calmly to children, express an interest in them as significant individuals, show a healthy regard for their opinions and care for their needs.

1.4   You speak courteously to parents and show genuine interest in their opinions, offering helpful comments about their child's academic and social progress.

1.5   You are positive about school life by what you say and make an effort to contribute your expertise and practical support in extra-curricular activities.

1.6   You make every effort to work in harmony with support staff, involve them in your planning where appropriate and use their expertise to enhance pupil learning.

1.7   You are willing to listen to advice and act upon it, offer suggestions about improving your teaching and draw on the effective practice of others.

1.8   You are familiar with the legal requirements for teachers, the school policies for behaviour and health and safety, and exercise sensible judgement about their implementation.

SUMMARY

Demonstrating professionalism as a trainee teacher encompasses far more than possessing the technical ability to teach. You need strong subject knowledge but also the skills and strategies to engage children in learning, enthuse them about the work and give them opportunities for success. You need to teach consistently but also to inject imagination and creativity into your lessons and empower children to do the same in their learning. You need to relate to colleagues socially but also prove that you are reliable, flexible and willing to learn so that you can improve your practice. You need to relate well to parents but also show that you genuinely care about their children and want them to be happy, motivated and successful.

Professionalism as a trainee teacher involves much more than conforming to a set of standards. It is behaving and responding in such a positive, responsible and determined way that, despite your inexperience, you are viewed and treated as an integral member of the staff team.

ANNOTATED FURTHER READING

Arthur, J., Davison, J. and Lewis, M. (2004) *Professional Values and Practice: Achieving the Standards for QTS*, Abingdon: RoutledgeFalmer. A comprehensive description of what needs to be known, understood and demonstrated to achieve each standard.

Browne, A. and Haylock, D. (eds) (2004) *Professional Issues for Primary Teachers*, London: Paul Chapman. A text that deals thoroughly with the key professional issues faced by student teachers and practising teachers.

Day, C. (2004) *A Passion for Teaching*, Abingdon: RoutledgeFalmer. A powerful amalgam of ways in which teachers can bring commitment, enthusiasm, intellect and emotional energy into their teaching and relationships in school.

Fenstermacher, G.D. (2004) 'The concept of manner and its visibility', in E.C. Wragg (ed.) *The RoutledgeFalmer Reader in Teaching and Learning*, pp. 123–35, Abingdon: RoutledgeFalmer. Highlights the importance of teacher manner in fostering pupils' moral and intellectual development.

Nias, J. (1997) 'Would schools improve if teachers cared less?', *Education 3–13*, 25: 3, 11–22. A thought-provoking article about the implications of caring for effective teaching.

REFERENCES

Beveridge, S. (2004) *Children, Families and Schools: Developing Partnerships for Inclusive Education*, Abingdon: RoutledgeFalmer.

Department for Education and Employment (DfEE) (1999) *The Induction Period for Newly Qualified Teachers*, Sudbury: DfEE Publications.

Department for Education and Employment/QCA (1999) *The National Curriculum: Handbook for Primary Teachers in England Key Stages 1 and 2*, London: DfEE/QCA.

Department for Education and Skills/TTA (2002) *Qualifying to Teach: Professional Standards for Qualified Teacher Status and Requirements for Initial Teacher Training*, London: TTA.

Department for Education and Skills (2003) *Aiming High: Raising the Achievements of Minority Ethnic Pupils*, London: Crown Copyright.

Desforges, C. and Abouchaar, A. (2003) *The Impact of Parental Involvement, Parental Support and Family Education on Pupil Achievement and Adjustment: A Literature Review*, Research Report 433 for the DfES, London: Queen's Printer Copyright; www.dfes.gov.uk/research/ (accessed March 2006).

Eisenhart, M., Behm, L. and Romagno, L. (1991) 'Learning to teach: developing expertise or rite of passage?', *Journal of Education for Teaching*, 17: 1, 51–71.

Nias, J. (1989) *Primary Teachers Talking: A Study of Teaching at Work*, London: Routledge.

Teacher Training Agency (2004) Website for HLTA Standards: www.hlta.gov.uk (accessed March 2006).

2 Exploring the Nature of Learning and Teaching

Unit 2.1

Looking at Children

Tricia David

INTRODUCTION

This unit is intended to help you look at children – the general patterns of their development, but also how and why they may develop in different ways, and why it is important that you, as a teacher, know about child development as well as being knowledgeable about curriculum subjects and teaching strategies. We will also explore the current legislative context and how this impinges on your role as a teacher. Additionally, the unit will draw your attention to the influence of children's home lives and family relationships on their learning. You will be asked to *observe* and *listen to* children; to *reflect on your own childhood* – it may have predisposed you to think in certain ways; to explore how the *ecological niche* you inhabited was similar to and different from those of the children you meet in your training and work; and to remember that *each child is a unique person*.

OBJECTIVES

By the end of the unit you should be beginning to:

- recognise why teachers need to be knowledgeable about child development;
- understand patterns of children's development and know how and why they may vary;
- understand how an individual child's 'world' of family, friends, school and other contexts familiar to them influences their ability to 'make sense' of their learning;
- know about the United Nations Convention on the Rights of the Child and the recent Children Act in this country, and about some of their implications for schools and teachers;
- recognise that each child is a *person*, whatever their age.

WHY DO TEACHERS NEED TO KNOW ABOUT CHILD DEVELOPMENT?

One of the reasons why we, as teachers, need to know about the patterns of children's development is that we then have a notion of what children are capable of and what they may have already achieved. Another positive aspect in favour of your being well-informed about general patterns of development is that you will be able to reflect on your observations of the children in your class or school and explore, where necessary, why certain children's development may be delayed or different from that of their peers.

Less than half a century ago, the American psychologist William Kessen became fascinated by the ways in which societies shape children and their childhoods. He came to recognise, after visiting Communist China, that, with children's collusion, each culture 'invents' its children (Kessen 1979). Kessen and others were to cast doubt on the fixed and universal view of children's development that had held sway among developmental psychologists for some time. The idea that children follow fixed patterns of psychological development as well as physical growth underpins a pervasive understanding of them as *adults-in-the-making*, somehow unfinished and incapable.

Today we acknowledge the importance of both *nature* and *nurture*, seeing them as interdependent aspects of human development. Development itself is no longer regarded as a given, as simply a matter of maturation, but as a process that happens when the human body, especially the brain, receives appropriate nourishment, stimulation and challenge. In other words, nature and nurture are synergistic.

The problem with knowing only about certain theories and even research evidence about child development is that this may predispose you to have fixed views and expectations, rather than understanding that the time and place in which children live impacts on that development. Social, or cultural, constructions of childhood are now recognised as influencing children's psychological development (see, for example, James *et al.* 1998). For example, while children's teeth may erupt in roughly similar patterns irrespective of the country in which they are growing up, their ability to read fluently by the age of six will vary because of the understandings and expectations in that country. In England children are deemed to be failing if they cannot read relatively fluently by the end of KS1, while in most other European countries children are not learning to read in any formal sense until they are this age.

So knowing general patterns of development can help you relate appropriately to children at particular stages but we must always be aware of the pitfalls of applying child development theories too rigidly. After all, the theories are themselves constructed in specific cultural contexts and as such are therefore likely to reflect the understandings and assumptions about children held in that society or community (David *et al.* 2003).

This short unit cannot do justice to all that has been written about children's development. Information about theories and research relevant to this age group comprises a vast body of work. What I intend to do therefore is to outline key aspects of development between birth and eleven years of age and provide references to relevant follow-up texts.

However, here are some more 'health warnings' about overly rigid thinking concerning development. First, although I am using global phases in what follows, any suggestion of 'stages' should immediately ring alarm bells, because children's development is individual. Physical growth, under healthy conditions, may mean that children progress to adult stature and sexual maturity in much the same patterns, irrespective of where they live, so that, for example, most children at age two are half their ultimate adult height and girls reach their adult height earlier than do boys. Nevertheless, it is important to note that poverty impacts on both physical health and psychological development (Wilkinson 1994; Penn 2005). There may also be differences between children as a result of congenital conditions, illnesses or disabilities which may predispose some children to find certain areas of learning more difficult than their peers do (Lewis 1996; Wall 2003).

Psychological development is neither continuous, smooth nor universal. It depends what the child's community expects of him or her – and even these expectations may be different for different children, boys/girls, rich/poor, black/white, born with a recognisable disability/not, etc. For example, Penn (2005) points out that in some Inuit tribes in Canada the young children are expert map makers. Konner (1991) relates how children under seven in parts of Cameroon will gather herbs, cut them up, mix and cook them for medicine for sick friends. Similarly, three hundred years ago Daniel Defoe argued that parents were irresponsible if they did not ensure their offspring had a trade by the age of five, by which they could earn a living should the parents die. Children are subjected to different assumptions and expectations in different communities. They live up or down to these assumptions and expectations, actively participating in the construction of these differing childhoods.

Our society is now very complex and there is much to learn during the years of childhood, thus the dominant construction of childhood in the Western/Minority World is one which has resulted in a definition of childhood that ranges from birth to eighteen and requires many years of schooling (or a legally accepted alternative). The context created by these conditions means that even the researchers and theorists working to further our understandings of children's development are affected by these assumptions and expectations.

Traditionally developmental psychologists tended to carry out research and to report their findings in ways which meant children's development was compartmentalised. More recently it is being acknowledged that although research focusing on one area, such as cognitive, emotional, physical or social development, reduces complexity in the investigation, it also reduces awareness of the complexity of real children's development. Recognising this complexity has made life more complicated for the researchers, and it means that as teachers we too need to note how children's emotional, social, physical and cognitive development are interrelated. Further, researchers (Deloache and Brown 1987, among others) have begun to point out that many published child development findings underestimate children's capabilities, either because the children were 'tested' in unnatural surroundings or because the type of research methods used excluded reporting on children's potential and achievements by those most familiar with them.

KEY ASPECTS OF CHILDREN'S DEVELOPMENT DURING THE YEARS FROM BIRTH TO THE END OF PRIMARY SCHOOL

Key theorists and researchers who have influenced thinking and practice in the field of Education during the early phases of life and learning are:

- Jean Piaget (1955), Lev Vygotsky (1978), Jerome Bruner (1986), Margaret Donaldson (1978) – on thinking.
- Urie Bronfenbrenner (1979), Albert Bandura (1992), Carol Gilligan (1982), Barbara Rogoff (1990), Michael Cole (1996) – on how contexts impact on development.
- Sigmund Freud (1991), D.W. Winnicott (1964), John Bowlby (1953), Judy Dunn (1993) on emotions.
- B.F. Skinner (1938), Jean Piaget (1955), Noam Chomsky (1975) – on language development.

(The references given are examples of their work. You will find many other books and articles by these prolific thinkers and writers. You might also look at David *et al.* 2003 and Penn 2005 for recent summaries and discussions of their work related to practice with young children. See, for example,

Bee 1989, Davies 1999 for fuller information about child development research and theory; see Morss 1990, Singer 1992, Burman 1994, Walkerdine 1999 for critiques of child development theories; and MacNaughton 2003, for explanations of the implications of numerous theories for teaching young children.)

Much of the research on how children develop has been carried out in the United States, so it is important that you are cautious in applying theories or research findings without also observing and listening to children to see if reality matches text. Fleer (2003) discusses this issue in relation to the application of theories to children from ethnic minorities. For this reason I will be asking you to carry out tasks in order to reflect on similarities and differences between real children's capabilities and what we are led to believe.

Task 2.1.1
Reflect on your own childhood

Think back to an event during your own childhood (between the ages of three and eleven). Why has the memory stayed with you? What did you learn from that event? Is it possible to derive a principle for your own teaching as a result of that experience?

From the moment a baby is born, possibly even during their time in the womb, they are learning about their world – their own, individual *ecological niche*, trying to make sense of it all. They will use all their senses to find out about the context in which they find themselves. Taste, smell, hearing and touch will be stronger than sight at first. Researchers (Karmiloff and Karmiloff-Smith 2001) have pointed out that before birth babies have been listening to the languages they hear in their homes, so that as neonates they are capable of differentiating the speech patterns of the languages that are familiar to them from those that are not. Neuroscientists (Gopnik *et al.* 1999) have amassed research evidence demonstrating how the baby's brain is a tangle of neurons that activate vigorously, making millions of connections – connections stimulated into action by sensory inputs, that is, by experiences. Clearly babies become more and more able to use this amazing facility for brain development as they become more able to control their own movements, first as they manage to control their eyes and head, then in sitting up to look at what is going on around them, later by crawling, standing and walking, and by talking and interacting. It is thought that babies come into the world 'programmed' to be social, to want human contact and interaction. Their curiosity about how the world 'works', whether that be in the objects they find and play with, or the people and what they do, means they are insatiable learners (see for example Gerhardt 2004; Robinson 2003). The DfES recently produced guidelines (DfES 2003) for practitioners who work with children from birth to three, in an effort to ensure that this first phase of learning is not wasted through either inappropriate adult-led formalisation or equally inappropriate, neglectful laissez faire.

By the time a child is three, they are usually very mobile, can express themselves and engage in imaginative play, know a great deal about their environments, and above all are sophisticated experts on the strengths and weaknesses of their parents, siblings and friends and can manipulate those closest to them by teasing or feigning crying. But this social adeptness at 'mind reading' means they also show empathy (Dunn 1993).

During the later part of this phase, known educationally as the Foundation Stage (three to five years old) in this country, this insatiable thirst for learning continues, unless attempts at independence and exploration have been thwarted. Children at this age are highly self-motivated and eager to be with other children, to learn through play and talk. Recent research (BERA 2003) suggests that the most appropriate teaching at this stage involves adults

- being good observers (so individual children's personal interests and learning styles can be taken into account);
- engaging in joint exploration and experimentation;
- being able to join in children's activities without taking over but, among other things, by extending learning through interaction, encouraging recall and metacognition, the provision of props and careful planning for further development of the play activity.

During the years from five to eleven children's body shape will have been changing, their heads taking up a smaller proportion of their height compared with the very early years. In babyhood, their relatively large heads accommodated their large 'plastic' human brain, a brain that is capable of learning and adaptation throughout life, with no truly critical periods. A *critical period* is one where an aspect of development may be arrested if particular stimuli are not presented to an organism. Although psychologists argue that humans do not have critical periods, they do suggest there may be *sensitive periods* when certain experiences maximise potential. The most important point about this is that human development can continue and omissions can be remedied. An example of this comes from research with refugee children (Rutter *et al.* 1998).

Children's rate of growth in height and weight slows down during the years from five to eleven, the most rapid growth having occurred between birth and two. Other bodily changes which continue from babyhood right through to adolescence include increases in the number of bones (a one-year-old has only three wrist bones, an adult has nine); the hardness and size of bones also increase. Similarly, as children grow their muscle tissue develops so that their strength increases. The layer of subcutaneous fat which started in the womb peaks at nine months and declines until around six or seven years of age. Looking at aspects of children's physical development draws our attention to the fact that they need to move around, requiring physical challenges to promote growth and to develop coordination through appropriate activities. Some researchers (e.g. Goddard Blythe 2000) argue that being expected to sit still for relatively long periods may be both painful and detrimental to young children.

Once they have been admitted to primary school, children's friendships, already important since the age of two, will become even more central to their lives and identity development. Peer groups, shared cultures, the growing interest in more organised games, and their influence can be observed in the playground.

Task 2.1.2
Observe a group of children in the playground

Hillman *et al.* (1990) found that children's freedom and mobility have been seriously curtailed during the last few decades. Many parents are afraid to allow their children to go out without supervision because of dangers on the roads and fear of abduction.

Observe a group of children playing – how is their play different from that you and your friends engaged in? What does this tell you about children's lives today? What do the similarities in their play to that of your generation tell you about children?

The researcher Barbara Rogoff (1990) built on the work of Vygotsky and Piaget to argue that a child's social world is the key to their development. In societies which encourage individuality and independence children will compete with siblings and peers, whereas communities which seek to develop interdependence will raise their children more communally, including them in most areas of life and not regarding the needs of the young as conflicting with their own. She thus concludes that opportunities for shared thinking and guided participation are important elements of apprenticeship in thinking and intellectual competence. Children need shared challenges with both other children and with adults. The idea of each human being as a 'lone learner' has been seriously undermined (see also Gipps and McGilchrist 1999). In a similar way, theories of language development have been subjected to critiques (Bloom and Tinker 2001) and most recently the *intentionality* of the child has been highlighted. This further promotes the idea that language and cognitive development are interconnected.

In other words, the importance of seeing children as competent, strong agents, participating in their families and communities, rather than as passive, helpless victims of circumstance totally dependent on adults, has emerged as a new model of childhood. This does not mean that you and I as adults no longer have responsibilities for children, in fact quite the reverse. The 1989 Children Act was the first in the UK to acknowledge that children's views, wishes and feelings must be taken into account by parents and professionals. Further, for the first time, UK legislation adopted the concept of parental responsibility, as opposed to parents' rights. These legal developments and the more recent 2004 Children Act, mean that the context in which you will be working with children is a rapidly changing one and is very different from the one you experienced as a pupil.

LEARNING AND PLAY

Play as a vehicle for learning has been seen largely as an approach to be adopted in early years settings, rather than in classrooms in KS1 and 2, in spite of recommendations concerning its efficacy for a wider age range (Moyles 2005). Nevertheless, it is important to note that researchers have suggested there are phases to play (Hutt *et al*. 1989). First a child behaves as if asking the question 'What does this do?' (of whatever material or experience they are exploring to gain knowledge) and this is known as the *epistemic* phase of play. After a period of serious investigation, the child will begin to act as if asking the question 'What can I do with this?', the *ludic* phase, which usually entails smiling, joking and having fun. Both phases are necessary in order that the child incorporates the new knowledge or skills gained in the first phase into their repertoire.

You will find that play approaches to learning have advantages over more didactic teaching but they do not preclude your sensitive involvement as teacher, being the 'scaffolder' of learning or 'model' for the 'apprentice' thinker (Nelson 1986; Rogoff 1990). When children are given opportunities to learn through play you will find that:

- children are intrinsically motivated to be involved;
- they pose 'questions' of play to themselves, rather than trying to find a 'right answer', so play is non-threatening, although it is frequently challenging;
- the children's 'ownership' and control of the situation, as learners, strengthens both their motivation and their learning;
- the 'what if' quality of play encourages creativity; rules can be invented and broken;
- social development is occurring during play;
- different forms of play exercise the body and mind;
- play is pleasurable!

(adapted from David and Nurse 1999: 171–2)

As children become older, during KS1, you will usually find that they begin to enjoy play with rules. Although younger children are able to take part in games with set rules, they do not always want to follow them and may not understand the need to do so. For example, Ceris (four) loved to play Happy Families (with cards depicting animals) but when asked refused to give another player either the Miss Mouse or Miss Rabbit cards. She would reply, 'Sorry, you can't have it because it's my favourite.' Meanwhile, Eliot (at seven) polices the board and card games he plays with his family, remembering intricate rules as laid down in the printed instructions.

OBSERVING CHILDREN

One of the most important skills we can develop as teachers is that of observation. You will become adept at remembering or recording (perhaps initially on post-it notes) what you have seen and heard individuals or small groups of children doing or saying. You can then reflect upon your notes and you will have evidence-based knowledge of each child's achievements. You can use this to provide for them to take the next steps in their learning.

One nursery educator was trying to help a group of two- and three-year old new entrants feel welcome, so she introduced a Teddy to them, saying he needed the children to look after him and show him around as he did not know the nursery. During a story session one of the children found a very small chair for the Teddy but after a few minutes another child nudged the chair, causing it to turn so that the Teddy was facing away from the educator and her book. One of the older girls drew the educator's attention to this, saying that the Teddy could not see the book, despite the fact that the girl herself could – evidence of this child's ability to spatially de-centre (see Donaldson 1978 for further discussion of early thinking skills).

Some of the most revealing observations of children's knowledge and thinking are gained when they are playing and have control of the activity. In play situations, especially during imaginative play, children are at their most eloquent, perhaps because they are relaxed rather than stressed. Löfdahl (2002) describes her observations of a group of four- and five-year-old girls playing in a home corner. One girl had become sceptical about Father Christmas and decides he should be dead because he is so old but so powerful he has managed to stay alive. They will finish him off. The two inside the 'house' pretend they will leave him a bowl of poisoned porridge. A third girl then organises 'presents' to be left while the two 'slept', so the poisoned porridge idea is abandoned.

You need to remember that children weave everything they have seen, heard and experienced – even (perhaps especially) aspects of life they do not fully understand, attempting to deal with issues of power – into their imaginative play. They are exploring their own and others' knowledge (epistemic play) and experimenting with it (ludic play). I remember when one of my daughters was just three she paused outside the pantry with her dolly pram and in a very self-assured tone, asked me to look after her baby so she could 'just go into this pub'. I was amused but also horrified at the thought that she might be playing the same game at the preschool she had begun to attend and hoped the practitioners would realise this was not something she had actually experienced!

Having said that, it is often during play that you may notice signs indicating that a child may be experiencing abuse. Discussing such an observation confidentially with the senior teacher responsible for Child Protection (usually the head or deputy head in a primary school) would be essential.

Task 2.1.3
Listening to children

Look at some of the strategies suggested by Clark and Moss (2001) for encouraging children to express their views and for adults to really hear them. In what ways can schools promote or prevent listening?

INDIVIDUAL CHILDREN AND THEIR FAMILIES

Partnership with parents has been common practice in early childhood settings and primary schools for almost half a century but interpretations of what this has meant can range from school/curriculum/ child focused to family focused collaboration (see Unit 8.2 Collaborating with Parents).

Children begin their learning in the very individual cultural contexts of their homes. Their initial understandings about life and learning are based on their interactions with their parents and other family members. You will need to develop positive relationships with children's parents and significant other family members because these are the people who know the children best – they can help you understand each child better – and in order that together you can give each child optimal support for learning. Your knowledge of their family, home and interests will help you enable each child's learning.

CHILDREN'S RIGHTS: UNIVERSAL LEGISLATION AND CHILDREN'S OWN VIEWS

Following the terrible disruption caused by the Second World War to huge numbers of children, the United Nations began work on a Declaration of the Rights of the Child. Subsequently most countries ratified the Convention on the Rights of the Child (United Nations 1989). This international legislation has influenced internal legal development in member states, such as the UK 1989 Children Act. Two of the central tenets of the 1989 Children Act, which began to impact on how children are viewed in society, are:

- children's views wishes and feelings must be taken into account in any decisions that affect them;
- professionals working in children's services must work effectively together, striving to keep children with their families, rather than taking them into care.

Both the UN Convention and subsequent Children Acts mean every child should be respected as a person with views, wishes and feelings which they must be enabled to express.

THE NEW CHILDREN ACT 2004 AND MULTIPROFESSIONALISM: THE ROLE OF THE SCHOOL

The main aim of the government in introducing a new Children Act which emphasises better inter-agency work across all services for children up to age 19, is that every child, whatever their background, shall have the support needed to:

- be healthy;
- stay safe;

- enjoy and achieve through learning;
- make a positive contribution to society;
- achieve economic well-being.

Task 2.1.4
The Children Act 2004

Download the document Every Child Matters: Change for Children in Schools from the website www.everychildmatters.gov.uk/main-policies/.
When you have read the document, decide what changes you would advise in a school familiar to you in order to fulfil the requirements and spirit of this Children Act.

SUMMARY

If we place children and their learning at the heart of the education process, bearing in mind the contemporary and possible future needs of society, what kinds of places might we envisage the schools of the future to be? Moss and Petrie (2002) have argued that we need to rethink services for children as children's spaces. Certainly the children in our nurseries and schools now, and their families, are very different from those of a generation ago. They are living in a fast-changing, post-industrial, technological society. Environmental issues may be the most urgent and threatening problems that face them. Alongside this, the main concerns of children of primary school age seem focused on their closest relationships, family members, family breakdown, and possible 'loss' (Cox, forthcoming). Schools are being asked to provide support for families (for example through out-of-hours care facilities), as well as maintaining their central *raison d'être* – children's learning. This means that as teachers you will be required to engage with a more holistic view of children than has been the case in the past, teaching them and supporting them and their families as they meet the challenges posed by twenty-first century tasks of childhood.

ANNOTATED FURTHER READING

www.everychildmatters.gov.uk/main-policies/. This website provides masses of information about the intended effects of the Children Act 2004. It includes outlines of how the thinking underpinning Every Child Matters affects early years provision, children and young people, the inauguration of a Children's Commissioner for England, improvements in inter-agency work to benefit children, the role of schools in children's trusts.

MacNaughton, G. (2003) *Shaping Early Childhood*, Maidenhead: Open University Press/McGraw-Hill Education, pp. 40–69. Chapter 3 sets out and critiques some of the child development theories which can be used to inform practice.

Strandell, H. (2000) 'What is the use of children's play: preparation or social participation?', in H. Penn (ed.) *Early Childhood Services. Theory, Policy and Practices*, Buckingham: Open University Press, pp. 147–57. Strandell writes about her research observations about boys engaging in play which may appear pointless to some adult eyes. She demonstrates that the boys are engaging in social play, 'sorting out' their relationships.

REFERENCES

Bandura, A. (1992) 'Social cognitive theory', in R. Vasta (ed.) *Six Theories of Child Development: Revised Formulations and Current Issues*, London: Jessica Kingsley Press.

Bee, H. (1989) *The Developing Child* (5th edition), New York: Harper & Row.

BERA Early Years SIG (2003) *Review of Early Years Research: Curriculum, Pedagogy and Adult Roles*, Southwark: BERA.

Bloom, L. and Tinker, E. (2001) *The Intentionality Model of Language Acquisition. Monograph of the Society for Research in Child Development*, 66(267): 4.

Bowlby, J. (1953) *Child Care and the Growth of Love*, Harmondsworth: Penguin.

Bronfenbrenner, U. (1979) *The Ecology of Human Development*, Cambridge, MA: Harvard University Press.

Bruner, J. (1986) *Actual Minds, Possible Worlds*, Cambridge, MA: Harvard University Press.

Burman, E. (1994) *Deconstructing Developmental Psychology*, London: Routledge.

Chomsky, N. (1975) *Reflections on Language*, New York: Pantheon Books.

Clark, A. and Moss, P. (2001) *Listening to Young Children: The Mosaic Approach*, London: National Children's Bureau.

Cole, M. (1996) *Cultural Psychology: A Once and Future Discipline*, Cambridge, MA: Belknap Press.

Cox, J. (forthcoming) 'Is Childhood in Crisis?', doctoral study, Canterbury Christ Church University College, Canterbury.

David, T. and Nurse, A. (1999) 'Inspection of under-fives' education and constructions of childhood', in T.David (ed.) *Teaching Young Children*, London: PCP-Sage.

David, T., Goouch, K., Powell, S. and Abbott, L. (2003) *Birth to Three Matters: A Review of the Literature*, Research Report 444. London: DfES.

Davies, D. (1999) *Child Development: A Practitioner's Guide*, London: The Guilford Press.

Deloache, J.S. and Brown, A.L. (1987) 'The early emergence of planning skills in children', in J. Bruner and H. Haste (eds) *Making Sense*, London: Cassell.

DfES (2003) *Birth to Three Matters. A Framework to Support Children in their Earliest Years*, London: DfES.

Donaldson, M. (1978) *Children's Minds*, Glasgow: Fontana.

Dunn, J. (1993) *Young Children's Close Relationships. Beyond Attachment*, Newbury Park, CA: Sage.

Fleer, M. (2003) 'Post-Vygotskian lenses on Western early childhood education: moving the debate forward', *European Early Childhood Education Research Journal*, 11(1): 55–68.

Freud, S. (1991) *Introductory Lectures on Psychoanalysis*, London: Penguin.

Gerhardt, S. (2004) *Why Love Matters: How Affection Shapes a Baby's Brain*, Hove: Brunner-Routledge.

Gilligan, C. (1982) *In a Different Voice: Psychological Theory and Women's Development*, Cambridge, MA: Harvard University Press.

Gipps, C. and McGilchrist, B. (1999) 'Primary school learners', in P. Mortimore (ed.) *Understanding Pedagogy and its Impact on Learning*, London: PCP/Sage.

Goddard Blythe, S. (2000) 'Early learning in the balance', *Support for Learning*, 15(4): 154–9.

Gopnik, A., Melzoff, A. and Kuhl, P. (1999) *How Babies Think*, London: Weidenfeld & Nicolson.

Hillman, M., Adams, J. and Whitelegg J. (1990) *One False Move … A Study of Children's Independent Mobility*, London: Policy Studies Institute.

Hutt, S.J., Tyler, S.J., Hutt, C. and Christopherson, H. (1989) *Play, Exploration and Learning*, London: Routledge.

James, A., Jenks, C. and Prout, A. (1998) *Theorizing Childhood*, Cambridge: Polity Press.

Karmiloff, K. and Karmiloff-Smith, A. (2001) *Pathways to Language*, Cambridge, MA: Harvard University Press.

Kessen, W. (1979) 'The American child and other cultural inventions', *American Psychologist*, 34(10): 815–20.

Konner, M. (1991) *Childhood*, London: Ebury Press.

Lewis, A. (1996) *Primary Special Needs and the National Curriculum*, London: Routledge.

Löfdahl, A. (2002) 'Children's narratives in play – "I put this rice pudding here, poisoned, so Santa Claus will come and eat it!"', *Early Childhood Practice*, 4(2): 38–47.

MacNaughton, G. (2003) *Shaping Early Childhood*, Maidenhead: Open University Press/McGraw-Hill Education.

Morss, J. (1990) *The Biologising of Childhood*, Hove: Lawrence Erlbaum Associates.

Moss, P. and Petrie, P. (2002) *From Children's Services to Children's Spaces*, London: Routledge.

Moyles, J. (Ed) (2005) *Just Playing?* (3rd edition), Maidenhead: Open University Press/McGraw-Hill.

Nelson, K. (1986) *Event Knowledge, Structure and Function in Development*, Hillsdale, NJ: Erlbaum.

Penn, H. (2005) *Understanding Early Childhood*, Maidenhead: Open University Press/McGraw-Hill.

Piaget, J. (1955) *The Language and Thought of the Child*, London: Routledge and Kegan Paul.

Robinson, M. (2003) *From Birth to One: The Year of Opportunity*, Buckingham: Open University Press.

Rogoff, B. (1990) *Apprenticeship in Thinking. Cognitive Development in Social Context*, Oxford: Oxford University Press.

Rutter, M. and the English and Romanian Adoptees (ERA) Study Team (1998) 'Developmental catch-up, and deficit, following adoption after severe global early privation', *Journal of Child Psychology and Psychiatry*, 39: 465–73.

Singer, E. (1992) *Child Care and the Psychology of Development*, London: Routledge.

Skinner, B.F. (1938) *The Behaviour of Organisms*, Englewood Cliffs, NJ: Prentice-Hall.

Strandell, H. (2000) 'What is the use of children's play: preparation or social participation?', in H. Penn (ed.) *Early Childhood Services. Theory, Policy and Practices*, Buckingham: Open University Press.

United Nations (1989) Convention on the Rights of the Child, New York: United Nations.

Vygotsky, L.S. (1978) *Mind in Society: The Development of Higher Psychological Processes*, Cambridge, MA: Harvard University Press.

Walkerdine, V. (1999) 'Violent boys and precocious girls: regulating childhood at the end of the millennium', *Contemporary Issues in Early Childhood*, 1(1): 3–22.

Wall, K. (2003) *Special Needs and Early Years: A Practitioner's Guide*, London: PCP/Sage.

Wilkinson, R.G. (1994) *Unfair Shares*, London: Barnardos.

Winnicott, D.W. (1964) *The Child, the Family and the Outside World*, Harmondsworth: Pelican.

Unit 2.2

Looking at Learning

David Wray

INTRODUCTION

Learning is paradoxical in nature. It can sometimes appear to be a very simple thing. All of us are learning all the time, after all, from the myriad of experiences we encounter in our daily lives. I go to a new restaurant and I learn that even smoked salmon can be spoilt if you serve it with too much dill sauce; I read the newspaper and learn a little more about how Chelsea are threatening to take over the English footballing world; I play on my son's X-box and finally learn how to outwit that alien that's been shooting me in every one of my previous tries. Learning is so simple that we do not question its presence in how we go about our daily activities, for it is as natural to our existence as eating and drinking. Yet, when we encounter difficulties in learning something, we no longer take the learning process for granted. It is only then that our awareness of how we learn is heightened. Learning can suddenly seem very difficult indeed. I remember trying numerous ways of learning Latin declensions at school until it suddenly struck me I could make a nursery rhyme of them. Lupus, lupe, lupum, lupi, lupo, lupo. This revelation worked so well I still have this (useless) knowledge pat even now.

Learning is taken for granted as a natural process. Yet, as simple a process as it seems, understanding how we learn is not as straightforward. The existence of numerous definitions and theories of learning and the significant and, at times, vitriolic debates between adherents of particular theories vouch for the complexity of the process. A look, more or less randomly, at educational psychology textbooks will illustrate the differences between the views of the 'experts' about what exactly learning is and how we learn. In David Fontana's *Psychology for Teachers* (Fontana 1985), for example, the author writes, 'Most psychologists would agree that learning is a relatively persistent change in an individual's possible behaviour due to experience' (p. 211). This definition reflects a behaviourist view of learning, for it equates learning with an outcome defined as behaviour. Contrast it with the remarks of Norah Morgan and Juliana Saxton in their *Teaching, Questioning and Learning* (Morgan and Saxton 1991: 7) as they argue that

> effective teaching depends upon recognizing that effective *learning* takes place when the students are active participants in 'what's going on'. And for effective teaching and learning to occur, teachers must structure their teaching to invite and sustain that active participation by providing experiences which 'get them thinking and feeling', 'get the adrenalin flowing' and which generate in students a need for expression.

And later: 'Learning springs from curiosity – the *need* to know' (p. 18). Here learning appears to be defined more by learner engagement with experiences, leading to thought, expression and knowledge – a much broader definition.

So, what is this simple, yet complex, thing called 'learning'? And does it matter how we define it? Will that actually make a difference to how we attempt to go about enabling it to happen in classrooms?

OBJECTIVES

By the end of this unit, you should be able to:

*   recognise and describe the main elements of the major theoretical approaches to learning;
*   understand the implications of each of these approaches for classroom teaching.

APPROACHES TO LEARNING

Although there are many different approaches to learning, there are three basic schools of thought about learning theory: behaviourist, constructivist (often referred to as 'cognitivist') and social constructivist. In this unit I will provide a brief introduction to each theory. For each, I will give a short historical introduction, followed by a discussion of the view of knowledge presupposed by the theory. Next, I will give an account of how learning and learner motivation are treated before concluding with some discussion of some of the implications for teaching embedded in each theory. A brief overview of the main points of the unit are given in Table 2.2.1.

BEHAVIOURISM

Brief history

Behaviourism began as a reaction against the introspective psychology that dominated the late nineteenth and early twentieth centuries. Introspective psychologists such as Freud and Jung maintained that the study of consciousness was the primary object of psychology. Their methods relied on introspection, that is, first-person reports of feelings and experiences, both conscious and subconscious. Behaviourists such as Watson and Skinner rejected introspective methods as being subjective and unquantifiable. Instead, they focused on objectively observable, quantifiable events and behaviour. They argued that since it is not possible to observe objectively or to quantify what occurs in the mind, scientific theories should take into account only observable indicators such as stimulus-response sequences. According to Skinner (1976: 23),

Table 2.2.1 An overview of the main features of learning theories

| | Learning theory | | |
	Behaviourism	Constructivism	Social constructivism
Knowledge	Repertoire of behavioural responses to environmental stimuli.	Knowledge systems are actively constructed by learners based on existing structures.	Knowledge is socially constructed.
Learning	Passive absorption of predefined body of knowledge by learner. Promoted by repetition and positive reinforcement.	Active assimilation and accommodation of new information to existing cognitive structures. Discovery by learners.	Integration of students into knowledge community. Collaborative assimilation and accommodation of new information.
Motivation	Extrinsic, reward and punishment (positive and negative reinforcers).	Intrinsic. Learners set their own goals and motivate themselves to learn.	Intrinsic and extrinsic. Learning goals and motives are determined both by learners and extrinsic rewards provided by the knowledge community.
Teaching	Correct behavioural responses are transmitted by the teacher and repeated by the students. The teacher reinforces these.	The teacher facilitates learning by providing an environment that promotes discovery and assimilation/ accommodation.	Collaborative learning is facilitated and guided by the teacher. Group work.

> The mentalistic problem can be avoided by going directly to the prior physical causes while bypassing intermediate feelings or states of mind. The quickest way to do this is to ... consider only those facts which can be objectively observed in the behaviour of one person in its relation to his prior environmental history.

For behaviourists such as Skinner, what happens in the mind during processes such as learning would forever be inside 'the black box' and thus not knowable. All that psychologists could do was to observe the behaviours resulting from such internal states.

What is knowledge?

Behaviourists such as Watson and Skinner viewed knowledge as a repertoire of behaviours. Skinner argued that it is not the case that we use knowledge to guide our action, rather 'knowledge is action, or at least rules for action' (p. 152). It is a set of passive, largely mechanical responses to environmental stimuli. So, for instance, the behaviourist would argue that to say that someone knows Shakespeare is to say that this person has a certain repertoire of behaviour with respect to Shakespeare (p. 152).

Knowledge that is not actively expressed in behaviour can be explained as behavioural capacities. For example, 'I know a Siamese cat when I see one' can be seen as effectively equivalent to 'I have the capacity to identify a Siamese cat although I am not now doing so' (p. 154). If knowledge is seen as a repertoire of behaviour, someone can be said to understand something if they possess the appropriate repertoire of behaviour. No reference to unobservable cognitive processes is necessary (pp. 156–7).

What is learning?

From a behaviourist perspective, the transmission of information from teacher to learner is essentially the transmission of the response appropriate to a certain stimulus. Thus, the point of education is to present the learner with the appropriate repertoire of behavioural responses to specific stimuli and to reinforce those responses through an effective reinforcement schedule (Skinner 1976: 161). An effective reinforcement schedule requires consistent repetition of the material. The material to be learned should be broken down into small, progressive sequences of tasks, and continuous positive reinforcement should be given. Without positive reinforcement, learned responses will quickly become extinct. This is because learners will continue to modify their behaviour until they do receive some positive reinforcement.

What does motivation involve?

Behaviourists explain motivation in terms of schedules of positive and negative reinforcement. Just as receiving food pellets each time it pecks at a button teaches a pigeon to peck the button, pleasant experiences cause human learners to make the desired connections between specific stimuli and the appropriate responses. For example, a learner who receives verbal praise and good marks for correct answers is more likely to learn those answers effectively than one who receives little or no positive feedback for the same answers. Likewise, human learners tend to avoid responses that are associated with negative reinforcements such as poor marks or negative feedback.

How should you teach?

Behaviourist teaching methods tend to rely on so-called 'skill and drill' exercises to provide the consistent repetition necessary for the effective reinforcement of response patterns. Other methods include question (stimulus) and answer (response) sequences in which questions are of gradually increasing difficulty, guided practice, and regular reviews of material. Behaviourist methods also typically rely heavily on the use of positive reinforcements such as verbal praise, good marks, and prizes. Behaviourists test the degree of learning using methods that measure observable behaviour such as tests and examinations.

Behaviourist teaching methods have proved most successful in areas where there is a 'correct' response or easily memorised material. For example, while behaviourist methods have proved to be successful in teaching structured material such as facts and formulae, scientific concepts, and foreign language vocabulary, their usefulness in teaching comprehension and composition, to name but two abilities demanded by current national curricula, is questionable.

As an example of this kind of teaching, some of you will have experienced the use of 'language laboratories' when you were learning a foreign language. In the language lab, you were often presented with stretches of discourse in the target language which you were required to repeat and then you were given feedback on the accuracy of this repetition. This experience has been demonstrated to improve learners' knowledge of the particular discourse form but not of how this should be adapted to other, real-life, situations. While I was in the sixth form at school, for instance, I worked with an enthusiastic language teacher who decided we should be introduced to Russian. Through extensive experience of language lab drills I learnt (by rote) how to greet someone in Russian (Zdrastvwe Olga, kak tee posavaesh?), how to acknowledge such a greeting (Spasiba, kharasho, a ti?) and how to respond

(Spasiba, kharasho) – these were spoken drills so I never did know how this was written down! Unfortunately, the first and only time I tried this out on a Russian speaker, he was not called Olga, and did not acknowledge my greeting in the 'right' way, and thus left me floundering! My language behaviour was not sufficiently adaptable to cope with the real-life situation.

Behaviourist theories of learning have had a recent renaissance in the field of behaviour management rather than in content and concept learning. Positive behaviour management is usually taken to involve rewarding acceptable behaviour in pupils (CBG – Catch them Being Good) and ignoring unacceptable. Thus, so the theory goes, pupils will be encouraged to repeat the acceptable behaviour and the unacceptable will gradually die away. Note that it has usually been argued that, theoretically, unacceptable behaviour, if met with a negative response by the teacher, may in fact be perceived by the pupil as having been rewarded (any attention being better than none for some pupils) and thus will not fade away but be continued. Ignoring it is better. This argument makes good sense theoretically but you might find it difficult to implement practically!

It is also true, of course, that the reward (positive feedback) that a pupil gains following unacceptable behaviour may come not from the teacher but from others in the class. The class clown tends to get his/her rewards from peers rather than from teachers.

Task 2.2.1
A behaviourist approach to teaching

Behaviourist approaches to teaching tend to rely on three basic principles:

1   break down the desirable end behaviour into small steps;
2   teach – that is, stimulate and reinforce – each of these steps in the learner;
3   reinforce increasingly long chains of behaviour until the full end behaviour is finally achieved.

• Think of a teaching event in which you might employ such a set of principles for your teaching. Share your suggestions with colleagues and discuss how applicable this approach might be to teaching.
• Before reading the following section of this unit, discuss with your colleagues what you consider to be the main limitations of behaviourism as a theory of learning.

CONSTRUCTIVISM

Brief history

A dissatisfaction with behaviourism's strict focus on observable behaviour led educational psychologists such as Jean Piaget to demand an approach to learning theory that paid more attention to what went on 'inside the learner's head'; an approach that focused on mental processes rather than observable behaviour – cognition rather than action. Common to most constructivist approaches is the idea that knowledge comprises symbolic mental representations, such as propositions and images, together with a mechanism that operates on those representations. Knowledge is seen as something that is actively constructed by learners based on their existing cognitive structures. Therefore, it relates strongly to their stage of cognitive development. Understanding the learner's existing intellectual framework is central to understanding the learning process.

The most influential exponent of constructivism was the Swiss child psychologist Jean Piaget. Piaget rejected the idea that learning was the passive assimilation of given knowledge. Instead, he proposed that learning is a dynamic process comprising successive stages of adaptation to reality during which learners actively construct knowledge by creating and testing their own theories of the world. Piaget's theory has two main strands: first, an account of the mechanisms by which cognitive development takes place; and second, an account of the four main stages of cognitive development through which all children pass.

The basic principle underlying Piaget's theory is the principle of equilibration (balancing): all cognitive development progresses towards increasingly complex but *stable* mental representations of the world. Such stability is threatened by the input of new ideas and so equilibration takes place through a process of adaptation. One of the reasons why humans have often been quite resistant to new ideas is this in-built need for stability in their concepts of the world. Think about the centuries during which people were convinced that the sun orbited the earth, rather than vice versa. It was not until evidence of the falsity of such a belief was overwhelming that most people made the destabilising mental shift to a new set of ideas about the world.

Such adaptation might involve the assimilation of new information into existing cognitive structures or the accommodation of that information through the formation of new cognitive structures. As an example of this, consider what happens when you enter a novel situation, say, going into a new restaurant. Normally, although you have never been in this particular restaurant before, you will have experience of many similar environments, and thus know what to expect. You know the sequence of events (waiter brings menu, leaves you for a while, returns to ask for your order; if it's a posh restaurant a different waiter asks you what wine you would like to drink with the meal, etc.): you know what is expected of you. The 'new' aspects of this restaurant (location, orientation of the room, design of the menus, particular specialist dishes, where the loos are, etc.) are simply new elements of information which you need to assimilate into your mental maps of the world (Piaget used the term 'schema' to refer to one of these mental maps – the plural is variously written as 'schemata' or 'schemas', depending on how classical your education was). If, less usually, this restaurant is way outside of your previous experience (suppose it's your first visit to a Japanese restaurant) then the process of learning might be more radical. There may be details about the cutlery, plates, order of the courses, appropriate drinks, etc. to come to terms with, and these new features need to be accommodated into an expanded schema of 'restaurant'. Thus, learners adapt and develop by assimilating and accommodating new information into existing cognitive structures.

Piaget also suggested that there are four main stages in the cognitive development of children. In their first two years, children pass through a sensori-motor stage during which they progress from cognitive structures dominated by instinctive drives and undifferentiated emotions (they do not care who picks them up as long as they satisfy the basic physical drives of hunger, comfort, etc.) to more organised systems of concrete concepts and differentiated emotions (not anyone will do as a food provider – it has to be Mum or Dad). At this stage, children's outlook is essentially egocentric in the sense that they are unable to take into account others' points of view. The second stage of development lasts until around seven years of age. Children begin to use language to make sense of reality. They learn to classify objects using different criteria and to manipulate numbers. Children's increasing linguistic skills open the way for greater levels of social action and communication with others. From the ages of seven to twelve years, children begin to develop logic, although they can only perform logical operations on concrete objects and events. In adolescence, children enter the formal operational stage, which continues throughout the rest of their lives. Children develop the ability to perform abstract intellectual operations, and reach emotional and intellectual maturity. They learn how to formulate and test abstract hypotheses without referring to concrete objects. Most importantly, children develop the capacity to appreciate others' points of view as well as their own.

Piaget's theory was widely accepted from the 1950s until the 1970s. Then researchers such as Margaret Donaldson began to find evidence that young children were not as limited in their thinking as Piaget had suggested. Researchers found that, when situations made 'human sense' (Donaldson's term) to children, they could engage in mental operations at a much higher level than Piaget had predicted. His theory, particularly that aspect related to the above stages of development, is not now as widely accepted, although it has had a significant influence on later theories of cognitive development. For instance, the idea of adaptation through assimilation and accommodation is still widely accepted, and incorporated into what is now known as 'schema theory', which we will revisit in the next unit of this book.

What is knowledge?

Behaviourists maintain that knowledge is a passively absorbed repertoire of behaviours. Constructivists reject that claim, arguing instead that knowledge is actively constructed by learners and that any account of knowledge makes essential references to the cognitive structures within the learner's mind. Knowledge comprises a complex set of mental representations derived from past learning experiences. Each learner interprets experiences and information in the light of their existing knowledge, their stage of cognitive development, their cultural background, their personal history, and so on. Learners use these factors to organise their experience and to select and transform new information. Knowledge is therefore actively constructed by the learner rather than passively absorbed; it is essentially dependent on the standpoint from which the learner approaches it.

What is learning?

Because knowledge is actively constructed, learning is defined as a process of active discovery. The role of the instructor is not to drill knowledge into learners through consistent repetition, or to goad them into learning through carefully employed rewards and punishments. Rather, the role of the teacher is to facilitate discovery by providing the necessary resources and by guiding learners as they attempt to assimilate new knowledge to old and to modify the old to accommodate the new. Teachers must thus take into account the knowledge that the learner currently possesses when deciding how to construct the curriculum and to present, sequence, and structure new material.

What does motivation involve?

Unlike behaviourist learning theory, where learners are thought to be motivated by extrinsic factors such as rewards and punishment, constructivist learning theory sees motivation as largely intrinsic. Because it involves significant restructuring of existing cognitive structures, successful learning requires a major personal investment on the part of the learner. Learners must face up to the limitations of their existing knowledge and accept the need to modify or abandon existing beliefs. Without some kind of internal drive on the part of the learner to make these modifications, external rewards and punishments such as marks are unlikely to be sufficient.

How should you teach?

Constructivist teaching methods aim to assist learners in assimilating new information to existing knowledge, and to enable them to make the appropriate modifications to their existing intellectual frameworks to accommodate that information. Thus, while constructivists accept some use of 'skill and drill' exercises in the memorisation of facts, formulae and lists, etc., they place much greater importance on strategies that help learners actively to assimilate and accommodate new material. For instance, asking learners to explain new material in their own words can help them to assimilate this material by forcing them to re-express the new ideas in their existing vocabulary. Similarly, providing pupils with sets of questions to structure their reading can make it easier for them to relate the ideas in the reading to previous material by the highlighting of certain aspects of the text. These questions can also help pupils to accommodate the new material by giving them a clear organisational structure of ideas. Pre-reading questions such as this are referred to by researchers into reading as 'advance organisers'. An extreme example of their usefulness can be seen in the following activity.

Task 2.2.2
Using schema to construct meaning

1   Read the following passage, then close this book and try to tell someone else what the passage was about.

The procedure is actually quite simple. First you arrange things into different groups. Of course one pile may be sufficient depending on how much there is to do. If you have to go somewhere else due to lack of facilities that is the next step, otherwise you are pretty well set. It is important not to overdo things. That is, it is better to do too few things at once than too many. In the short run this may not seem important but complications can easily arise. A mistake can be expensive as well. At first the whole procedure will seem complicated. Soon, however, it will become just another facet of life. It is difficult to foresee any end to the necessity for this task in the immediate future, but then one can never tell. After the procedure is completed one arranges the materials into different groups again. Then they can be put into their appropriate places. Eventually they will be used once more and the whole cycle will then have to be repeated. However, that is a part of life.

2   Now read the passage again in order to answer the following questions:

• Outline the steps in the process of washing clothes as they are listed in the passage.
• Can you see any end to the necessity for this task in the immediate future?

You should have found that having the questions there to guide your reading made it possible for you to understand a passage which, previously, was incomprehensible. What has happened here is that the questions have 'switched on' the appropriate schema in your mind, allowing details to be assimilated.

Because learning is largely self-motivated in constructivist theory, a number of methods have also been suggested which require pupils to monitor their own learning. For instance, the regular use of check-up tests and study questions can enable pupils to monitor their own understanding of material. Other methods that have been suggested include the use of learning journals by pupils to monitor their progress and highlight any recurring difficulties. (Modern web logs, or 'blogs', are an electronic version of such journals which are just beginning to be used in classroom learning.)

Constructivists also tend to place a great deal of emphasis upon practical activity, involving the physical manipulation of objects, in teaching such subjects as mathematics and science. Challenging and pushing forward pupils' ideas is much more likely to happen with this kind of hands-on experience and is well expressed in the proverb much beloved of constructivist learning theorists: 'I hear, I forget; I see, I remember; I do, I understand.'

SOCIAL CONSTRUCTIVISM

Brief history

Social constructivism is a variety of constructivism that emphasizes the collaborative nature of much learning. Social constructivism was developed by the Soviet psychologist, Lev Vygotsky. Vygotsky rejected the assumption made by constructivists such as Piaget that it was possible to separate learning from its social context. He argued that all cognitive functions originate in, and must therefore be explained as products of, social interactions and that learning was not simply the assimilation and accommodation of new knowledge by learners; it was the process by which learners were integrated into a knowledge community. According to Vygotsky (1978 – this date refers to the translation into English of Vygotsky's work, which was in fact published in the original Russian in the 1930s: 57):

> Every function in the child's cultural development appears twice: first, on the social level and, later on, on the individual level; first, between people (interpsychological) and then inside the child (intrapsychological). This applies equally to voluntary attention, to logical memory, and to the formation of concepts. All the higher functions originate as actual relationships between individuals.

What is knowledge?

Constructivists such as Piaget saw knowledge as actively constructed by learners in response to interactions with environmental stimuli. Vygotsky emphasised the role of language and culture in cognitive development. According to Vygotsky, language and culture play essential roles both in human intellectual development and in how humans perceive the world. Humans' linguistic abilities enable them to overcome the natural limitations of their perceptions by imposing culturally defined meaning on the world. Language and culture are the frameworks through which humans experience, communicate, and understand reality. Vygotsky uses an example to illustrate this. When we look at the following symbol we see a clock.

Imagine though how a person would perceive this object who has never seen a clock before. He/she would be reduced to describing it, in Vygotsky's words, as 'something round and black with two hands' (p. 39). (Notice that here Vygotsky actually understates his own case since in order to describe the two lines in the object as 'hands' you have to have a concept of clock in the first place!) The essential element that transforms this object into 'clock' is its cultural usage. Vygotsky's point is that language and the conceptual schemes that are transmitted by means of language are essentially social phenomena. As a result, human cognitive structures are essentially socially constructed. Knowledge is not simply constructed, it is co-constructed.

What is learning?

Vygotsky accepted Piaget's claim that learners respond not to external stimuli but to their interpretation of those stimuli. However, he argued that constructivists such as Piaget had overlooked the essentially social nature of language. As a result, he claimed they had failed to understand that learning is a collaborative process. Vygotsky distinguished between two developmental levels: the level of *actual development* is the level of development that the learner has already reached, and is the level at which the learner is capable of solving problems independently. The level of *potential development* (the 'zone of proximal development') is the level of development that the learner is capable of reaching under the guidance of teachers or in collaboration with peers. Learners are capable of solving problems and understanding material at this level that they are not capable of solving or understanding at their level of actual development. The level of potential development is the level in which learning takes place. It comprises cognitive structures that are still in the process of developing, but which can only develop under the guidance of or in collaboration with others.

What does motivation involve?

For behaviourists, motivation is essentially *extrinsic* – it depends on positive or negative reinforcement from outside. Constructivist motivation is essentially *intrinsic* – it derives from the learner's internal drive. Social constructivists see motivation as both extrinsic and intrinsic. Because learning is essentially a social phenomenon, learners are partially motivated by rewards provided by the knowledge community. However, because knowledge is actively constructed by the learner, learning also depends to a significant extent on the learner's internal drive to understand.

How should you teach?

If learning is social, then it follows that teaching should ideally use collaborative learning methods. These require learners to develop teamwork skills and to see individual learning as essentially related to the success of group learning. This should be seen as a process of peer interaction that is mediated and structured by the teacher. Discussion can be promoted by the presentation of specific concepts or problems and guided by directed questions, the introduction and clarification of concepts and information, and references to previously learned material. More specific discussion of collaborative teaching and the linked strategies of modelling and scaffolding will be found in the following unit.

SUMMARY

The point made at the beginning of this unit was that learning is such a familiar and everyday thing that it is somewhat surprising that defining it has caused such huge debate. But understanding the main principles of these debates is absolutely crucial if you are to successfully plan for and implement effective learning in your classroom. Learning is what you are mainly there to bring about, so clearly what you think learning is makes a difference to the way you teach. It is unfortunately the case, however, that some teachers never really give this issue much thought. Learning is so obviously important that it becomes unproblematic. But teachers like yourself, sufficiently interested to read books and units like this one, will know that our intentions as teachers, our *theories* about teaching and learning, do make a difference to how we act in classrooms.

In this unit, I have reviewed the main theoretical approaches to learning and tried to pull out their practical implications. In many ways, you can be an effective teacher if you view learning mainly from a behaviourist, constructivist, or social constructivist viewpoint: it is not your choice of theory that makes the difference. What matters is that your strategies for teaching and your teaching actions match the theory you hold about learning. Coherence between your theories and your practices will be much more successful in enabling learning than thinking one thing but doing another.

ANNOTATED FURTHER READING

Margaret Donaldson's book *Children's Minds* was an immensely significant book when it was first published. It brought together recent research into children's learning which gave a fundamental challenge to Piagetian views that learners were limited by the current conceptual development stage they were operating in. It was also noteworthy for being one of the most readable accounts of learning and development ever written.

Joyce, B., Calhoun, E. and Hopkins, D. (1997) *Models of Learning – Tools for Teaching*, Buckingham: Open University Press. A very useful outline of different models of learning. The writers isolate four 'families' of teaching based on the types of learning they promote: information processing; social/building a learning community; personal; and behavioural.

One of the most comprehensive and readable introductions to the study of learning is David Wood's *How Children Think and Learn*. Wood is very good at relating the theoretical notions he describes so well to their practical implications for teaching. He concludes by arguing that, 'for some time to come, I suspect that the most valuable resources within the classroom will be found in human form', by which he means you – the teacher.

REFERENCES

Donaldson, M. (1978) *Children's Minds*, London: Fontana.
Fontana, D. (1985) *Psychology for Teachers*, London: Macmillan.
Joyce, B., Calhoun, E. and Hopkins, D. (1997) *Models of Learning – Tools for Teaching*, Buckingham: Open University Press.
Morgan, N. and Saxton, J. (1991) *Teaching Questioning and Learning* London: Routledge.
Skinner, B.F. (1976) *About Behaviorism*, New York: Vintage Books.
Vygotsky, L. (1978) *Mind in Society*, London: Harvard University Press.
Wood, D. (1988) *How Children Think and Learn*, Oxford: Blackwell.

Unit 2.3

From Learning to Teaching

David Wray

INTRODUCTION

In the previous unit we examined several important theories of learning, from behaviourism to social constructivism. It will probably have occurred to you that, in planning for the learning you hope and intend will take place in your classroom, you are guided not by a single theory of learning but in fact by elements of all these theories. There are useful elements within each of the theories reviewed in the previous unit, and indeed in other theoretical explorations of learning. Planning for teaching is not as simple as just deciding on the particular learning theory you wish to subscribe to. There are, however, a number of important insights into learning which can be used to underpin approaches to teaching and it is the purpose of this unit to outline these insights and then to develop some principles for teaching which can be derived from them.

OBJECTIVES

After reading this unit you should be able to:

- discuss some important insights into the nature of learning and recognise the implications of these for teaching;
- describe the basic elements of an apprenticeship approach to teaching, justify such an approach in terms of its foundation in research and theory, and suggest practical examples of the implementation of such an approach.

INSIGHTS INTO LEARNING

Four basic insights into the nature of the learning process have come from research over the last twenty years or so. Each of these has important implications for approaches to teaching.

Learning is a process of interaction between what is known and what is to be learnt

It has become quite clear that, in order to do any real learning, we have to draw upon knowledge we already have about a subject. The more we know about the subject, the more likely it is that we shall learn any given piece of knowledge. Learning which does not make connections with our prior knowledge is learning at the level of rote only, and is soon forgotten once deliberate attempts to remember it have stopped.

Learning has been defined as 'the expansion and modification of existing ways of conceiving the world in the light of alternative ways' (Wray and Medwell 1991: 9). Such a constructivist approach to learning places great emphasis upon the ways in which prior knowledge is structured in the learner's mind and in which it is activated during learning. Theories about this, generally known as schema theories as they hypothesise that knowledge is stored in our minds in patterned ways (schema), suggest that learning depends, first, upon the requisite prior knowledge being in the mind of the learner and, second, upon it being brought to the forefront of the learner's mind.

As an example of this, in the field of learning through reading, try the following activity.

Task 2.3.1
Schemas and reading

Look at the following story beginning:

> The man was brought into the large white room. His eyes blinked in the bright light.

Try to picture in your mind the scene so far. Is the man sitting, lying or standing? Is he alone in the room? What sort of room is it? What might this story be going to be about?

Now read the next extract:

> 'Now, sit there,' said the nurse. 'And try to relax.'

Has this altered your picture of the man or of the room? What is this story going to be about?

After the first extract you may have thought the story would be set in a hospital, or perhaps concern an interrogation. There are key words in the brief beginning which trigger off these expectations. After the second extract the possibility of a dentist's surgery may enter your mind, and the interrogation scenario fade.

Each item you read sparks off an idea in your mind, each one of which has its own associated schema, or structure of underlying ideas. It is unlikely, for example, that your picture of the room after the first extract had a plush white carpet on the floor. You construct a great deal from very little information.

Learning from the material you read is exactly like this. It is not simply a question of getting a meaning from what is on the page. When you read, you supply a good deal of the meaning to the page. The process is an interactive one, with the resultant learning being a combination of your previous ideas with new ones encountered in this text.

As another example of this, consider the following sentence:

Mary remembered her birthday money when she heard the ice-cream van coming.

Without trying too hard you can supply a great deal of information to the meaning of this, chiefly to do with Mary's intentions and feelings, but also to do with the appearance of the van and its driver's intentions. You probably do not immediately suspect him as a potential child molester! Notice that most of this seems so obvious that we barely give it much conscious thought. Our schemas for everyday events are so familiar that we do not notice it when they are activated.

Now compare the picture you get from the following sentence:

Mary remembered her birthday money when she heard the bus coming.

What difference does this make to your picture of Mary, beyond the difference in her probable intentions? Most people say that she now seems rather older. Notice that this difference in understanding comes not so much from the words on the page as from the complex network of ideas which these words make reference to. These networks have been referred to as schemas, and developments in our understanding of how they operate have had a great impact upon our ideas about the nature and teaching of reading comprehension.

Task 2.3.2
The impact of varying the schema

Try out the 'Mary' sentences above on some pupils you have access to (say between the ages of 6 and 11). Do they have the same responses to the sentences as you do? If not, then this probably suggests that they have not yet developed the background schemas that you use in reading the sentences.

If they do make similar responses to you, you can extend the activity by using further variations on the original sentence. What schemas does the following activate, for example?

Mary remembered her gun when she heard the ice-cream van coming.

Or the following?

Mary remembered her stomach when she heard the ice-cream van coming.

Ask the pupils to think of their own variations and to explain the different impressions each leaves on the reader.

We have explored this issue through the example of reading, but the same interaction between the known and the new happens in any kind of learning. Many teachers have had the experience of asking a young child the apparently simple, mathematical question:

What is the difference between 6 and 9?

The answer they receive might be 3, or 'one number is upside down', or 'my brother is 9 and he's older than me 'cos I'm 6', depending upon the schema which is activated by the word 'difference'.

You may also have heard the story of the newly qualified teacher who began work with a class of 5–6-year-olds in a rural school. She decided to begin her work with the class by using a topic she was reasonably confident they would be familiar with, so she showed them a picture of a cow. She asked the class, 'Now, who can tell me what this is?' but, to her consternation, not one of them could give her an answer, all of them looking faintly puzzled by the picture. After several equally fruitless attempts to get an answer to this simple question, she eventually became somewhat exasperated. 'Surely *somebody* can tell me what this is? You see them every day.' Eventually one little boy raised his hand, not to give her an answer but to ask if he could look more closely at the picture. Baffled by now, she allowed him to come closer. He studied the picture for several moments before announcing in a tentative voice, 'I *think* it's an Aberdeen Angus cross heifer'.

In this case the children actually possessed much more background knowledge – a richer schema – than the teacher. Their subsequent learning around this topic would be considerably different from that the teacher had planned.

Learning is a social process

Ideas about learning have progressed significantly away from Piaget's purely 'lone scientist' view of learners as acting upon their environments, observing the results and then, through reflection, modifying or fine-tuning their schemas concerning these environments. Modern learning theory gives much greater recognition to the importance of social interaction and support and has a view of the learner as a social constructor of knowledge. In collaboration with others, learners establish:

- shared consciousness: – a group working together can construct knowledge to a higher level; than can the individuals in that group each working separately. The knowledge rests upon the group interaction;
- borrowed consciousness: – individuals working alongside more knowledgeable others can 'borrow' their understanding of tasks and ideas to enable them to work successfully.

From a social constructivist perspective, the most important tool for learning is discourse. A lot of research has been carried out to try to understand the qualities of discourse that enhance its effectiveness. Raphael and her colleagues, for example (Raphael *et al.* 1992), have studied the discourse used by primary-aged pupils as they engaged in discussions about the books they had read. The question leading this research was: how do discussions about books influence 10–11-year-old pupils' ability to talk about literature? A great deal was revealed in the research about the role played by the constitution of the groups, the books they discussed, and the writing activities they were asked to complete as a follow-up. For example, it was found that the books chosen needed to have the potential for controversy and the power to elicit emotional responses. Furthermore, writing activities that allowed pupils more flexibility in their responses were more beneficial and led to more interesting discussions than those that demanded more structured responses. Finally, Raphael's research identified some of the more useful roles the teacher could play in such book discussions, such as modelling ways in which they could articulate their personal responses to literature.

The crucial role that the teacher plays in promoting the co-construction of knowledge in classrooms was also shown in the research of Forman *et al.* (1995) who studied the discourse of 11–12-year-old pupils and their teacher as they discussed mathematical problems. The classic pattern of classroom discussion has been found to consist largely of teachers initiating an exchange (usually by asking a question), a pupil responding (answering the question), and a teacher giving feedback on that response. This pattern is known as the Initiation – Response – Feedback (IRF) exchange and has been shown to account for up to 75 per cent of normal classroom discussion. In the Forman study, however, it was found that the pupils, rather than the teacher, were often engaged in evaluating each other's contributions, while the contributions of the teacher were often for the purpose of expanding upon pupils' contributions to the discussion. Similar patterns of discourse have been found in the sequence of research projects reported in Kumpulainen and Wray (2002), and suggest that group discussion, in changing the traditional patterns of classroom discourse, allows and encourages much greater involvement of pupils in learning.

Learning is a situated process

We learn everything in a context. That is not controversial. But modern learning theorists also suggest that what we learn is the context as much as any skills and processes which we use within that context (Lave and Wenger, 1991). Psychologists have sought in vain for 'generalisable skills' and all teachers are familiar with the problem of transfer of learning. Why is it that a child who spells ten words correctly in a spelling test is likely to spell several of these wrongly when writing a story a short while afterwards? And why, to give an example from my own teaching experience, can a 10-year-old boy, who in class is absolutely hopeless with number work, maintain an extended, sensible discussion about horse-racing odds with peers in the playground? 'It's 9 to 4 on but it's going to soften.' Do *you* understand that statement? What will the odds move to if they 'soften'? Is it 9 to 5 on, or 10 to 4 on? This mathematically challenged pupil had no problem with numbers of this kind. The answer to these conundrums is simply that the learning of skills such as spelling and number knowledge is so inextricably bound up with the context of learning that it cannot easily be applied outside of this context.

Traditionally education has often assumed a separation between learning and the use of learning, treating knowledge as a self-sufficient substance, theoretically independent of the situations in which it is learned and used. The primary concern of schools has often seemed to be the teaching of this substance, which comprised abstract, decontextualised, formal concepts. The activity and context in which learning took place were thus regarded as ancillary to learning – they were useful in terms of motivating the learners but not fundamental to the nature of the learning.

Recent investigations of learning, however, challenge this separation of what is learned from how it is learned and used. The activity in which knowledge is developed and deployed is now seen as an integral part of what is learned. Learning and cognition, it is now possible to argue, are fundamentally situated.

As an example of this, consider the work of Miller and Gildea (1987) on vocabulary teaching in which they describe how children are taught words from dictionary definitions and a few exemplary sentences and compare this method to the way vocabulary is normally learned outside school.

People generally learn words in the context of ordinary communication. This process is startlingly fast and successful. Miller and Gildea note that by listening, talking, and reading, the average 18-year-old has learned vocabulary at a rate of 5,000 words per year (13 per day) for over 16 years. By contrast, learning words from abstract definitions and sentences taken out of the context of normal use, the way vocabulary has often been taught, is slow and generally unsuccessful. There is barely enough classroom time to teach more than 100 to 200 words per year. Moreover, much of what is taught turns out to be almost useless in practice. Miller and Gildea give the following examples of pupils' uses of vocabulary acquired this way:

- Me and my parents correlate, because without them I wouldn't be here.
- I was meticulous about falling off the cliff.
- Mrs. Morrow stimulated the soup.

Given the method, such mistakes seem unavoidable. Teaching from dictionaries assumes that definitions and example sentences are self-contained 'pieces' of knowledge. But words and sentences are not self-contained in this way. Using language would be almost impossible without the extra help that the context of an utterance provides. Take all the words in English which directly refer to other words or elements of context – termed by linguists 'indexical' words. Words such as here, now, next, tomorrow, afterwards and all pronouns are not just context-sensitive; they are completely context-dependent. Even words that seem to carry content rather than point to other words – words like 'word' – are situated. I give you my word that a word, unless it is the Word of God, means what I choose it to mean – is, in a word, context-dependent, each of these 'words' meaning something quite different.

Experienced readers implicitly understand that words are situated. They, therefore, ask for the rest of the sentence or the context before committing themselves to an interpretation of a word. And then they go to dictionaries with situated examples of the usage in mind. The situation as well as the dictionary supports their interpretation. But the pupils who produced the sentences listed had no support from a normal communicative situation. In tasks like theirs, dictionary definitions were assumed to be self-sufficient. The extra linguistic props that would structure, constrain, and ultimately allow interpretation in normal communication were ignored.

All knowledge is like language. Its constituent parts refer to parts of the world and so are inextricably a product of the activity and situations in which they are produced. A concept, for example, will continually evolve every time it is used, because new situations, negotiations, and activities inevitably recast it in a slightly different form. So a concept, like the meaning of a word, is always under construction. All learning is temporary and contextually situated. I remember being very puzzled in one of my early secondary school science lessons to be informed we were going to make a 'solution'. This sounded interesting: I had envisaged science as being exactly that – finding solutions to the problems of the natural world. When making the solution turned out to be simply a matter of mixing some blue crystals with water and watching them disappear, I could not help asking the teacher what that was the solution to!

Task 2.3.3
Using words with various meanings

Think of some further examples of words and/or concepts which have a multiplicity of meanings depending on the contexts in which they occur. How might you go about teaching some of this diversity of meaning to your pupils?

Learning is a metacognitive process

While reading some particularly densely written background material before writing this unit I noticed that it was becoming increasingly difficult for me to concentrate on what I was reading. My mind kept drifting to other, lighter, topics and several times I came to with a jerk to realise that I had understood nothing of the several paragraphs I thought I had 'read'. This was a metacognitive experience, and my comprehension monitoring had alternately lapsed and kicked into action. These terms are probably unfamiliar to many people, yet the processes to which they refer have been increasingly demonstrated to be of special importance in learning and in the operation of many intellectual activities. What do these terms mean?

There are two stages in the development of knowledge: first, its automatic unconscious acquisition (we learn things or how to do things, but do not know that we know these things), and second, a gradual increase in active conscious control over that knowledge (we begin to know what we know and that there is more that we do not know). This distinction is essentially the difference between the cognitive and metacognitive aspects of knowledge and thought. The term metacognition is used to refer to cognition about cognition: thinking about your own thinking.

Metacognition can be differentiated into metacognitive knowledge and metacognitive experience. Metacognitive knowledge is the relatively stable information which we have about our own thinking processes. This knowledge may be about ourselves, about the tasks we are faced with and about possible strategies for tackling them. I may know, for example, that I have to read things at least twice before I will understand them, that it is much easier to understand texts if they are about a topic about which I already know something, or that it will help me remember information if I jot down key points as I read it.

Metacognitive experience refers to the mechanisms used by active learners as they regulate their own attempts to solve problems. These might include:

- checking the outcome of what has already been attempted;
- planning the next moves in response to a problem;
- monitoring the effectiveness of these attempted actions;
- testing, revising and evaluating strategies for learning.

Although it has been demonstrated that even quite young children can monitor their own activities when working on a simple problem, learners of any age are more likely to take active control of their own cognitive activities when they are faced with tasks of medium difficulty. This is not surprising since it seems logical that with an easy task there is no need to devote too much attention to it, and with a task which is too hard, there is a tendency to give up.

As an example of metacognition in action, we can consider the activity of reading. Good reading has been described as follows:

> A good reader proceeds smoothly and quickly as long as his understanding of the material is complete. But as soon as he senses that he has missed an idea, that the track has been lost, he brings smooth progress to a blinding halt. Advancing more slowly, he seeks clarification in the subsequent material, examining it for the light it can throw on the earlier trouble spot. If still dissatisfied with his grasp, he returns to the point where the difficulty began and rereads the section more carefully. He probes and analyses phrases and sentences for their exact meaning; he tries to visualise abstruse descriptions; and through a series of approximations, deductions, and corrections he translates scientific and technical terms into concrete examples.
>
> (Whimbey 1975: 91)

While it is, of course, true that all readers do not follow precisely this sequence of actions, recent theories of reading have suggested similarly strategic models for the process. Most characterisations of the reading process include skills and activities which involve what is now termed 'metacognition'. Some of the metacognitive activities involved in reading are:

- clarifying your purposes for reading, that is understanding the aim of a particular reading task;
- identifying the important aspects of a text;
- focusing attention on these aspects rather than on relatively trivial aspects;
- monitoring on-going activities to determine whether comprehension is taking place;

- engaging in self-questioning to check whether your aims are being achieved;
- taking corrective action if and when failures in comprehension are detected.

Reading for meaning therefore inevitably involves the metacognitive activity of comprehension monitoring, which entails keeping track of the success with which your comprehension is proceeding, ensuring that the process continues smoothly and taking remedial action if necessary.

Although mature readers typically engage in these processes as they read for meaning, it is usually not a conscious experience. Skilled readers tend to proceed on automatic pilot until a triggering event alerts them to a failure or problem in their comprehension. When alerted in this way they must slow down and devote extra effort in mental processing to the area which is causing the problem. The events which trigger such action may vary widely. One common triggering event is the realisation that an expectation held about a text has not been confirmed by actual experience of the text. For example, in reading a sentence such as the following, 'The old man the boats'; the fourth and fifth words will probably cause a revision of your sense of understanding and therefore take longer to process.

Realising that you have failed to understand is only part of comprehension monitoring; you also have to know what to do when such failures occur. This involves making a number of strategic decisions such as:

- reading on: reading more of the text to see if more information can be gained;
- sounding out: examining letters and sounds carefully (this strategy is used most often by younger readers);
- making an inference: guessing a meaning on the basis of textual clues and previous knowledge;
- re-reading: reading the difficult section again;
- suspending judgement: waiting to see if the text provides more clues.

Numerous research studies have examined the operation of metacognition in children's reading, that is, their monitoring of their own comprehension. Overall, there has been a remarkable consistency in the findings of these studies and it seems that

> Young children and poor readers are not nearly as adept as older children/adults and good readers, respectively, in engaging in planful activities either to make cognitive progress or to monitor it. Younger, less proficient learners are not nearly as 'resourceful' in completing a variety of reading and studying tasks important in academic settings.
>
> (Garner 1987: 59)

The above description has focused on reading, but this only parallels what we know about the importance of metacognition in all areas of learning. Self-awareness appears to be an essential ingredient in success in school. As John Holt put it,

> Part of being a good student is learning to be aware of the state of one's mind and the degree of one's understanding. The good student may be one who often says that he does not understand, simply because he keeps a constant check on his understanding. The poor student, who does not, so to speak, watch himself trying to understand, does not know most of the time whether he understands or not.
>
> (Holt 1969: 23)

This is a fundamental problem for young children: being much less aware of the operations of their own minds, and much less able to introspect to find out how their minds are working, they are thus less able to exert any conscious control over their own cognition. There is a strong implication that learning can be improved by increasing learners' awareness of their own mental processes.

PRINCIPLES FOR TEACHING

Arising from these insights we can derive some clear principles for teaching:

- We need to ensure that learners have sufficient previous knowledge/understanding to enable them to learn new things, and to help them make explicit these links between what they already know and what they are learning.
- We need to make provision for group interaction and discussion as teaching strategies, both in small, teacher-less groups and in groups working alongside experts.
- We need to ensure meaningful contexts for learning, particularly in what are often called basic skills. This implies some kind of negotiation of the curriculum for learning. What is a meaningful context for teachers cannot be assumed automatically to be a meaningful context for learners.
- We need to promote learners' knowledge and awareness of their own thinking and learning. This might be done by, for example, encouraging them to think aloud as they perform particular cognitive tasks.

TOWARDS A MODEL FOR TEACHING

Palincsar and Brown (1984) described a teaching procedure which began from the principles just outlined and which was based upon the twin ideas of 'expert scaffolding' and what they referred to as 'proleptic' teaching: that is, teaching in anticipation of competence. This model arose from the Vygotskian idea that children first experience a particular cognitive activity in collaboration with expert practitioners. The child is first a spectator as the majority of the cognitive work is done by the expert (parent or teacher), then a novice as he/she starts to take over some of the work under the close supervision of the expert. As the child grows in experience and capability of performing the task, the expert passes over greater and greater responsibility but still acts as a guide, assisting the child at problematic points. Eventually, the child assumes full responsibility for the task with the expert still present in the role of a supportive audience. Using this approach to teaching, children learn about the task at their own pace, joining in only at a level at which they are capable – or perhaps a little beyond this level so that the task continually provides sufficient challenge to be interesting. The approach is often referred to as an apprenticeship approach. In the apprenticeship approach to reading, for example, the teacher and child begin by sharing a book together with, at first, most of the actual reading being done by the teacher. As the child develops confidence through repeated sharings of the book, he/she gradually takes over the reading until the teacher can withdraw entirely.

In mathematics learning Taylor and Cox (1997) have researched the effects of such apprenticeship approaches. They developed what they termed a 'socially assisted learning approach' which involved teachers modelling the ways they solved mathematical word problems, then encouraging learners to engage in such problem-solving using several devices, such as the use of a reflection board in which teachers and pupils could share publicly their representation of a problem, peer collaboration, reflective questioning, scaffolding and quizzes. The pupils experiencing this approach did significantly better on word problem tests than a control group who just received their normal mathematics teaching. When they analysed in a more detailed way the interactions of the teachers and the pupils, the researchers found that the support offered by the teacher was not a function of the number of questions or statements the teacher made but rather that these questions/statements came at the right time, when they served to scaffold understanding.

In explaining their results, Taylor and Cox (1997) speculated that success with this type of learning was a result of shared ownership of the learning, in which were expectations that:

- all members of the group worked on the same aspect of the problem at the same time;
- members externalised their thoughts, including possible wrong approaches and answers;
- members came to agreement among themselves before proceeding; and
- as the teaching proceeded, more of the control of the activity was transferred from the adult to the children.

There appear to be four stages to the teaching process implied by these models.

Demonstration

During this stage, the expert models the skilful behaviour being taught. There is some evidence that learning can be assisted if this modelling is accompanied by a commentary by the expert, thinking aloud about the activities being undertaken. One relatively simple procedure is that of the teacher modelling how he/she tackles the skills he/she is teaching, for example, reading or writing in such a way that the learners have access to the thought processes which accompany these activities.

Joint activity

The expert and the learner share the activity. This may begin by the expert retaining responsibility for the difficult parts while the learner takes on the easy parts, while in some teaching strategies prior agreement is reached that participants will take turns at carrying out sections of the activity. The expert is always on hand to take full control if necessary. One of the best examples of this joint activity is that known as 'paired reading' (Morgan 1986) in which the teacher (or parent) and the learner read aloud in unison until the learner signals that he/she is ready to go it alone. The teacher withdraws from the reading but is ready to rejoin if the learner shows signs of difficulty such as prolonged pausing or reading errors.

Supported activity

The learner undertakes the activity alone, but under the watchful eye of the expert who is always ready to step in if necessary. In our work on the reading and writing of non-fiction (Wray and Lewis 1997) we have found that this is the stage in the process which is most often neglected and teachers tend to move too rapidly from heavily supporting the children's work to asking them to work without support. Consequently, this is the stage at which most of our practical teaching strategies, such as writing frames, were aimed. Such scaffolding strategies play a key role in the teaching approaches implied in the National Literacy Strategy.

Individual activity

The learner assumes sole responsibility for the activity. Some learners will, of course, move much more rapidly to this stage than others and the teacher needs to be sensitive to this. It is, arguably, equally as damaging to hold back learners by insisting they go through the same programme of support and practice as everyone else as it is to rush learners through such a programme when they need a more extensive programme of support.

Task 2.3.4
Using staged interactive teaching

Think of a skill you have taught in a primary school (or are planning to teach). Can you focus your teaching of this skill around the four steps of demonstration, joint activity, supported activity and individual activity? Jot down some notes on how you might use each of these stages in your teaching of this skill.

When you have done this activity, compare your approach to some of the examples given in Wray and Lewis 1997.

SUMMARY

In this unit I have outlined four major insights which can be derived from a study of learning. These are that:

- learning is a process of interaction between what is known and what is to be learnt;
- learning is a social process;
- learning is a situated process;
- learning is a metacognitive process.

Using these insights I have suggested four key principles for teaching. These are:

- we need to ensure that learners have sufficient previous knowledge/understanding to enable them to learn new things, and to help them make explicit these links between what they already know and what they are learning;
- we need to make provision for group interaction and discussion as teaching strategies, both in small, teacher-less groups and in groups working alongside experts;
- we need to ensure meaningful contexts for learning, particularly in what are often called basic skills;
- we need to promote learners' knowledge and awareness of their own thinking and learning.

These principles are, I have argued, best exemplified by what can be termed an 'apprenticeship' approach to teaching. There are many elements in the National Literacy and Numeracy Strategies which illustrate the use of such principles. I hope you will be able to see applications for these principles in all your teaching. The apprenticeship approach has, after all, been used for years to teach all sorts of material to all sorts of people in the world outside school – 'just plain folks' in the terms used by some researchers. Its rediscovery by school teachers was long overdue.

ANNOTATED FURTHER READING

Lave, J. and Wenger, E. (1991) *Situated Learning: Legitimate Peripheral Participation*, Cambridge: Cambridge University Press. This book contains an exploration of learning as participation in communities of practice. According to the authors, participation moves from the periphery to the 'centre'. Learning is, thus, not seen as the acquisition of knowledge by individuals so much as a process of *social* participation. This is a seminal text which opened up the concept of situated learning.

Wray, D. (1994) *Literacy and Awareness*, Sevenoaks: Hodder and Stoughton. If you would like to know more about the concept of metacognition and, in particular, its relation to the teaching of literacy, this book represents a very good start. It includes chapters on metacognition and understanding in reading, awareness and writing, and language awareness.

REFERENCES

Forman, E.A., Stein, M.K., Brown, C. and Larreamendy-Joerns, J. (1995) 'The socialization of mathematical thinking: the role of institutional, interpersonal, and discursive contexts', Paper presented at the 77th annual conference of the American Educational Research Association, San Francisco.

Garner, R. (1987) *Metacognition and Reading Comprehension*, Norwood, NJ: Ablex.

Holt, J. (1969) *How Children Fail*, Harmondsworth: Penguin.

Kumpulainen, K. and Wray, D. (2002) *Classroom Interaction and Social Learning*, London: RoutledgeFalmer.

Lave, J. and Wenger, E. (1991) *Situated Learning*, Cambridge: Cambridge University Press.

Miller, G.A. and Gildea, P.M. (1987) 'How children learn words', *Scientific American*, 257(3): 94–9.

Morgan, R. (1986) *Helping Children Read*, London: Methuen.

Palincsar, A. and Brown, A. (1984) 'Reciprocal teaching of comprehension-fostering and comprehension-monitoring activities', *Cognition and Instruction*, 1(2): 117–75.

Raphael, T., McMahon, S.I., Goatley, V.J., Bentley, J.L. and Boyd, F.B. (1992) 'Research directions: literature and discussion in the reading program', *Language Arts*, 69: 55–61.

Taylor, J. and Cox, B.D. (1997) 'Microgenetic analysis of group-based solution of complex two-step mathematical word problems by fourth graders', *Journal of Learning Science*, 6: 183–226.

Whimbey, A. (1975) *Intelligence Can Be Taught*, New York: Dutton.

Wray, D. and Lewis, M. (1997) *Extending Literacy*, London: Routledge.

Wray, D. and Medwell, J. (1991) *Literacy and Language in the Primary Years*, London: Routledge.

Unit 2.4

Developing Your Teaching Skills

Samantha Twiselton

INTRODUCTION

> Any subject can be taught to any child at any age in some form that is honest and powerful.
> (Bruner 1972: 122)

This is a bold claim and quite daunting to anyone contemplating the skills that might be needed for effective primary teaching. Yet it is actually quite useful in helping us to understand what should be involved. This chapter will look at the skills and knowledge required for you to be able to create and support successful learning experiences. It will focus in particular on the range of different factors that effective teachers need to consider when they decide what to do in the classroom.

OBJECTIVES

By the end of this unit you should be beginning to:

- understand the importance of being aware of the underlying structures that underpin learning objectives;
- understand some of the different types of knowledge involved in effective teaching;
- be able to relate these to the decisions informing teachers' actions in the classroom;
- develop strategies to help your own decision making in the classroom.

KNOWLEDGE AND LEARNING – FOR THE PUPIL AND THE TEACHER

According to Bruner and many others, learning involves the search for pattern, regularity and predictability. We can only make sense out of the confusion of information continuously bombarding our senses if we can *relate* the pieces of information to each other in some way. If a young child is presented with some bricks and the task of building a tower, this is only likely to be possible if s/he has had some other similar experiences to draw on (e.g. experimenting with bricks and learning something about how they balance, building other simple structures, etc.).

Input from a teacher should help children in the formation and discovery of the patterns and rules that are most likely to help them: a) make sense of the experience and b) generalise it to other experiences. Complex tasks can be broken down into manageable smaller problems so that the learner can detect patterns and regularities that could not be discovered alone. So a task like building a tower with bricks can be made possible by the presence of a teacher who helps the pupil through decisions and actions in small steps, while still holding 'the bigger picture' of the ultimate goal of the tower in mind.

Bruner's claim in the opening quotation is linked to the idea that the ultimate aim of teaching a subject is to help children understand the basic principles that help define it, give it identity and allow other things to be related to it meaningfully. The 'fundamental ideas' of a subject are defined as those ideas that have the greatest breadth of applicability to new problems. An effective teacher will have an excellent grasp of these fundamental concepts and will be able to break down tasks in ways that will make them achievable while still remaining consistent with the core ideas that underpin them. This means that core ideas are developed in nucleus as early as possible and are returned to with ever increasing complexity and sophistication in a 'spiral curriculum' as children's experience and understanding makes them ready for it.

So what does this mean in terms of the knowledge base required by you as a teacher and how this should be applied in the classroom? This can be a very alarming question for someone learning to be a primary school teacher as there are so many different subjects in the primary curriculum, each having its own detailed requirements.

QUALITY VERSUS QUANTITY

The answer to this problem may be helped by Sternberg and Horvath's (1995) attempt to define what is involved in teacher expertise. They comment that there are a number of studies (e.g. Chi *et al.* 1981; Larkin *et al.* 1980) that show that it is not so much the *amount* of knowledge that the expert possesses but *how it is organised* in the memory. In general, experts are sensitive to the deep structures of the problems they solve – they are able to group problems together according to underlying principles. This supports Bruner's model. It seems that the key to being able to teach, for example, history or mathematics is not so much your knowing endless information about the subject, as your understanding some of the key underlying principles and concepts that underpin it.

This is very much supported by my own study (Twiselton, 2000, 2003, 2004) of the types of knowledge and understanding that primary student teachers develop as they go through their Initial Teacher Education programme. I found that (partly dependent on how far through the programme they were) these students could be placed into one of three main categories (or points on a continuum) – *Task Manager*, *Curriculum Deliverer* or *Concept/Skill Builder*. The Task Managers (who were likely to be near the beginning of ITE) viewed their role in the classroom in terms of task completion, order and business – without any explicit reference to children's learning. The Curriculum Deliverers did see themselves as there to support learning – but only as dictated by an external source – a scheme, curriculum or lesson plan – and they struggled to give a rationale for *why what was being taught mattered* in any other terms. In contrast, the Concept/Skill Builders (likely to be at or near the end of ITE) were aware of the wider and deeper areas of understanding and skill needed by pupils that underpinned their learning objectives. Of the three types, the Concept/Skill Builders were much more likely to be able effectively, consistently and responsively to support learning at every stage of the learning experience. The most outstanding quality that separated the Concept/Skill Builders from the other two categories was their ability to see the 'bigger picture' and give a rationale for what they were attempting to do in terms of key principles and concepts.

Task 2.4.1
Connecting teaching and learning to the bigger picture

1   Choose the subject in which you feel most confident – *e.g. 1: English; e.g. 2: science.*
2   Choose a key area within it – *e.g. 1: poetry reading and writing; e.g. 2: solids, liquids and gases.*
3   Write the key area in the middle of a piece of paper and write words and phrases you associate with it around the edge – *e.g. 1: rhyme, rhythm, verses, language play, imagery; e.g. 2: evaporation and condensation, state, materials, properties.*
4   In a different colour write key words and phrases for all the ways in which this area is important – *e.g.1: it gives a pattern and meaning to chaotic experiences, it expresses emotion, it entertains, it conveys images, it communicates powerful ideas; e.g. 2: the changing properties of materials allow us to manipulate our environment, we can manufacture things using these changes, life on land requires the fresh water produced by evaporation and condensation.*
5   Look at the words and phrases in the two different colours you have used. Is it possible to connect them? *e.g. 1: rhyme and rhythm help to entertain and impose pattern and meaning, imagery is an effective way of communicating powerful ideas; e.g. 2: evaporation and condensation are important examples of key processes we use to manipulate the environment.* If so, you are connecting the 'what' with the 'why' in the way the Concept/Skill Builders were doing.
6   Consider the implications for how these aspects of the subject should be taught to pupils. How can you ensure that they are presented with the 'why' sufficiently?

The next stage is to work out what other factors will be involved and how this translates into classroom practice. Figures 2.4.1 and 2.4.2 provide some examples of how a similar approach can be taken through planning in Key Stage 1 and Key Stage 2. The commentary shows how the teaching can be directed by the underpinning rationale for the learning objectives.

OTHER TYPES OF TEACHER KNOWLEDGE

Any attempt to define all the different kinds of teacher knowledge required in effective practice is bound to hit the problem that the list can be infinitely extended. However, it is worth noting that most people agree that however you describe it, the knowledge base is wide-ranging and varied and that different kinds of knowledge are required at different times. Tochon and Munby (1993) studied expert and novice teachers and found that a key characteristic that distinguished the experts was their ability to draw on a wide range of different kinds of knowledge (e.g. the subject, the plan, the individual

DESIRED LEARNING OUTCOMES	
T5/6	Recite stories with predictable and repeating patterns and describe story settings and incidents
S2	Use awareness of grammar to decipher new words
W3	Hear initial and final phonemes

KEY LANGUAGE	USE OF ICT
Setting, character, phoneme, alliteration.	Clicker

ASSESSMENT [make reference to each section of the lesson]

Shared – yellow group – word choices.
Guided – red group – ability to make sentence orally and in writing.
Plenary – green group – explanation of choices.

USE OF OTHER ADULTS: *Mrs X to support green group in use of clicker.*

ANTICIPATED MISCONCEPTIONS/DIFFICULTIES: *Support with spelling strategies – reluctance to attempt unknown words – encourage to 'have a go' – use 'magic line'.*

ACTIVITIES		COMMENTARY
Introduction Approx. timing – 10 minutes	Introduce text. Look at cover – predict what the characters are thinking (whiteboards). Discuss title – explain that we are going to be spending the week thinking about stories with a repeating pattern. Discuss why people like repeating patterns and why such stories are enjoyable. Explain that we are going to be looking at repeating texts so that we can have a go at writing our own later in the week.	*It is important that pupils are helped to understand the purposes of the texts they look at.* *It is also helpful if there is a concrete goal (e.g. writing their own story based on this one) that is introduced at the beginning and can give meaning and purpose to the week's activities.*
Whole Class Work Use of additional support Approx. timing – 20 minutes	Read Bear Hunt – encourage joining in. Cover up words with post-its – time out for words it could be. Show me – ideas. Look at sound effects – time out for more words beginning with 'sw', etc. *Additional support – Mrs X focused observation of yellow group word choices on feedback sheet.*	*It is important to emphasise those aspects of the text that define it and make it enjoyable – joining in with repetition is a good way to do this.* *Explain that sound effects might be used in the story the children write – it will be useful to have a bank of words and ideas they can use later.*
Guided Group **Red group** Approx. timing – 20 minutes	1 Introduce Rosie's walk – explain similar to Bear Hunt in some ways. 2 Strategy check – matching phonemes. 3 Look through text – tell a partner how is same? 4 Review/discuss. 5 Look at text – compare with Bear Hunt – how different? What do we like about each one? 6 Review.	*Frame the whole discussion within the idea of eventually being able to take the best ideas from each book and use them in their own story. Remember to keep emphasising the features that make the text enjoyable.*
Independent Work Approx. timing – 20 minutes	Introduce independent work with whole class. Draw pictures for each stage of story. In pairs: blue group, green group – add simple captions underneath. Yellow group – clicker – put pictures in right order – find captions and paste.	*Explain that the independent work will help with planning their own stories later in the week.*
Plenary	Focus – green group. Blu-tack sentences on blackboard – green group read aloud.	*Explain that the captions will help when thinking of sentences for own stories later in the week.*

Figure 2.4.1 Lesson plan – Year 1/2 – Monday

DESIRED LEARNING OUTCOMES	
T3	To investigate how characters are presented through dialogue, action and description and through examining their relationship with other characters
S4	To adapt writing for different audiences

KEY LANGUAGE	USE OF ICT
Characterisation, empathy, perspective, imagery.	

ASSESSMENT [make reference to each section of the lesson]

Shared – yellow group – word choices.
Guided – red group – ability to make sentence orally and in writing.
Plenary – green group – explanation of choices.

*USE OF OTHER ADULTS: **Mrs X to support green group.***

*ANTICIPATED MISCONCEPTIONS/DIFFICULTIES: **Support with spelling strategies – reluctance to attempt unknown words.***

ACTIVITIES		COMMENTARY
Introduction Approx. timing – 15 minutes	**Look at cover – predict what the characters are thinking (whiteboards). Use freeze frame and thought tracking to follow this up. Could include a hot seat activity.** **Map out Bear Hunt – focus on one character – list words for each section to show how he is feeling.**	*In introducing the text yesterday it will have been important to explain it is going to be used to help consider how characters' perspectives change through the story so that pupils can write own story showing this.*
Whole Class Work Use of additional support *Mrs X focused observation of yellow group word choices on feedback sheet.* Approx. timing – 20 minutes	**Read opening passages from 'The Shrieking Face' – look at how author builds up images of how Angus is feeling – time out – show me – write up key words, phrases, sentences.** **Ask for ideas for similar language for Bear Hunt character:** **Teacher demo – 'He was feeling brave and adventurous – like a warrior going into battle.'** **Time out – paired ideas – supported composition.**	*It is important that the discussion focuses on the effective use of language for conveying characters' perspectives. Pupils need to keep alive that the purpose is to help them use language effectively in their own stories.*
Guided Group Approx timing – 15 minutes	**Red group – write opening sequence to new version – emphasise figurative language – use examples from shared work as starting point.**	*Keep the reader's needs in mind at all times – read aloud and check for effectiveness.*
Independent Work Approx. timing – 15 minutes	**Write key words on a story plan for each stage of the story. Write opening sequence.**	*It is important that the pupils understand that this is going to be continued later in the week.*
Plenary – 10 minutes	**Focus – green group.** **Blu-tack sentences on black board – green group read aloud – consider effectiveness.**	*The focus should be on effectiveness and audience.*

Figure 2.4.2 Lesson plan – Year 5 – Tuesday

pupil, the context etc.) in making one teaching decision. The novices tended to think about one thing at a time and to stick quite rigidly to their plan, regardless of whether the pupil responses, the context etc. supported this.

Lee Shulman (1987) has classified the knowledge base of teaching into seven categories: content knowledge (better known to us as subject knowledge), general pedagogical knowledge, curriculum knowledge, pedagogical content knowledge, knowledge of learners and their characteristics, knowledge of educational contexts, and knowledge of educational ends. Others (e.g. Turner-Bisset 1999) have expanded this list. The important thing for student teachers to note is not so much the items on the list (though these are useful) but the fact that they are so varied. It is the *drawing together and combining* of these varied factors that is important.

This is supported by both TTA studies in effective numeracy (1997) and literacy (1998) teachers. The Medwell *et al.* (1998) study found that the subject knowledge of the effective literacy teachers was only fully identifiable when it was embedded within a teaching context: 'Our interpretation of what we have observed is that the effective teachers only knew their material by how they represented it to children … through experience of teaching it, their knowledge seemed to have been totally embedded in pedagogic practices' (Medwell *et al.* 1998: 24). They also found that the effective teachers tended to have more coherent belief systems linked to the importance of communication, composition and understanding. This links with Bruner's views about the key components that are the fundamentals of the subject. In the parallel effective numeracy teachers study (1997), Askew *et al.* characterised effective numeracy teachers as being 'connectionist-oriented'. They claimed that the highly effective teachers believed that being numerate required having a rich network of connections between different mathematical ideas.

COMBINING KNOWLEDGE

In Sternberg and Horvath's (1995) study of teaching expertise three key features are identified. The first is *knowledge* and we have already considered their claim that the organisation of the knowledge around principles is the central factor. The second and third features are *efficiency* and *insight*. Efficiency is closely linked to experience in that the claim is that experts are much faster at processing information and making well-informed decisions, partly because what is initially effort-full and time-consuming becomes effortless and automatic with practice. This is obvious, and one of the most comforting pieces of advice that can be given to student teachers is that as time goes on many things that are difficult now become much easier. However, it is worth noting that Sternberg and Horvath also claim that experts typically spend a greater proportion of time trying to understand the problem whereas novices spend more in actually trying out different solutions. Sometimes deciding the best response through more detailed analysis is a much more efficient way of dealing with it than rushing in without clear judgement.

It can be argued that *insight*, Sternberg and Horvath's third feature of teacher expertise, involves a combination of the first two (knowledge and efficiency). Insight involves distinguishing information that is relevant to the problem solution from that which is irrelevant. This obviously provides the expert teacher with an insight into the situation, which will enable her/him to: a) make the most efficient use of the time available and b) draw on the most useful areas of knowledge.

My study of student teachers (mentioned above) also involved examining how expert teachers operate. I did this through observing them teach, making detailed notes of their actions and words, and interviewing them closely afterwards about how they decided what to do. The following extract is

Task 2.4.2
Analysing assessment cycles

1   Read through the observation notes and use the ASSESSMENT/RESPONSE column to make a note of any points at which the teacher (X) appears to be making an assessment or acting on the basis of an assessment made.
2   Repeat this with the observation notes below on p. 76 (from a different teacher).
3   What are the differences you notice between the two teachers?

OBSERVATION NOTES	ASSESSMENT/RESPONSE
9.23 X is talking to child (C1) about her picture of a ladybird: "Do you want to do some writing to tell everyone about this?" (C1 nods) "What shall we write?" C1: "The ladybird is sitting on a leaf" X: "Excellent. Which side shall we start?" C1 "Over here" 9.25 X: "You go ahead and write it and show me in a minute" X is explaining the spiders web pattern to a child (C2) 9.27 X: "Can you make the lines go all along the web? It's very important you start at the left and finish on the right because we are practising for writing. Where's the left? Where will you start?" (C2 shows her; she observes closely as C2 starts the web.) X: "Lovely, don't forget to keep your pencil on the line. Nice and slow." 9.30 X: "What a lot of lovely writing. I can see some of the letters of your name. Where's the 'm'?" C1: Here and here X: "You've done those beautifully. Can you read me your writing now?" C1: "The ladybird is sitting on the leaf. She has lots of children and they like flying." 9.32 X: "Wow! You've added more to it! You told me earlier on that there was an 'l' at the beginning of ladybird. Where might the 'l' have gone here?" (C1 points randomly and vaguely) X: "Can you read it again and point to the words at the same time?" (C1 moves her finger along the line from left to right, but there is no attempt to match up the writing with what she is saying.) 9.34 X: Now I'll write my writing. Where shall I start?" (C1 shows her, X writes the words and reads them as she does so) X: "Let's read it again together." They read it, X gently holds C1's finger and helps her to point to the words as they read.	

OBSERVATION NOTES	ASSESSMENT/RESPONSE
10.10 TT to C1: What does that say? (points from left to right over the label) No answer from C1 TT: What does it start with? C1: It's a drink TT: Yes, but what does it start with? C1: Don't know TT: It's milk! 10.12 TT to the whole group: Take it in turns to choose a card – see if you can match it. C2 takes a card TT: What does that say? (C2 is looking at the picture) C2: Chocolate TT: Good girl! Put it in the right place. 10.14 C3 takes a card with a sandwich label TT: What does that say? Have you got that? C3: It says pizza TT: It's not pizza. What does it say? It says sandwich! 10.17 C1 takes a card TT: What does that card say? (no answer) TT: W.... C1 Watermelon TT: Brilliant! 10.19 C2 takes a card TT: What does it say? C2: Ice-cream TT: Have you got ice cream? (TT points to game card) C2: No 10.20 TT: Well done!	

an example of the notes taken and Task 2.4.2 helps with understanding how this can be analysed to show how effective teachers constantly assess the situation in order to make the most effective response.

The second set of observation notes were taken from a student teacher (TT) during her first placement. The differences are notable. The student teacher assesses in a limited way and only uses a narrow range of strategies. The expert teacher is constantly assessing and responding and she uses a range of strategies in doing this. This supports Sternberg and Horvath's claims that effective teachers demonstrate knowledge, efficiency and insight through their ability to quickly process and analyse a learning experience and draw on a range of conceptual principles to make the best decisions for action.

SUMMARY

Teaching is a very complicated business and effective teaching requires a wide range of types of knowledge and a large number of skills. In this unit I have tried to elaborate on some of the more important components of teaching skills and to explore the implications of these for your teaching. It is important to close this unit with a reminder of the importance of quality over quantity. It is not the amount you know, or the number of teaching skills you have some competence in that are crucial. Your depth of knowledge and level of confidence in your skills is of much more importance. As you experience teaching, keep asking yourself the 'why' question and keep your eyes and ears open to children's responses. Deeper knowledge and surer confidence in your actions will follow if this becomes your natural mindset.

ANNOTATED FURTHER READING

Askew, M., Brown, M., Rhodes, V., William, D. and Johnson, D. (1997) *Effective Teachers of Numeracy*, London: Teacher Training Agency. This study was commissioned by the TTA as an enquiry into the characteristics (skills, knowledge and beliefs) of teachers identified as effective in teaching numeracy, and, indirectly, as an evidence base for the establishment of the Standards for the award of Qualified Teacher Status in the area of numeracy teaching. Its most significant finding was that the effective teachers of numeracy were those able to see and explain to pupils the rich connections between areas of numerical knowledge.

Medwell, J., Wray, D., Poulson, L. and Fox, R. (1998) *Effective Teachers of Literacy*, London: Teacher Training Agency. This was the parallel TTA study exploring the characteristics of effective teachers of literacy. One of its most important findings was that teacher subject knowledge in literacy was not a simple matter of what teachers knew about language. How they knew it, and the contexts in which they could apply it were of much more significance.

Shulman, L.S. (1987) 'Knowledge and teaching: foundations of the new reform', *Harvard Educational Review*, 57(1): 1–22. Lee Shulman might fairly claim to have invented the field of teachers' subject knowledge and his work has been the inspiration for numerous studies in a range of subject areas.

REFERENCES

Askew, M., Brown, M., Rhodes, V., William, D. and Johnson D. (1997) *Effective Teachers of Numeracy*, London: TTA.

Bruner, J. (1972) *The Relevance of Education*, Trowbridge: Redwood Press.

Chi, M.T.H., Feltovich, J.P. and Glaser, R. (1981) 'Categorization and representation of physics problems by experts and novices', *Cognitive Science*, 5(2): 121–52.

Larkin, J., McDermott, J., Simon, D. and Simon, A. (1980) 'Expert and novice performance in solving physics problems', *Science*, 208: 1335–42.

Medway, J., Wray, D., Poulson, L. and Fox, R. (1998) *Effective Teachers of Literacy*, London: TTA.

Shukmna, L.S. (1987) 'Kowledge and teaching: foundations of the new reform', *Harvard Educational Review*, (57(1): 1–22.

Sternberg, R. and Horvath, J. (1995) 'A prototype view of expert learning', *Education Research*, 24(6): 9–17.

Tochon, F. and Munby, H. (1993) 'Novice and expert teachers' time epistemology: a wave function from didactics to pedagogy', *Teaching and Teacher Education*, 2: 205–18.

Twiselton, S. (2000) 'Seeing the wood for the trees: the National Literacy Strategy and Initial Teacher Education; pedagogical content knowledge and the structure of subjects', *Cambridge Journal of Education*, 30(3): 391–403.

Twiselton, S. (2003) 'Beyond the curriculum: learning to teach primary literacy', in E. Bearne, H. Dombey and T. Grainger (eds) *Interactions in Language and Literacy in the Classroom*, Milton Keynes: Open University Press.

Twiselton, S. (2004) 'The role of teacher identity in learning to teach primary literacy', *Education Section Review: Activity Theory*, Special Edition.

Turner-Bisset, R. (1999) 'Knowledge bases for teaching', *British Educational Research Journal*, 25(1): 39–55.

3 Planning and Managing Learning

Unit 3.1

Approaching Long- and Medium-term Planning

Jane Medwell

INTRODUCTION

The focus of this unit is longer-term planning: the termly and yearly plans you will use to prepare your teaching across the curriculum. This sort of planning includes long-term planning expressed as school policies and medium-term planning expressed as termly or half-termly planning sheets. Planning at this level is the basis of all your teaching but it is not something you will easily encounter during your initial training. You should take every opportunity to look at, discuss and question the medium- and long-term plans you encounter.

OBJECTIVES

By the end of this unit you should:

- understand the difference between long-term and medium-term planning;
- understand the purposes of long- and medium-term planning;
- know the key features of long- and medium-term plans;
- understand the range of issues considered when making long- and medium-term plans;
- be confident in interpreting medium-term plans.

THE IMPORTANCE OF LONG-TERM PLANNING

Long-term planning can often seem like a 'given' in school. When you go to a school placement the planning is already there in the form of national curriculum documents and school policies. This may even already have been translated into medium-term plans. However, it is important that you understand how long- and medium-term plans are developed and it is important that you can question the assumptions upon which such plans are based.

Long-term plans for a Key Stage are usually determined through whole-staff discussion, a process in which you may not be able to be involved. If you do not contribute to long-term planning, then you will always teach what, and how, someone else has chosen, instead of participating in those decisions yourself. One of the most important parts of your NQT year will be the opportunity to participate in policy reviews.

WHAT ARE YOU PLANNING?

Long-term planning is the process whereby the school team decides how the curriculum is taught across the whole school or Key Stage. It shows:

- exactly what the school curriculum is;
- how the curriculum is covered in terms of breadth and depth;
- how the curriculum is structured within year groups and across Key Stages;
- how much time is allocated to each area of the curriculum in each year group.

The curriculum to be covered in state-maintained schools in England at FKS, KS1 or KS2 includes the statutory content of the National Curriculum for the relevant Key Stage. At Foundation Key Stage this includes the Early Learning Goals and at KS1 and 2, the programmes of study and statements of attainment.

The documents of the National Curriculum are available on the National Curriculum website (<www.nc.uk.net>) and give a broad outline of the content of the curriculum, but not how it is to be taught. This is the role of long-term planning in schools.

For each subject and for each Key Stage, programmes of study set out what pupils should be taught, and attainment targets set out the expected standards of pupils' performance. Schools choose how they organise their school curriculum to include the programmes of study. Teachers' planning for schemes of work usually starts with the programmes of study and the needs and abilities of their pupils. Level descriptions can help to determine the degree of challenge and progression for work across each year of a Key Stage.

Some key issues taken into consideration when planning long term are:

- *breadth* – so that pupils experience the full range of curriculum areas and the key skills discussed above as well as any additional skills and learning identified as important in the school curriculum;
- *depth* – so there are opportunities for in-depth learning and the chance for children to really develop their own understandings;
- *coherence* – so that natural and meaningful links within and between some subjects are recognised and developed to help children learn as purposefully as possible;
- *relevance* – so that pupils' activities relate to previous learning and so that they can understand how the learning is relevant to them;

- *differentiation* – so the needs and progress of pupils are catered for;
- *progression* – so learning develops through sequenced activities as children go through each term and school year, without undue repetition.

Task 3.1.1
Beginning to plan a topic

This task aims to get you to consider a popular topic such as healthy living, where it appears in the NC and how this might be taught to children at KS2.

Go to the National Curriculum online at <www.nc.uk.net> and look at the KS2 PSHE guidance. Identify the programme of study under Knowledge, Skills and Understanding.

Developing a healthy, safer lifestyle
3) Pupils should be taught:
what makes a healthy lifestyle, including the benefits of exercise and healthy eating, what affects mental health, and how to make informed choices

This is only a small part of the PSHE curriculum (which does not have statements of attainment).

Now identify what areas of the curriculum are related to this PSHE programme of study. Look at the programmes of study and attainment targets for Science at KS2 and PE at KS2.

HOW WILL YOU PLAN TO TEACH THE CONTENT?

The content of the statutory curriculum and the needs of the children are two defining factors in what you teach. In long-term planning you also have to consider:

- how much time is allocated to each area of the curriculum in each year group;
- how the curriculum is structured within year groups and across Key Stages.

How much time to allocate to learning in each subject, theme or key skill is an important area for negotiation. The working week in school includes activities such as collective worship and assemblies as well as lessons. It will not be possible to include every learning experience that teachers would like. For instance, a KS2 English co-ordinator might suggest the following allocation of time for English for all KS2 children:

- an hour for literacy study every day (5 hours);
- ten minutes for daily handwriting practice (50 minutes);
- twenty minutes for reading a story or poem to children every day (1 hour 40 minutes);
- 20 minutes per week for speaking and listening;
- time for setting and doing spelling tests (30 minutes);
- a weekly drama session in the hall (40 minutes);
- a daily 15-minute silent reading time for all pupils (1 hour 15 minutes).

All these are worthy activities but if all were to be timetabled, the English part of the curriculum could consume more than ten hours of a week in which there are only around 25 teaching hours! Each subject can always justify more time, and national targets, such as the aspiration of two hours physical education a week, must be taken into account. This is why long-term planning requires decisions about school priorities and about the use of time for cross-curricular work.

Although the time available for teaching and learning is finite, there are a number of ways to plan this time so that it is used effectively and helps children to make links between their different areas of learning. Dividing school time rigidly into 'subjects' so that each subject has a weekly allocation may not be the most effective way to use the time. For instance, rather than having a timed 'lesson' for developing the spiritual, moral, social and cultural (SMSC) lives of children, most schools plan to address this through a range of provision: school assemblies, collective worship, RE and whole school activities, as well as the rules and ethos of the school. This does not mean that SMSC 'just happens' or that it is a less important aspect of school life than other subjects. The school has a clear policy and a detailed medium-term plan is derived from it. But it has decided that the best way to address SMSC is not through a weekly 'lesson'.

Some schools decide to 'block' subjects, so that children will have a meaningful block of time for a subject but may not have this subject every week of the year. Children may, for example, do art for one half-term and DT the next, or history one term and a geography topic the next. In this way, the material can be studied, explored and learnt in depth, with an integrity and relevance that would not be possible in 15 minutes per week.

In Foundation Stage and KS1 it is very common to find that time is planned around the topic that is the focus of children's learning, with sessions not clearly 'labelled' as particular subjects. The curriculum planning is used to ensure a balanced curriculum but the need for activities to make sense to the children is more important than the need for labels.

Another example of planning across the curriculum might be the introduction of the teaching of a modern foreign language at KS2. Some schools address the allocation of time for MFL by scheduling a regular MFL slot for each class, or simply arranging a club out of school time. Other schools will 'block' MFL teaching so that children do it more intensively in a particular term of the school year. In some schools the Y6 children have a very intense MFL programme in the last term of school, after SATs and at the same time as transition to secondary school is considered. Other schools will look for opportunities for cross-curricular approaches. They might have a regular MFL lesson for all children but also integrate MFL into the school curriculum through assemblies about other cultures, writing to twin schools in English, answering the register in other languages and learning about the target country in geography. This does not actually eat up more curriculum time than the timetabled lesson but, through careful planning, gives the children a much broader experience. Decisions about how to allocate time to MFL will depend not only on the learning goals and time available but also on who will teach this aspect of the curriculum and what resources are needed. This is true across the curriculum.

In considering how to structure the curriculum within year groups and across Key Stages you will have to consider the possibilities and resources available to you. The use of expensive resources that must be shared, such as IT suites and halls, is an important consideration. Teacher time and expertise is also a valuable resource that needs to be planned effectively. A teacher who is particularly qualified or expert in a subject like music, a foreign language or sport might well spend a good part of their time teaching a whole range of classes. This does not apply only to individual teachers who already have a particular skill or knowledge. Many schools ask teachers to develop particular specialisms, so that their teaching energy can be used effectively. It may also be useful for teachers to concentrate on a smaller range of subjects so that they can consolidate expertise and make planning and assessment manageable. Some schools will plan to make the teaching (including planning and assessment) manageable by using sets across classes or Key Stages, or by having teachers teach different parts of the curriculum to a range of classes. These sorts of decisions can help to make good use of expertise and to make the learning meaningful and relevant to children. When considering such arrangements, a school staff will weigh them against the lack of continuity caused by a change of teacher and the demands of moving children around between lessons.

The long-term planning undertaken by a school will be expressed through its policies, prospectus and development plan. You need to read these documents carefully. You will notice these documents will have review dates and will be regularly considered by staff so that changes to long-term planning can be made. There are some decisions that will be very clear to you as you work in school but may not be written down – this can include the organisation of sets and groupings and the timing of the school day. If you choose your moment well, mentors and teachers will be happy to discuss these important, but often unwritten parts of school policy.

ASSESSMENT AND TARGET SETTING IN LONG-TERM PLANNING

One aspect of school planning that is relatively difficult to observe but has a real influence on long-term planning is school target-setting. This happens at a number of levels. At national level in England, there are targets for the proportion of 11-year-olds achieving level 4 in English and mathematics National Curriculum tests at the end of Key Stage 2. Schools, with the help of their Local Education Authority, are required to set targets for the proportions of their pupils reaching these targets. Within school, further targets are set for particular Key Stages and year groups.

School senior managers use the SAT results and the optional tests in English and mathematics to monitor pupils' progress towards these targets. SAT results are available to schools as summaries of data that can be used with the pupil assessment tracker to help heads and teachers set targets for schools, Key Stages and individual year groups. These targets are negotiated with the head, subject co-ordinator and teachers so that everyone is clear not only what is to be achieved, but what action can be taken to help children reach their targets. Such actions might include changes to staffing, such as changing the proportion of teaching assistance or special needs support, the provision of resources or timing of booster classes and other interventions. These decisions exemplify how national targets become school targets and influence long-term and medium-term planning. When you are in school, ask your mentor about the school's targets and your class teacher about class targets.

How the school assesses is also a matter for long-term planning. All schools required to follow the National Curriculum are also required to undertake statutory assessment and report to parents annually (although the arrangements are different in England, Wales and Scotland). However, schools also have to decide how they will conduct their assessment for learning so that it is most useful and underpins teaching, without generating unnecessary work or disrupting teaching. The school will have an assessment policy which is certainly worthy of your attention.

MEDIUM-TERM PLANNING

Medium-term plans will address the National Curriculum and the policies of the school but will be much more specific than long-term planning. Medium-term planning might be half-termly or termly planning. Plans will be subject or theme specific, but also demonstrate links to other subjects. They will give you much more detail about:

- the organisation and timetable of the particular class, and of any sets or other teaching arrangements;
- learning objectives for the class and sets;
- learning experiences and activities that will take place in the term or half-term;

- continuity and progression in learning – the way the learning is paced and broken up into manageable units.

Teachers have access to a good deal of support in their medium-term planning in the form of government schemes of work and frameworks of objectives which, although not statutory, are very widely used. The KS1 and KS2 *Frameworks for Teaching Literacy and Mathematics* usually form a part of the school's medium-term planning, although they are not statutory. The objectives in these frameworks are ideal for medium-term planning and can be grouped carefully so that some are addressed repeatedly and some just once. These objectives are designed for medium-term planning and you would not expect to be able to address them in a single lesson. They are objectives for a sequence of lessons and more than one objective might be addressed in a single lesson.

The National Primary Strategy publishes medium-term plans for maths and English for each year group, based on the literacy and numeracy objectives. These plans are very useful in grouping objectives in ways that make sense – for example, so that you plan to teach imperative sentences during a unit of work on instructions, rather than trying to teach a less appropriate sentence type. However, most teachers do not use these ready-made plans unadapted, as the plans cannot take account of the children in a particular class and their prior experience. Even so, the published plans are a very useful tool for shaping your own medium-term plans and the web-based format is helpful. As well as the frameworks, you would also need to consider other aspects of maths and English work and include planning for speaking and listening, and cross-curricular links between English and Maths and other subjects. It would be unfortunate to ignore the real opportunities for literacy and oracy offered by the study of geography, history or science, for instance.

The schemes of work for foundation subjects and MFL (QCA/DfES) are also not statutory but are widely used. They demonstrate one way of organising medium-term plans for non-core subjects and are used flexibly in most schools. Schools often adapt these to meet their specific needs, local situation or available resources.

Task 3.1.2
Using schemes of work to plan

Look at the DfES standards site, which contains the schemes of work available to schools www.standards.dfes.gov.uk.
Follow up PSHE, the healthy living statement from the programme of study for Science and PE.

- What units of work for Science are relevant in each KS2 year (Y3, 4, 5, 6)?
- What PE units are relevant?
- Examine how the units are structured to ensure that the knowledge, skills and understanding are addressed as well as breadth of study.
- What Science and PE units of study would you specifically identify for a Y4 class, if you were aiming to teach the PSHE PoS about healthy living?

You can take this investigation further by looking at the literacy schemes of work and suggesting ways to link the Science unit studied to the text types studied in each term, or look at the ICT scheme of work to find links between Science and use of ICT.

The medium-term plan will be written well before the start of the term or half-term it applies to. In most cases it will be written by a group of teachers – either a Key Stage or year group team. The plan may well be based upon, or use elements from, a previous year's plan but will never be simply copied again. The meetings where plans are written, or those where plans are reviewed, are some of the most useful meetings you can attend.

The role of the medium-term plan is:

- to provide the detailed framework for classroom practice in a way that can be understood by everyone involved and can be scrutinised by co-ordinators, heads and inspectors (or taken up by a supply teacher, if necessary);
- to identify the nature of work to be covered during the term or half-term and ensure that it covers the requirements set out in the long-term plan;
- to reflect the broad principles laid down in the school's policy for the subject and curriculum and ensure that agreed routines and teaching take place;
- to detail the knowledge, skills and processes to be taught during the half-term or term;
- to involve all staff concerned with its teaching in both its writing and subsequent review;
- to give clear guidance about the range of teaching styles and assessment techniques to be used.

For you, as a trainee, the medium-term plan has an additional role. It is there for you to discuss with your mentor, teacher, curriculum co-ordinators and teaching assistants. A detailed discussion of the medium-term plan is a very focused way of learning about how the class operates and is the first step in moving towards your responsibilities as a teacher. If you are able to discuss the medium-term plan for one subject with the teacher, you can then identify how you might be involved. Is there an activity you can plan, for instance?

The most important elements of a medium-term plan are:

- title of the unit of work and identified curriculum areas;
- objectives or learning outcomes: concepts, knowledge, skills and attitudes (related to the NC PoS or Early Years curriculum);
- key learning questions derived from objectives for pupils. These are not as simple as you might imagine. You must be well-informed in the subject area and anticipate areas of uncertainty or confusion;
- relevant attainment targets, level descriptions and a clear note of what you expect the majority of the class to achieve;
- broad aspects of differentiation such as how you differentiate for different sets or groups;
- key vocabulary for pupils;
- broad comments about activities: showing progression and organisation;
- identified assessment tasks: summative and formative. These might include 'formal assessment tasks' such as a particular piece of writing, a quiz or a mind map at the end of a unit of work but will also include the lesson outcomes as you go through the unit. These are important formative assessment opportunities.

In addition to these content-specific medium-term plans, most teachers have very carefully elaborated, but often unwritten, plans for the non-subject based parts of the curriculum. You need to learn routines, resources, the rules of behaviour, standards and processes of marking, and tokens of reward. You should know how your teacher works with the teaching assistants and how plans and assessments are shared amongst the teaching team. These aspects of class work may be enshrined in policies, but you may need to learn them through observation and discussion. These aspects of the curriculum, the unwritten curriculum, facilitate children's learning and knowing them marks you out as a teacher.

**Task 3.1.3
Influences on planning**

Think back to the last piece of medium-term planning in which you were involved. Try to isolate any aspects of the unwritten curriculum applying in your class which influenced your medium-term plans in any way. Examples of features you might suggest include:

• availability of teaching assistants/other adults in the classroom;
• physical aspects of the classroom, e.g. ready availability of a sink;
• rewards systems operating in the class/school. For each feature, describe how it influenced your planning, and what you might have done (or did do) to moderate the effects of this influence.

SUMMARY

Planning, teaching and assessment are often described as a cycle, because each process is dependent on the others. Teachers devote a considerable amount of their time and energy to planning effectively, something that has now been recognised in teachers' working conditions. There is no perfect teaching plan because there is no ideal class. Long-term plans are based on a National Curriculum that has had widespread national discussion, but still needs to be made relevant and workable in the context of each school, through planning the curriculum, resources and teaching. Even when long-term plans are established, the medium-term plan has to take account of the particular class and situation. Having clear medium-term plans is a very good basis for writing the short-term plans you will be teaching from, but it does not mean those medium-term plans are set in stone. You will find that sometimes teaching does not follow the expected plans, or some outcomes are not what you expect. All teachers make changes to their medium-term plans. They may change the rate at which they address issues, omit or add items, or alter the manner or order in which topics are addressed. These changes do not indicate poor medium-term planning – they show that the teacher is making clear assessments of children's performance and evaluating the teaching techniques, pace and strategies necessary for the children to make progress.

ANNOTATED FURTHER READING

Medwell, J. (2005) *Successful Teaching Placement*, Exeter: Learning Matters. This book covers in much greater detail issues of planning for work with pupils at various stages. It also discusses the implementation of these plans and strategies for successful teaching.

The DfES Standards site http://www.standards.dfes.gov.uk/schemes3/. This site now hosts the DfES/QCA schemes of work for the various subjects in the primary curriculum. The site states that,

Many schools take the schemes of work as the starting point for their plans. They make their own decisions about how to make best use of this resource, remembering that the schemes are not statutory. Schools can use as much or as little as they wish and are free to devise their own ways of meeting the requirements of the national curriculum.

There is also guidance here on how to plan with the schemes and adapt units of work.

The QCA site http://www.qca.org.uk/8680.html. This now includes a section entitled Customise your curriculum, which is designed specifically to give

> examples of how teachers are taking ownership of the curriculum, shaping it and making it their own, by:
>
> - embedding aspects of English and mathematics in other subjects – giving pupils opportunities to use basic skills in rich, relevant and motivating contexts;
> - adapting units from the schemes of work – adjusting plans to better meet their children's needs;
> - combining units from different subjects – making learning more coherent, connecting essential skills, knowledge and understanding.

REFERENCES

Department for Education and Skills (undated) *The Standards Site – Primary National Strategy (Literacy)* http://www.standards.dfes.gov.uk/primary/literacy/.

Department for Education and Skills (undated) *The Standards Site – Primary National Strategy (Mathematics)* http://www.standards.dfes.gov.uk/primary/mathematics/.

Department for Education and Skills (undated) *The Standards Site – Schemes of Work* http://ww.standards.dfes.gov.uk/schemes3/.

Unit 3.2

Approaching Short-term Planning

Jane Medwell

INTRODUCTION

The focus of this unit is short-term planning: the weekly and daily planning you will do to prepare your teaching across the curriculum. Planning at this level is one of your most onerous tasks during training but it is one of your greatest learning experiences. As you build up your responsibility for planning you will develop a real understanding of its central importance in teaching. This unit also refers to your use of ICT in teaching and underlines the importance of planning for this.

OBJECTIVES

By the end of this unit you should:

- understand the difference between medium-term and short-term planning;
- understand the purposes of short-term planning;
- know the key features of short-term plans;
- be able to critically evaluate examples of short-term planning;
- feel more confident to write some of your plans during your school experience.

THE IMPORTANCE OF SHORT-TERM PLANNING

All teachers undertake short-term planning for their teaching. They will do weekly and, sometimes, daily plans. As a trainee you will do both weekly and daily plans. You will base these on the medium- or long-term plans available to you in schools during your placement or, later in your training, on medium-term plans you may have made yourself. A short-term plan is your tool for adapting the broad objectives of the medium-term planning for the learning needs of your class. This means you may have to add or omit parts of the medium-term plan, rearrange the order in which work is done and plan the way you teach, in detail, so that all the children can learn.

The most obvious reason for planning your lessons carefully is to ensure that you offer children engaging and appropriate lessons. You have to ensure that your lessons address the teaching you have foreseen in medium-term plans in such a way that all the children in the class can understand and explore the issues. As each child is different, you have to plan lessons that present information in ways suitable for all. This is the role of differentiation.

As a trainee, the creation of short-term plans also has a formative role for you and is a key training experience in itself. By writing a short-term plan you are 'rehearsing' your lessons, anticipating challenges and working out exactly what you will do. By evaluating each short-term plan as the basis for the next, you are learning lessons from what you and the children have done. A cycle of planning, assessment, modification and more planning is the basis for children's learning. It is also the basis of yours!

Finally, short-term plans are also a way for you to be accountable, as a teacher and a trainee. Teachers write weekly plans so that they, or other teachers, can work from them and adapt them, but also so that head teachers, colleagues, inspectors and outside agencies can scrutinise and work with the plans. You will write plans so that your teacher and teaching assistants can understand the plans and their roles in them. Teachers and mentors will be able to examine and advise you about these plans and those assessing your performance can gain insights into your professional thinking. If nothing clse, this is good practice for an Ofsted-inspected future!

PLANNING FORMATS

The format of your plans will depend on a number of factors, including the age group you are teaching, your course requirements and school practices where you are teaching. You will probably find that completing some sort of grid on the word processor is easiest but it is not essential – clarity is the main issue. There is no single, perfect planning format and you may find that you want to adapt your format to meet your training needs.

Teachers will usually have a weekly plan for each subject at Key Stage 1 and 2, although the strong links across the curriculum may dictate a topic or integrated plan. In early KS1 and the Foundation Key Stage the weekly plan will usually be written by at least the teacher and teaching assistant. It may involve a larger team. It will address all the areas of development and will usually be planned around a theme. A good weekly planning format will include most or all of the following:

- weekly objectives related to daily tasks;
- references to the relevant curriculum documents;
- task objectives;
- texts, ICT and other resources to be used;
- a summary of each activity for each group, identifying differentiation;

- specific roles for teaching assistants;
- key points for plenary sessions;
- assessment points.

Weekly plans will break down learning and teaching in such a way that the children can achieve the learning objectives. This is a difficult skill because, as well as knowing everything necessary for medium-term planning, to do weekly plans you need to know what the children have already done, know and can do; the pace the children work at; their individual needs; and the likely response of the children to what you are planning. You will 'predict' these elements of the teaching for the week but will find that you have to change or amend these weekly plans in response to the children's learning. This is good practice and shows you are using assessments to inform your plans. It is a good idea to amend weekly plans by hand, so that observers can *see* that you are doing this.

Figure 3.2.1 shows an example of a format suitable for planning a sequence of lessons. Annotations under the figure give further details about the kinds of material you might include in each section of the plan.

Experienced teachers may teach from their weekly plans and as you gain experience you may too. When you start teaching you will plan your early lessons and parts of lessons on the basis of the teacher's weekly plans. As your placement progresses, you will be required to write weekly plans (or sequences of lesson plans) for core subjects. You may do this as part of a teaching team but you will be expected to make a significant contribution and to lead the planning at this level before you can achieve the standards for the award of QTS.

One very important aspect of planning that is best addressed through weekly plans is the issue of routine activities such as guided group or individual reading and writing, story telling, registration, distribution of maths games or books, story reading, book browsing, spelling tests, handwriting practice, tables practice, mark making, weather recording, show and tell and action rhyme times. These routines are easy to overlook but they are very important. Patterns of activity that are known to both child and adult are soothing, familiar and powerful learning activities. Your weekly plan needs to be checked to ensure these activities represent the balance you want and that they are planned.

LESSON PLANNING

On the basis of weekly plans, you can construct detailed, daily plans. The format depends on the age of the children and what you are planning for. The key elements that you should include are:

- class/group taught;
- time and duration of lesson;
- objectives for the session or lesson;
- reference to the relevant curriculum documents;
- texts, ICT and other resources to be used;
- structure and timings of the lesson;
- summary of each activity for each group, identifying differentiation and what you expect teacher and children to do;
- specific roles for teaching assistants and, usually, a plan for the teaching assistant;
- details of teacher and child activity;
- key vocabulary to be used;
- key questions to be asked;
- key teaching points;

Term/Year:			Teaching Group:		
Curriculum Subject/Theme/Area(s) of Learning:					
Broad Learning Objectives	**Learning Objectives**	**Key Activities**	**Resources**	**Cross-curricular Aspects**	**Planned Method of Assessment**

Broad Learning Objectives: • specific references to Early Learning Goals, NC, NNS, NLS, agreed syllabus for RE
Learning Objectives: stating anticipated achievement in one or more of the following: • attitudes (show…)   • skills (be able to…)   • knowledge (know that…)   • understanding (develop concept of…)   These form the basis of assessment and are judged through planned outcomes
Activities should: • enable Learning Objectives to be met   • include a variety of experiences that progressively develop children's learning   • recognise pupils' diverse needs (including pupils with SEN, more able and gifted pupils, and pupils with EAL)   • take account of pupils' gender and ethnicity
Resources should be: • influenced by Learning Objectives   • listed in detail   • considered with health and safety in mind   • related to displays where relevant
Opportunities to develop significant and planned attitudes, skills, knowledge and understanding *across* the curriculum in (e.g.):   • English   • ICT   • PSHE/Citizenship   • other NC subjects/areas of learning where significant
Anticipated Evidence: • to demonstrate achievement of Learning Objectives, and to inform assessment and record keeping (may be observational, verbal, written or graphic evidence, depending on activity)   • to reflect a *range* of assessment methods

Figure 3.2.1 An example format for planning a sequence of lessons

- identified outcomes (how will you assess whether the children have achieved their learning objective?);
- note of pupils' previous experience;
- cross-curricular links;
- identified health and safety issues (such as glue guns, the need to wear coats etc.);
- an evaluation section;
- key points for plenary sessions;
- assessment points – who are you assessing and what do you want to know?
- timings.

You may begin your training by doing lesson plans for every session you teach and, later, when you have more experience, move to teach from your weekly plans. However, always do individual lesson plans when your lesson is being observed because it helps the observer to see your thinking (and you to do it!). You should also do lesson plans when you are teaching new ideas, are unsure of yourself or the children or have a specific training target in mind. For instance, if you find it hard to manage time in your lessons with KS2 you will find that planning your lessons in detail, writing predicted times on the plans and reviewing them afterwards really helps you to improve this.

PLANNING AN EFFECTIVE LESSON

The research about planning is varied. Brophy and Good (1986) stressed that effective teachers demanded productive engagement with the task, prepared well, and matched the tasks to the abilities of the children. Effective lessons tend to be those with a clear structure, shared understandings about what is to be learnt and why, where all children can do the activities and use the learning time effectively and the teachers assess progress and evaluate the lessons. All these elements of a successful lesson can be addressed through your planning by focusing on your: lesson structure, management, lesson objectives, differentiation for learning and your use of evaluation of lesson plans. All these features will help you to make a lesson engaging and interesting.

Successful lessons have clear beginnings and strong conclusions with a certain amount of 'academic press' – that is impetus to complete tasks within the given time. The suggested use of time in literacy and numeracy hours reflects this research finding. There is nothing magic about the time allocations of the literacy and numeracy hours but they were a result of careful consideration of how learning time could be divided up. You may not use this lesson structure but you should always make sure you have a strong, clear structure to a lesson and that the children know what this is. In this way the children can learn to use time effectively and experience 'academic press'.

Time spent learning, itself, is a significant factor in the effectiveness of lessons, with research suggesting that the most effective teachers are those who maximise learning time by reducing off-task chatter and managing the class effectively (Silcock 1993). Transitions from whole class to group work, effective distribution of resources, and strategies for behaviour management are all parts of lessons where time can be saved through effective planning, thereby maximising learning time for pupils.

Learning to manage the pace of your lessons, so that the teaching and learning are lively and challenging but not rushed, takes time. It is fairly well established that the efficiency of experienced teachers allows them to perform complex procedures in a fraction of the time taken by novices – this is why you need to plan things experienced teachers do not even think about! If you find it difficult to maintain the pace of a lesson, you may want to plan in five-minute intervals and note down the times on your lesson plans.

Task 3.2.1
Scrutinising weekly planning

Scrutinising weekly planning

To do this task you will need a weekly plan and medium-term plan from your placement. Ensure you know the answers to these questions:

- Which parts of the medium-term plan does the weekly plan address?
- Which parts of the relevant curriculum documents does this refer to?
- How long will each lesson or session in the weekly plan be?

Focus on one part of the weekly plan, perhaps English, maths, or science:

- What resources are needed for the lessons in the weekly plan?
- What is the balance of whole class, group and individual work for this week?
- What are the class management challenges for this week?

Discuss your chosen element of weekly planning with your teacher. Possible topics for discussion include:

- How do you ensure that the learning is accessible to all the children in the class?
- How do you differentiate for children who have SEN, EAL or are in the gifted and talented register?
- What arrangements are made to include children with Individual Education Plans (IEPs) or targets?
- What role will a teaching assistant or other adult play in these lessons and how will they know what to do?
- What do you do if the children do not make the predicted learning gains in one week?
- Will any of these sessions present particular management challenges?

What are the 'routine' activities in this week? Fill in the chart below and add other activities.

Activity	When	How long/ often	Resources	Content	Teacher action	Pupil response
welcome/ weather etc.						
show and tell						
action rhymes/poems						
story times						
spelling test						
tables practice						
register						
handwriting						

Learning objectives are probably the most important points on a lesson plan. You should be absolutely clear about what you want the children to learn, understand or do as a result of your lesson. These lesson objectives must be reasonable and achievable. You may want to reference NC/PNS objectives on your lesson plan but phrase your lesson objective accurately so that the children can achieve it. A single lesson may address or contribute to an NNS or NLS objective or to the achievement of an Early Learning Goal, but no lesson will completely cover one of these big objectives.

Most importantly, you must make sure your lesson objectives are meaningful. This means they must make sense in terms of the curriculum so that children are not simply learning a set of assorted skills and knowledge that may (or may not) make sense later. It also means that objectives must be clear to and understood by the children. A study of teachers of literacy (Wray *et al.* 2002) found that effective teachers made sure that even young children understood the wider role of tasks in their learning. You will undoubtedly write up lesson objectives somewhere in the class such as the interactive whiteboard, a sheet of paper or a chart but unless you discuss these objectives with children and ensure the children know what they are learning and why, written objectives are just additional wallpaper.

Your questioning is an important part of your teaching. The need to ask a range of open and closed questions has been well documented. Brophy and Good (1986) make recommendations from their review of research which include the need to ensure that questions are clear, that all children are asked questions, that the pace of questioning is adjusted to the task and that children are given sufficient wait time to answer. They also stress that it is important for questions to elicit correct answers, although, as new material is learnt, the error rate will inevitably rise as a result of children being stretched. More recent characterisations of teaching have stressed the importance of teachers demonstrating, or modelling, the learner behaviour they wished to teach. This includes reading aloud to students, modelling comprehension strategies, modelling writing processes and thinking aloud as you solve mathematical problems. Modelling is a key feature of the National Primary Strategy. Plan the key points you want to make to the class, the key questions and main skills you want to model. In this way you can make sure you teach what you intend to teach.

Differentiation is the way you plan to meet the diverse learning needs of pupils. You will teach the knowledge, skills and understanding in ways that suit the pupils' abilities and previous experience. Differentiation is represented in different forms in your planning:

- *Presentation* – plan to use a variety of media to present ideas, offer vocabulary or extra diagrams to those who need more support. You will find ICT particularly helpful in preparing different types of presentation on paper, audio tape, screens or interactive whiteboards;
- *Content* – select appropriately so that there is content that suits most children, with additional content available to some. For instance: some children may do six calculations where others complete ten. ICT, using the internet, can offer you a range of content;
- *Resources* – use resources that support pupils' needs such as writing frames, language master word banks or Spellmaster machines for poor spellers. For children with EAL you might need to ensure that target vocabulary is available in a written form;
- *Grouping* – group pupils of similar ability for targeted support or pair children with a more able pupil, teaching assistant or language support teacher;
- *Task* – match tasks to pupils' abilities. This can mean different tasks for different pupils. It is sometimes a good idea to offer different tasks that address the same objectives to different pupils so that they can achieve success;
- *Support* – offer additional adult or peer assistance, from a TA, language support teacher or more experienced child;
- *Time* – giving more or less time to complete a given task can make the task more suitable to the particular pupils.

Differentiation sounds simple, but demands really good knowledge of the content, the children, resources and a range of teaching strategies. You will achieve appropriate differentiation by working closely with the teacher so that you find out what strategies are available and work for these children. Key resources to plan into your lessons will be TAs, language support staff and the Individual Education Plans written for children with special needs.

Evaluation is a part of planning and also allows you to show you are able to improve your performance through self-evaluation. Evaluation means considering:

- how well the children achieved the learning objectives (assessment);
- how well you planned, taught and managed teaching in relation to your training targets.

Evaluations will usually be brief and will usually focus on two aspects: what you did and what the children learnt. The most useful evaluations focus on particular aspects of your teaching and are the basis of your own training targets. You may be keen to record positive evaluations but less keen to focus on improvement. However, you should develop your ability to analyse your teaching, especially when you can see an area for improvement. When your evaluation comment identifies work to be done, always say what you propose to do in response. The very best planning is that which clearly uses evidence from children's previous attainment and leads on to influence the planning and teaching of the next session or lesson. This sort of evidence may be the annotations to a lesson plan you make in response to previous evaluations.

BUILDING PLANNING EXPERIENCE

Your early plans on a teaching experience may not be for whole lessons but for short parts of lessons or sessions such as a whole class phonics game, a guided reading session for a small group of children or a mental/oral starter in a maths lesson. Planning these parts of lessons gives you the chance to pay attention to detail and really concentrate on some important aspects of using plans such as:

- ensuring you make your key points clearly;
- maintaining a pace that is brisk and engaging but not so fast that the children are lost;
- effective questioning and interactive teaching;
- using resources such as the interactive whiteboard or phonics objects.

Planning parts of lessons and teaching them is a good start to building up responsibility for whole lessons (see Task 3.2.2 on p. 98).

PLANNING FOR OTHER ADULTS IN THE CLASS OR SETTING

To ensure you work well with teaching assistants or other adults in class, you may use a set format to present clear expectations of what you would like the teaching assistant to do. This will usually include space for the TA to write assessment notes about how well the children achieved the objective. These notes may well affect your future planning.

Figure 3.2.2 on p. 99 shows an example of a planning format suitable for use with a teaching assistant.

Task 3.2.2
Planning a mental/oral starter

Use the planner below to observe a mental/oral starter taught by your teacher. Then plan and evaluate a mental/oral starter or shared literacy session. This may be more detailed than you are used to but using such detail will help you to construct the mental 'scripts' you need to manage this complex task.

Planner for a mental/oral starter, shared reading or shared writing session

Date	Group/class
Duration	NC/PNS reference
Resources	Key vocabulary

Activity

Questions

Less confident	Confident	More confident

Assessment

Less confident	Confident	More confident

Evaluation

Date .... **Lesson Focus** ....

Activity (a brief account of the activity and the TA's role in any whole class introduction, shared reading mental and oral etc.)
Resources needed
Key vocabulary to use
Key questions to use

Objectives

1

2

3

For completion by the TA after group work

Names		can do	needs help
	1		
	2		
	3		
	1		
	2		
	3		
	1		
	2		
	3		
	1		
	2		
	3		
	1		
	2		
	3		

Figure 3.2.2   An example of a planning format for a teaching assistant

Task 3.2.3
Involving a teaching assistant

Arrange a specific time to talk to the TA in your placement class about a lesson in which he/she has assisted. Find out the following:

• What does the TA think the objective of the session was?
• What did the TA understand his/her role to be?
• What key vocabulary did he/she use?
• What resources did he/she prepare?
• How did the TA know what to say and do?
• What additional information would he/she like about class tasks?

When you have this information you will be able to use it to direct your communication with the TA in your lessons.

PLANNING AND ICT

ICT can assist you in your planning in two main ways. First, the computer is an invaluable tool for planning itself because it can help with the process and content of planning. Word processing allows you to produce and amend your plans swiftly and effectively. (Alternatively you can easily spend every evening colour coding, cross referencing and wasting time.) The internet also offers you thousands of ready-made plans for almost any topic. These will not be instant solutions to the problems posed by your next lesson because they do not meet the needs of your particular class. However, they do present you with a spectacular range of ideas and formats. You need to use them, but not rely on them.

The second way that ICT can be useful is as a subject for your planning. If you are planning to use an interactive whiteboard for your mental/oral starter in a maths lesson, you can make the lesson visually attractive (so that all eyes are attracted to it and are not distracted elsewhere). The content can be tailored to meet the whole range of abilities and the children can come out and be fully involved in the learning. You might use your computer to produce worksheets for some groups of children whilst others use calculators or roamers. To conclude the lesson, your plenary session might include the IWB or a demonstration using a projected calculator. The ICT can make the lesson more effective, but only if you plan it carefully.

When you think of using ICT do not concentrate only on the computer. Children can use audio or video recording to do speaking and listening, reading and writing activities. If children are presenting findings from group work, the OHP might be the most accessible technology. Do not overlook the use of TV and radio materials. Like computer programs, they are produced specifically for schools, have helpful teaching guidance and can be very useful if planned carefully.

SUMMARY

Planning is one of the most time-consuming processes you will engage in but planning well will help you to become a successful teacher. All successful teaching relies on teachers producing lessons that engage and motivate the children. This is partly down to selecting the right content and partly down to the way the content is dealt with. These issues are planning issues. Use your plans to rehearse and evaluate your lessons and you can appear confident, happy and interesting to your class of children.

ANNOTATED FURTHER READING

Gipps, C., Hargreaves, E. and McCallum, B. (2000) *What Makes a Good Primary School Teacher?*, London: RoutledgeFalmer. This accessible book offers an account of the range of teaching, assessing and feedback strategies used by individual 'expert' primary teachers and how they know or decide which strategy to bring into play, and when.

The Primary National Strategy site http://www.standards.dfes.gov.uk/. This site contains the frameworks for literacy and numeracy as well as plenty of 'exemplified units of work', that is, medium- and shorter-term plans for teaching.

The TeacherNet site http://www.teachernet.gov.uk. This site offers access to over 2,000 lesson plans and has invaluable advice about many aspects of planning.

Wray, D., Medwell, J., Poulson, L. and Fox, R. (2002) *Teaching Literacy Effectively*, London: Routledge Falmer. This books reports the findings of the 'Effective Teachers of Literacy' project and includes several findings relating to the importance of good planning.

REFERENCES

Brophy, J. and Good, T. (1986) 'Teacher behaviour and student achievement', in M.C. Wittrock (ed.) *Handbook of Research In Teaching*, London: Collier Macmillan.

Silcock, P. (1993) 'Can we teach effective teaching?', *Educational Review*, 45(1): 13–19.

Wray, D., Medwell, J., Poulson, L. and Fox, R. (2002) *Teaching Literacy Effectively*, London: Routledge Falmer.

Unit 3.3

Managing Classroom Behaviour

Roland Chaplain

INTRODUCTION

This chapter introduces you to a framework for developing behaviour management strategies. The effective management of pupil behaviour depends on a range of interrelated factors, such as the organisational climate and aims of the school; your personality, social competence and beliefs about the causes of behaviour; the academic and social development and dispositions of your pupils; and group dynamics.

OBJECTIVES

By the end of this unit you should understand:

- the multilevel nature of behaviour management in school;
- the value of a proactive Classroom Behaviour Management Plan;
- the importance of structural and organisational factors and interpersonal tactics in managing pupil behaviour;
- ways of responding to challenging behaviour.

FROM WHOLE SCHOOL ISSUES TO CHALLENGING PUPILS

Managing classroom behaviour should not be viewed in isolation from other areas of behaviour management in school. Figure 3.3.1 illustrates the multilevel nature of behaviour management moving from whole school issues through classroom management to working with challenging individuals.

Inconsistency between the levels offers pupils the opportunity to manipulate the system. Being an excellent class teacher means nothing if chaos reigns around you – the after-shock eventually gets through.

Schools are required to produce 'policies designed to promote good behaviour and discipline on the part of its pupils' (School Standards and Framework Act, 1998, 61.4) which should reflect the expectations of a school community, inform practice, highlight valued behaviour and thus contribute to the school's organisational climate. The importance of behaviour policies in developing effective schools has been acknowledged (Elton Report, 1989) and more recently required by legislation (Education Act (No. 2), 1986; Education Act, 1996; Education Act, 1997; and School Standards and Framework Act, 1998). Chaplain (1995) suggested that behaviour policies should reflect the views and aspirations of *all* stakeholders in a school's community including pupils, parents, staff and managers.

When the behaviour policy is well thought out, understood and consistently applied by all adults responsible for pupils, it can significantly reduce or eliminate many minor disruptive behaviours almost 'automatically'. There are a number of familiar school-wide routines (for example, assemblies, dress, timetable, movement, lining up, reporting, sanctions, rewards) which serve to visibly reinforce what the school values. The whole school policy sets the standard for all levels of behaviour management providing uniformity and predictability for pupils and teachers alike. However, teachers are individuals and classrooms each have their own 'climate' which makes them distinctive – but preferably within an overall consistent framework.

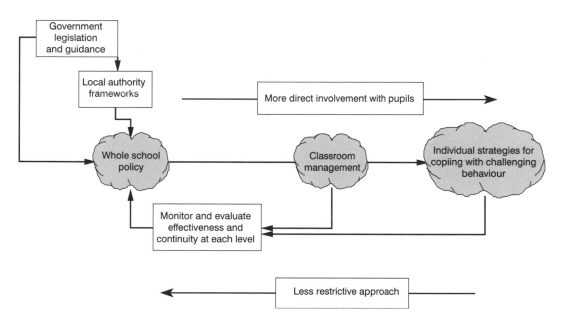

Figure 3.3.1   The multilevel model of behaviour management

Note: The whole school policy is the standard against which both classroom management and individual strategies are compared. As the management function moves from left to right so does the level of intrusiveness or direct control over student behaviour.

Task 3.3.1
Whole school behaviour policy

Obtain a copy of the behaviour policy from your school and consider:

- Are the core school rules explicit?
- To what extent do they match your own expectations for pupil behaviour?
- What rewards exist for those pupils who behave as expected and what sanctions exist for those who do not?
- Is there a clear hierarchy of rewards and sanctions?
- Compare your school's policy with that of another trainee – in what ways are they similar?

TEACHER STRESS, PUPIL BEHAVIOUR AND CLASSROOM CONTROL

Research has consistently reported pupil misbehaviour as a significant stressor for teachers (Borg 1990; Chaplain 1995; Dunham and Varma 1998; Kyriacou and Sutcliffe 1978). However, whilst teachers usually rate extreme behaviour (physical and verbal assault, for instance) as their biggest concern, such behaviour is not an everyday occurrence in the regular classroom. In contrast, low level disruptive behaviours (e.g. talking out of turn, getting out of their seats, not having equipment, fiddling with pens) are a familiar experience for many teachers (Elton Report, 1989), the cumulative effect of which can be very stressful. These 'daily hassles' (Kanner *et al.* 1981) are usually offset by 'daily uplifts' most notably in the form of positive feedback from pupils – arguably the most rewarding aspect of teaching.

Task 3.3.2
Understanding disruptive behaviour

- What disruptive behaviours cause you most concern?
- List them in order of priority, then write alongside the frequency you have observed or experienced them.
- Consider the type of behaviour in relation to its frequency to understand its potential effect.

CAUSAL EXPLANATIONS OF MISBEHAVIOUR

What do you consider are the main causes of pupil misbehaviour:

- *within pupils* – personality, part of growing up, children are: intrinsically naughty; need to be managed; have no respect for authority?
- *within school* – irrelevant curriculum, teachers' incompetence, poorly managed schools, teachers' attitudes?
- *within the community* – poor parenting, poverty, lack of discipline in the home/community/ society?

Consider the implications of selecting particular categories. *Within pupils* and *within the community* factors are least under your control, thus not useful in helping you to cope. In contrast *within school* factors are controllable by teachers and therefore easier to change. If you found yourself blaming factors outside your control you are not alone – Lawrence *et al.* (1986) found 78 per cent of teachers blamed misbehaviour on issues outside their control. I will therefore emphasise those factors which you can best control and demonstrate how by developing a Classroom Behaviour Management Plan (CBP) you can develop organisational, structural and interpersonal behaviours to produce a well-managed classroom.

MANAGING YOURSELF

Verbal and non-verbal behaviours are the bread and butter of teaching, however, they are not always under your direct conscious control. You may plan to communicate something to someone but when under pressure fail because of emotional interference or lack of confidence. You have, no doubt, noticed other people's habits when feeling under pressure – looking nervous, coughing, fidgeting, or playing with their hair. I have observed teachers using the utterance 'ssh' or 'erm' when trying to gain the attention of the class – to no avail. They are busily 'ssh-ing' but the pupils carry on talking. When informed of this they often deny it – until, that is, they watch the video which surprises them as they were not *aware* of this happening. They can remember pupils misbehaving, but nothing about their ineffective *habit*. We are all aware of being told to 'ssh' as a young child and it may indeed work effectively for some teachers – the problem arises when such overlearned 'automatic' responses are ineffective and we do not realise it. Other ineffective strategies retained from childhood which may emerge when we feel under pressure include shouting, screaming and losing our temper. Overcoming such behaviours requires first becoming aware of them (e.g. video yourself), identifying and overlearning alternative effective methods, and practicing them when not under pressure – taking an active role in self regulation to enhance coping.

The degree to which you feel able to influence important events in your life (locus of control – Rotter, 1966) is central to effective coping. People who believe they can influence important events (internals) tend to cope better than those who believe other people make important decisions for them and who eventually feel powerless (externals). I have met many trainee teachers who are reluctant to change classroom seating arrangements, despite being aware that existing arrangements are not working for them. Their reason for not asking to make changes is usually because they feel that as it is someone else's classroom, to do so would be wrong. However, their teachers/mentors are often as surprised as me that the trainees did not make such changes. The situation could be brought under the trainee's control merely by asking if it's OK to move things around to help them teach more effectively.

Belief in your capability to manage behaviour (teacher efficacy) affects how you cope with disruptive behaviour. A positive teacher efficacy means we think, feel and behave in a more confident manner and expect to cope effectively (Woolfolk and Hoy 1990), making pupils feel secure and more likely to respond positively. Teachers are required to be *an authority* (knowledge) and *in authority* (able to manage pupils). The latter requires social competence (interpersonal skills and emotional control), something we can control and develop further with attention, effort and practice. We can also manipulate the classroom environment to reduce pressure on our personal resources.

I recently observed a trainee teaching a maths lesson which involved the four rules. She admitted to being anxious (after the lesson) about teaching maths and had decided to write down all her workings on a card which she held in her hand, checking everything before responding to children's answers or writing examples on the board. However, this behaviour prevented her from maximising interaction with the class (limited eye contact, staying near the whiteboard, talking with her back to the class) because she kept looking at the card. As the lesson progressed she began confirming pupils' answers to the most elementary calculations from her card (for fear of getting them wrong). Her anxiety arose from her (false) beliefs in her capability in maths, given the examples were all within her ability.

Teacher efficacy then affects your thinking, emotions, social behaviour and hence your ability to cope. To overcome this problem she was advised to write worked examples on a flip chart before the lesson (covering the answers with 'post it' shapes). With the answers available but covered, she was able to scan the room, move to different parts of the classroom (getting pupils to remove the 'post its') and so maintain the flow of the lesson.

Self awareness and self monitoring then provide a useful starting point for considering how *all* your behaviours contribute to how you manage your class. Changing how you think, feel and behave is not necessarily an easy process and may feel uncomfortable but the potential benefits make it worthwhile.

Self regulation in the classroom requires attention to what you say and how you say it and checking you are being understood; looking and feeling confident; self belief; and communicating your authority and status as a teacher through verbal and non-verbal behaviour (Chaplain 2003).

Task 3.3.3
Identifying personal strengths and weaknesses

- make an audit of your resources (personal strengths) and concerns about teaching;
- indicate ways in which you perceive them as a resource/concern;
- now identify which factors you believe you can change and those outside your control;
- consider what changes to make and how to deal with the unchangeable.

DEVELOPING A CLASSROOM BEHAVIOUR MANAGEMENT PLAN (CBP)

A CBP is not dissimilar to your lesson plan but should focus on:

- how you will organise your classroom for different lessons, including seating arrangements which *minimise off-task* behaviour;
- producing a classroom behaviour management profile – tactics to deter disruption (preventative); responses to pupils who occasionally slip off-task (reorientation); and responses to more persistent off-task behaviour (reactive) (see Table 3.3.1);
- rewards and sanctions you will use;
- your verbal and non-verbal behaviour;
- contextual priorities, e.g. challenging behaviour.

It should be informed by, and reflect the expectations of, the school behaviour policy and as such will differ to varying degrees between schools. Check, for instance, that any rewards/sanctions you plan to use are acceptable within your particular school.

How you structure your CBP is a matter of personal choice – you may have a separate plan or alternatively integrate with your general lesson plan. Do remember to keep a separate detailed record of different strategies you have tried and their success rate.

MAKING AN EARLY IMPACT ON YOUR CLASS

We form impressions of other people in a few seconds (Ambady and Rosenthal 1993) which then often remain unchanged for long periods of time. Hence the first part of your CBP should consider the type of impression you wish to make. In your early visits to the classroom you will be observing, which can feel uncomfortable as pupils are inquisitive and will want to know all about you, weighing you up and some seeing what they can get away with. You will want to settle in and get to know the ropes but do not be too friendly with the pupils, as you will eventually have to establish your authority with the whole class. This is not to suggest you should be standoffish or hostile; just pace yourself and remember to convey your status and authority as a teacher. Your first lesson may be relaxed with pupils being quite passive (Ball 1980) but at some point they will test your ability to establish and maintain behavioural limits, so making sure you are clear about your expectations is paramount.

It is essential to pay attention to detail, especially in your early lessons. Your CBP should include details of how you will:

- convey and reinforce your behavioural expectations (rules and routines);
- use verbal and non-verbal behaviours to control the class – especially at critical points in the lesson (see Table 3.3.1, p. 108);
- reward positive responses (see Table 3.3.2 , p. 109);
- apply sanctions to negative responses (Table 3.3.2). Sanctions and rewards should be arranged hierarchically with a clear progression;
- organise the physical layout of the classroom.

These procedures are not exclusive to early lessons since they represent good professional practice. Both your learning plans and CBP will be modified over time as you become more practised, experiment and rise to new challenges.

CONVEYING YOUR EXPECTATIONS: RULES AND ROUTINES

All lessons have similar patterns, for example: getting attention of the class, conveying information, managing feedback, moving equipment and moving pupils, monitoring and responding to unwanted behaviour. Whether your teaching is enhanced or undermined by any or all of the above depends on devising and applying appropriate, enforceable and effective rules and routines. Rules set the limits to pupils' behaviour (Charles 1999). Whilst whole school (core) rules are designed primarily to produce harmonious relationships among pupils, the main purpose of classroom rules is to maximise pupil engagement with learning (Savage 1991). Effective rules provide pupils with a physically and psychologically safe predictable environment (Chaplain 2003) and work in a preventative way to establish and keep order and maintain momentum through the lesson. To gain maximum effect rules should be:

- *Positively worded* – tell pupils what they *can do* rather than what they *cannot do*, e.g. 'be nice' as opposed to 'don't be nasty'. Negatively framed rules are not effective long term (Becker *et al.* 1975).
- *Few in number* – long lists of rules will not be remembered: focus on key concerns. Canter and Canter (1976) suggest four: follow directions; keep hands, feet and objects to yourself; no teasing or name-calling; no swearing. I would recommend no more than five.
- *Realistic* – do not have rules which are not enforceable or achievable by the class or individuals.
- *Focused* – on key issues such as personal safety, safety of others, cooperation and facilitating learning.
- *Applied consistently* – intermittent or selective reinforcement of rules will render them ineffective. Consider this example, if putting hands up to answer questions is a rule and you respond positively to those pupils who shout out a very competent answer, then reprimand someone else for shouting out who does not give sophisticated answers, you are sending out mixed and unhelpful messages to pupils about how much you value them.

Table 3.3.1 Sample classroom behaviour management profile

Preventative	Reorientation	Reactive
Establishing and practicing rules and routines	Gaze – sustained eye contact to inform pupils you are aware of what they are doing	Caution – inform what will happen should the unwanted behaviour persist
Being clear about what you want – reinforcing and checking for understanding	Posture and gesture – use to complement gaze e.g. raised eyebrow, raised first finger, hands on hips	Remove privileges e.g. ban from use of the computer or miss a trip
Being alert to changes based on perceptions of pupils' non-verbal and verbal behaviours (e.g. too quiet/too loud, eye movements, looking out of window)	Space invasion – the closer you are to pupils the more control you will have – do not hide behind your desk or 'glue' yourself to the whiteboard – the classroom is your domain to move around as you wish	Require pupil to complete extra work during breaktimes
Scanning – think about positioning in respect of being able to see the whole class at all times to quickly respond to potential disruption	Restate rules – remind pupils about what is expected	Time out as arranged with colleague or manager in advance – avoid having disruptive pupils wandering around the school: it is no help to anybody
Going up a gear in anticipation of a disruptive event e.g. new pupils, time of year	Use individual encouragement to get pupils back on task – 'You have been doing really well so far...'	Contract – agree with pupil specific expectations and record successes – review and adjust as necessary
Being enthusiastic even when you're not!	Name dropping – we are all sensitive to hearing our name even when there are several conversations going on – mentioning a non-attentive pupil's name whilst you are talking will usually get their attention. Supplement this, if necessary, with gestures	Removal from class temporarily – working elsewhere in school or with another class
Manipulating classroom layout e.g. planned seating arrangements	Praising peers in the vicinity of someone off-task can be effective provided the pupil values being praised by you – usually most effective with younger pupils	Suspension from school
Using appropriate reward systems for on-task behaviour	Humour – pupils like teachers with a sense of humour so make use of yours – but not by ridiculing pupils, and ensure it is appropriate to pupils' level of development	
Awareness of pupils' goals	Maintain the flow of the lesson by carrying on teaching whilst moving round the room, using non-verbal gestures and removing anything being played with (e.g. pens) to avoid being distracted from what you have to say	
Getting lesson timings right		

Table 3.3.2 Examples of hierarchical rewards and sanctions

Rewards	Example	Sanctions	Example
*Verbal praise private	Quiet word: 'John, that's excellent.'	Gesture	Raised first finger, thumbs down
*Verbal praise public	Teacher and class applaud individual	Prolonged gaze	Hold eye contact (with frown)
Public display of positive behaviours	Star/points chart – cumulative points gets postcard to parents	Rule reminder	'What do we do when we want to ask a question?'
Classroom awards	Certificates, badges or superstar of the day/week award	Physical proximity	Move closer to pupil – perhaps stand behind him/her saying nothing
Contact home (either for accumulated star /points or exceptional good behaviour)	Notes/cards/phone calls	Verbal reprimand	'I am very unhappy with your behaviour.'
		Public display	Remove points from star chart
		Separate from group in class or keep back at playtime	Adjust length of time to suit needs/age of pupil
Special privileges	Helping around school, attending an event	Record name	Write name on board
		Removal from classroom	Teach outside normal teaching area
Tangible rewards	Book token, sweets, pens	Refer to SMT	Send to deputy (as per school policy)
		Contact parents	Letter/phone home
School award	Certificates, tokens	Invite parents to school	For informal/formal discussion
		Behavioural contract	Short, focused on specific expectations
		Separation from group	Individual teaching or special class
		Suspension	For an agreed period
		Review contract	As a basis for return
		Exclusion	

Note: *Initially praise could be for every positive occurrence, over time change to intermittent to maintain effectiveness. Praise should be warm and natural, appropriate to pupil's level of development, varied and creative.

When taking over a class from another teacher it is important to consider their expectations in relation to your own and whether this will affect the way in which you establish your rules. If you adopt the rules of the existing teacher, do not assume the pupils will necessarily respond in the same way to you – they will not inevitably associate you with a particular rule, so make sure you inform them of what you expect even if it means repeating what you believe they already know.

Make sure you display your rules prominently and keep reminding pupils about them. Be creative, perhaps using cartoons or pictures to liven up your display.

Task 3.3.4
Developing classroom rules

- Can you think of 4 or 5 rules which embody your behavioural expectations?
- Look again at the school behaviour policy; are your expectations similar?
- Discuss how your classroom teacher/mentor established his/her rules with your class.
- Do you feel confident applying them?

REWARDS AND SANCTIONS

Rules alone do not guarantee good behaviour. They need to be linked to consequences – which means *consistently* rewarding pupils who follow the rules and applying sanctions as a deterrent to those who do not. Both types of consequence should follow a hierarchical sequence (Table 3.3.2) with which you should be familiar – avoid using higher order rewards or sanctions prematurely. Furthermore, when threatening sanctions offer the opportunity to respond positively. For example, 'Joe, you have left your seat again despite knowing the rule. Now you can either sit down and stay there or stay in at break for 5 minutes.' However, should they continue to ignore the rule say 'Joe, you are already staying in for 5 minutes, now either sit down or you will be staying a further 5 minutes.' Whatever sanction you threaten be sure to carry it through, otherwise you will be guaranteeing a repeat at a later date since you have rewarded unwanted behaviour. Share the rewards for positive behaviour with the whole class. This may require some sophisticated social skills to encourage more withdrawn pupils to contribute and more enthusiastic ones to wait their turn without disengaging them from learning. For example, 'Thanks for putting your hand up all the time Henry, however, I am going to ask someone else to answer this one.'

For rewards and sanctions to be effective they need to be fit for purpose – the reward must be something the pupils like and the sanction(s) something they do not like. It is unwise to assume that *you* know what pupils like or do not like. You may not have liked being sent to see the head but some pupils do since it provides them with attention or status and gets them out of class. One way of discovering what pupils value is to ask them to complete an *'All about me'* sheet in which they indicate their favourite subjects, hobbies, music, sport and learning styles. Plan to start each new day on a positive note whatever happened the day before – feeling negative in advance focuses attention on negative behaviour which is self defeating.

USING ROUTINES TO MAXIMISE ON-TASK ACTIVITY

Schools like most organisations operate through a series of established routines. Whilst rules provide the framework for the conduct of lessons, they are few in number; teachers therefore rely on a large number of routines to provide the link between expectations and action. Routines are usually organised around times, places and contexts. Effective teachers spend considerable time in their early encounters with their classes teaching them routines (Emmer *et al*. 1994) which when practised become automatic, leaving more time for teaching. Jones and Jones (1990) found that up to 50 per cent of some lessons were lost to non-teaching routines such as getting out equipment and marking work, so efficient routines provide a real learning bonus. The following paragraphs consider some examples of common routines in more detail.

Entering the classroom – how pupils enter your classroom sets the scene for the lesson – charging noisily into a room is not the best way to start a lesson so consider how you might control this initial movement. One way is to greet your pupils at the door, look pleased to see them and remind them what they are expected to do when they go into class. Physically standing by the door reduces the likelihood of pupils charging in but if they do call them back and make them repeat the procedure correctly.

Getting the attention of the class – can be achieved in various ways using verbal or other noises or using silence:

- *Using noises* – such as, ringing bells, tapping the desk, clapping, asking pupils to show their hands or sit up straight. Which method you choose depends on your personal style and school policy. However, make sure that you explain to the pupils beforehand what the signal is and what you want them to do when they hear it. I recently witnessed a teacher working with a 'lively' class use a tambourine to gain attention part way through the lesson, but omitted to let pupils know beforehand. Whilst it made everyone jump (including me), it was not associated with any required behaviour. A more effective method would have been to tell the class in advance, 'Whenever I bang the tambourine I want you all to stop what you are doing and look at me'.

- *Using silence* – some teachers find they can gain attention using non-verbal signals such as; folding their arms, hands on hips, raising eyebrows or frowning. It is a very powerful technique but requires you to feel confident about your presence. Puppets can also be effective attention-getters. A large figurative hand puppet, like those used for counting and phonics, can also be used to settle pupils (see <puppetsbypost.com>). Introduce the puppet and say that he/she will only come out if everyone is quiet – because he/she suffers from headaches or is nervous. If the noise level gets too high put the puppet away. Hermit crab or snail puppets which only emerge if people are well-behaved are also excellent! Pupils are usually very attentive and empathetic towards puppets and so they can be used to aid their socio-emotional development. We have had excellent results using them with pupils from foundation stage to Year 6.

Briefing – take time to make sure pupils understand exactly what is required from them at each stage of the lesson – unless you want those pupils who find it hard to pay attention wasting time asking other pupils what they should be doing. Taking time in your first lessons may be difficult if you are anxious about being in the spotlight – if this is so use prompts to remind yourself to speak slowly and carefully (perhaps writing SLOW on your lesson notes). Write instructions, key words and questions on the board to support your verbal inputs – *do so before the lesson* so that you can maintain eye contact and scan the whole class whilst briefing them. You might also consider using consistent colour coded writing to differentiate instructions, key words, questions, etc. so that pupils recognise more easily what is expected of them.

Distributing equipment – there can be a dilemma deciding when to issue equipment. If done in advance it can cause a distraction with pupils fiddling with it whilst you are talking, whereas issuing it after you have finished talking can disrupt a settled group. Choosing which one to use depends on how the class responds to you and each other. If you issue equipment in advance, make sure you tell pupils beforehand not to touch the equipment, rather than having to correct afterwards. Always check all your equipment before the lesson; do not assume people will have returned the electrical experiment kit complete with full batteries and wires untangled – otherwise you may find yourself spending 20 minutes sorting it out, giving pupils the opportunity to misbehave.

Moving bodies – sometimes not considered when planning lessons; however, keeping control of pupils on the move both in and out of the classroom requires careful planning if it is to be efficient and safe. Again make sure you specify in advance exactly what you require people to do (including supporting adults). If moving a class to a different location, think before the lesson about the group dynamics in the same way you would plan a learning activity. Plan where to position yourself in relation to the group to maintain your view of everyone you are responsible for. Use reinforcement to point out those individuals who are behaving correctly to encourage the other pupils to copy them.

Checking for understanding – throughout your lesson to be sure that pupils are clear about what is expected. Where appropriate, support your verbal instructions with written ones. Avoid repeatedly asking the same child or group and encourage all pupils to ask relevant questions if in doubt.

Task 3.3.5
Establishing classroom routines

- Think about the routines you consider important in your classroom and make a list.
- How do you plan to get the pupils to learn them?
- When in school test their efficiency – do they work? Could they be improved?

CLASSROOM LAYOUT

There is evidence to demonstrate a correlation between seating arrangements and pupil behaviour. For example, sitting boys with girls tends to reduce disruption (Merret 1993); children organised in rows tend to be less disruptive than when organised in groups (Wheldall and Lam 1987). However, these findings need to be considered in relation to other evidence such as the nature of the learning task and the level of academic and social functioning of the children.

Movement around the classroom should be free flowing. Where this is not the case there is a potential for disruption as some individuals take up every opportunity to push past, nudge, or dislodge the chair or whiteboard of other pupils with minimal effort (for a more detailed discussion see Chaplain 2003).

Task 3.3.6
Making the most of the physical environment

- Consider the layout of your classroom; is there sufficient room to move easily between the furniture?
- Make a drawing of the classroom and cut out the various pieces of furniture; try moving them around to see which arrangement gives the least disrupted flow around the room.
- Where is the best place to stand to address the whole group? (Do not assume it is by the whiteboard.)
- Monitor your movement during a lesson (video record or ask someone to record your movements) – do you spend equal amounts of time with each group?

COPING WITH CHALLENGING BEHAVIOUR

Whilst having well thought out rules and routines will provide a secure structure for most pupils, some will persistently challenge your authority. Challenging behaviour ranges from physical and verbal aggression to defiance and refusal to work. The members of such groups are not homogeneous and range from pupils with temporary difficulties to those with persistent difficulties such as Attention Deficit Hyperactivity Disorder (ADHD) or other Behavioural, Emotional or Social Difficulty (BESD) who may require specialist interventions.

There are a number of important general points to make in respect of coping with challenging behaviour. First, avoid interpreting such behaviour as a personal 'assault' – pupils seldom behave this way because they hate you and you will gain nothing from getting angry (this does not mean you should not reprimand pupils in an assertive way). Second, don't become obsessed with fitting pupils to descriptive categories – focus on understanding *their behaviour* and record carefully what they do and when they do it – making sure you *include positive* behaviour, however infrequent. Keep a record of positive behaviours which not only provides an uplift when times are tense but also gives useful insight into the pupil's currency – i.e. what motivates them to behave appropriately.

Keep things in perspective and do not lose your sense of humour. Dealing with challenging individuals can lead you to view the situation as being increasingly serious which inhibits problem solving and creativity. It is not uncommon for teachers to reach the point of questioning their own ability and losing confidence. This is reflected in their behaviour and pupils quickly recognise the change, making a difficult situation worse. Finding humour in the situation is often sufficient to influence events positively (Molnar and Lindquist 1989). Focus on controlling your emotions and on believing that the situation can be coped with, if not completely controlled. Even situations that are so awful that you have to grin and bear it – it won't last for ever. Do not be afraid to ask for help with extreme pupils. If you anticipate a negative reaction (e.g. temper tantrum) to a particular event arrange for a supportive adult to be around in advance of that time. Fortunately, such occurrences are rare and most can be dealt with by adopting appropriate tactics, some of which I have outlined below.

Dealing with challenging behaviour requires attention to several issues including:

Being consistent with whatever approach you adopt. Challenging pupils are looking for structure and security and will repeatedly challenge you until they realise you mean business. They act like people playing slot machines and will keep pressing your buttons until they hit the jackpot (make you angry) – do not let them; keep calm and focused. Remember there are no quick fixes so prepare for the long haul!

Classroom organisation – seating arrangements – position challenging pupils near the front so that there are no pupils between them and you to distract or provide an audience for a confrontation. This also allows you to maintain close proximity whilst addressing the class, making monitoring and controlling their behaviour easier, e.g. through direct eye contact and using hand gestures. Putting these children with groups for all activities is likely to create disruption as they will cause arguments and fights, often making the bullets for others to fire. This is not to suggest that they should live in isolation but think about the nature of the learning task and (classroom permitting) try having them working on separate tables for individual tasks.

Learning – carefully organise their time and the sequencing/size of their learning tasks. If concentration is an issue, break down their learning into smaller achievable progressive units, vary the tasks, emphasise visual learning, use colours and shapes to help them organise their work and change their tasks frequently. It is also helpful to have a clock visible and indicate how long they are required to stay on-task for; the clock provides a visual reference point and helps maintain focus. Specify exactly what you want them to do.

Support – where you have adult learning support in class, plan in advance what action each of you will be responsible for should the pupil start misbehaving. Determine who will deal with the pupil and who will look after the rest of the class to eliminate ambiguity and inconsistency.

Changing behaviour – Focus on observable behaviour; avoid describing a pupil as 'always badly behaved'. List the behaviours causing concern then gather detailed observations of what occurs before the unwanted behaviour (antecedent), the behaviour itself and what happens afterwards (consequence), along with how frequently it occurs (see Figure 3.3.2).

Use your observations to hypothesise why the pupil is behaving in this way. In Figure 3.3.2 it could be the antecedent (asking Joan to put her toys away) or the consequences (other pupils laughing when she defies you). Next decide what you want Joan to do instead of being defiant, and what to reward her with for behaving appropriately. The process requires attention to detail which is outlined in Figure 3.3.3. For a fuller description of this and other approaches see Chaplain 1995; Chaplain and Freeman 1998; Chaplain 2003.

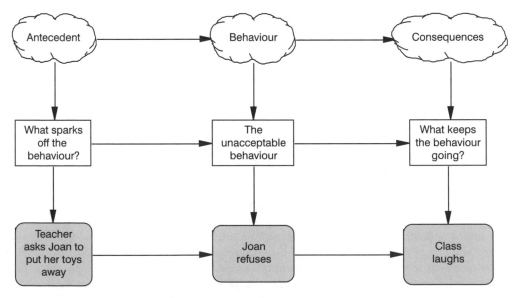

Figure 3.3.2 An A–B–C model of behaviour

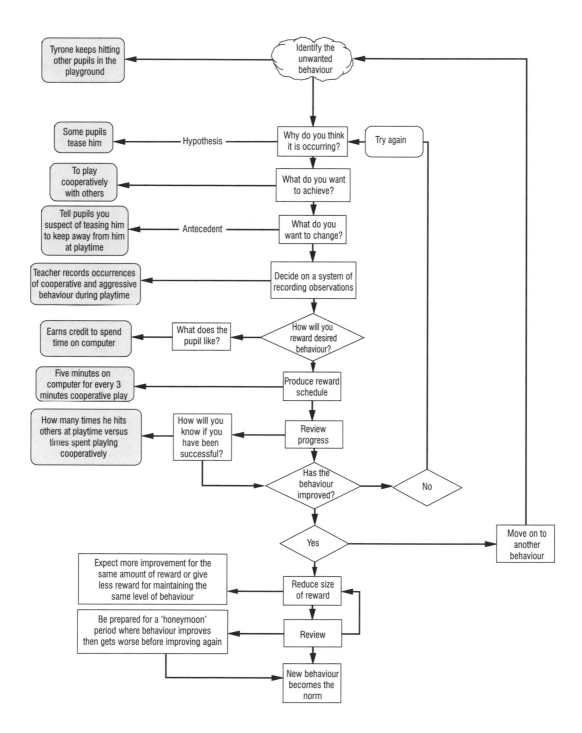

Figure 3.3.3 Behaviour change cycle

SUMMARY

This unit has briefly covered some key factors to consider when developing your Classroom Behaviour Management Plan. It is essential to keep in mind that effective classroom behaviour management is strongly influenced by whole school attitudes and practices as well as your interpersonal skills and classroom organisation. Additional reading has been provided to assist you in extending your knowledge of the areas covered.

ANNOTATED FURTHER READING

Canter, L. and Canter, M. (2001) *Assertive Discipline: Positive Behavior Management for Today's Classroom*, Los Angeles: Canter and Associates. Although aimed at the USA market this text offers helpful guidance on developing a discipline plan and managing difficult behaviour.

Chaplain, R. (2003) *Teaching Without Disruption in the Primary School: A Model for Managing Behaviour*, London: RoutledgeFalmer. A comprehensive account of the theory and practice of behaviour management including whole school issues, classroom management and how to cope with difficult pupils.

Porter, L. (2000) *Behaviour in Schools: Theory and Practice for Teachers*, Buckingham: Open University Press. A useful sourcebook reviewing some key theories on behaviour management, their underlying philosophy and recommended practices.

Robertson, J. (1996) *Effective Classroom Control: Understanding Teacher–Student Relationships*, London: Hodder and Stoughton. Advice on establishing and maintaining authority in the classroom with an emphasis on non-verbal communication.

REFERENCES

Ambady, N. and Rosenthal, R. (1993) 'Half a minute: predicting teacher evaluations from thin slices of behaviour and physical attractiveness', *Journal of Personality and Social Psychology*, 64: 431–41.

Ball, S.J. (1980) 'Initial encounters in the classroom and the process of establishment', in P. Woods (ed.) *Pupil Strategies*, London: Croom Helm.

Becker, W.C., Englemann, S. and Thomas, D.R. (1975) *Classroom Management*, Henley-on-Thames: Science Research Associates.

Borg, M.G. (1990) 'Occupational stress in British educational settings: a review', *Educational Research*, 10: 103–26.

Canter, L. and Canter, M. (1976) *Assertive Discipline: A Take Charge Approach for Today's Educator*, Los Angeles: Lee Canter Associates.

Chaplain, R. (1995) 'Stress and job satisfaction: a study of English primary school teachers', *Educational Psychology*, 15(4): 473–91.

Chaplain, R. (2003) *Teaching Without Disruption in the Primary School: A Model for Managing Behaviour*, London: RoutledgeFalmer.

Chaplain, R. and Freeman, A. (1998) *Stress and Coping*, Cambridge: Pearson Press.

Charles, C.M. (1999) *Building Classroom Discipline from Models to Practice*, 6th edition, New York: Longman.

Dunham, J. and Varma, V. (1998) *Stress in Teachers: Past Present and Future*, London: Whurr Publishers.

Elton Report (1989) *Discipline in Schools: Report of the Committee Chaired by Lord Elton*, London: HMSO.

Emmer, E.T., Evertson, C.M., Clements, B.S. and Worsham, M.E. (1994) *Classroom Management for Secondary Teachers*, 3rd edition, New Jersey: Prentice Hall.

Jones, V.F. and Jones, L.S. (1990) *Comprehensive Classroom Management*, 3rd edition, Needham: Allyn and Bacon.

Kanner, A.D., Coyne, J.C., Schaever, C. and Lazarus, R.S. (1981) 'Comparison of two modes of stress measurement: daily hassles and uplifts versus major life events', *Journal of Behavioural Medicine*, 4: 1–39.

Kyriacou, C. and Sutcliffe, J. (1978) 'Teacher stress: prevalence sources and symptoms', *British Journal of Educational Psychology*, 48: 159–67.

Lawrence, J., Steed, D. and Young, P. (1986) *Disruptive Pupils – Disruptive Schools?* London: Routledge.

Merret, F. (1993) *Encouragement Works Best*, London: David Fulton Publishers.

Molnar, A. and Lindquist, B. (1989) *Changing Problem Behaviour*, San Francisco, CA: Jossey-Bass.

Rotter, J.B. (1966) 'Generalised expectancies for internal versus external control of reinforcement', *Psychological Monographs*, 91: 482–97.

Savage, T. (1991) *Discipline for Self Control*, New Jersey: Prentice Hall.

Wheldall, K. and Lam, Y.Y. (1987) 'Rows versus tables II. The effects of classroom seating arrangements on classroom disruption rate', *Educational Psychology*, 7(4): 303–12.

Wheldall, K and Olds, P. (1987) 'Of sex and seating: the effects of mixed and same-sex seating arrangements in junior school classrooms', *New Zealand Journal of Educational Studies*, 22, 71–85.

Woolfolk, A.E. and Hoy, W.K. (1990) 'Prospective teachers' sense of efficacy and belief about control', *Journal of Educational Psychology*, 82: 81–91.

Unit 3.4

Managing Group Work

Roy Corden

INTRODUCTION

Teaching and learning occurs most successfully in discursive classrooms where, through investigation and the sharing of perspectives, children may be brought to new levels of understanding. The National Literacy Framework describes successful teaching as 'discursive, characterised by high quality oral work' and 'interactive, encouraging, expecting and extending pupils' contributions' (DfEE 1998: 8). Similarly, the National Numeracy Strategy states that 'high-quality direct teaching is oral, interactive and lively ... in which pupils are expected to play an active part by answering questions, contributing points to discussion, and explaining and demonstrating their methods to the class' (DfEE 1999: 11). However, interactive discourse involves a combination of children thinking aloud, being open to each other's ideas and collaborating in the expression of both shared and conflicting thoughts. The development of children's metacognition is an essential element of successful interactive discourse: that is, their ability to monitor, control and reflect on their own use of language. It is this process of objectifying in language what we have thought and then reconsidering it, which allows us to develop our understanding (Bruner 1986). However, dialogic discourse which is characterised by sustained interaction where children explore ideas, and reflect on and explain their thought processes in a corporate, whole class context is not a prominent feature in our schools (see Alexander 2000 for an international comparison). Indeed, in examining changes in primary practice over a twenty-year period, Galton *et al.* (1999) concluded that the pattern of classroom interaction in primary schools has remained fairly constant. The survey found that whole class teaching was dominated by low level questioning and children, although apparently organised into small groups, still worked individually. Further research by Hardman *et al.* (2003) found that, rather than promoting higher levels of interaction, teachers rarely encouraged or extended children's contributions either during whole class or small group work. For successful classroom interaction to occur, a collaborative climate must be established where children feel part of a learning community in which problems are solved and understandings are developed through collective cognitive action.

OBJECTIVES

By the end of this unit you should:

- know how to introduce and develop group work successfully within the classroom;
- understand the purpose and organisation of different groups;
- be aware of the different phases and associated language during group interaction;
- be able to evaluate group interaction and monitor progress.

TYPES OF TALK

Spoken language is influenced by context, audience and purpose: where the communication is taking place, who we are communicating with and to what purpose will shape how we interact, what we say and how we say it. In presentation talk, usually done in whole class scenarios, the language will be relatively rehearsed, polished and quite formal. Although, after working in groups, children may present their findings to others, group work is largely concerned with process talk. This kind of exploratory language is unrehearsed, untidy and characterised by false starts, repetition, pauses, overlaps and interruptions. An Early Learning Goal is for children to 'Use talk to organise, sequence and clarify thinking, ideas, feelings and events' (QCA 2000: 58). In the following transcript Foundation Stage children use exploratory language as they discuss how best to grow nasturtium seeds.

Amelia   We can put them in the sand … the tray … they'll … [interrupted].

Chanese   In the window's best …'cos … [interrupted].

Richie   But what shall we put 'em in?

Chanese   Pots we have to put 'em in … [interrupted].

Amelia   No … no … no we don't 'cos we can choose … we can choose.

Zak   Boxes'll be best … them little boxes … we can put some soil … [interrupted].

Richie   Or … or … not soil … not soil … cotton wool … be best.

Zak   No no no … 'cos seeds grow in soil don't they?

Chanese   Well that's what we've got to find out … I mean … we've … [interrupted].

Zak   Yeah but they're more going to grow in soil I think.

When organising group work in the classroom it is important to have clear teaching objectives and to recognise the kinds of talk that particular tasks are likely to elicit. Examples of the different kinds of talk are shown in Figure 3.4.1, p. 120.

MANAGING SMALL GROUP WORK

Although group seating has been a prominent feature of classroom organisation in primary schools, research has consistently confirmed that a great deal of group work is either ineffective or inappropriate (Galton *et al.* 1980; Galton *et al.* 1999). Appropriate and properly organised group work encourages

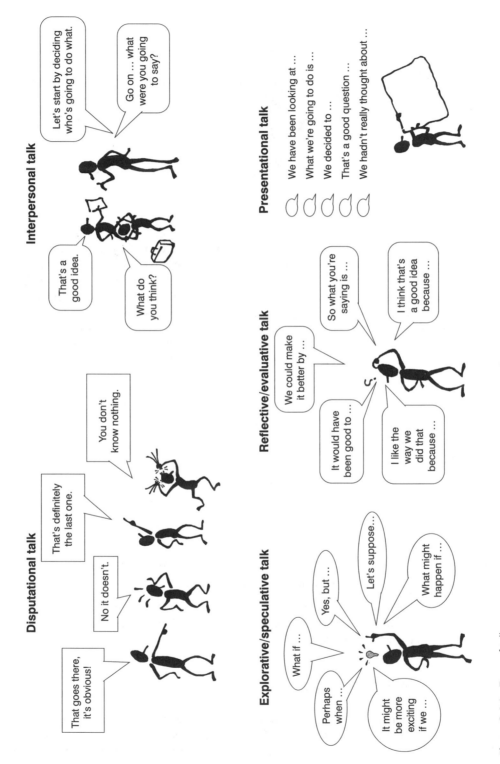

Figure 3.4.1 Types of talk

exploratory language where pupils engage in sustained discourse to speculate, challenge, reason, justify, reflect and evaluate. However, children need to understand why they are being asked to work collaboratively, to see the relevance of what they are doing and recognise that, as group members, they have both individual and collective responsibilities. Moreover, for group work to be successful it needs to be matched carefully to learning purposes and organised accordingly.

GROUP TYPES AND PURPOSES

Group work places both social and cognitive demands on children and different kinds of tasks will elicit different kinds of responses. It is important, therefore, to ensure that groups match tasks and purposes.

- *Resource group*   Pupils sit together to share resources but work to achieve individual objectives.
- *Cooperative group*   Pupils work on separate but related tasks to achieve a group objective.
- *Collaborative group*   Pupils work together on a task to achieve a group objective.

Other types of groups

- Friendship
- Mutual interest
- Mixed interest
- Targeted (jigsaw/rainbow)
- Mixed attainers
- Selected attainers

Task 3.4.1
Organising different groups

In small groups or with talk partners, identify occasions when you might organise the class into different kinds of groups. Discuss your experiences of how primary classrooms are generally organised. Evaluate how well you think groups were matched to purposes and discuss what changes you might make.

When planning for small group work you need to have an awareness of the kinds of tasks being presented to children because these will have an impact on the process and the expected outcome:

Discussion task: where there is an onus on process and the sharing of ideas. The subject matter is likely to be interpretative or controversial, for example a poem, narrative text, magazine article or newspaper report. The outcome may be a group decision or consensus or the development of individual interactive skills and cognitive understanding.

Problem-solving task: where a number of alternatives may be critically evaluated, for example a sequencing, prediction or deletion activity. The outcome may require a group consensus or individual decisions that are reached after group discussion.

Production task: where children work collaboratively to produce a group response, for example, the dramatisation of a text, or adaptation of a text for film. Jigsaw activities where children work on different aspects of a topic to achieve a group goal, such as writing an information book about Ancient Egypt, is an example of a production task.

In designing tasks, you need to consider the cognitive demands and social skills required to undertake activities cooperatively. Devising activities that are appropriate for cooperative rather than individual outcomes is a challenge. However, once the learning purpose is determined, and it is clear that group work is appropriate, the necessary organisation becomes clearer. It is advisable to begin cooperative group work with simple production tasks, where children are clear about the procedure and the expected outcome before moving on to introduce collaborative problem-solving activities which demand more abstract discussion. Structured activities with well-defined rules will help to keep pupils on task. Task and context demands should be increased gradually as children develop their skills and confidence.

Questions to ask about a task

- What are the social and cognitive demands of the task?
- Is the task suitable for cooperative/collaborative working?
- What kind of group is most suitable for the task?
- How will the task be introduced and children's curiosity and enthusiasm aroused?
- Are the resources and materials suitable and sufficient?
- What is my (teacher's) role during the task?
- Are the children clear about the task in terms of process (how they are to work) and product (what they are expected to produce)?
- What response/feedback/reward will be given on completion of the task?

INTRODUCING GROUP WORK TO THE CLASS

At the Foundation Stage, children are required to 'Interact with others, negotiating plans and activities' (QCA 2000: 48). Such activity requires skill, understanding and an appreciation of what working with others entails. Children are often told to discuss and collaborate but receive little guidance or explanation (Kutnick *et al.* 2002). It is essential to model the discussion process, make the ground rules explicit and clarify roles and expectations. Successful group work depends on the children's willingness to make it work. They are more likely to cooperate, with you and each other, if they know why they are doing something and appreciate the benefits of what they are doing. A little time spent on activities to develop children's appreciation and understanding will reap rewards.

Getting children to value group work

Children often do not understand the point of group work so getting them to value it as a way of learning is important. One simple activity is to show an illustration such as the one in Figure 3.4.2. The children are asked, initially, to see if they can detect the hidden figure. However, they are instructed to work independently and silently. After a period of time they are then encouraged to talk. Children exchange ideas and in so doing speculate, explain, reason, expand and justify. Children can then compare how they felt when asked to do the task individually as opposed to collaboratively.

Figure 3.4.2   Getting children to value group work

Establishing ground rules

It is important to establish ground rules for group discussion and interaction. One way of achieving this is through a snowball group activity:

- children individually write three rules for group work;
- individuals join talk partners to share ideas and choose four rules;
- pairs join together in small groups to share ideas and choose five rules;
- two or more groups join together to share ideas and choose six rules;
- whole class shares ideas and decides on a class charter for group work.

Stages in group discussions

Group discussion tends to go through various stages. However, this varies considerably depending on the type of group, purpose of task and children involved. My own observations of group work have shown that successful interaction is often unpredictable and the discourse characterised by false starts, hesitations, repetition, backtracking and constant changes of direction. However, from the ORACLE and CLIP research projects Tann (1981) and Robertson (1990) both identify progressive phases from orientation and norm establishment through to conflict, productivity and conclusion. I particularly like Tuckerman and Jensen's (1977) rhythmical nomenclature of forming, storming, norming, performing and adjourning.

Forming

This is where group members come together and get to know each other and sort out their various roles.

Storming

At this stage children will attempt to ease into the group work situation and to impose work patterns that suit them personally. This may result in some social bartering and conflict may occur between individual group members. At this stage children may question the relevance of group work and show resentment at having to work together in this way.

Norming

This stage is reached when children develop a shared understanding of the task and perceive the purpose of working together in a group. Expectations of behaviour are clarified and agreed upon and a set of 'norms' for each group is recognised.

Performing

This is the most productive and usually the longest stage where children focus on the task in hand and begin to interact effectively. Children will use language *socially* to maintain interpersonal relations and *cognitively* to achieve the learning goal.

Adjourning

As the name suggests this is the concluding stage where the discussion is drawn to a close and children may reflect on and learn from their experiences.

THE ROLE OF THE TEACHER

In this general pattern there are clear implications for you, as the teacher (Corden 2000). At the forming stage children may be anxious especially if it is the beginning of a new school year or if they have to interact with peers with whom they do not normally work. You need to explain the task clearly, provide unambiguous directions and discuss, with the children, the reasons for working together in a group. It is at the storming stage where most disruption is likely to occur. Children may jockey for position, some individuals try to impose their particular ways of working on the group and others question or reject the whole notion of working in this way. You need to anticipate the challenges, be proactive and discuss, with the children, ways of working before starting the task. Children can be supported at the norming stage by you clarifying the nature of the groups and the purpose of the task at the start of the lesson. Establishing an agreed set of ground rules for group work and displaying these for the children to see can facilitate proceedings. It is at the performing stage where you need to interact skilfully and sensitively, taking on different roles and acting contingently to scaffold but not inhibit or control the discussions. Discussions can deteriorate, fizzle out or simply reach an abrupt end where children fail to perceive their purpose or value. At this stage a period for reflection and evaluation is necessary. When adjourning, children should consider the quality of their interaction and assess how successful they have been in completing the task.

Ensuring participation

Ensuring that all pupils participate in group work is a major consideration. Some children can opt out of work and allow others to complete a task. Children will often do this if the task is challenging and other members of the group are evidently more able. High achievers can also refuse to participate fully if they feel the task is too easy or is moving too slowly for them. Sometimes those children who are enthusiastic and seem prepared to do most work eventually feel exploited and do not contribute effectively. Other children simply go through the motions of working but operate independently and do not collaborate or exchange ideas. Attention seekers are those children who move around the classroom and interrupt the work of others. Children who can seem eager to participate in whole class debates may prefer to work individually rather than as collaborative group members. Intermittent workers are those who tend to work when they know they are being observed but will move off task whenever an opportunity arises.

In some activities, assigning roles to children can be counterproductive and may inhibit the natural flow of ideas. However, group discussion can easily deteriorate into what Mercer (1996: 225) calls disputational talk, where group members simply argue their own viewpoint but don't consider those of others. Learning to speak and learning to listen when someone else is speaking begins in the early years through role play. More formal group work at Key Stage 1 can be supported by children having a resource such as a glove puppet which symbolises 'holding the floor'. When anyone wears it everyone else in the group must listen carefully to what they have to say. Others must indicate that they want the puppet next and it is gradually passed around the group. At Key Stage 2 a number of talk-tokens can be issued to group members, which can then be spent when anyone wishes to speak.

For some kinds of group discussion to be of value it needs to be informed interaction, where children bring to the task essential background experience and knowledge. In such cases the discussion can be facilitated if children are given specific roles. Providing role cards can help ensure that children work productively (see Figures 3.4.3 and 3.4.4, pp. 126 and 127).

CLASSROOM LAYOUT AND RESOURCES

When children are appropriately organised into groups they are likely to use language to explore, speculate, interrogate and hypothesise. Within a collaborative environment children can construct knowledge, reach understandings and formulate meanings as they not only consider and evaluate materials which are put to them, but also formulate questions, consider options and develop a sense of involvement in and responsibility for their own learning. However, research into the organisation of primary classrooms has shown that group work is often used merely as an expedient seating arrangement with children working independently and with no apparent reason for them to be seated in groups. It is essential that group work be seen as part of an organisational repertoire and only used when it is appropriate to do so.

Different kinds of talk have implications for classroom layout. There may be times when you want to address the whole class and will need to ensure that all children can make eye contact with you. It is possible to organise effective contexts for talk in a classroom by adapting the layout to reflect different working patterns (see Hastings and Chantrey Wood 2002). Effective storage of resources creates an orderly working environment which can be more easily adapted than one with excessive clutter. Clearly defined resource areas or 'resource islands' in the classroom can minimise unnecessary movement. Establishing procedures where children take responsibility for accessing and returning resources will ensure the classroom remains tidy and that resources are available and used efficiently.

Mentor

It is your job to:
- Help and support your group.

You will need to:
- Help in a positive and supportive way.
- Explain the task clearly to the other members of your group.
- Ask others in your group what they don't understand about the task.
- Try to explain the task in small parts.
- Show the group how you would try to work out the problem, but don't do it for them.

Reporter

It is your job to:
- Report to other groups on behalf of yours.

You will need to:
- Work with the scribe to organise a report about what you have done. Include:
  - What your question was.
  - Whether or not you found a solution.
  - The solution, if there was one.
  - Strategies used to find the solution.
  - Any difficulties you had.
- Speak to the other groups using a loud, clear voice.
- Answer any questions that the other group, or teacher, has about what you are saying.

Scribe

It is your job to:
- Scribe for the other members of the group.

You will need to:
- Organise the writing equipment your group will need (pens, paper etc.).
- Make useful notes.
- Write down what your group work out.
- Maybe re-write any information that needs to be clearer to others.
- Organise the information you have written.
- Write the solution clearly.
- Work with the reporter at the end of the task to organise a report about your work.

Leader

It is your job to:
- Lead the other members of your group.

You will need to:
- Make sure that everyone in the group has their say.
- Make sure that everyone listens when someone is speaking.
- Make suggestions about how to do the task if people are not sure.
- Organise a vote if necessary.
- Stay calm, even if others are getting excited.

Figure 3.4.3 Role cards

Mentor

'How about if I put it this way …'
'You add this and this, what does it make?'
'This is a way we could do it …'
'If we do this, can you see that it links to what we did before?'
'I'll explain it to you.'
'In other words …'
'Let's try it another way.'
'How would you work it out?'
'Which bit don't you understand?'

Reporter

'This is what we have been doing …'
'In our group we had to find a solution to …'
'We found out that …'
'We started by making a guess …'

Scribe

'Shall I write that down?'
'This is what I have written so far …'
'Could you say that again please?'
'Is this a good idea? Do you think I should record it?'
'Does this make sense …?'

Leader

'We all need to cooperate.'
'What would you like to say?'
'Does that make sense?'
'I think this is a fair way …'
'I think we need to …'
'Can we all listen to …'
'Can we speak one at a time?'
'Is there anything else anyone wants to say?'
'Shall we have a vote?'
'Are we agreed on …?'

Figure 3.4.4 Language cards

Task 3.4.2
Designing a classrom context for talk

In small groups or with talk partners, choose one of the group discussion and interaction teaching objectives (PNS 2003). Discuss how you might organise the classroom to meet your purpose. Draw a sketch of your classroom then join another pair. Exchange ideas and justify your choice of design.

EVALUATING THE QUALITY OF GROUP INTERACTION

In order to assess the quality of group interaction you need to be clear about your objectives because purpose of task and type of group will influence the outcome. In each of the following examples the task is for children to interrogate and evaluate a text. The teacher is looking for evidence of collaborative interaction, exploratory language and development in children's understandings.

Task 3.4.3
Evaluating a group interaction

In small groups or with talk partners discuss the quality of interaction in transcripts one and two. Consider what skills pupils are using to develop the discourse. Discuss how the social interaction is helping to enhance the pupils' learning.

Transcript one

1 Kirsty	So, shall we read through and make a note of all these first?
2 Shabina	Yeah he thinks he's useless … he says [reading from the text] 'why are you so useless?'
3 Kirsty	OK … if I write all this down for now then and //
4 Jay	He calls him Fuzz [laughing].
5 Kirsty	= then we can talk about it.
6 Shabina	You what … why?
7 Kirsty	I dunno … 'cos he's got a beard I suppose.
8 Jay	I'm gonna say Conrad doesn't respect his dad … thinks his dad is a nut … a nutty old tramp.
9 Beckie	Conrad does not think much of his dad … he thinks his dad is useless [writing this down].
10 Jay	Is that what you're putting.
11 Shabina	I'm putting that he doesn't have any respect for his dad.
12 Beckie	Shab, are you writing out bits from the book?
13 Shabina	Yeah, some bits like where Conrad or his dad say things to each other.

14 Jay	This is daft … as if you could make a tank!
15 Kirsty	But do you think he's really going to make a tank or is he just going to imagine it … [reading from the text] … it says 'Somewhere out there in his imagination'.
16 Jay	Well, just put what you think … I think it's daft.

Transcript two

1 Beckie	I think he's made Snyder seem more nasty by how he's made the others.
2 Shabina	Yeah, like the others are … nice … nicer.
3 Kirsty	Like Mrs Mutterance … [reading from the text] 'she was white haired and small and entirely round'.
4 Jay	Yeah, and she wore funny fingerless mittens and sucked sweets.
5 Shabina	Yeah, it's how he's described them … but he's made Mrs Mutterance and Amy both small and I reckon he's done that on purpose.
6 Beckie	That's what I mean … to make Snyder seem more horrible …
7 Jay	To make Snyder seem more threatening … more scary… 'cos yeah … here it says her face was white and solemn.
8 Kirsty	'A kittenish concern in the large dark eyes' [reading from the text].
9 Shabina	Suppose he's saying she's just like a kitten … like a kitten is … small //
10 Kirsty	But not just small.
11 Shabina	= like … a kitten … because anything can hurt a kitten.
12 Jay	Not anything.
13 Kirsty	No but kittens trust people, don't they … I think he's trying to make Amy seem like someone who you could hurt dead easy.
14 Beckie	Yeah…oh yeah … 'cos look … Wallace … he calls Snyder an old monster man … so don't you think that's good … he's making Amy a little kitten and Snyder a monster.
15 Jay	And here … back here it says he was like a bear … [reads from the text] 'his shadow a bear on the wall'.
16 Beckie	Because she's like an old mother cat … all fat and cuddly.
17 Jay	So, are you saying she's weak and scared as well?

In transcript one Kirsty (1) attempts to develop group collaboration by suggesting a collective interrogation of the text but she meets with limited success. She volunteers to be the scribe for the group and there is an assumption that discussion will ensue. At this stage there is every indication that Kirsty is correct. Shabina (2) accepts Kirsty's suggestion and refers to the text for evidence to support a claim and Jay draws attention to the derogatory term Conrad uses to describe his father. However, this exploratory interaction is short-lived and soon a decisive transition takes place as Jay and Shabina's utterances (8, 10 and 11) signal the onset of an individualised independent work pattern. When Kirsty (15) does attempt to initiate some collaborative discussion by asking *do you think*, she is rejected.

In transcript two the contrast between the talk in the activity on *Conrad's War* and that arising through the same pupils discussing *London Snow* could not be sharper. The girls begin their discussion by focusing on the main characters in the story. The talk evolves in a fully collaborative manner and could be described as truly exploratory, indicated by linguistic markers such as *what if*, *suppose*, *I reckon*, *but don't you think*, *so are you saying*, *yeah but*, *how do you know* and *perhaps*. The talk is also naturally but deliberately managed by the group as they clarify the task, exchange views, challenge, reason, justify and extend ideas. Beckie (1) initiates discussion with an exploratory utterance marked by *I think* and Shabina (2) maintains the initiative by offering supporting evidence from the text. All participants engage in collaborative activity as they extend Beckie's initiative. Kirsty and Jay (3 and 4) investigate the text in an attempt to substantiate Beckie's hypothesis. Beckie (6) reaffirms her view and shows an implicit appreciation of the others' contributions. Jay and Kirsty (7 and 8) respond by again seeking evidence from the text to support Beckie's point. Shabina (9) extends the discussion by offering a hypothesis, signalled by the linguistic mode-marker *suppose*. Kirsty accepts Shabina's point and develops it by offering an additional perspective. Kirsty's utterance (13) is particularly noteworthy because it illustrates the truly collaborative nature of the discussion in both social and cognitive terms. *I think* indicates an exploratory mode and the linguistic hedge *don't they* suggests tentativeness and an invitation for others to agree or disagree with her contribution. Beckie (14) agrees with Kirsty's hypothesis and extends it by referring to the text. The hedge *don't you think* again illustrates a tentativeness and willingness to engage in debate. Another characteristic of collaborative discussion, the use of conjunctions to begin utterances, is now evident. In turn, *and*, *because* and *so* (15, 16, 17) serve as cohesive devices and indicate that the pupils are not merely offering individual and disparate contributions but are focusing on and collectively extending an issue.

The difference in the quality of discourse from the same children undertaking similar tasks highlights how important it is for you and the children to have a shared understanding of objectives and expectations. This is not to say that you should predetermine outcomes and although speaking and listening should be taught explicitly it should be developed in contexts where discourse serves a real purpose. Teaching objectives, classroom activities and example work sequences for group discussion are provided by the Primary National Strategy (2003). In planning work sequences there are specific organisational strategies and teaching techniques you can use to develop the quality of interactive discourse in your classroom and these are explained in the PNS leaflet and poster pack.

MONITORING PROGRESS AND ACHIEVEMENT IN GROUP WORK

The Primary National Strategy (2003) identifies progression in speaking and listening and offers a suggested format for recording achievement. Self assessment should also form a part of the overall monitoring system and children should be encouraged to evaluate their own and each other's contributions. You can use these on-going formative evaluations for diagnostic and planning purposes and also to make summative assessments when necessary. Some recording formats are shown in Figures 3.4.5, 3.4.6 and 3.4.7.

Name:

Group:

I listened to what others in the group said			
I gave my ideas			
I answered when people asked me questions			
I helped others in the group to speak			
I helped the group to work well			

I think I was especially good at…

I think I could be better at…

I think the group was good at…

I think the group could be better at…

Figure 3.4.5 Self assessment (Key Stage 1)

Name:

Group:

I helped to plan/organise the way we worked			
I helped the discussion by sharing my ideas with others			
I listened and thought carefully about what others said			
I took on the role of (_____)			
I encouraged and supported others by responding constructively to ideas			
My contribution helped the group to complete the task			
I challenged people's ideas and suggested alternative views/actions			

I think I was especially good at…

I think I could be better at…

I think the group was good at…

I think the group could be better at…

Figure 3.4.6 Self assessment (Key Stage 2)

Date: _____

Speaking and listening objective: _____

Context/Activity: _____

Names	Comment

Figure 3.4.7 Teacher assessment

SUMMARY

Effective teaching and learning is underpinned by interactive discourse. The Primary National Strategy (2004) recognises the learning potential of peer group discussions that offer children opportunities to explore, reason, justify, speculate and evaluate as they develop cognitive understandings. Children who are organised into collaborative partnerships in the classroom are more likely to have the confidence to take risks, offer tentative thoughts and explore hypothetical avenues. Within a secure cooperative environment children can actively construct knowledge, consider options and formulate meanings. However, seating children together will not automatically result in productive, collaborative discussion. Children need to understand the purpose of group work and appreciate the benefits of collaboration. They need to know and accept the ground rules and to recognise individual and collective responsibilities. As the teacher you need to be aware that different kinds of tasks are likely to elicit different responses and to match group organisation to purpose. Above all, you need to establish an enquiring, reciprocal climate for learning in your classroom where you model effective discourse through your own interaction with children.

ANNOTATED FURTHER READING

Broadhead, P. (1997) 'Promoting sociability and cooperation in nursery settings', *British Educational Research Journal*, 23(4): 513–31. This article explores the issue of sociability in children aged 4–5 years. It examines the potential of various activities to develop problem-solving and interactive dialogue.

Grugeon, E., Dawes, L., Smith, C. and Hubbard, L. (2005) *Teaching Speaking and Listening in the Primary School* (3rd edition), London: David Fulton. In this Chapter 2, 'Talk in the early years', the authors re-assert the value of talk at home and in the early years classroom. Practical activities for promoting talk are described.

Hardman, F. and Beverton, S. (1995) 'Developing collaborative group work in the primary school: the importance of metacognition', *Reading*, July: 11–15. This article discusses the importance of developing children's understanding of discourse strategies. It suggests that skills such as turn-taking and active listening need to be explicitly taught and modelled by teachers.

Lyle, S. (1996) 'An analysis of collaborative group work in the primary school and the factors relevant to its success', *Language and Education*, 10(1): 13–31. This article draws on ten years of classroom research and argues that collaborative learning needs careful planning of tasks and classroom organisation. Particular attention is drawn to the role of the teacher, group structure and composition and group members' previous experiences.

REFERENCES

Alexander, R. (2000) *Culture and Pedagogy: International Comparisons in Primary Education*, Oxford: Blackwell.

Bruner, J. (1986) *Actual Minds, Possible Worlds*, Cambridge, MA: Harvard University Press.

Corden, R. (2000) *Literacy and Learning through Talk*, Buckingham: Open University Press.

DfEE (1998) *The National Literacy Strategy: A Framework for Teaching*, London: DfEE.

DfEE (1999) *The National Numeracy Strategy*, London: DfEE.

Galton, M., Simon, B. and Croll, P. (1980) *Inside the Primary Classroom*, London: Routledge.

Galton, M., Hargreaves, L., Comber, C., Wall, D. and Pell, A. (1999) *Inside the Primary Classroom Twenty Years On*, London: Routledge.

Hardman, F., Smith, F, Wall, K. and Mroz, M. (2003) *Interactive Whole Class Teaching in the Literacy and Numeracy Lessons*, University of Newcastle Upon Tyne. A Report for the Economic and Social Research Council.

Hastings, N. and Chantrey Wood, K. (2002) *Reorganizing Primary Classroom Learning*, Buckingham: Open University Press.

Kutnick, P., Blatchford, P. and Bains, E. (2002) 'Pupil groupings in primary school classrooms: sites for learning and social pedagogy', *British Educational Research Journal*, 28(2): 187–206.

Mercer, N. (1996) 'The quality of talk in children's collaborative activity in the classroom', *Learning and Instruction*, 6(4): 359–77.

Primary National Strategy (2003) *Speaking, Listening, Learning: Working with Children in Key Stages 1 and 2*, London: DfES.

Primary National Strategy (2004) *Excellence and Enjoyment: Learning and Teaching in the Primary Years Professional Development Materials*, London: DfES.

QCA (2000) *Curriculum Guidance for the Foundation Stage*, London: DfEE.

Robertson, L. (1990) 'Cooperative learning à la CLIP', in M. Brubacher, R. Payne and K. Rickett (eds) *Perspectives on Small Group Learning*, Oakville, Ontario: Rubicon.

Tann, S. (1981) 'Grouping and group work', in B. Simon and J. Willocks (eds) *Research and Practice in the Primary Classroom*, London: Routledge.

Tuckerman, B. and Jensen, M. (1977) 'Stages of small group development revised', *Group and Organisational Studies*, 1: 419–27.

Unit 3.5

Organising Your Classroom for Learning

Peter Kelly

INTRODUCTION

In this unit I link approaches to organising learning environments to views about how learning takes place. Learning is complex, and no one view can fully capture this complexity. However, each view of learning is helpful in understanding and planning for particular aspects of learning. I argue that a balanced approach to classroom organisation draws on each view of learning. Thus we should use different approaches to promote different types of learning.

OBJECTIVES

Having read this unit you should be able to:

- recognise the link between views about how learning takes place and approaches to organising your classroom;
- know the key approaches to organising your classroom;
- recognise the scope and limitation of each of these approaches;
- identify appropriate approaches for particular learning objectives.

ORGANISING LEARNING

How you organise your classroom says a great deal about how you view your children's learning. Colleagues, parents and, perhaps most importantly, children will read much about what you value from those features of classroom life for which you are responsible: the areas of the curriculum you choose to link and focus on, the lessons and activities you plan, the roles you ascribe to other adults in your classroom, how you group and seat the children, the decisions you allow children to take, the resources you provide and the ways in which you make them available, your use of display and of opportunities to learn outside the classroom and school, and so on.

Consider the range of options available to you in relation to just one of these: groupings. Children can be taught as a whole class, in groups or individually. In groups they might work collaboratively or be provided with differentiated individual tasks. Such tasks might be differentiated in terms of the level of challenge of the task or the level of support the group receives, and so on. Such features are not simple alternatives: those you choose to use and the circumstances in which you choose to use them will say something about your beliefs as a teacher, even if these are largely tacit and the decisions you make intuitive.

There is a lot of advice available on classroom organisation. This has not always been the case. It was not until the 1960s that the traditional model of teaching – that is, a teacher standing at the front of the classroom with the children sitting facing, working on the same task at the same time - was challenged. Progressive approaches, developed largely from the ideas of Jean Piaget, suggested children should be free to work at different speeds and in different ways, learning from first-hand experiences through active exploration and personal discovery. But traditionalists argued such approaches were largely ineffective: there were things which children needed to be taught like spelling and grammar which could not be discovered or left to chance. Thus began an enduring and polarised educational debate.

More recently a loose consensus has prevailed which recognises that certain approaches favour certain kinds of learning rather than one approach being best. Nevertheless the range of approaches suggested can appear daunting. In fact it is relatively straightforward if you remain mindful of one thing: how you organise your classroom depends on how you believe children will learn in your classroom.

This unit considers classroom organisation in relation to four views of learning: basic skills acquisition; constructing understanding; learning together; and apprenticeship approaches.

Basic skills acquisition

Once a favourite of traditionalist knowledge transmission approaches, direct teaching dominates approaches to basic skills teaching in the National Literacy Strategy (NLS) and National Numeracy Strategy (NNS) in England. Originally conceived somewhat behaviouristically as teacher demonstration and student imitation leading to a period of consolidation and practice, in these strategies direct teaching has been the recipient of a Vygotskian makeover, becoming an interactive approach where the importance of high-quality dialogue and discussion between teachers and pupils is emphasised. However this has been an issue with many teachers who have been less ready to move away from a teacher demonstration and student imitation model towards a more interactive one.

Learning as constructing understanding

Originating in the ideas of Jean Piaget, constructivists see learners as theory builders, developing understandings to make sense of their observations and experiences, and modifying these understandings in the light of subsequent observations and experiences so that they become more generally useful and closer to accepted viewpoints. This perspective has had a huge impact on some curriculum areas, particularly science where a cottage industry grew in the 1980s researching the alternative understandings and misunderstandings, termed 'alternative frameworks', which children have of the phenomena they encounter. Phil Adey and Michael Shayer's Cognitive Acceleration through Science Education (CASE) has adapted and extended the constructivist approach. By challenging children's misunderstandings of phenomena the CASE approach aims to develop the structure of their thinking.

Social learning

Social constructivists like Jerome Bruner cite the ideas of the Russian theorist Lev Vygotsky in positing a central role for talking and listening in learning. Making sense and developing understanding, they assert, are essentially social processes which take place through talk. The National Oracy Project identified a whole range of ways in which participation with others in activities involving discussion can improve learning: it supports learners in constructing new meanings and understandings as they explore them in words; it allows learners to test out and criticise claims and different points of view as they speak and listen to others; and importantly, talk provides raw material for learners' own thinking, because for Vygotsky, thought is an internal, personal dialogue.

Learning as an apprenticeship

The work of social anthropologists such as Jean Lave and Etienne Wenger has illuminated how people learn in everyday contexts. This has led them to reconsider school learning in socio-cultural terms. Thus, there are many metaphors that we can adopt for our classrooms: the writer's workshop, the artist's studio, the scientist's laboratory, and so on. In each case, this view suggests, the children act as craft apprentices, engaging in the authentic activities of the community to which the metaphor pertains. So for children to think as, for example, historians, they have to be helped to act like historians by doing what historians do. The same is, of course, true for scientists or practitioners in any other area of enquiry.

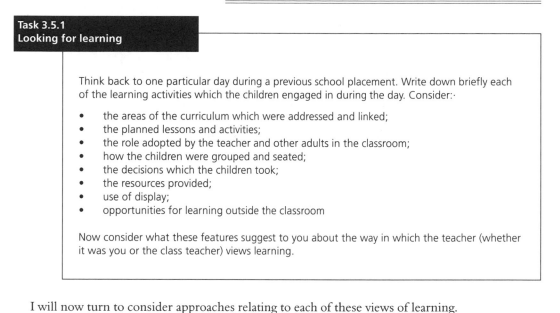

Task 3.5.1
Looking for learning

Think back to one particular day during a previous school placement. Write down briefly each of the learning activities which the children engaged in during the day. Consider:·

- the areas of the curriculum which were addressed and linked;
- the planned lessons and activities;
- the role adopted by the teacher and other adults in the classroom;
- how the children were grouped and seated;
- the decisions which the children took;
- the resources provided;
- use of display;
- opportunities for learning outside the classroom

Now consider what these features suggest to you about the way in which the teacher (whether it was you or the class teacher) views learning.

I will now turn to consider approaches relating to each of these views of learning.

CLASSROOM APPROACHES

Basic skills and direct interactive teaching

The NLS and NNS in England promote direct interactive teaching. As a whole class approach, this allows children to benefit from direct involvement with their teacher for sustained periods. But direct teaching and interaction are also important during individual, paired and group work.

The role of dialogue is emphasised: children are expected to play an active part in discussion by asking questions, contributing ideas and explaining and demonstrating their thinking to the class. However, many studies have found that teachers spend the majority of their time either explaining or using tightly structured questions. Such questions are mainly factual or closed in nature, and so fail to encourage and extend child contributions or to promote interaction and thinking.

New technologies have had, in recent years, a significant impact on direct interactive and whole class teaching. These include interactive whiteboards, data projectors, and remote devices such as infra-red keyboards and graphics tablets.

Good direct interactive teaching, as exemplified in some of the best examples of Literacy and Numeracy teaching using the NLS and NNS, is achieved by balancing different approaches:

Directing and telling

Sharing teaching objectives with the class, ensuring that children know what to do, and drawing attention to points over which they should take particular care.

Explaining and illustrating

Giving accurate, well-paced explanations, and referring to previous work or methods.

Demonstrating

Giving clear, well-structured demonstrations using appropriate resources and visual displays.

Questioning and discussing

Ensuring all children take part; using open and closed questions; asking for explanations; giving time for children to think before answering; allowing children to talk about their answers in pairs before contributing them to the whole class; listening carefully to children's responses, responding constructively; and challenging children's assumptions to encourage thinking.

Exploring and investigating

Asking children to pose problems or suggest a line of enquiry.

Consolidating and embedding

Through a variety of activities in class and well-focused homework, opportunities are provided to practise and develop new learning; making use of this learning to tackle related problems and tasks.

Reflecting and evaluating

Identifying children's errors, and using them as positive teaching points by exploring them together; discussing children's reasons for choosing particular methods or resources; giving oral feedback on written work.

Summarising and reminding

Reviewing during and towards the end of a lesson that which has been taught and what children have learned; identifying and correcting misunderstandings; making links to other work; and giving children an insight into the next stage of their learning.

Direct interactive teaching approaches focus on knowledge and skills transmission and acquisition through active learning and interaction. In this they leave little room for learners to construct their own understandings of phenomena. This is where the following approach is useful.

Constructing understanding

Constructivists believe learners build their understandings of the world from their experiences and observations. They suggest that children bring many misconceptions and misunderstandings to the classroom from their experiences of the world, and assert that the best way to change such misunderstandings is to challenge children to change them themselves through hands-on explorations. For example, in science children may, from their experiences at home, have formed the misconception that clothes make you warmer. An investigation where chocolate is wrapped in fabric could be used to see if this causes the chocolate to melt. Such information might challenge the children's misconception, and the children would need to restructure their thinking to accommodate the new information that the chocolate is not warmed up; rather it is prevented from cooling or warming as the outside temperature changes.

However one of the problems here is that it is assumed children will recognise the need to change their thinking or even that they will want to do it. An approach which takes the constructivist approach further is CASE. This can be used to formalise the thinking and restructuring process as it contains certain key elements which many teachers have adopted or adapted in their own classrooms:

Concrete preparation

The problem is stated in terms which are understandable to the children; that is, so that they see it as a problem. For example, you might ask the children to talk to the person next to them and think about clothes they might choose to take on holiday to a very cold country and why.

Cognitive conflict

Children are encouraged to consider a range of possible explanations for causes and effects that may interact in complex ways with each other. For example, children investigating types of clothing (identifying features such as fabric type, thickness and shape) and their suitability for a cold location could consider which feature or combination of features is central.

Social construction

Now the children work together on the challenging activity to construct new joint understandings. In this, although the teacher asks probing questions to focus debate, the children do most of the thinking. So the children might share each others' discussions and try to come to a consensus.

Metacognition

In this process the children are helped to become conscious of their own reasoning in order to understand it. In putting pupils in charge of their own learning it is important to enable them to articulate their own thinking and learning processes.

Bridging

This is the conscious transfer of the new ideas and understandings from the context in which they were generated to new but related contexts. Thus the children could apply their new shared understanding of clothing in cold countries to hot countries.

This approach focuses largely on the learning of the individual. Social learning approaches, which follow, focus more on what can be achieved by a group working together, with the view that what is done together the individual will eventually become able to do alone.

Social learning

Establishing ground rules

Before engaging in social learning approaches, a number of ground rules need to be established with children. Rules to stop interruptions of all those involved in group work, adults or children, should be negotiated first. Thus children needing help might be encouraged to take greater responsibility for their learning by seeking support elsewhere, or by doing alternative work until support is available.

Such independent and self-directed learners can be referred to as autonomous. The American educationalist Susan Bobbit-Nolan considers three levels of autonomy. The first is when learners have autonomy or control over the strategies which they use to carry out a task without the guidance of their teacher. Thus in mathematics a teacher might teach a variety of strategies for children to undertake three-digit multiplication. The children can then choose which one to use in tackling a problem. Similarly, children might choose the form of recording to use for a science exploration and so on. At the second level, learners have control over the content of the curriculum, the things to be studied and learned, the objectives of learning. Thus children might decide to explore something in its own right or set their own goals for their learning. They might choose an area or theme on history to research, an assignment to write, an experiment to do, or a book to read. This is learning for pleasure, following tangents, and satisfying curiosities. At the third level, learners are able to judge things for themselves, after taking evidence and various views into account. Thus the children might make informed decisions about changes to school routines such as playtimes, spending money on new items for class or elections to the school council. They might tackle controversial issues in school and debate these, looking at the perspectives of different parties. This third level of autonomy goes beyond simply independence in accessing resources or completing the teacher's work, and has been called 'intellectual autonomy'. Learners who have intellectual autonomy think for themselves, link their thinking to their experiences and open their minds to new ideas.

Discussions during group work should be democratic: everyone has the right to a say, and for their contribution to be valued. This means that participants should:

- listen attentively to the contributions of others without interrupting;
- speak to each other, looking at the person to whom they are responding;
- take turns and allow everyone an equal opportunity to speak;
- be sensitive to each others' needs;
- try to see things from other people's points of view, even if they disagree with their position;
- give reasons for their views;
- and be prepared to change their viewpoint in the light of new information, and accept others doing the same.

Further, children should understand that it is disrespectful to others if they monopolise the talk or if they ridicule or are unkind about others or their views. Of course, it is often most effective when the children are allowed to come up with rules such as these themselves: with prompting they can be encouraged to address the key areas. A good place to develop these together with a regard for these democratic ways of working is the school council.

Collaborative group work

Group tasks are most effective when children need to share their knowledge, skills and understandings to a common end through some form of problem solving or open-ended task. In their activity, children's talk will centre initially on their actions, but should be moved towards their understandings.

Research has suggested that the ideal size for groups engaging in collaborative work is four – pairs are too small for generating lots of ideas, threes tend to form a pair and exclude the third member, and groups bigger than four become harder for the children to manage so it is less likely that everyone will be fully included. Similarly mixed gender and mixed ability groups tend to be more inclusive, focused, and generate the widest range of viewpoints and ideas.

There are two basic forms of task organisation for collaborative work: 'jigsaw' and 'group investigation'. The former requires each group member to complete a sub-task which contributes to the whole group completing the assigned task. This might be the production of a picture, diagram or piece of writing about, say, Roman villas for a group display on that topic. In the second, all of the group work together on the same task, with each member of the group being assigned a different role. So the children might create a small dramatic episode portraying life in a Roman villa. Each child would play a different character, and, in addition, one child might take on the role of director.

So, for example, a group might work together on a 'jigsaw task' to produce a leaflet welcoming newcomers and informing them about the school. Each child might survey a different group of children from across the school to find out what information newcomers would need and benefit from. Particular attention would be paid to the experiences of any newcomers to the school. Then the group would make decisions together about which areas to address, in what format, etc. Each child could then be allocated the task of developing an aspect of the leaflet, with these being finally brought together for the finished document.

Dialogical enquiry

Dialogical enquiries are discussions in which learners, through language and sometimes supported by written notes and prompts, jointly engage in:

- working towards a common understanding for all;
- asking questions and suggesting ideas relating to the evidence on which proposals are based;
- looking at issues and problems from as many different perspectives as possible;
- challenging ideas and perspectives in the light of contradictions and evidence so as to move the discussion forward.

Examples include book clubs or reading circles, where children discuss their reading and produce new books together. Similarly writing conferences are extremely valuable, in which writers discuss their writing with their peers. Of course, having such shared dialogues about texts will improve participants' ability to engage in such dialogues alone.

Other opportunities exist in developing home–school learning partnerships in children's work. Thus in one example, parents of a particular group of young children read the same book with their children at home one evening. During the shared reading, parents wrote down the children's responses to the stories on post-it notes and fixed them to the relevant pages. Next day these notes became the starting points for discussion between the teacher and the group.

With older children, each child in a group reading the same book together might individually write a piece predicting the next stage of the story. This writing might provide the starting point for a group discussion about the evidence for each prediction, likelihood and plausibility of each prediction and the groups preferred outcome. Such a discussion could equally be based on individual group members writing initially from the perspective of one of the characters of the story and providing that character's point of view. The discussion could then consider the story from this variety of perspectives.

In terms of interpretation of data, such discursive enquiries are important because they can link the process of enquiry to the big ideas of the subject. So, for example, in science, following an investigation of the conditions in which plants grow best, rather than children simply describing the conditions which are most favourable to healthy plant growth, the discussion can focus on ideas about why this might be the case. Perhaps the children's text of the data collected can be compared in their discussion to other writing they have done which has attempted to explain findings.

Learning through apprenticeship

Apprenticeship models of learning require groups of children to engage in the actual or authentic activities of particular groups. So, for science, children work as scientists, engaging in an enquiry for which the answer is not already known, using the key ideas and tools of science and sometimes working in partnership with others from the local community. For example, Year 5 and 6 children might set up a weather station or get involved in monitoring environmental changes in an environmental awareness campaign. In doing this they might involve members of the wider community, contact experts at the Met Office for advice, and so on.

There are many other possibilities for authentic activities in schools. So, in mathematics Year 1 and 2 children might conduct a traffic survey in order to provide evidence for a letter to the council for some form of traffic control outside school, and Year 5 and 6 children might be helped to cost and plan a residential visit, whilst children in Years 3 and 4 could run a school stationery shop – ordering, pricing and selling goods in order to make a small profit. Similarly in geography children in Key Stage 2 might survey and research the school population growth using various indicators such as local birth rates, and could be encouraged to identify the implications of their findings. Finally children from across the school could be involved in making a CD for sale following their composition of various items for a particular event such as a school anniversary.

Sometimes it is important to look at particular areas of study in many different ways. For example, in an essentially historical study of the Battle of the Somme in 1916, older children could engage not only in an historical enquiry based approach, be it text or computer based or involving the examination of original artefacts, but also by looking at events through the eyes of poets and novelists, or through the eyes of geographers or scientists. As such the work of others might be explored, and the children might engage in original work themselves not only in writing and poetry but also through the media of music, dance, drama and painting. This would provide the children with a very full and rich learning experience.

The approaches described in this unit are summarised in Table 3.5.1.

Task 3.5.2
Planning for learning

Consider how you might plan a series of lessons in one subject area so that a variety of the above approaches is used. For example, in science looking at life processes in Years 1 and 2:

- constructing understanding: growing sunflowers from seed in class, exploring the conditions in which these grow best;
- group work, discussion: separate groups investigate the effects of one factor on plant growth, making hypotheses beforehand and discussing findings after;
- authentic activity: set up a garden centre in school, so that the children can grow a variety in time to sell at the summer fair;
- interactive direct teaching: the children are taught how to write clear instructions so that they can provide buyers at the summer fair with instructions for caring for their plants.

Try doing this for another area of learning, for example data handling in mathematics for Year 4.

Table 3.5.1 An overview of approaches for organising your classroom

Approaches to Organising your Classroom	Learning Focus	Broad Learning Objectives	Strengths	Challenges
National Literacy and Numeracy Strategies (DfES)	Basic skills acquisition	NLS and NNS objectives	An interactive approach where the importance of teacher modelling and high-quality dialogue between teachers and pupils is emphasised	Many teachers have had difficulty adopting fully interactive direct teaching; tendency to be used at whole class levels rather than with individuals or groups; little emphasis on learner's own starting point
Many primary science schemes (including Nuffield Primary Science); Cognitive Acceleration in Science Education (Phil Adey and Michael Shayer)	Constructing understanding	To develop enquiry and investigative process skills; to develop children's own understandings of phenomena; to apply understandings to new contexts	Starts from children's ideas and perspectives, building on these using direct hands-on experience	Assumes children will notice experiences which don't fit their understandings, challenge their understandings and be able to restructure these to accommodate the new experiences
Group Work; Discussion; Dialogical Enquiry	Social learning	To develop collaborative and speaking and listening skills; to see things from different points of view; to develop critical and creative thinking; to develop children's own understandings of phenomena	Supports learners in constructing new meanings and understandings as they explore them together in words; allows learners to test out and criticise claims and different points of view as they speak and listen to others; and provides raw material for learner's own thinking	Require children to have certain basic skills and obey certain ground rules; sometimes difficult to organise; works best when children show areas of autonomous learning
Authentic Activity and Enquiry	Apprenticeship	To encourage children to act and see the world as scientists, historians, archaeologists, poets, and so on	Outward looking, considering learning as something which takes you outside the classroom; inspiring and motivating	Requires significant time to allow it to happen; often needs access to good quality resources; teachers need to feel confident and have some expertise in the area of activity or enquiry or be able to get in someone who has

SUMMARY

Learning is complex, so much so that no one view of learning can fully express this complexity. It is only by considering learning in a variety of ways that we can begin to gain a fuller understanding of its nature, and it is only by planning for such a variety of approaches to address learning as has been described in this unit that we can provide rich and inclusive classroom experiences for our children.

ANNOTATED FURTHER READING

For a substantive analysis of pedagogy (which Alexander suggests is the act of teaching and the way we discuss this) and recent government interventions in primary education see: Alexander, Robin (2004) 'Still no pedagogy? Principle, pragmatism and compliance in primary education', *Cambridge Journal of Education*, 34(1): 7–33.

There are many National Literacy and Numeracy Strategy materials discussing the nature of interactive direct teaching. An interesting critique can be found at: http://www.literacytrust.org.uk/Pubs/hardman2.html.

A more detailed consideration of social learning and apprenticeship approaches, together with a wide range of examples and many suggestions for enhancing practice is provided in: Kelly, Peter (2005) *Using Thinking Skills in the Primary Classroom*, London: Sage.

REFERENCES

Adey, P., Shayer, M. and Yates, C. (1995) *Thinking Science*, London: Nelson.
DfEE (1999) *The National Literacy Strategy*, Sudbury: DfEE Publications.
DfEE (1999) *The National Numeracy Strategy*, Sudbury: DfEE Publications.
Lave, J. and Wenger, E. (1991) *Situated Learning: Legitimate Peripheral Participation*, Cambridge: Cambridge University Press.
Norman, K. (1992) *Thinking Voices: The Work of the National Oracy Project*, London: Hodder and Stoughton.

Unit 3.6

Planning for Learning Outside the Classroom

Simon Catling

WORKING OUTSIDE THE CLASSROOM

Opportunities for learning outside the classroom are generally valued. Almost every primary school child studies in their school grounds on various occasions in different subjects during the year. Annually, several million off-site primary pupil visits take place. Providing experience for young children to learn through activities in the real world is important to primary teachers.

OBJECTIVES

By the end of this unit you should be able to:

- appreciate the value and benefits of out-of-classroom learning;
- identify opportunities in your own planning and teaching where you can use out-of-classroom learning;
- plan effectively for out-of-classroom learning.

CAMEO 1

Jenni's Year 2 class are in the school grounds. As part of a springtime cross-subject focus on growth and change in nature, she is using observational work in art. The children are using pencils, chalk or charcoal to make sketches of plants and buds. They are taking digital photographs, and will follow up this work by creating colour paintings from their sketches and photographs. Jenni argues that using opportunities in their well-established school grounds enhances the children's learning through close observation, working *in situ* rather than bringing natural items into class, and challenging them to use good quality resources from a young age. She says these challenges enable them to concentrate and focus their interest.

CAMEO 2

Phil's class is in the local high street doing fieldwork for their local geography study. Working with teaching assistants and parents, the Year 5 children are examining how well the local council, shops and other businesses have provided access for those with disabilities or infirmities. The children are mapping the accessibility of doorways, the help or hindrances of street furniture, and so forth, and using a rating scale to judge the quality of access. They work in groups, with a designated area to map. They are taking digital photographs of good and poor examples they see, to be used later in a display showing their findings and outlining their proposals for action. The children partly planned this fieldwork, which included developing awareness of the risks of undertaking studies along a street that many of them knew well. During his risk assessment Phil took photographs to show the children so they could discuss potential hazards and how they could safely undertake their tasks. Phil uses sites outside school because he feels that for geography, science and history it is vital to go into the real world around them. He argues that children can 'see further' by going outside because such fieldwork extends their observations in a disciplined and 'disciplinary' way.

Task 3.6.1
Out-of-classroom learning

Consider your own experience studying outside, whether with a class and teacher before or during your course, or as a primary or secondary school student.

- describe an activity you did, where you did it and for how long;
- list what you think you were intended to learn;
- reflect on what you feel you really learnt from this out-of-class activity.

THE VALUE OF OUT-OF-CLASSROOM LEARNING

There is strong support for the view that learning outside the classroom is vital for all children, adding value to their classroom experiences; that well planned and taught, such learning enhances children's knowledge, understanding and skills across subjects; and that it fosters children's motivation, self-confidence and interpersonal learning (House of Commons Education and Skills Committee 2005). While clear arguments have been made for the value of younger children's learning in the school

- Off-site fieldtrips are often memorable for children, even into adulthood;
- younger children seem well-motivated when working outside the classroom;
- for many children out-of-classroom activities enhance their knowledge and understanding of the topic(s) studied;
- where children undertake environmental studies and/or become involved in school-based 'green initiatives' over time using the school grounds and/or off-site visits, their knowledge, understanding and valuing of the environment develops positively;
- fieldtrips to particular sites may enhance children's positive attitudes to that site/area;
- younger children's social and interpersonal skills can improve through ecological and field studies, particularly where they engage in collaborative tasks requiring co-operation, perseverance, initiative, reliability and leadership qualities; these tasks can also enhance children's self-esteem and self-confidence;
- children's involvement in school grounds 'greening' activities may have an overall positive impact on their general cognitive achievement.

Figure 3.6.1 The impact of out-of-classroom learning on younger children

grounds and off-site, there is limited *research* into its benefits. Reviewing studies into the impact of fieldwork, visits off-site, working in the school grounds and outdoor adventure activities, Rickinson *et al.* (2004) drew several tentative conclusions (Figure 3.6.1, above).

Rickinson *et al.* (2004) examined the opportunities and gains that out-of-classroom learning offers, as have others (e.g. Braund and Reiss 2004; Scoffham 2004). Their study noted various *foci* for learning outside, several *benefits* of such studies, and a range of *sites* that might be used (see Figure 3.6.2, p. 150). You should note that the *foci* and *benefits* refer to cognitive outcomes, values and attitudes, *and* personal and interpersonal learning.

The aims and value of out-of-classroom learning are:

- providing experiential and active learning in the environment;
- motivating children through stimulating and enjoyable experiences;
- initiating or extending enquiry skills through 'real world' investigations;
- developing observational, recording and analytic skills *in situ*;
- developing knowledge and understanding in a 'real world' context;
- encouraging and enabling children to work co-operatively;
- fostering a 'feel' for the environment, through examining values and attitudes.

There are challenges in undertaking out-of-classroom activities. Figure 3.6.3 on p. 151 indicates some of these. Such challenges need to be resolved when organising working outside the classroom. You need to remember that risk assessments and health and safety regulations are for your security as a teacher as well as for the children's safety. Planning out-of-classroom learning requires understanding the benefits such opportunities provide and finding ways to overcome the potential difficulties considerately and safely. Appreciating the value of out-of-classroom learning sets a positive basis for achieving this.

Examples of *foci* for out-of-classroom learning about:

- the natural environment, e.g. the school 'wild area';
- human settlements, e.g. a local village or urban area study;
- community activities, e.g. bulb planting in green spaces;
- nature-society interactions, e.g. visits to nature reserves;
- environmental issues, e.g. contentious planning proposals and developments;
- oneself, e.g. in making a residential visit with peers for the first time;
- others, e.g. through working together on small-group fieldwork tasks;
- new skills, e.g. using quadrants learnt through activities led by field centre staff.

Examples of *benefits* resulting from out-of-classroom learning:

- greater understanding of enquiry-based research, e.g. from investigating stream flow, erosion, transportation and deposition;
- greater information about the local environment, e.g. through recognising historical features;
- increased knowledge and understanding of geographical processes, e.g. people's use of shops;
- recognition of personal values and feelings, e.g. in relation to your neighbourhood;
- fostering attitudes to the future of an environment, e.g. a relic woodland, or to one's personal treatment of the environment;
- developing new or improved skills, e.g. in orienteering and communication;
- developing or reinforcing positive behaviours, e.g. in taking care not to leave litter or in working with others in community activities;
- personal development, e.g. in building self-confidence through completing new challenges.

The possible *sites* for out-of-classroom activities include:

- school grounds;
- rural/suburban/urban areas around school;
- rural/suburban/urban areas in contrasting localities;
- wilderness areas;
- rivers, streams, ponds, lakes, canals;
- rural or city farms, botanic gardens;
- parks, allotments, gardens;
- industrial sites, heritage sites, castles, country houses;
- museums, science centres, National Park centres, zoos;
- field study centres, nature study centres.

Figure 3.6.2 Opportunities provided by learning outside the classroom

Task 3.6.2
Taking children out of the classroom

Using your own experience (see Task 3.6.1) and the information in Figures 3.6.1, 3.6.2 and 3.6.3:

- List your reasons for including out-of-classroom activities in your own teaching. What do you really want the children to learn from working outside the classroom, in the school grounds and beyond? Consider how such benefits link across the curriculum.
- Choose one out-of-classroom activity you might want to do and outline the benefits for the children that you would plan it for. Note the challenges that you need to overcome and how you might achieve this.

Challenges	Possible concerns
Time	Organising out-of-classroom activities requires time and forethought, whether going into the school grounds, the neighbourhood or a distant locality. It may require rearranging the timetable.
Resources	Visits to museums and similar venues involve costs that may need to be obtained from parents. Taking children outside involves organising other adult support, and informing them about the activities they will supervise. Time is needed to walk to nearby sites, and public or private transport bookings must be made in advance. There is overseeing the children on the bus/coach, having sick bags, etc.
Safety and health concerns	You must be fully acquainted with the school's and local authority's guidance on health and safety and follow procedures. Teachers and parents have heightened concerns about how safe children will be, whether from traffic, walking, farm visits, etc.
Personal confidence in taking children out	Taking children out requires confidence. A particular concern is managing children's behaviour. Going into the school grounds, locally or further afield, means knowing what these places are like, what can be studied and how safely, and setting suitable challenges in the children's tasks.
Risk assessment	You must make a risk assessment of a potential, even familiar, site. Making judgements about risks involves taking responsibility for decisions about the possible hazards and ways to overcome them.
Regulations and requirements	The number of forms to complete and the regulations to check can be numerous. It may include obtaining permission from the head teacher/governors *and* someone in the LEA.

Figure 3.6.3 Possible challenges to out-of-classroom learning opportunities

ORGANISING FOR LEARNING OUTSIDE THE CLASSROOM

This section discusses matters you need to consider and organise when working with children outside the classroom (Braund and Reiss 2004; Hoodless *et al.* 2003; Kimber and Smith 1999; Richardson 2004; Richmond 1997).

Deciding why to go out of the classroom

First you must consider *why* you might take the children out of the classroom for teaching and learning activities. As with all activities, this is about what you want the children to learn and why using the school grounds or going off-site will enhance the children's learning. You need to consider:

- How will working outside/off-site meet your *learning objectives/outcomes*?
- Where does it fit into the *sequence* of activities planned for the study topic?
- How does it contribute to the focus of study *at that time*?
- What *relevant children's experience* does it draw on or develop? Or does it provide new experiences?

Deciding where to take the children

Having decided to go outside, you must consider *where* you will take the children. You may look at a particular area or features in the school grounds for a science investigation; you might take the children into the local area as part of an enquiry they have planned; or you could involve the children in an historical re-enactment at a country house working with its education staff. In each case you need to have answered the following questions:

- Where is the most appropriate *location/site/centre* to take the children for the learning you are planning?
- Is it possible to take the children there *when* you want to (visits to centres, zoos, museums, etc. need booking *well* in advance)?
- What *alternative sites* are there (if you cannot get your first choice)?

Meeting the school's policies for taking children outside

Before undertaking work outside, you *must* check who is responsible for giving permission (usually the head teacher) and what the school's policy is. Primary schools have policies for off-site visits and health and safety matters. Figure 3.6.4 indicates what you should find in a school visits policy. This policy states how the school complies with government and Local Education Authority regulations for such visits, and gives the particular requirements the school has added relevant to its particular circumstances, for instance about what happens for a child unable to accompany a visit off-site.

Working in the school grounds means complying with good practice and common sense approaches to planning and organising your classroom teaching and to managing behaviour. The school will have a view on the support of other adults to work with you. You will need to check this with the head teacher if there is no statement in the school's visits policy.

When taking the children off-site for activities, for however long, there are organisational matters to check. Use the *checklist* in Figure 3.6.5, particularly for when you are planning a visit to a site some distance away, and need to travel by public transport or coach.

CHECKING THE SITE

When you take the children into the school's grounds, you must check that the sites you use are appropriate and accessible. You should check if other staff intend to take children outside when you plan to.

A school visits policy should tell you about:

- the value of working outside and off-site;
- ways in which off-site studies support work across the curriculum;
- possible sites and locations for working: in the grounds, off-site locally, at more distant locations, and about centres to visit;
- local Education Authority and school regulations and organisational requirements, such as permission forms, adult:pupil ratios, health and safety matters, letters to parents, etc.;
- making site visits and undertaking risk assessment;
- fieldwork resources;
- countryside and urban codes for environmental care.

Figure 3.6.4   Elements of a school visits policy

Checklist items	Date started	Date completed
1 Check school policies for off-site visits		
2 Identify reasons and objectives for working off-site		
3 Obtain permission from head teacher/governors/LEA		
4 Select location(s) for visit		
5 Check date(s)		
6 Undertake site visit and complete risk assessment forms		
7 Book visit with those who run the site/centre		
8 Book transport and check timings (as required)		
9 Collect payments (if required) and keep accounts		
10 Write to parents about visit and request signed permission slips (unless already covered by school's approach)		
11 Introduce visit, purpose and activities to children; involve children in planning aspects of their work		
12 Brief teachers, teaching assistants and other adults; allocate responsibilities for children and roles in case of emergency		
13 Know emergency procedures; access mobile phone; leave lists of participants, route and contact points in school		
14 Organise resources/equipment and responsibility for return		
15 Make payments (as needed)		
16 Write letters of thanks (from children/yourself)		
17 Evaluate visit; note modifications for future site use		

Figure 3.6.5 A checklist for planning off-site work

If you plan to undertake fieldwork or a visit off-site you must make a *reconnaissance* visit to the location first, whether it is a local site, a museum, a field centre or anywhere else, and have completed a *risk assessment form*, if necessary. This is essential because you must establish such matters as:

- the suitability of the site (does the museum have what you want the children to study?);
- its safety (are the pavements wide enough?);
- booking the education staff (what will they do; how will they work with the children at the field centre?);
- are the facilities suitable (accessible toilets, somewhere to eat, a place to shelter in rain?).

You should use the school's risk assessment form and complete it as required. Figure 3.6.6 (p.154) shows an example. If you are uncertain about how to judge the probability and severity of the risks, ask more experienced staff for help. You may find that there is a completed risk assessment form for your proposed site and that you are not required to complete a new one. You must still make a site visit; it is useful practice to undertake your own risk assessment and compare it with the school's.

Use these questions to find out the school's approach to taking children out of the classroom:

- What is the school's policy on out-of-classroom activities and off-site visits?
- Do you need agreement to take children out of the classroom to work in the school grounds? If so, from whom?
- From whom do you need permission to take children off-site, locally or further afield?
- Who can help you make bookings for visits and help you ensure that you have met all the needs and requirements for organising visits?
- What do you do to visit the site, check its suitability and availability, and complete a risk assessment form?

RISK ASSESSMENT FORM				
Visit site:				
RA undertaken by:				
Date:		Season for proposed visit:		
No. persons on visit: Adults:		Pupils:		
Location [Mark on map]	Possible Safety/Health Hazards	Risk Probability	Risk Severity	Precautions/Actions: to reduce/remove Risk

Overall Risk:

Decision to visit:

Signed:	Head teacher approval: Date:

Risk Assessment Guidance		
Level of Risk	Probability of happening	Severity of outcome
Low [L]	Not likely or very rare occurrence	None or very slight perhaps involving minor First Aid
Medium [M]	Possible but might happen only occasionally	Chance of injury occurring
High [H]	Likely to happen often	Possible hospitalisation, or causes fatality/disability

Figure 3.6.6   A risk assessment record

Task 3.6.3
Examining a school's out-of-classroom/visits policy

Obtain or read through a school's visits policy (and its health and safety policy) to see what it states about working with children outside the classroom and off-site. Use the information in Figure 3.6.4 (p. 152) as a guide. Check the guidance on permission, ratios, organisation and risk assessment. Make your own list of points to check in other school visits policies.

Planning teaching and learning outside the classroom

Planning a teaching session out of the classroom requires the same level and quality of planning as for any lesson. It is important to consider your teaching approach and the types of activities that the children will do. Figure 3.6.7 outlines five teaching approaches used in out-of-classroom studies (Kimber and Smith 1999). When deciding your approach be clear about your purpose and the level of children's active learning involvement that you want. Consider the merits of each approach.

It is important to lead into the fieldwork or visit lesson/day, not least to ensure the children come appropriately dressed for the activities they will do. In an *enquiry-based research* approach the children will have been involved in planning some or all of their tasks. For their study of a wasteland site, they might have identified, with their teacher, the specific questions and topics they will pursue at the site, have agreed the teams to undertake the tasks, and have organised the way they will measure, evaluate the quality and describe the potential of the site, so that they can bring back useful information for analysis and future planning. This may have taken two or three lessons prior to the fieldwork.

The fieldwork or visit itself needs to be carefully planned, whether it lasts half an hour or much of the day. Figure 3.6.8 on p. 156 provides an example of a lesson plan. There may be more detail in this plan than you usually provide, but it is important to be thorough, since planning for work outside the classroom and off-site is done less frequently. This example includes some key points that need to be planned into the lesson. Look particularly at the lesson sequence.

When planning to take children out of the classroom, consider these questions:

- What do you want them to learn?
- How can and will you organise the lesson?
- Have you borne in mind safety aspects?
- Have you the adult support you need?
- Have you planned for the time available?

Site investigation: children undertake observations, measurements and recording to find out information, e.g. about particular artefacts in a museum, the use of shops in a local street, or river flow.

Enquiry-based research: children engage in planning the studies they undertake, the focus of and approaches to investigations, and the recording and follow up, e.g. researching how a particular site is managed, or using interview questions they devise to investigate the roles of people in a religious centre.

Problem solving: children tackle a particular problem identified at a site, e.g. evidence in relation to a particular event in the past, mapping an area, or identifying ways to improve a site.

Re-enactment: children use role play or dramatic recreations of people's lives, probably in costume, from a time in the past or at another place elsewhere in the world. This requires orientation to the context at the start and debriefing at the end about what has been learnt.

Guided walk: children are guided around a site, e.g. a museum or historic building or on an urban or rural trail, where particular features, etc. are pointed out or they observe and record on a worksheet.

Figure 3.6.7 Five teaching approaches to use in out-of-classroom studies

Subject: Geography – Local Area Study   **Children**: 26 – Year 5

Context and focus: What does street furniture   **Time/Duration**: 2 hours 15 minutes
tell about the place it is in?

Learning outcomes – Children will be able to:
- identify different categories of street furniture;
- record the location of the street furniture accurately on a large-scale map;
- give reasons for their judgements about the purpose and usefulness of street furniture.

Background to the current lesson:
- fifth lesson in local study unit, first off-site;
- children have fieldwork experience in school grounds and off-site;
- children have recorded on maps but not used quality ratings.

Risk assessment outcome: Overall accident risk low
- wide pavements to sites and along streets selected;
- traffic at time of day less heavy;
- large open space to meet at the centre of area, toilets nearby.

Lesson sequence [Introduction, Main Activity, Conclusion]:
Introduction (20 minutes)
1. Check children understand purpose of fieldwork: annotate a local map for types of street furniture, rating for usefulness, using key and rating scale agreed.
2. Review, through discussion, variety of street furniture they expect to see: signs (directions, information), posts (traffic lights, lighting), advertising notices (hoardings, A-stands), furniture (seats, benches), and safety fixtures (bollards, railings).
3. Check children have maps, keys, rating scales, clipboards. Ensure partners paired up, children know which adult they're overseen by (five groups), and understand how to undertake tasks. Check they know their survey area. Toilet check.

Main activity (1 hour 30 minutes)
4. Go out as a class, each group with an adult, walk to open space by bank (15 minutes). Check all present. Groups/adults move to areas.
5. On each street, group identifies street furniture; maps/rates. Pairs state rating judgements; group agrees fair quality rating; record. In turn, pairs take photographs of selected street furniture. Repeats for two streets (45 minutes)
6. At set time, regroup at open space. Count children. Children list three points on back of map about helpfulness or not of street furniture observed (15 minutes).
7. Return (15 minutes).

Conclusion (25 minutes)
8. Pairs check maps/notes, ensure legible, and symbols and rating judgements clear.
9. Plenary, pairs comment on variety/usefulness of street furniture. Discuss purpose, value, environmental impact of street furniture.

Next lesson:
Same groups share information, prepare maps, ratings, comments on judgements about usefulness of street furniture in area surveyed; prepare report on role, quality, effectiveness of street furniture surveyed.

Support/differentiation:
Two TAs, two parent helpers responsible for groups of four children. Children in mixed pairs. Two children (slow at recording) with same TA. Two children (concentration and behaviour support) with me. Two children (ESL) with TA.

Assessment opportunities [observed by adults]
- Do children identify a variety of street furniture types (use categories)?
- Do children mark locations accurately on map (recording)?
- Can children give reasons for some ratings (making judgements)?

Resources:
- A4 map: survey streets;
- street furniture key, rating key;
- clipboards, digital cameras.

Cross-curricular links:
- literacy – speaking and listening;
- thinking skills – making judgements.

Figure 3.6.8 An example of a fieldwork lesson plan

Following up work undertaken outside the classroom

The lesson plan in Figure 3.6.8 includes follow-up activities. These help to settle the children when they return to class and encourage them to think about key points from their research. You should do this, if only for a few minutes, when you arrive back before lunch or the end of the day, before the children disperse. As one in a series of lessons on the topic, you should plan to follow up out-of-classroom work over one or more lessons.

It is important for you to have considered:

- How do I use the enthusiasm generated by the work outside the classroom?
- How will the children work on the information they have gathered?
- What types of outcome do I want to see?
- What resources and support do they need to complete their work?

Evaluating the experience

You should always evaluate out-of-classroom studies. You may have collected new information from a museum, a field centre or a mosque to add to topic resources. You need to know what the children feel they gained from the experience. Such matters are important because you must appreciate how out-of-classroom learning has been beneficial for the children, how effectively it fitted into your planned learning sequence, whether the site is worth using again, and in what ways you might improve future out-of-classroom activities. You can evaluate the experience immediately, to record key points straightaway, and at the end of the topic, when you judge how well such activities contributed overall to the children's learning. The questions to consider include:

- What was your own and the children's response to the out-of-classroom experience?
- What were the benefits and limitations of what you did?
- What would you change and why?

Task 3.6.4
Planning for out-of-classroom learning

Either for a unit you have taught *or* for one you might teach, *evaluate* or *plan* a sequence of three lessons:

- the lead-in lesson to the out-of-classroom studies;
- the lesson in the school grounds or off-site;
- the follow-up lesson after the out-of-classroom work.

Use the questions at the end of each sub-section to help you in your evaluation or planning.

SUMMARY

Learning outside the classroom is essential for every child. Using the school grounds and off-school sites, nearby and distant, enhances each primary curriculum subject. Some subjects, such as geography and science, require children to work outside to gather data for their studies at various times, but work in English, mathematics, history, RE, art, design & technology and ICT benefits from children using real world experiences in their studies. In PE the outdoor environment, for sport and more adventurous activities, is an essential teaching and learning site.

Planning work outside the classroom must be based on a clear understanding and appreciation of its value. Teaching using the school grounds and off-site remains popular and is valued by primary teachers, even though there are safety concerns and organisation challenges. Teachers persist with out-of-classroom activities because they see the motivational and the cognitive and affective learning value for children.

- Consider carefully why and when to take the children out of the classroom.
- Know the regulations and requirements that have to be met.
- Visit every site you use before you take the children, however well you know it, and complete a risk assessment.
- Know why and where out-of-classroom learning fits into the sequence of lessons and the children's learning, how you lead into the activities and how you follow up what has been done.
- Thorough and careful planning and organisation enhances the experience for yourself and the children, and enables you to manage their behaviour in a motivating context.
- Evaluate the children's experience and its place in a unit's learning sequence.
- Judge the benefits and limitations of your out-of-classroom teaching and apply your learning in future.

ANNOTATED READING LIST

Braund, M. and Reiss, M. (eds) (2004) *Learning Science Outside the Classroom*, London: RoutledgeFalmer. This text provides a thorough outline of the ways science education can be enhanced through taking children into the school grounds and to water habitats, museums and field centres. It covers planning and safety matters.

DfES (1998) *Health and Safety of Pupils on Educational Visits*, London: DfES. This handbook (updated periodically) provides guidance and information about organisation and safety planning for visits.

Hoodless, P., Bermingham, S., McCreery, E. and Bowen, P. (2003) *Teaching Humanities in Primary Schools*, Exeter: Learning Matters. Chapter 10 provides an informative, case-study based approach to planning out-of-school teaching.

Scoffham, S. (ed.) (2004) *Primary Geography Handbook*, Sheffield: Geographical Association. Chapter 10 outlines effective approaches to fieldwork teaching. The book includes many examples of ways to work with children in the school grounds and off-site, locally and further afield.

WEBSITES

Use these terms to search for websites providing information on places to visit and on fieldwork organisation: 'field study', 'field trips', 'field visits', and 'field work'. They will lead you to sites providing a wide variety of out-of-classroom activities.

Consult the following websites:
- English Outdoor Council: www.englishoutdoorcouncil.org
- Geographical Association: www.geography.org.uk
- Learning Through Landscapes: www.ltl.org.uk
- School Journeys Association: www.sja-online.org

REFERENCES

Braund, M. and Reiss, M. (eds) (2004) *Learning Science Outside the Classroom*, London: RoutledgeFalmer.

Hoodless, P., Bermingham, S., McCreery, E. and Bowen, P. (2003) *Teaching Humanities in Primary Schools*, Exeter: Learning Matters.

House of Commons Education and Skills Committee (2005) *Education Outside the Classroom*, London: The Stationery Office.

Kimber, D. and Smith, M. (1999) 'Field work, visits and work outside the classroom', in Ashley, M. (ed.), *Improving Teaching and Learning in the Humanities*, London: Falmer.

Leeder, A. (2004) *Tips for Trips*, London: Continuum.

Richardson, P. (2004) 'Fieldwork', in Scoffham, S. (ed.) *Primary Geography Handbook*, Sheffield: Geographical Association.

Richmond, K. (1997) *Planning School Visits and Journeys*, London: Collins Educational.

Rickinson, M., Dillon, J., Teamey, K., Morris, M., Young Choi, M., Sanders, D. and Benefield, P. (2004) *A Review of Research on Outdoor Learning*, Preston Montford: Field Studies Council.

Scoffham, S. (ed.) (2004) *Primary Geography Handbook*, Sheffield: Geographical Association.

4 Approaches to the Curriculum

Unit 4.1

The Aims of Primary Education

Richard Bailey

INTRODUCTION

This unit focuses on the aims of primary education. It encourages the reader to reflect upon aims that are inherent within different philosophies of education, as well as to consider their own views of the aims of primary education.

OBJECTIVES

By the end of this unit you should have:

- a greater understanding of the aims of education and their relevance to practitioners;
- reflected upon the relationship between educational aims and educational practice, and be familiar with some well-known historical examples;
- considered the specific aims of primary education, as well as the values that underpin them;
- thought about your own philosophy of primary education, and be aware of the practical implications of philosophical thinking in education.

WHAT ARE AIMS, AND WHY DO WE NEED THEM?

You might think that discussions of educational aims are not very practical or useful. You might think that they are overly theoretical, when what you really need as a trainee teacher are workable strategies to help you survive in the classroom. I hope that it will become clear by the end of this unit that this is a mistaken view, as any sensible discussion about educational practice is always built on top of a foundation of aims. A teacher who is skilled in a technical sense but who lacks a clear sense of their subject or lesson will almost certainly offer the pupils an unsatisfactory experience. The same can be said for education as a whole.

Aims define the point of an activity: what it seeks to achieve; where it should go.

The difficulty is that there is no simple, overriding aim of education to which all of us – teachers, parents, academics, policy-makers – can agree and aspire towards. There are numerous possible aims. Taken individually, these aims often seem legitimate and reasonable. Placed together, however, it often becomes apparent that some aims are incompatible with others. For example, in introducing its educational reforms in England and Wales in the 1980s, the Government identified a number of principles, such as: educational standards and excellence, parental choice and participation, professional accountability, market forces and consumer satisfaction, economy, efficiency and effectiveness (Le Métais, 1995). Some have suggested that there are real tensions between pairs of these principles, or between them and other widely accepted principles. For example, the call for parental choice and the promotion of market forces may be incompatible with the demand for equality.

Skills and competencies are important if one wishes to become a good teacher. But they are really very little more than tools used to help realise some goal. Without this goal – this *aim* – the tools become rather pointless.

The solution to this apparent problem is not like the solution to a crossword puzzle, in which you simply need to find the correct answer. This is because educational aims are inseparable from educational *values*. Values are concerns about what ought to be. A value can be understood as a belief which need not rely on facts or evidence. Values like freedom, equality, the importance of the unique individual, the importance of community, of family, the defence of one's society, and social justice go beyond mere statements of fact towards more ambitious, yet more ill-defined, aspirations.

To make this point more clearly, turn to Task 4.1.1.

Task 4.1.1
Which aims?

An international review of the stated aims of educational systems from around the world came up with the following composite list (Tabberer, 1997):

Excellence	Individual development
Social development	Personal qualities
Equal opportunity	National economy
Preparation for work	Basic skills
Foundation for further education	Knowledge/skills/understanding
Citizenship/community/democracy	Cultural heritage/literacy
Creativity	Environment
Health/physical/leisure	Lifelong education
Parental participation	

Give this list to friends and family and ask them to select what reflects most closely, for them, the main aims of education. Which aims are most frequently selected? Which are not selected at all?

If you are working in a school, ask to see a policy document that contains that school's aims. How do these aims reflect the list?

What is your view? Which aims do you think capture your personal philosophy?

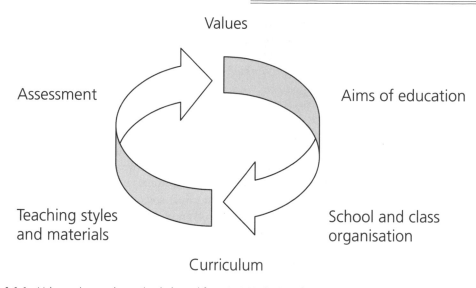

Figure 4.1.1 Values, aims and practice (adapted from Le Métais, 2004)

Ultimately you, as a professional, will have to come to some judgement for yourself, as will every teacher. Clearly not all judgements are equally valid; we might well question the judgement of a teacher for whom the purpose of primary education is to bring about unconditional obedience to space aliens! However, at some stage, every teacher needs to ask him/herself, 'what am I trying to achieve?', 'what are my goals as a teacher?', 'what are my aims?'.

Values influence our aims, which, in turn, influence every aspect of the education we offer our pupils. Figure 4.1.1 illustrates one way about thinking of the relationship between values, aims and practice.

Values and aims direct decisions about school and class organisation (are pupils grouped according to age, ability or interest? How much say do parents and outside groups have? What is the nature of the authority of the teacher? Who is in charge?). Decisions of this sort will influence the type of curriculum offered (subject-based or theme-based? Broad and balanced or narrow and specialist? Which subjects receive most time, which receive least?), and these questions influence the selection of appropriate teaching styles and materials (teacher-centred or learner-centred? Memorising facts or problem-solving? Teacher as authority, as friend, as resource?). Finally, the type of assessment strategies employed, if they are to have any purpose at all, need to reflect the aims of the education process.

In this era of national curricula and national strategies, it might seem surprising to be asked to reflect on the aims of education. Surely they are a given. And, of course, it would be a foolish trainee teacher who carried on oblivious to the policies and requirements of central Government. But if we consider its stated aims, it is apparent why teachers' perspectives still have a role.

The National Curriculum for England does not commit itself to aims specifically for primary education. It does, however, give two broad aims for the curriculum, as a whole:

- The school curriculum should aim to provide opportunities for all pupils to learn and to achieve;
- The school curriculum should aim to promote pupils' spiritual, moral, social and cultural development and prepare pupils for the opportunities, responsibilities and experiences of adult life.

(DfEE/QCA 1999)

As they stand, these aims seem quite broad, and could reflect almost any educational system in the world. It is possible, however, to imagine some practices that would conflict with these aims, such as those that excluded sections of the pupil population, or those that offered only a narrow range of experiences. To some extent, then, you are working in a context in which aims are already in place, if only at a rather general level.

There are good reasons to suppose, however, that talk of aims will be relevant to you throughout your training. As a citizen, you have the same right as everyone else to hold and express your view on what education is for, and to contribute to the communal discussion about the aims and character of education. As a teacher, you have an even greater responsibility to be clear with yourself and others what your aims are, and be prepared to argue and defend them (Haydon 1995). It is very difficult to identify universally shared values and aims. Committed professionals need to make decisions at each stage of the teaching process about how to interpret their values and aims in terms of practice. For this reason, we do not have one type of school, with one type of curriculum, teaching approach and assessment. And we do not have one narrow, prescriptive set of aims, to which all teachers must comply.

So, in response to the charge made at the beginning of this unit that talk of aims is not very practical, we are able to respond that we cannot even begin to decide what we should do in a particular situation without some idea of what it is we want to achieve.

AIMS AND PRACTICE: SOME HISTORICAL EXAMPLES

The point has already been made that educational practice cannot be separated from notions of aims. In order to exemplify this, we will consider the educational theories of three influential thinkers: Plato, Jean-Jacques Rousseau and John Dewey. These thinkers have been selected because each has had a significant influence on how people think about the ways education should be conceived and carried out. Also, they have the virtue of coming from different places and times from our own. This distance should make it easier for us to talk about aims and practice, without being constrained by our assumptions of the way education *ought to be*.

Plato

The ancient Greek philosopher Plato (428–348 BCE) wrote about education in a number of his works, but his best known treatment is in the book that has come to be known as *The Republic* (Bloom, 1991). Plato, a student of Socrates and the teacher of Aristotle, is said to have founded the first university – his Academy, near Athens.

Much of Plato's work is presented in the form of dialogues, or question and answer discussions in which a student, or 'seeker', is led to uncover gaps in his/her reasoning by a teacher, or 'expert'. This method of teaching has come to be known as the 'Socratic Method' (after Plato's teacher), and characterises the presentation of educational ideas in *The Republic*, as well as Plato's view that such dialogues are a powerful method for developing a student's understanding and comes through questioning, not teaching. Although this might at first appear a somewhat progressive teaching style, Plato makes it clear that the teacher–student relationship is not one of equals – the teacher is in control.

To understand Plato's educational theory, it is necessary to understand his views of politics. For him, the central issue is that of justice or right-living; the just person lives a life of harmony. This harmonious life expresses itself in two ways. First, as a member of a community, the just person lives a life that is appropriate to his/her social group. Soldiers, farmers, leaders and manufactures all contribute to the just state, but each needs to stay in their place in the order: they need to know their place.

Second, just as the state needs order and harmony, so does the individual. We all have appetites and passions, as well as a capacity for reason and reflection. The different elements within us relate directly to the different roles within the state: our appetites (which equate to the producers) and our passions (the soldiers) must remain under the control of the higher, rational part (the leaders). When our appetites and passions overtake our reason, we become disturbed and disordered, just as a state becomes unstable if the lower orders take control from their leaders.

For Plato, then, the aim of education is to produce certain types of people, the just, and a certain type of state, the just society, in which each of the different elements keeps its proper place in the order. And how can we recognise where different people fit in this order? Plato's view is that humans are made up of a body that is perishable and a soul which is immortal. Some souls are better than others. In Plato's terms, some of us have gold in our souls, whilst other progressively less worthy people have iron and bronze. The highest function of education, therefore, is to develop those with souls of gold (Moore 1974) and to lead them to see beyond superficial appearances towards an understanding of another level, the world of eternal, changeless reality.

So, how does this view of education translate into practice? First, if there really are different qualities of people, it follows that they will require different forms of schooling. Second, young children of quality who are not yet ready for the strains of philosophical training need to develop their senses, their love of beauty, order and harmony. Third, as children get older, they need to be inspired by tales of heroes and great leaders. Fourth, they need to ensure that their bodies are strong enough to house their souls, so the young need a period of rigorous physical training. Finally, only once the few have shown themselves to be fit will they be taught the secrets necessary for leadership. Only if these steps are followed will the state be kept safe, harmonious and just.

Rousseau

Jean-Jacques Rousseau (1712–78) was born in Switzerland and grew up in France. His book *Emile* is generally regarded as the most significant text on education since Plato's *Republic*. Rousseau lived shortly before the French Revolution, and his writing is often credited as being influential in setting the intellectual scene for that great political change. He worked variously as an engraver, a music teacher, a private tutor and a writer.

Rousseau's 'other' great book is *Social Contract*, which begins with the famous and chilling lines: 'Man was born free, and he is everywhere in chains' (Cranston 2004). This quotation captures his view that we are born good, but are corrupted by the evils of society. Rousseau called for an abandonment of the French society of his day, which he thought corrupt and unjust, and the emergence of a new kind of society, based on the real interests and engagement of its members (as opposed to just the aristocrats). The government, in this new system, would be based on what he calls the 'General Will', the rational, informed will of all members of society, guided by principles of 'liberty, equality and fraternity'. There is always a danger in such democratic structures that individuals and minority groups are exploited. So, Rousseau was forceful in advocating freedom of thought, independence and individualism of members and, of course, education.

Rousseau's *Emile* is a call for 'a return to nature', and his goal of education is the 'natural man' and an educational system 'according to nature'. Quite what he means by 'nature' is a matter of some interpretation. Certainly there is a strong 'green' element in Rousseau's writing. However, he means much more than modern environmentalism. In some parts of *Emile*, it seems that nature equates to the way things are in the natural world, within which children live as human animals. So, Rousseau stresses the importance of treating a child as a child, and not as a mini-adult (as was the fashion of his day). Children, he argued, do not share the faculties and needs of adults, so should not be treated as if they did. Ultimately, childhood should be characterised by a life of experience, rather than knowledge, of sensation rather than reason. In another part of Emile, it seems that Rousseau has a somewhat different understanding of the term 'nature'. In these cases, he places much greater emphasis on the natural person as one who has yet to be corrupted by society. A third view, offered by Rousseau's critics, is that his natural man is really the middle-class citizen of his new society, who is independent of thought, yet able to play a constructive part in society, without being overtaken by it (Moore 1974).

The relationship between Rousseau's views of childhood and education, and modern, so-called, 'child-centred' or progressive education is clear. It is not surprising, then, that he has been blamed by some traditionalists for the anti-intellectual, anti-social forms of schooling that they claim have become endemic in recent decades. This is, perhaps, a little harsh, as Rousseau clearly recognised the need for both intellectual and social engagement; he stressed, however, that studying from books, initiation into academic disciplines and learning about the social world should occur when the individual is mature enough to benefit from them and not be corrupted by them. Before that time, during childhood, s/he should be educated using personal experience.

Dewey

John Dewey (1859–1952) was born in an America evolving into a major industrial nation, yet still influenced by the ethos of the frontier, with its emphasis on enterprise, independence and merit. He is acknowledged as one of the most influential educational philosophers of modern times, and, although he is sometimes portrayed as Rousseau's intellectual heir, and the father of modern child-centred education, he really marks a different tradition altogether.

Like both Plato and Rousseau before him, Dewey's views on education were greatly influenced by his views on children's nature. Born in the year that Charles Darwin published *Origin of Species*, Dewey saw humans as active, problem-solving creatures, who are continually seeking to overcome challenges from their environment. By the time they enter school, they have already experienced a great deal, and bring with them innate instincts to communicate, construct, inquire and express themselves. Children also bring their interests, and it is a basic task of the teacher to make use of these interests and instincts by guiding the child's activities at school. Dewey divides childhood into three developmental stages: the period of 'play', which is characterised by spontaneous child-led activity; the 'techniques' period, during which the child learns to follow simple procedures; and the period of 'reflective attention', when an overtly critical problem-solving is developed. At each stage, the emphasis is on the child's activity, which gradually becomes more specific and outcome-orientated as the child grows older.

Underlying Dewey's philosophy is the aim of educating a certain type of person: an individual fit for a democracy. However, unlike the writers we met earlier, he is very suspicious of any theory of education that has an 'end' in mind, whether it be Plato's *Ruler* or Rousseau's *Natural Man*. For Dewey, education cannot really have an aim beyond itself: the end point of education is more education. This does not mean that Dewey thought of education as distinct from society; on the contrary, he was keen for schools to prepare for life in the 'real world'. Therefore, schools should present their students with real problems, which stem from their own interests. Many of these problems may originate in the social settings in which children work co-operatively and collaboratively. Education according to Dewey, therefore, is fundamentally concerned with developing children's innate interests and abilities by leading them to operate in the world of practical problems.

Task 4.1.2
Educational aims and philosophies

Reflect upon the different visions of education offered by Plato, Rousseau and Dewey. Each has a distinctive view of education, and of its aims. Also, each, whether implicitly or explicitly, has a view of the role of *primary education* within their vision.

Outline the aims of primary education within each of these approaches. Can you recognise aspects of these aims in modern education and schooling? Consider, in particular, these contexts:

- the Foundation Stage;
- independent 'preparatory' schools;
- self-proclaimed 'child-centred' schools;
- the school with which you are most familiar.

WHAT ARE THE AIMS OF PRIMARY EDUCATION?

Is there a quintessential character of 'primary' education? Are there aims that are special to the primary phase that set it apart from other aspects of pupils' learning and experience? One writer, reflecting on changing practices of the years and different approaches around the world, has been led to ponder: 'We encounter so little uniformity of practice that we might feel inclined to ask whether the word "primary" is anything more than a label denoting a stage of compulsory schooling' (Alexander 1984: 11). Can that be all that is special about primary education: the age of the pupils? Or is there something else; is there something special and distinctive about the primary phase?

Historically, there have been some discrete traditions associated with primary education (see Alexander 1984; Pollard and Tann 1997):

- *The elementary tradition*
  This is a form of educational practice and provision associated with a concentration on the so-called '3Rs' (reading, 'riting and 'rithmetic), and with a strict approach to discipline.
- *The developmental tradition*
  This approach emphasises the ways in which children develop physically, socially, emotionally and intellectually as a basis for planning and organising learning.
- *The preparatory tradition*
  This tradition sees primary education as a 'preparation' for later schooling, during which children learn the more traditional subject-based knowledge.

To some extent, these traditions need not be mutually exclusive. It is quite possible to envisage a school claiming to support all three approaches. For example, it might claim to be respectful of children's developmental needs, whilst still recognising their need to learn the basics of literacy and numeracy, as well as the foundations of good behaviour, so that they are prepared for the more traditional business of secondary schooling. But this would miss the purpose of the classification, which is to reflect upon the dominating aim, the driving purpose that defines and, to some extent, restricts what is offered in the name of primary education. Our imagined school might very well claim to represent all three traditions, but the true test comes when time and resources are limited, or when external inspectors demand evidence of its achievement. Does the school push forward its exemplary record in reading, writing and arithmetic, and flawless disciplinary record, or does it claim that it has devised a curriculum that is responsive and respectful of each child's developmental needs, which means that not all children can read or add-up because they are not all ready for these skills, or does it boast of its outstanding SAT results or high success rate in winning places in selective secondary schools?

Task 4.1.3
School aims and educational traditions

Part 1 You have already been asked to read your school's policy documents. To which tradition do you think they most closely belong? What language in the policy document leads you to your conclusion?

Part 2 Collaborate with colleagues on your course, and share your gathered policy documents. Which themes are most evident, which are least evident?

THINKING ABOUT YOUR OWN PHILOSOPHY OF PRIMARY EDUCATION

> Education as such has no aims. Only persons, parents and teachers, etc. have aims, not an abstract idea like education.
>
> (Dewey 1916: 107)

Studies suggest that most teachers enter the profession with a strong sense of values and aims (Thomas 1995). You are probably the same. I hope that you have had the opportunity to reflect upon your own values and aims, and perhaps you have reconsidered them or modified them in some way. In reflecting on your own conceptions of the aims of primary education, two points need to be stressed. First, your aims come from somewhere; just as Plato, Rousseau and Dewey all reflect aspects of their culture and time in their philosophies of education, we cannot separate ourselves from our upbringing, schooling and cultural values. Whilst we might like to think that we generate our views through raw intelligence and reason alone, the reality is that our individual beliefs often reflect our upbringing, previous experiences and social background. This is why we can find it difficult to change our aims, as their source can date back many years, and be closely associated with our conception of ourselves as people. Second, we need to remember that our aims will influence what we do, both inside and outside of the classroom. Our aims are revealed in our behaviour and, thus, in our teaching (Pollard 2002).

So aims are serious matters, and deserve critical examination. The final task encourages you to do precisely this.

Task 4.1.4
Stepping behind the 'Veil of Ignorance'

For the final task, you are going to be asked to carry out what philosophers call a 'thought experiment', which is an attempt to solve a problem using the power of your imagination and reasoning. This experiment comes from the philosopher John Rawls whose book *A Theory of Justice* (1972) explored the fundamental principles of justice. Rawls was aware that we all have backgrounds, prejudices and vested interests which may distort our apprehension of these fundamental principles, so he proposed a way in which we could imagine how to choose these principles if we knew nothing about our present situation. This is what he calls the 'original position':

> I assume that the parties are situated behind a veil of ignorance. They do not know how the various alternatives will affect their own particular case and they're obliged to evaluate principles solely on the basis of general considerations. First of all, no one knows his place in society, his class position or social status; nor does he know his fortune in the distribution of natural assets or abilities, his intelligence and strength, and the like … It is taken for granted, however, that they know general facts about human society. They understand political affairs and the principles of economic theory; they know the basis of social organisation and the laws of human psychology. In fact, the parties are presumed to know whatever general facts affect the choice of the principles of justice.
>
> (Rawls 1972: 136–7)

Now, step behind the 'veil of ignorance', and consider the aims of primary education. Knowing nothing about your background, your place in society and your personal aspirations, outline a set of aims that reflect your interpretation of a reasonable and just primary education system.

SUMMARY

To some extent, all teachers have to work within a framework of aims, prescribed by the National Curriculum, but there is plenty of room for the development and articulation of your personal views and philosophy. Aims help give teachers a sense of direction and purpose in their professional work; different aims are associated with different teaching practices, curriculum organisation and assessment procedures. As such, they deserve serious consideration and examination.

ANNOTATED FURTHER READING

Pollard, A. and Tann, S. (1997) *Reflective Teaching in the Primary School: A Handbook for the Classroom*, London: Continuum. This practical textbook has become something of a classic. Although it covers a great amount of material of relevance to primary practitioners, its implicit demand that we reflect upon our action and the thinking behind it, makes this a valuable resource for those wishing to consider aims in real-life contexts.

Pring, R. (2004) *Philosophy of Education: Aims, Theory, Common Sense and Research*, London: Continuum. A challenging, thought-provoking series of chapters, examining different aspects of educational theory, and introducing the reader to a range of relevant authors and texts.

Walker, D.F. and Soltis, J.F. (2004) *Curriculum and its Aims*, New York: Teachers College Press. This book from the US offers an accessible introduction to the issue of educational aims. It uses case studies to exemplify the practical implications of different theoretical positions, and offers a useful further reading section.

REFERENCES

Alexander, R. (1984) *Primary Teaching*, Eastbourne: Holt, Rinehart and Winston.

Bloom, A. (tr.) (1979) *Emile: or, On Education*, New York: Basic Books.

Bloom, A. (tr.) (1991) *The Republic of Plato*, New York: Basic Books.

Cranston, M. (tr.) (2004) *Jean-Jacques Rousseau: The Social Contract*, London: Penguin.

Dewey, J. (1916) *Democracy and Education*, New York: Free Press.

DfEE/QCA (1999) *English National Curriculum Handbook*, London: HMSO.

Haydon, G. (1995) 'Aims of education', in S. Capel, M. Leask and T. Turner (eds) *Learning to Teach in the Secondary School*, London: Routledge.

Le Métais, J. (1995) *Legislating for Change: School Reforms in England and Wales, 1979–1994*, Slough: NFER.

Le Métais, J. (2004) 'Values and aims in curriculum and assessment frameworks', in S. O'Donnell, C. Sargent, R. Brown, C. Andrews and J. Le Métais (eds) *INCA: The International Review of Curriculum and Assessment Frameworks Archive*, London: QCA.

Moore, T.W. (1974) *Educational Theory: An Introduction*, London: Routledge and Kegan Paul.

Pollard, A. (2002) *Reflective Teaching*, London: Continuum.

Pollard, A. and Tann, S. (1997) *Reflective Teaching in the Primary School: A Handbook for the Classroom*, London: Continuum.

Rawls, J. (1972) *A Theory of Justice*, Oxford: Clarendon Press.

Tabberer, R. (1997) 'Primary education: expectations and provision', in S. O'Donnell, C. Sargent, R. Brown, C. Andrews and J. Le Métais (eds) *INCA: The International Review of Curriculum and Assessment Frameworks Archive*, London: QCA.

Thomas, D. (1995) *Teachers' Stories*, Buckingham: Open University Press.

Unit 4.2

The National Context for the Curriculum

Maureen Lewis

INTRODUCTION

Prior to the introduction of the National Curriculum (NC) in 1998, the school curriculum was largely determined at local level but throughout the 1970s and 1980s public debate about education, schools and the curriculum grew. This debate culminated in the introduction of a statutory National Curriculum by the Department for Education and Science in 1988, which heralded an era of increasingly centralised control of education. During the last decade or so the NC and other non-statutory guidance (and the support structures and assessment associated with these) have become part of the mechanism by which government education policy becomes enacted within schools.

A school's curriculum involves a complex interplay of beliefs, attitudes, skills, knowledge and understanding. It is no surprise therefore that what is taught in our schools and how it is taught is a matter of debate between those who subscribe to different values, have different aims for education, have different views on the kind of knowledge that the curriculum should contain or who question whether a National Curriculum is needed at all (see Kelly 2004, for detailed discussion of such issues).

The National Curriculum Handbook for Primary Teachers (DfEE and QCA, 1999) defines the curriculum as 'all the learning and other experiences that each school plans for its pupils' (p. 10). This definition, as with most issues connected to the curriculum, is disputed and alternative definitions exist, but for this unit we will use this official definition. Throughout this unit we will be discussing the National Curriculum and non-statutory guidance for England. For details of the National Curriculum in Wales and Northern Ireland see http://www.accac.org.uk and http://www.ccea.org.uk. For details of the National Curriculum for Scotland see Unit 4.3.

OBJECTIVES

By the end of this unit you should:

- understand the rationale and context for the emergence of a National Curriculum;
- be familiar with the current aims, structures and content of the National Curriculum;
- have examined the implementation of the non-statutory, National Strategies for Literacy and Numeracy as a case study of moving from policy into curriculum practice;
- have considered the advantages and disadvantages of a statutory National Curriculum;
- have reflected on possible future developments of the National Curriculum.

THE EMERGENCE OF A NATIONAL CURRICULUM

The 1944 Education Act did not lay down any requirements for the school curriculum (other than the inclusion of religious education). This gave schools and individual teachers great freedom to determine what was taught. There have been many significant educational and political changes during the last fifty years that have affected this position and some of the key events relating to the curriculum are outlined below.

The rise of progressive education

In the 1950s and 1960s, the 11+ examination was widely used to assess children at the end of their primary years and children were then selected to attend grammar schools or secondary modern schools. In 1953 the first secondary comprehensive (non-selective) school opened and gradually some LEAs began to abandon the 11+ examination. Changes to both the primary and secondary curriculum such as the introduction of 'modern maths', the use of 'Nuffield science' and the introduction of 'creative writing' in English began to be made. In 1964, 'The Schools Council for the Curriculum and Examinations' was created and worked closely with teachers on projects and publications around curriculum development. In 1967 the 'Plowden Report' (Central Advisory Council for Education, 1967) argued for an active and experiential curriculum for primary schools. This report both reflected and gave further impetus to changes that were happening within schools, some of which were moving towards progressive and child centred approaches. Although the extent of progressive practice within primary schools in the 1960s and 1970s is difficult to quantify, this shift in thinking and practice brought to the fore the tensions between child centred views of education and more traditional, performance based views.

The 'Great Debate'

The rise of progressive educational ideas and practices led to a public debate via parliamentary questions, newspaper articles and publications such as the 'Black Papers' – *The Fight for Education* (Cox and Dyson 1969a) and *The Crisis in Education* (Cox and Dyson 1969b). These papers attacked new practices such as the introduction of mixed ability classes, the use of competency based assessment and the spread of informal and 'play' based approaches in primary schools. They argued that such developments were leading to a decline in education standards. The 'Black Papers' created a furore and the authors were criticised by their opponents for their lack of conceptual clarification and lack of research evidence to support their claims. The debate around declining standards was particularly fiercely contested and in 1974 the government set up 'The Assessment Performance Unit' to monitor standards in mathematics, English and science. and to provide statistical evidence on this.

In response to the continuing debate, in 1976, the then Prime Minister opened what he called 'The Great Debate' on education in a speech, in which he discussed the need for changes in education. The major concerns at the time centred around beliefs that:

- there was a general decline in educational standards;
- the curriculum had become overcrowded;
- there was an imbalance in the subjects being studied (too many students taking humanities and not enough studying science and technology);
- there were variations in approaches to the curriculum between schools;
- the curriculum did not meet the demands of a modern society.

Task 4.2.1
Concerns about the curriculum

Look at the list of concerns about the curriculum in 1976. Discuss the following questions:

- Which of these concerns are under discussion in relation to today's schools?
- What would you consider to be robust evidence to prove or disprove these concerns?
- Do you consider that any of the concerns listed have been 'solved' or become less pressing since 1976?

Following the 'Great Debate', the DES issued *Circular 14/77* which required all LEAs to produce detailed statements of their curricular policies. This was followed in 1980 by an Education Act which gave more power to LEAs in controlling the curricular provision in their schools and required schools to make public their curricula.

After the election of a new government in 1979, the idea of a 'core curriculum' which gave greater attention to 'the basics' began to be promoted. Critics saw this as a narrowing of the curriculum, with the potential for a split between 'the basics' and the rest of the curriculum (which could be seen as less important). Throughout the 1980s public and political attention continued to focus on the curriculum. HMI published a series of papers called *Curriculum Matters* discussing the curriculum in a range of subjects; in 1984 the 'Schools Council' which had worked closely with teachers to develop the curriculum was replaced; and a further quango was established – 'The Council for the Accreditation of Teacher Education' (CATE) – to bring initial teacher training under more direct central control.

These decades of intense debate and increasing official control of the curriculum culminated in the Education Reform Act of 1988 which introduced a National Curriculum for the first time. The NC contained the statutory statements and non-statutory guidance concerning the curriculum every child should study between the ages of 5 and 16. It set out the structural details of how the National Curriculum would operate:

- core and foundation subjects to be studied by all pupils;
- attainment targets defining progress through knowledge, skills and understanding in every subject;
- programmes of study – the content, skills and processes to be taught during each key stage;
- assessment arrangements for assessing each pupil at or near the end of key stages.

'The National Curriculum Council' (NCC) and the 'Schools Examination and Curriculum Council' (SEAC) were set up to oversee the new curriculum. These quangos later changed to the 'School Curriculum and Assessment Authority' (SCAA) and latterly to the 'Qualifications and Curriculum Authority' (QCA).

In 1999 the National Curriculum was revised. The subject content was slimmed down and citizenship was included for the first time; the aims, purposes and values were stated explicitly and further non-statutory guidance and learning across the curriculum guidelines were included. This revised document – *The National Curriculum Handbook for Primary Teachers in England* (DfES/QCA 1999) – is currently in force. Figure 4.2.1 shows the content and assessment of the current National Curriculum and its division into Key Stages.

In the same year, the 'Foundation Stage' was introduced as a distinct phase for children aged 3–5 years. The Education Act, 2002, extended the National Curriculum to include the Foundation Stage and the six areas of learning outlined in *Curriculum Guidance for the Foundation Stage* (QCA, 2000) became statutory for nursery and reception classes and early years settings receiving education grant funding. A national assessment system for the Foundation Stage, replacing local baseline assessment schemes, was also introduced. In addition to the statutory National Curriculum, further non-statutory National Strategies for English and Mathematic, giving detailed termly curriculum objectives and advice on how to deliver these objectives, were introduced in 1997 and 1998.

THE AIMS AND STRUCTURES OF THE NATIONAL CURRICULUM

Values, aims, purposes and principles

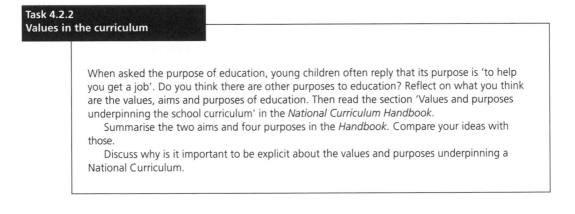

Task 4.2.2
Values in the curriculum

When asked the purpose of education, young children often reply that its purpose is 'to help you get a job'. Do you think there are other purposes to education? Reflect on what you think are the values, aims and purposes of education. Then read the section 'Values and purposes underpinning the school curriculum' in the *National Curriculum Handbook*.

Summarise the two aims and four purposes in the *Handbook*. Compare your ideas with those.

Discuss why is it important to be explicit about the values and purposes underpinning a National Curriculum.

At Foundation Stage the curriculum document sets out a list of aims along with a set of principles for early years education.

Programmes of study, attainment targets, level descriptors

The *programmes of study* are legally binding statements that set out:

- the knowledge, skills and understanding that must be taught;
- the breadth of study – the contexts, activities, areas of study and range of experiences through which the knowledge, skills and understanding are taught.

Key Stage	Age	Year	Statutory curriculum 2005	Other non-statutory areas and non-statutory guidelines	Statutory assessment
Foundation Stage	3–4		Statutory document – *Curriculum Guidance for the Foundation Stage* **6 areas of learning** • Personal, social and emotional development • Communication, language and literacy • Mathematical development • Knowledge and understanding of the world • Physical development • Creative development Each area of learning has set of related **early learning goals**		The Foundation Stage Profile (reception year)
	4–5	R			
Key Stage 1	5–6	1	Statutory document – *The National Curriculum Handbook for Primary Teachers in England* **Core subjects** – English, mathematics, science	• Personal, social and health education (PHSE) • MFL • Key skills – problem solving, communication, application of number, information technology, working with others, improving own learning and performance	Teacher assessment and national tests and tasks in English and mathematics (summer term Y2)
	6–7	2			
Key Stage 2	7–8	3	**Foundation subjects** – design and technology, information and communications technology, history, geography, art and design, music, physical education **Additional statutory areas** – religious education. Content determined by LEA or faith foundation. QCA national framework available, citizenship **General teaching requirements** – apply across all subjects and include inclusion, use of language, ICT, and health and safety	• Thinking skills – enquiry, information processing, reasoning, creative thinking, evaluation	National tests in core subjects (summer term Y6)
	8–9	4			
	9–10	5			
	10–11	6			
Key Stage 3	11–12	7	As Key Stages 1 and 2 with addition of a modern foreign language (MFL)	As Key Stages 1 and 2 but MFL now statutory	National tests in core subjects (summer term Y9)
	12–13	8			
	13–14	9			

Figure 4.2.1 Content and assessment of the current National Curriculum

For example, in Key Stage 2 Science, the knowledge, skills and understanding pupils should be taught includes:

> the effect of light, air, water and temperature on plant growth (SC2, PoS 3a), and under breadth of study it is required that they do this through:
>
> - a range of domestic and environmental contexts that are familiar and of interest to them;
> - looking at the part science has played in the development of many useful things using a range of sources of information and data, including ICT-based sources;
> - using first-hand and secondary data to carry out a range of scientific investigations, including complete investigations.
>
> (Defa and QCA 1999: 85)

Attainment targets set out the criteria for the knowledge, skills and understanding that pupils are expected to have by the end of each Key Stage. Most attainment targets are divided into eight progressively more challenging level descriptors.

These level descriptors provide the basis for making judgements about pupil performance, and the expected attainment at each Key Stage is shown in Figure 4.2.2. There will always be some pupils who may move more slowly or more quickly through the levels because of their particular abilities and aptitudes.

Range of levels at which the great majority of pupils are expected to work		Expected attainment for the majority of the pupils at the end of the Key Stage	
Key Stage 1	1–3	At age 7	2
Key Stage 2	2–5	At age 11	4
Key Stage 3	3–7	At age 14	6

Figure 4.2.2 National Curriculum attainment target levels

National tests (see Units 7.1 and 7.2) at the end of each Key Stage (and teacher assessment at Key Stage 1) are used to assign levels. Schools inform parents of the individual results of these formal tests for their child and the overall school results are made public. Teachers also use the levels to assess children's work and moderate standards within the school.

Task 4.2.3
Attainment targets and assessment

Select one core subject and one foundation subject and examine the attainment target level descriptors for these. In each subject you have chosen, track one skill or one strand of knowledge through the level descriptors and note how it becomes more complex.

If you have access to children's work, consider where you would place this in terms of the level descriptors.

Discuss what you think are the advantages and disadvantages of assessing children's work in this way.

Schemes of work and other National Curriculum support materials

Schools are expected to show how they will deliver the National Curriculum through outlining their planning in schemes of work. There is no statutory way in which a school must set out its schemes of work, and head teachers and teachers can plan their own schemes to take account of their own context and the choices available to them within the curriculum. For example, the breadth of study in history allows schools to select from seven possible ancient civilizations to study.

To support teachers in understanding how the programmes of study can be translated into practical schemes of work, QCA provides exemplar schemes of work in all subject areas except for English and mathematics (where support with planning is provided via the National Strategies). Many schools have used these schemes of work to ease the planning burden and to familiarise themselves with the planning process. As they have become increasingly familiar with the programmes of study, schools have begun to develop and adapt the schemes of work.

The personalisation of centrally provided support materials is now officially encouraged. In *Excellence and Enjoyment* (2003) – the DfES statement of its vision for primary education– schools are encouraged to be more innovative and creative and use the freedom they have to plan a more flexible curriculum. On the QCA website and on the *National Curriculum in Action* website, there are examples of how to adapt and combine units along with case studies showing the many different ways the programmes of study can be translated into practice. While many teachers find these resources helpful, critics see them as a way of controlling and strengthening the official approach to the curriculum. On the other hand, the encouragement for schools to be more flexible has been welcomed by most educationalists as evidence of a changing ethos after several years of increasingly centralised control.

THE NATIONAL STRATEGIES – A CASE STUDY OF POLICY INTO CURRICULUM PRACTICE

The implementation of the National Strategies for English and mathematics is illustrative of the ways government education policy becomes enacted within schools. As with the introduction of the National Curriculum, the National Strategies were conceived as a response to perceived low standards of attainment in reading and mathematics and concerns about how these were taught in school (see, for example, Ofsted 1996).

When the Labour government took power in 1997, it had already set up a 'Literacy Task Force' whilst in opposition and was thus ready to launch a National Literacy Strategy from September 1998, building on a pilot project run the preceding year. It also quickly moved to set up the National Numeracy Strategy. As part of the new public service agenda the launch of the strategies was linked to clear 'accountability' targets by which success would be measured. For literacy this was that by 2002, 80 per cent of eleven-year-olds should achieve the expected level (Level 4) for their age group in the national tests for English. In 1996, prior to the NLS, 57 per cent of 11-year-olds reached Level 4 in English. In 2002 the figure was 75 per cent. Although the test scores rose substantially, the targets were missed. Commitment to meeting the targets was such that the then Education Minister resigned, in part because of this failure. Such actions give powerful messages to schools about the importance placed on raising standards.

As well as targets against which the progress of individual schools could be judged, there were also carefully structured systems put in place to ensure the Strategies were taken up by schools. Writing in *Education Week* (November, 2000), Michael Barber, the architect of the delivery of the Strategies, acknowledged that 'implementation involves an integrated system of "pressure and support"' and listed the following as key elements for ensuring policy became practice:

- *A long term national project plan* for both literacy and numeracy, setting out actions, responsibilities, and deadlines.
- *A substantial investment* sustained over the lifetime of the Strategies and skewed toward those schools which need the most help.
- *A project infrastructure* involving national direction from the Standards and Effectiveness Unit of the Department for Education disseminated via regional directors, LEA Strategy Managers and LEA consultants who deliver training and offer targeted support. There are also school-based, expert teachers who model best practice for their peers.
- *A detailed teaching framework* and an expectation that every class will have a daily mathematics lesson and literacy hour.
- *A professional-development programme* consisting of centrally provided courses and materials to use for school-based professional development and curriculum support.
- *The provision of 'intensive support'* to schools where it was deemed the most progress was required, and early intervention and catch-up programmes for children who had fallen behind.
- *Regular monitoring* by Ofsted and LEAs and *external evaluation* by Ofsted and a team from the University of Toronto (OISE) .
- *A national curriculum for initial teacher training*, requiring all providers to prepare trainee primary teachers to teach the daily mathematics lesson and the literacy hour.

Given this 'assertive, relatively controlling, and responsive set of strategies' (Barber 2000) for implementation, it is no surprise that the majority of schools adopted the National Strategies into their curriculum in some form or other (see for example Ofsted's first evaluation report 1999, Fisher and Lewis 2002), even though they are not statutory and they were criticised by those who objected to increased government control of *how* teachers teach. They also criticised the perceived loss of teacher professionalism, the negative impact an emphasis on literacy and numeracy had on the rest of the curriculum, and expressed subject reservations about aspects such as the teaching of reading methods advocated by the Strategy (see, for example, Frater 1999).

The implementation of the National Strategies demonstrates how a perceived need for educational reform influences government policy – that standards will be raised by reforming how a curriculum subject is taught – and how this policy in turns leads to curriculum change through a detailed teaching programme, advice on how to deliver it and mechanisms to encourage participation.

THE ADVANTAGES AND DISADVANTAGES OF A NATIONAL CURRICULUM

Now you have looked at why the National Curriculum was created, how it is structured and assessed and considered a case study of how government curriculum policy becomes practice you will probably have begun to form your own opinions on whether a national approach to the curriculum is a good idea. Those who support the introduction and continued development of a National Curriculum and non-statutory guidance argue that it has a crucial role to play in addressing several educational issues. These include:

- *Providing an entitlement curriculum* for all pupils regardless of ability. The National Curriculum applies to all children and there is guidance on inclusion for children with special education needs, those for whom English is an additional language and pupils with disabilities.
- *Ensuring progress and continuity*, through subjects, between key stages and across schools.

- *Addressing inequality of provision* and educational opportunity between schools, by ensuring schools do not offer widely varying curricula.
- *Raising standards.* The National Curriculum levels provide a measure against which individual progress and attainment can be judged. They also provide national assessment data against which schools can be judged in comparison to schools with similar intakes.
- *Improving communication, transparency and accountability.* Parents and the wider public know what is taught in schools and the progress that can be expected. Schools must report on the progress of individuals to parents. Governments and LEAs can monitor the results of investments in professional development and curriculum innovations. Education is very costly and governments and the public have a right to know if their money is being spent effectively.

Those who have concerns about the role of a National Curriculum point to:

- *A lack of conceptual clarity* in the aims and purpose of the National Curriculum and a particular view of the nature of knowledge and how it is acquired and measured.
- *The ideological dominance of the official views* and discourse. For example, at subject level an emphasis on Standard English, or at the conceptual level the implicit message that this is the only and correct approach to the curriculum.
- *A diminution in teacher professionalism and autonomy* with teachers increasingly told what to teach and how to teach it leaving no space for professional judgement.
- *Restrictions on pupil choice and creativity.* The curriculum leaves little space for pupils to pursue areas of particular interest or go outside the prescribed curriculum. Critics argue about whether this prepares children for the kind of flexible, self-motivating environments in which many will spend their adult working lives or whether it allows them to develop as fully-rounded individuals.
- *The crowded nature of the curriculum* which can lead to superficial understanding in order to achieve coverage.
- Concerns regarding *the reliability of national tests* and their impact on what is taught.

Task 4.2.4
Do we need a National Curriculum?

Consider the arguments for and against a National Curriculum. Which, to you, seem the most compelling? On balance do you consider we should retain, abandon or modify our National Curriculum?

A CURRICULUM FOR THE TWENTY-FIRST CENTURY

Curriculum development never remains static for long, and, as society changes, the kind of curriculum it wants and needs in its schools is likely to change also. In 2005, QCA launched a debate about the future of the National Curriculum on its 'Futures' website asking:

- What forces for change should influence the development of our national curriculum?
- How should we adapt our system to meet the needs of the time?
- How do we guarantee an entitlement for all learners and at the same time allow scope for innovation and personalization in the ways we organise learning?

(QCA 2005)

In the last few years there have already been some interesting developments around national curricula in this country and in other countries. In this country there have been the messages about schools curriculum freedoms contained in *Excellence and Enjoyment* (DfES, 2003) and the growing interest in the aspects of learning currently to be found in the 'Learning across the National Curriculum' section of the current curriculum document. These aspects of learning include:

- Key skills – problem solving, communication, application of number, information technology, working with others, improving own learning and performance.
- Thinking skills – enquiry, information processing, reasoning, creative thinking, evaluation.

Primary National Strategy continuing professional development materials that have gone to primary schools – *Excellence and Enjoyment: Learning and Teaching in the Primary Years* (2004) – devote two study units to looking at what these aspects of learning involve and how they can be developed across the curriculum. The focus is on the process of learning as well as the subject content. This development coincides with a growing interest from many primary schools in re-examining the learning process. Campaigns to promote 'learning to learn' and research and development into this are underway from a range of organisations and academics (for example, the Campaign for Learning, ESRC's 'Learning to Learn Research Project', Claxton, 2002). Similarly, national organisations (such as the Royal Society of Arts) and individuals are working with schools to develop more creative approaches to the curriculum (see Units 5.1 and 4.4).

At the same time, governments around the world are looking critically at their national or state curricula. In Tasmania, for example, the new national curriculum *Essential Learnings* is focused not around subject divisions but around five curriculum organisers – Thinking, Communicating, Personal Futures, Social Responsibility and World Futures (see http://www.education.tas.gov.au/ocll/). All these developments point to a new phase of curriculum development.

SUMMARY

This brief overview of the development of the National Curriculum shows the move from teacher and school autonomy to an increasingly centralised control of the curriculum. This centralising and homogenising process developed over several decades and was the focus for intense discussion throughout this time. Such discussion continues to this day and what should be taught and who decides remain contested areas. As society continues to evolve and change, new demands are made on the curriculum. Debates now focus on what is needed to be an effective learner in the new 'knowledge society' (Hargreaves 2003) and qualities such as flexibility and creativity are seen as important, as well as factual knowledge and skills.

After several years of a centrally controlled, content driven curriculum, schools are again being encouraged to develop some degree of autonomy within their curricula. Keeping an entitlement curriculum for all and maintaining standards within greater freedoms may be the next challenge for curriculum development.

FURTHER ANNOTATED READING

Colwill, I. (2005) *What has the National Curriculum ever done for us?* Downloadable from www.qca.org.uk/ futures/. In this article the Director of QCA curriculum division argues that the purposes of the National Curriculum are essentially democratic. He elaborates on the purposes of a National

Curriculum and discusses how future revision needs to take place. This article gives a useful insight into 'official' thinking about the curriculum.

Kelly, A.V. (2004) *The Curriculum. Theory and Practice*, 5th edition, London: Sage. Kelly summarises the findings of curriculum research, and considers the nature and development of the curriculum and the importance of examining curriculum development. He takes a critical look at recent curriculum development and the introduction of the National Curriculum.

Moon, B. (2001) *A Guide to the National Curriculum*, Oxford: Oxford University Press. A useful overview of the National Curriculum, its rationale, development, structures and assessment.

Pollard, A. and Triggs, P. (2000) *What Pupils Say: Changing Policy and Practice in Primary Education*, London: Continuum. A view of the curriculum from the pupils' perspective. This book looks at the impact of the introduction of the National Curriculum on pupils and their experiences in the classroom.

REFERENCES

Barber, M. (2000) 'Large-scale reform is possible', *Education Week*, 25 November 2000. Accessed at http://www.edweek.org/ew/articles/2000/11/15/11barber.h20.html.

Campaign for Learning: http://www.campaign-for-learning.org.uk.

Central Advisory Council for Education (1967) *Children and Their Primary Schools* (*The Plowden Report*), London: HMSO.

Claxton, G. (2002) *Building Learning Power: Helping Young People Become Better Learners*, Bristol: TLO.

Cox, C.B. and Dyson, A.E (eds) (1969a) *The Fight for Education. A Black Paper*, Manchester: Critical Quarterly Society.

Cox, C.B. and Dyson, A.E (eds) (1969b) *Black Paper Two: The Crisis in Education*, Manchester: Critical Quarterly Society.

DfEE and the QCA (1999) *The National Curriculum Handbook for Primary Teachers*, London: HMSO.

DfES (2003) *Excellence and Enjoyment: A Strategy for Primary Schools*, London: DFES.

Economic and Social Research Council: http://www.tlrp.org/proj/phase11/phase2f.html.

Fisher, R. and Lewis, M. (2002) 'Examining teaching in the literacy hour', in Fisher, R., Brooks, G. and Lewis, M. (eds) *Raising Standards in Literacy*, London: Routledge.

Frater, G. (1999) 'National initiatives for literacy: two cheers', *Education 3–13*, 27(1): 3–11.

Hargreaves, A. (2003) *Teaching in the Knowledge Society*, Buckingham: Open University Press.

Kelly, A.V. (2004) *The Curriculum. Theory and Practice*, 5th edition, London: Sage.

Office for Standards in Education (1996) *The Teaching of Reading in 45 Inner London Primary Schools: A Report by Her Majesty's Inspectors in Collaboration with the LEAs of Islington, Southwark and Tower Hamlets*, London: Ofsted.

Office for Standards in Education (1999) *National Literacy Strategy – an Evaluation of the First Year*, London: Ofsted.

Primary National Strategy (2004) *Excellence and Enjoyment: Learning and Teaching in the Primary Years*, London: PNS/DfES.

Qualifications and Curriculum Authority (2000) *Curriculum Guidance for the Foundation Stage*, London: QCA.

Qualifications and Curriculum Authority (2005) *Futures: Meeting the Challenge*. Accessed at http://www.qca.org.uk/11493.html.

Unit 4.3

The Scottish Context for the Curriculum

Susan Ellis

No curriculum can be regarded as being final.
(Frank Adams, 2003, p. 378)

INTRODUCTION

We all accept that the curriculum needs to define and frame that which is most important for children to learn and teachers to teach. The challenges involved in such a task are threefold. First, reaching a common agreement about what is important and fundamental can be problematic. Politicians, local authorities, teachers, children, parents and employers may all have different views. The second challenge is to find a curriculum framework that provides support and direction but also allows flexibility so that the curriculum can respond to changes in the social context of education and changes in our understandings of how best to support children's learning. The third challenge is to ensure that the curriculum intentions are not lost during implementation. Recent experience in Scotland indicates that this final challenge is perhaps the hardest to meet. This unit outlines some of the implications of the current 5–14 Curriculum and Assessment Guidelines in Scotland, and the proposed changes that will be in place by 2007.

OBJECTIVES

By the end of this unit you should be able to:

- explain the process of curriculum development in Scotland, who shapes the curriculum and how this is done;
- describe the 5–14 curriculum that currently operates, why it was formed and how it has been operationalised by local authorities and primary school teachers;
- describe proposed changes to the current curriculum and how they may impact on the curriculum in the future;
- Consider how aspects of the Scottish context could impede or facilitate change.

CURRICULUM POLICY IN SCOTLAND

Scotland has its own legislative framework for education. National Policy is framed by the Scottish Executive Education Department (SEED) and education is the formal responsibility of the First Minister, who is answerable to the Scottish Parliament.

There is no legally enforceable 'National Curriculum' in Scotland and all curriculum and assessment guidelines are non-statutory. This means that the curriculum in Scotland is not a rigid, centrally determined programme. What *is* statutory, is that the Minister for Education and Young People, local authorities and schools work together to improve the quality of school education, and that they report on their progress to the people of Scotland. The Standards in Scotland's Schools Act (2000) places a duty on Scottish Ministers to set, from time to time, national priorities in education. Education authorities must use these to frame their own objectives, which form the context for the schools' development plans, interpretations and delivery of the curriculum.

The National Priorities give a general sense of direction for educational policy and curriculum development (see Figure 4.3.1).

Curriculum policy and development is shaped by several bodies. SEED publishes the national 5–14 Guidelines for Curriculum and Assessment. Periodically, it also publishes additional advice in the form of 'Aspect Inspection' reports, based on evidence from school inspections and international studies. These help schools and local authorities to identify and address issues, including curriculum issues, and to ensure appropriate teaching content and effective methodologies for teaching and learning. SEED is also responsible for advising the Minister for Education and Young People about national issues in education.

The Scottish Qualifications Authority (SQA) is responsible for national qualifications and tests in primary and secondary schools. It actively develops and promotes summative and formative assessment in schools. Decisions about what is to be tested, and the questions and tasks used for testing obviously influence how curriculum guidelines are interpreted, and SQA officials work closely with officials from SEED on matters of curriculum advice.

Learning and Teaching Scotland (LTS) is a non-executive public body providing national advice on curriculum policy and practice. It has responsibility for national research and development work and for keeping the national curriculum and assessment guidelines under review. It also supports national staff development initiatives and produces resources for use by teachers in schools.

The current National Priorities

1   To raise standards of educational attainment for all in schools, especially in the core skills of literacy and numeracy, and to achieve better levels in national measures of achievement, including examination results.
2   To support and develop the skills of teachers, the self discipline of pupils and enhance school environments so that they are conducive to teaching and learning.
3   To promote equality and help every pupil benefit from education, with particular regard paid to pupils with disabilities and special educational needs, and to Gaelic and other lesser used languages.
4   To work with parents to teach pupils respect for self and one another and their interdependence with other members of their neighbourhood and society and to teach them the duties and responsibilities of citizenship in a democratic society.
5   To equip pupils with the foundation skills, attitudes and expectations necessary to prosper in a changing society and to encourage creativity and ambition.

Figure 4.3.1   National Priorities. Source: http://www.nationalpriorities.org.uk/schools/schools/html

The management of school education rests with the 32 local authorities in Scotland. Local authorities are expected to interpret and deliver national priorities and curriculum guidelines in a way that meets local needs, whilst taking account of advice from SEED, SQA and LTS. Most local authorities support head teachers and teachers by producing planning frameworks, guidelines and resources for key curricular areas.

The curriculum in schools is the formal responsibility of the head teacher, who prepares development plans for the local authority to show how the school is developing its curriculum in line with local and national priorities. The head teacher must ensure that teachers deliver an appropriate and balanced curriculum, with appropriate monitoring and reporting.

Policy on testing

Pupils sit 5–14 national tests in reading, writing and mathematics when the teacher judges them to have attained a particular level. Local Authorities commonly use achievement in the 5–14 tests to negotiate targets for improving attainment in individual schools and for identifying issues across schools. Local authorities monitor the success of their schools and part of the monitoring process is the school's ability to meet or exceed its targets.

National standards in maths, science, reading and writing are surveyed on a 4-year cycle by the Assessment of Achievement Programme (AAP), which reports on national performance standards and their changes over time. Scotland also participates in several international studies of achievement, which allow educational policies and practices to be examined against globally-defined benchmarks. The Program for International Student Assessment (PISA) studies the attainment of 15-year-old students in maths, literacy and science in OECD countries; the Progress in International Reading Literacy Study (PIRLS) provides data on how nine and ten-year-olds perform in reading, and the Trends in International Mathematics and Science Study (TIMSS) does this for mathematics and science.

Task 4.3.1
The shape of the curriculum in Scotland

Using the information given so far, draw a diagram to show how the curriculum is shaped and developed in Scotland. Compare your diagram with that of a colleague.

THE 5–14 CURRICULUM

In Scotland, pupils enter school in the year of their fifth birthday. There is one intake per year, in August, and the ages of children in P1, the youngest class, range from four years six months to five years six months. Children leave primary school when they are eleven years six months to twelve years six months.

The 5–14 Guidelines for Curriculum and Assessment apply to all stages of the primary school and the first two stages of secondary schooling. They were originally designed to offer a framework for curriculum content and planning, rather than a definitive specification of what should be covered in each curricular area. Initially, the Guidelines divided the primary school curriculum into five broad areas:

- English Language (covering attainment outcomes of Talking; Listening; Reading; Writing)
- Maths (covering attainment outcomes of Information Handling; Number, Money and Measurement; Shape Position and Movement)
- Environmental Studies (covering attainment outcomes of Science; Social Subjects; Technology)
- Religious and Moral Education (covering attainment outcomes of Christianity; Other World Religions; Personal Search)
- Expressive Arts (covering attainment outcomes of Art and Design; Drama; Music; Physical Education)

Then, in 2000, more areas were added:

- ICT
- Health Education
- Personal and Social Development
- Modern European Languages
- Latin

There are also guidelines to detail the Structure and Balance of the Curriculum, Assessment and Reporting.

Each 5–14 document is set out in the same way. A rationale explains the basic structure of the curricular area, framed as attainment outcomes, and explains broad approaches to teaching and learning. Then, a section describes progression within each outcome by detailing possible teaching content. The content is framed as 'strands', each of which has attainment targets describing minimum competencies for six levels of attainment, A–F. Finally, 'Programmes of Study' provide brief exemplifications of how each strand might be addressed at each of the levels.

The 5–14 guidelines frame curriculum content in terms of levels rather than year or age-groups. In one year-group there will be children working at different levels, and the teacher must differentiate work appropriately.

The structure and balance guidelines recommend that schools devote 15 per cent of curriculum time to mathematics, 20 per cent to language (including modern languages from P6), 15 per cent to expressive arts, 15 per cent to religious and moral education (including personal and social development and health education) and 15 per cent to environmental studies. The remaining 20 per cent flexibility time is often used for language teaching, particularly in the early primary years.

Although the 5–14 guidelines are not statutory, they are used by Her Majesty's Inspectorate for Education (HMIE) as the basis for school inspections, and inspection reports are published. Inspection reports do not identify specific staff, but most primary schools are small and it is easy to work out to whom inspectors are referring when they report on the quality of planning, teaching and learning in a particular year group. As a result, most primary schools implement the 5–14 guidelines to the letter. Teachers use planning frameworks devised by the local authority or school management to ensure that all attainment targets are addressed. A few authorities tell schools which schemes and teaching resources to use, but most allow schools to choose. Generally one finds a mixture of schemes and resources, some published by the local authority, some by LTS and some commercially produced.

Specific priorities in Scotland are literacy and numeracy. In 2002, SEED published an overview of the national guidance, resources and initiatives across pre-school, primary and secondary literacy education and set an agenda for future work. The main issues identified were:

- raising attainment amongst pupils experiencing poverty and injustice;
- promoting links between pre-school, primary and secondary schools;
- improving standards in the 12–14 age group;

- • addressing gender disparity in attainment;
- • encouraging local authorities to share good practice.

These issues are being addressed through three key mechanisms: 'Closing the gap' (by promoting equality, inclusion and diversity and reducing structural inequalities of opportunities and outcomes); 'Building capacity' (by ensuring that the teaching workforce has the capacity to deliver high quality services); and 'Ensuring excellence' (by setting clear standards and evaluating and reporting on the quality of outcomes).

Introduction of the 5–14 Guidelines

Prior to 5–14, curriculum advice was developed by COPE (the Committee on Primary Education) and its sub-committees, subject to final approval by the Consultative Council on the Curriculum. Primary teachers had a free choice about what they taught, and how. However, it was difficult to ensure that curriculum recommendations were discussed and adopted by schools. A major report for the Scottish Education Department noted that, six years after the Primary Memorandum (which had been a key curriculum initiative), 'few head teachers had done anything to formulate a policy for the planned implementation of the approaches suggested' (SED 1971: 16).

There are many reasons why schools can be slow to adopt new initiatives. There can be a passive resistance: Eisner notes that 'experienced teachers tend to ... ride out the wave of enthusiasm, and then just float until the next wave comes' (1992: 616). There can also be a tendency to recognise aspects that concur with current practice, and overlook or dismiss newer ideas. Certainly, when the English Language 5–14 Guidelines were published in 1989, the emphasis on talking and listening was greeted with genuine surprise, despite policy documents since 1965 advocating the importance of planned contexts for talk.

Prior to the introduction of the 5–14 Guidelines, policy makers were concerned about unacceptable variability in assessment practices, in attainment and in reports to parents. There was a lack of curricular continuity, breadth and progression and of continuity between primary and secondary school curricula (Adams 2003).

The 5–14 Guidelines were established to address these concerns. Scotland had always had a history of consensual curriculum development and there was disquiet about the concept of centrally determined curriculum guidelines. It was described as 'a shift in policy-making style in Scotland, from debate followed by consensus to consultation followed by imposition' (Rodger, quoted in Adams, 2003, p. 371). As a result, the new 5–14 guidelines were based on a consensual understanding of 'existing good practice' rather than adopting a more theoretical or research-based framework; they were born of 'evolution, rather than revolution'. The consensual approach meant that the Guidelines had a reasonably good fit with the knowledge-base and resources already in place in local authorities. The downside was that they did not ask fundamental questions of existing assumptions or practice. For example, changes in the teaching of reading came not from 5–14, but from the Early Intervention initiative sponsored by SEED (Ellis and Friel 2003)

Another problem was that each curricular area was developed by a separate working party of specialists. Each group considered its own subject, with scant regard to cross-curricular themes or connections. This encouraged a compartmentalised curriculum and meant that primary schools abandoned integrated approaches such as the Scottish Storyline methodology (Bell 2003), which could provide curricular coherence and harness children's interests and emotions. Moreover, no one had an overview of the whole curriculum, which led to serious curriculum overload.

THE CURRENT CURRICULUM

The pressure for accountability created in the wake of the Guidelines ensured that curriculum policy was taken seriously and the 5–14 Guidelines have improved equity and attainment. However, the pressure for accountability has also resulted in teachers, schools and local authorities overemphasising schemes and worksheets to evidence coverage and progression. Forward planning became a mechanism for mapping activities onto attainment targets and strands, rather than a serious opportunity to consider the most appropriate learning priorities and contexts for the class.

Despite their non-statutory status, the interpretation of the guidelines has become increasingly literal, which has magnified their weaknesses. Dividing every subject area into discrete outcomes, each split into strands and then further into tiny slivers of attainment targets, has fragmented the curriculum in a way that was never envisaged. The framework has discouraged integration and has not prompted teachers to consider how to contextualise work and help pupils to see connections and links. The sheer number of work programmes to be covered has led to time pressures, which have created stress and squeezed opportunities for play, self-directed learning, extended writing and problem-based learning. There are so many discrete schemes to be covered that teachers feel they have no time to treat their pupils as social beings: 'I'm so busy teaching talking and listening, I don't have time to discuss what the children did at the weekend' (Ellis and Kleinberg, 1997, p. 3). Teachers feel that they have little time to re-visit, consolidate or explore ideas in depth. The pace and quantity of work has diverted average teachers from developing more complex models of teaching and learning and frustrated the best, who know that they could teach in a more effective way.

The use of test results to measure the success of schools and local authorities has led to a reliance on teaching resources that specifically mirror the national test formats, with mechanistic teaching approaches and superficial content. When the writing tests were recently changed, one popular local authority scheme had to be re-written because the teaching content was focused on the old test content and criteria.

In short, the 5–14 Guidelines have encouraged teachers to focus on the teaching content and on attainment. These are good things. However, they have been implemented in a way that does not encourage a learning environment that is intellectually and emotionally engaging for children or for teachers.

Task 4.3.2
Curriculum change: teachers and training

Find some reasonably experienced primary teachers to interview. Ask them about the curriculum developments they have experienced during their career. How did the changes affect their work with the pupils? Their planning or thinking about teaching? What did they think of them at the time? How do they feel about them now? What are the current curriculum issues? How do these teachers feel about them?

A CURRICULUM FOR EXCELLENCE

In 2004, Peter Peacock, the Minister for Education and Young People, wrote:

> The curriculum in Scotland has many strengths.... However, the various parts were developed separately and, taken together, they do not now provide the best basis for an excellent education for every child. The National Debate showed that people want a curriculum that will fully prepare today's children for adult life in the 21st century, be less crowded and better connected, and offer more choice and enjoyment.
>
> (SEED 2004: 6)

This is an extraordinarily brave and frank statement for any government minister to make. It indicates a genuine desire to make the education system work for children and reflects a confidence in the willingness and ability of the Scottish educational community to deliver effective change.

The 5–14 curriculum in Scotland is undergoing a major review. In 2002, SEED initiated a National Debate on Education. Consultation showed that people valued the curriculum for its flexibility, combination of breadth and depth, quality of teaching and the quality of materials that support teaching. They did not want a more centralised, uniform curriculum. They did, however, want a less crowded curriculum, one that would make learning more enjoyable and with better connections between the pre-five, primary, secondary and post-secondary stages.

In 2003 a Curriculum Review Group considered the policy implications of this for education across the 3–18 age-group. It published its recommendations in *A Curriculum For Excellence* (SEED 2004). Those that will impact most significantly on the primary curriculum are:

- to introduce a single curriculum for 3–18 year olds, supported by a simple and effective structure for assessment; and
- to de-clutter the primary curriculum to free up more time for young people to achieve and to allow primary teachers the freedom to exercise judgement on appropriate learning.

The starting point for *A Curriculum For Excellence* is that children learn through experiences in the family and community, as well as at school and that the curriculum must recognise and use this. It argues for a curriculum that 'speaks' to different groups, teachers, pupils, parents and employers, and recognises what they need. It should give teachers clear aims for teaching, the flexibility to apply professional judgements in planning and teaching, and allow time and space for innovative and creative teaching and learning. It should give children a clearer focus on the purpose of learning activities (leading to better achievement), more choice, better progression and more enjoyment of learning.

To do this, curriculum guidance should cover what is taught, and how, but be streamlined to provide specific detail where it makes sense and remove the unnecessary detail in expressive arts and environmental studies to allow flexibility. It should enable a smooth transition from pre-school to primary by promoting pre-school learning approaches such as play, in the primary curriculum.

A group called the Curriculum for Excellence Programme Board is now considering how to implement the recommendations of the Curriculum Review Group and is due to report in 2007. When the new *Curriculum for Excellence* comes into effect, it will have to deliver on all four purposes of education that were identified by the Curriculum Review Group.

Scottish curriculum development tends to be a process of evolution rather than revolution. Brian Boyd has noted that 'Scotland has never been extreme with its educational innovations; ... [the Scottish approach] has always been to integrate innovation firmly into traditional approaches' (Humes and Bryce, 2003: 111). The 'practice-driven' approach in two recent national curriculum development projects illustrates this: *Assessment is for All* (promoting formative assessment in the classroom) and

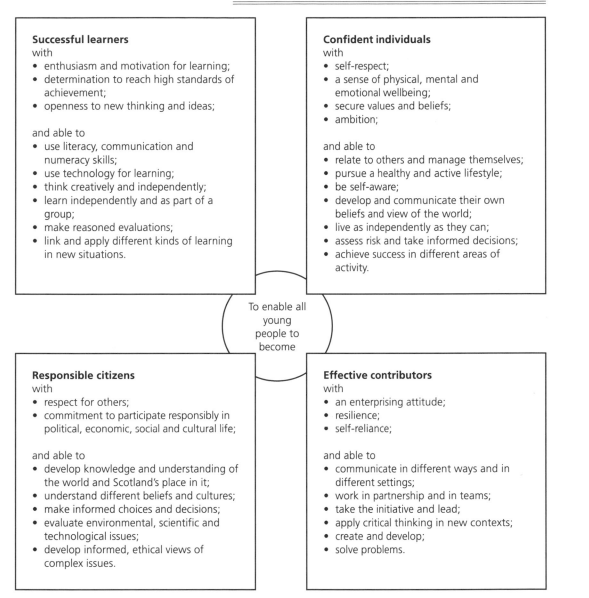

Successful learners
with
- enthusiasm and motivation for learning;
- determination to reach high standards of achievement;
- openness to new thinking and ideas;

and able to
- use literacy, communication and numeracy skills;
- use technology for learning;
- think creatively and independently;
- learn independently and as part of a group;
- make reasoned evaluations;
- link and apply different kinds of learning in new situations.

Confident individuals
with
- self-respect;
- a sense of physical, mental and emotional wellbeing;
- secure values and beliefs;
- ambition;

and able to
- relate to others and manage themselves;
- pursue a healthy and active lifestyle;
- be self-aware;
- develop and communicate their own beliefs and view of the world;
- live as independently as they can;
- assess risk and take informed decisions;
- achieve success in different areas of activity.

To enable all young people to become

Responsible citizens
with
- respect for others;
- commitment to participate responsibly in political, economic, social and cultural life;

and able to
- develop knowledge and understanding of the world and Scotland's place in it;
- understand different beliefs and cultures;
- make informed choices and decisions;
- evaluate environmental, scientific and technological issues;
- develop informed, ethical views of complex issues.

Effective contributors
with
- an enterprising attitude;
- resilience;
- self-reliance;

and able to
- communicate in different ways and in different settings;
- work in partnership and in teams;
- take the initiative and lead;
- apply critical thinking in new contexts;
- create and develop;
- solve problems.

Figure 4.3.2 Purposes of the curriculum from 3–18, *Curriculum for Excellence*

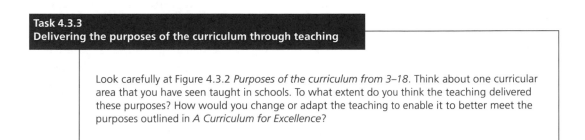

Task 4.3.3
Delivering the purposes of the curriculum through teaching

Look carefully at Figure 4.3.2 *Purposes of the curriculum from 3–18*. Think about one curricular area that you have seen taught in schools. To what extent do you think the teaching delivered these purposes? How would you change or adapt the teaching to enable it to better meet the purposes outlined in *A Curriculum for Excellence*?

Building Bridges (promoting better links between the primary and secondary school curricula) work through local authority-based action research projects to buy teachers time to enable them to apply new ideas and discuss their experiences with colleagues (LTS, 2004).

For all the criticisms of 5–14 contained in the above Ministerial response, it is highly likely that the existing 5–14 Guidelines will be used as the starting point for change. The argument is pragmatic: there are many ways to organise the curriculum, all with strengths and weaknesses. Complete re-organisation takes time and saps energy and confidence as teachers abandon old terminology and frameworks and learn new ones. It is more efficient and effective to adapt and re-focus the current frameworks in a way that will prompt local authorities and schools to use them differently. Certainly, the basic principles of the *Curriculum for Excellence* are remarkably similar to those of the 5–14 Guidelines.

The experience of implementing the 5–14 Guidelines shows that national curriculum policy needs to pay as much attention to the process of implementation as to initial structures and frameworks. To be successful, the *Curriculum for Excellence* initiative will need to find a way to orchestrate the many different influences that could support or destroy its spirit.

It will need to encourage a much more complex definition of what is meant by a balanced curriculum. The 5–14 Guidelines assume that balance lies in the curriculum content and can be measured as time. However, a definition of balance that sees it in terms of balance for the child (adapting to the different learning styles or the knowledge, interests and experiences that children bring to school) or balance for the school (accounting for the school environment and social context, as well as teacher expertise) is just as valid and would discourage mechanistic interpretations. Support for this shift may not be difficult to achieve. The 5–14 Guidelines have been heavily criticised for their narrow interpretation of balance and prior to 5–14, COPE rejected a simple arithmetical approach (Adams, 2003).

There needs to be greater recognition that higher test scores do not necessarily mean a higher quality of education. It is not that national testing should be abandoned, but that we need a broader discussion of test results at national and local levels. If the performance of schools and teachers is seen only in terms of numeracy and literacy test results, the broader qualities sought by the *Curriculum for Excellence* will get marginalised.

A clear view of the nature of accountability in national, local authority and school contexts will also be important. A culture of criticism and blame encourages a defensive, mechanistic curriculum as teachers and head teachers seek protection by 'following guidelines to the letter'. The changing nature of HMIE inspections to self-evaluation against nationally published performance indicators may address this. To fully change the culture, we need a move towards research-orientated schools, in which serious curriculum innovation and evaluation is part of the job for teachers, head teachers and local authorities. Only this would provide the professional basis necessary for serious collaboration between SEED, local authorities and teachers and is essential if education is to be seen and understood as a complex process with many outcomes, rather than a one-dimensional commodity. Currently, funding is often ring-fenced for priorities determined by SEED. It can be difficult for schools and local authorities to set their own agenda for curriculum innovation.

If the *Curriculum for Excellence* is successful, it is likely to produce a more diverse education system. Preventing the politicisation of the curriculum may be difficult. Public accountability means that local authorities and schools must account for their actions and all public bodies now pay careful attention to how they are reported in the press. The temptation will be for each local authority to promote its own initiatives as 'the best solution', reducing complex analyses to newspaper headlines. This will not help reflection and careful decision-making. Rational discussion and genuine debate, which acknowledges the complexity of the issues, will be crucial.

Academic research on the curriculum has tended to focus either on debating national policy or on the content and design features of specific programmes and their impact. Work on scaling-up educational reform shows that the contexts in which programmes are implemented are at least as important as their design features (Datnow *et al.* 2002). 'Educators know experientially that context matters most in the "chemistry" that makes for educational effectiveness' (Eisner 2004: 616). Given this, we know surprisingly little about the nature of educational decision-making below the level of national policy. How and why do local authority staff or head teachers adopt particular resources and innovations? What evidence-base is used? Who do they consult? Which aspects of the local context are considered, and how much weight do they afford to each? Decision-making could be better supported with a clearer understanding of the informal and formal influences exerted by peer groups, others in the educational hierarchy (above and below), previous experiences of teaching, external consultants, research, commercial companies and by the parents or children. This may lead to more robust decisions.

Teachers will also need to be allowed to see their job differently. The image of the primary teacher as an isolated adult, focused solely on young children is changing. The career structure reached following recommendations in the McCrone Report (2000) promotes a more social and research-based view of teaching. It recognises that teachers need to discuss their practice with others and that time must be available for this. However, time is not enough. We need upfront acknowledgement that teaching is both an art and a profession, and primary teachers need to develop a strong and assertive professional voice for talking about their work. They need to be prepared to engage in a more open and honest dialogue with head teachers and local authority staff about how the curriculum is delivered and which local implementation policies are enabling and which are not. As artists, teachers need to openly discuss the timing, selection and balance of ideas with parents and children as well as each other and accept that sometimes they may not get it right.

We all need to recognise that teachers' learning is social and emotional as well as cognitive. Continuing professional development needs to enhance teachers' professional judgement and dialogue, alongside their knowledge, and ensure that head teachers actively support this process. Good leadership in schools needs to be seen in terms of building capacity at all levels, including the capacity of weak teachers. As one Scottish head teacher recently explained,

> Weak teachers are not made competent by being given work programmes or criticism; they just clam-up and become passive. They need to talk, talk and talk some more about how they are teaching the children in their own class and get specific, tailored advice and help, including practical support and demonstrations, with explanations linked to that.

(Ellis 2005)

SUMMARY

The discussion of curriculum guidelines and how they are implemented can seem awfully dry and boring. There is a great temptation for student teachers to focus on the immediate job of teaching the children without thinking about the big picture. It is part of every teacher's professional responsibility to think about what is most important in education, and to ensure that the curriculum is working to deliver this. The key points from this unit are that curriculum guidelines are only one aspect of a complex, dynamic picture and that the process of implementation is crucial.

ANNOTATED FURTHER READING

Bryce, T.G.K. and Humes, W.M. (eds) *Scottish Education: Second Edition Post-Devolution*, Edinburgh: Edinburgh University Press. This is the most comprehensive text on Scottish Education. Each chapter is designed to give an overview of the key features and issues.

Kirk, G. and Glaister, R. (1994) *5–14: Scotland's National Curriculum*, Edinburgh: Scottish Academic Press. Small and useful, this text will explain the wider context of the 5–14 Guidelines.

SEED (2004) *A Curriculum for Excellence*, Edinburgh: HMSO. A highly readable document that sets out the framework for the new curriculum.

REFERENCES

Adams, Frank R. (2003) '5–14: origins, development and implementation', in Bryce, T.G.K. and Humes, W.M. (eds) *Scottish Education: Second Edition Post-Devolution*, Edinburgh: Edinburgh University Press.
Bell, S. (2003) *The Scottish Storyline Method*. Retrieved 6 March 2005 from http://www.storyline.org.
Datnow, A., Hubbard, L. and Mehan, H. (2002) *Extending Educational Reform: From One School to Many*, New York: RoutledgeFalmer.
Eisner, E.W. (1992) 'Educational reform and the ecology of schooling', *Teachers College Record*, 93(4): 610–27.
Eisner, E.W. (2004) 'Artistry in teaching', *Cultural Commons*, http://www.culturalcommons.org/eisner.htm. Accessed: 28 February 2005.
Ellis, S. (2005) 'Making literacy thrive in schools: a case study from Scotland', *Voice & Vision*, 23(2): 4–7. Almaty: National Reading Association of Kazakhstan.
Ellis, S. and Friel, G. (2003) 'English language', in Bryce, T.G.K. and Humes, W.M. (eds) *Scottish Education: Second Edition Post-Devolution*, Edinburgh: Edinburgh University Press.
Ellis, S. and Kleinberg, S. (1997) 'Helping teachers support young children in science inquiries', *Education 3–13*, 25(3): 59–64.
Humes, W.M. and Bryce, T.G.K. (2003) 'The distinctiveness of Scottish education', in Bryce, T.G.K. and Humes, W.M. (eds) *Scottish Education: Second Edition Post-Devolution*, Edinburgh: Edinburgh University Press.
LTS (2004) *Assessment is for Learning: Teachers' Projects*, http://www.ltscotland.org.uk/assess/projects.asp. Accessed 27 February 2005.
LTS (2004) *Building Bridges in Literacy and Numeracy P6–S2*, http://www.ltscotland.org.uk/literacyandnumeracy/. Accessed 27 February 2005.
McCrone, G. (2000) *Report of the McCrone Inquiry into Professional Conditions of Service for Teachers*, Edinburgh: HMSO.
SED (1971) *Primary Education: Organisation for Development*, Edinburgh: HMSO.
SEED (2004) *A Curriculum for Excellence*, Edinburgh: HMSO.

Unit 4.4

The Curriculum

Dominic Wyse

INTRODUCTION

The nature of the primary curriculum has come under intense scrutiny over the last 15 years. In spite of all the controversy and change since 1988 you will see that the curriculum model remains largely the same as the first statutory curriculum from 1862. Once again progressivism is on the march and there are some optimistic signs that things like creativity will begin to play a much more important part in primary education. The unit concludes with a vision for the future primary curriculum.

OBJECTIVES

By the end of this chapter you should:

- understand the aims of the curricula at Foundation Stage and Key Stages 1 and 2;
- appreciate that the history of the curriculum is an important aspect of continuing debates;
- begin to think about how teachers make professional decisions about the curriculum in the best interests of the children that they teach;
- have some ideas about how a future curriculum might look.

As part of your preparation for school experience you will have become more familiar with national curricula: the early years are covered by the *Curriculum Guidance for the Foundation Stage* (age 3 until the beginning of the term after the child's fifth birthday; this is usually nursery and reception settings); for the later years *The National Curriculum: Handbook for Primary Teachers in England* (age 5–11: Year 1 to

Year 6; there is another handbook for National Curriculum secondary education). In spite of the importance of the National Curriculum in relation to what all primary teachers must teach, you may find that once you start your school experience the document is rarely referred to. This is because schools' long-term and medium-term planning has often been discussed, agreed and written down over a considerable period of time. Once this thinking has been translated from the National Curriculum into teaching plans, the official documents are not really needed so much. This can make it difficult for student teachers to appreciate the links between the National Curriculum and school planning.

Another area where it is sometimes difficult to see the links with the statutory documents is the extent to which some of the important opening statements of national curricula are genuinely reflected in classroom practice. These opening statements, such as principles and values, should be very important because in theory it is these which guide everything else in the documents, and in practice.

The Foundation Stage guidance starts with a definition of terms: 'The term curriculum is used to describe everything children do, see, hear or feel in their setting, both planned and unplanned.' (QCA/DfES 2000: 1) Although this is a welcome reflection of the idea that learning in the early years is not differentiated from the idea of 'work' in the way that it is in later years, it is possible that this definition imposes too much control on the lives of the children. What if they don't want 'everything' in their lives at school to be regarded as part of the formal curriculum?

The opening paragraph of the Foundation Stage guidance sets a familiar political theme which has dominated curriculum development since 1988: 'standards'.

> This guidance is intended to help practitioners plan to meet the diverse needs of all children so that **most will achieve** and some, where appropriate, will go beyond **the early learning goals** by the end of the Foundation Stage.
>
> (QCA/DfES 2000: 5, emphasis in original)

The early learning goals in the Foundation Stage are assessed by the Foundation Stage profile which is a precursor to the statutory tests/exams at 7, 11, 14, and 16. Many people remain unhappy that the children of England are tested more than any other country in the world.

The section on 'Aims for the Foundation Stage' features a series of ten bullet points (see Table 4.4.1). One of the positive aspects of these aims is that part of what was once called the 'hidden curriculum' is explicitly represented. The personal and social domain is firmly embedded in the curriculum and appears first in the list of 'areas of learning' (QCA/DfES 2000: 26):

- personal, social and emotional development;
- communication, language and literacy;
- mathematical development;

Table 4.4.1 The aims of the Foundation Stage

Aims for the Foundation Stage	Domain
Personal, social and emotional well-being	Personal
Positive attitudes and dispositions towards their learning	Personal
Social skills	Social
Attention skills and persistence	Personal
Language and communication	Personal and social
Reading and writing	Cognitive
Mathematics	Cognitive
Knowledge and understanding of the world	Cognitive
Physical development	Personal
Creative development	Cognitive

- knowledge and understanding of the world;
- physical development;
- creative development.

But while the conceptual organisation into broad areas of learning is helpful, the traditional emphases are still obvious. Reading, writing, mathematics and science are priorities but creativity appears at the bottom of the list. The order of a list may not seem to be particularly significant but you will see that it reflects a common trend over more than 100 years.

Unlike the National Curriculum which locates speaking and listening after reading and writing, in the Foundation Stage guidance communication and language comes before literacy. It is certainly true that language development is an essential part of learning and as such should be an important feature of the curriculum. However, the special place of speaking and listening as something which is naturally acquired and the medium through which learning and teaching takes place makes it unique. Although this is quite controversial, in view of the fact that speaking and listening was neglected for many years, I think that it may be necessary to re-evaluate the balance between the modes. A more clearly specified language curriculum should differentiate with rigour between language features which are likely to be naturally acquired, those which might benefit from more directed teaching as part of the English curriculum and those which should be covered as part of all curriculum subjects. If this were to be done there would be a slight reduction in the curriculum content for the subject English. This would be consistent with research evidence which shows that reading and writing are not acquired as naturally as speaking and listening and benefit more from direct teaching.

When we turn to the National Curriculum it is clear from the outset that there are other differences between it and the Foundation Stage guidance. Even the concept curriculum is defined differently. You will remember that at the Foundation Stage 'The term curriculum is used to describe everything children do, see, hear or feel in their setting, both planned and unplanned'. The National Curriculum says 'The school curriculum comprises all learning and other experiences that each school plans for its pupils. The National Curriculum is an important element of the school curriculum' (QCA/DfES 2000: 1). The main difference here is that the curriculum is only the *planned* elements whereas in the Foundation Stage it includes the unplanned elements. There is no logical reason why curriculum should be defined differently in these two phases and this reflects different influences at work when these curricula were written. The suggestion that the National Curriculum is only 'an important element' rather than the complete curriculum is potentially rather significant, but in practice schools have consistently struggled to fit the National Curriculum into their timetables at all. In addition the subjects are grouped differently and the National Curriculum has a heavier focus on the cognitive domain.

The two aims for the National Curriculum are taken from the Education Act 1996 (see Table 4.4.2). You can see from point 5 that religious education and religious worship are singled out in the legal requirements for schools in England and Wales. We need to question whether the wording of the

Task 4.4.1
Religious education, religion and the curriculum

The Church of England and the Catholic Church have had a profound influence on the English education system including involvement in funding of schools; the legal necessity for a daily act of worship; and the place of Religious Education as a subject. Given that in most other countries this is not the case, and in some the National Curriculum is completely secular, to what extent do you think the influence of religion is a positive aspect of the curriculum in England?

Table 4.4.2 The aims of the curriculum

General duties in respect of the curriculum.	**351.** - (1) The curriculum for a school satisfies the requirements of this section if it is a balanced and broadly based curriculum which-
	(a) promotes the spiritual, moral, cultural, mental and physical development of pupils at the school and of society, and
	(b) prepares pupils at the school for the opportunities, responsibilities and experiences of adult life.
	(2) The Secretary of State shall exercise his functions with a view to securing that the curriculum for every maintained school satisfies the requirements of this section.
	(3) Every local education authority shall exercise their functions with a view to securing that the curriculum for every maintained school which they maintain satisfies the requirements of this section.
	(4) The governing body and head teacher of every maintained school shall exercise their functions with a view to securing that the curriculum for the school satisfies the requirements of this section.
	(5) The functions referred to in subsections (2) to (4) include in particular functions conferred by this Part in relation to religious education, religious worship and the National Curriculum.

two aims are appropriate for twenty-first-century England. For example, is pupils' 'spiritual' development correctly positioned as the first priority of the first of the two aims? White (2004) analyses the extent to which the National Curriculum actually does reflect its aims. I would emphasise the fact that it is not clear at all that the second aim, to prepare children for adult life, is being met.

Following the aims, the next section of the National Curriculum handbook for teachers covers the 'four main purposes of the National Curriculum' (p. 12). The first of these is 'to establish an entitlement'. When the National Curriculum was first proposed there was overwhelming resistance to the fact that it should be introduced at all, as Haviland (1988) showed. However, one of the strong arguments mounted in favour of the National Curriculum was that pupils across England and Wales were receiving an uneven education which could include considerable repetition of subject matter, a situation that could be exacerbated if children moved areas to different schools. There were also well-founded claims that some groups of children, particularly minority ethnic ones, were subject to low expectations reflected in the curricula that were delivered to them. A national curriculum was seen as a solution to these problems because it would ensure that all children had an *entitlement* to a continuous and coherent curriculum (another one of the four purposes). But exposing children to the *same* curriculum does not necessarily lead to the fulfilment of their entitlement. I would argue that a curriculum that is informed by pupils' interests, needs, and rights is more likely to give them their entitlement than a uniform one which is legally imposed. Despite the resistance to the National Curriculum, it was introduced in 1988. Following many complaints that it was over-burdening schools it was revised in 1993 but the revisions did little to reduce the load. The current version remains very similar to the previous versions and to understand the reasons for this we need to look back in time.

HISTORY OF THE CURRICULUM

The idea of the curriculum being dominated by the three Rs (reading, writing and arithmetic) is a very old one. In 1862 parliament finally agreed a legal document called 'The Revised Code of 1862'. This introduced the idea that children over the age of seven would be examined in the three Rs by an inspector. Children were grouped by age into different 'standards' which had certain requirements (see Table 4.4.3).

Teachers were paid 8 shillings for each child who passed the examination of the 3 Rs in their standard. A failure in any one of the 3 Rs would mean that the grant was reduced by 2 shillings and 8 pence. Four shillings was awarded for general merit and attendance. This system known as 'payment by results' had two main problems: a) the stress on the children due to the examination system; b) the focus on the 3 Rs resulting in a very narrow curriculum (Curtis and Boultwood 1964). Payment by results was suspended from 1895 to be replaced by more freedom for primary teachers represented by the Education Act 1902 and the publication of the significant handbook 'Suggestions for the Consideration of Teachers and others concerned in the work of Public Elementary Schools'. Until 1926 the legal powers established in the Elementary Code meant that the Board of Education held the right to approve the school

Table 4.4.3 The curriculum specified by the Revised Code of 1862

	Standard I	Standard II	Standard III	Standard IV	Standard V	Standard VI
Reading	Narrative in monosyllables	One of the narratives next in order after monosyllables in an elementary reading book used in the school	A short paragraph from an elementary reading book used in the school	A short paragraph from a more advanced reading book used in the school	A few lines of poetry from a reading book used in the first class of the school	A short ordinary paragraph in a newspaper, or other modern narrative
Writing	Form on black-board or slate, from dictation, letters, capital and small, manuscript	Copy in manuscript character a line of print	A sentence from the same paragraph, slowly read once, and then dictated in single words	A sentence slowly dictated once by a few words at a time, from the same book, but not from the paragraph read	A sentence slowly dictated once, by a few words at a time, from a reading book used in the first class of the school	Another short ordinary paragraph in a newspaper, or other modern narrative, slowly dictated once by a few words at a time
Arithmetic	Form on black-board or slate, from dictation, figures up to 20; name at sight figures up to 20; add and subtract figures up to 10; orally from examples on the black-board	A sum in simple addition or subtraction, and the multiplication table	A sum in any simple rule as far as short division (inclusive)	A sum in compound rules (money)	A sum in compound rules (common weights and measures)	A sum in practice or bills of parcels

curriculum and timetable through the work of inspectors. In 1926 the regulations were revised and any reference to the subjects of the curriculum was removed (Cunningham 2002).

It wasn't until much later, in the 1960s, that government began to take a strong interest in the curriculum once more. The establishment of the School's Council was followed by Prime Minister James Callaghan's Ruskin College speech which clearly signalled government's intention to take more control of the curriculum. As you saw at the beginning of the unit and in Unit 4.2 this control of the curriculum was maximised in the Education Act 1996 and has steadily increased to the present day through the imposition of the national literacy and numeracy strategies and latterly the Primary National Strategy. As I remarked in a previous publication, the primary school, which had once been called a 'secret garden' because nobody could easily get access, has become a national park.

Cunningham (2002) points out that Local Education Authorities (LEAs) teachers' centres were an important catalyst for new ideas and practices and he claims that their influence has been unduly neglected by historians of the teaching profession. The year 1902 marked the beginning of progressivism which through the first 70 years of the twentieth century was increasingly influenced by courses provided by LEAs. From my own point of view I still remember the excitement of taking part in courses run by the Inner London Education Authority (ILEA) and later involvement in the Language in the National Curriculum (LINC) project while working in Bradford, and subsequent courses run by Kirklees authority when I worked in Huddersfield. However, I'm not sure that the progressive ideas emerging from teachers' centres were as universally influential as has been suggested. Let me take an example from the teaching of English. 'The real book approach' is a progressive approach to the teaching of literacy which has frequently been blamed for alleged poor standards in reading, but the number of teachers who use such an approach is frequently exaggerated. Research has shown (Wyse 1998) that at various periods in time only about 4 per cent of schools have confirmed that they use such progressive approaches to the teaching of literacy. Simpson (1996) confirms this figure in his comment that in spite of the Plowden report's claim that many of the old beliefs about primary teaching had been 'blown away', only 4 per cent of schools had rejected streaming, which was in contradiction to the report's recommendations. This lack of change in teacher practice continued in spite of the fact that LEA teachers' centres and universities may have promoted progressive educational ideas. Alexander (1995: 258) recognised this when he spoke about the 'change in the collective culture of schools contrasting with continuity in the privacy of classrooms.' And he later voiced the view that

> English primary education in 2000 is nineteenth-century elementary education modified – much modified, admittedly – rather than transformed. Elementary education is its centre of gravity. Elementary education provides its central point of reference. Elementary education is the form to which it most readily tends to regress.
>
> (Alexander 2000: 147)

One of the most damaging aspects of this is the separation of core and foundation subjects which Alexander (2004) has called a crude '"basics" and the rest' curriculum which you saw was first statutorily implemented in the Revised Code of 1862.

A NEW PROGRESSIVISM: CREATIVITY

The period since the Education Reform Act 1988 which first established the concept of a National Curriculum has been a bleak time. Heavy prescription through the National Curriculum, National Strategies, testing, targets and league tables of test results have resulted in an impoverished curriculum. Amidst this stormy landscape, a lifeline emerged in the unexpected form of another government report.

The National Advisory Committee on Creative and Cultural Education (NACCCE) was established in February 1998 to make recommendations on the creative and cultural development of young people through formal and informal education. There were some powerful messages in the report:

> The real effect of the existing distinction between the core and foundation subjects now needs to be carefully assessed in the light of ten years' experience. It appears to have reduced the status of the arts and humanities and their effective impact in the school curriculum.
>
> (National Advisory Committee on Creative and Cultural Education 1999: 75)

As a way of reducing the curriculum content and addressing the neglect of subjects such as music and art the report recommended: 'In order to achieve parity, the existing distinction between core and foundation subjects should be removed' (p. 87). Unfortunately this recommendation was not followed when the National Curriculum 2000 was put into place. The NACCCE report seemed to strike a chord with many people in education who were deeply unhappy about the mechanistic and bloated curriculum that had been followed since 1988. In spite of overwhelming support for its message, politicians were not quick to act.

Excellence and Enjoyment: A Strategy for Primary Schools (Department for Education and Skills (DfES) 2003) subsumed the literacy and numeracy strategies and was the third major national strategy from the period between 1997 and 2003. It came on top of an unprecedented number of government interventions in primary education. In spite of teachers' feelings of 'intervention overload' it was anticipated keenly because of the growing consensus that educational policy in England was too prescriptive and that this was impacting negatively on creative teaching and creative learning. It was hoped that fundamental reforms might result in a more appropriate level of professional autonomy for teachers including the opportunity to teach more creatively with fewer constraints.

The primary strategy document does indeed include words like 'freedom' and 'empowerment' and, on page 18, for the first time after the executive summary, the word 'creativity' appears:

> 2.11 Some teachers question whether it is possible to exercise their curricular freedom, because of the priority the Government attaches to improving literacy and numeracy. But as OfSTED reports have shown, it is not a question of 'either', 'or'. Raising standards and making learning fun can and do go together. The best primary schools have developed timetables and teaching plans that combine creativity with strong teaching in the basics.
>
> (p. 18)

It is true that it is not impossible to teach creatively and to help children learn creatively in spite of government constraints but there is a more important consideration: is the primary strategy the *best* way to achieve creativity? Is it reasonable that government should place more responsibility on primary schools and teachers without admitting their own failure to ensure an appropriate balance to the curriculum since 1997?

The primary strategy fails to resolve the problems that have bedevilled the primary curriculum for a very long time. The continued place of the National Strategies is a case in point. There is no question that the frameworks for teaching from the National Literacy and Numeracy Strategies have added to the burden on the curriculum. However there are important differences between the two. The most significant difference is that the numeracy framework covers all the programmes of study for mathematics in the National Curriculum whereas the literacy framework only covers reading and writing; speaking and listening is mainly covered separately. The conceptual confusion of the literacy framework has also led to many more difficulties for teachers.

The Primary Strategy fudges the important question about the continued place of the literacy strategy in the primary curriculum. On the one hand we are told: 'The National Literacy and Numeracy

Strategies, though they are supported strongly, are *not statutory* and can be adapted to meet schools' particular needs'. (*op. cit.*p. 16, emphasis added) But on the other hand,

> The Literacy and Numeracy Strategies have, according to all those who have evaluated them, been strikingly successful at improving the quality of teaching and raising standards in primary schools. But we need to *embed the lessons of the National Literacy and Numeracy Strategies more deeply.*
>
> (*op cit.* p. 27, emphasis added)

The claim that the NLS Framework for Teaching has been called strikingly successful by all those who have evaluated it is totally unsubstantiated, even by the government's own evidence. The government commissioned a team from the University of Toronto to carry out an independent evaluation of the strategies; the first report was lukewarm at best about the impact of the pedagogy of the literacy strategy:

> Clearly it would be naïve to conclude that the instructional and other practices included in NLNS were the sole causes of the gains being made [in test results]. For example, as we have discussed in several other sections of this report:
> *   There is, at best, uneven evidence that such practices can be counted on to 'produce' numeracy and literacy gains;
>
> (Earl *et al.* 2000: 36)

The second report affirmed this position by the claim that 'the strategies themselves are a unique blend of practices whose effects, to our knowledge, have never been carefully tested in real field settings' (Earl *et al.*, 2001, p. 81). The idea that the literacy strategy has been completely successful is laid to rest in the final report: 'we recognise...that both strategies have been contentious' (Earl *et al.*, 2003, p. 34). Remarkably, even OfSTED who have relentlessly applied pressure on schools and universities to adopt the pedagogy of the NLS in the past, have recognised that all is not well and have prioritised as their first action point that government should 'Undertake a critical review of the NLS, paying particular attention to the clarity and usefulness of the framework as a tool for improving standards in literacy across the whole curriculum' (Office for Standards in Education (OfSTED) 2002: 4). This is something that I had argued for in a number of publications (Wyse 2000, 2001, 2003a; Wyse and Jones 2001).

The NLS Framework for Teaching is too prescriptive and hinders creativity. Evidence that government has responded to the growing complaints about the prescription in the curriculum is shown in the superficial changes of language evident in the Primary Strategy document but not in substantial action.

One of the most significant things to emerge following the NACCCE report was the Creative Partnerships initiative. The Department for Media, Culture and Sport (DMCS), Department for Education and Skills (DfES) and the Arts Council started funding Creative Partnerships in 2002. This released £110 million to support the development of 'creative learning' in approximately 900 primary and secondary schools in 36 areas of the country. The main aim has been to provide school children across England with the opportunity to develop creativity in learning and to take part in cultural activities of the highest quality.

To a certain extent the success of Creative Partnerships represents progressivism beginning to take hold of the curriculum once more. The idea of putting creativity at the heart of the curriculum by teaching more holistically, thematically and by breaking down the barriers of the core subjects in particular, is in some ways reminiscent of early periods of progressivism. You may even hear some cynics suggesting that this is just another example of ideas coming in and out of fashion. While this is partially true it fails to show understanding of the fact that this new creativity is built on a history of curriculum development and for that reason can never be identical to previous versions. Evidence of this is shown by Spendlove and Wyse (2005) whose research revealed teachers' complaints that even with the extra funding from Creative Partnerships the main barriers to creative teaching and learning were the statutory ones: the National Curriculum and the associated testing and inspection system.

Task 4.4.2
Thinking about national curricula

- What changes would you like to see made to the curriculum?
- What are your views about a subject-led curriculum?
- Has the emphasis on English and maths since 1997 been a reasonable one?
- In what ways are teachers developing a more creative curriculum?
- Which aspects of the curriculum are you excited about teaching? Which ones are you less confident about? What will you do to improve your confidence?

THE FUTURE OF THE PRIMARY CURRICULUM

One of the most important things about the curriculum in future is that the model needs to be relevant from the early years up to the end of schooling and should genuinely prepare students for higher education and lifelong learning. As we have seen in this unit the current model for early years differs from the model for primary years; the Literacy Strategy model differs from the Numeracy Strategy model. I propose the following curriculum model as a starting point for thinking about the curriculum (see Figure 4.4.1).

A curriculum model that reflects learning and teaching throughout life needs to put the individual's 'self' at the centre. It is the individual person's motivation to learn and their interests which will sustain learning throughout life. A new curriculum will need to encourage teaching which explicitly encourages pupils to find areas of work that motivate them and to pursue these in depth, even at the very earliest stages of education. Children's rights to participate in all matters that affect them should not be an abstract item in the programmes of study for citizenship but a daily reality in their lives (see Wyse 2003b for a discussion of the United Nations Convention on the Rights of the Child and the

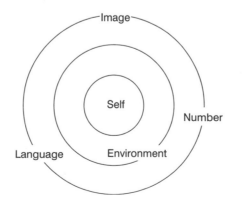

Figure 4.4.1 Proposed curriculum model

condemnation the UK's report received from the UN Committee on the Rights of the Child). Role play and drama will be a recurrent medium for reflecting on the self and others. Physical development including health will be nurtured as part of this focus.

The environment in which learning takes place is vital to sustain the self. In spite of futuristic claims about learning electronically from home, a place called school will still be the main arena for learning but it should be one that is not a grimy, damp, cold, boomy Victorian building: it should be architecturally inspiring. It should be a place where the crafts of life, such as the preparation and sharing of food and the performing of and listening to music, are centre stage. The social interaction provided by the home and community will form an integrated link with the social interaction provided by the school's curriculum. Sights, sounds and exploration of the world, beginning with the immediate surroundings, will form part of the environmental curriculum. Investigations will take place, problems will be solved, and things will be made. All of this will be set in the context of active participation in working towards a sustainable environmental future for the world.

Learning centred on images – both still and moving: icons; logos; signs; symbols – will no longer be neglected in view of the dominant role these things have in our daily lives, and which have done for many years. The counting and categorisation of entities ultimately leading to the beautiful abstraction of mathematical symbols will remain a powerful focus for learning about number. Language in all its linguistic contexts, including text and talk, will also remain a powerful focus and one which unites all other aspects of this curriculum.

Information Technology (IT) will not be a subject. Do we have P and P, or paper and pencils, as a subject in the curriculum? No. Information technology will be central to the work of schools just as any other basic resource is. It will not be used as the latest solution to all our problems but it will whenever appropriate enrich the possibilities for learning and teaching, and its natural influence will continue to grow.

Is my suggestion that we abandon the current subject dominated core/foundation curriculum particularly radical? Not really. As one example of practice, the Royal Society for the Encouragement of Arts, Manufactures and Commerce (RSA) has been working with schools developing their 'Opening Minds' curriculum for a number of years. Opening Minds is a curriculum that more than 500 schools have trialled. It is not based on subjects but a series of 'competences' that students are expected to acquire through curriculum content decided by schools. The RSA's conference in 2005 asked the question 'How special are subjects?' (RSA 2005; Wyse 2005). There was strong agreement from nearly all participants and speakers that not only were other models practically possible but also there was an urgent need for changes to be made to the National Curriculum. As another example of alternative curricula, the primary curriculum developed by the International Baccalaureate Organisation (IBO) organises its curriculum around six themes. Consider, also, higher education which offers hundreds of subjects, and continues to add new ones, that combine a range of understanding and skills which would benefit from preparation by a different curriculum model in schools. However, the reason that these changes have not been made before, and why the curriculum is still entrenched in the nineteenth century, is that it requires our political leaders to have the knowledge, understanding and courage to change legislation and revolutionise the primary education system in order to bring it into the twenty-first century.

Task 4.4.3
Looking at different models of the curriculum

Look at a curriculum model that is different from the National Curriculum such as the IBO primary curriculum available from http://www.ibo.org/. Discuss the similarities and differences, and agree some changes that you would like to see made to the National Curriculum as a result of your consideration of alternatives.

SUMMARY

In this unit we have discussed the aims of the curriculum at the Foundation and Key Stages 1 and 2 together with understanding how teachers make professional decisions about the curriculum for their pupils. It is recommended therefore that you build on these discussions by reading the two articles and one book recommended below in the annotated further reading in order to widen your knowledge and understanding of the primary school curriculum.

ANNOTATED FURTHER READING

Alexander, R. J. (2004) 'Still no pedagogy? Principle, pragmatism and compliance in primary education', *Cambridge Journal of Education*, 34(1): 7–33. Robin Alexander has made an important contribution to the field of primary education and this paper summarises a number of important themes which he has developed through his research.

Bayliss, V., Bastiani, J., Cross, M., James, L. and Wyse, B. (2003) *Opening Minds: Taking Stock*, London: Royal Society for the Encouragement of Arts, Manufactures and Commerce. An evaluation of a small sample of the schools who have used the RSA's Opening Minds curriculum. Shows how it can be done in practice and some of the potential pitfalls.

Kelly, A. V. (2004) *The Curriculum: Theory and Practice*, 5th edition, London: Sage. An excellent overview of issues which combines comprehensive definitions with necessary political analysis. The comments about the increase in political interference with the curriculum revealed through the author's reflections about the five editions of this book are fascinating.

REFERENCES

Alexander, R.J. (ed.) (1995) *Versions of Primary Education*, London: Routledge.

Alexander, R.J. (2000) *Culture and Pedagogy: International Comparisons in Primary Education*, Oxford: Blackwell.

Alexander, R.J. (2004) 'Still no pedagogy? Principle, pragmatism and compliance in primary education', *Cambridge Journal of Education*, 34(1): 7–33.

Bayliss, V., Bastiani, J., Cross, M., James, L. and Wyse, B. (2003) *Opening Minds: Taking Stock*, London: Royal Society for the Encouragement of Arts, Manufactures and Commerce.

Cunningham, P. (2002) 'Progressivism, decentralisation and recentralisation: local education authorities and the primary curriculum, 1902–2002', *Oxford Review of Education*, 28(2–3): 217–33.

Curtis, S.J. and Boultwood, M.E.A. (1964) *An Introductory History of English Education since 1800*, 3rd edition, London: University Tutorial Press.

Department for Education and Skills (DfES) (2003) *Excellence and Enjoyment: A Strategy for Primary Schools*, Suffolk: DfES.

Earl, L., Fullan, M., Leithwood, K., Watson, N., Jantzi, D., Levin, B., *et al.* (2000) *Watching and Learning: OISE/UT Evaluation of the Implementation of the National Literacy and Numeracy Strategies*, Nottingham: DfEE Publications.

Earl, L., Fullan, M., Leithwood, K., Watson, N., Jantzi, D., Levin, B., *et al.* (2001) *Watching and Learning 2: OISE/UT Evaluation of the Implementation of the National Literacy and Numeracy Strategies*, Nottingham: DfEE Publications.

Earl, L., Watson, N., Levin, B., Leithwood, K., Fullan, M., Torrance, N., *et al.* (2003) *Watching and Learning: OISE/UT Evaluation of the Implementation of the National Literacy and Numeracy Strategies*, Nottingham: DfES Publications.

Haviland, J. (1988) *Take Care, Mr Baker!* London: Fourth Estate.

Kelly, A.V. (2004) *The Curriculum: Theory and Practice*, 5th edition, London: Sage.

National Advisory Committee on Creative and Cultural Education (1999) *All Our Futures: Creativity, Culture and Education*, Suffolk: DfEE Publications.

Office for Standards in Education (OfSTED) (2002) *The National Literacy Strategy: The First Four Years 1998–2002*, London: OfSTED.

QCA/DfES (2000) *Curriculum Guidance for the Foundation Stage*, London: QCA Publications.

Royal Society for the Encouragement of Arts, Manufactures and Commerce (RSA) (2005) *How Special are Subjects? Are They the Best Way to Structure a Curriculum or Can We Do Better?* London: Creative Partnerships/RSA.

Simpson, D. (1996) 'Progressivism and the development of primary education: an historical review', *History of Education Society Bulletin*, 58 (Autumn): 55–63.

Spendlove, D. and Wyse, D. (2005) 'Definitions and barriers: perspectives on creative learning', Paper presented at the Documenting Creative Learning symposium, 23 April, University of Cambridge.

White, J. (ed.) (2004) *Rethinking the School Curriculum: Values, Aims and Purposes*, London: Routledge Falmer.

Wyse, D. (1998) *Primary Writing*, Buckingham: Open University Press.

Wyse, D. (2000) 'Phonics – the whole story? A critical review of empirical evidence', *Educational Studies*, 26(3): 355–64.

Wyse, D. (2001) 'Grammar. For writing? A critical review of empirical evidence', *British Journal of Educational Studies*, 49(4): 411–27.

Wyse, D. (2003a) 'The National Literacy Strategy: a critical review of empirical evidence', *British Educational Research Journal*, 29(6): 903–16.

Wyse, D. (ed.) (2003b) *Introduction to Childhood Studies*, Oxford: Basil Blackwell.

Wyse, D. (2005) 'Two tears for the primary curriculum', Paper presented at the How Special are Subjects? conference, 6 April, Royal Society for the Encouragement of Arts, Manufactures and Commerce (RSA), London.

Wyse, D. and Jones, R. (2001) *Teaching, English, Language and Literacy*, London: RoutledgeFalmer.

5 Recent Developments in Primary Education

Unit 5.1

Creativity in the Curriculum

Teresa Grainger and Jonathan Barnes

INTRODUCTION

> The more prescriptive a curriculum, the greater the need to be explicit about creativity and not leave it to chance.
>
> (Design Council in NACCCE 1999: 83)

> Teachers and school leaders have to recognise that the development of creativity in pupils is an essential part of their job, and that an appropriate climate has to be established.
>
> (OFSTED 2003: 11)

These two quotations indicate the need for the profession to attend to the creative development of the young and to avoid viewing creativity as merely the latest educational bandwagon or yet another thing to add to schools' lists of priorities. In a world dominated by technological innovations, creativity is a critical component; human skills and people's powers of creativity and imagination are key resources in a knowledge-driven economy (Robinson 2001), and as social structures continue to change, the ability to live with uncertainty and deal with complexity is essential. So organisations and governments all over the world are now more concerned than ever to promote creativity (Craft 2001, 2005). It develops the kinds of skills that young people need in a rapidly changing and uncertain world and it can improve their self-esteem, motivation and achievement.

Creativity is now positioned more centrally in the curriculum; 'creative development' is named as an Early Learning Goal in the Foundation Stage curriculum (DfEE 2000)and 'creative thinking' as a key skill in the NC (DfEE 1999). In addition, explorations of creative teaching and teaching for creativity are growing in number (see for example Jeffrey and Woods 2003; Jeffery and Craft 2004; Grainger *et al*. 2004) and teachers themselves are seeking innovative ways of shaping the curriculum in response to children's needs, statutory requirements and the creativity agenda.

However, working with an overloaded curriculum in a culture of accountability, you are no doubt already aware that the backwash of the assessment system markedly affects classroom practice. Such pressure can limit opportunities for creative endeavour and may tempt you to stay within the safe boundaries of the known, offering a curriculum largely framed and developed by others, rather than one framed and developed by you in response to your children's needs and interests. Recognising the tension between the incessant drive for measurable standards and the development of creative teaching is a good starting point, but finding the energy and enterprise to respond flexibly to this reality is the real challenge. In order to do so, you need to be convinced that creativity has an important role to play in education and realise that you can contribute to the shifting agenda both personally and professionally. You may also need to widen your understanding of creativity and creative practice in order to teach creatively and teach for creativity.

OBJECTIVES

By the end of this unit you should have:

- an increased understanding about the nature of creativity;
- an awareness of some of the features of creative primary teachers;
- a wider understanding of teaching for creativity;
- some understanding of how to plan for creative learning.

CREATIVE PRACTICE

The class is full of focused learners, whose voices express urgency and interest as they collaborate in groups to create three-dimensional representations of two Egyptian gods. Earlier that morning, at this primary school in Northampton, these six- and seven-year-olds had discussed the many options available to them, generated ideas and listened to others and were now in the process of turning these into action. They operated independently of their teacher, finding resources in their own room or in others, monitoring their achievements in the time available (they knew they would have at least one more session to complete this challenge), and constantly evaluating and discussing their work. The groups created a wide variety of representations, and new ideas that emerged during the creative process were also added, celebrated and critically appraised. Later in this half term's unit of work on the Egyptians, the children wrote instructions for making these images and added them to their huge class book, which also contained DVDs of the various cross-curricular activities undertaken and showed the total transformation of their classroom into an Egyptian museum. However, their ability to recall, explain, and discuss the finer points of this creatively planned and executed project two terms later was an even richer testimony to the excellence, enjoyment and learning achieved by all.

In this school, as in many others recently, the staff have been working to adopt a more creative approach to the primary curriculum and have placed creative teaching and learning at the heart of their practice. Influenced by an understanding of the nature of creativity, by government documents which encourage a more flexible stance (DfES 2003), by HMI reports which highlight the significant achievements of creative schools (OfSTED 2003) and by involvement in creative partnerships of many kinds, teachers are increasingly finding more innovative ways of teaching primary school children and are planning more explicitly to develop children's creativity.

SO WHAT IS CREATIVITY?

Creativity is not confined to special people or to particular arts-based activities, nor is it undisciplined play. It is however, notoriously difficult to define. It has been described as 'a state of mind in which all our intelligences are working together'…involving 'seeing, thinking and innovating' (Craft 2000: 38) and as 'imaginative activity fashioned so as to produce outcomes that are both original and of value' (NACCCE 1999: 29). Creativity is possible wherever human intelligence is actively engaged and is an essential part of an effective education: it includes all curriculum subjects and all children, as well as teachers and others working in primary education. Indeed it can be demonstrated by anyone in any aspect of life, throughout life.

It is useful to distinguish between high creativity and ordinary creativity, between 'Big C Creativity' (exemplified in some of Gardner's (1993) studies of highly creative individuals, such as Picasso, Einstein and Freud), and 'little c creativity' which Craft (2000, 2001) highlights. This latter form focuses on the individual agency and resourcefulness of ordinary people to innovate and take action. Csikszentmihalyi suggests that each of us is born with two contradictory sets of instructions: a conservative tendency and an expansive tendency, but warns us that

> If too few opportunities for curiosity are available, if too many obstacles are put in the way of risk and exploration, the motivation to engage in creative behaviour is easily extinguished.
>
> (Csikszentmihalyi 1996: 11)

In the context of the classroom, developing opportunities for children to 'possibility think' their way forwards is therefore critical (Craft 2001). This will involve you in immersing the class in an issue or subject and helping the children ask questions, take risks, be imaginative and playfully explore options as well as innovate. At the core of such creative endeavour is the child's self determination and agency as an active thinker to find and solve problems. From this perspective, creativity is not seen as an event or a product (although it may involve either or both), but a process or a state of mind involving the serious play of ideas and possibilities. This generative, problem finding/problem solving process may involve rational and non-rational thought and may be fed by the intuitive, by daydreaming and pondering, as well as by the application of knowledge and skills. In order to be creative children do need considerable knowledge in a domain, but 'creativity and knowledge are two sides of the same psychological coin, not opposing forces' (Boden 2001: 102) and imaginatively enrich each other.

Imaginative activity can take many forms; it draws on a more varied range of human functioning than linear, logical and rational patterns of behaviour (Claxton 1997). It is essentially generative and may include physical, social, reflective, musical, aural or visual thinking, involving children in activities which produce new and unusual connections between ideas, domains, processes and materials. When children and their teachers step outside the boundaries of predictability and are physically engaged, learning through their minds and bodies, eyes and ears, this provides a balance to the sedentary and, too often, abstract nature of school education. In less conventional contexts, new insights and connections may be made through analogy and metaphor. The two modes of creative thinking, the 'imaginative-generative' mode which produces outcomes, and the 'critical-evaluative' mode which involves consideration of originality and value (NACCCE 1999: 30), both operate in close inter-relationship and need to be consciously developed in the classroom.

Claxton and Lucas (2004) suggest that the process of creativity involves the ability to move freely between the different layers of our memories to find solutions to problems. They propose a metaphor of the mind based on the concept of three layers of memory which impact upon our thinking: an upper layer or *habit map*, a map of repeated patterns of behaviour; an *inner layer* comprising individual conscious and unconscious memories; and an *archetypal layer* laid down by our genes. Others see the creative mind as one which looks for unexpected likenesses and connections between disparate domains (Koestler 1964; Bronowski 1976). Csikszentmihalyi (1996) suggests, however, that creativity does not happen inside people's heads, but in the interaction between an individual's thoughts and the socio-cultural context.

It is clear that creativity is not bound to particular subjects. Indeed, it depends in part on interactions between feeling and thinking across different subject boundaries and ideas. It also depends upon a climate of trust, respect and support, an environment in which individual agency and self determination are fostered, and ideas and interests are valued, discussed and celebrated. Yet we have all experienced schools that fail to teach the pleasure and excitement to be found in science or mathematics for example, or who let routines and timetables, subject boundaries and decontextualised knowledge dominate the daily diet of the young. In such sterile environments when formulae for learning are relied upon and curriculum packages are delivered, children's ability to make connections and to imagine alternatives is markedly reduced. So too is their capacity for curiosity, for enquiry and for creativity itself.

Task 5.1.1
Reflecting on ownership and control in learning

Relevance, ownership and control of learning, as well as innovation, have all been identified as key issues in creative teaching and learning in children (Jeffrey and Woods, 2003). Imaginative approaches involve individuals and groups in initiating questions and lines of enquiry so that they are more in charge of their work; such collaboration and interaction helps to develop a greater sense of autonomy in the events which unfold.

To what extent have you observed children taking control of their learning, making choices, and demonstrating ownership of their own learning? Think of some examples and share these in small groups. To what extent was the work also relevant to the children? Were they emotionally or imaginatively engaged, building on areas of interest, maintaining their individuality and sharing ideas with one another? If you have seen little evidence of these issues, consider how you could offer more opportunity for relevance, ownership and control of learning in the classroom.

CREATIVE TEACHING AND TEACHING FOR CREATIVITY

The distinction between creative teaching and teaching for creativity may be a helpful one in that it is possible to imagine a creative teacher who personally enters creatively into the classroom context, yet fails to provide for children's creative learning.

Responsible creative professionals are not necessarily flamboyant performers, but teachers who use a range of approaches to create the conditions in which the creativity of others can flourish. Creative teachers also make use of their own creativity, not just to interest and engage the learners, but also to promote new thinking and learning. Their confidence in their own creativity will enable them to offer the children stronger scaffolds and spaces for emotional and intellectual growth.

Research undertaken in an HE context, with tutors teaching music, geography and English, suggests that creative teaching is a complex art form, a veritable 'cocktail party'(Grainger, *et al.* 2004). The host gathers the ingredients (the session content), and mixes them playfully and skilfully (the teaching style), in order to facilitate a creative party that is enjoyable and worthwhile (the learning experience). Whilst no formula was, or could be established for creative teaching, some of the ingredients for personally mixing a creative cocktail were identified, albeit tentatively, from this work. It is clear, however, that the elements are not in themselves necessarily creative, but that the action of creatively shaking and stirring the ingredients and the individual experience of those attending are critical if the 'cocktail party' is to be successful. The intention to promote creative learning appeared to be an important feature in this work.

The session content (the cocktail ingredients), included the themes of placing current trends in a wider context and extensive use of metaphor, analogy and personal anecdotes to make connections. The teaching style (the mixing of the cocktail), included the themes of multimodal pedagogic practices, pace, humour, the confidence of the tutors and their ability to inspire and value the students. In relation to the learning experience (the cocktail party), the themes included involving the students affectively and physically and challenging them to engage and reflect. Together these represent some of the critical features of creative teachers and creative teaching which combine to support new thinking.

Task 5.1.2
Is teaching a kind of cocktail party?

Consider the metaphor of teaching as cocktail party for a moment. In what ways do you think this metaphor captures the vitality of teaching, the dynamic interplay between teachers, children and the resources available? Select one or two of the features, for example, humour or use of metaphor or personal anecdotes. Do you make extensive use of either of these features? Remember as the research indicates, such features need to be employed with others in a flexible experiential encounter at the 'cocktail party'.

Consider your current tutors or previous teachers. Which are/were the most creative teachers? Do they/did they create successful cocktail parties in which you felt valued and were given the space to engage fully, to take risks, make connections and develop deep learning? How do/did they achieve this?

PERSONAL CHARACTERISTICS OF CREATIVE TEACHERS

It is difficult to identify with any certainty the personal characteristics of creative teachers, although common elements observed in research studies and commented upon by writers in the field (e.g. Jones and Wyse 2004; Craft, 2003; Beetlestone, 1998; Csikszentmihalyi, 1996; Fryer 1996) include the following:

- enthusiasm, passion and commitment;
- risk-taking;
- a clear set of personal values;
- willingness to be intuitive and/or introspective;
- gregariousness and introspectiveness;
- a deep curiosity or questioning stance;
- awareness of self as a creative being.

This list encompasses many of the personal qualities you might expect in any good teacher, except perhaps the last. As Sternberg (1999) suggests, creative teachers are creative role models themselves; such professionals continue to be self-motivated learners, who value the creative dimensions of their own lives and make connections between their personal responses to experience and their teaching. In addition, a clear set of values, reflecting fair-mindedness, openness to evidence, a desire for clarity, and respect for others are important and among the attitudinal qualities embedded in creative teaching. So too is a commitment to inclusion, a belief in human rights and equality. Such attitudes and values have a critical role in creative teaching and are perhaps best taught by example.

FEATURES OF A CREATIVE PEDAGOGICAL STANCE

The intention to promote creativity is fundamental; you will need to place children in situations which help them make connections and then build on these, creating a climate of enquiry, of ideas and of sensible risk-taking. You will also need to plan to develop their independence and ability to work as a community. There are a number of features of a creative pedagogical stance which you may want to consider in relation to your teaching and observation of other creative professionals.

A learner-centred ethos

Creative teachers tend to place the learners above the curriculum and combine a positive disposition towards creativity and person-centred teaching which actively promotes pupils who learn and think for themselves (Craft 2000). Relaxed, trusting educator–learner relationships exist in creative classrooms and the role of the affect and children's feelings play a central role in learning in such contexts. A creative ethos will also involve you showing patience and openness and reinforcing children's creative behaviour, celebrating difference, diversity and innovation as well as learning to tolerate mild or polite rebellion (Gardner 1999). If you adopt such a person-centred orientation you will be shaping the children's self-esteem and enhancing their intrinsic motivation and agency.

A questioning stance

Creativity involves asking and attempting to answer real questions. The creative teacher is seen by many writers as one who uses open questions and who promotes speculation in the classroom encouraging deeper understanding and lateral thinking. In the context of creative teaching, both teachers and children need to be involved in this process of imaginative thinking, encompassing the generation of challenging and unusual questions and the creation of possible responses (Cremin 2004).

Creating space, time and freedom to make connections

Creativity requires space, time and a degree of freedom. Deep immersion in an area or activity allows options to remain open, and persistence and follow-through to develop. Conceptual space allows children to converse, challenge and negotiate meanings and possibilities together. In recent Primary National Strategy research, teachers worked with more extended and coherent units of work, and through employing both film and drama raised both standards and boys' creativity in writing (Bearne *et al.* 2004).

Employing multimodal teaching approaches

A variety of multimodal teaching approaches and frequent switching between modes in a play-like and spontaneous manner supports creative learning. The diversity of pattern, rhythm and pace used by creative teachers is particularly marked (e.g. Woods 1995), as is their use of informed intuition. As you teach, opportunities will arise to use your intuition and move from the security of the known; give yourself permission to go beyond the 'script' you have planned, allow the children to take the initiative and lead you. Afterwards consider the effect of this more responsive approach: did the children exert their autonomy, were they more fully engaged and intrinsically motivated?

Prompting full engagement, ownership and ongoing reflection

In studying an area in depth, children should experience both explicit instruction and space for exploration and discovery. Try to provide opportunities for choice and be prepared to spend some time developing their self-management skills so they are able to operate independently. Their full engagement can be prompted through appealing to their own interests and passions, by involving them in imaginative experiences, and by connecting learning to their lives (Grainger *et al.* 2005). You will find that as the children realise their questions make a difference, they will begin to ask more, ponder longer and reflect upon other ways to achieve a task or represent their learning. A semi-constant oscillation between engagement and reflection will become noticeable in the classroom as you work to refine, reshape and improve learning. The ability to give and receive criticism is also an essential part of creativity and you will need to encourage evaluation through supportive and honest feedback.

Modelling risk-taking and enabling the children to take risks too

The ability to tolerate ambiguity is an example of the 'confident uncertainty' to which Claxton (1997) refers when discussing creative teachers, those who combine subject and pedagogical knowledge, but also leave space for uncertainty and the unknown. You will gain in confidence through increased subject knowledge, through experience and reflection, but your assurance will also grow through taking risks and having a go at expressing yourself. Risk-taking is an integral element of creativity, and one which you will want to model and foster. The children too will need to feel supported as they take risks in safe non-judgemental contexts.

To be a creative practitioner you will need more than a working knowledge of prescribed curriculum requirements. You will need a secure pedagogical understanding and strong subject knowledge, supported by a passionate belief in the potential of creative teaching to engage, inspire and educate. Such teaching depends in the end upon the human interaction between teacher and student and is also influenced by the environment

CREATING ENVIRONMENTS OF POSSIBILITY

You may have been to a school where creativity is planned for, where there is a clear sense of shared values and often a real buzz of purposeful and exciting activity. Such schools have a distinctive character which impacts upon general behaviour, relationships, physical environment and curriculum. An ethos which values creativity will, according to most definitions, promote originality and the use of the imagination, and encourage an adventurous attitude to life and learning. In such environments of possibility, packed with ideas and experiences, resources and choices, as well as time for relaxation and rumination, physical, conceptual and emotional space is offered.

The social and emotional environment

Taking creative risks and moving forward in learning is heavily dependent upon an atmosphere of genuine acceptance and security. As Halpin notes,

> pupils [should be able to] feel confident enough to take risks and learn from failure instead of being branded by it. ...they should react positively to self help questions like: 'Am I safe here?' 'Do I belong?' 'Can I count on others to support me?'
>
> (Halpin 2003: 111)

The sense of well-being which offers a positive answer to these questions is promoted in creative schools by respecting individuals and involving children in activities which affirm both their individuality and their common humanity. Children's well-being now forms an important part of school self-evaluation (OFSTED 2004), school inspection requirements (DfES 2005) and the guidance related to the Children Act (HM Government 2005). A secure ethos in the context of the creative school may, however, display apparently contradictory characteristics. It is likely to be at the same time:

- highly active and relaxed;
- supportive and challenging;
- confident and speculative;
- playful and serious;
- focused and fuzzy;
- individualistic and communal;
- understood personally and owned by all;
- non-competitive and ambitious.

Since Plato, many have argued that there are links between involvement in creative acts and a general sense of well-being. More recent research in cognitive neuroscience (Damasio 2003) and positive psychology (Seligman 2004; Fredrickson 2003) has suggested that simply feeling 'happy' promotes optimum conditions in both mind and body, and also ensures constructive and secure relationships. This has led some to make arguments for a thorough re-evaluation of curricula, in favour of educational programmes which offer frequent, planned and progressive creative opportunities across every discipline (Barnes 2005; see also Unit 4.2).

The physical environment

The physical environment in a school which promotes creativity is likely to celebrate achievement and individuality. Jeffrey and Woods (2003) have shown it can affect every aspect of the environment which is not only stimulating, but is also a valuable teaching resource. Children's views on this are important and deserve to be taken into account (Burke and Grosvenor 2003). Recent projects have shown how creative thinking in the context of focused work on improving the school building, grounds or local areas, can achieve major citizenship objectives and high level arts and literacy targets in an atmosphere of genuine support and community concern (Barnes 2005).

Active modes of learning and problem solving approaches which include independent investigation require accessible resources of various kinds, so the richer and more multifaceted a range you can offer the better. This supports genuine choice, speculation and experimentation, happy accidents and flexibility. As well as good quality equipment and resources for each discipline, schools may want to 'collect' the following:

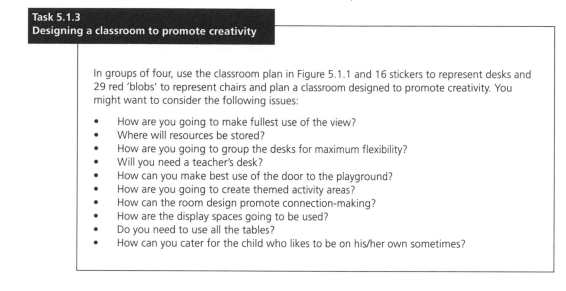

Task 5.1.3
Designing a classroom to promote creativity

In groups of four, use the classroom plan in Figure 5.1.1 and 16 stickers to represent desks and 29 red 'blobs' to represent chairs and plan a classroom designed to promote creativity. You might want to consider the following issues:

- How are you going to make fullest use of the view?
- Where will resources be stored?
- How are you going to group the desks for maximum flexibility?
- Will you need a teacher's desk?
- How can you make best use of the door to the playground?
- How are you going to create themed activity areas?
- How can the room design promote connection-making?
- How are the display spaces going to be used?
- Do you need to use all the tables?
- How can you cater for the child who likes to be on his/her own sometimes?

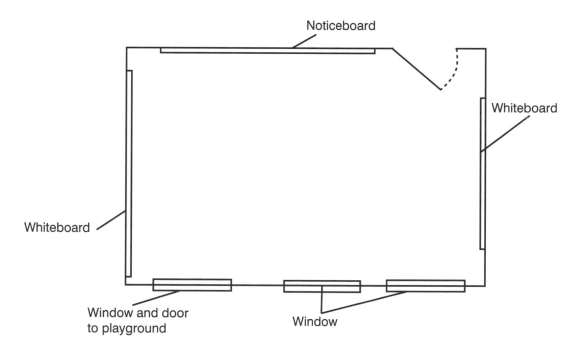

Figure 5.1.1   Constructing a 'thinking classroom'

- objects (like crockery, etchings, machines and containers) chosen to suggest links between subjects;
- games and toys (commercial or home-made) to add amusement, challenge and variety;
- items (like religious objects, fabrics, art and craft, foods, plants) representing the range of cultures in school and society;
- tools and artefacts (e.g. mystery objects from the local museum service) to encourage deeper thinking;
- creative professionals (like hairdressers, architects, artists, town planners, website designers, advertisers, window dressers) from the community willing to work with pupils;
- tools (such as those used by geography, maths, ICT, science and D/T) which promote the use of hands and bodies;
- products which reflect current technologies;
- communications technologies to aid understanding and engagement.

PLANNING FOR CREATIVITY

The NC, with its reminders about linking subjects and programmes of study, is open to imaginative interpretation, and can support cross-curricular planning and creative practice across Foundation and KS1 and 2. Recent documentation from the government in England clearly promotes a broader approach to curriculum planning, supporting not only excellence and enjoyment, but also transferable learning, creativity and confidence (DfES 2003). Such a holistic approach needs to build on insights from research if it is to ensure progression and raise standards.

Ten suggestions from research

- Create a *positive*, *secure* and *comfortable* atmosphere (Bentley and Seltzer 1999);
- ensure a range of *practical, creative* and *analytical* activities for each child (Sternberg 1997);
- have *clear goals* and individualised targets a little above current ability (Csikszentmihalyi 2002);
- use a manageable number of *relevant subjects* to throw light on the topic (Gardner 1999);
- build *emotionally significant links* to the life of each child, engage all the senses and use tools and objects to support and promote thinking (Woods 1995; Damasio 2003);
- involve developmentally appropriate *progression* in skills, knowledge and understanding (Thompson *et al.* 2004);
- refer to a wider framework which includes *concepts, content* and *attitudes* (Grainger *et al.* 2004);
- emphasise individual and cooperative *thinking* and *learning* throughout (Bruner 1996; Craft 2000);
- provide supportive *assessment* procedures which build security and include time and tools for reflection (Adey and Shayer 2002);
- offer a wide range of opportunities to discover *engagement, enjoyment* and other *positive emotions* (Fredrickson 2000, 2003).

Key Stage 1 teachers have generally retained a cross-curricular element in their planning; those in Key Stage 2 are now considering the advantages of more creative curriculum approaches. Many now plan coherent learning experiences where 'school subjects [are seen as] resources in the construction of the curriculum, rather than determinants of its overall structure and emphasis' (Halpin 2003: 114).

They plan in teams and maximise the relevance of their curriculum to the local community and the children's lives, using the rich physical, human and cultural resources of their locality and preparing significant shared experiences for children to interpret in individualised ways.

Teachers are also beginning to work from the Key Skills and the thinking skills at the front of the NC, perceiving these to offer the permission and structure needed to support medium-term planning for creativity. Their challenge, like yours, is to take account of individual differences in learning, help each child become a self-regulated learner, and ensure appropriate coverage of subject-specific content. The curriculum map (Figure 5.1.2) is one attempt to balance these demands. As a medium-term plan it seeks to combine guidance from research with the detailed expectations of the NC. It builds upon the Key Skills, namely:

- communication;
- application of number;
- information technology;
- working with others;
- improving own learning and performance;
- problem solving.

It highlights the thinking skills identified in the NC, namely:

- information processing;
- reasoning;
- enquiry;
- creative thinking;
- evaluation.

It also takes into account other cross-curricular aspects, such as:

- financial capability;
- enterprise education;
- education for sustainable development;
- PSHE/citizenship;
- statement of values.

INTEGRATING THE KEY SKILLS

Classrooms in which the Key Skills are explored through subjects are characterised by activity, security, inclusivity and the equal treatment of different ways of understanding. At different times there could be different centres within the room where children can develop an idea musically, physically, spatially, socially or practically on their own or in groups. Allowing children to work on a given theme in their areas of strength promotes connections as different groups make and share links between the subject disciplines and real life experience.

Communication

Reading, writing, speaking and listening should be encouraged in meaningful contexts across all school experience, but there are many other means of communication. We communicate multimodally through

Theme	What's the problem? (Problem solving skills)	How can we organise it? (Working with others)	How is it going to help children's learning? (Improving own learning)	How are we going to include opportunities for maths? (Application of number)	How am I going to help my children see themselves as thinkers? (Thinking skills)	How am I going to use ICT? (Information technology)
A visit to the site of the new bypass						
Art making close-up drawings of small aspects of the site and then make them into giant abstract paintings	We've got to plan an exhibition of our half term's work on the new road	Group sculpture Group installation Group display	Reflection: What do I think worked best? Critical evaluations looking for ways to improve	Framing pictures, allocating resources by weight (e.g. clay) Scaling up and down	Creative thinking: 'How can I make this drawing into a giant painting?'	Creating titles using MS Word, modified photography/video as background information for display
Design/Technology making a model of the new road	We've got to make a model of our ideas for making the bypass less ugly	Group projects based upon a model of the new road	Identifying refinements/applications. Thinking about different people's points of view	Scale drawing Measuring components Measured designs	Reasoning and enquiry thinking: What do different people think? What would improve this place?	Recording using digital camera
English using the road to generate a debate/writing a road story	We've got to work out the pros and cons of building a bypass around our village	Questionnaires Group evaluations Debates Role play	'What would happen if...?'; 'Are there any other ways this can be done?' and 'What will it be like when...?'	Using numbers to make the arguments, numbers of people affected, traffic, animals etc.	Information processing, evaluation thinking: What do we think about this issue?	Word processing Stimulus material from the web
Work in the school locality for the school website						
Geography discovering what the locality is like now	We have to prepare an introduction to our local area for the school website	Field work Role play an issue related to change in the locality Group map making	What do different kinds of people think of living here? What are the problems? What are the benefits?	Mapping Traffic survey Using maps at different scales Making graphs	Creative thinking: How can we represent this area on a map? Enquiry thinking: What do we like/dislike about our locality?	Current information from the www CD ROM/GIS satellite images and packages like DigitalWorlds
History finding out about the locality in the past	We have to make a history page for the school website	Class discussion on issue in history, e.g. Separate Girls and Boys entrance.	Imagine what it was like then. Consider different perspectives	Presenting of numerical data. Comparing dimensions of school hall/classrooms with old plans	Information processing: deciding on which information to include and which to leave out	Making links to Census and other historical information on web, collect and evaluate different sources
Mathematics presenting the facts and figures about the locality	We've got to present statistics about the local area for our project	Teams challenged to make the clearest graph	'What are we going to need to think about if this graph is to be clear?'	Applying number to real situations	Creative thinking: new presentation ideas Information processing	Using calculators, different measures, collecting data
Modern foreign language making the school website attractive to people from other countries	Designing a welcome page for visitors from other European countries	Role play in foreign language	Appreciating the perspective of outsiders	Counting in foreign languages, simple mathematical problems in French, Spanish or German	Evaluation: Why might this be a good thing?	Translators Foreign sites Background information on the web CD ROM packages
Work in the school grounds to find and investigate mini beasts						
Music making music to accompany a mini beast film	Our film needs music which help people understand the life and wonder of tiny creatures	Group composition, children work in groups to make music for slugs, ants, woodlice, centipedes etc.	How can we make this more surprising, how can we use patterns, silence, symmetry in our music? How could we improve it?	Beats in a bar Number patterns in music (Gamelan) Drumming patterns Repeating patterns	Creative thinking: using sound to represent animate objects	Digital keyboards Altered environmental sounds using CD, Mini disc, video DVD on insect life Making own video
Physical education making a mini beast dance, movement or body sculpture	We have to make a dance or movement on the theme of insects	Group planning and performance of dance/movement routines. Group decisions on body sculpture	Negotiating movement/dance decisions, evaluating/planning improvements	Numbered sequences e.g. dance movements Sale of tickets to performances	Creative thinking: using body movements and shape to suggest mini beast movement and life	Use of music examples from the web or CD/video of skills/stimulus Make DVD of final product
Religious education asking the big questions	Thinking about the significance of the natural world. Expressing feelings in poems, lists, music or painting	Paired discussion, 'Why do you think God made insects?' Are there any things we can't see?	Thinking about the purpose/sustainability/quality of life issues. The seen and unseen world	Significant numbers, 3, 7, 12 Numbers in nature	Reasoning: asking the why question Evaluation: asking why this is valuable	Stimulus for reflection, other cultures views on insects (eg San ('Bushmen') and the Mantis) Record reflections for DVD
Science finding out about classification, mini beast life and sustainability	We want to find out more about mini beasts' habitats, life cycles, food and how we can classify them	Individual group responses to various Science problems: classification, preferred habitats, life cycle, food	Making and testing hypotheses	Fibonacci series, numbers in natural objects, petals, leaves, sea shells, classification. Moral considerations	Information processing, reasoning, enquiry, evaluation: all involved	Variety of life. Take close up photos and video footage of insects in their habitat

Figure 5.1.2 An example of a curriculum map

play, pictures and symbols, music, number, dance and mime, in facial expressions and body language. Schools can maximise upon alternative modes of communication by offering children different ways to present their learning; understanding in PE may be better communicated in movement, for example, or in history by an exhibition of artefacts.

Application of number

Number is one of the languages through which children can understand curriculum themes. In topics centred on design/technology, art and PE they can practically apply concepts of weight, measurement, symmetry and balance. In geography and history, distance, graphs, statistics, scale and time are keys to understanding the wider world. A theme illuminated by the perspectives of music, RE, MFL, English or science may need number to help children understand sonic, spiritual, linguistic and natural patterns around them.

Information technology

The challenge is to ensure that ICT supports the progressive development of skills, knowledge and understanding across the curriculum. A class in rural Kent for example, used digital cameras to record significant aspects of their locality and classified these into four categories: 'natural life', 'our historic environment', 'working in our village' and 'what's changing?'. The development of their understanding could be traced in the discussions, selections and poster presentations which accompanied this activity. In other contexts, teachers use digital sound technology and the internet to provide children with opportunities to make new connections.

Working with others

Groupwork on real-life, curriculum-based challenges can help to develop emotional literacy. The capacity to relate, to empathise and experience both leadership and 'followership', as well as cope with disputes and disappointments are all evident in real group work where pupils need to cooperate fully in order to achieve their goals.

Improving own learning and performance

Reflection has been shown to make a marked influence on learning. In general, questions like 'What do you think we are going to have to think about?', 'What could you do if you have problems?', 'How do you know that?', 'What might make this easier?' 'How are we going to do this?', 'What might happen if…?' and 'Are there other ways this can be done?' can stimulate creative thinking. But learning and performance are improved not just by thinking, but also by applying progressively more challenging subject skills to the topic.

Problem-solving

If children are given authentic situations to interpret, real challenges to meet, and relevant contexts to work within they will operate in 'problem-solving' mode and generate new understanding in the process (Perkins, 2000). A Reception class for example was taken to the beach and groups were set the task of describing to their French sister schools what the place was like, without words. The children discussed the problem, shared solutions and embarked upon drawing, collecting, recording sounds, taking photos and making music. On their return to school their next problem was how best to send their work to France.

Task 5.1.4
Planning problem-solving activities

In groups, plan a short field trip very near to a school you know. Generate four 'problems' which children might safely be faced with in this context. Suggest the skills which would be needed to approach these problems and activities designed to help solve them. Decide on the Key Skills and curriculum areas this activity would address.

SUMMARY

Creative teaching is a collaborative enterprise which capitalises on the unexpected and variously involves engagement, reflection and transformation, patterned at such a rate as to invite and encourage a questioning stance and motivate self-directed learning. Creative learning involves asking questions, exploring options and generating and appraising ideas as you take risks and imaginatively think your way forwards and make new or innovative connections. We trust you will choose to teach creatively and promote creativity through your planning, building, in choice and autonomy, relevance and purpose in environments of possibility both inside and outside the primary classroom.

ANNOTATED FURTHER READING

Craft, A. (2000) *Creativity Across the Primary Curriculum: Framing and Developing Practice*, London: RoutledgeFalmer. This is an inspiring read, practically based but informed by theory and research. Anna Craft explores core principles and the different subjects and considers ways in which teachers can develop a more 'creative mindset' towards the curriculum and pedagogy. A breakthrough when it was published, this book is both accessible and thought-provoking.

Halpin, D. (2003) *Hope and Education: The Role of the Utopian Imagination*, London: RoutledgeFalmer. A very accessible, passionate but philosophically sound argument for putting the hope back into education. Professor Halpin concentrates on the need to change educators' attitudes towards a more child-centred, creative and culturally sensitive curriculum. In his mind, establishing an ethos of security where no child feels 'a loser' is central to promoting creativity.

Scoffham, S. (ed.) (2004) *Primary Geography Handbook*, Sheffield: The Geographical Association. This subject-based handbook for teachers has a wealth of well-tried and practical examples of creativity applied to geography. Chapters on 'Young geographers', 'Geography, creativity and place', 'Geography and the emotions' and 'Making geography fun' show how creative teaching and promoting creative thinking in children is central to a subject not usually thought of as being creative.

REFERENCES

Abbs, P. (2003) *Against the Flow*, London: Routledge.

Adey, P. and Shayer, M. (2002) *Learning Intelligence: Cognitive Acceleration from 5 to 15 Years*, London: Open University Press.

Barnes, J. (2005) ' "You could see it on their faces...": the importance of provoking smiles in schools', *Health Education*, August 2005.

Bearne, E., Grainger, T. and Wolstencroft, H. (2004) *Raising Boys' Achievements in Writing*, Joint Research Project United Kingdom Literacy Association and the Primary National Strategy, Baldock: United Kingdom Literacy Association.

Beetlestone, F. (1998) *Creative Children, Imaginative Teaching*, Buckingham: Open University Press.

Boden, M. (2001) 'Creativity and knowledge', in A. Craft, B. Seffrey and M. Liebling (eds) *Creativity in Education*, London: Continuum.

Bronowski, J. (1976) *The Origins of Knowledge and Imagination*, New Haven, CT: Yale University Press.

Burke, C. and Grosvenor, I. (2003) *The School I'd Like: Children and Young People's Reflections on an Education for the 21st Century*, London: Routledge.

Claxton, G. (1997) *Hare Brain, Tortoise Mind: Why Intelligence Increases When You Think Less*, London: Fourth Estate.

Claxton, G. and Lucas, B (2004) *Be Creative: Essential Steps to Revitalize Your Work and Life*, London: BBC.

Craft, A. (2000) *Creativity Across the Primary Curriculum: Framing and Developing Practice*, London: RoutledgeFalmer.

Craft, A.(2001) 'Little c: creativity in craft', in A. Craft, B. Jeffrey and M. Liebling (eds) *Creativity in Education*, London: Continuum.

Craft, A. (2005) *Creativity in Schools: Tensions and Dilemmas*, London: Routledge.

Craft, A. and Jeffrey, B. (2003) 'Teaching creatively and teaching for creativity: distinctions and relationships', *Educational Studies*, 30(1): 77–87.

Cremin, M. (2004) 'The role of the imagination in classroom drama', unpublished dissertation, Canterbury Christ Church University College, Canterbury.

Csikszentmihalyi, M. (1996) *Creativity: Flow and the Psychology of Discovery and Invention*, New York: Harper.

Csikszentmihalyi, M. (2002) *Flow: The Classic Work on How to Achieve Happiness*, London: Rider.

Damasio, A. (1995) *Descartes' Error*, New York: Quill.

Damasio, A. (2003) *Looking for Spinoza: Joy, Sorrow and the Feeling Brain*, Orlando, FL: Harcourt.

DfEE/QCA (1999) *National Curriculum for English Programme of Study*, London:DfEE/QCA.

DfEE/QCA (2000) *The Curriculum Guidance for the Foundation Stage*, London: QCA/DfEE.

DfES (2003) *Excellence and Enjoyment: A Strategy for Primary Schools*, Nottingham: DfES.

DfES (2004) *Every Child Matters: Change for Children in Schools*, http://publications.teachernet.gov.uk/eOrderingDownload/DfES-1089-2004.pdf (accessed 22/02/06).

DfES/OFSTED (2005) 'A new relationship with schools', http://publications.teachernet.gov.uk/eOrderingDownload/1288-2005DOC-EN.pdf (accessed 22/02/06).

Fisher, R. (1999) *Head Start: How to Develop your Child's Mind*, London: Souvenir Press.

Fisher, R. (2003) 'Thinking skills, creative thinking', *Junior Education*, May, p. 29.

Fredrickson, B. (2000) 'Cultivating positive emotions to optimise health and well being', *Prevention and Treatment*, 3(7) (March 2003), available at www.journals.apa.org/pt/prevention/volume3/pre0030001a.html (accessed 21/02/06).

Fredrickson, B. (2003) 'The value of positive emotions', *American Scientist*, 91(4): 330–5, available at www.lsa.umich.edu/psych/peplab/pdf/AMSCI_2003-07Fredrickson.pdf (accessed 21/02/06).

Fryer, M. (1996) *Creative Teaching and Learning*, London: Paul Chapman.

Gardner, H. (1993) *Frames of Mind: The Theory of Multiple Intelligences*, 2nd edition, London: HarperCollins

Gardner, H. (1999) *The Disciplined Mind*, New York: Simon and Schuster.

Gardner, H. (1999) *Intelligence Reframed*, New York: Basic Books.

Gardner, H. (2000) *Intelligence Reframed: Multiple Intelligences for the 21st Century*, New York: Basic Books.

Goleman, D (1999) *Working with Emotional Intelligence*, London: Bloomsbury.

Grainger, T. (2003) 'Creative teachers and the language arts: possibilities and potential', *Education 3-13*, 31(1): 43–8.

Grainger, T., Barnes, J. and Scoffman, S. (2004) 'Creative teaching: a creative cocktail', *Journal of Education and Teaching*, 38(3): 243–53.

Grainger, T., Goouch, K. and Lambirth, A. (2005) *Creativity and Writing: Developing Voice and Verve in the Classroom*, London: Routledge.

Halpin, D. (2003) *Hope and Education: The Role of the Utopian Imagination*, London: Routledge.

Jeffrey, B. and Craft, A. (2004) 'Teaching creatively and teaching for creativity: distinctions and relationships', *Educational Studies*, 30(1): 77–97.

Jeffrey, B. and Woods, P. (2003) *The Creative School: A Framework for Success, Quality and Effectiveness*, London: RoutledgeFalmer.

Jones, R. and Wyse, D. (2004) *Creativity in the Primary Curriculum*, London: David Fulton.

Koestler, A. (1964) *The Act of Creation*, London: Penguin.

NACCCE (1999) *All Our Futures: The Report of the National Advisory Committee on Creative and Cultural Education*, London: DfEE/DCMS.

Nikerson, R.S.(1999) in Sternberg, R. (ed.) *The Handbook of Creativity*, Cambridge.

OFSTED Framework for Inspection (2005) http://www.ofsted.gov.uk/publications/index.cfm?fuseaction=pubs.displayfile&id=3862&type=pdf (accessed 22/02/06).

Perkins, D. (2000) *The Eureka Effect: The Arts and Logic of Breakthrough Thinking*, New York: Norton.

Robertson, I .(1999) *Mind Sculpture*, London: Bantam.

Robertson, I. (2002) *The Mind's Eye*, London: Bantam.

Robinson. K. (2001) *Out of Our Minds*, London: Capstone.

Seligman, M. (2004) *Authentic Happiness*, New York: Free Press.

Seltzer, K. and Bentley, T. (1999) *The Creative Age: Knowledge and Skills for the New Economy*, London: Demos.

Starko, A. (2001) *Creativity in the Classroom*, London: Lawrence Erlbaum.

Sternberg, R. (1997) *Successful Intelligence: How Practical and Creative Intelligence Determine Success in Life*, New York: Plume.

Sternberg, R. (ed.) (1999) *The Handbook of Creativity*, Cambridge: Cambridge University Press.

Woods, P. (1995) *Creative Teachers in Primary Schools*, Buckingham: Open University Press.

WEBSITES

DfEE/DCMS (1999) *All Our Futures: Creativity, Culture and Education*, http://www.dfes.gov.uk/naccce/index1.shtml (accessed online April 2005).

HM Government (2005) *The Education Act 2005-04-12*, http://blackboard.cant.ac.uk/courses/1/ED03DEPRODE/content/_68689_1/Ed_20Act_2005_202005097.pdf (accessed online April 2005).

OFSTED (2003) *Expecting the Unexpected,* http://www.ofsted.gov.uk/publications/.

Unit 5.2

Thinking Skills

Robert Fisher

We need to think better if we are going to become better people.

(Paul, aged 10)

INTRODUCTION

In recent years there has been growing interest across the world in ways of developing children's thinking and learning skills (Fisher 2005). This interest has been fed by new knowledge about how the brain works and how people learn, and evidence that specific interventions can improve children's thinking and intelligence. The particular ways in which people apply their minds to solving problems are called *thinking skills*. Many researchers suggest that thinking skills are essential to effective learning, though not all agree on the definition of this term. If thinking is how children make sense of learning, then developing their thinking skills will help them get more out of learning and life. This unit looks at the implications of research into ways to develop thinking children, thinking classrooms and thinking schools.

OBJECTIVES

By the end of this unit you should:

- understand 'thinking skills' and their role in learning;
- understand some key principles that emerge from research into teaching thinking;
- know the main approaches to developing children's thinking;
- see how you might integrate a 'thinking skills' approach into classroom teaching.

WHAT ARE THINKING SKILLS?

Thinking skills are not mysterious entities existing somewhere in the mind. Nor are they like mental muscles that have a physical presence in the brain. What the term refers to is the human capacity to think in conscious ways to achieve certain purposes. Such processes include remembering, questioning, forming concepts, planning, reasoning, imagining, solving problems, making decisions and judgements, translating thoughts into words and so on. Thinking skills are ways in which humans exercise the *sapiens* part of being *homo sapiens*.

A skill is commonly defined as a practical ability in doing something or succeeding in a task. Usually we refer to skills in particular contexts, such as being 'good at cooking' but they can also refer to general areas of performance, such as having a logical mind, good memory, being creative and so on. A thinking skill is a practical ability to think in ways that are judged to be more or less effective or skilled. They are the habits of intelligent behaviour learned through practice, for example children can become better at giving reasons or asking questions the more they practice doing so.

If thinking skills are the mental capacities we use to investigate the world, to solve problems and make judgements then to identify every such skill would be to enumerate all the capacities of the human mind and the list would be endless. Many researchers have attempted to identify the key skills in human thinking, and the most famous of these is Bloom's taxonomy (see Figure 5.2.1).

Bloom's taxonomy of thinking skills (what he called 'the cognitive goals of education') has been widely used by teachers in planning their teaching. He identifies a number of basic or 'lower order' cognitive skills – knowledge, comprehension and application – and a number of higher order skills – analysis, synthesis and evaluation. Figure 5.2.1 shows the various categories identified by Bloom and the processes involved in the various thinking levels.

	Cognitive goal	*Thinking cues*
1	Knowledge (knowing and remembering)	Say what you know, or remember, describe, repeat, define, identify, tell who, when, which, where, what
2	Comprehension (interpreting and understanding)	Describe in your own words, tell how you feel (interpreting and understanding) about it, what it means, explain, compare, relate
3	Application (applying, making use of)	How can you use it, where does it lead, apply what you know, use it to solve problems, demonstrate
4	Analysis (taking apart, being critical)	What are the parts, the order, the reasons why, the causes/problems/solutions/consequences
5	Synthesis (connecting, being creative)	How might it be different, how else, what if, suppose, putting together, develop, improve, create in your own way
6	Evaluation (judging and assessing)	How would you judge it, does it succeed, will it work, what would you prefer, why you think so

Figure 5.2.1 Bloom's taxonomy (from Bloom and Krathwohl, 1956)

You could plan or analyse many learning activities in terms of Bloom's categories. For example when telling a story, a teacher might ask the following kinds of questions:

1   Knowledge   *What happened in the story?*
2   Comprehension   *Why did it happen that way?*
3   Application   *What would you have done?*
4   Analysis   *Which part did you like best?*
5   Synthesis   *Can you think of a different ending?*
6   Evaluation   *What did you think of the story? Why?*

Bloom's taxonomy built on earlier research by Piaget and Vygotsky that suggested that thinking skills and capacities are developed by *cognitive challenge*. Teachers need to challenge children to think more deeply and more widely and in more systematic and sustained ways. Or as Tom, aged 10 put it: 'A good teacher makes you think ... even when you don't want to.' One way in which you, as a good teacher, can do this is by asking questions that challenge children's thinking.

Task 5.2.1
Questions for thinking

Choose a story, poem, text or topic that you would like to use with children as a stimulus for their thinking. Using Bloom's taxonomy create a series of questions to think about and discuss after you have shared the stimulus with them. List your questions under Bloom's six categories: knowledge, comprehension and application, analysis, synthesis and evaluation.

WHY ARE THINKING SKILLS IMPORTANT?

Thinking skills are important because mastery of the 'basics' in education (literacy, maths, science etc.), however well taught, are not sufficient to fulfil human potential, or to meet the demands of the labour market or of active citizenship. Countries across the world are recognising that a broad range of competencies are needed to prepare children for an unpredictable future. These 'higher order' thinking skills are required, in addition to basic skills, because individuals cannot 'store' sufficient knowledge in their memories for future use. Information is expanding at such a rate that individuals require transferable skills to enable them to address different problems in different contexts at different times throughout their lives. The complexity of modern jobs requires people who can comprehend, judge and participate in generating new knowledge and processes. Modern democratic societies require their citizens to assimilate information from multiple sources, determine its truth and use it to make sound judgements.

The challenge is to develop educational programmes that enable all individuals, not just an elite, to become effective thinkers because these competencies are now required of everyone. A 'thinking skills' approach suggests that learners must develop awareness of themselves as thinkers and learners, practise strategies for effective thinking and develop the habits of intelligent behaviour that are needed for lifelong learning. As Paul, aged 10, put it: 'We need to think better if we are going to become better people.'

WHAT DOES RESEARCH TELL US ABOUT THINKING?

Research in cognitive science and psychology is providing a clearer picture of the brain and the processes associated with thinking (Smith 2002). This brain research has some important implications for teachers. For example we now know that most of the growth in the human brain occurs in early childhood: by the age of six, the brain in most children is approximately 90 per cent of its adult size. This implies that intervention, while the brain is still growing, may be more effective than waiting until the brain is fully developed. Cognitive challenge is important at all stages, but especially in the early years of education.

Psychologists and philosophers have helped to extend our understanding of the term 'thinking', including the importance of *dispositions*, such as attention and motivation, commonly associated with thinking (Claxton 2002). This has prompted a move away from a simple model of 'thinking skills' as isolated cognitive capacities to a view of thinking as inextricably connected to emotions and dispositions, including 'emotional intelligence', which is our ability to understand our own emotions and the emotions of others (Goleman 1995).

There is also a growing realisation that we need to teach not only cognitive skills and strategies but also develop the higher 'metacognitive' functions involved in metacognition. This involves making learners aware of themselves as thinkers and how they process/create knowledge by 'learning how to learn' (see sections on 'Self Awareness' in the Primary National Strategy, DfES 2004).

Metacognition involves thinking about one's own thinking. Metacognition includes knowledge of oneself, for example of what one knows, what one has learnt, what one can and cannot do and ways to improve one's learning or achievement. Metacognition also involves skills of recognising problems, representing features of problems, planning what to do in trying to solve problems, monitoring progress and evaluating the outcomes of one's own thinking or problem-solving activity.

Metacognition is promoted by helping pupils to reflect on their thinking and decision-making processes. Metacognition is developed when pupils are helped to be strategic in organising their activities and are encouraged to reflect before, during and after problem-solving processes. The implication is that you need to plan time for debriefing and review in lessons to encourage children to think about their learning and how to improve it. This can be done through discussion in a plenary session, or by finding time for reflective writing in their own thinking or learning logs.

The human mind is made up of many faculties or capacities that enable learning to take place. Our general capacity for understanding or *intelligence* was once thought to be innate and unmodifiable. As a child once put it: 'Either you've got it or you haven't.' The notion of inborn intelligence which dominated educational practice until the mid-twentieth century was challenged by Vygotsky, Piaget and others who developed a constructivist psychology based on a view of learners as active creators of their own knowledge. Some researchers argue that intelligence is not one generic capacity but is made up of multiple intelligences (Gardner 1993). Howard Gardner's theory of multiple intelligence has had a growing influence in recent years on educational theory and practice, although not all are convinced of its claims. Whether intelligence is viewed as one general capacity or many, what researchers are agreed upon is that it is modifiable and can be developed.

Key principles that emerge from this research include the need for teachers and carers to provide:

*   *cognitive challenge*, challenging children's thinking from the earliest years;
*   *collaborative learning*, extending thinking through working with others;
*   *metacognitive discussion*, reviewing what they think and how they learn.

This research and the pioneering work of Feuerstein, who created a programme called Instrumental Enrichment, Matthew Lipman, who founded Philosophy for Children, and other leading figures such as Edward de Bono, creator of 'lateral thinking', have inspired a wide range of curriculum and programme developments (Fisher 2005). These include a range of teaching approaches that you could use, including 'cognitive acceleration', 'brain-based' approaches (such as 'accelerated learning') and 'philosophical' approaches that aim at developing the moral and emotional as well as intellectual aspects of thinking – caring and collaborative as well as critical and creative thinking. These are discussed below.

By the end of the twentieth century there was a widespread realisation that 'key' or 'core' skills of thinking, creativity and problem-solving lay at the heart of successful learning and should be embedded in primary and secondary school curricula. When the DfEE in England commissioned Carol McGuinness to review and evaluate research into thinking skills and related areas, key points that emerged from her study were that:

- pupils benefitted from being coached in thinking;
- not one model, but many approaches proved effective;
- success was due to pedagogy (teaching strategies) not specific materials;
- strategies were needed to enable pupils to transfer thinking to other contexts;
- teachers needed professional support and coaching to sustain success.

McGuinness (1999: 13) points out that the most successful interventions are associated with a 'strong theoretical underpinning, well-designed and contextualised materials, explicit pedagogy and teacher support'.

In England the revised National Curriculum (DfES 1999) included thinking skills in its rationale, stating that thinking skills are essential in 'learning how to learn'. The list of thinking skills identified in the English National Curriculum is similar to many such lists: information processing, reasoning, enquiry, creative thinking and evaluation. Any good lesson or learning conversation will show evidence of some or all of these elements. They focus on 'knowing how' as well as 'knowing what', not only on curriculum content but on learning how to learn. Figure 5.2.2 shows how they can be related to Bloom's taxonomy.

The National Curriculum in England, as elsewhere, is no longer to be seen simply as subject knowledge but as being underpinned by the skills of lifelong learning. Good teaching is not just about achieving particular curriculum objectives but also about developing general thinking skills and learning behaviours. Since the McGuiness review and the explicit inclusion of thinking skills in the National Curriculum, interest in the teaching of thinking has burgeoned in the UK. Research has shown that interventions work if they have a strong theoretical base and if teachers are enthusiastic and well-

Thinking skills	Bloom's taxonomy
Information processing	Knowledge, comprehension
Enquiry	Application
Reasoning	Analysis
Creative thinking	Synthesis
Evaluation	Evaluation

Figure 5.2.2 Thinking skills in the National Curriculum

trained in the use of a programme or strategy. Teachers are developing 'teaching for thinking' approaches in new directions, integrating them into everyday teaching to create 'thinking classrooms', and developing whole school policies to create 'thinking schools'.

Task 5.2.2
Identifying thinking skills

Identify in a lesson plan, or observation of a classroom lesson, the thinking skills that are being developed as general learning objectives. Look for evidence that the children are engaged in information processing, reasoning, enquiry, creative thinking and evaluation.

The following proforma could be used for recording the evidence:

Identifying thinking skills
What thinking skills are pupils developing and using in this lesson? Identify examples of:

Information processing
- Finding relevant information
- Organising information
- Representing or communicating information

Reasoning
- Giving reasons
- Making inferences or deductions
- Arguing or explaining a point of view

Enquiry
- Asking questions
- Planning research or study
- Engaging in enquiry or process of finding out

Creative thinking
- Generating ideas
- Imagining or hypothesising
- Designing innovative solutions

Evaluation
- Developing evaluation criteria
- Applying evaluation criteria
- Judging the value of information and ideas

HOW DO WE TEACH THINKING IN THE CLASSROOM?

Researchers have identified a number of teaching strategies you can use to help stimulate children's thinking in the classroom. These approaches to teaching thinking can be summarised as:

- cognitive acceleration approaches;
- brain-based approaches;
- philosophical approaches;
- teaching strategies across the curriculum.

Cognitive acceleration approaches

CASE

Philip Adey and Michael Shayer developed the original Cognitive Acceleration Through Science Education (CASE) project in the 1980s and early 1990s for Key Stage 3 Science. Their work now extends into other subjects and age groups and has perhaps the best research and most robust evidence of the impact of thinking skills in the UK (for a summary see Adey and Shayer 2002).

The following is a typical format of a CASE lesson for thinking that builds-in time for cognitive and metacognitive discussion:

1   Concrete preparation   stimulus to thinking, introducing the terms of the problem
2   Cognitive conflict   creates a challenge for the mind
3   Social construction   dialogue with others, discussion that extends thinking
4   Metacognition   reflection on how we tackled the problem
5   Bridging   reviewing where else we can use this thinking and learning

CASE lessons have also been developed for young children, called 'Let's Think!' which aims to raise achievement by developing Year 1 pupils' general thinking patterns and teachers' understanding of children's thinking.

During 'Let's Think!' lessons young children work with a teacher in groups of six and each activity takes about 30 minutes. The session is completely oral, with discussion based on a range of objects. At the beginning of the session the teacher helps agree a common language to describe the objects being used. Having established the vocabulary and the concepts involved, the teacher sets the challenge of the activity. One popular activity in this schema is called the 'hoop game' when children are required to put orange toy dinosaurs in one hoop and T-Rex dinosaurs in another hoop. The challenge is that one of the dinosaurs is an orange T-Rex. This is very perplexing for our pre-operational children because they have to utilise two pieces of information about the dinosaur and find a solution to the problem. The children work together as a group to come to a solution or a number of possible solutions to solve the task. They discuss their ideas and make suggestions. The teacher guides them, without being obvious, towards the idea of overlapping the hoops and putting the wayward dinosaur in the intersection.

As in other discussion-based approaches children are encouraged to state whether they agree or disagree with each other by giving a reason. For example, they are taught to say, 'I think... because' or 'I disagree with you because...'. The activities are designed as problems to be solved thus creating a context for developing thinking. Children are given a challenge, are required to work collaboratively, to plan and evaluate their own and others' thinking strategies, and the teacher then gets the children to think about their thinking (metacognition) through asking such questions as 'What do you think we are going to have to think about?' and 'How did you get your answer?' rather than 'Is your answer correct?'. Of course you do not need the 'Let's Think!' materials to apply this teaching strategy to any area of the curriculum.

What the 'Let's Think!' approach aims to do is to accelerate cognitive development between two types of thinking. The first type of thought is what Piaget (1953) called 'pre-operational', when children still find it difficult to engage in what adults perceive as rational thought. The next stage, which Piaget described as 'concrete operational', involves manipulating at least two ideas in order to produce a third, new idea, which is what the sessions encourage the children to do. 'Let's Think'! aims to accelerate the transition between the two types of thought in order to help pupils make better sense of their learning and improve general achievement. They do this, as you might, by ensuring their teaching includes cognitive challenge, collaborative activity and children thinking about how they think and learn.

'Thinking maths' lessons for primary children are part of a related project called CAME (Cognitive Acceleration of Mathematics Education). These lessons involve discussion-based tasks in maths that aim to develop children's conceptual thinking rather than the mechanics of doing the maths. They differ from open-ended investigations in that each lesson has a specific concept to develop. The activities are planned to generate group and whole class discussion rather than written work with an emphasis on how did you get your answer rather than what is the answer. As the CAME approach suggests, if your emphasis in teaching is 'How did you get your answer?' rather than 'Is your answer correct?', it is a far more productive way of generating children's thinking and learning.

'Brain-based' approaches

Accelerated learning

Many educationalists are influenced by recent research into how the human brain works and draw on some of the implications of this research for teachers and schools. 'Accelerated learning' and 'Multiple intelligence' approaches all draw on these broad ideas together with research into learning styles. The common feature is the reliance on brain research to inspire teaching techniques in the classroom.

There are many theories of learning styles. They are rooted in a classification of psychological types and the fact that individuals tend to process information differently. Different researchers propose different sets of learning style characteristics, but many remain unconvinced by their claims that children learn best through using one preferred style (Coffield *et al.* 2004).

'Accelerated learning' approaches include applying VAK – visual, auditory and kinaesthetic – learning styles to teaching:

- visual – learning best through pictures, charts, diagrams, video, ICT etc.;
- auditory – learning best through listening;
- kinaesthetic – learning best through being physically engaged in a task.

For example, in teaching her class to spell a word a teacher might show them how to chunk the word into three pieces, and emphasise this by using different colours for each section of the word, and to visualise it in their heads. She might also ask them to write the word in the air with their fingers. 'Accelerated learning' emphasises the importance of including a range of learning experiences, visual, verbal and physical, in your teaching, so that children are challenged to think in different ways.

These and other 'brain-based' teaching strategies such as 'BrainGym' (which uses simple but challenging aerobic exercises to focus the mind and stimulate the brain) offer much scope for your own research in the classroom.

De Bono

According to Edward de Bono we tend to think in restricted and predictable ways. To become better thinkers we need to learn new habits. His teaching strategy known as 'thinking hats' helps learners try different approaches to thinking. Each 'thinking hat' represents a different way to think about a problem or issue. Children are encouraged to try on the different 'hats' or approaches to a problem to go beyond their usual thinking habits (de Bono 1999). The 'hats' or thinking approaches, together with questions you might ask, are as follows:

White hat	=	information	*What do we know?*
Red hat	=	feelings	*What do we feel?*
Purple hat	=	problems	*What are the drawbacks?*
Yellow hat	=	positives	*What are the benefits?*
Green hat	=	creativity	*What ideas have we got?*
Blue hat	=	control	*What are our aims?*

De Bono claims the technique is widely used in management but little research has been published on its use in education. Some teachers have found it a useful technique for encouraging children to look at a problem or topic from a variety of perspectives. It encourages us, and our children, to think creatively about any topic and to ask: 'Is there another way of thinking about this?'

Philosophical approaches

A pioneer of the 'critical thinking' movement in America is the philosopher Matthew Lipman. Originally a university philosophy professor, Lipman was unhappy at what he saw as poor thinking in his students. They seemed to have been encouraged to learn facts and to accept authoritative opinions, but not to think for themselves. He became convinced that something was wrong with the way they had been taught in school when they were younger. He therefore founded the Institute for the Advancement of Philosophy for Children (IAPC) and developed with colleagues a programme called Philosophy for Children, used in more than 40 countries around the world.

Lipman believes that children are natural philosophers because they view the world with curiosity and wonder (Lipman 2003). Children's own questions form the starting-point for an enquiry or discussion, which can be termed 'philosophical'. The IAPC has produced a number of novels, into every page of which, strange and anomalous points are woven. As a class reads a page, with the teacher, the text encourages them to raise queries. These questions form the basis of guided discussions. The novels provide a model of philosophical enquiry, in that they involve fictional children engaging in argument, debate, discussion and exploratory thinking.

Stories for thinking

Many resources have been developed in recent years to adapt Matthew Lipman's approach to Philosophy for Children to the needs of children and teachers in the UK. 'Stories for Thinking' is one such approach (Fisher 1996). The aim, through using stories and other kinds of stimulus for philosophical discussion, is to create a *community of enquiry* in the classroom (see www.sapere.org.uk).

In a typical 'Stories for Thinking' lesson the teacher shares a 'thinking story' with the class. They have 'thinking time' when they are asked to think about anything in the story that they thought was strange, interesting or puzzling. After some quiet thinking time the teacher asks for their comments or questions, and writes each child's question on the board, adding their name after their question. The children then chose from the list of questions which one they would like to discuss. The teacher then invites the children to comment, and sees who agrees or disagrees with particular comments made. If children do not give reasons or evidence from the story for their opinions the teacher asks 'Why do you think that?' or 'Have you got a reason for that?'.

When asked the value of a 'Stories for Thinking' lesson one child said: 'You have to ask questions and think hard about the answers.' Another said: 'Sometimes you change your mind and sometimes you don't.' A third reply was: 'It is better than just doing reading or writing because you have to say what you really think.'

Teachers note that in 'Stories for Thinking' lessons, in which they may also use poems, pictures, objects or other texts for thinking, the children have become more thoughtful, better at speaking and listening to each other, at asking questions and using the language of reasoning, more confident in posing creative ideas and in judging what they and others think and do and are more confident about applying their thinking to fresh challenges in learning and in life (Fisher 1999, www.teachingthinking.net).

What stories or other forms of stimulus could you use to really engage your children in thinking? How could you create an enquiring classroom?

Task 5.2.3
Creating a thinking classrom

What would a thinking classroom look like?

1   Collect words to describe what a thinking classroom might look like. These might include some reference to the teacher's behaviour, children's behaviour, classroom environment or kinds of activity that help children to think and learn well.
2   Sort your ideas into small groups and give each group a heading that you think appropriate.
3   Choose one idea from each group and consider how you could develop this in your classroom.

TEACHING STRATEGIES ACROSS THE CURRICULUM

A growing number of programmes and strategies aim to help teachers develop children's thinking and learning across the curriculum, such as TASC (Thinking Actively in a Social Context) and ACTS (Activating Children's Thinking Skills). It is difficult to evaluate the success of these and other interventions because of the many variables involved in the teaching situation. There is much scope here for your own research into teaching strategies in the classroom and for developing new strategies.

A number of specific teaching strategies have been identified to help stimulate children's thinking in different subject areas and many of these are included in the Primary National Strategy guidance for teachers (DfES 2004). For example 'Odd One Out' is a teaching technique to identify pupils' understanding of key concepts in different subjects. A teacher might in a numeracy lesson put three numbers on the board, such as 9, 5 and 10; or in science three materials; or in English three characters to compare and contrast – then ask the children to choose the 'odd one out' and to give a reason. Teachers who use this strategy claim it can reveal gaps in the knowledge that she has taught and the knowledge and vocabulary that the children are then able to use. The children think of it as a game and are used to thinking up examples and ideas which show their thinking in different curriculum subjects. This approach encourages creative thinking and reasoning (Higgins *et al.* 2001). Can you think of three things and give reasons why one, two or each of them might be the odd one out?

Concept mapping

Many approaches include the use of thinking diagrams, 'graphic organisers' or 'concept maps' as an aid to making thinking visual and explicit.

Concept mapping is an information-processing technique with a long history. Tony Buzan developed this technique into a version he calls Mind Mapping (Buzan 1993). Concept maps are tools that help make thinking visible – and involves writing down, or more commonly drawing, a central idea and thinking up new and related ideas which radiate out from the centre. By focusing on key ideas written down in children's own words, and then looking for branches out and connections between the ideas, they are mapping knowledge in a manner which can help them understand and remember new information. A simple concept map might be used to map out the connections between characters in a story. Children might also draw maps from memory to test what they remember or know. Teachers have found concept maps helpful in finding out or revising what children know and the technique is especially popular when used in pairs or groups. Children can learn from the technique from an early age and many find it motivating. As one young child put it: 'Concept mapping gets you to think and try more.' Concept mapping is a useful teaching and revision technique for extending thinking and making it visually memorable (Caviglioni and Harris 2000).

When you are planning your next topic or activity with children think of ways of making your own or your children's thinking visible, for example by creating a 'mind map' of a story, a process or collection of ideas.

Computers and thinking

Research shows that there are several ways in which ICT could particularly enhance the teaching and learning of thinking skills. There is evidence that the use of computers can lead to improved information-processing skills. ICT enables multiple and complex representations of information, allowing learners for example to think with a richer knowledge base. As James, aged 8, said: 'I didn't know there was so much to know!'

Educational software can act like a teacher to prompt and direct enquiry through asking questions, giving clues and suggesting avenues of investigation. It can also act as a resource while learners discuss and explore ideas, prompting reflection around a simulation for example. Networks via the internet and including video-conferencing, can allow children to engage directly in collaborative learning and knowledge sharing with others who are not physically present.

The main criticism of the computer as a tutor model is that directed computer teaching does not allow children to be creative learners, able to think and make connections for themselves, and so is unlikely to support the development of higher order thinking. This can be transformed, however, by collaboration around ICT activities, which has been shown to have the potential to enhance the learning of transferable thinking skills.

Effective collaborative learning still needs to be structured. Learners should be taught how to reason and learn together before they are asked to work collaboratively with ICT, because having to articulate and explain strategies to others is more likely to lead to transfer than just doing things without thinking or talking them through. For example, working with LOGO is not just manipulating a screen turtle. It is about reasoning and developing effective problem-solving strategies that can be achieved much better with a learning partner or small group through discussion. In the lesson plenary, by reflecting on this process of collaborative problem solving, the teacher can help children to 'bridge' their thinking from their experience with LOGO or another computer program to different areas of the curriculum.

Computers can help develop children's thinking skills when used as part of a larger dialogue about thinking and learning (Wegerif 2002). The challenge for you as a teacher is to find ways to use the computer to encourage thinking with and discussion between children.

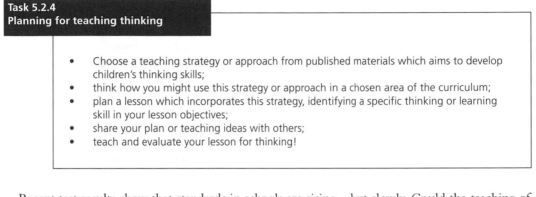

Task 5.2.4
Planning for teaching thinking

- Choose a teaching strategy or approach from published materials which aims to develop children's thinking skills;
- think how you might use this strategy or approach in a chosen area of the curriculum;
- plan a lesson which incorporates this strategy, identifying a specific thinking or learning skill in your lesson objectives;
- share your plan or teaching ideas with others;
- teach and evaluate your lesson for thinking!

Recent test results show that standards in schools are rising – but slowly. Could the teaching of thinking provide a key to raising achievement? The experience of many teachers suggests that when pupils are taught the habits of effective thinking they grow in confidence, their learning is enriched and they are better prepared to face the challenges of the future. Children think so too – as Arran, aged 9, put it: 'When you get out in the real world you have to think for yourself, that's why we need to practise it in school.'

Good teaching is about helping children to think for themselves, which is why it is both a challenge and an adventure.

SUMMARY

In recent years there has been much research into ways of developing children's thinking and learning skills. This has been informed by growing knowledge about how the brain works, how people learn and how teaching approaches can help improve children's ability to think and learn. 'Thinking skills' is a term often used to refer to the many capacities involved in thinking and learning. These skills are seen as fundamental to lifelong learning, active citizenship and emotional intelligence. Research shows that thinking is developed through cognitive challenge, and opportunities for collaborative work and metacognitive discussion. Successful approaches to teaching thinking include cognitive acceleration, brain-based and philosophical approaches. These and other teaching strategies can help raise standards of achievement and create thinking children, thinking classrooms and thinking schools.

ANNOTATED FURTHER READING

Fisher, R. (2005) *Teaching Children to Learn*, 2nd edition, Cheltenham: Stanley Thornes. This book is a practical guide to teaching strategies that develop thinking and learning skills and provide a framework for active learning in the primary classroom.

Fisher, R. (2005) *Teaching Children to Think*, 2nd edition, Cheltenham: Stanley Thornes. This book discusses the nature of thinking and thinking skills and explores the development of thinking skills programmes and how they can be implemented in the classroom.

McGuinness, C. (1999) *From Thinking Skills To Thinking Classrooms: A Review and Evaluation of Approaches for Developing Pupils' Thinking*, London: DfEE (Research Report RR115). Download a Word version of this report: http:www.dfes.gov.uk/research/data/uploadfiles/RB115.doc. The aim of this

Government review was to evaluate research into thinking skills and consider how this research might translate into classroom practice.

Wegerif, R. (2002) *Literature Review in Thinking Skills, Technology and Learning*, www.nestafuturelab.org. This review examines the role of technology in supporting the teaching of thinking skills, summarising research into the use of technology as a 'mind tool' for developing collaboration and communication.

REFERENCES

Adey, P. and Shayer, M.(2002) *Learning Intelligence*, Buckingham: Open University Press.
Bloom, B. and Krathwohl, D.R. (1956) *Taxonomy of Educational Objectives, Handbook 1: Cognitive Domain*, New York: David McKay.
Buzan, T. (1974/1993) *Use Your Head*, London: BBC Publications. See also www.mind-map.com.
Caviglioni, O. and Harris, I. (2000) *Mapwise: Accelerated Learning Through Visible Thinking*, Stafford: Network Educational Press.
Claxton G. (2002) *Building Learning Power: Helping Young People Become Better Learners*, Bristol: TLO.
Coffield, F., Moseley, D., Hall, E. and Ecclestone, K. (2004) *Should We Be Using Learning Styles. What Research Has to Say to Practice*, London: Learning Skills and Development Agency.
de Bono, E. (1999) *Six Thinking Hats*, London: Penguin.
DfEE (1999) *The National Curriculum: Handbook for Primary Teachers in England*, London: QCA.
DfES (2004) Primary National Strategy (www.standards.dfes.gov.uk).
Fisher, R. (1996) *Stories for Thinking*, Oxford: Nash Pollock.
Fisher, R. (1997) *Games for Thinking*, Oxford: Nash Pollock.
Fisher, R. (1997) *Poems for Thinking*, Oxford: Nash Pollock.
Fisher, R. (1999) *First Stories for Thinking*, Oxford: Nash Pollock.
Fisher, R. (2000) *First Poems for Thinking*, Oxford: Nash Pollock.
Fisher, R. (2001) *Values for Thinking*, Oxford: Nash Pollock.
Fisher, R. (2003) *Teaching Thinking: Philosophical Enquiry in the Classroom*, London: Continuum.
Fisher, R. (2005) *Teaching Children to Learn*, 2nd edition, Cheltenham: Stanley Thornes.
Fisher, R. (2005) *Teaching Children to Think*, 2nd edition, Cheltenham: Stanley Thornes.
Gardner, H. (1993) *Multiple Intelligences: The Theory In Practice*, New York: Basic Books.
Goleman, D. (1995) *Emotional Intelligence*, New York: Bantam.
Higgins, S., Baumfield, V. and Leat, D. (2001) *Thinking Through Primary Teaching*, Cambridge: Chris Kington.
Lipman, M. (2003) (2nd edn) *Thinking in Education*, Cambridge: Cambridge University Press.
McGuinness, C. (1999) *From Thinking Skills to Thinking Classrooms: A Review and Evaluation of Approaches for Developing Pupils' Thinking*, London: DfEE (Research Report RR115).
Piaget, J. (1953) *The Origins of Intelligence in Children*, London: Routledge.
Smith, A. (2002) *The Brain's Behind It*, Stafford: Network Education Press.
Wegerif, R. (2002) *Literature Review in Thinking Skills, Technology and Learning*, www.nestafuturelab.org.

Unit 5.3

Learning Through Dialogue

Elizabeth Grugeon and Lorraine Hubbard

INTRODUCTION

This unit looks at current issues concerning speaking, listening and learning in the primary school. It discusses why there is a need to change pedagogic practices so that the dialogue that takes place in the classroom between teachers and pupils and between pupils themselves can become a powerful learning tool. It explores different approaches and strategies for introducing and supporting collaborative learning in small groups and suggests a number of ways in which you may begin to develop a range of skills which will enable you to encourage effective discussion and dialogic talk in your classroom. This may entail a reconsideration of your own role as teacher. As Alexander suggests, 'if we want children to talk to learn – as well as learn to talk – then what they say probably matters more than what teachers say' (2004: 19).

OBJECTIVES

By the end of this unit you should be beginning to:

- understand the need to change pedagogic practices;
- understand the meaning of dialogue and dialogic talk;
- understand why this will have a productive effect on children's learning and
- develop a range of skills to introduce dialogic talk in your classroom.

IS THERE A PROBLEM?

We want to start this unit by looking at some of the issues and considering why these may be problematic. You could begin by imagining that you are in a classroom observing a lesson.

Teacher	Now I want you all to think about the story we were reading yesterday. Can anyone remember what it was called? Sit down, please, Sam. No, we don't call out. I am looking for someone who is sitting quietly with their hand up. Yes, Alison, can you *tell* us the title?
Alison	The Iron Man?
Teacher	Good girl, that's right, it was called The Iron Man, wasn't it? Can anyone remember what happened to the iron man? Where did he come from? Where did he go? Yes, Danny, can you tell us?
Danny	Fell off the cliff.
Teacher	That is right, he walked up to the edge of the cliff and he fell off, well done!

This is not a real example but one we made up to illustrate a common routine of question and answer: elicitation, repetition and reformulation. You will notice who does most of the talking and might like to ask yourself what sort of message this gives to children about the importance of their talk. You might also ask yourself why teachers seem to need to reformulate children's answers and praise them for simply doing what they have been asked to do. This pattern of classroom talk, in which the teacher controls the discourse, asking the important questions, repeating children's answers and offering praise does not seem likely to advance children's thinking or develop their talking skills. The prevalence of this kind of routine has long been a matter of concern and this has come to a head quite recently.

By 2002 (that is 5 years after the National Literacy Strategy Framework for Teaching was introduced), there was a general feeling that children's competence in speaking and listening was being held back. Research (English *et al.* 2002) showed that on average only 10 per cent of oral contributions by children aged 5 to 7 in the literacy hour were longer than three words and only 5 per cent longer than five words. Similar research (Elmer and Riley 2001) showed that teachers of 7 to 11-year-old children were not asking sufficiently challenging questions and further research claimed that longer interactions between teachers and children had dramatically declined since the introduction of the literacy hour.

> Teachers spent the majority of their time either explaining or using highly structured question and answer sequences. Far from encouraging and extending pupil contributions to promote higher levels of interaction and cognitive engagement, most of the questions asked were of a low cognitive level designed to funnel pupils' response towards a required answer... Most of the pupils' exchanges were very short, with answers lasting on average 5 seconds and were limited to three words or fewer... It was very rare for pupils to initiate the questioning.
>
> (Smith *et al.* 2004: 408)

Their data forced them to conclude that, '"top-down" curriculum initiatives like the NNS and NLS, while bringing about a scenario of change in curriculum design often leave deeper levels of pedagogy untouched' (p. 409). They suggest that there is a need for different approaches in order to change habitual classroom behaviours and that changing pedagogic practices is the major challenge to the future effectiveness of the strategies. In this unit we look at some of the suggestions for speaking, listening and learning that are already changing classroom practice in the primary school.

MAKING CHANGES

Guidance appeared in schools at the end of 2003. This new material aimed to ensure that spoken language, including drama, would be specifically taught and that there would be explicit links between the literacy objectives in the NLS Framework. More significantly, for the first time, there would be a specific rationale for progression in each of the four strands: speaking, listening, group discussion and drama.

A far more structured approach to speaking and listening was offered than we have seen hitherto; a far more detailed account of the relationship between speaking, listening and learning. A new concept, teaching through dialogue or dialogic talk was introduced:

> Teaching through dialogue enables teachers and pupils to share and build on ideas in sustained talk. When teaching through dialogue, teachers encourage children to listen to each other, share ideas and consider alternatives; build on their own and others' ideas to develop coherent thinking; express their views fully and help each other to reach common understandings. Teaching through dialogue can take place when a teacher talks with an individual pupil, or two pupils are talking together, or when the whole class is joining in discussion.
>
> (DfES/QCA 2003: 35)

DEFINING THE TERMS

What do we mean by dialogue? How do we learn through dialogue? In this unit, we hope to define this term and consider why it is so important for children's learning and your teaching.

'Talk in learning is not a one-way linear communication but a reciprocal process in which ideas are bounced back and forth and on that basis take children's thinking forward' (Alexander 2004: 48). In dialogue, ideas are bounced back and forth, participants are equal partners striving to reach an agreed outcome and trying out and developing what Mercer has described as the joint construction of knowledge or becoming involved in a process of 'inter thinking' (Mercer 2000). You can do this in dialogue with your pupils; pupils can do it with each other in a process of 'joint enquiry' (Barnes and Todd 1995). In order to create a dialogic repertoire in the classroom, 'It is not sufficient..., to repeat or reformulate a pupil's contribution: what is said needs actually to be reflected upon, discussed, even argued about, and the dialogic element lies partly in getting pupils themselves to do this' (Alexander 2004: 20).

DIALOGIC TALK – PROMOTING EXTENDED TALK AND THINKING

The lack of extended talk and opportunity to articulate ideas has a limiting effect on children's thinking skills which has been recognised as a problem that needs to be tackled. The research carried out by Robin Alexander has had considerable impact on print and video materials for the classroom. This material has a new focus: the relationship between speaking and listening and children's learning. Rather than a teacher's questions eliciting brief responses from pupils, we see that dialogic talk is a type of interaction where teachers and pupils make substantial and significant contributions.

The child as a powerful thinker

While sequences of Alexander's dialogic talk are not necessarily easy to achieve in the Early Years classroom, nevertheless, all children need 'involvement in thoughtful and reasoned dialogue' (Mercer 2003: 76) which should become a part of their oral repertoire. Larson and Peterson (2003: 309) indicate that 'early childhood educators should give children ample opportunities to participate in extended discourse forms, including narratives, explanations, pretend talk, and other forms of complex conversations, in order to achieve successful school-based outcomes'.

As you develop your teaching, you will probably feel the need for some basic approaches to encourage dialogue, such as opening questions of the type 'Can you tell me what you have been doing?'. Then, of course, you need to listen to the child. This might sound obvious, but during the course of a busy day in the classroom it is easy to forget, especially as talk is the easiest, most used and most accessible form of communication.

The help which we give to children in order to further their learning is often called scaffolding, a term coined by Bruner. But Eve Gregory (1996: 21) warns us that, as learning is different across cultures, so the scaffolding we provide should also take account of this difference.

Rethinking classroom talk

The new approach requires you to consider making changes in the way you interact with children: there are features of language that are distinctively oral and do not occur in a written form and which need to be explicitly addressed in the classroom. We have to take on board the collaborative nature of meaning-making and the oral exploration of ideas. There is the importance of variation and range of spoken language and the need to teach children how to use this repertoire effectively. You may find that children successfully explore the nuances of spoken language in drama and role-play.

Task 5.3.1
Your talk in the classroom

You might like to discuss some of the following:

- What sort of questions will challenge children cognitively?
- How can you model the kind of language and subject vocabulary that you want them to use?
- How will you encourage children to express their ideas and views?
- What strategies can you use to extend dialogue?
- How can you ask children to explain their thinking when they give the wrong answer?

Questions and answers

If we think of dialogue as a vehicle for a process of joint inquiry through which learners construct meaning, then questions and answers are vital. In dialogic talk the questions asked by children are as important as the questions asked by the teacher, as are the answers given. You are not using questions solely for the purpose of testing pupils' knowledge but also to enable them to reflect, develop and extend their thinking. And when you have asked questions you need to pay attention to the children's answers: ' there's little point in framing a well conceived question and giving children ample "wait time" to answer it, if we fail to engage with the answer they give and hence with the understanding or misunderstanding which that answer reveals' (Alexander 2004: 19). You can use questioning to lead children through a line of reasoning by responding to their answers. This may mean spending rather longer on individual children's responses while you help them to explore their understanding. In a whole class setting this may mean fewer children making an oral contribution but it gives you a chance to model the types of language that children should be using to solve problems, test evidence, analyse ideas and explore values.

Carol Smith expands these ideas and gives further ideas about ways in which you can think about your questioning. She suggests that when teachers speak to children about their work, asking questions is the most commonly used strategy to assess their learning and progress, but that should not be the sole objective. If these questions are 'kept open', they can lead into other areas of discussion and further questions, positively encouraging further thinking. She feels that,

> the best way to support children in developing their ability to respond to open or semi-open questions is to encourage them to prepare their own questions either for the plenary in the literacy hour or for other groups to respond to in guided/independent times.

> (Smith 2005)

In order to develop dialogic talk in the classroom, to make learning through speaking and listening more effective, she recommends that we should give children more time to think before expecting a response:

> We often expect an immediate answer from children, asking 'reliable' children with their hands up. The quality of response will always be better if time is given for individual thought to a whole range of questions. The use of 'talk partners' in both literacy and numeracy can give children an opportunity to think answers through, sometimes with the aid of a 'white board.' By allowing children plenty of time at first, to think their answers through, you might find they need much less time, as their experience deepens, to discuss and arrive at their answer.

> (Smith 2005)

She also develops the use of 'talk partners'.

> Ideas can be shared first with a partner, a teaching assistant or small group; after a little more time, the quieter child will feel able to speak in front of the whole class. Review times during a teaching session help everyone to clarify their thoughts and ideas and frequently spur on those children having difficulty with self-motivation.

> (Smith 2005 :90)

EXPLORATORY TALK

This is a very useful term, introduced by Barnes (1976) and developed by Mercer (2000). It is the kind of talk that we should aim to develop. When children engage in exploratory talk we can hear them thinking aloud: hypothesising and speculating. Children speak tentatively, using words and phrases like 'perhaps', 'if', 'might', 'probably'; they give reasons to support their ideas, 'because' and seek support from the group by using tag questions, 'wouldn't it?'. They are evidently listening to each other or to you, the teacher, and considering their response.

When we engage in exploratory talk we are almost certain to be working in a small group with our peers; we will be sharing a problem, and constructing meaning together. We will be exchanging ideas and opinions, considering and evaluating each other's ideas, building up shared knowledge and understanding as we collaborate as equals. We are thinking together (Dawes 2005: 108). When children are working in this way their reasoning becomes apparent in their talk. However, this kind of talk does not come naturally to children; they need to be guided by their teachers to understand the value of collaborative talk. Our students often tell us that they have seen very little small group work going on in classrooms; on their brief school placements they find it difficult to carry out tasks involving small group work because of the children's lack of experience.

Dawes reminds us:

> Teachers often specify 'exploratory talk' as the sort of talk that they would particularly want to encourage between children working in groups, at the computer or during any other task. However, disappointingly little exploratory talk may take place unless children know that this is an aim for their work together. Children may not be aware that the best use of speaking and listening is as a tool for exploring one another's ideas, or to reason together.
>
> (Dawes 2005: 107)

Interthinking

The concept of interthinking is an important aspect of learning through dialogue.

> Having to say what you mean – thinking aloud – is a way of making your thoughts clear to yourself: having to explain and describe things to a partner is a way of developing a shared understanding of ideas. If your partner is prepared to accept your initial suggestion, without you having to justify or defend it, you have no stimulus to engage critically with your own thoughts. Also, you have no alternative suggestions to produce the creative friction from which new ideas arise. This *interthinking* – the joint engagement with one another's ideas to think aloud together, solve problems or make mutual meaning – is an invaluable use of spoken language (Mercer 2000). Children need to learn how to do this, and need lots of opportunities to practice.
>
> (Dawes 2005: 108–9)

Encouraging exploratory talk: teaching ground rules for talk

Exploratory talk is difficult enough for adults to achieve and it cannot be assumed that it will come naturally to children. Simply grouping children to work together will not necessarily help them to develop talking skills. Unless children know what we mean by 'discussion', and have the skills to engage one another in speaking and listening, they may gain little of educational value from the talk or the activity. However, a group of children who are aware of the importance of talk have a real advantage.

Children who are expected to work together in a small group need to be taught how to talk to one another. They need direct instruction in the talk skills which will enable them to get the best out of their own thinking and that of all the other members of their group. They have to understand and share the aims for their talk. They come to recognise that if all the group can agree on a set of rules, 'ground rules for talk', then talk can proceed in a way which will make the whole group, and its individuals, more likely to achieve success and develop new ways of thinking. Ground rules for discussion are to do with active listening, thoughtful speaking and respectful collaboration. These are some of the ground rules for exploratory talk:

- everyone in the group is encouraged to contribute;
- contributions are treated with respect;
- reasons are asked for;
- everyone is prepared to accept challenges;
- alternatives are discussed before a decision is taken;
- all relevant information is shared;
- the group seeks to reach agreement.

Of course, you will want the children you are teaching to talk about this and draw up a similar list in their own words. You can put it up on the wall or print it out as a reminder for small groups when they are working on their own.

Problem solving

'Investigations and problem-solving activities are efficient in helping pupils to apply and extend their learning in new contexts' (OFSTED Handbook 1995: 69). You may need to consider how we can address this explicitly in the classroom. One way is through group collaborative talk: collaborative talk in order to solve a science or technology problem is an example of children using talk in order to learn. Often in these contexts the nature of the talk is untidy; for example, sentences will be unfinished, words repeated, and considerable interruptions will take place. Children need to be in groups for this kind of activity and it must be a task which requires them to talk to each other.

Task 5.3.2
Talk in small groups: a classification game

You might like to try this out for yourself when you have an opportunity:

- Give each group plenty of small pieces of paper and a topic each – animals, plants, food, TV programmes. Each group should not know the topic titles you have given to the other groups.
- Each group writes down examples of the category on the separate pieces of paper. For example, the animals group would write down the name of an animal on each piece of paper.
- The group sorts and then classifies the names. *You would need to ask the group why they have organised their examples in this way.*
- Exchange papers with another group. *Will this group classify differently? Can they guess the title you gave the other group?*

Discussion and comment

There are no right answers, which in itself is a learning experience, but the level of reasoning, justifying, speculating, hypothesising, specifying and persuading is considerable from this kind of task. However, this is an activity which is worth further exploration and analysis. Why would we do such a lesson in terms of the curriculum? The aim would be to widen the children's talk repertoire and improve their communication skills and an activity such as this would encourage the children to communicate effectively. They would need to choose their words in order to justify their standpoint and to learn the conventions of discussion, e.g. turn-taking and reasoning.

Dialogue in the home

In the close and more equal relationship of their homes, with parents and siblings and other carers, young children are confidently using dialogue to find out about their world. They regularly ask questions, 'why?', 'where is he gone?'; they initiate ideas and activities, 'let's go out'; and they speculate about the world, 'what would happen if…?' You might like to consider why this kind of dialogue seems to disappear when they enter school.

The richness of talk in the home has been well researched and documented, most notably by Brice-Heath (1983), Tizard and Hughes (1984), Wells (1987) and in the *Early Years Language Project* in Devon which started work in 1986. A typical transcript from this project reveals a four-year-old in conversation with his mother. The family lived in a dockland area of a major city and spoke in the local dialect. They are talking about Ross starting school:

M	Yeah, well, that's what you go to school for to learn how to write things down and how to read and how to spell, i'n'it?
R	You can't spell.
M	Can.
R	No you can't.
M	I can.
R	When you was four you couldn't spell.
M	No, that's why Mummy went to school, to learn, that's why you go to school, i'n'it?
R	To learn.
M	Mmm.
R	Did you go to school to learn?
M	Mmm.
R	You don't now do you?
M	No, don't go t'school now.

Ross and his mother are using the language of their speech community to further Ross's knowledge about school. It is an example of what Tizard and Hughes would call 'a passage of intellectual search'. Ross, by making challenging statements, is trying to make sense of an important aspect of school life. Ross and his mother are communicating well and 'the basics' are there. What we need to remember is that home talk might well be different but it is not deficient.

Discussion and comment

Is the language spoken in this extract different from what we would expect in school? In what ways? Perhaps you feel that there is a more even 'balance of power' between the two speakers because of the close relationship between mother and child. The child is exploring something that puzzles him. Would he be able to do this in a busy classroom?

Into school: talk in the early years

Of course, teachers cannot attempt to replicate the one-to-one conversation which happens in the home, yet if the 'basics' of communication are there, teachers are well able to build on these. The guidance for the foundation curriculum (DfEE/QCA 2000) sets out its aims on language and communication in the Early Learning Goals and refers specifically to speaking and listening: 'Conversation, open-ended questions and thinking out loud are important tools in developing vocabulary and in challenging thinking' (p. 23). Further guidance is given in the stepping stones. Children with English as an additional language are specifically addressed and the importance of building on their language experiences at home.

Ourselves

A popular topic with young children is 'Ourselves'. A good starting point for this is for the teacher to bring in a photograph of herself as a baby and tell stories of her own family. The next step is for the children to bring into school photographs of themselves when they were babies and any toys, clothes or books that might still be in the family. Topics like this are rich in learning potential and often expand to include parents and other areas of the curriculum. Their great strength is that they build on the child's own background, knowledge and experience. You will find that it will help to focus on the spoken language; although a great deal of talk occurs naturally in an Early Years classroom, it is useful and fun to have specific lessons on talking about talk. You might ask the children to consider the kinds of language they used when they were very young:

- How did you ask for a drink when you were a baby?
- What did you use for 'thank you' and 'please'?
- What do you say now?
- How do you ask for a drink at school?
- How do you greet your friends/teacher/head teacher?
- Can we write it down? What do you notice?

The teacher's skill and sensitivity enables the children to reflect on their own language and perhaps on the wider issues of speaking and writing; for example, this is what we all *say*, but what would we *write*? Particular aspects that need to be addressed are adaptation to listeners and context and an introduction to some of the features which distinguish Standard English from the patterns of speech practised so far by the child.

The issue here is that the children are talking about the language itself; they are learning about language through talking about language and acquiring a metalanguage. As teachers, we are surrounded by constant talk in a busy reception class, so it is easy to forget its importance; there's a danger of not giving talk its due attention. Speaking and listening are not incidental but require definite planning.

Talk opportunities in the classroom

By the end of Year 6, most children will be expected to achieve a level of competency in speaking and listening.

> Talk in the classroom is crucial to learning. It is where answers to puzzling questions can be found. It is where thoughtful argument and discussion make way for the understanding of new skills and difficult concepts. It is where difficult issues, which emerge from the children's literacy work, their maths or science investigations, history or RE studies, can be talked through. It is where children listen to and respect the views of each other and where everyone's learning is empowered by talking about what they have learned. It is where children can be supported in raising their own questions about their learning.
>
> (Smith 2005: 86)

By the time most children reach Year 3, they will have come to understand the appropriateness of different kinds of talk in different contexts. By placing a greater emphasis on group discussion and interaction children should now be given far greater opportunities to talk, discuss and share ideas. By giving children the language of argument and persuasion, we can give them the tools to be more effective and articulate at expressing their views in a democratic way. From Years 3 to 6 you should have introduced them to the idea that there is an agreed set of rules for this kind of talk.

Task 5.3.3
Ground rules for talk

> You might find it useful when you next set a problem-solving task for a group of children to get them to discuss and record their own rules which they will use while they are carrying out the task. At first they may be puzzled by this and unsure what you want. You will need to plan very carefully to ensure that they discuss the importance of talk and listening in their own learning. Just as you have had to train yourself to listen to children, they have to learn to listen attentively to each other to take the group task forward.

SUMMARY

To introduce effective dialogic talk in your classroom you may want to think about the different ways you plan to involve talk in your teaching. In many cases, your talk will focus on organisation, the content of your lesson and questions which will show you how well the children are understanding that content. When you include speaking and listening in your planning, however, remember that engaging in dialogue with children involves a process of joint inquiry and the construction of meaning. You will need to think about the kind of questions you ask, and how you are going to respond to the children's answers so that you can extend their thinking. This is also the case when children work together in small groups; they will also need to adjust the way they talk together and will be helped by an introduction to ground rules for talk and a discussion of the importance of talk to their learning.

ANNOTATED FURTHER READING

Alexander, R. (2004) *Towards Dialogic Teaching: Rethinking Classroom Talk*, Cambridge: Dialogos UK. This is a short booklet which explains the rationale for dialogic teaching, the international research which has led to this and the current research taking place in the UK to implement the changes that are implied in this document.

Dawes, L., Mercer, N. and Wegerif, R. (2000) *Thinking Together: A Programme of Activities for Developing Thinking Skills At KS2*, Birmingham: The *Questions* Publishing Company. This practical book discusses the aims of the *Thinking Together* approach; how and why to teach the thinking together lessons; how to plan for group work and improve the quality of talk in the classroom. It has a very useful section which will help you to introduce ground rules for talk followed by suggestions for a number of lessons.

Dawes, L. and Sams, C. (2004) *Speaking and Listening Activities for Learning at Key Stage 1*, London: David Fulton Publishers. Talk Box provides an effective way of teaching children about speaking and listening in the Early Years. It will help you to understand how to introduce ground rules for exploratory talk to young children. A number of ideas for lessons will show you how to use the Talk Box to encourage children's reasoning and decision-making.

Grugeon, E., Dawes, L., Smith, C. and Hubbard, L. (2005) *Teaching Speaking and Listening in the Primary School*, 3rd edition, London: David Fulton Publishers. This book gives a comprehensive review of current issues and classroom practice. It includes information about using ICT, drama, storytelling, guided reading, planning and assessment for talk in both Key Stages.

http://www.thinkingtogether.org.uk. This site includes further information about the Thinking Together approach.

REFERENCES

Alexander, R. (2004) *Towards Dialogic Teaching: Rethinking Classroom Talk*, Cambridge: Dialogos UK.
Barnes, D. (1976) *From Communication to Curriculum*, Harmondsworth: Penguin.
Barnes, D. and Todd, F. (1995) *Communication and Learning Revisited*, London: Heinemann.
Brice-Heath, S. (1983) *Ways with Words: Language, and Work in Communities and Classrooms*, Cambridge: Cambridge University Press.
Bruner, J. (1986) *Actual Minds, Possible Worlds*, Cambridge, MA: Harvard University Press
Corden, R. (2000) *Literacy and Learning Through Talk. Strategies for the Primary Classroom*, Buckingham: Open University Press.
Dawes, L. (2005) 'Speaking, listening and thinking with computers', in Grugeon, E., Dawes, L., Smith, C. and Hubbard, L. (eds) *Teaching Speaking and Listening in the Primary School*, 3rd edition, London: David Fulton Publishers.
Dawes, L. and Sams, C. (2004) *Speaking and Listening Activities for Learning at Key Stage 1*, London: David Fulton Publishers.
Dawes, L., Mercer, N. and Wegerif, R. (2000) *Thinking Together: A Programme of Activities for Developing Thinking Skills at KS2*, Birmingham: The *Questions* Publishing Company.
DfEE (1998) *The National Strategy: Framework for Teaching*, London: DfEE.
DfEE/QCA (2000) *Curriculum Guidance for the Foundation Stage*, London: DfEE/QCA.
Elmer, C. and Riley, J. (2001) 'P is for possibly', *The Primary English Magazine*, 7(1): 23–5.
English, E., Hargreaves, L. and Hislam, J. (2002) 'Pedagogical dilemmas in the National Literacy Strategy', *Cambridge Journal of Education*, 32(1).
Gregory, E. (1996) *Making Sense of a New World: Learning to Read in a Second Language*, London: Paul Chapman Publishing.
Grugeon, E., Dawes, L., Smith, C. and Hubbard, L. (2005) *Teaching Speaking and Listening in the Primary School*, 3rd edition, London: David Fulton Publishers.

Hubbard, L. (1990) Unpublished MPhil thesis, University of Exeter.

Larson, J. and Peterson, S.M. (2003) 'Talk and discourse in formal learning settings', in Hall, N., Larson, J. and Marsh, J. (eds) *Handbook of Early Childhood Literacy*, London: Sage.

Mercer, N. (2000) *Words and Minds: How We Use Language to Think Together*, London: Routledge.

Mercer, N. (2003) 'The educational value of "dialogic talk" in whole class dialogue', in *New Perspectives on Spoken English in the Classroom: Discussion Papers*, London: QCA.

OFSTED (1995) *The Ofsted Handbook: Guidance on the Inspection of Nursery and Priamry Schools*, London: HMSO.

Qualification and Curriculum Authority (QCA)/Department for Education and Skills (DfES) (2003) *Speaking, Listening and Learning: Working With Children in Key Stages 1 and 2*, London: HMSO.

Smith, C. (2005) 'Developing children's oral skills at Key Stage 2', in Grugeon, E., Dawes, L., Smith, C. and Hubbard, L. (eds) *Teaching Speaking and Listening in the Primary School*, 3rd edition, London: David Fulton Publishers.

Smith, F., Hardman, F., Wall, K. and Mroz, M. (2004) 'Interactive whole class teaching in the National Literacy and Numeracy Strategies', *British Educational Research Journal*, 30(3): 395–411.

Tizard, B. and Hughes, M. (1984) *Young Children Learning*, London: Fontana.

Wells, G. (1987) *The Meaning Makers: Children Learning Language and Using Language to Learn*, London: Hodder and Stoughton.

Unit 5.4

Citizenship in the Primary School

Cathie Holden

INTRODUCTION

Laws for our town:

- Everyone is allowed to go skateboarding in the park but it is your responsibility if you get hurt.
- Everyone can use the church, synagogue or mosque.
- You must pick up all your litter, keep in the speed limit, use seatbelts and look after our river.
- You must not smoke.
- If you break these rules you will be fined 500 euros.

The nine-year-olds who came up with these 'laws' were devising their own town for the future. They had to plan their town taking into consideration environmental issues and the needs of the community. As well as physically planning the town they had to think about how the town would be governed, the rights of its citizens and laws they would need. This required them to learn about basic rules and laws in their own community and to consider what it was they valued and wanted to protect in their new communities. Whilst this lesson has links to geography (the local area) and religious education (values) it was neither of these: it was a discrete or 'stand-alone' lesson on education for citizenship.

Education for citizenship is a new area of the curriculum and offers both challenges and opportunities for teachers.

OBJECTIVES

By the end of this unit you should understand:

- what citizenship education is;
- why we need it;
- the importance of an active learning and participative approach;
- the variety of ways in which it can be taught;
- the role of the teacher in dealing with controversial issues;
- how it can be assessed.

WHAT IS EDUCATION FOR CITIZENSHIP?

Education for citizenship (CE) is about preparing children for the responsibilities of adult life in a global society. In secondary schools it exists as a separate subject but in primary schools in England it is one of four strands within Personal, Social, Health and Citizenship Education (PSHCE). It is closely related to these other three areas but rather than focusing on the personal (e.g. welcoming refugee children into the school, or learning about healthy eating) the focus is on society, so that children might analyse different approaches in the media to refugees or might look at competing demands on the health service. Thus education for citizenship aims to help children make links between their own lives and the wider world and understand the part they can play both now and in the future as active citizens. Within the primary school CE aims to help children develop an understanding of the following key areas:

- topical issues (moral, social or cultural) and events;
- democracy and the role of the individual within this;
- why and how rules and laws are made;
- their community and the part they can play within this;
- the range of identities (ethnic, religious, regional) within the UK;
- human rights and responsibilities;
- how conflict can be resolved (in the community, in the wider world);
- the role of voluntary and pressure groups acting for change.

WHY DO WE NEED EDUCATION FOR CITIZENSHIP?

The last decade has seen a movement across Europe, the United States, Canada and Australia for the inclusion of education for citizenship. This has arisen for a number of reasons. First, the increasingly diverse nature of many countries (including the UK) and the rise of racism and intolerance have pinpointed the need for children to understand multiple identities and the contribution of different ethnic groups to society. This includes an understanding of the harm caused by racism and a respect for cultural heritages different from their own.

Second, there has been a decline in the number of young people engaged in democratic processes, with many not bothering to vote in national or European elections. This is perhaps not surprising given that (in the UK) young people could previously leave school with no knowledge of voting, elections or how parliament works. This is not healthy for any democracy, and is not healthy for young people themselves. Thus CE includes as central, learning about democratic processes – in school and at a local and national level.

Third, there is a realisation that we need to educate children to live in a global society where there are increasing social and environmental challenges. Primary children, interviewed in 2004, spoke of their concerns about environmental problems, crime, violence and social inequality on both a local and global scale and discussed the actions of politicians (Holden 2006). Research by Claire (2001) indicates how young children in inner-city London are aware of the effects of poverty and migration on their own lives, talking from experience about religious and racial intolerance and economic injustices. Schools have a duty to listen to these concerns, to clarify misconceptions and to help children understand the complexities of interdependence and globalisation.

Cogan and Derricott (2000), summarising an international survey into the characteristics of effective citizens of the twenty-first century, conclude that we will need people who can:

- work co-operatively with others;
- develop social justice principles to guide own actions;
- think in a critical and systemic way;
- appreciate and learn from cultural differences;
- evaluate problems in the wider community and global context;
- resolve conflicts non-violently;
- change lifestyles to protect the environment;
- recognise and defend human rights;
- dare to strive for a fairer future;
- participate in democratic politics.

You will see that their list is not about passive citizens who just 'know about' human rights or the environment, but is instead about pro-active people who defend the rights of others, who change their lifestyles to protect the environment and who actively participate in politics. This notion of the 'active citizen' is central to the current approach to CE.

Finally, in the UK, there have been calls for more adventurous and creative approaches within the primary curriculum, with more emphasis on speaking and listening and more opportunities for children to be involved in their school (e.g. *Excellence and Enjoyment*, DfES 2003). Education for citizenship can provide many of these opportunities.

WHY IS ACTIVE LEARNING CENTRAL TO CITIZENSHIP?

If one of the aims of citizenship education is to encourage children to be active participants then the methods we use must be interactive, encouraging debate and discussion. We cannot teach children to listen to others, to co-operate, to respect each other's views and to value democracy if we operate classrooms where children are not respected and their concerns are not listened to. Didactic and passive methods will not make for lively and informed debate. Advice on the teaching of citizenship in England suggests an active-learning approach:

> It is vital that pupils are provided with structured opportunities to explore actively aspects, issues and events through school and community involvement, case studies and critical discussions that are challenging and relevant to their lives. It is difficult to conceive of pupils as active citizens if their experience of learning in citizenship education has been predominantly passive.

> (QCA 1998: 37)

What does this look like for you as a teacher? It means trying to ensure that you help your children to:

- develop the confidence to voice their own opinions;
- develop their skills in recognising the views/experience of others;
- develop their skills in critical thinking and in forming arguments;
- develop their skills of co-operation and conflict resolution;
- trust in their creative powers;
- develop skills of democratic participation;
- gain experience of taking action for change.

(Clough and Holden 2002: 6)

All of the examples that are given in the rest of this unit have active learning at their core, and include the following kinds of activities:

- small group discussions followed by plenary sessions to clarify thinking;
- open-ended collaborative enquiries on topical and controversial issues;
- role-play and simulations;
- visits to the community or working with community members;
- participating in democratic processes of change (within the school or within the community).

Having established that CE needs to be active and participatory, we now need to look at where there are opportunities for this kind of approach. A session in maths where children move physically to represent how division works may be active learning but it is not citizenship. So citizenship is about active learning *plus* appropriate subject knowledge and we will now look at where opportunities for the citizenship content can be found.

WHERE CAN CITIZENSHIP BE TAUGHT?

CE can be covered in different ways:

- as a part of another curriculum subject;
- as part of PSHE;
- as a discrete or stand-alone subject;
- through the ethos of the school, whole school activities and events.

Citizenship as part of another curriculum subject

Perhaps the easiest way of incorporating citizenship in your teaching is to take your existing lesson plans or schemes of work and see how they can be adapted. Many teachers are surprised to find that they are covering some of the aspects already and that often only a few adjustments are required. It is often a case of looking out for the controversial, the topical or links to the present day.

The following tasks will help you to see how you might go about this.

Task 5.4.1
Citizenship at Key Stage 1

Look at the KS1 QCA unit of work on Ourselves and consider how you might develop this to teach about ethnic diversity within the UK and help children respect other cultural heritages. One way would be to include the stories of children who have come to live in the UK from other countries. Choose a story from the many fiction and non-fiction books available: Letterbox library (www.Letterboxlibrary.com) is a good place to start. Then consider how you might develop the unit to include past--present links which help you cover one of the areas of citizenship (above). For example, you could use stories of children who lived in the past, looking specifically for issues of justice and injustice, such as child labour in Victorian times.

Task 5.4.2
Citizenship at Key Stage 2

Choose a unit of work in geography and referring to the key areas of citizenship (above), identify what you would consider the citizenship links to be. For example, if you were studying coasts with Year 4, a possible citizenship link would be the rights and responsibilities of people in the management of coasts now and in the future. This could involve children looking at proposed developments, people's responses to them, the work of pressure groups and how to resolve conflicts of interest.

Once you have identified a citizenship link with your unit of work, think of possible activities for the children which are interactive and have local (and possibly global) links. Make sure that you identify clear learning objectives for both citizenship and geography.

These two tasks will have helped you appreciate that current curriculum topics or areas can be extended to include education for citizenship. A village school with a vertically grouped class of Reception and Years 1 and 2, took their topic of Toys and looked for global links and for opportunities to promote co-operation and conflict resolution. The citizenship elements included games from other countries (e.g. Ebele's Favourite: A book of African games) and games which involved co-operation and sharing. Children used the big book 'Play on the line' about the right to play and collected toys to send to refugee children on the edge of the Sahara Desert (www.saharatoys.org.uk).

In another school, teachers have looked at their teaching of RE, history and geography over the course of a year and specifically included a citizenship lesson in each unit of work. Table 5.4.1 shows their thinking for Year 2 and Year 5.

This approach can be adopted with other subjects. Thus an English lesson on persuasive writing might be extended to include a study of different newspapers' reporting of issues relating to asylum seekers. You could also extend your children's speaking and listening skills by using real-life situations – for example asking the children to interview a community member or their local MP. This would involve making decisions on what topics to raise and what makes a good question. In science, children can look at different forms of energy and current controversies about which types of energy are safe. They can look at cloning, GM crops and other topical controversial issues such as global warming and pollution. There are many opportunities for children to take action themselves (recycling, reducing energy consumption) thus participating as active citizens. They can also learn about organisations which are working for change in the environmental field, such as Greenpeace.

Table 5.4.1   Citizenship links to the humanities

Year 2		
RE		
RE theme: What does it mean to belong?	CE links: Global diversity: children of the world	Resources: Oxfam, Save the Children
History		
History theme: Children in Victorian times	CE links: Children's rights now and then: the right to play and to education	Resources: UNICEF
Geography		
Geography theme: Katie Morag's Island Home	CE themes: Accessibility: making the island accessible to all visitors, including those with disabilities	Resources: Katie Morag's Island Home, visit from disability officer

Year 5		
RE		
RE theme: How do beliefs influence action?	CE links: Active citizenship: making the world a better place – locally and globally	Resources: Charities working for change
History		
History theme: Tudors	CE links: Power and democracy: the rights of leaders, the death penalty then and now	Resources: Amnesty International
Geography		
Geography theme: Water – its effects on landscape and people	CE themes: The world's water: rights and responsibilities (accessibility, conservation)	Resources: 'Waterliterate' www.wateraid.org.uk

Citizenship as a discrete or stand-alone subject

Some schools have decided that certain areas of the citizenship curriculum are best covered as stand alone lessons, particularly when it comes to teaching about democracy and the law as it is often difficult to find ways of incorporating these areas into current units of work. This approach is being increasingly adopted by secondary schools for the same reason.

Task 5.4.3
Inviting visitors

Your school has decided to invite in the local MP as part of a citizenship week. You have been asked to organise this. You are keen to avoid a session where the MP talks 'over the heads' of the children on topics which are not relevant to them. How might you

- incorporate the visit of the MP into a unit of work on democracy?
- ensure that the session with the MP is interactive and relevant?
- involve the children in organising the visit?

A Year 4 class invited in their local MP after a unit on the community (as part of their citizenship work). They had spent a morning walking round their local city, visiting the council offices and the town hall and were aware of the importance of their MP representing their city in Parliament. Prior to the MP's visit, the teacher had the children work in threes to come up with three questions for the MP. All the questions were put up on the whiteboard and the children voted for which they thought were the best questions and why. The task of asking the questions was divided among the children, whilst others were assigned to meet him and show him round the school. Other children informed the local press. Some of the questions that the children chose to put to the MP were:

- Why don't we pay more to the people who give us food from other countries?
- Have you helped anyone in different countries?
- Why did the fight in Afghanistan start in the first place?
- Why don't we have more recycling bins?
- What can you do about the traffic?
- Why do you go to Parliament?
- Do you care very much about your country?

In another school, the teacher was doing a unit of work on the local area in geography. She wanted to follow this up in discrete citizenship lessons to look at the local area in the future, drawing on the pupils' aspirations for their community. As part of this she wanted to teach about the value of laws and rules in a community by getting the children to think about how their community of the future would be governed. This lesson is again one which follows active learning principles: there is opportunity for drawing, planning, speaking and listening, collaborative group work and empathy. There are opportunities for the teacher to assess these citizenship skills as the children engage with the task. The following was planned for two lessons.

The children's laws at the opening of this unit come from this lesson. Further lesson plans for primary citizenship can be found in Clough and Holden (2002), from which this activity is adapted, and Claire (2004).

My town, my future

Purpose

- To plan a community for the future, based on current concerns.
- To consider the physical and social needs of a community.
- To help children understand the role of the law in protecting communities.

Preparation

You will need a large sheet of sugar paper for each group and felt-tip pens.

Procedure

Start the class thinking about what makes a good town and what facilities are needed in relation to their own town or city. Draw on knowledge from local study:

- What do we like about our town (city)?
- What would we choose to show visitors?
- Which areas need improving?
- What is currently being planned for our town?
- What do we need here that we don't have?

Explain to the class that even now councillors and town planners are making decisions that will affect their town (or village or city) in a few years' time, planning new estates, roads and services. Others (councillors, politicians) are making decisions about laws and regulations which will affect people's way of life. For the purpose of this activity, children are to have the chance to plan a new town for twenty years hence or they can re-model their existing town. Money is not an issue but environmental issues must be considered.

Questions to consider:
- What facilities do young people need in a town or city?
- What do the elderly need?
- What about people with physical disabilities?
- What about the needs of other groups (e.g. newcomers, families)?

In addition to considering the needs of different groups, you can ask children to think about the transport system they want, meeting places, places of worship, schools etc.

After they have drawn the plans for their town, ask each group to agree on what *laws* they want in their community in order to protect people's rights and have the town function effectively. What punishments or sanctions would there be for those who break these laws? When all groups have completed their towns and laws, pin them on the walls for all to see or ask each group to explain in turn why their new town would be a good place to live.

Plenary

- How have you taken into account the needs of different groups?
- In what ways was your town environmentally friendly?
- Would you like to live in these towns? Why?
- What rules or rights did people have?
- How were these enforced?
- How different are these to current laws?

Citizenship as part of PSHE

Many schools will deliver citizenship through PSHE but you need to take care if you adopt this approach to ensure that the citizenship element is properly covered. First take time to see how PSHE is being taught in your school.

PSHE can be delivered in a number of ways, some of which may appear invisible to the new teacher. For example, learning to share, line up quietly, look after children new to the school and even eating with a knife and fork would all be part of social and moral education. Moral issues may also be covered in assemblies and in RE, healthy eating may be part of science, and many stories in literacy will offer opportunities for discussion on sensitive issues. But perhaps the most commonly used vehicle for PSHE is circle time. You will probably be familiar with this but if not, do ask to sit in on a circle time session on your next visit to school. In this, children sit in a circle and take turns to give their opinion on a given topic, with the conversation often being controlled by use of a special object which children hold when it is their turn to speak (Mosley 1996). This can be an excellent forum for discussion of many social and moral issues but if it is to move beyond PSHE and relate to citizenship, it must move beyond the personal. Circle time on bullying in the playground, or relationships between friends, for example, would be PSHE rather than citizenship. It would become citizenship if the focus were a current topical issue or an issue affecting the wider community. Thus a circle time on keeping healthy at a personal level would be PSHE but a class debate on whether the government should pay for expensive new drugs or put the money into care of the elderly would be citizenship.

Some schools use thinking circles, based on the work of Fisher (2001), as a basis for discussing citizenship issues. This moves beyond circle time as it allows for more in-depth group conversations and models the processes of deliberative discussion. With this technique, the teacher presents a story or moral issue (current or past), after which children reflect individually on a number of key questions, discussing these in small groups and then as a class. Children are taught to look for evidence to back up their statements, to question others and to review their thinking.

If children are used to thinking circles for discussing moral dilemmas, then when an event happens in the news or a controversial issue arises, the children (and the teacher) know how to discuss it. Children used to looking at current events from a number of points of view are learning how to come to informed decisions. Children can also be encouraged to bring their own concerns to the thinking circle and to formulate their own questions. The skills learnt in a thinking circle can then be transferred to role-play and more formal debates.

Citizenship through the ethos of the school

Although this way of delivering citizenship comes last here, it is perhaps the most important. When you visit schools you can often get a feel straight away for the ethos of the school and this will very much relate to citizenship. In a school where there is a strong citizenship ethos you are likely to find that:

- the children are treated with respect;
- their work is displayed with care;
- they are given responsibility around the school;
- they have a voice in the running of the school (e.g. through the school council);
- they have played a part in making the school rules;
- they feel valued and listened to;
- the school has active links with the local community.

It is obviously very difficult for you as a new teacher to influence the ethos of a school but a good place to start is the school council.

Task 5.4.4
School councils

Ask if you can sit in on the school council. Observe how the meeting is run and how decisions are reported back and proposals carried forward. Is there a school council notice board or do the class representatives report back to their classes? When do council meetings take place? In children's time or in school time? How are children elected onto the council? If possible talk to both school councillors and those who are not on the council to see what they think about it. Do they feel that their concerns are addressed effectively? Do they feel they have a voice?

There are many useful materials on effective school councils – both starting one up and improving existing ones. A good starting place is www.schoolscouncil.uk. If your school does not have a council, you might wish to start one (and older staff will often welcome a younger energetic person doing this!) but do take care to consult with staff and governors and make sure you have everyone's support.

You can also take the principles of school councils into your classroom, ensuring that children can air their concerns and that they are addressed. You can create opportunities within your classroom to involve the children in setting the classroom rules, sharing responsibilities and displaying work.

Apart from school councils, many schools will hold whole school events which offer opportunities for citizenship links. For example, the school may raise money for Red Nose Day or for another charity. The important thing here is to be sure that the children understand why they are raising this money, what the charity is doing and in particular what the recipients of the funds are doing to help themselves. There is a danger with fund-raising for charity that children see themselves as the benefactors, bringing in old toys for 'poor children', rather than being helped to understand the reasons why these children may be poor and what is being done to alleviate their plight. When children are fully engaged with charities (and allowed to have a say in which charities they choose), they can be great advocates for change and feel that they are making a positive contribution. Many charities now provide background information written for children, on their work, for example www.oxfam.org.uk and www.savethechildren.org.uk.

Other whole school activities may involve children visiting the elderly, helping in the school grounds or befriending new children. All of these offer scope for going 'behind the scenes' to understand the situation. Thus a visit by children to the elderly to help with their Christmas party might also be an opportunity to look at funding for and care of the elderly. Befriending new children to the school can be a chance to look at why people move, migration in general and the support services available to newcomers. What is at the heart of all these approaches is an open mind, a creative approach to the curriculum and an awareness of the opportunities provided by citizenship education.

HANDLING CONTROVERSIAL ISSUES: THE ROLE OF THE TEACHER

Whether you find yourself incorporating an aspect of citizenship into a history lesson or leading circle time on a sensitive issue like refugees, you are bound to encounter controversy. In fact it is often the controversial aspect of a curriculum subject that provides the citizenship element. Citizenship and controversy go hand in hand.

For this reason it is important for you to know where you stand. The original document which was the basis for the citizenship curriculum said that central to citizenship education was the need for children to debate topical and controversial issues in the classroom.

> Controversial issues are important in themselves and to omit informing about and discussing them is to leave a wide and significant gap in the educational experience of young people.
>
> (QCA 1998: 6)

This can be a cause for concern for many teachers, especially those new to the profession. You may worry that your own contributions or those of children in your class may be biased and reflect strongly held opinions which may be difficult to manage. For this reason there is clear guidance to teachers on different strategies for managing debate in classrooms. QCA (1998) recommends three possible approaches:

- the neutral chair approach;
- the balanced approach;
- the stated commitment approach.

You may use a combination of these approaches as the need arises. You may remain neutral, letting children put the various viewpoints, you may give a view (not necessarily your own) to ensure a balance of opinions is heard, or you may give your own view as a means of encouraging pupils to agree or disagree. What is important is that pupils are 'offered the experience of a genuinely free consideration of difficult issues' (QCA 1998: 60) and that issues are analysed 'according to an established set of criteria, which are open to scrutiny and publicly defensible' (p. 61). In other words, it is up to your professional judgement which approach you take so long as there are clear ground rules established which the children know about and which are fair to all.

If discussing controversial issues is part and parcel of life in your classroom and if an established set of criteria are in place, then when 'tricky' issues surface (e.g. 9/11) both you and the children will know how to listen to different views, to debate and discuss, rather than being worried about how to approach such controversial topics.

ASSESSMENT

It is important that citizenship does not become a subject where we just assess children's subject knowledge (e.g. about how parliament works or the rights of the child) as this would negate everything that has been said about the importance of developing the skills of enquiry, discussion and participation. At the current time QCA is working on exemplar materials to help teachers assess attainment in citizenship education so look out for advice on this.

Meanwhile Tables 5.4.2 and 5.4.3 illustrate the work of one teacher who is keen to develop ways to assess the skills of citizenship and to provide information for her Year 6 children to take to secondary school on transfer. Table 5.4.2 is for the teacher to use with individual pupils – you will see that the evidence comes from observing the child in group work rather than from written work. Table 5.4.3 is for the child to fill in (with guidance) to take to the secondary school so that their new teacher can know what they have covered and what their interests are. In this case it makes sense to combine information on both citizenship and PSHE on one form.

Table 5.4.2 An assessment tool for use in primary schools

Skills Area	Very Good	Good	OK	Needs Work	Evidence
Demonstrates an understanding of the issues					
Contributes to the discussion					
Argues points logically					
Considers the values involved					
Listens to others					
Is prepared to change his/her mind					
Works in a team					
Is prepared to compromise					

SUMMARY

Citizenship education is one of the challenges of the new century. It brings the past and present together, and it brings the current and the controversial into the classroom. It helps educate children who are informed, who are sensitive to the views of others and who can give their opinions based on evidence. Many teachers have welcomed this new initiative as it is a chance to go 'beyond the basics' and teach creatively about issues of importance to both children and teachers. As one PGCE primary student said when interviewed about teaching citizenship:

There's teaching the stuff that you have to teach but there's also educating children about life and about the real world and real issues and that's something which I feel is really important, it's close to my heart and something which I want to do.

Table 5.4.3   PSHCE information to go with Year 6 child to secondary

Name: *Comments from child*	*Comments from teacher/other adult*
Positions of responsibility held:	
Involvement in the school and wider community *(e.g. paired reading, people I help, clubs I'm involved in):*	
PSHE programmes covered *(e.g. bullying, drugs education, sex education):*	
Citizenship education covered *(e.g. work on human rights, fairtrade, democracy, organisations working for change):*	
Personal reflections on my ability to contribute to whole school changes, make choices, stand up for what I think is right and cope with challenges:	
Any issues that I feel strongly about *(e.g. things happening locally or globally):*	

ACKNOWLEDGEMENTS

With thanks to Karen Thomson, Cockington Primary School, Torquay and Gill Taylor, University of Exeter.

ANNOTATED FURTHER READING

Claire, H. (ed.) (2004) *Teaching Citizenship in Primary Schools*, Exeter: Learning Matters. A very useful book which covers all aspects of citizenship, including early years and links to history and geography.

Clough, N. and Holden, C. (2002) *Education for Citizenship: Ideas into Action*, London: RoutledgeFalmer. This book covers the 7–14 age range and has lesson plans which can be used directly in the classroom along with follow-up activities. Each chapter also summarises the latest thinking around particular themes, e.g. community, political literacy.

Young, M. and Commins, E. (2002) *Global Citizenship: The Handbook for Primary Teaching*, Cambridge: Chris Kington. As the title suggests, the emphasis is on global citizenship and the book has many useful ideas for teaching about other cultures and countries whether in separate citizenship lessons, through geography or through assemblies.

www.oxfam.org.uk/coolplanet/. This website is excellent for all aspects of global citizenship with many teaching ideas.

www.citized.info. This website has been set up especially for trainee teachers and teachers new to citizenship. There are lesson plans, schemes of work and a newly established forum for NQTs to discuss citizenship teaching. There is a specific primary section.

REFERENCES

Claire, H. (2001) *Not Aliens: Primary School Children and the Citizenship/PSHE Curriculum*, Stoke-on-Trent: Trentham.
Claire, H. (ed.) (2004) *Teaching Citizenship in Primary Schools*, Exeter: Learning Matters.
Clough, N. and Holden, C. (2002) *Education for Citizenship: Ideas into Action*, London: RoutledgeFalmer.
Cogan, J. and Derricott, R. (2000) *Citizenship for the 21st Century: An International Perspective on Education*, London: Kegan Paul.
DfES (2003) *Excellence and Enjoyment: A Strategy for Primary Schools*, Nottingham: DfES.
Fisher, R. (2001) *Values for Thinking*, Oxford: Nash Pollock.
Holden, C. (2006) 'Young people's concerns', in Hicks, D. and Holden, C. (eds) *The Challenge of Global Education: Key Principles and Effective Practice*, London: Routledge.
Mosley, J. (1996) *Quality Circle Time*, Wisbech: LDA.
QCA (1998) *Education for Citizenship and the Teaching of Democracy in Schools*, London: QCA.

Unit 5.5

Gifted and Talented

Deborah Eyre

INTRODUCTION

> We need to take particular steps to serve the needs of gifted and talented children.
>
> (DfES 2003: 41)

The idea that gifted and talented children need particular consideration during their primary schooling is one that has only recently been formally recognised. Yet, it has long been recognised that one of the greatest challenges for any primary teacher is to manage the learning needs of the various children in their class, especially when those children have very differing abilities.

Gifted and talented children is the term applied to those children who are achieving, or have the potential to achieve, at a level substantially beyond the rest of their peer group. It does not mean just the infant Mozart or the child Einstein, but rather refers to the upper end of the ability range in most classes. Every primary teacher therefore needs to know how to teach the gifted and talented and to be familiar with the techniques for creating high levels of intellectual challenge in the classroom. On the whole these children can be some of the most rewarding to teach and provided that you create a classroom in which they can thrive, they will generally repay you handsomely. Conversely if they are under-challenged they can become disruptive and difficult.

This unit is designed to help you to create a classroom that meets the needs of your gifted and talented children by creating an intellectually lively and challenging learning environment. By creating this kind of environment to meet the needs of your gifted children you will also provide benefits for the whole class and raise overall expectations. In this unit we will consider how to identify the gifted or talented children in your class, ways to create an overall learning environment that encourages high levels of achievement, and techniques for planning challenging tasks.

WHO ARE THE GIFTED AND TALENTED?

Identifying who is gifted or talented is not as important in the primary school as making provision for them. You need to concentrate on making the right provision and then it is easy to spot who is gifted. The reason for this is that giftedness is not something that we are born with and will always be evident whatever the circumstances; it is rather more complicated than that. Current thinking suggests that we are born with certain predispositions and that they give us the capacity to excel in particular areas. But this does not mean we will automatically excel, only if we develop those predispositions. For predisposition we might substitute the more commonly used educational term, potential.

An easy way to think about giftedness is as an equation.

$$\text{potential} + \text{opportunities/support} + \text{personal drive} = \text{high achievement (giftedness)}$$

Therefore, for giftedness to emerge, children must meet the right opportunities and be given appropriate support throughout their entire childhood. It is not a question of 'pushing' or 'hot-housing' but, instead, of coaching and supporting. Not holding children back by having preconceived ideas about what a six-year-old or a ten-year-old can/should do, but equally not pushing them forward at a rate that makes them uncomfortable.

Therefore the main focus in primary education should be in creating the right opportunities, offering appropriate support and helping the child to develop a desire to learn and to achieve. Also to act as a 'talent spotter' recognising indicators of outstanding ability as and when they begin to emerge. As you will already know, most researchers think that ability is multi-dimensional, so you don't have to be good at everything, just outstanding at something, to be considered gifted.

It is important to keep in mind that children defined as gifted or talented are simply normal children with all the usual personality characteristics of their age group. They are diverse in their personalities and interests and it is no more possible to attribute an extensive range of personality characteristics to gifted children than it would be to children with, say, dyslexia. Don't be surprised if you find you have a gifted child in your class who is naughty or immature; giftedness is simply about intellectual ability and that is only one aspect of any child. As far as intellectual characteristics are concerned, most gifted and talented children are of above average ability generally, but have specific areas of outstanding strength.

IDENTIFYING THE GIFTED AND TALENTED

Outstanding ability in some areas, or in some children, can be detected very early. If, in Foundation Stage, you have a child who uses an extensive vocabulary and exhibits an easy facility with language then they will stand out from others in the class. Equally, a child who when introduced to simple number patterns then makes up much more complex ones of his or her own, e.g. using large or negative numbers, is obviously mathematically able. These types of children who stand out from their peers are known in the literature as 'precociously gifted' and are usually identified early.

A second group of children start to emerge when they start school. In primary school some children with the potential to perform highly will start to forge ahead of others as soon as school introduces them to high quality learning opportunities in the formal curriculum. They will readily acquire the knowledge, skills and concepts associated with their domains of strength. For these individuals identification becomes a relatively straightforward process because the gap between their performance and that of their peers grows rapidly. They will be the 'star performers' in your class. They may well be recognisable in Foundation Stage or Key Stage 1 but will almost certainly be on the gifted and talented register by Key Stage 2.

The 'precociously gifted' and 'star performers' usually identify themselves but there are other indicators that can help you as a teacher to spot who else might be gifted. One of the best early indicators is not so much about outstanding performance relative to others, but rather about substantial interest. The child who is fascinated by music or number or language and seeks to play games with it. (Linguistically able children often, for example, make up terrible jokes using word puns.) As formal school progresses, each stage brings a chance for children to collide with new opportunities and to discover their areas of particular strength. Playfulness is not restricted to Foundation Stage; you may be playful at any stage; in fact the more skilled you become in an area the more scope there is to play. Once you know that a story has to have a beginning, a middle and an end you can start to create ones that don't! A key technique for teaching gifted and talented children is to encourage them to be intellectually playful. Teach them the rules and then help them to move beyond them.

Task 5.5.1
Talent spotting

Spend a few minutes thinking about the children in your class. Can you identify any who fit the categories we have looked at? Do you have any 'precociously gifted'? Who are your 'star performers'?

Over a day or two observe your class and see if you can spot any intellectually 'playful' children.

Families play a large part in the intellectual development of young children. Any signs of ability or 'playfulness' will be nurtured in most families, especially if the area of interest coincides with the interests of other members of the family. If a pair of professional musicians find their child shows an interest in music they will encourage and support its development in quite a structured way. Equally a family of academics might encourage questioning or investigation. An entrepreneurial family will encourage entrepreneurship, and so on. This means that it is hard for you as a teacher to discern between raw potential and nurtured achievement. Howe (1995) suggests that in the right circumstances anyone can be coached to become gifted. This may be an extreme view but nevertheless help from home can assist those with potential to appear 'precocious' and perhaps more worrying can lead to some children being seen as gifted in their early years of schooling when in fact they are really just well-coached. These children will inevitably begin to find schooling more difficult as they move through school when the conceptual demands increase and their performance will become less remarkable.

The reverse of parent support is of course the results of lack of parental support. Gifted children from homes where intellectual support and opportunity is lacking are more reliant on the school making those opportunities and support available. These children will not show up in the 'precociously gifted' category and will never be your 'star performers' unless you as a teacher take action. You need to spot their 'playfulness' or insightful comments and structure their learning to help them make rapid progress in the formal curriculum. It is your job to look below the surface, especially with children from disadvantaged backgrounds.

Five ways to spot gifted children

- assessment of achievement through a variety of assessment measures (precocious);
- particularly at Foundation Stage and KS1, children who are interested in an area and actively seek to pursue it, enjoying it for its own sake (playful);
- pupils who appear to master the rules of a domain easily and can transfer their insights to new problems (precision);
- pupils who observe their own behaviour and hence utilise a greater variety of learning strategies than others (self regulation);
- pupils who exhibit any of the characteristics above plus a tendency towards non-conformity in the given domain (originality).

A very real problem in identifying gifted and talented children in primary school is confusion between the acquisition of skills and real intellectual ability. Giftedness is about cognitive ability, the ability to think. Skills are important but not all gifted children acquire basic skills quickly and this can hold back intellectual development.

In considering this you may find it helpful to think of a particular skill, e.g. learning to read, as being like learning to drive. The length of time it takes you to pass your driving test is not an indicator of how good a driver you will eventually be. You can't be an expert driver without acquiring the basic skills (passing the test) but it is how you apply those skills later that makes the difference. So too in school. Acquiring the skills is important but it is how you 'use and apply' them that differentiates between acceptable and outstanding performance.

> Jack, aged seven, is a linguistically gifted child with an exceptional vocabulary. He learned to talk at 12 months and never makes grammatical errors. He never needs to redraft his ideas because he has immense fluency with language. However, he finds some of the skills associated with learning to read (decoding text) or to write (forming letters) difficult even though he is expert at plot and character. This discrepancy is because the aspects he finds difficult require visual or physical coordination which is not an area of strength for him. He needs support in these. This mismatch between ability and skill can lead to a very frustrating period for some gifted children as they are accustomed to learning easily. If they are not helped to master basic skills then underachievement is inevitable. However, once these 'tools' are acquired then progress is very rapid. This inability to master some of the basic skills quickly, is one of the reasons that some gifted children are not recognised at primary school. Jack may well have been overlooked if his teacher had not been 'talent spotting'.

We have talked very little about the role of SATs or other tests in the identification process. They are of course crucial and an integral part of the school's methodology for identifying gifted children. If a child performs well on the test then that should be seen as a key indicator. However, it is also important to look beyond test data especially in Foundation Stage and Key Stage 1. Tests should be seen as one indicator rather than the sole indicator. Evidence-based teacher assessment is crucial in this process, so use the tests, but also keep your antenna alert for undiscovered talent.

Creating the learning environment

Gifted and talented children are first and foremost children and much of what they need is exactly the same as for other children. They need to be treated like other children and expected to behave accordingly. If the following is the basis by which you set your classroom climate for all children then gifted children will also thrive.

Gifted and talented children need to:

- have a secure environment in which they feel happy to display ability;
- experience intellectual challenge, sometimes having to struggle to achieve;
- take risks and sometimes make mistakes;
- relax and have fun;
- comply with the class rules and code of conduct;
- know that they can ask searching questions and get a considered response;
- receive praise when they do well;
- be recognised as individuals with strengths and weaknesses;
- be able to discuss things meaningfully with the teacher.

Creating a secure environment

Each of the items in the above list are particularly important for gifted and talented children. The secure environment is perhaps the most important of all. Gifted children who are achieving highly do stand out, and this can cause difficulties. Sensitive children will notice that they stand out and may not find it easy. It is not 'cool to be bright'. In some schools, and in some classrooms, gifted children will learn that drawing attention to what you know leads to being called 'clever clogs' or earns you the reputation as the class 'boffin'. If you are a sensitive child this can be very damaging and such children soon learn to hide their ability and in some cases deliberately underachieve in order to remain unnoticed. Less sensitive children may continue to draw attention to themselves and become socially ostracised. Gifted children do need to learn how to manage their ability so that they do not continually show off and try to outperform everyone else, but equally they should not have to be ashamed of their ability. It is something to celebrate. If you are really committed to celebrating diversity in your classroom then it should be easy to accommodate the gifted and talented children. Circle time, for example, is a good way of addressing the needs of gifted individuals and also can be used to help them to recognise the different strengths other children have.

If you are trying to 'talent spot' then it is essential that you create a classroom climate where children are happy to reveal their ability. The best way to do this is to focus all your children on learning and deliberately draw attention to the different strengths individuals in the class bring to the class's learning. More generally make it clear that everyone is expected to do their best and it is evidence of achievement through hard work that is rewarded not just achievement. A piece of research (Eyre *et al*. 2002: 10) looking at primary school teachers who were very good at teaching gifted and talented children, found that all the successful classrooms were positive, pacey and purposeful with a focus on hard work, fun and recognition of individual effort and achievement. They were not classrooms characterised by serious and earnest endeavour but rather a context where children and teachers enjoyed the challenge of learning and the satisfaction of progress and success.

A classroom with high expectations

Of course in order for gifted children to both emerge and to excel you have to have high expectations regarding what you think can be achieved. The learning objectives must be ambitious and clear and you need to ensure that the children are aware of them. Gifted children make intellectual connections between what they are learning now, what they learnt before and the long-term learning objective. They like you to take them into your confidence and for you to tell them not only what is going to happen but also why you are doing it and where it is leading. By Years 5 and 6 many gifted children will want an overview of the term or at least the half-term because this information helps them to gain control of their learning and become more independent. If they know you are going to do the Greeks then they may begin to read about them. They may line up their relatives to make sure they give them relevant presents for Christmas and they are likely to help you make the lessons more engaging. Of course you do not need to have a special conversation with your gifted and talented about the overall scheme of work, just tell the whole class.

A key element in creating a good learning environment is learning to value each child as an individual and knowing their strengths and weaknesses. Even the most gifted children are better at some things than others and they often suffer from people expecting them to be able to do everything equally well. They may find it hard to ask for help and some will be real perfectionists who find even minor failures hard to take. You can help here by creating an approach where 'having a go' is highly valued, even more than 'getting it right'. Make comments like, 'That's a really good suggestion, I can see why you thought that but …'. 'I used to think … but then I found out' etc. Encourage children to take intellectual risks and not worry if they are wrong. Einstein said that clever people are those who make their mistakes fastest. Help your class to see that making mistakes is good if we examine them carefully and learn from them. It helps us move forward. Try using some examples of famous people who made big mistakes on the way to discovering great things. (Science can provide particularly good examples since science is about refuting or confirming existing theories.)

Teacher/pupil interaction

Gifted and talented pupils like to work with people who have greater levels of expertise than themselves. In school this is usually the adults, and especially the teacher. It can also, in many schools, be other children of similar ability. Gifted children value teachers who habitually discuss things with their class and who are willing, on occasion, to discuss something in depth with the individual. To make this happen it is important to focus on four areas:

- teacher questions;
- pupil questions;
- teacher explanation;
- pupil explanation.

Teacher questions can stimulate thinking and are a very useful way to differentiate for the most able. Try directing a series of particularly searching questions towards a confident child who you know to be gifted and let everyone listen as the argument is developed.

Task 5.5.2
The power of questions

Discuss with your tutor your questioning technique. How frequently do you ask open questions which require children to think or offer an opinion? Most teachers ask too many closed questions which are designed merely to confirm whether the child understands rather than open up new thinking.

Look at how to improve your questioning skills. (Wragg and Brown 1993, is a good starting point, as is the guidance from the literacy and numeracy strategies.)

Asking the right questions is a two-way process and as children move through primary school you need to help them to become questioners. They need to pose questions and query findings, not take information at face value. This can begin very early and 'book talk' is a good way to engage with this agenda. If you begin by saying what questions could we ask about this book and doing this quite regularly then your gifted children will start to pose similar questions when they read. Aidan Chambers' book entitled *Tell Me* (1993) has a great set of ideas for this. This technique works equally well with a historical picture or a map. Any stimulus can be used in this way to get children thinking. In GCSE history, original sources are used and students judge the reliability of the source. This kind of technique can easily be used in Key Stage 2 and even younger. All children can take part when this is a general classroom activity but with your gifted children you should encourage, and later expect, them to take this analytical approach to all their work not just when you have set up a particular task. For gifted pupils it should become a way of thinking not just an activity.

In a similar way you can use your teacher explanations to create thinking. Don't just describe and convey information. Try to set it as a query or use it to make connections with previous learning. Encourage your gifted children to describe what they have learnt/found out in such a way as to make it appealing to others – perhaps for a specific audience, e.g. a younger class or the school governors. Explanations that have a real purpose are much more engaging than feedback sessions.

Classroom management

The key to meeting the needs of all the children in your class, including the gifted, is time management. Well-established classroom routines create the space for one-to-one work with individuals. Make sure the classroom is laid out in such a way as to enable children to collect materials independently. Ensure that you prevent disruptive behaviour by having a clear code of behaviour and a consistent approach to dealing with misbehaviour. Make sure your instructions are clear and unambiguous. Create ways of working in the classroom that everyone adheres to, e.g. where to put books for marking. Most of all, always make sure you have planned carefully and have everything you need for the lesson.

WAYS TO CHALLENGE GIFTED CHILDREN IN THE PRIMARY CLASSROOM

Much of what constitutes good classroom provision generally is also good provision for the gifted. You need to ensure that these elements are in place generally in your classroom before looking at specific challenges for the gifted:

- careful planning;
- clear learning objectives;
- target setting;
- high expectations;
- variety of approach;
- assessment for learning;
- good evaluation.

Gifted children need to be challenged both by the way in which they are required to operate in class and by the tasks they are given to do. These two elements support each other. In designing tasks for gifted and talented children it is useful to consider what we know about their learning (Shore 2000: 173).

- Gifted pupils do not seem to use strategies that others never use;
- gifted pupils differ from others in the creativity and extent to which they draw upon a repertoire of intellectual skills that are nonetheless available to others;
- they demonstrate expert performance by using metacognition, strategy flexibility, strategy planning, hypothesis, preference for complexity, extensive webbing of knowledge about both facts and processes
- they think like experts even though they may lack some of the skills of experts.

So there is nothing that is unique to the gifted children in your class. The above does, however, give some good clues on designing tasks to challenge the gifted. If gifted children think like experts then consider what experts in the subject consider to be important and try to include it. If gifted children are original and creative in their solutions to problems give them tasks that encourage this and don't be surprised if they fail to give you the text book answer. If they see learning as a complex interwoven web then help them to make those connections and allow them to complexify the original task to make it more interesting and demanding. Try differentiation by self, i.e. they suggest ways in which the core task set for the whole class could be made more demanding. Don't forget they are the ones with the brains: don't do everything for them.

Tasks to help children engage in advanced thinking

It is helpful to consider what, in addition to the acquisition of the knowledge, skills and concepts that we hope all children will achieve, we should expect of gifted children. The following are behaviours you should seek to engender:

- greater reflection;
- exploration of a variety of viewpoints;
- consideration of difficult questions;
- formulation of individual opinions;
- problem solving and enquiry;
- connections between past and present learning;
- regular use of higher order thinking (analysis, synthesis and evaluation);
- independent thinking and learning.

How might you do this? A good way is by designing enquiry-based tasks:

- think independently – what do you think was the reason?
- reflect – why do you think that happened?
- recognise connections in learning – can you think of another time when that happened? Or – compare these two accounts.
- explore ideas and choose a 'best' solution – which of these would be the most appropriate for …?
- justify ideas – which of the following would be best, give reasons for your choice?
- explain ideas using appropriate technical language – yes that's right, that is called a …
- solve problems and recognise the strategy used – what made that successful?
- think about real problems – how could we stop mud getting on the classroom carpet?
- encouragement to use a wide vocabulary – can you find a better word for …?
- order and marshal ideas – tell me/draw/write the different steps you took to do that experiment.
- explore conflicting ideas – was Robin Hood a good man?

This enquiry-based approach helps gifted children to develop the higher level thinking skills that will enable them to perform at an advanced level. There are a variety of hierarchies of thinking skills in the education literature but all share a view that the higher order thinking involves concepts such as comparison, analysis, reworking of ideas (synthesis), invention and evaluation of worth/value. The unit in this book by Robert Fisher (Unit 5.2) looks in more detail at general use of thinking skills. When creating challenge for the gifted simply focus on the top level skills.

These kinds of enquiry-based tasks are a good way to create challenge for the gifted but they do not always have to be given to a specific group of children. Sometimes the task may require advanced reading or mathematical skills and therefore can only be offered to a specific group, but often enquiry tasks can be designed with challenge for the gifted in mind but then made available to all. The gifted will simply offer better, more sophisticated and more original solutions. This brings us back to identification. If you offer these types of tasks to all children then the outcomes may surprise you. You may 'talent spot' potentially gifted children you had not recognised before.

Breadth, depth and pace

There are three ways in which you can plan for gifted children to experience learning outside of that made available to all. You can add breadth, depth or pace to the normal curriculum on offer.

Breadth (sometimes called enrichment) can be defined as adding additional material at broadly the same cognitive level. For example, studying more about a particular period of history or reading more widely around the core subject. It does not require the acquisition of new skills but may emphasise the opportunity to 'use and apply' existing ones. Breadth can also include learning a completely new subject in addition to those studied by others. An example here might be Key Stage 2 after-school Latin Club. Breadth is useful because using and applying learned skills is a good way to consolidate them and also creates a context for devising original ideas. Introducing children to new areas can also help children discover their abilities by widening their horizons and since this is a key role for primary schools, adding breadth to the curriculum for all children (as well as those identified as gifted) should be seen as a key strategy in challenging the gifted and talented.

In adding breadth to the curriculum the greatest risk is inevitably overload. If you want your gifted children to experience additional learning then also consider what you could excuse them from. Gifted children are no more industrious than others and don't like having extra work.

Depth (sometimes called extension) refers to an increase in cognitive level achieved by taking the existing focus of work and going into greater depth. It usually involves learning new material including new skills and concepts. Good classroom provision should include a mix of breadth, depth and pace but perhaps depth is the most important. It is about learning how to think intellectually. There are many ways to achieve depth but here is an example you might like to try. Take a solvable puzzle, e.g. a crossword or a word search, and first ask all the class to solve it and then ask the gifted children to create one of their own. In order to create a puzzle you need to consider how the puzzle works and this requires you to deconstruct it. Talk about how it functions and why it works. Can they make one? Can they make one that is even better than the one they solved? Why is it better? This takes you into much deeper territory. Equally you might add depth by selecting an area that experts value but which does not appear in the primary curriculum. Historiography is a good example here. If you have very able children in Key Stage 2 looking at the Victorians then you might take a Victorian (maybe from your local area) who was considered as a hero in his or her time and is now less valued (or vice versa) and consider how the society in which we live shapes our view of history. Use some first-hand resources like newspaper articles. These are very easy to access on the web.

A practical way to increase depth is by bringing experts into the classroom, using people from the wider community, from museums or science centres, using authors or academics, using parents or local experts. These events are great for all children but think carefully about whether a proportion of the time could be spent with a smaller group developing high level skills or exploring more advanced concepts.

Pace is about moving through the existing curriculum faster than other children and is sometimes called acceleration. (Acceleration should not be confused with accelerated learning which is something quite different.) In practice, whatever strategies you adopt will involve the gifted children moving ahead of their peers in the formal curriculum and this is entirely appropriate. In general planning you should always look at the more advanced levels in the National Curriculum as a key way of creating challenge for the gifted and talented. The National Curriculum is a spiral curriculum and so concepts reoccur and skills are revisited. When planning a lesson you should consider what would be the next learning objective in this area and would it be suitable to include it in this lesson for some children.

The best provision for gifted children is through a mix of depth, breadth and pace. When planning the scheme of work it is usually easy to see which might work best but ensure that you do not rely too heavily on any single one.

Task 5.5.3
Task design

Create three tasks for use in your classroom. Task 1 must add breadth, task 2 depth and task 3 pace. Implement them and then reflect on the following with your tutor:

- why you chose them;
- how you created them;
- who in your class experienced them and why;
- how they worked in practice;
- what you have learned from the process.

There is no single way to create challenge for your gifted and talented but make sure you aim high and use resources that will help you to create well-informed, thinking children. The following ideas may get you started:

- Investigate or problem-solve using a 'plan/do/review' approach.
- Work from difficult texts or intensively on one text.
- Use a variety of texts/pictures/artefacts, to compare and contrast.
- Record in an unusual way. Use fewer words rather than more.
- Role-play. Think from someone else's point of view.
- Provide choice in how children handle the content.
- Create tasks that require decision-making.
- Create tasks with no single correct answer.
- Provide the answer; they set the questions.
- Create an element of speed. Journalistic deadlines.
- Introduce technical language. Speak and think like an expert.

SUMMARY

Meeting the needs of gifted and talented children is part of meeting the needs of all. By focusing on high expectations and talent spotting you may well find more gifted children than you expect and at the same time create a learning environment that is challenging and fun for all. The aim for a primary school is to ensure that their gifted and talented children reach secondary school with a desire to learn and the skills to do so, so that they can go on to achieve highly.

ANNOTATED FURTHER READING

Eyre, D. (1997) *Able Children in Ordinary Schools*, London: David Fulton Publishers. This is a practical handbook for teachers and head teachers looking to improve provision in schools. It includes chapters on management and classroom practice.

Eyre, D., Coates, D., McClure, L. and Wilson, H. (2002) *Effective Teaching of Able Pupils in the Primary Classroom*, Birmingham: National Primary Trust. This short book describes the practice of five teachers who are considered to be very good at challenging gifted children in their classroom.

Eyre, D. and McClure, L. (eds) (2001) *Curriculum Provision for the Gifted and Talented in the Primary School*, London: David Fulton Publishers. An edited book with chapters detailing help and ideas on teaching English, maths and science.

Friedman, R.C. and Shore, B.M. (eds) (2000) *Talents Unfolding: Cognition and Development*, Washington, DC: American Psychological Association. A substantial edited volume covering the work of some of the key international research in gifted and talented education.

DfES and QCA websites, gifted and talented sections.

REFERENCES

Chambers, A. (1993) *Tell Me*, Stroud: Thimble Press.

DfES (2003) *Excellence and Enjoyment*, London: Department for Education and Skills.

Eyre, D., Coates, D., McClure, L. and Wilson, H. (2002) *Effective Teaching of Able Pupils in the Primary Classroom*, Birmingham: National Primary Trust.

Howe, M. (1995) 'What can we learn from the lives of geniuses?', in Freeman, J. (ed.) *Actualizing Talent*, London: Cassell.

Shore, B.M. (2000) 'Metacognition and flexibility: qualitative differences in how gifted children think', In Friedman, R.C. and Shore, B.M. (eds) *Talents Unfolding: Cognition and Development*, Washington, DC: American Psychological Association.

Wragg, E.C. and Brown, G. (1993) *Questioning*, London: Routledge.

6 Diversity and Inclusion

Unit 6.1

Inclusive Approaches

Janet Tod and Simon Ellis

INTRODUCTION

Inclusion remains firmly on the educational agenda for the twenty-first century and is likely to be central to the development of your practice. This unit will explore inclusion and inclusive education within the context of Special Educational Needs (SEN) and disability by looking at: key principles, policy initiatives, and development of inclusive practice.

OBJECTIVES

By the end of the unit you should have:

- an increased understanding of the rationale for inclusion in schools;
- an awareness of the policy initiatives that inform inclusive approaches for schools;
- reflected upon how to develop your own pedagogy with regard to inclusion;
- increased your range of strategies for achieving increased inclusion.

KEY PRINCIPLES

Educational inclusion is a term that lacks adequate theorising or consensus about what it means in practice (Wearmouth *et al.* 2005). Central to the ideology of inclusion is the belief that education makes a powerful contribution to the social construction of inclusive communities and an inclusive society. Inclusive education is concerned with human rights in that it promotes access to, and participation in, an appropriate mainstream community based education. It offers the promise of increased opportunity to engage in lifelong learning and employment.

Although the concept of inclusion is not new (Clough 1998), policy changes for Special Educational Needs (SEN) have undoubtedly been triggered by the United Nations Educational, Scientific and Cultural Organisation (UNESCO) Salamanca Statement (1994). This followed a World Conference on Special Needs Education which called for inclusion to be the 'norm'.

Research indicates that most teachers endorse the ideology of inclusion (Avramidis and Norwich 2002) and are enthusiastic about developing their practice in this area. However there are issues to be faced within the practical context of the classroom. Perhaps you have asked yourself some of the following questions:

- How can I 'get through' the learning outcomes prescribed by the National Curriculum Key Stages (which seem quite challenging and fast-paced) and at the same time set the pace and objectives needed for learners with SEN?
- If inclusion is about human rights and I have a pupil who is disrupting others in the class, does the individual right of a pupil to be included take precedence over the right of the rest of the class to learn?
- Do children with severe and complex learning needs really learn best in a mainstream class? Surely they need some form of specialist provision and would be better off in a special school.
- How can inclusion work for a pupil who is deaf and partially sighted? I have a pupil who is finding it difficult to communicate with his peers at playtime. His parents want him to go to a school where he can make friends easily *and* learn – I am tending to agree with them.
- As we have Teaching Assistants who know more about SEN than I do, isn't it better for them to deal with SEN pupils on an individual basis?

All these questions and reflections are relevant to you as you progress with your learning and teaching in the primary school. They are questions that should be aired with your mentors and colleagues. Inclusion does of course tend to be regarded as 'the right thing to do' and it is this moral imperative than often makes teachers feel guilty about saying anything negative about inclusive policies and practices.

When you are reflecting upon your concerns about the practical difficulties of inclusion it is important for you to also think about some potential drawbacks of non-inclusive approaches. These may include:

- An acceptance by teachers that academic and social learning outcomes are necessarily 'limited' for some pupils by virtue of the pupil's genetic inheritance and/or social circumstances. Such a stance *assumes* that we can reliably identify 'potential to learn' and make educational decisions on behalf of the individual concerned. These decisions may involve placement in separate and/or different provision and may reduce the opportunity for the pupil concerned to access a mainstream curriculum and neighbourhood peer interaction.
- Non-inclusive approaches for SEN pupils may endorse a view that an emphasis on basic self-help and communication skills is a more 'appropriate' education for some individuals.
- Protection from, rather than participation in, the life and learning of same age mainstream peers.
- Exposure to the notion that difference/diversity from the 'norm' is somehow a weakness that has to be pitied and provided for within a protective framework.
- By segregating pupils with SEN/disability from mainstream and community activities there is a lost opportunity for all children to experience the benefits of learning and socialising with a

range of different individuals. This may result in a fear and unease about relating to 'different' individuals being continually reproduced as a societal norm.

- By constantly trying to identify and teach to a 'mythical average' teachers do not extend their professional expertise and have to seek help from 'specialists'; incidentally, the notion that there is a distinct pedagogy for specialist teaching for SEN/disability is not supported by research (Norwich and Lewis 2001).
- Pupils with SEN are still cited as being at risk of social exclusion (Parsons 2003) ten years after the original SEN *Code of Practice* (DfE 1994). Children with SEN are four times more likely to be excluded from mainstream school than other pupils (BBC/DfES 2005).

It is important to remember that a positive attitude to inclusion has an impact on the process of developing inclusive teaching strategies (Halliwell 2003). However as a member of the teaching profession you cannot be positive about inclusion just because you are told it is the right thing to do; you need to understand the different perspectives on inclusion – ideological, political, sociological and educational – and experience the processes and outcomes of inclusion in your school contexts. You will develop increased understanding over time and come to appreciate that inclusion is a process that is influenced by a range of factors and has different meanings and outcomes for those involved, e.g. it may have a different meaning for a parent than a policy maker and be judged accordingly. The following exercise is designed to enable you to understand these different perspectives on inclusion within your school.

Task 6.1.1
Is your school inclusive?

Do you think your school is inclusive? Think about the process by which you made that judgement. If you were asked to gather evidence about the impact of inclusion in your school, what evidence would you look for and why?

In reflecting upon whether your school is inclusive you probably became aware that there are many different indicators to be considered, i.e. indicators linked to policy development, changes in practice, and the experiences of the individual learner. In thinking about inclusion from your perspective it should now be clear that inclusion is a complex construct rather than a single indicator that you are required to achieve.

POLICY INITIATIVES

In looking at policy initiatives for inclusion there appear to be two key agendas:

- one agenda for making mainstream schools more responsive to increasing diversity – we will refer to these as 'generic' inclusion policies;
- the other agenda to provide guidance for those pupils who may require *'additional to and different from'* provision (DfES 2001a) as a result of special or additional educational needs (AEN). We will refer to these as 'SEN specific' policies.

'Generic' inclusion policy development:

With respect to policy that applies to *all* pupils the following documentation will be relevant to the development of practice in your school:

1   *Excellence for All Children: Meeting Special Educational Needs* (DfEE 1997) and

2   *Meeting Special Educational Needs: A Programme of Action* (DfEE 1998). These two policies embraced the principle of inclusion and set the scene for subsequent guidance and policy designed to develop inclusive practice within schools.

3   *The National Curriculum: Handbook for Primary Teachers in England* (DfEE/QCA 1999). The National Curriculum inclusion statement (DfEE/QCA 1999) emphasises the importance of providing effective learning opportunities for *all* pupils and sets out three principles essential to the development of a more inclusive curriculum:
    * setting suitable learning challenges;
    * responding to pupils' diverse needs;
    * overcoming potential barriers to learning and assessment for individuals and groups of pupils.

4   *The Index for Inclusion: Developing Learning and Participation in Schools* (Booth *et al.* 2000) was published by CSIE (Centre for Studies in Inclusive Education). The DfEE funded distribution of the *Index* to every school and LEA in England. The *Index* is a tool for a process of self-evaluation of policy and practice. It is designed to be used as a contribution to a process of school review involving all staff, governors, students, parents and carers. The *Index* is organised under three dimensions, each with two subsections. Each of these leads to a list of indicators that can be used to guide the self-evaluation process. The three dimensions are :
    * *Dimension A:* creating inclusive cultures;
    * *Dimension B:* producing inclusive policies;
    * *Dimension C:* evolving inclusive practice.

Dimension C, which is particularly relevant to this unit has as its purpose:

> This dimension is about making school practices reflect inclusive cultures and policies of the school. It is concerned with ensuring that classroom and extra-curricular activities encourage the participation of all students and draw on their knowledge and experience outside the school. Teaching and support are integrated together in the orchestration of learning and the overcoming of barriers to learning and participation. Staff mobilise resources within the school and learning communities to sustain active learning for all.
>
> (Booth *et al.* 2000: 45)

This statement captures the underpinning philosophy of inclusive education and the materials contained within the *Index* support schools in developing their own policies and practices.

5   *Inclusive Schooling* (DfES 2001b) provided practical advice to schools and LEAs on the operation of the inclusion framework and set out seven principles of an inclusive education service:
    * inclusion is a process by which schools, local education authorities and others develop their cultures, policies and practices to include pupils;
    * with the right training, strategies and support nearly all children with special educational needs can be successfully included in mainstream education;
    * an inclusive education service offers excellence and choice and incorporates the views of parents and children;
    * the interests of all pupils must be safeguarded;
    * schools, local education authorities and others should actively seek to remove barriers to learning and participation;

- all children should have access to an appropriate education that affords them the opportunity to achieve their personal potential.

   Mainstream education will not always be right for every child all of the time. Equally just because mainstream education may not be right at a particular stage it does not prevent the child from being included successfully at a later stage.

   (DfES 2001b: 2)

6   *Every Child Matters* (DfES 2003, 2004a, 2004b) has served to set educational inclusion within the broader context of radical change in the whole system of children's services including explicit shifting from intervention to prevention with services working together more effectively. The procedures set out in *Every Child Matters* are designed both to protect children and maximise their potential. The overall aim is to reduce the numbers of children who experience educational failure, engage in offending or antisocial behaviour, suffer from ill health, or become teenage parents (DfES 2003).

   Every Child Matters identifies five outcomes that are key to well-being in childhood and later life:

   - *being healthy:* enjoying good physical and mental health and living a healthy lifestyle;
   - *staying safe*: being protected from harm and neglect;
   - *enjoying and achieving:* getting the most out of life and developing the skills for adulthood;
   - *making a positive contribution:* being involved with the community and society and not engaging in antisocial or offending behaviour;
   - *economic well-being:* not being prevented by economic disadvantage from achieving their full potential in life.

   These five outcomes are central to the programme of change outlined in *Every Child Matters* and are at the heart of the Children Act 2004 which provides the legislative foundation for the programme.

In looking at the development of 'generic' policies for inclusion the key consistent messages for class teachers are that:

- teachers plan for the diverse needs of *all* pupils in their class;
- meeting diverse needs, including SEN, is the responsibility of all teachers.

This is a significant change from the era of 'integration' that followed the DES 1978 Warnock Report and subsequent 1981 Education Act. During this era, class teachers typically planned for the majority of pupils and then sought additional resources and approaches for their SEN pupils (e.g. IEPs Individual Education Plans) through a staged approach to SEN as set out in the 1994 DfE *Code of Practice* framework.

If inclusion is to be viewed as a *process* that requires 'specialist provision' to be critically re-examined and located within the repertoire of mainstream schools and their teachers, then it follows that interim 'SEN specific' policies will be needed to protect the learning needs of pupils with SEN during the period when mainstream teachers are being trained, and schools are developing their policies and practices for inclusion.

'SEN specific' policies

The revised *Special Educational Needs Code of Practice* (DfES 2001a) sought to further emphasise themes from the National Curriculum inclusion statement:

> All schools through their cycle of observation, assessment, planning and review make provision for increased curriculum differentiation, curricular adaptations, and pastoral or disciplinary procedures dependent on the individual child's strengths and weaknesses. A variety of approaches should be employed to maximise the achievement of all pupils. These kinds of arrangements apply to all children and are not part of special educational provision.
>
> (DfES 2001a: 47)

In confirming that these elements are part of normal teaching, the *Code of Practice* placed the emphasis on the level of *additional* and *different* action necessary, through School Action and School Action Plus and associated Individual Education Plans (IEPs) to ensure that individual SEN pupils make adequate progress. The *Code of Practice* sets out clearly its definitions of adequate progress and makes it clear that judgements about reasonable progress should be made based on what it is reasonable for the particular child to achieve.

The Special Educational Needs and Disability Act (2001) amended the Education Act 1996 and transformed the statutory framework for inclusion into a positive endorsement of inclusion. It delivered a strengthened right to a mainstream education for children with SEN. This Act places a duty upon schools not to discriminate against a person with a disability in any aspect of school life.

Removing Barriers to Achievement (DfES 2004c), with its aim of making 'education more innovative and responsive to the diverse needs of individual children, so reducing our reliance on separate SEN structures and processes and raising the achievement of the many children – nearly one in six – who have SEN' (p. 5) is grounded in the priorities of *Every Child Matters*. In *Removing Barriers to Achievement* a model is presented that confirms key messages from both the *Code of Practice* and the National Curriculum inclusion statement that all teachers are teachers of pupils with SEN.

In reflecting upon policy development for education you can see that there is a consistent message to schools and their teachers to develop their policies and practices for inclusion. Perhaps paradoxically, but to protect the needs of pupils with SEN, additional SEN documentation has retained the commitment to inclusion but has required classroom teachers to provide *additional* and *different* provision for some pupils. More recently, through *Every Child Matters* and *Removing Barriers to Achievement,* there appears to be a growing synthesis between policy for SEN and generic inclusion guidance.

It seems reasonable to conclude that the thinking behind the government's provision of both generic and SEN guidance within the overall framework of inclusion was that inclusion is a process that takes time to develop. As teachers become more confident and competent in planning for diversity the less will be the need for provision that is '*additional and different*'.

DEVELOPMENT OF INCLUSIVE PRACTICE

In this section of the unit we attempt to provide some broad, practical advice on inclusive practice at the classroom level. It is important to recognise, however, that inclusive practice encompasses all aspects of school life, and consequently practices, in one part of the school; or in one aspect of school life contribute, either positively or negatively, to the development of inclusive practice in the school as a whole. There is a consistent message within policy and guidance materials that inclusive practice in individual classrooms can only be developed effectively within an agenda of whole school commitment and engagement to improving access and participation for all pupils. This is emphasised by the materials and processes inherent in the *Index for Inclusion* (Booth *et al.* 2000).

You will note that within your school and within policy documentation there are strategies for inclusion and SEN as illustrated by Tables 6.1.1 and 6.1.2. Consistent use of strategies such as these should enable you to develop your teaching skills in such a way that you increasingly meet the learning needs of a wider range of pupils. Indeed, this is central to inclusive teaching. However, there will be some pupils who need 'additional and different' teaching (DfES 2001a) as prescribed within the framework of the *Code of Practice*. Table 6.1.2 describes, in general terms, some of the approaches that have been developed to meet the needs of these pupils.

It is noteworthy that a number of the strategies within Table 6.1.2 for pupils with SEN represent extensions of, or a more focused usage of, generic strategies within Table 6.1.1. A number of these strategies are likely to benefit all pupils. Likewise, the strategies within Table 6.1.1 will be appropriate for many pupils with SEN. This is a point endorsed by research that questions whether there is a distinctive pedagogy for special education (Norwich and Lewis 2001; Davis and Florian 2004).

In developing your teaching you may want to consider whether you are offering a compensatory or complementary approach to your pupils with SEN. You will note from Table 6.1.2, taken from the DfES (2001a) *Code of Practice*, that the term 'help' is used frequently (e.g. in the 'cognition and learning' quadrant of the grid, 'help' is used in six out of the nine strategies listed). You may want to consider how you could interpret 'help' in this instance so that your pupil is enabled to make progress *and* develop his/her independence.

Table 6.1.1   A checklist of general strategies to facilitate inclusion

- Plan your lesson from the perspective of setting suitable learning challenges, overcoming barriers and responding to diverse needs.
- Consider in your planning if all pupils have the underlying skills needed to access the activities within the lesson, e.g. if the activity requires group discussion, do pupils have the necessary skills to work in this way?
- Make learning objectives explicit – tell your pupils what you want them to learn by the end of the lesson, and let them know how this relates to prior learning.
- Plan for predictable occurrences, e.g. pupils without equipment, latecomers, pupils who have missed prior learning due to absence, pupils who miss parts of the lesson due to following specialised programmes out of class, etc.
- Break lessons down into shorter 'episodes' by offering pupils a range of small tasks with clear learning targets.
- Make use of formative assessment (Clarke 2001) to monitor individual pupil progress and identify future steps in learning.
- Use a variety of presentation styles to maximise the chances of engaging all pupils in the lesson.
- Keep your instructions clear and short.
- Teach 'self help' strategies for pupils to use if they are stuck – knowing what to do when you don't know what to do is an important learning behaviour!
- Have supportive resources available – e.g. word banks, visual/written reminders of sequence of the task, etc.
- Plan additional adult support to promote access, engagement and participation, not dependence.
- Mix individual and group work.
- Make sure praise is consistently used and is available for effort, achievement and pro-social behaviour as well as attainment.
- Plan seating and grouping to reflect the type of learning that is intended to take place.
- Take the opportunity to review, summarise, assess, secure and reinforce learning after small tasks within lessons and at the end of the lesson.

Table 6.1.2   General strategies for pupils with SEN

Children with SENs relating to communication and interaction	*Children with SENs relating to cognition and learning*
• flexible teaching arrangements; • help in acquiring, comprehending and using language; • help in articulation; • help in acquiring literacy skills; • help in using augmentative and alternative means of communication; • help to use different means of communication confidently and competently for a range of purposes including formal situations; • help in organising and coordinating oral and written language; • support to compensate for the impact of a communication difficulty on learning in English as an additional language; • help in expressing, comprehending and using their own language, where English is not the first language.	• flexible teaching arrangements; • help with processing language, memory and reasoning skills; • help and support in acquiring literacy skills; • help in organising and coordinating spoken and written English to aid cognition; • help with sequencing and organisational skills; • help with problem solving and developing concepts; • programmes to aid improvement of fine and motor competencies; • support in the use of technical terms and abstract ideas; • help in understanding ideas, concepts and experiences when information cannot be gained through first-hand sensory or physical experiences.
Children with SENs relating to behaviour, emotional and social development	*Children with SENs relating to sensory and/or physical needs*
• flexible teaching arrangements; • help with development of social competence and emotional maturity; • help in adjusting to school expectations and routines; • help in acquiring the skills of positive interaction with peers and adults; • specialised behavioural and cognitive approaches; • rechannelling or refocusing to diminish repetitive and self-injurious behaviours; • provision of class and school systems which control or censure negative or difficult behaviours; • provision of a safe and supportive environment.	• flexible teaching arrangements; • appropriate seating, acoustic conditioning and lighting; • adaptations to the physical environment of the school; • adaptations to school policies and procedures; • access to alternative or augmented forms of communication; • provision of tactile and kinaesthetic materials; • access to different amplification systems; • access to low-vision aids; • access in all areas of the curriculum through specialist aids, equipment or furniture; • regular and frequent access to specialist support.

In planning to achieve increased synthesis between generic 'good teaching' and 'SEN specific strategies', it might be useful to examine how generic strategies can be made '*additional and/or different*'. As an example, if you take the generic strategy 'make learning objectives explicit' from Table 6.1.1 you could give a visual format of the learning objective(s) to some of your pupils who had language, communication and/or memory difficulties. This interweaving of generic 'good teaching' strategies with 'specialist' SEN strategies is fundamental to the development of your inclusive teaching.

INCLUSIVE TEACHING

The inclusion statement within the National Curriculum (DfEE/QCA 1999) sent a clear message that differentiation for a wide variety of needs and the planning of lessons to ensure access and participation was part of normal teaching. The depiction of these three elements (i.e. setting suitable learning

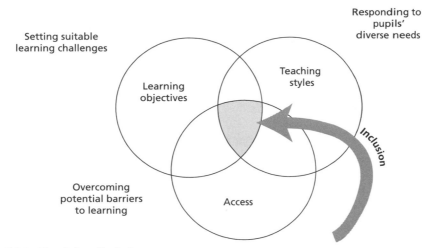

Figure 6.1.1 The circles of inclusion

challenges, responding to pupils' diverse needs and overcoming barriers to achievement) in a Venn diagram in subsequent DfES materials (DfES 2002) is significant as it conveys the message that inclusive practice relies on all three elements being present. For you as a teacher the challenge in developing your practice is to address the three elements as outlined in Figure 6.1.1.

The National Curriculum inclusion statement (DfEE/QCA 1999) sets out examples of approaches that might be undertaken within the three areas and reading these will provide a useful starting point.

SETTING SUITABLE LEARNING CHALLENGES

In setting suitable learning challenges you will need to place emphasis on giving every pupil in your class the opportunity to experience success in learning and to achieve as high a standard as possible (DfEE/QCA 1999). Setting suitable learning challenges involves identifying appropriate *learning objectives*.

Learning objectives within the framework of the National Curriculum can be thought of in terms of what the teacher intends the pupil to learn (DfES 2004d). For some pupils it will be inappropriate to work on the same tasks as other pupils in the class or the same learning objectives. In setting suitable learning objectives you may need to identify outcomes for particular individuals or groups, which are different from those set for the class as a whole. In taking this decision you need to be clear that, with appropriate access and teaching strategies, the child could not work on the same tasks and learning objectives as his/her peers. For example, some children with social, emotional or behavioural difficulties may lack skills in relation to their capacity to work as part of a group but may have the cognitive ability to meet fully the same learning objective as their peers. For these pupils, giving them work of an easier level just because they cannot cope with the method of delivery (i.e. group work) may lead to boredom and lack of challenge that could result in increased behavioural difficulties. Setting suitable learning challenges requires that you accurately assess the child's current level of attainment and make a judgement about the next step in learning. This may involve *tracking back*. *Tracking back* is a phrase used within some DfES documentation (e.g. DfES 2002) to describe the process of looking at earlier attainment targets in order to identify current learning objectives. The DfEE document *Supporting the Target Setting Process* (DfEE 2001), commonly referred to as the P scales, provides advice on identifying the next steps in learning for pupils operating below Level 1 of the National Curriculum.

Whilst by practical necessity you will need to notionally group pupils in order to make lesson planning and delivery manageable, you will of course need to be aware of each child as an individual learner, and be able to evaluate whether your inclusive teaching has enabled them, as individuals, to make the progress you have planned for them through the setting of appropriate learning objectives.

Responding to pupils' diverse needs

Children learn in different ways, often dependent on the curriculum content and/or the child's preferred modality, or style of learning. It is important therefore that you use a variety of teaching methods so as to match the unique needs of individuals or groups and to secure motivation and concentration. Some pupils may require tasks that are of a more structured nature, or activities that are broken down into sequences of shorter tasks to match their current concentration span. Some pupils may need to overcome difficulties with personal organisation so that they gradually become better equipped to tackle open-ended tasks or tasks requiring a problem-solving approach.

Whilst information is processed and received through all our senses, it is thought by some writers (e.g. Shaw and Hawes 1998) that pupils may have a preference towards one particular modality. This has led to emphasis within some schools on attempting to identify pupils' single learning styles rather than making use of multi-sensory approaches to learning that incorporate visual, auditory and kinaesthetic elements. Whilst using a variety of presentation styles that target visual, auditory and kinaesthetic channels is good inclusive practice, it is now questioned as to whether the selection of a particular style (e.g. kinaesthetic) for individual learners leads to improved learning (Coffield *et al.* 2003). A preferred learning style is simply that – a preference – and does not mean that individuals can only learn in one way (Hughes 1999) or that individuals use one learning style for all types of learning activity. In planning for individuals within group settings the central issues for your teaching style are: balance and emphasis. This coupled with the adoption of an evaluative stance (i.e. what teaching style is improving the learning for which pupils) should enable you to increasingly adapt your whole class teaching to meet the diverse learning needs of individual pupils within your class. Thus in spite of emerging research questioning the existence of learning styles, there is still a utility in emphasising a particular modality for a child who experiences difficulty, e.g. for a child with difficulties in concentration, an emphasis on practical activities involving increased movement may be helpful. Problems occur when the balance is lost and an assumption is made that a particular child only learns in one way, or that the way they are currently learning is the only way that they will ever learn.

In responding to diverse needs, other practical factors to consider include the clarity of verbal instructions, length of the session, the proportion of time spent listening and the proportion of time spent doing, the mixture of individual, partner and group work, and the mix of closed and open-ended tasks.

Overcoming barriers to learning

Providing access involves finding ways of 'bypassing' or overcoming barriers to learning. For a child with a hearing impairment this could take the form of a radio aid; for a child with dyslexia it may mean finding alternative ways to provide access to the written word by the use of tape recorded stories, visual planners, etc.; for a child with a receptive language impairment it may involve a teaching assistant giving extra support by going over the teacher's instructions with the child to check understanding. Central to inclusive practice is the idea that many of the approaches developed to support pupils with

SEN are effective as whole class strategies for all children. For example, providing written reminders and/or pictorial representations of the key points from your lesson introduction will help a child with receptive language difficulties but will benefit *all* children as they will be able to check independently what they need to be doing.

Task 6.1.2
Using the circles of inclusion

Using Figure 6.1.2, consider a pupil (or pupils) you have encountered and identify what you would need to do in each circle. How would you evaluate the *impact* of your teaching on pupil learning?

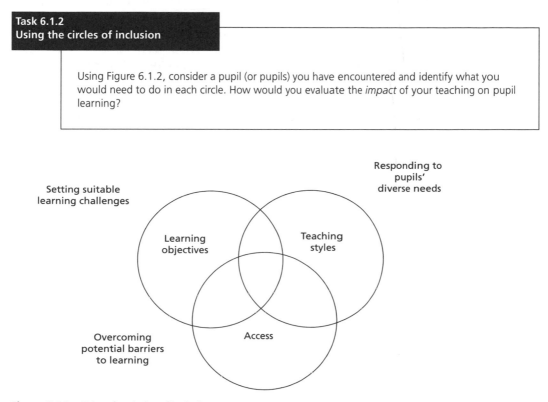

Figure 6.1.2 Using the circles of inclusion

SUMMARY

Educational inclusion has been developed more in response to a global moral imperative based on human rights than as an evidence-based rationale for an enhanced educational experience for all.

This unit has examined the philosophy and policy that underpins the development of school practices for inclusion. It can be seen that although the philosophy of inclusion offers a dominant ideological driver for developments in education, the realisation of many of the aims for individual learners, i.e. 'all children should have access to an appropriate education that affords them the opportunity to achieve their personal potential' (DfES 2001b: 2) is a challenge that has yet to be achieved.

Our review of policy noted that there has been a gradual development in educational policy from 'inclusion' as an agenda based on human rights, and to some extent rooted in 'place' i.e. mainstream community school, to one in which outcomes and experiences for *individuals* are seen as increasingly important. These are being viewed by policy makers not just in terms of individual 'well-being' but in terms of the longer-term costs and impact on society of low attainment and educational exclusion, linked to antisocial behaviour and long-term unemployment. It is for this reason that there is now a reduced emphasis on the *location* of inclusive education and more emphasis on the *process* and *impact* on individual outcomes and experiences.

Primary school teaching in an era of *Every Child Matters* places emphasis on the interdependence of family, school, and community strategies for improved educational outcomes for individual learners. There is an increasing demand for teachers to play a pivotal role in multi-agency working, early identification and intervention.

As a professional you have a unique opportunity to contribute to developing policy and practices for inclusion. Central to this development is the need for you to adopt a critical stance to emergent policy developments and to be clear about the 'purpose' of inclusion for the individuals you teach. In so doing you will develop an evaluative stance to your practice that will enable you to contribute to the creation of a much needed evidence base for the provision of effective strategies for inclusion for pupils with diverse learning needs.

ANNOTATED FURTHER READING

Cheminais, R. (2004) *How to Create the Inclusive Classroom*, London: David Fulton. This book provides checklists to monitor inclusive practice and should support you in creating a learner-friendly barrier-free classroom. It should help you to understand the impact on classroom practice of recent legislation and guidance as well as clarifying the roles and expectations of pupils, parents, SENCOs, teachers and school leaders.

Frederickson, N. and Cline, T. (2002) *Special Educational Needs, Inclusion and Diversity: A Textbook*, Buckingham: Open University Press. This book provides a comprehensive and detailed discussion of the major issues in special education. Whilst recognising the complex and difficult nature of many Special Educational Needs, the authors place a firm emphasis on inclusion and suggest practical strategies enabling professionals to maximise inclusion at the same time as recognising diversity.

Garner, P. and Davies, J. D. (2001) *Introducing Special Educational Needs*, London: David Fulton. This book should be useful to you as you undergo your teacher training as it features broad coverage of key aspects of SEN. It provides information on major SEN themes, key questions for you to consider on each topic, a selection of the most important readings, sets of reflection-based tasks, activities for completion during school placements, practical activities designed to be led by a tutor or mentor and a series of suggested topics for school-based assignments in SEN.

Gross, J. (2002) *Special Educational Needs in the Primary School: A Practical Guide*, Buckingham: Open University Press. This work is aimed at class teachers, heads and special needs coordinators. It should help you to build differentiation into planning lessons and schemes of work. It describes workable strategies for managing the most common behaviour difficulties and meeting special needs in language, literacy and mathematics. At a whole school level, it offers practical guidance on reviewing special needs policies, assessment, record keeping, and the management of roles and resources.

REFERENCES

Avramidis, E. and Norwich, B. (2002) 'Teachers' attitudes towards integration /inclusion: a review of the literature', *European Journal of Special Needs Education*, 17(2): 129–47.

BBC/DfES (2005) 'More children banned from schools', http://news.bbc.co.uk/1/hi/education/4122408.stm.

Booth, T., Ainscow, M., Black-Hawkins, K., Vaugh, M. and Shaw, L. (2000) *Index for Inclusion: Developing Learning and Participation in Schools*, Bristol: CSIE.

Clarke, S. (2001) *Unlocking Formative Assessment: Practical Strategies for Enhancing Pupils' Learning in the Primary Classroom*, London: Hodder and Stoughton.

Clough, P.(1998) *Managing Inclusive Education: from Policy to Experience*, London: Paul Chapman.

Coffield, F.C., Moseley, D.V.M., Hall, E. and Ecclestone K. (2003) *Should We Be Using Learning Styles? What Research Has to Say to Practice?* Report B, Newcastle upon Tyne: LDSA/University of Newcastle upon Tyne.

Davis, P. and Florian, L.(2004) *Teaching Strategies and Approaches for Pupils with SEN: A Scoping Study*, Briefing Paper RB516, Nottingham: DfES.

DES (1978) *Report on the Commission of Special Education* (Warnock Report), London: HMSO.

DfE (1994) *The Code of Practice on the Identification and Assessment of Special Educational Needs*, London: DfE.

DfEE (1997) *Excellence for All Children: Meeting Special Educational Needs*, London: HMSO.

DfEE (1998) *Meeting Special Educational Needs: A Programme of Action*, London: DfEE.

DfEE/QCA (1999) *The National Curriculum: Handbook for Primary Teachers in England*, London: DfEE/QCA.

DfEE (2001) *Supporting the Target Setting Process*, Nottingham: DfES.

DfES (2001a) *Special Educational Needs Code of Practice*, London: DfES.

DfES (2001b) *Inclusive Schooling: Children with Special Educational Needs, Guidance on Pupil Support and Access*, Nottingham: DfES.

DfES (2002) *Including All Children in the Literacy Hour and Daily Mathematics Lesson*, Nottingham: DfES.

DfES (2003) *Every Child Matters*, Nottingham: DfES.

DfES (2004a) *Every Child Matters: Next Steps*, Nottingham: DfES.

DfES (2004b) *Every Child Matters: Change for Children*, Nottingham: DfES.

DfES (2004c) *Removing Barriers to Achievement*, Nottingham: DfES.

DfES (2004d) *Learning and Teaching for Children with Special Educational Needs in the Primary Years*, Nottingham: DfES.

Halliwell, M. (2003) *Supporting Children with Special Educational Needs*, London: David Fulton.

Hughes, M. (1999) *Closing the Learning Gap*, Stafford: Network Educational Press.

Norwich, B. and Lewis, A. (2001) 'Mapping a pedagogy for special educational needs', *British Journal of Educational Research*, 27(3): 313–26.

Parsons, C. (2003) 'Confronting disaffection: the will to punish and pay the price', paper presented at the At Risk National FORUM conference 23–25 February, Myrtle Beach, SC. http://www.behaviour4learning.ac.uk/viewArticle.aspx?contentId=376.

Shaw, S. and Hawes, T. (1998) *Effective Teaching and Learning in the Primary Classroom*, Leicester: The SERVICES Ltd.

UNESCO (1994) *The Salamanca Statement and Framework for Action on Special Needs Education*, New York: UNESCO.

Wearmouth, J., Glynn, T. and Berryman, M. (2005) *Perspectives on Student Behaviour in Schools: Exploring Theory and Developing Practice*, London: RoutledgeFalmer.

Unit 6.2

Providing for Differentiation

Eve Bearne

INTRODUCTION

Differentiation is one of those 'iceberg' terms in teaching – what you see on the surface covers something much bigger. But not only does it have underlying complexities, it is also one of those concepts which teachers assume that 'everyone knows' what it means. However, there is no clear consensus about what the term means and implies. It is linked in many teachers' minds with 'mixed ability teaching' but there is still considerable debate about what it might look like in the classroom and just what 'ability' is. Some place greater emphasis on curriculum provision whilst others see differentiation as more linked with individual progress. As with many classroom issues, the answer often lies in the combination of providing a suitable curriculum to ensure progression for all learners whilst catering for individual needs.

OBJECTIVES

By the end of this unit you should be able to:

- see the links between differentiation, diversity and difference;
- see the importance of providing a differentiated approach to the curriculum for a diverse range of learners;
- understand the main approaches to differentiation;
- develop some practical strategies to provide differentiated approaches to learning.

What does differentiation mean to you? How would you depict it? Draw a sketch or diagram and write a few words of explanation to describe differentiation. You might then compare your ideas with others in your group and with the examples in Figures 6.2.1, 6.2.2 and 6.2.3 and discuss with your tutor the range of descriptions of differentiation gathered by the group. A group list would be a good starting point for a definition.

So what does differentiation look like?

Figures 6.2.1–3 show examples of how some teachers see differentiation.

Figure 6.2.1 shows how learning objectives relate to individuals. The teacher describes this as: 'Making one thing accessible to all, through an acknowledgement of different learning styles and experiences and a knowledge of individuals' "baseline" knowledge and skills.'

Figure 6.2.2 shows three different ways of reaching a learning destination. The teacher came across this in an in-service session and felt it aptly summarised her views. Route A is by bus where the passenger depends on the driver; Route B shows how a traveller might choose between a range of different vehicles; in Route C the traveller gets to the destination her/his own way. The teacher writes: 'The transport enables all students to access the curriculum through means which suit their individual needs.'

Figure 6.2.3 shows a swimming pool. The teacher writes: 'Differentiation is ensuring that every child can find their depth in every lesson but also challenging them to swim. If we don't support/ encourage child A to take chances she will never leave the shallows.'

The first teacher emphasises providing for the different qualities, knowledge and experiences of every learner whilst aiming for common learning objectives for all; the second recognises the importance of developing pupils' independence; the third sees it as important to create an environment which allows learners to feel secure enough to push themselves further. These descriptions indicate the variations which experienced teachers may have in mind as they consider differentiation. They also share a concern to provide for individual differences within a common curriculum.

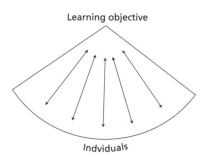

Figure 6.2.1 Description of differentiation – Teacher 1

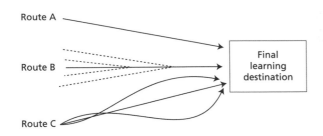

Figure 6.2.2   Description of differentiation – Teacher 2

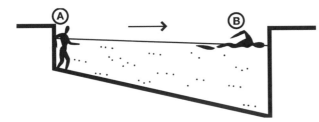

Figure 6.2.3   Description of differentiation – Teacher 3

DIFFERENTIATION, DIFFERENCE AND DIVERSITY

In general terms, differentiation is about how far the curriculum is appropriate for groups of learners with particular needs. This does not only mean considering special educational needs, including the group defined as gifted and talented, but takes into account the differences between what a young learner at the Foundation Stage may need in contrast to an appropriate curriculum for pupils at Key Stage 2. Such a general approach would also consider differences between schools, settings and their communities. For example, a school where there are many multilingual pupils will adjust its curriculum to make the most of its linguistic diversity; or a school where pupils have to travel long distances may adopt specific approaches to home–school liaison. In this general sense differentiation means providing an appropriate curriculum, within national guidelines, for the particular school.

In its more specific usage, differentiation refers to provision of learning opportunities and activities for individuals in particular classrooms. This often includes a concept of 'matching' the task or activity to the child's experience, knowledge and skills and in official terms, differentiation is often linked with inclusion. There are, of course, many links between the two concepts (see Unit 6.1) but while inclusion is largely concerned with equity in terms of individual rights and curriculum entitlement, differentiation focuses on the management of teaching and learning, including:

- identifying pupils' knowledge, experience, skills and learning preferences;
- planning for a variety of ways into learning;
- classroom organisation for learning;
- using resources (material and human);
- responding to the outcomes of activities or units of work and assessment of achievement in order to plan for future learning.

The Education Reform Act of 1988 legislated for every pupil's entitlement to a curriculum which is broad, balanced, relevant and 'subtly' differentiated. In 1992 the National Curriculum Council referred to providing a curriculum suitable for 'differences in the abilities, aptitudes and needs of individual pupils' (NCC 1992: 67). Over ten years later, the official definition of inclusion is to provide 'effective learning opportunities for all pupils' (QCA 2005). Its key principles stress teaching in a way which takes account of the diversity of pupils' learning needs and preferences. In other words, differentiation needs to be thought of in terms of how the curriculum might cater for and build on differences in the needs of specific groups of pupils as well as the diversity of the learners in the classroom; and how teaching can accommodate the range.

Taking account of difference and diversity can be a complex matter. Differentiation which genuinely allows for diversity will need to consider:

- differences in learning styles, strategies or preferences;
- particular strengths and difficulties in some areas of the curriculum;
- physical and medical differences;
- variations in fluency of English, which may not be the first language;
- gender differences;
- the range of previous experiences brought to the classroom.

as well as the fact that any learner might use a range of approaches to learning according to the task, the context or the time of day.

Providing for the needs of different learners means having some sense of where they are in their learning at any specific time. This in turn implies having some sense of where you want them to be. It means that before planning for any unit of work or series of activities the teacher will need to have a clear idea of learning objectives. This should be accompanied by useful pupil records of progress so that the learning can be matched to individuals or groups. Very often this will include grouping pupils. This is a very common classroom practice to manage teaching and learning, but the reasons for grouping have to be clear. Some activities require grouping pupils according to their common achievements in a recognised teaching programme; an example of this is guided reading where grouping is determined by a perceived common level of reading competence. At other times, teachers will opt for 'mixed ability' groups.

Grouping pupils can be a little more tricky than may at first appear since even if learners can be grouped according to common qualities, they may not form genuinely homogeneous groups. It is by no means a simple matter to group according to ability because it begs the question 'ability in what?'. There is a danger in making generalised judgements. It is all too easy to assume that someone who has difficulty with spelling, reading, writing or numeracy is 'less able'. Such convenient definitions are best avoided; they are inaccurate and misleading and, in the end, give no help either to the teacher or the pupil. It is better to be precise and to describe the skills rather than the pupil, for example, less fluent in reading but accurate in mental mathematics.

Not only does each person's 'ability' vary according to the task or curriculum area, it also varies according to what the teacher makes it possible for the pupil to achieve. Observing pupils at work – in PE, art, design and technology or as they work together on the computer, and listening to their talk in science or maths, for example – can reveal a great deal about the learning strengths and needs of particular pupils. Such observations help to provide descriptions of what learners can do which avoid unhelpful labels and over-generalisations.

Task 6.2.2
Reflecting on your own abilities

Think about your own 'abilities'. Are you good at everything? Some people are very good at reading the spaces and patterns of team sports, whilst others read music as fluently as print. Some find mental calculations in mathematics easy; some are good at constructing things in three dimensions; some express ideas elegantly through dance; others are successful at solving abstract problems. What are your strengths? What areas of your learning need, or have needed, support? Make a few notes then compare your reflections with others in your group. How diverse are you as a group of learners? Discuss with your tutor the implications this diversity has for planning teaching and learning.

IDENTIFYING THE RANGE OF LEARNERS

Learning styles have been analysed and categorised by cognitive psychologists for some time, but they are now receiving even more attention, probably led by industrial and workplace studies and often following the thinking of Howard Gardner's 'multiple intelligences' (1999; 1993). Various accelerated learning projects (see, for example, Rose and Nicholl 1997; Smith 1996) focus on the ways in which people learn. A common formulation is to see learners as more likely to adopt visual, auditory or kinaesthetic approaches to learning. However, whilst it is interesting to consider the range of learning styles, strategies and skills, there is a danger in being too eager to categorise the learner. Labelling pupils may not be particularly helpful as this can take attention away from teaching approaches and the importance of contexts for learning. Added to that, hard and fast categorisations can ignore the fact that many learners use a variety of approaches to learning according to circumstances, prior learning and experience and what is on offer in terms of teaching. Rather than seeing these qualities as fixed, like the colour of one's eyes, it is better to take account of diversity in planning for teaching but also to aim to extend the range of learning approaches through specific teaching.

Differences in learning styles, strategies or preferences

Having offered those reservations, it is important to see learners as individuals with particular strengths and preferences. Some may approach learning by taking in whole concepts and then attending to detail, while others build from detail to broad concepts. The versatile learner is the one who has been able to develop both kinds of learning to fit specific purposes. Some learners show more of a tendency to take intellectual risks in learning while others are much more cautious. While any learner may show a predisposition towards a more innovative or a more speculative approach, it might be valuable to develop the ability to decide when it is best to be adventurous and when it is better to be more carefully decisive. Some read pictures or diagrams more readily than verbal or symbolic texts; some prefer words or numbers; some learn better by ear than by eye; some learn best through practical experience; some find the social aspects of learning crucial. Whatever the learner's preferences or predispositions, however, it is important to remember that none of these approaches is necessarily 'better' than another.

Task 6.2.3
Identifying your learning preferences

Have a look at these comments on their own learning made by a range of 9 and 10-year-olds. What do they tell you about their learning preferences?

- I worked it out by thinking about what we'd done last time.
- I can't be bothered to work out all those fiddly bits.
- I like to find out all the facts from the internet.
- Being under pressure helps me to learn.
- It helps me if I know what to do.
- We've been shown how to do different investigations so I use the best way of doing it.
- I like maths when things are hard.
- I have a big blackboard of words in my mind that I know how to spell.
- I like to make models and inventions.
- I like trying things out … I don't like being interrupted when I've got a good idea.
- I want to learn how to be a good social person … a good group would be a boff, two friends and me.
- If it's got writing on it, I'll read it.

You may find it tricky to tie some of these down. That is perfectly understandable and simply serves to demonstrate the problems of trying to make hard and fast categorisations of learners. However, they should help you discuss with your tutor the issues about 'learning styles'.

Pupils' particular strengths and difficulties

Specific strengths or difficulties with learning can often be associated with pupils who give cause for concern. This can be because the pupil's learning may not be thriving, or because the teacher feels that more could be done to support or extend particular learners. 'Cause for concern' may include pupils with statements of special educational need, but it can be wider than that. One teacher described the range of pupils who caused her concern as:

K. Who was having difficulty with written work and not providing evidence of learning via written tasks or presentation. This pupil speaks Hindi as well as English.

L. Who was having difficulty with 'owning' information and tended to re-hash knowledge rather than remembering and using it in imaginative writing or similar creative activities.

M. Who was achieving an excellent standard of written work and could remember facts of historical events, but showed no real sense of empathy.

N. Who was achieving an excellent standard of written and spoken work and needed to be extended and stretched.

(Reynolds, 1996: 168)

A 'special educational need' can mean that we have to provide for those who take readily to school-based learning and those who excel at some aspects of the curriculum as well as catering for those who find learning difficult or burdensome.

Identifying pupils who might be described as gifted and talented is an aspect of diversity which has come to prominence over the last few years. However, it is not always easy to pinpoint learners who might come within this category. Unit 5.5 provides a full overview but to make sure that these pupils are not forgotten when thinking about differentiation, they need to be included briefly here. Very able children often show outstanding potential or ability in one area or in several or all areas of the curriculum. This might not be in traditional academic learning but could be in physical, creative, spatial, mechanical or technical learning. Pupils' overall abilities could be so well developed that they operate significantly in advance of their peers or a pupil might show outstanding talent in just one area of learning again outstripping others of their age. Whether their abilities are in a range of areas or just one, such pupils require extra provision of learning experiences in order to support and extend the identified ability.

Generally, however, it is often the 'strugglers' who come to attention first in the classroom. You might have observed pupils who:

- have low self-esteem;
- are capable, but frustrated because they don't have the means, vocabulary, strategies or techniques to write what they want to say;
- do not yet speak English fluently;
- only skate on the surface of text when reading aloud and don't understand what they're reading;
- 'can't think what to write' because they are paralysed by fear of failure; have poor techniques; do not value their own experience; lack motivation;
- are restless: wanderers, diverters;
- can write with technical accuracy but do not seem to have their own voice;
- are naturally slow at working;
- have hearing loss/sight loss/difficulties with manual dexterity;
- are too proud to ask for help;
- have language or neurological disorders;
- have so many ideas they find it hard to follow one through.

> **Task 6.2.4**
> **How do teachers provide support for different learners?**
>
> Select one or two of the descriptions above and consider how pupils displaying these characteristics might be supported and moved on in their learning. If possible, recall any strategies you have observed teachers using, or that you have used yourself. Discuss with your tutor the practical implications of offering support for strugglers. Add to this list as you consider bilingual/multilingual learners and gender issues. What strategies have you seen teachers use to cater for language diversity and for gender differences?

Bilingual/multilingual pupils

Again, it is important to avoid generalisations. Bilingualism is perhaps best seen as a continuum of proficiency in speaking more than one language which varies according to the social contexts of language use, for example with peers who speak the same language, with peers who don't, with older people or relatives, at school, work or worship (see Unit 6.5). Everyone, including apparently monolingual people, uses a set of language variations, so it is worth trying to find out about:

- the languages/dialects used in school, in lessons, break time and with friends;
- the languages used in the home;
- any language classes attended out of school.

Gender

Issues of gender often focus on boys' underachievement although concerns about boys' achievements in learning generally are not new. Whilst any underachievement is a proper concern for everyone involved in education – parents, teachers and pupils – it is wise not to take on generalised observations about boys, girls and learning without asking a few questions or gathering first-hand information. Contexts differ and pupils' attitudes, motivation and achievements will be influenced by a variety of home, classroom and school-based factors. Careful observation and monitoring are essential so that teaching approaches can be developed which will support boys' – and girls' – achievements (see Unit 6.4).

APPROACHES TO DIFFERENTIATION

Considering diversity involves not only looking at the qualities and potential of different learners, but also at the provision which is made to support and build on that potential. Different individuals learn best in certain settings or environments and through different means or approaches. As you have already considered, some learners find diagrams, maps and webs useful in shaping up and in representing ideas; some read pictures more accurately than written text; some think best in sequences, using lists to help organise ideas and actions; others have a more random or spontaneous way of dealing with things. For sustained work some people need background noise, others need absolute silence. The next move after identifying the range of learners is to identify the range of contexts and opportunities for learning which are on offer and which seem successful and effective.

Creating a school environment for learning

It is at whole school level that the aspects of differentiation which balance issues of equity and entitlement with access to the curriculum are most apparent. If differentiation means taking account of the diversity of pupils' experiences, knowledge and approaches to learning, then the environment is critical in allowing or blocking access to learning. In reviewing provision at whole school level, it is worth considering first of all how hospitable to diversity the physical setting is. Figure 6.2.4 offers a checklist. You might think that these aspects of differential provision seem peripheral, but they are, in fact, a reflection of the general approach to diversity which will operate in the provision of learning, too.

- Are the notices accessible to those who read iconic or pictorial texts more readily than print?
- Are the languages of the school community genuinely represented?
- Is there access for those whose mobility is hampered?
- How is pupils' work presented and displayed? Is there 'only the best' – or a wider representation?
- How accessible is the library or resource centre – what provision has been made for diversity here? Does it have books of maps, photographs, technical magazines and manuals?
- How does the school reflect an environment for different subjects? Is pupils' work in maths, science, design and technology displayed as much and as frequently as art work and written work?

Figure 6.2.4   The school as hospitable to diversity – review

Task 6.2.5
Observing school approaches to differentiation and diversity

This task and the following two ask you to make some observations in a school. If you are not likely to be making a school visit soon, you will need to complete the review by thinking back to a school that you are familiar with. When you have completed the review in Figure 6.2.4 discuss your notes with one or two colleagues. What differences did you find between the schools? What similarities? How can you account for these?

A second means of finding out the school approach to differentiation is to look at school policy documents. Ask the school for a copy of their general policy about differentiation. Look at the policy for one specific area of the curriculum. What guidance does it give about differentiation?

You may have found some gaps as well as some useful guidance. With your tutor, outline some guidelines which might be included in a school or particular subject policy to support appropriate differentiation.

The classroom environment

A good starting point for reviewing differentiated provision is to start with the question: What messages does the classroom give about the status or value given to the diversity of the pupils? Fig. 6.2.5 provides a checklist of the classroom setting since the physical environment reflects the thoughts of the teacher about what provision for diversity means.

It is worth remembering, however, that the physical context for learning is only part of the environment. Even more significant in supporting the diverse needs of learners is the environment of opportunity, expectation and challenge offered by the teacher. This might include:

- modelling and demonstrating processes and approaches;
- offering pupils chances to experiment and try things out for themselves;
- creating an environment where failing is seen as part of learning and is a stepping stone to trying again;
- building on successes.

- Are there special areas for activities – technical, practical, role play, listening, working on the computer, problem solving?
- What do the displays suggest about accessibility to different approaches to learning? Are there pictures, diagrams, written texts, maps, photographs, three-dimensional objects?
- What about the pupils' input into displays and the visual environment? Is the work or display material all selected and mounted by the adults?
- Is there variety in the curriculum areas on display?
- How does the classroom operate as an environment for inclusion? What about the height of shelves and displays and the use of space?
- What messages about gender and culture are signalled by the materials and books used?

Figure 6.2.5   The classroom as hospitable to diversity – review

Task 6.2.6
Reviewing how the classroom environment provides for diversity

Complete the review of the physical environment of the classroom in Figure 6.2.5 and observe how your teacher creates an environment of opportunity, expectation and challenge. Discuss with your tutor the relationship between the tangible environment of the physical setting and the intangible environment of the teacher's attitudes and aspirations for the pupils.

To be able to provide adequately for diversity means thoughtful and continuing intervention in learning based on a positive view of what the range of learners in the classroom can achieve. It is often assumed that intervention for learning is about teachers 'doing things' in the classroom. In fact, the most effective intervention happens before a teacher ever reaches the classroom – in the process of planning and organising activities and approaches.

Managing groups

Flexible planning for differentiation raises issues about how groups are constituted and how they might be varied. Strategies to organise groups may depend on social factors as well as learning objectives so that pupils might be grouped according to:

- friendship patterns;
- expertise or aptitude relative to the task or subject;
- a mix of abilities relative to the task or subject;
- gender;
- home language;
- pupils' own choices;
- the content of the activity.

Whenever teachers plan for the management of learning there is an implicit question about classroom control. This is fundamental to productive group work so that it is important to teach pupils how to work productively in groups. This might mean:

- negotiating ground rules for turn-taking and dealing with disagreements;
- giving written prompts to guide discussion;
- developing ways of time-keeping for fair chances to contribute;
- using role play and simulations;
- reviewing and evaluating with the pupils the ways in which they managed (or did not manage!) to work together.

Task 6.2.7
Observing group work

Either by observing during a day in your current school or by remembering a particular classroom, make notes about the ways in which work is organised:

- Is there a balance between whole class teaching, group work, paired work and individual work?
- Are the children working *in* groups or *as* groups?
- Following one pupil, note the variations in groups which that child is involved in during the day.

Compare your observations with others' in your group. From your discussions, make a list of the criteria used by the teachers to decide on how to group the pupils. Was it always by perceived ability? Discuss with your tutor the advantages and disadvantages of grouping according to any specific criterion.

All the observations you make in school will help you to think about how best to manage group work in your own teaching (see also Unit 3.4).

Provision – planning for input and activities

For certain activities, differentiation is unnecessary, although attention to diversity will be important. In drama work, for example, activities are likely to be 'open access'; in PE, differentiation will be decided by criteria which will be different from those for maths. In planning work for classes and groups, teachers make decisions about learning objectives: the facts, concepts, strategies they want the class to learn in the course of the teaching unit in each subject area; what experiences they want them to have; what attitudes they want them to develop. As a starting point they will draw on their previous knowledge of the pupils' existing knowledge, concepts, skills and experiences. In terms of input, decisions might be made about factual information, the concepts and the vocabulary which will be used to help learners grasp content and ideas. At this point it is important to start with what the learners already know in order to build on existing knowledge. At the same time planning will identify what new information or concepts individuals and the group as a whole might now be introduced to.

In planning for specific learning outcomes, teachers may differentiate by providing different tasks within an activity to cater for different levels of ability. In its worst manifestation this version of differentiation is represented by three different worksheets – one with mostly pictures and few words; one with more words more densely packed and one picture; and a third with lots of words and no pictures. This kind of 'worst case' practice gives very powerful negative impressions to all the learners in the classroom. It is more like division than differentiation. While recognising that these things are done with the best intentions in order to cater for the range of pupils it is wrong to assume that ability is linked only with reading print text. Also, if differentiated tasks assume that certain individuals or groups will only be able to cope with a limited amount of new information this can run the risk of excluding pupils who might be able to cope with more ambitious learning objectives. The challenge to the teacher is to find ways of framing tasks which can not only genuinely stretch all the learners, but which might provide for the variety of ways in to learning.

These teachers describe their approaches to differentiated input and tasks:

> When I plan for a unit of work I make sure that I include visual stimuli and IT, some activity-based and some print-based tasks and some group and individual work.

I try to vary the teaching approaches between and within lessons, scaffolding and extending where appropriate. When the children work in literacy groups I might ask them to do a storyboard on one day and some writing on another. That means that I can move around the groups and support and extend where necessary. In whole class teaching I'll use a drama strategy for one activity and scaffold the learning, adjusting as I notice how individuals are doing. I might also read aloud to them for another so that they have a common experience.

I try to word questions differently on their activity sheets. I might use a general open question then provide additional bullet points and examples to support those who need more structure to help them think but I'll also put some more challenging questions so that those who need extending can push themselves further.

Resources and support

While it is important to identify a range of material resources to cater for the preferences of all learners – for example, computers, tape recorders, videos, pictures, photographs, maps, diagrams and print – it is also important to acknowledge and use the range of human resources available in the classroom, for example, learning support assistants. However, support need not only be seen in terms of the adults in the classroom, or peer support; it might also mean use of IT or other tools for learning. Perhaps the most critical element in considering this area of provision for diversity is to do with teacher time. There is never enough time to give the individual support which a teacher almost inevitably and continuingly wants to offer. Group and paired work, self-evaluation, support from adults or other pupils, collaborative revising and proof-reading all help in offering differentiated support.

These teachers describe their approaches to differentiating by support:

> I find that I do differentiate by support, although with the older pupils I teach it has to be done subtly to avoid upsetting individuals. I tend to use paired work a lot, basing the pairs on different things – sometimes I suggest the pupils choose their own learning partners, at other times I select a more confident mathematician, for example, to work with someone who finds some of the concepts difficult. But I do think it's important to avoid making social divisions. In group work I'll sometimes select groups according to having someone who is more confident in literacy to take notes working with others who may not be quite so fluent and I also make the criteria for working in groups explicit so that everyone feels valued whatever role they take on.
>
> Of course, the TA [teaching assistant] is an important part of differentiated support but I don't really like the usual practice of putting her with the least able group – whatever that means. It's not good for her because it doesn't stretch her professionally and it means that I don't get to work with them and give them some focused support. We discuss things at the beginning of the week and sometimes she'll be working with the high fliers – she's particularly interested in science so I tend to ask her to work with the able scientists quite often. At other times I'll work with them and she'll work with other groups. She's also very good with IT so she might work with individuals at certain times either to bring their IT skills up to scratch or to push the really experienced pupils.

Outcome, response and assessment

Many teachers favour differentiation by outcome but this can be seen as a less organised way to cater for the range. If differentiation by outcome is to be genuinely effective it has to be allied with a response to help move learners on and that response has to be based on a clear view of the learning outcomes aimed for in a series of lessons or a unit of work. This teacher explains why she prefers to differentiate at this stage of the teaching process:

> I find differentiation by outcome the easiest because it leaves less room for error – any surprises about an individual's achievement won't have hindered learning, I mean mistakes can be made with provision if a child knows more or less than judged by the teacher, or the format of the activity has inhibited comprehension. Differentiation by outcome allows for more open-ended learning where pupils find their own level and their learning benefits from some more differentiated follow-up/reflection in order to further develop individual skills.

Outcomes can be both tangible and intangible. Tangible (written, diagrammatic, craft or artwork, displays of physical activities or drama activities) products provide obvious opportunities for assessment across a range of areas and kinds of ability. However, intangible outcomes are equally open to observation and assessment: increased confidence; the ability to carry out a particular operation or to present ideas orally; new-found enthusiasm or the articulation of concepts which have been understood; the use of a language to talk about the subject or learning itself (metalanguage). Equally, response need not always be written. The end points of learning are often used to assess how well pupils have achieved, but if assessment is to inform future teaching and learning, then there may be a need for a diversity of kinds of assessment and variation in times when those assessments are carried out. Response to the outcomes of learning, by teachers and pupils, makes the process of learning explicit and acknowledges different abilities. Response also encourages learners themselves to evaluate their work and leads towards future progress.

Teachers are continually making assessments and judgements – minute by minute, hour by hour, day by day – as they work alongside pupils. Those assessments are based on implicit criteria of what counts as success and will necessarily be adjustable to take into account all the learners in the classroom. That is a teacher's professional expertise but it is important to make criteria explicit. In doing so, a teacher can check that s/he is using a differentiated range of types of assessment which will accurately describe the achievements of a diverse set of learners (see Units 7.1 and 7.2).

SUMMARY

Differentiation involves providing a curriculum which allows for the progress of all learners but will specifically cater for the needs of different groups of pupils and the diverse strengths, needs and abilities of individual learners. It involves planning for teaching approaches which will build on the knowledge, concepts, skills and prior experiences of the pupils in the class. It also means balancing knowledge of the range of learners with the content of learning and managing and evaluating teaching and learning to try to move all learners on successfully. Judgements about lesson content, pace of learning, levels of challenge, management of groups in the classroom, use of support, and response to individuals and groups for successful differentiation are part of the developed expertise of teachers. You are just starting on that professional journey; thoughtful observation and planning will help you to begin effective, supportive and stimulating differentiation.

Task 6.2.8
Planning for differentiation

You may want to carry out this task with a partner. Decide on a series of lessons or unit of work for one subject area which you might be responsible for in your next classroom teaching. In the grid below note some strategies that you might use as you plan for differentiation at each stage of the learning process.

Subject:	Learning objectives:
Stage of the learning process	Strategies for effective differentiation
Planning for provision: tasks and activities	
Grouping	
Resources	
Support	
Outcome	
Response	
Assessment	

ACKNOWLEDGEMENTS

My thanks to Shaun Holland, Ben Reave, Sara Tulk, Rowena Watts and children from primary schools in north Essex.

ANNOTATED FURTHER READING

Bearne, Eve (ed.) (1996), *Differentiation and Diversity in the Primary School*, London: Routledge. There aren't many books which specifically deal with differentiation in the primary school. This book is an edited collection which provides a series of chapters on a range of themes and curriculum areas and is written mostly by classroom teachers. There are sections on definitions of differentiation; differentiation and literacy; mixed ability and the range of learners; issues of assessment; and a final section on school policy for differentiation. Although it was written some time ago, the content is still highly relevant and there are good practical suggestions as well as more reflective chapters.

Hart, S., Dixon, A., Drummond, M.J. and McIntyre, D. (eds) (2004) *Learning Without Limits*, Maidenhead: Open University Press. This book isn't specifically about differentiation but questions easy judgements about 'ability' and ability grouping. It is based on classroom research with years 1–11 and in a series of case studies describes how teachers have developed alternative approaches to some of the limiting classroom practices based on ability judgements.

The magazine *Special Children*, published by Questions Publishing Co. monthly, is a source of up-to-date, relevant, classroomly and thoughtful articles, and the journal *Support for Learning* provides a range of articles about inclusive approaches to support productive differentiation.

REFERENCES

Gardner, H. (1993) *Frames of Mind: The Theory of Multiple Intelligences*, 2nd edition, London: Fontana Press.

Gardner, H. (1999) *Intelligence Reframed: Multiple Intelligences for the 21st Century*, New York: Basic Books.

National Curriculum Council (1992) *Starting Out with the National Curriculum*, York: NCC.

Qualifications and Curriculum Authority: National Curriculum online *Statement on Inclusion*, http://www.nc.uk.net/nc_resources/html/inclusion.shtml. Accessed 18 August, 2005.

Reynolds, J. (1996) 'An ear to the ground: learning through talking', in Eve Bearne (ed.) *Differentiation and Diversity*, London: Routledge.

Rose, C. and Nicholl, M.J. (1997) *Accelerated Learning for the 21st Century*, London: Piatkus.

Smith, A. (1996) *Accelerated Learning in the Classroom*, London: Network Educational Press.

Unit 6.3

Education for Cultural Diversity and Social Justice

Hilary Claire

This unit is for *everyone* planning to teach in British primary schools, whether you have considerable experience of minority ethnic groups and different religions and identify yourself with a minority group; whether you grew up with a strong sense of 'white English' identity and have limited experience of other cultures, religions and ethnicities; whether you will teach in multicultural inner city areas or in mainly white schools.

OBJECTIVES

In this unit you will consider:

- how multicultural education relates to education for social justice;
- some do's and don'ts for a multicultural classroom;
- what inclusion of minority ethnic children means in practice;
- acknowledging and tackling racist stereotypes, bullying and name calling;
- the overt curriculum, cultural diversity and education for social justice.

INTRODUCTION

Diversity is a fact of our national and global world. Britain has been multicultural since the Romans came here two thousand years ago. Though 'white Europeans' form the majority in Britain, they are the minority globally. Ethnicity and skin colour are not interchangeable even though 'ethnic minority' has become code for 'people of colour'. Everyone, indigenous white Protestants included, has ethnicity, related to culture, regionality and religion. Now, using contemporary definitions, about 7.9 per cent of the British population belongs in a variety of 'minority ethnic groups', the result of British imperialism and colonialism in the nineteenth century and first half of the twentieth century, human rights legislation through which refugees and asylum seekers have entered Britain, and membership of the European Union (see www.statistics.gov.uk/census2001). The largest group is Irish (www.cre.gov.uk), followed by people originating in the Asian subcontinent. Increasingly, mixed heritage children contribute significant numbers in our schools. Minorities have traditionally settled near one another in Britain, for mutual support and work. So in some areas there are quite large settlements of particular groups, though in others, minority individuals can be more isolated.

DIVERSITY, INCLUSION AND ENTITLEMENT: MULTICULTURALISM AND COUNTERING RACISM

We all belong to a common humanity but this does *not* mean you will 'treat all children the same'. They are not: and being 'colour blind' means ignoring people's cultural and ethnic identities. However, this unit will not attempt to provide you with answers about specific cultural requirements, nor will it offer suggestions for 'celebrating diversity'. Rather it concentrates on tackling racism.

Minority ethnic children are entitled to equal access and inclusion through both overt and hidden school curricula. The National Curriculum and the Race Relations Amendment Act (2000) put schools under a legal obligation to promote good race relations and provide full equality of opportunity for all pupils. Inclusion is not something which is 'done to' minority or marginalised pupils. It's about everyone's attitudes, values and personal qualities and a school's response to all its pupils. Effective inclusion means that in school and out in the world, all pupils feel and behave in ways that show that *they and everyone else belongs*.

Multicultural education which 'celebrates diversity' is an important part of responding to diverse communities. Any child in Britain, growing up in a nation and a world of ethnic, cultural and religious diversity, needs to learn to understand and respect different cultures and beliefs and not concentrate solely on white European/Christian achievements and customs. We are educating children for a future in which the old barriers of distance and geography will be even more ephemeral, in which world events will impact on us all, wherever we live. Children in rural England as well as in Coventry or Birmingham need to know about the variety of cultures and communities in Britain and in the wider world.

Celebrating diversity, with its positive connotations, goes some way towards inclusion and ensuring entitlement, but it is by no means sufficient to ensure equality of access or outcome. This is because minority children's experience may be profoundly affected by ignorance, stereotyping and racism. Research shows that these are more likely to go unchallenged in mainly white areas where teachers think 'there is no problem here' (Jones 1999).

Britain is part of Europe and part of the world; recognising and tackling racism in schools is part of broader concerns with human rights and social justice, recognising the necessary response of education to economic, social and political globalisation. It's worth remembering that Britain has signed up to both the Convention of Human Rights and the Convention of the Rights of the Child. You might start there, when you work with children. Figure 6.3.1 illustrates how these concepts fit together.

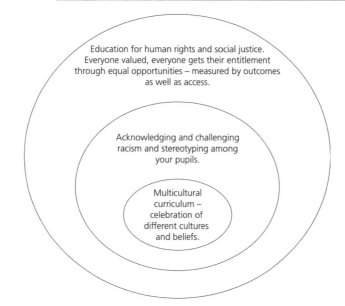

Figure 6.3.1   Concepts for a classroom based on education for social justice

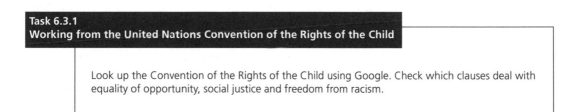

Task 6.3.1
Working from the United Nations Convention of the Rights of the Child

Look up the Convention of the Rights of the Child using Google. Check which clauses deal with equality of opportunity, social justice and freedom from racism.

Providing *access* to a full curriculum does not, of itself, ensure entitlement and equal opportunities. *Outcomes* are the test of success; if results suggest that some groups are underachieving, then we must consider possible obstacles to progress. Recent statistics show that though class and gender remain the main variables in pupil success, ethnic origin is also significant. Official statistics show that other than pupils of Indian origin, *middle class white girls and boys* achieve much better than pupils from the main minority groups. We don't yet have detailed comparative statistics for the most recent newcomers, but anecdotal evidence suggests that they too may be underachieving.

Over the years, there have been a number of explanations for group underachievement, from 'blaming the victim', considering the curriculum, to accusations of institutional racism in education, and personal racism in teachers. Strategies to deal with the situation have also shifted, recognising that schools cannot cure the ills of society, but they can at least be part of the solution.

MULTICULTURALISM – GOING BEYOND TOKENISM

It is important to go beyond projects which exoticise minority communities, or highlight the ways in which they are different from the majority. In some schools minority communities only get a look in through curriculum work in RE, focusing on festivals and specific beliefs. Best practice is not the occasional celebration after which you revert to a monocultural curriculum, but always looking for opportunities to include different ethnicities in the ordinary range of resources and activities. There are some excellent books, particularly for the younger children, for example about grandparents, birthdays and weddings, which include a range of people doing ordinary things.

SOME DO'S AND DON'TS

Aim for a more inclusive approach through *all* the curriculum subjects, not just RE. For example, in art, and design and technology, children might learn about cultural and scientific achievements from outside Europe – the Taj Mahal built by Shah Jehan, the Great Wall of China, Great Zimbabwe, the Egyptian or the Mayan pyramids; sculptors from Mesopotamia (now Iraq) who made the magnificent friezes commemorating their rulers' victories; the bronzes and sculptures of Benin craftworkers in the sixteenth century; the magnificently decorated monasteries carved into the mountains in Ethiopia, built by early Coptic Christians. The mathematical knowledge of Middle Eastern people who established our number system, scientific inventions of African Americans like Garrett Morgan (who invented traffic lights), the survival and tracking skills of Australian Aborigines or South African San people all help children appreciate cultural achievements from many different peoples and places. You can use Arabic symmetrical designs, the patterns on African kente or batik textiles to teach geometry. Bring in fruits and vegetables from around the world to draw, paint and cook, including in mainly white, rural areas. Nowadays, many children are as familiar with Indian and Chinese takeaway food as they are with McDonald's – use the ingredients for work in KS1 on the senses. When you choose significant people in KS1 history, don't just rely on Florence Nightingale and Brunel. Teach children about Gandhi, Martin Luther King, Rosa Parks. From nursery through to upper primary, search out stories and picture books from the wider world, or those featuring minority children in central and not marginal roles. In some areas you may have to go beyond the school library for resources representing minority children and adults in positive roles. Letterbox Library's catalogue, which specialises in multicultural fiction and non-fiction for children, will help.

Don't wait till Travellers arrive in your classroom before considering how to make their children feel welcome. Consult the Traveller Support Unit in your local LEA. Remember that there may be significant hostility in the outside community, which your class may internalise, and help them understand different life choices, and some of the difficulties faced by Travellers.

Because you will be concerned with general attitudes, not just responding to specific minority individuals in the class, displays around the school should give clear messages that neither Britain, nor the world is all 'white'. Taking care to avoid stereotypes, show people from different ethnic backgrounds doing a variety of things in the world of work and academia, whether or not there is a significant minority group in your area. In geography or work on 'homes' or 'jobs' show Africans in Western dress living in large cities, and not just in rural settings in round thatched cottages. When you do discuss (for example) thatched cottages, remember that they offer sustainable and practical solutions to local conditions. Avoid pejorative language, such as 'mud hut', 'coloured', 'Eskimo', 'Bushmen' or 'Red Indian'. Exercise caution about posters showing people in the developing world as victims of famine or poverty, with implications that people in the rich West are superior and always in the patronising position of 'helping'. Be vigilant about linking projects that consolidate rather than challenge prevalent racist stereotypes.

Most minority children (apart from refugees) are born in Britain, and to ask 'where do you come from?' implies that they are not British and don't belong. Instead, you could plan an inclusive activity in which everyone tells each other where they have family connections or have visited, and what languages they speak and understand. Mark this up on a world map and you could find that many white English children also have connections around the world, or understand languages other than English. If you are part of the white majority, don't talk about 'us' and 'them', implying that minority groups are not part of 'us'. In fact, get out of the habit of 'us' and 'them' thinking, on the way to being inclusive. Learn how to pronounce unfamiliar names – by asking! Say 'first names', not 'Christian' names – for obvious reasons – and never refer to people as 'ethnics' or 'multicultural'.

Don't target individual representatives of a minority group to 'teach' the rest of the class, or inadvertently suggest that you are particularly concerned with one individual, by looking directly at them when you talk about their culture or faith. This is embarrassing for children who don't want to stand out as different. Parents may be willing to come and talk about specific customs but this will depend on existing attitudes towards minorities in the school and community. Good relationships are essential, in which all parents already feel quite comfortable and welcome in school to talk about their children's progress, or attend assemblies. Otherwise they will not necessarily be willing to come to do a special session cooking or showing how to wear a sari. If you want to 'celebrate diversity', for example in music or food, it is better to include a wide variety of cultures, to prevent a minority group feeling like exotic outsiders.

Remember that well-meant sporadic actions can backfire; minority children certainly recognise where they are being included, but they are also sensitive to tokenism. For example, a Year 4 Muslim child I interviewed (Claire 2001) said her school talked about Eid as 'Muslim Christmas' and only ever mentioned Islam when there was a specific festival. Otherwise, she said, 'it was all Christian, Christian, Christian!'.

Multicultural education if it's approached well, is a necessary part of responding to ethnic diversity in the local community and in the national and international domain. But, there is a health warning if multiculturalism is the sum total of the school's initiatives.

CHALLENGING RACISM AND EDUCATION FOR SOCIAL JUSTICE

Multicultural education is 'feel good' – as the term 'celebratory' suggests. However, 'knowing about' a culture or religion, sharing in the celebrations and so on does not necessarily deal with people's hostility and prejudice against those perceived as 'other'. The occasional session about a festival, learning a Caribbean song, or making Diwali lights really has little to do with combating racism. In fact, inadvertently, prejudice and stereotypes may be reinforced, confirming that some people are really 'not like us' at all.

Education for social justice may involve controversial issues, since it goes beyond celebratory multicultural education, both in its aims and its approaches. *It acknowledges and tackles stereotypes, prejudice and racism* both locally and in the wider world. It also concerns itself with promoting democratic practices and equality, which may mean that in addition to racism it addresses sexism, and inequalities due to globalisation and poverty.

Acknowledging racism and stereotyping

Russell Jones' research in *Teaching Racism or Tackling it?* (1999) shockingly revealed the extent of unacknowledged racism in white primary schools and how teachers turned a blind eye to overt racist behaviour and talk. Other projects confirm that some schools do not acknowledge the extent of racism in the community outside the school, the racial dimensions in specific episodes inside school involving people of colour (including teachers and trainees), and treat inappropriate behaviour or victimisation just like any other instance of bullying. The DfES series of pamphlets *Aiming High* explains why calling someone Paki, chocolate bar, Al Qaeda, Chinkie, or any other current pejorative name is serious and offensive: it is linked to discrimination and unequal access to jobs and housing, victimisation in communities, and violence and hostility to minority groups which can escalate in very unpleasant ways.

There are two different things to consider: first, the presence of small numbers of minority children, who may feel marginalised, invisible, or be bullied. The second is to counter damaging negative stereotypes about minority groups, that may go unchallenged or even be reinforced in the local majority culture.

Racist attitudes are based on negative stereotypes which identify a person within a group because of e.g. their colour, religion or cultural practices. Colour is not the only factor in racism and stereotyping. Jews, Irish, Travellers and white asylum seekers from Eastern Europe have all at one time been – or still are – negatively stereotyped. Some negative stereotypes are a hangover of history, for instance against opponents in World Wars, or because Imperialism and colonialism set up white Europeans as superior to colonised people. Currently, many Muslims find themselves lumped together with terrorist groups, despite explicit efforts to distance themselves. Stereotypes at their worst dehumanise people, set them up as 'other' and deny not just their individuality, but membership of a common humanity where everyone shares the same feelings, fears, hopes and potential. Negative stereotypes can affect even the youngest children or they may be directed at their family. Whichever, they affect individuals' experience, self-esteem and life chances, and undermine every child's entitlement to achieve their full potential.

Insular or prejudiced attitudes in some communities may be even more challenging than knowing how to respond appropriately in a class with many different cultures and beliefs, since children in mainly white areas may be more prone to stereotyping groups with whom they have little personal contact. In some mainly white areas, Travellers may be the target for negative attitudes. Some Commission for Racial Equality (CRE) research showed that Irish people are also regularly subjected to prejudice and stereotyping. Recent research into attitudes among primary children in mainly white areas revealed that even where there are virtually no Muslim people, Islamophobia, linked to current fears about 'terrorism', may be growing. Refugees may inspire controversy, perhaps because of much negativity in tabloid newspapers. You may need to do some quite specific work about why people seek asylum, using fiction or non-fiction to help children understand the human stories behind fleeing one's country (e.g. Rutter 1998) and follow this through with work about the many former refugees who have enriched their adopted countries. But moralising seldom alters anyone's mind. Citizenship/ Circle Time may be the occasion for opening up debate, using the ground rules and procedures for dealing with contentious issues.

TACKLING NEGATIVE ATTITUDES IN THE CLASSROOM

Work on multiple identities

We all have multiple identities (Parekh 2000) and though ethnicity, language, culture and religion are extremely important parts of our identities, so is membership of groups which cut across these. An activity to challenge stereotypical thinking involves asking children to group themselves according to a variety of different characteristics and interests. As they form sets of children who like certain music, or sports teams, or books or food, they see that despite external differences they have much in common.

You can also organise games where children move into groups if they speak more than one language, or have visited another country, or have relatives or friends abroad. Such groupings recognise diversity but look for commonalities with the majority community.

Name calling and bullying of minority ethnic children

Name calling is probably the most frequent expression of racial hostility in schools. It's not the words themselves, but the power of hurtful, negative connotations. Abusive name calling about minority groups happens in all-white schools as well as multicultural ones. If children don't realise that this is unacceptable – and why – then they need the boundaries stated clearly, and they need help with understanding the repercussions for those being abused, even if they are not there. In both multicultural and monocultural classes you will need to be alert to the language children use, often quite casually. Then you must make a decision about how you will deal with the underlying racism. Your school has probably declared itself a zero tolerance zone for racist talk. But moralising tends not to work in the face of opposing attitudes, and forbidding things is not education, it's just controlling the symptoms. Racist language should be disallowed not just in support of children who are victimised and those children who are already conscious of social justice, but also for those who are waiting for a lead. Lastly, you should challenge racist language and the thinking behind it, because you hope to undermine some of the more inflexible views and make the unacceptability of such talk clear. For those children whose own families are openly racist, it is hard to counter entrenched attitudes and not possible to control what goes on outside the school boundaries. But if we didn't believe education could change things, we wouldn't be doing the job, so what comes after zero tolerance and the pep talks is crucial. Do take heart from the number of people who will tell you that their teachers made them rethink and ultimately reject some negative attitudes in their own community.

If you have very few minority children in your class, you should be especially vigilant about bullying which may be happening out of sight or earshot. If you suspect this, try an anonymous 'Auntie Aggie' box, where anyone can post a note – perhaps post your own anonymous note to get a discussion going. Teachers have stories of a white child refusing to sit with a black child, saying 'he smells', or of a lone individual who is never chosen for teams. Isolated children may be marginalised, suffer from low self-esteem and feelings of not belonging. Some recent research showed that Asian boys can be bullied because of perceptions that they are not macho and good at football. Sensitise yourself to the ways in

---

Task 6.3.2
Monitoring the experience of marginalised children

Next time you are in school, take some time to watch specific children who might be vulnerable, in the playground and on those occasions when children choose partners or group members. Isolation and marginalisation can be a signpost for more overt bullying away from teachers' eyes. Who is being left out? Who is hanging around on the side lines? Can you find out why some children are popular and others are not? Does the school's equal opportunities policy have anything to say about bullying and name calling? How is this monitored and dealt

which children use overt racism or racist language as part of their bullying behaviour. If children of different ethnicities have got into conflict, try asking just what they are accusing each other of.

Your own confidence about dealing with racism

If you are going to raise such issues in your classroom you need to feel confident about your own rationale for dealing with prejudice and negativity. You may want to do some reading at your own level about how racism affects people, and about institutionalised racism. You will also need skills of managing rational debate and controversy (see Crick 1998, Claire 2004).

Second, you need to know where to get information to counter the misconceptions that prejudiced people call up in their justifications. The web is a good source to deal with 'the numbers game' – fed by the tabloid press – which is often used in claims about how many refugees, Travellers, or people from minority groups are responsible for e.g. housing shortages, crime, or exploiting the NHS or Social Security.

The overt curriculum

Your curriculum response to racism will vary depending on the age and emotional experience of the children, and the context but do remember that foresight and 'inoculation' are better than reaction. With younger children, life-size Persona Dolls who are brought into the classroom and whisper their story, or their feelings to the teacher, who speaks for her/him, are extraordinarily effective in raising issues and getting children to consider the plight of children who are victimised or labelled (Brown 2001). Persona Dolls are now being used with older primary children too and if you can't get a doll, the video made for teachers is useful for upper primary children. Ask whether your LEA has a Theatre in Education project to help mainly white children consider issues through the eyes of the actors. Along those lines, you might choose a picture book to get discussion going about discriminating against children because of colour or religion – such as *Black Like Kyra, White Like Me* (Judith Vigna) or *The Christmas Menorahs* (Janice Cohn) (both from Letterbox Library). Teachers in Key Stage 2 have been able to raise issues about racism starting with the story of Anne Frank, or books like *A Candle in the Dark* (Adele Geras) about children who escaped from the Nazis to England, or Beverley Naidoo's classic *Journey to Jo'burg,* set in South Africa under apartheid.

In addition to story books which introduce ideas about discrimination, including to the youngest children, where animals often stand in for people, quite young children can consider issues through the lives of significant figures as part of the KS1 history curriculum. Through learning why we remember Harriet Tubman, Sojourner Truth, Mary Seacole, Bessie Coleman or Gandhi, you can introduce positive black/minority figures, and also discuss the discrimination they encountered.

With older children, teachers have used the lives of Nelson Mandela, Mary Prince, Joe Louis and Josephine Baker, or an event like the name calling against the English footballers in the Madrid stadium (2004) to move into discussion of contemporary racism and discrimination against different communities. The history curriculum gives direct opportunities to raise questions of racism, for example through learning about the experience of Caribbean immigrants post-World War 2.

Other examples are:

- For a special assembly based on 'Significant People', Year 2 learned about Gandhi's challenge to British rule in India through studying the Salt March in 1930.

- Year 4 History, Britain since the 1930s: following work on Anne Frank, children discussed contemporary refugees and asylum seekers, the murder of Stephen Lawrence (1993) and the subsequent campaign led by Doreen and Neville Lawrence.

Task 6.3.3
Researching who you might teach about to promote understanding of social justice

> Use the web to find out a bit about some of the people mentioned above and consider how you might use their lives to develop children's appreciation of damaging effects of racism.

Teacher attitudes and expectations

Teachers' rather than children's attitudes are unfortunately sometimes at issue. Teachers are part of wider society; it can take courage to look hard at one's own attitudes and acknowledge one's own prejudices. Sadly, a variety of stereotypes about minorities co-exist in the majority white society. Where such attitudes are played out in negativity to some children, for example in being more punitive, expecting them to behave in certain ways, or having lower expectations, children are denied equal opportunities and their entitlement. You might work with a friend and take notes about each other's behaviour in class, for example who you praise and address positively, who you tell off by name, who you choose to answer questions or do special jobs. In my own research, white as well as black children reported that some playground supervisors were harder on black kids than whites, that they didn't wait to find out what had actually happened, but pounced on a few black kids who they had already decided were to blame. Some Year 6 Muslim boys told me that once a supply teacher had put them all together on one table and then treated them 'as if we were all the thickos'. Some white children in another school considered a teacher racist who always chose whites to do errands.

Some white students fear that minority children (or their parents) might accuse them of racism if they find it necessary to discipline them. Remember that the statistics show that black children, particularly Caribbean boys, *are* more prone to negative discipline or exclusion than others and that the accusations are sometimes warranted. Children from minority communities are well aware of how racism has worked against them. If necessary, talk to another member of staff, preferably at senior level, get feedback about what happened, and be prepared to admit you mishandled something.

Your strength is to show you have been taking care with the curriculum approaches which have been outlined in this unit, not only 'celebrating diversity', but promoting social justice and equality. If you are genuinely fair, just, even-handed in all situations, and it is as plain as it can be that you do not discriminate or have favourites you will be able to deal with accusations of racism.

In thirty years teaching in England, I have found the presence of many different ethnicities in our schools, communities and nation hugely enriching for our personal and professional lives. I hope that you will be able to share my experience.

SUMMARY

In this unit you have considered the layers that lead to education for social justice. So-called multicultural education is only the first, albeit necessary stage towards inclusion and providing equal opportunity for all children. Multicultural education must be embedded in the daily curriculum and be more than the occasional celebration of festivals and different cultures. Education for inclusion and social justice also means acknowledging and being able to tackle racism directly and through the curriculum. As well as understanding how stereotyping and misinformation support prejudice, teachers need the professional skills and confidence to address racism effectively, when it occurs between children. Lastly, these two layers need to be embedded in a wider curriculum approach which concerns itself with social justice across the range of equality issues. It isn't possible to address cultural diversity or racism in a social, economic or historical vacuum. The inclusive classroom and school will acknowledge our connections to one another in an interdependent global village.

ACKNOWLEDGEMENTS

I would like to thank the following colleagues for advice and critical comment, though I take responsibility for the final result: Peter Barton, Paul Bracey, Pat East, Valerie Hardman, Cathie Holden, Balbir Sohal, Linda Whitworth, Claudette Williams.

ANNOTATED FURTHER READING

Claire, H. (ed.) (2004) *Teaching Citizenship in Primary Schools*, Exeter: Learning Matters. Chapters on issues of social justice, teaching controversial issues and worked through curriculum examples in different subjects taking an inclusive approach.

Dadzie, S. (2000) *Toolkit for Tackling Racism in Schools*, Stoke on Trent: Trentham Books. One of the best 'handbooks' giving practical ideas for school and classroom.

DfES Ethnic Minority Achievement site – (http://www.standards.dfes.gov.uk/ethnicminorities). A wide range of clear and relevant guidance and information and many links to other government sites. Look for *Aiming High* publications for material on refugees, minority groups including in mainly white schools, and gypsies/travellers.

Siraj-Blatchford, I. (1994) *Early Years – Laying the Foundations for Racial Equality*, Stoke on Trent: Trentham. A very clear discussion of what to do and how to promote equality in Early Years settings.

REFERENCES

Brown, B. (2001) *Combating Discrimination: Persona Dolls in Action*, Stoke on Trent: Trentham.
Claire, H. (2001) *Not Aliens: Primary School Children and the PSHE/Citizenship Curriculum*, Stoke on Trent: Trentham.
Crick, B. (1998) *Education for Citizenship and the Teaching of Democracy in Schools*, London: QCA (pp. 56–61 for guidance on teaching controversial issues).
Jones, R. (1999) *Teaching Racism or Tackling it?*, Stoke on Trent: Trentham.
Parekh, B. (2000) *The Future of Multi-ethnic Britain*, Report of the Commission on the Future of Multi-ethnic Britain, Runnymede Trust with Profile Books.
Rutter, J. (1998) *Refugees – A Resource Book for Primary Schools*, London: Refugee Council.

WEBSITES

www.emaonline.org.uk: site for ethnic minority achievement – a resource base for teachers developed by Birmingham, Leeds and Manchester LEAs with funding from the DfES, containing many practical ideas and links. (Click on *Good practice* on the home page and then on *Education* in the list entitled *Sectors*.)

http://www.education.ed.ac.uk/ceres/Resource/AEfiles/AE13.htm lists books about equality and early years/primary education.

www.letterboxlibrary.com Letterbox Library multicultural and non sexist resources for children and teachers.

Unit 6.4

Responding to Gender Differences

Elaine Millard

INTRODUCTION

This unit discusses the influence of gender on attitudes to schooling in general and the development of literacy in particular. While working your way through it, you will be asked to think carefully about the way in which society conveys its messages about what it means to be a boy or a girl and the strategies that you might adopt for ensuring that all pupils are encouraged to develop effective learning skills irrespective of gender.

OBJECTIVES

By the end of this unit you should:

- be clear about what is meant by gender, differentiating its role from that of sex and understanding its interaction with race and class;
- have an informed opinion of the role played by gendered cultural capital in determining school success;
- be able to identify some common patterns of behaviour that militate against individual pupils' school performance and know how to combat them;
- begin to connect children's experiences of home with school learning;
- have gained more insight into the role children's own (gendered) interests can play in motivating learning.

BACKGROUND TO THE ISSUE

> Boys are doing badly at all stages of education: they fall behind girls early on – and stay there. This massive under-achievement challenges all those who educate them, says Professor Ted Wragg. In the sixth annual TES/Greenwich lecture – and as a new millennium dawns – he outlines a 10-point plan to lift performance.
>
> (TES 1997)

> Girls' Achievement: Girls appear to be outperforming boys in many important categories of educational achievement, according to a recent federal study.
>
> The report – produced by the U.S. Department of Education's National Center for Education Statistics – says that 4th grade girls outperformed their male peers on reading and writing assessments, that girls are less likely than boys to repeat a grade and to drop out of high school, and that female high school seniors tend to have higher educational aspirations than their male counterparts.
>
> But the report points out that young women are still under represented in some fields of study, such as computer science, engineering, and physical sciences.
>
> (*Education Week* 2004: 15)

It has not been possible to be involved in education in the Anglophone nations (Australia, Canada, USA, UK) at the turn of the twenty-first century, either as a student or educator, without having encountered in some shape or form the strident public debate concerning the 'under performance' of boys. Boys' underachievement in education in schools in general, and in literacy in particular, has become a global concern, evoking an anxious response from governments across the Western world. In England in the primary school, girls' literacy levels are significantly better than those of boys and although national strategies have been in place to support boys' achievement, they have not yet 'caught up' though reading levels are better than those in writing.

From the way these differences are reported, you might be forgiven for thinking that not a single boy in your class will be able to achieve his best in the system as it stands. The anxiety over boys' achievements has been further fuelled by some male commentators who, speaking up for the importance of reforming boys' education, have suggested that schooling has become overly feminised, through the dominance of female teachers (Bleach 1998) and does not cater for the particular needs of boys (Hannan 1999; Biddulph 1997). They have recommended remedies such as the abandonment of coursework; boys only classes, or boys paired with girls to discipline boys' learning; the recruitment of greater numbers of male primary teachers to create 'role models' and a more 'boy friendly' curriculum. The general feeling in these accounts of the problem is that boys were being held back by the system. This is portrayed vividly in an account of the well-known educationalist, Ted Wragg's views on the subject reported in the TES, accompanied by an image entitled 'Chained males – How boys are held back'. This shows boys in short-trousered school uniforms, dragging a ball and chain behind them. At the time of its publication these views could be taken either as providing a practical summary of issues raised earlier by research, or contributing to one of the periodic national moral panics such as that in the early 1980s about falling reading standards. You can find Wragg's views and recommendations by searching the Archive section of the TES website (www.TES.co.uk) citing the date of its publication (16 May 1997).

The difficulty for most of the scholars engaged in previous gender research (Epstein *et al.* 1998; Arnot *et a*l. 1999; Skelton 2001) is that these strategies assumed fixed differences in the learning styles of boys and girls and made no attempt to look at the issue of masculinity itself. Moreover, by focusing attention back on boys, the real achievements made by girls in the two previous decades were ignored.

Despite differences in perception and emphasis, it is agreed by most commentators that some boys and some girls are in need of different approaches to teaching and learning than is currently provided for them in school and that the key to understanding the boys issue is rooted firmly in the cultural differences inscribed in femininities and masculinities. Without this understanding the teacher is trapped in the competing victims scenario, where either boys' or girls' needs take primacy at any given time, and so one group is always seen as underprivileged.

As someone preparing to teach, you will need to be circumspect in your judgements and have a more solid basis for supporting all your pupils' learning than the ready assumption of gender stereotypes that predominate in the popular press and in some books of advice on managing boys' schooling. Therefore, before you consider what researchers and curriculum advisers have had to say on the topic, I would like you to think through the importance of gender from your own standpoint.

Task 6.4.1
Thinking about the influence of gender on people's experiences

Jot down your ideas on the following topics, then, either compare your responses with fellow student teachers, or with someone in your school of a different generation from yourself. Look for the similarities and differences in your experiences.

Your schooling:
- How far do you think that boys and girls of your own generation have been given equal opportunities to succeed in school?
- Were there any times at school that you thought you were treated differently from members of the opposite sex?
- Did boys and girls of your generation share similar career aspirations?
- Did boys and girls of your generation behave as well as each other, or as badly as each other in school?
- Which family members were most proactive in helping you learn to read?
- Do male and female members of your family share the same interests, particularly in reading tastes?
- Have you observed any difference in the treatment of boys' and girls' achievements and behaviours in school today?

About teaching:
- Did equal numbers of men and women of your acquaintance 'always want to be a teacher'?
- Now you have chosen to teach, what do your friends think of your choice? Do you think they would respond differently if you were of the opposite sex?
- Do men and women choose similar subjects as their specialism in school – who, for example, is in charge of literacy, who is in charge of ICT?

Comments

As someone who has been researching the effects of gender on schooling for over twenty years, I would hope that all of you found few real differences in the access to education for all and a sensitivity to individual needs of boys and girls of whatever race, class or gender. You may however have noted that there are still many differences in how boys and girls, men and women position themselves in relation to education, and may have views on how this influences their achievement in school and future employment. This unit will look at the issues that lie behind the questions and offer you ways of understanding the role that gender plays in shaping an individual's experience of school and engagement with her or his own education.

The irony of the 'moral panic' about boys' performance at school is that it draws its arguments from a theoretical basis for understanding differences in educational aspirations and achievements that is firmly grounded in the feminist perspective and a pro-woman lobby which some of the commentators seek to challenge. In the 1970s and 1980s the focus was on girls' underachievement, rather than any perceived problems with boys, though looking back at examination results, the difference in boys' achievements in English literature and foreign languages was already marked.

As Carrie Paechter has suggested, at the time girls were 'the other sex' or 'a boy gone wonky' (1998: 7) and their achievements were often compared unfavourably with that of boys of the same age or simply left unacknowledged as in their preferred sports or ways of learning. Hilary Wilce, writing for the TES in 1995, when the boy issue began to be raised, summed up the conditions that prevailed for girls in school at that time:

> Boys dominated the playgrounds, the computers, the Bunsen burners, and teachers' time and attention; men dominated the headships and pay scales. A majority of all teachers, men and women, said science classes mattered less for girls than boys, while girls were less likely than boys to get the remedial help they needed.
>
> (TES 1995)

Definitions

The first issue to clarify is the definition of *gender* as it is employed in the debate, distinguishing it from *sex*. Whereas the term *sex* is used to identify the biological differences between male and female, *gender* is used to designate the patterns of behaviour and attitude attributed to members of each sex that are an effect of education, culture and socialisation. Whereas *sex* is conventionally categorised by binary oppositions of male and female, *gender* has a less determined division embracing a spectrum of experiences and ways of self presentation so that one may adopt a feminine gender without being biologically female and vice versa. This means that each individual is responding to what is seen within a particular culture and context to be appropriate to itself while emphasising patterns of difference between the sexes rather than seeking to establish similarity and correspondence.

Put simply, *sex* is a biological given but *gender* is socially and culturally constructed. All the evidence supports the idea that boys and men are more concerned to establish themselves as not female, than vice versa.

Gender regime

A gender regime refers to the accepted understandings of masculinity or femininity as practised in a particular community or institution, such as the family, peer culture or school. Kessler *et al.* (1985) showed that young people were caught up in overlapping gender regimes. Perhaps the most powerful influence of all being the peer group who define what is 'cool' for either sex.

Habitus

Related to this concept is Pierre Bourdieu's theory of the *habitus* (Bourdieu, 1990); that is, taken-for-granted ways of thinking which although socially constructed are so ingrained through embodied action they appear natural – 'durably incorporated in the body'.

You can find a more detailed discussion of both these concepts in *Differently Literate* (Millard 1997: 20–3)

Cultural capital

This is a further concept from Bourdieu and refers to the advantages bestowed on individuals from their own family and community environment which they in turn develop. It incorporates difference in the cultural understandings shaped by gender, class, ethnicity and religious affiliations.

Identity work

Sex and gender are key components of personal identity and arguably the first fact that we register about someone we encounter, whether casually in the street or more permanently as with friends, colleagues and partners. Our upbringing and social interactions all provide us with strong messages about what it is to be a man or a woman and how we should present ourselves and interact socially. Carrie Paechter (1998) gives a very full account of the interrelationship of these two categories. It may help you to read her chapter on 'Gender as a Social Construct' in *Educating the Other.*

For those of you not able to access this book here are some of her key points:

- Much of what we take for granted as 'natural' in Western society, as regards sex and gender, is socially constructed and male-centred.
- In the majority of cases gender identity is related to biological, but this is not a necessary relation and in some cases, the two are unrelated.
- Biological explanations have been used to support prevailing social inequalities by naturalising gender roles.
- Differences in gender roles involve a power relation in which 'masculine' activities are given higher status than feminine ones: what these activities are will vary.
- Because of the power relation inherent in constructed gender differences, masculinity is more precarious, and therefore more defended than femininity; this leads to there being more restricted behavioural possibilities for males than for females.

(Paechter 1998: 52)

For us as educators, it is clear that school plays a significant role in shaping children's sense of self and it is important to take account of the role it plays in reinforcing, or as Marland has suggested, even emphasising gender as well as ethnic and social differences (1983).

Task 6.4.2
Relating adult/child interactions to gender

Consider some of the ways in which adults have been shown to interact with children and think about their consequences for learning, filling in the right hand column with your views. Two have already been completed to provide examples, however, please think of your own explanations for these items:

Boys and girls are treated very differently by adults through their earliest interactions.	*Gender differences are reinforced by this and boys and girls begin to emphasise their differences from each other.*
Boys are encouraged to be more active than girls and participate more frequently in boisterous play.	*Boys find sitting down for any length of time tedious and tend to fidget and 'mess about' during carpet time.*
Boys and girls are provided with different kinds of toys which reinforce these differences.	
Girls are provided with more opportunities for quiet play.	
Girls are provided with a wider range of writing and drawing.	
Girls are often dressed in ways which inhibit active play (pink is quite difficult to keep clean!).	
Girls spend more time working with, and talking to adults.	
The early reading of boys and girls, particularly as manifested in comics and popular culture, conveys different messages about what it is to succeed (see for example *Bob the Builder*).	
Young boys are bought more computer hardware and software and the software that is available is highly gendered.	

Task 6.4.3
Testing underlying assumptions

Collect a range of catalogues for mail order or Argos shops and look at the images of the toys for sale. Note who is shown to be playing with particular items. If you are working with a class of children, organise them into same sex groupings of 3-4 and ask them to cut out items they would choose to buy for themselves. Ask them to add any sound effects that might be included in their play. When I have undertaken this activity with older groups of students we have identified that boys are often shown using more active, noisy and aggressive toys, such as weapons, cars or space gadgets, girls, more nurturing and quieter items, such as soft toys, design and sketching materials or domestic equipment for small or large scale play.

Or collect a range of cards for a particular age range of children (5-8) and compare the activities portrayed in the images.

Or observe children in the playground at lunchtime or break. What kinds of activities are involved? Who sits quietly chatting to friends? Do girls and boys play team games together when unsupervised?

Look at the books chosen for reading at home by Year R or Year 1. Can you see any patterns in the titles and contents of the preferred readers? Which suggest a gendered choice?

If you work with older age groups you could use this technique to analyse the way men and women are reported in newspaper articles. It has been noted by others that women are often noted for their appearance, whilst men for their actions.

Look at the verbs used for the actions of men and women – are there key differences in the choice of vocabulary?

GENDER AND SCHOOL DISCIPLINE

In broad generalities many boys find accommodating to school a far more difficult proposition than most girls. In particular, working class boys and black boys find school regimes oppressive and often seek to subvert the power of their teachers and other authorities. This has been described by a number of sociologists who have identified key groups of boys who create their identities in opposition to schooling (Willis 1977; Mac an Ghaill 1994; Connell 1995; Martino and Meyenne 2001).

The findings of a wide range of studies related to behaviour are summed up below:

- Teachers find boys more disruptive in school and the attention they demand holds back girls.
- Boys' peer culture endorses 'messing about' in class – it is 'uncool' for them to be seen to work and the dominant groups mock boys who wish to study.
- Boys are less diligent about completing homework (particularly 'learning' or 'reading' work).
- Boys use diversionary tactics to disrupt classroom management.
- Teachers more frequently tolerate boys who regularly behave badly finding their irreverent attitudes attractive.
- Boys are reprimanded more often than girls – it is estimated that the ratio of praise to blame is as low as 1:3 for boys.
- Boys seek to occupy the 'action zone' in the lessons they enjoy, gaining more opportunities for interaction with teachers (Randall 1987; Shilling 1991).
- Girls are more quietly inattentive and may slip out of teacher's sight.
- Boys' disruptive behaviour annoys girls and prevents them from working as well as they intend.
- Boys' name calling can deter less dominant boys and most girls from feeling happy participating in ideas and comments.

Think about whether these findings match your own experience and decide what implications they have for your disciplinary practice. Discuss your ideas with your tutor and other teachers in training. Identify areas you might concentrate on in specific lessons.

Comment

One of the issues often raised by boys when they are consulted is that they are 'picked on' more than girls and it is clear from classroom observational research that teacher's gaze is frequently directed at the boys, focusing on their behaviour and using questioning as a closed disciplinary tactic (have you been listening?) rather than a heuristic strategy (can you find your own solution to this problem?).

In managing classroom behaviour you will need to show your fairness in dealing with both boys and girls in similar ways. Your 'ground rules' for the behaviour you expect should be applicable to all and when you deviate from them you need to be able to give a clear explanation of what has made you change your rules.

GENDER AND LITERACY

The following are points summarised from research evidence taken from *Differently Literate* (Millard 1997) with additional comments related to girls' needs:

- Boys and girls have different reading tastes and girls' reading matches more closely the demands of an English curriculum.
- Both genders' tastes need to be taken into account when selecting reading materials. It is important that girls' tastes are not overshadowed by supporting boys.
- Boys prefer oral and aural work to writing.
- Girls also need to be encouraged to be confident in oral presentation.
- Girls' writing shows evidence of more 'literary' influences, boys often draw on film or oral narrative patterns.
- Different styles of narrative and alternative ways of creating meaning such as PowerPoint presentations, web logs and simple poster presentations will help the overall development of boys and girls.
- Girls have greater concern for presentation in all forms of language work.
- Clear design rather than handwriting alone should be a way of judging presentation.
- Girls present work more neatly and therefore more legibly.
- Girls often do more than is required of them, boys the bare minimum.
- More emphasis to be placed on more finished pieces and fewer set pieces would encourage both genders to see writing as important.
- Boys are often embarrassed by the requirement to reveal aspects of self and personal experience. This is a difficult issue. Research has shown that boys are interested in discussing their own concerns but these need handling sensitively. English offers the opportunity of discussing important issues through a third person.
- The subject matter of the language curriculum can appear irrelevant, trivial and sometimes too childish.
- All children's interests and preoccupations deserve a place in schooling – see section on popular culture below.

There is no space here to look in detail at the pedagogy focused on writing. In my research studies (Millard 1997, 2000, 2003), I have concerned myself with difference in boys' and girls' approaches to writing, demonstrating that more boys than girls make use of visual forms to create meaning. It is important to understand each individual's preferences for making meaning and allow for a variety of ways of both planning and presenting texts. The work on text types and ways of framing writing which informs much of the National Literacy Strategy has proved very effective in supporting all children's written work, and, I would argue, that of boys in particular. Your task is to match the genre you are teaching to the pupils' interests and preferences in a process I have termed *fusion* (Millard 2000).

GENDER AND ORAL WORK

- Boys enjoy confrontation, competition, disputation and argument.
- Many boys' homophobic attitudes limit what can be said in group work.
- Girls find it easier than boys to work collaboratively.
- Teachers direct more questions at boys in whole groups so boys contribute most frequently.
- Boys' talk is often competitive and disruptive of classroom management.
- Boys dominate even in small mixed groups.
- Boys have developed a wide range of attention-seeking behaviours and their oral contributions can be diversionary.
- Both girls and quiet boys have problems in asserting their voices against more dominant boys.
- Boys tend to take charge of groups, however they often leave the written part of the work to girls and take charge of oral presentations.

A ROLE FOR POPULAR CULTURE

Although English and language work in school concerns itself largely with what is judged by adults to be appropriate works of literature written specifically for children, out of school pleasurable narratives are available in a much wider range of texts which include comics, magazines, television, film, videos, computer games and so on. Many of these texts are interconnected with each other so that a film, a comic, a computer game and a popular book may share a common narrative source and main characters. These narratives have wide currency with all groups of children and are important in the development of friendships and peer groups (Dyson 1997; Marsh 2003; Marsh and Millard 2003).

There are disadvantages to these materials as they are often more marked by gendered interests than materials commonly available in school and their commercial interests deliberately frame them to appeal specifically to boys and girls, reinforcing stereotypical ideas of typical interests; for example, football and Star Wars for boys, romance and Barbie dolls for girls. However, because of their wide circulation and the personal interest invested in them they provide a very rich source of ideas for writing and discussion and cannot be kept out of children's writing for long. As Marsh argues:

> Popular culture, media and new technologies offer a myriad of opportunities for deconstructing these representations of gender and developing critical literacy skills, skills which are essential in order to challenge the stereotypes which perpetuate literacy myths, including those relating to underachievement.

(Marsh 2003: 73)

Elsewhere, Jackie Marsh and I (Marsh and Millard, 2003) have discussed the role that popular media can play in creating motivation, particularly amongst pupils who find most school work unappealing (more frequently boys). They also allow for a discussion of whether the stereotypes contained in them properly represent difference. You need to be aware of your own classes' popular interests and use them to draw them into all aspects of language work (see Dyson, 1997; Marsh, 2003; Millard, 2005).

GENDER AND CHOICE

In Western cultures, girls can participate in activities which are seen as masculine e.g. football, computing, more readily than boys can take up interests which are labelled feminine e.g. French, dance. Tomboys have more credibility than cissies! One of the problems associated with reading is that it appears to many boys to be associated with the feminine. This is because it is mothers and other female family members who for the most part help with early reading, and book choice in school sometimes seems skewed to the kind of psychological story in which nothing very exciting happens (Millard, 1997).

Boys and masculinity

Some further definitions:

Hegemonic masculinity

Hegemony is the term introduced by Gramsci to refer to prevalent ideas that have become naturalised, are accepted without question and are used to explain things-as-they-are within a particular society. In the Western world there is a prevailing view in many quarters that accepts gender as a binary division, biologically given, and endorses masculinity as having a dominant, assertive role. Hegemonic masculinity is present in the narratives of popular novels and films, perhaps found at its extremes in such characters as the one played by Jack Nicholson in *One Flew Over the Cuckoo's Nest,* Randall P. McMurphy, who 'fights and fucks too much' and challenges feminine authority invested in the big nurse, Ratched.

Hegemonic masculinity in schools works similarly to establish a male peer-group culture based on sports and overt challenges to authority; it often rejects schooling as uncool and endorses messing about in class and achieving through effortless ability (Mac an Ghaill 1994, Connell 1995, Martino and Meyenne 2001). Mac an Ghaill caricatured this version of masculinity as being dominated by the three 'f's (fighting, fucking and football, 1994: 58, 108–9) . Its binary opposite has been labelled 'emphasised femininity' (Connell 1995). Connell suggests that the cultural ideal that is celebrated for women is about sociability, fragility, passivity and above all compliance with male desire. Emphasised femininity is constructed in a subordinated relationship to hegemonic masculinity in ways that reinforce masculine power.

It can be argued that one of the main reasons for girls' outstanding achievements in education has been the result of changing conceptions of femininity in society as a whole, brought about by the work of feminists outside as well as inside education.

By contrast there has been little attempt in this country to challenge the traditional roles of men in society or to understand the role that hegemonic (dominant) masculinity plays in creating or limiting boys' educational opportunities.

Raising the issue of how boys are limited by prevailing views of what it is to be a man needs a sensitive approach and is perhaps best introduced as the issue arises in the course of other work.

It is also useful to discuss with the boys from time to time how the world works for them.

Task 6.4.4
Some questions to ask the boys

The following are adapted from a collection of secondary school Australian boys' views, collated for the Australian Council of the Commonwealth by Martino and Pallotta-Chiarrolli (2001). They could be used with older boys at the end of primary school to elicit their attitudes and open discussion.

- What is it like growing up as a boy today? Think about both the adventurous possibilities and the pressures of 'being a guy'.
- Why do boys take risks and think drinking and smoking prove they are cool? Is it only boys who do this?
- Is it all right for boys to talk about their feelings? Can girls be good friends?
- On a scale of one to ten how do you rate your life in school? Does being a boy bring any special pressures there?
- How does the word 'different' get used about some boys? Can it make you feel vulnerable or inferior? (*Note: in the Australian study difference was used to explore the use of homophobic language as well as racial stereotyping.*)

You will find the responses, which have been taken from a wide-ranging survey, in *Boys' Stuff, Boys Talking About What Matters* (Martino and Pallott-Chiarolli 2001). Although it is older boys who have been given a voice, their views, carefully chosen, will interest younger boys who look up to older boys and young men as models. Here is an example:

> You're supposed to go to the footy, you're supposed to drink a six-pack every week and you're supposed to watch action movies over and over again. I don't like football, I don't like cricket, and I can cook. I think being a man is whatever you want it to be.
>
> Andrew

Comment

For example, in relation to pupils who are behind in reading, both boys and girls benefit from early intervention and skilled individual specialist help, not just boys; particularly as research has shown that girls are less likely than boys to get the remedial help they need.

Both boys' and girls' interests should be catered for and discussions held about the qualities of different genres; it is equally important that girls are helped to exercise choice and judgement about their own work, preferred learning styles and competencies.

Boys' behaviour may present teachers with greater difficulty but the rules made for good classroom management should encompass and treat both girls and boys fairly and equally.

I have focused much of this discussion of gender through asking you to think about the current emphasis on boys' needs. It is important to keep in mind the needs of girls. My own view is that most of the points raised about gender are as relevant to the sound development of girls as well as boys.

Some girls need:

- confidence building and their expectations raised;
- greater encouragement to participate in whole group situations;
- more strategies for dealing with challenging and confrontational behaviour;
- opportunities for working co-operatively with boys;
- a challenge to their set reading patterns, with a wider range of reading and writing activities;
- particular attention to quiet learners' oral skills;
- better access to ICT in school.

Teachers' awareness of gender does need to be raised but this awareness should also involve an understanding of how girls may be disadvantaged and supported too. I would like you to think carefully about your own influence in the classroom.

Ask someone whom you trust in school to:

- monitor your ways of communicating in the classroom and discuss your own use of inclusive language;
- monitor your interactions with children making a note of who you ask to answer questions, and who you ask to help with a range of tasks.

Ask yourself if you are providing your class with a range of texts and activities which reflect both genders' interests. Are there particular issues related to ensuring equal access to learning you need to address?

SUMMARY

Our culture, despite the many changes that have improved the position of women in society, is one that is still saturated with notions of gender difference, often with an assumption that there are 'natural' attributes of the sexes with which it is best not to meddle, even if these result in poorer orientation to schools and schooling. In helping you to think otherwise about the role of gender in education, I have therefore emphasised the importance of helping you to develop a pedagogy which is rooted in the socio-cultural lives of children and is sensitive to their previous experiences and preferred ways of learning.

ANNOTATED FURTHER READING

Many of the concepts on which this unit is based can be found in Millard, E. (1997) *Differently Literate: Boys, Girls and the Schooling of Literacy*, London: Falmer Press. You will find it helpful in guiding you on how to find out about your classes' interests in reading and writing. In particular it recommends collecting Stories of Reading – asking your classes to write about their own journeys into reading.

You will find ways of developing your practice in many of the areas discussed in Skelton, C. and Francis, B. (eds) (2003) *Boys and Girls in the Primary School*, Buckingham: Open University Press. This includes chapters on the following issues: working with children to deconstruct gender; the role of gender in the playground; aspects of transfer; issues of identity, status and gender; gender and special educational needs; literacy, gender and popular culture (Marsh) and gender equity in science.

The website: Boys, Girls and Literacy – National Literacy Trust http://www.literacytrust.org.uk/ Database/Boys contains a very helpful research index which helps you to follow through issues in gender.

REFERENCES

Arnot, M., David, M. and Weiner, G. (1999) *Closing the Gender Gap*, Cambridge: Polity Press.
Biddulph, S. (1997) *Raising Boys*, London: Thames.
Bleach, K. (1998) *Raising Boys' Achievement in Schools*, Stoke-on-Trent: Trentham Books.
Bourdieu, P. (1990) *The Logic of Practice*, Cambridge: Polity Press.
Connell, R.W. (1995) *Masculinities*, St Leonards, NSW, Australia: Allen & Unwin.
Dyson, A.H. (1997) *Writing Superheroes: Contemporary Childhood, Popular Culture, and Classroom Literacy*, New York: Teachers College Press.
Epstein, D., Elwood, J., Hey, V. and Maw, J. (eds) (1998) *Failing Boys: Issues in Gender and Achievement*, Buckingham: Open University Press.

Gorard, S., Rees, G. and Salisbury, J. (1999) 'Reappraising the apparent underachievement in boys at school', *Gender and Education*, 11: 441–54.

Hannan, G. (1999) *Improving Boys' Performance*, Oxford: Heinemann Educational Publishing.

Mac an Ghaill, M.(1994) *The Making of Men*, Buckingham: Open University Press.

Marland, M. (1983) *Sex Differentiation and Schooling*, London: Heinemann.

Marsh, J. (2003) 'Superhero stories: literacy, gender and popular culture', in C. Skelton and B. Francis (eds) *Boys and Girls in the Primary School*, Buckingham: Open University Press.

Marsh, J. and Millard, E. (2003) *Literacy and Popular Culture in the Classroom*, Reading: Reading and Language Centre Publications.

Martino, W. and Meyenne, B. (eds) (2001) *What About the Boys? Issues of Masculinity in Schools*, Buckingham: Open University Press.

Martino, W. and Pallotta-Chiarolli, M. (eds) (2001) *Boys' Stuff, Boys Talking About What Matters*, St Leonards, NSW, Australia: Allen & Unwin.

Millard, E. (1997) *Differently Literate: Boys, Girls and the Schooling of Literacy*, London: Falmer Press.

Millard, E. (2000) 'Aspects of gender: how boys' and girls' experiences of reading help to shape their writing', in J. Evans (ed.) *The Writing Classroom: Aspects of Writing and the Primary Child*, London: David Fulton Books.

Millard, E. (2003) Transformative pedagogy: towards a literacy of fusion, *Reading, Literacy and Language*, 37(1): 3–9.

Paechter, C. (1998) *Educating the Other: Gender Power and Schooling*, London: Falmer Press.

Randall, G. (1987) 'Gender differences in pupil–teacher interactions in workshops and laboratories', in M. Arnot and G. Weiner(eds) *Gender under Scrutiny*, London: Hutchinson in association with the Open University.

Shilling, C. (1991) 'Social space, gender inequalities and educational differentiation', *British Journal of Sociology of Education*, 12(1): 23–44

Skelton, C. (1998) 'Feminism and research into masculinities and schooling', *Gender and Education*, 10: 217–27.

Skelton, C. and Francis, B. (eds) (2003) *Boys and Girls in the Primary School*, Buckingham: Open University Press.

TES (1995) 'Different drums for gender beat', Hilary Wilce (15 September) http://www.tes.co.uk/search.

TES (1997) 'Oh boy', Editorial (16 May) http://www.tes.co.uk/search.

Willis, P. (1977) *Learning to Labour; How Working Class Kids Get Working Class Jobs*, London: Saxon House.

Unit 6.5

Responding to Linguistic Diversity

Anny Northcote

INTRODUCTION

The languages which we hear and see around us in our communities and classrooms in Britain enrich society and contribute to developing all children's understanding of the wider world. Society is made up from the languages and cultures of the individuals and communities within it. Statistics show that nearly 10 per cent of pupils in UK schools speak languages other than English which amount to some 300 languages (www.multiverse.ac.uk). The multicultural society we live in should be as much recognised and supported within the education system as anywhere else.

OBJECTIVES

By the end of this unit you should have:

- a greater understanding of responses to linguistic diversity in education;
- an understanding of the meaning of linguistic diversity;
- an understanding of bilingual children's range of linguistic skills;
- an awareness of practical strategies to support bilingual learners in the classroom.

HISTORICAL RESPONSES TO LINGUISTIC DIVERSITY

In the UK the response to children and their families speaking languages other than English has been predominantly regarded as a problem by successive governments. Even today, with advances made in our understanding of how children best acquire an additional language, there is still the demand that English should become the first language of families with other mother-tongues. The former Education and Home Secretary David Blunkett said that Asian families should speak English in their own homes because 'learning English enables parents to converse with their children in English… and to participate in wider modern culture. It helps overcome the schizophrenia which bedevils generational relationships' (www.blink.org). Apart from this being a highly provocative statement, what Mr Blunkett failed to understand was the benefits of maintaining the first language to support the acquisition of English and the fact that the majority of families use a range of languages in the home, including English.

The idea that bilingual families should speak in English at home stems from a notion, prevalent in the 1960s, that children and their families need to be assimilated into the wider society through conforming to the language and culture of that society. To achieve this, bilingual learners new to English were withdrawn from the 'normal' classroom context to 'special' English classes (Levine 1990) or Language Centres. This took them away from their peers and a natural environment in which they could hear and engage in the new language. The focus was solely on learning new language skills which ignored the actual linguistic competence of the learner (Levine 1990). Children new to English were marginalised and without full access to the curriculum. There was at this time the danger of perceiving 'immigrant' children as deprived, disadvantaged and handicapped due to their own background and unfamiliarity with the wider society's language and culture (Gregory 1996).

There was a shift in the 1970s which acknowledged a linguistic and cultural pluralism within the expanding move to comprehensive education. In 1975 The Bullock Report entitled *A Language for Life* presented a comprehensive study of language and English learning and teaching. This included a very powerful chapter on the importance of a child's home language which stated that

> no child should be expected to cast off the language and culture of the home as he crosses the school threshold, nor to live and act as though school and home represent two separate and different cultures which have to be kept firmly apart.

(DES 1975: 286)

The next decade saw some advances in recognising bilingual learners in their acquisition of a new language within a more positive understanding of a multicultural society; one which recognised cultural and linguistic diversity. The support for bilingual learners became more sustained and specialist, though all teachers were considered to be responsible for the learning and language needs of the bilingual students. Mother-tongue teaching was introduced in some areas, particularly in the early years, but this was limited and seen predominantly as part of a transition from the home language to English. The Swann Report *Education for All* in 1985 reported that there were still major concerns around the lack of progress in the advance of a pluralist society which recognised diversity, achievement and minority ethnic communities.

Since the 1988 Education Act, Ofsted reports (DfES 1995, 1999, 2003) have continued to identify underachievement of some minority ethnic pupils.

Recent legislative change did come about as a result of the enquiry into the death of Stephen Lawrence (Macpherson Report 1999). This led to the Race Relations (Amendment) Act 2001 which gives a statutory general duty for public authorities to promote race equality. In schools this means that there should be an improvement in the educational experience of all children, in particular those belonging to minority ethnic groups. In practice, all schools must have in place policies which promote and monitor the attainment of children from all racial groups. Even schools who may not have many or any bilingual learners in their school community still need to be prepared. Any policy should also include an approach for all children to understand race equality as part of their education.

There is also funding from EMAG, the Ethnic Minority Achievement Grant (DfES 1999) to employ LEA teams, teachers and assistants to work with minority ethnic groups, particularly those at risk of underachieving such as speakers of EAL and refugee children. Responsibility lies with you as the class teacher to provide an appropriate curriculum for all children, working in collaboration with the EMAG funded teams and teachers. In schools where there are only a small number of bilingual learners, such additional support may not be available. Therefore you need to be familiar with ways to plan for and support bilingual learners, whatever the context.

WHAT IS LINGUISTIC DIVERSITY?

There has been much debate about the term linguistic diversity. All children use a range of language when communicating with family members, friends and teachers whatever the first language. Standard English taught in school is one of these. Of course linguistic diversity is diverse in itself and varies from school to school. In some areas there will be schools with a wide range of languages spoken by a large number of children. There will be schools where there is one main language other than English spoken by the majority and schools where there may only be a few speakers of a minority language other than English. The combinations are varied but the key is that we live in a culturally and linguistically diverse country and if you can acknowledge that your language is central to your identity, so is everybody else's.

| Task 6.5.1 |
| Language survey |

Find out about languages spoken in a school you know. What do you know about the languages? Choose one of them and explore what is the story of migration behind the speakers of the language now settled in your area. Are there spoken dialects which differ from the written standard? How and where do children study their home language? Does the language relate to their religion and is this always the case? Be careful not to make assumptions or apply the same conclusion to all speakers of a certain language.

BILINGUALISM AND BILINGUAL LEARNERS

This is a complex area within which definition has merited a great deal of debate (see Baker 2001). The key aspect for the purpose of this unit is to consider the individual bilingualism of each learner within the educational context. When we talk about a child being bilingual this does not necessarily mean that the speaker is fully competent and fluent in at least two languages. Whilst this 'balanced bilingualism' may be one end of the continuum it is more likely that children in school may have varying levels of operating in two language domains. Children new to English do not have 'no language', as is sometimes said by teachers, but are highly proficient users of at least one language which is referred to as the first or home language in this unit. The term bilingual is intended to focus you on the potential of the learner and to avoid negative labels such as non-English speakers. This more positive approach can also be seen in the shift from the term English as a second language (ESL) to EAL, English as an additional language, in which English is seen in addition to an already well-established knowledge and understanding of at least one other language. Also you need to remember that bilingual learners are not a homogeneous group.

The rest of this unit explores the issue of linguistic diversity in our schools and classrooms and considers your knowledge and understanding of such diversity and in particular how to support bilingual learners. The approach is one which starts from what bilingual children already know about language and the actual language which they bring to the classroom. Not only does this establish the foundation for the learner acquiring the new language but also adds to the knowledge and understanding of language for all children. Questions frequently asked by student teachers are explored through what research tells us and what this might mean in action. There are ideas for the classroom as well as tasks for you to enhance your own research into the issues which affect and interest you in particular.

ACKNOWLEDGING CHILDREN'S FIRST LANGUAGE IN THE CLASSROOM

There is a considerable body of research which explores the relationship between acquisition of the first language and that of an additional language, particularly when that language is acquired subsequently rather than simultaneously. Cummins and Swain (1986) explore this relationship through a theory of interdependence which suggests that second language acquisition is influenced by the extent to which the first language has developed. If the first language is strong, acquisition of the second may be relatively easy.

Lambert (1974) considers that learning an additional language within the same set of cognitive and social factors as those of acquiring the first language, leads to 'additive bilingualism'. Positive values and high status given to the first language, provides an enriched context in which the second language is an additional tool for thought and communication. The learner is able to build on what they implicitly know about language and how to use it and adapt or adopt this to the new language. Opposite to this is 'subtractive bilingualism' in which skills in the first language are not deemed as a basis for acquiring the second language and a new set of linguistic skills have to be learnt. The value placed on the first language is low. Subtractive bilingualism can lead to a diminishing of the first language whilst at the same time not allowing the additional language to be fully developed. This may result in difficulties in acquiring the additional language and prevent children being able to show their true cognitive level. Their capacity and potential for learning may be wrongly viewed in a negative light. Therefore the concepts of additive and subtractive bilingualism are important when discussing the relationship between first and subsequent language acquisition. This also opens the debate on the positive cognitive aspects of being bilingual. The ability to speak two or more languages has been shown to contribute to cognitive understanding; to thinking, reasoning and problem-solving skills as well as to more confidence in social intercultural contexts (Baker 2001).

In fact there is evidence that support for the first language of bilingual learners at academic levels is key to academic success in the additional language.

Older children who arrive in the classroom at the early stages of acquiring English, but with a strong command of their first language and possibly literate in this, are generally found to acquire an additional language more rapidly than those who are not as skilled. Once concepts are developed making connections becomes easier – the new language gives new labels to the well-established concepts. In reality it can be hard to engage children in the classroom in their first language, particularly where there are small numbers of bilingual learners or a range of languages, spoken by individual children rather than groups. However, if you understand the role first language plays in the acquisition of an additional language, then you have to do something to make the experience of learning a positive one, building on the bilingual learners' linguistic backgrounds in their learning of English. The ethos of the classroom plays an important role here and recognising a child's bilingualism and therefore enhancing self-esteem, can go some way to showing the child's identity is important and diversity is beneficial for all children. As a teacher who encourages diversity and open discussion between adults and children and amongst peers you will see that when children use their first language with each other in the classroom there is a positive effect on their learning. A school which values the languages and cultures of the community will find that the bilingual children are more likely to be successful in their acquisition of English and in their learning (Ofsted 2003). All this is not just for the benefit of the bilingual learners but for all children and adults. It increases language and cultural awareness, supporting communication between groups and encouraging a positive response to a multicultural society. Where there are few bilingual learners in a school it may seem daunting to consider their needs but the same principles can apply. An example of integrating a new bilingual child into the classroom where there are no other bilingual learners can be seen in the case study below.

> *Year 1 and 2 class (Spring Term)*
> Marco is a five-year-old Italian boy who started school in the UK in the previous Autumn Term. He was new to English when he arrived. At that time his mother spoke a little English and gave good support which has continued.
>
> Marco settled well socially in class and soon began visiting friends out of school time.
>
> The classroom context presented lots of opportunities for play and modelling of spoken English by peers and adults. Marco really enjoyed himself in this context and particularly enjoyed retelling stories which he soon began to do in English.
>
> The teacher included lots of resources in Italian in displays and other materials. The whole class became interested in Marco's language. They supported Marco well, sometimes using Italian words such as 'comprende?'
>
> Student teacher, Bath Spa University College 2005

SUPPORTING HOME LANGUAGES IN THE CLASSROOM

- Allow and encourage children to speak and work in their own language;
- learn some key vocabulary and phrases such as numbers, days of the week, hello/goodbye, and encourage the other children to do this too;
- explore stories, books and poetry through the first language and introduce the English version with props, puppets or through drama;
- encourage talk partners to use home languages in whole class and group work;
- create a graphics/writing area with different scripts, giving all children opportunities to practise the range of symbols using different materials.

For more fluent bilingual learners, continue to explore texts using the home language with peers or adults. Similarly encourage students to use the first language as well as English when engaged with investigative and problem-solving tasks.

Task 6.5.2
Observing spoken language

Observe the use of language(s) of a bilingual learner in the classroom and playground. Record the different ways the child uses language to communicate with peers and adults. Does the context influence the child's confidence when speaking? What do your observations tell you about the child's understanding and use of home language and English?

LEARNING A NEW LANGUAGE IN CONTEXT

Children learn a language because they need to communicate. They do this best from their peers in a context where language is used to find things out, get things done, question, show understanding and express thoughts and feelings. Modelling by peers and teachers has been shown to be the most effective way to engage children new to a language. Visual support and practical activities which are intellectually challenging provide a context for the language in which speakers and listeners can then take an active role.

Language Centres which new arrivals may have attended in the past to learn English were phased out in the 1980s. Although there has been a call through the new Nationality, Immigration and Asylum Act for such centres to be re-opened, Ofsted itself has not found any reason to endorse this. Thirty-seven schools and eleven LEAs were inspected to evaluate the impact of the arrival of pupils from asylum-seeking families (Ofsted 2003). There were plenty of examples of good practice in place to address the needs of the students and their families in all areas including learning English. Many asylum-seeking children inspired their classmates and teachers because of the seriousness with which they treated education. Even though they spoke little or no English initially, nearly all made at least satisfactory progress and many progressed well in a short time (TES 2003).

Also in response to the possibility of withdrawal, a survey by Save the Children and Glasgow City Council found that mainstream schooling was the highlight of young refugees' difficult lives. More than 75 per cent of the 700 questioned said their experience at school was positive, allowing them to make friends, socialise, play and learn English.

TEACHING BILINGUAL CHILDREN IN A LINGUISTICALLY DIVERSE CLASSROOM

Acquiring an additional language has similarities to acquiring the first language. Learners of school age start by picking up words before putting them together in two or three word phrases as they tackle the syntactic structure of the new language. The similarities are important but it is also important to recognise the differences. The most important of these is that bilingual learners already know implicitly how a language works and are generally proficient users. They will also have conceptual understanding similar to that of their peers, and will relate the language to the context. Bilingual learners are not less intelligent or linguistically disadvantaged (Baker 2001). On the contrary – they have a skill in being able to speak and possibly read and write in more than one language as their understanding of English progresses. Not speaking English must not be viewed as a disability and should not be equated with SEN.

However it is important to recognise that some bilingual learners may have specific educational needs, not linked to their additional language acquisition. Children giving cause for concern need to be assessed carefully, preferably including professionals who know and understand the language and culture of the student (Hall 2001).

Learning through play and experimentation is a successful approach for all young children and gives a strong context in which opportunities for the new language can be used for social and intellectual engagement. In the Foundation Stage this should be common practice which can be enhanced through a range of resources which reflect the linguistic and cultural diversity of the community. Stories are also central to the primary curriculum and an excellent resource for supporting bilingual learners, particularly when supported by visuals, available on video, DVD or audio cassette, preferably in the home language as well as English.

Don't be surprised if some bilingual learners choose not to speak at these early stages. A silent period is quite common and of course during this time the child is engaging and, most importantly, listening. Bilingual learners acquire a new language most successfully if there is a meaningful context for learning to take place, within which they can listen, experiment, hypothesise, adapt or adopt the language. In some cases in KS1 and particularly in KS2, you may need to reassess your planning and teaching approaches, providing more opportunities for investigative and problem-solving tasks, using visual and physical resources.

SUPPORTING BILINGUAL LEARNERS WHO ARE AT DIFFERENT STAGES OF LEARNING ENGLISH

This is a very common and likely scenario. As for all children, learning contexts should be carefully planned with the intention to build on the strengths of the learner and address their specific needs which will vary from one bilingual student to another.

One aspect to consider is how to group children and frequently teachers may place the new student with speakers of the same language. Whilst it may be appropriate to have a student new to English working alongside a student with the same home language but more proficient in English, other factors need to be taken into consideration, such as experience, friendship, gender and interest. It is also important to consider the 'new' child's approach to learning. Recent research (Chen and Gregory 2004) shows how two Chinese girls, one, aged 9, new to Britain, the other born here and now 8, work together. It sheds light on how children may perceive learning a new language and, when given the chance, control their learning. The newly arrived older girl's insistence on what she wants to know and how she wants to learn may come from her previous experience of schooling, as well as her wish and determination to take on a new language. The younger girl's need to act as translator and teacher stretches her language abilities, allowing her to become more aware of her own bilinguality. Chen and Gregory argue that the interaction can only be successful if there is an element of trust, respect and reciprocity between the two girls which has to be in a setting which facilitates such interaction. They see the learning context, not as one in which the 'able' English speaker scaffolds the other but one in which a synergy is created, in which the roles of the more experienced and the novice are more complex.

Placing bilingual children together in one group is rarely appropriate and is in fact a form of withdrawal in the classroom rather than inclusion. Labelling them as 'the EAL group', which seems to be quite common practice, is demeaning and misguided. To understand this you need to consider further what has been stated previously – that children learn best when engaged in activities with speakers of English who can model the language appropriate to the task and to the cognitive level of the child. A collaborative approach to learning is one which is recognised as good practice for all children, and a stimulating learning environment which allows for children to take risks can give positive support for the bilingual learner. However, although some of their learning needs may be similar to those students whose first language is English, they also have different linguistic needs, particularly at the early stages, by the fact they are learning through another language and come from cultural backgrounds and communities where there may be differing expectations of education. This means that even if you only have one or two bilingual learners in your class, it's still important to find out about them and consider their needs.

Another important factor is how you assess children's development of English. The first thing to note is that no formal assessment should be done too early and even then any assessment of language has to start from the understanding of the child acquiring English as an additional language. All LEAs and schools should have descriptors which show the developmental steps against which to build a picture of each bilingual learner's achievements in the new language.

However, at the heart of this must be an understanding that proficiency in understanding written texts takes longer than the spoken language and this will vary depending on each child's age, educational background and other factors.

Cummins (1984a, 1984b) distinguishes between 'basic interpersonal communicative skills' (BICS) and 'cognitive and academic language proficiency' (CALP). BICS refers to the oral fluency of the bilingual learner which may take up to two years to achieve. CALP is more concerned with the demands of the curriculum particularly in terms of literacy skills which take longer, between five and seven years. This is somewhat dependent on when a bilingual learner begins to acquire a new language and whether or not they are already literate in the first. The main point is that you will often hear teachers say that a bilingual student is good at speaking and listening but in spite of this fluency finds writing and reading tasks harder than monolingual peers.

In summary, you need to consider several areas when planning for bilingual learners (Gravelle 2000). The social, cultural, linguistic and cognitive aspects need to be teased out alongside the learner's previous experience. The demands of the task need to then be considered for you to decide what support is needed.

WHAT CAN I DO TO SUPPORT THE BILINGUAL LEARNERS IN MY CLASS?

For children new to English:

- give them time to adjust to the new situation and to tune into the new language – don't pressurise them to speak but include them in the established routines and activities of the class, making them feel welcome;
- allow them to be silent if they choose to and know that this is fine;
- ensure activities are considered for their linguistic content – but keep the conceptual element at an appropriate challenging level for their age. Ensure activities are considered in terms of their cultural content and relate to previous learning and social experiences;
- centre activities around spoken English until confident that the child is able to engage with written texts through their own reading and writing. This may be quite soon with children in KS2 who are already literate;
- ensure that activities include active participation of the learners. Stories, songs, rhymes, turn-taking games, investigative and problem-solving tasks with good quality support materials provide opportunities to engage the child and give a scaffold for the linguistic component;
- consider supportive grouping with children who will provide a language model and be encouraging in a collaborative learning context;

- always have high expectations – look at what children can do, are interested in and enjoy.

For children more advanced in spoken English but who need further support with accessing written texts, particularly in KS2:

- give plenty of opportunities to discuss language and linguistic devices in a way which build on the children's own interest in a range of fiction and non-fiction texts, and their own reading and writing;
- engage in language play such as jokes, riddles, jingles and tongue-twisters which give an understanding of the subtleties and nuances of language and develop a colloquial fluency;
- set up discussion groups around literature which encourage children to focus on the text to support their comments and questions;
- consider close work with subject-related texts.

Task 6.5.3
Planning and teaching to support bilingual learners in English

Plan a sequence of activities (FS) or a unit of work (KS1/2). Consider the points above which are relevant to your context and plan two or three tasks to support the different bilingual learners in your class.

WHAT ABOUT PARENTS AND THEIR EXPECTATIONS?

Partnership between home and school is crucial to ensure bilingual learners and their families get the best support they can for academic success. All parents want their children to do well in school and for families settling in a new country, where the majority language is not their home language, there is an added dimension to achieving that success. All schools will have an admissions policy which should include gathering information about the child's linguistic and educational background which should be available to you.

Learning to speak, read and write English is high on the list of priorities for bilingual families and one role of the school is to discuss with parents how that is done and the support they can give. Being aware of the issues around how their children acquire English is often a relief to parents who think maintaining their home language may be disadvantageous to learning English. We need to show it is not, whilst at the same time encouraging parents to engage in the learning processes their children are familiar with, such as through reading and maths activities in the home.

However, some parents of bilingual learners may not feel comfortable coming into school and there needs to be some positive engagement to change such a situation. A tried and tested approach is sharing stories, culture, customs and bookmaking workshops involving children and their parents writing stories in different languages. Projects which involve the community groups which bring together parents and teachers to discuss issues as well as research into the children's range of literacy practices, have revealed a great deal about the children's language and literacy experiences outside of school which are rich and varied (Gregory 1996; Sneddon 1996).

AN INCLUSIVE CURRICULUM

What this unit has aimed to do is give you some insight into the positive opportunities bilingual learners and a linguistically diverse classroom can offer. The National Curriculum (DfES 1999) recognises some of the issues explored here and states that teachers should ensure access to the curriculum and assessment. The current emphasis in the Primary Strategy (DfES2003) is one which offers an inclusive curriculum based on three principles:

- setting suitable learning challenges;
- responding to pupils' diverse needs;
- overcoming potential barriers to learning and assessment for individuals and groups of pupils.

Such an approach in relation to bilingual learners needs:

- a whole-school commitment to raising achievement through inclusion;
- recognition and understanding of the knowledge, culture, previous education and language which bilingual pupils bring to school and the learning context;
- support for pupils to access the curriculum, adapting where necessary;
- partnership in teaching and learning.

SUMMARY

However, how we address and support the needs of bilingual learners is a politically charged arena. Underachievement of certain minority ethnic groups continues to be an issue and in spite of all the research into heightening our understanding of how students acquire an additional language, there have been no major structural changes to support this. We do not live in a culturally neutral society or one that is free from prejudice and racism. Socio-economic status is also a strong determiner of success and this range of causal factors cannot be solely tackled within education.

This picture makes it more important that the curriculum and the types of interaction we can establish in schools and classrooms should be there to promote academic success for all children. An integration into the mainstream, whilst clearly positive, must be done systematically and with appropriate resources, including bilingual teachers and assistants, if we are serious about supporting bilingual learners to achieve their potential. Therefore, a greater understanding amongst all teachers of bilingual children, their linguistic and cultural backgrounds, their families and communities is essential if any sense of social equity can be turned into positive achievement.

Therefore as new teachers soon to enter the profession it is crucial that you are aware of the issues in order to support your own planning for bilingual learners. It is not as daunting a task as is sometimes perceived. As discussed in this unit it is not about a separate curriculum for children with a learning disability, but about an enhanced curriculum for all children within which there are varied opportunities for children to extend their linguistic repertoire.

A greater understanding about how bilingual learners acquire an additional language and develop literacy skills gives insight into how all children learn to read and write and how talk in educational contexts is part of an extended literacy curriculum. As it was stated at the beginning of this unit, the range of languages spoken in this society and the cultures and communities in which they thrive can only enrich our schools and the lives of all children to become more tolerant and understanding of the backgrounds, linguistic and cultural, which present us with such diversity.

ANNOTATED FURTHER READING

Baker, C. (2001) *Foundations of Bilingual Education and Bilingualism*, 3rd edition, Clevedon: Multilingual Matters. Primarily a theoretical text which discusses comprehensively issues of bilingualism, learning and diversity as well as educational policies

Gravelle, M. (ed.) (2000) *Planning for Bilingual Learners*, Stoke on Trent: Trentham Books. This very practical book considers a framework for planning to support bilingual learners in the mainstream classroom. There are good classroom studies on new arrivals, promoting first languages, stories and writing and bilingual learners and numeracy.

Multiverse Exploring Diversity and Achievement, www.multiverse.ac.uk. An Initial Teacher Education resource, supported by the TDA, this website covers a wealth of resource material to enhance the educational achievement of pupils from diverse backgrounds. This includes research articles, debates and ideas for the classroom. Look here for the current statistics for languages spoken in your LEA. www.multiverse.ac.uk

REFERENCES

Baker, C. (2001) *Foundations of Bilingual Education and Bilingualism*, 3rd edition, Clevedon: Multilingual Matters.

Chen, Y. and Gregory, E. (2004) '"How do I read these words": bilingual exchange teaching between Cantonese-speaking peers', in E. Gregory, S. Long and D. Volk (eds) *Many Pathways to Literacy*, London: RoutledgeFalmer.

Cummins, J. (1984a) *Bilingualism and Special Education: Issues in Assessment and Pedagogy*, Clevedon: Multilingual Matters.

Cummins, J. (1984b) 'Wanted: a theoretical framework for relating language proficiency to academic achievement among bilingual pupils', in C. Rivera (ed.) *Language Proficiency and Academic Achievement*, Clevdon: Multilingual Matters.

Cummins, J. and Swain, M. (1986) *Bilingualism in Education*, London: Longman.

DES (1975) *A Language for Life* (The Bullock Report), London: HMSO.

DES (1985) *Education for All* (The Swann Report), London: HMSO.

DfES (1999) *Raising the Attainment of Minority Ethnic Pupils*, London: OFSTED.

DfES (2003) *Aiming High: Raising the Achievement of Minority Ethnic Pupils*, London: OFSTED.

Gillborn, D. and Gipps, C. (1996) *Recent Research on the Achievements of Ethnic Minority Children*, London: Ofsted.

Gravelle, M. (ed,) (2000) *Planning for Bilingual Learners*, Stoke on Trent: Trentham Books.

Gregory, E. (1996) *Making Sense of a New World*, London: Paul Chapman Publishing.

Gregory, E., Long, S. and Volk, D. (2004) *Many Pathways to Literacy*, London: RoutledgeFalmer.

Hall, D. (2001) *Assessing the Needs of Bilingual Learners Living in Two Languages*, 2nd edition, London: David Fulton Publishers.

Lambert, W.E. (1974) 'Culture and language as factors in learning and education', in F.E. Aboud and R.D. Meade (eds) *Cultural Factors in Learning and Education*, Bellingham, WA: 5th Western Washington Symposium on Learning.

Levine, J. (ed.) (1990) *Bilingual Learners and the Mainstream Curriculum*, London: Falmer Press.

Sneddon, R. (2003) 'What language do you speak at home?', in *The Best of Language Matters*, London: CLPE.

7 Assessment

Unit 7.1

Assessment and Learning: Summative Approaches

Kathy Hall and Kieron Sheehy

INTRODUCTION

In this unit you will have the chance to reflect on *what summative assessment* is, *its uses* and *its potential impact on learners.* You will also be able to consider some aspects of current policy on assessment. We start by considering some basic questions about summative assessment and by linking it with formative assessment. We will go on to identify purposes of summative assessment as well as sources of assessment evidence and we will explain what counts as good evidence of learning. We also consider SATs in the context of summative assessment and we finish by inviting your views on current assessment policy.

OBJECTIVES

By the end of this unit you should be able to:

- define summative assessment and be able to relate it to formative assessment;
- explain why it is important to assess learners in a variety of contexts and know the kinds of assessment tasks that are effective in generating good evidence of learning;
- identify ways in which schools might use summative assessment information to feed back into teaching and learning;
- describe some aspects of the national policy on assessment and offer an informed opinion about the current emphasis on different assessment purposes and approaches.

WHAT IS ASSESSMENT AND WHY DO IT?

Assessment means different things in different contexts and it is carried out for different purposes. There is no simple answer to what it is or why we do it. Indeed one of the most important messages that we would like you to take away from this unit is that assessment is not a simple or innocent term. Assessing learning is not a neutral or value-free activity – it is always bound up with attitudes, values, beliefs and sometimes prejudices on the part of those carrying out the assessment and on the part of those being assessed. When we make assessments of children's learning we are always influenced by what we bring with us in terms of our previous experiences, personal views and histories. Children's responses to assessment are influenced by what they bring with them – their previous experiences and their personal views.

SUMMATIVE ASSESSMENT SUMS UP LEARNING

Most recent sources on assessment refer to two important types. One is summative assessment, the other is formative assessment. Sometimes summative assessment is termed 'assessment of learning' (AoL) and in recent times formative assessment is associated with 'assessment for learning' (AfL). These newer terms are useful as they give an insight into the purpose of assessment that is involved in each case. In the next unit (Unit 7.2) the area of formative assessment is addressed in more detail.

As the term implies, summative assessment tries to sum up a child's attainment in a given area of the curriculum. Summative assessment is retrospective: it looks back at what has been achieved, perhaps over a term, year or key stage. Formative assessment, on the other hand, is prospective: it looks forward to the next steps of learning. However, debate continues over whether and how summative and formative assessment should be distinguished (Threlfall 2005). As we explain in a moment, we consider that the use to which assessment information is put is also helpful in determining whether it is labelled summative or formative.

SOURCES OF ASSESSMENT EVIDENCE

Assessing learning is about collecting information or evidence about learners and making judgements about it. The evidence may be based on one or more of the following:

- what learners say;
- what learners do;
- what learners produce;
- what learners feel or think.

The information or evidence may come from learners' responses to a test, such as a spelling test; a classroom activity, such as a science investigation; a game or a puzzle; a standard assessment task, or a test like the SATs. It may come from a task or activity that is collaborative, that is one where several pupils work together on the same problem. It may come from a task that pupils do on their own without interacting with other children.

We suspect that you will have observed children and made judgements about them in many of those settings; you may have noted down some of your observations and/or shared them with the class teacher or tutor when you were on teaching practice.

PURPOSES OF SUMMATIVE ASSESSMENT

As a new teacher you will be meeting children who you have not taught, or may not have even met previously. In these situations you might wish to gain an overview of each pupil's progress. This is particularly so when children are transferring between different stages of schooling and the classwork is different. Summative assessment is used frequently in these contexts because, in obtaining a summary of what learners know or can do, it helps the teacher to decide what to teach next.

Summative assessment is carried out for several purposes. One purpose is to provide you with a summary of learners' achievement that will inform your future teaching and of course your planning for future learning. (This is close to the notion of formative assessment described in the next unit.) A second purpose is to provide valid and accurate information that can be shared with parents about their children's progress. A third purpose for summatively assessing learning is to provide a numerical measurement which can be used in league tables – the purpose being to make schools accountable. Before reading on, try to put these purposes in order of importance for yourself as a classroom teacher.

We suspect this exercise is not that simple to do. Assessing learners for the purpose of helping you to plan your teaching can't easily be accommodated alongside assessing learners for the purpose of rendering the school or class accountable through the publication of league tables. League tables call for assessment methods which are reliable in that they are comparable across all schools and across the country as a whole and valid in that they offer an account of what is considered important to know at various stages of schooling. As Black *et al.* (2003: 2) note these are 'exacting requirements'. Reliability and comparability are not major issues if, on the other hand, you are seeking evidence to help you decide what to teach next.

For the purpose of generating league tables, as Black *et al.* (2003) note, the main assessment methods are formal tests (not devised by teachers). These are usually isolated from day to day teaching and learning, and they are often carried out at special times of the year. In contrast, assessments designed to inform your teaching are usually more informal, they may be integrated into your ongoing teaching, and they are likely to be carried out in different ways by different teachers. In the light of the previous sentence, you may well wonder what the difference is between summative and formative assessment, and indeed some research challenges the distinction in the first place (Threlfall 2005). However, in line with the work of Black and Wiliam (1998) we are reluctant to label the latter as formative assessment.

As we see it, the salient feature of formative assessment is that learners themselves use the information deriving from the assessment to bridge the gap between what they know and need to know (see Hall and Burke, 2003 for a full discussion). Collecting information to inform your teaching is in itself no guarantee that learners will use this information to move forward in their learning.

PRODUCING GOOD EVIDENCE OF ACHIEVEMENT

It is important to appreciate that summative assessment can take a variety of forms – it need not, indeed should not, just be a written test. In addition, it is important for you as a teacher to try to anticipate how pupils might respond to the demands of an assessment task. In 1987 Desmond Nuttall wrote a paper describing the types of tasks or activities that are good for assessing learning. Such tasks, he says, should be concrete and within the experience of the individual; they should be presented clearly; and they should be perceived by the pupils as relevant to their current concerns.

Being able to respond to a task in a variety of ways, e.g. making, doing, talking, writing, allows learners to demonstrate their learning in a variety of ways. The value of varied approaches to assessing learning is that they help learners really show what they know or can do. For example, a learner who is not a very skilled writer may be better able to demonstrate their historical knowledge through talk or through a combination of written work and oral work. Think about your own history as a pupil – do you feel that a written test enabled you to demonstrate what you really knew? Would other ways have been more appropriate for assessing your competence in different curriculum areas?

The use of a variety of ways of assessing learning (often referred to as multiple response modes) allows adults to have evidence of learning from a variety of contexts thus avoiding making judgements about learning based on single sources of evidence, like say in a pencil-and-paper test. This results in information that is more accurate and trustworthy than results deriving from just one assessment in just one situation. You could say that it is more valid and dependable. By looking across several instances in which a child uses, say, reading, the teacher and teaching assistant get valuable information about that child as a reader.

Judgements based on the use of a variety of sources of assessment information are of course more demanding on time and resources. This means teachers and policy makers have to consider the appropriate balance to obtain between validity and trustworthiness of assessment evidence on the one hand and manageability and cost on the other.

TICK SHEETS AND PORTFOLIOS

Some teachers use 'tick sheets' to summarise a child's achievements at a point in schooling. This type of assessment is also summative. What is your view of this approach in the light of the previous section about good assessment evidence?

The tick sheet, yes/no approach might be manageable for very busy practitioners and could provide a useful overview of a child's learning. However, it is likely to be too crude to offer a really meaningful account of learning and usually it offers no source of evidence or little evidence regarding the context in which the assessment took place. Mary Jane Drummond, an expert on early years education, says that a tick sheet approach may hinder the production of a 'rich respectful account' (Drummond 1999: 34) of a child's learning.

Portfolios offer a useful way of keeping evidence of learning. For example, your pupils might have an individual literacy portfolio into which they put lists of books read, written responses to stories, non-fiction writing, drawings or paintings in response to literature and so on. They may include drafts of work as well as finished pieces of writing. You might then use this evidence to write short summary accounts of your pupils which in turn could be used as a basis of discussion at a parents' evening.

As well as individual portfolios, some schools keep 'class' or 'school' portfolios where they put samples of pupil work. They may annotate the samples with reference to context and the standards met. So, for example, contextual annotations might include the date, whether the piece of work was the result of pupils collaborating or an individual working alone, whether the teacher helped or whether it was done independently. Annotations about the standard met might include a grade or a score and a comment indicating how closely the work met a national curriculum standard or level description (discussed below). This kind of portfolio sometimes acts as a vehicle for teachers to share their interpretation of the standards, not just amongst themselves but also with parents and with pupils.

SUMMATIVE ASSESSMENT AND TEACHER ASSESSMENT

As well as the external testing regime of standard assessment tests (SATs), teachers assess and report on their pupils via Teacher Assessments. They are required to 'sum up' their pupils' attainments in relation to National Curriculum levels – this is known as Teacher Assessment (TA). As we noted earlier, in order to offer defensible and trustworthy accounts of their attainment, you need to assess pupils in a variety of contexts and in a variety of ways. But any assessment is only as good as the use to which it is put. Some writers refer to this concept as 'consequential validity' as what is considered important are the consequences of the assessment – what happens to the assessment information once it is collected. Is it used to inform teaching, to enable the production of league tables or to summarise achievement for parents or the next teacher?

Assessment information, including that obtained via SATs and especially via TA, can be used in a way that supports teaching and learning. We will explain this with reference to the way some teachers use level descriptions.

Level descriptions are used in all four parts of the UK. They are summary statements that describe the types and range of performance which pupils are expected to demonstrate at various stages in their schooling. Teachers have to judge which level 'best fits' a child's performance for each area of the curriculum. Judging which level best fits a child's performance involves cross-checking against adjacent levels in a scale and considering the balance of strengths and weaknesses for each particular child.

What use is made of level descriptions? Does the process of allocating levels to pupils' achievements inform teaching and learning? A study conducted in six different schools in six different LEAs in the north of England sought to understand how primary teachers were using level descriptions (Hall and Harding, 2002). On the basis of many interviews over two years with teachers and LEA assessment advisers and observations of assessment meetings, two contrasting approaches to the process of interpreting and using level descriptions in schools were identified. The approaches are described as *collaborative* and *individualistic*.

To illustrate, we will describe just two of the schools – East Street and West Street (not their real names) – which show these contrasting tendencies.

East Street School is a large inner city primary school of 400+ pupils, all but 5 per cent of whom are from ethnic minority backgrounds. East Street has an assessment community which is highly collaborative with teachers, parents and pupils having many opportunities to talk about assessment and how and why it is done. The staff frequently meet to discuss the purposes of assessment in general and of their ongoing teacher assessment in particular. They talk about what constitutes evidence of achievement in various areas of the curriculum and they compare their judgements of samples of pupil work. They use a range of tools, such as school portfolios and sample material from QCA, to help in their assessment tasks and to ensure that they are applying the level descriptions consistently. They strive to include pupils, parents and other teachers as part of that assessment community.

West Street School is a larger-than-average primary school serving a varied socio-economic area in a northern city. Pupils are drawn from a mixture of privately owned and council maintained housing and the school has a sizeable number of pupils from educationally disadvantaged backgrounds. West Street reluctantly complies with the demands of national policy on assessment. Teachers here work largely in isolation from each other in interpreting and implementing assessment goals and, especially, in interpreting level descriptions and using portfolios and evidence. There is no real attempt to involve interested groups, like parents and pupils, in assessment discussions. The staff tend to view national testing as an unhelpful, arduous intrusion.

What all of this tells us is that schools vary a great deal in how they implement national assessment policy. Some teachers reluctantly comply with the policy while others make it work for the benefit of all interested parties in the school. To be more precise, some teachers use level descriptions in a way that supports assessment *for* learning and assessment *of* learning.

To become a collaborative assessment community, staff need time to develop their expertise. They need time to talk about and share their practices in a culture that shares the expectation that adults too are valued learners.

Task 7.1.1
Applying level descriptions in summative assessment

- Study Figure 7.1.1 which summarises the assessment approach in East Street and West Street schools.
- Suggest some reasons for the difference in approach in the two schools.
- Practice in most schools is probably somewhere in between these two. Make a note of practices listed in East Street that you are aware of from your experience in school recently.

	Collaborative (East Street School)	**Individualistic** (West Street School)
GOALS	Compliant and accepting	Reluctant compliance and resistance
PROCESSES	1 Level Descriptions – interpretation is shared 2 Portfolio – in active use 3 Exemplification Materials – owned by teachers; a mixture of school-devised and QCA materials 4 Evidence – planned collection; variety of modes; assessment embedded in teaching and learning; emphasis on the process 5 Common language of assessment 6 Commitment to moderation (cross-checking of interpretations of evidence)	1 Level Descriptions – little or no sharing of interpretations 2 Portfolio – dormant 3 Exemplification Materials – QCA not used; commercially produced materials used by some individuals 4. Evidence – not used much; assessment often bolted on to learning and teaching; emphasis on products 5 Uncertainty/confusion about terms 6 Weak or non-existent moderation
PERSONNEL	Whole school Aspirations to enlarge the assessment community to include pupils, parents and other teachers	Y2 teachers as individuals. No real grasp of the potential for enlarging the assessment community
VALUE SYSTEM	Assessment seen as useful, necessary, and integral to teaching and learning; made meaningful through collaboration	Assessment seen as 'imposed' and not meaningful at the level of the class teacher

Figure 7.1.1 Assessment communities and assessment individuals

SUMMATIVE ASSESSMENT AND SATS

Summative assessment does not just refer to the kinds of end of key stage assessment carried out in schools all over the country in Years 2 and 6. While those external tasks and tests, known as SATs, are indeed summative, they are not the only kind of summative assessment that goes on in schools. However, because of their 'high stakes', i.e. the school's ranking in league tables depends on them, they are accorded very high status in practice in schools and people sometimes make the mistake of assuming that summative assessments means SATs. Table 7.1.2 illustrates the range of SATs undertaken by pupils in English primary schools in 2004.

- Foundation Stage Profile (5 years old)   ALL STUDENTS
- KS1 Tests (7 years old)   ALL STUDENTS
  English, Maths
- Optional Tests (8 years old)   NEARLY ALL STUDENTS
  English, Maths
- Optional Tests (9 years old)   NEARLY ALL STUDENTS
  English, Maths
- Optional Tests (10 years old)   NEARLY ALL STUDENTS
  English, Maths
- KS2 Tests (11 years old)   ALL STUDENTS **Results Published**
  English, Maths
- Year 7 Progress Tests   Low Attainers

Figure 7.1.2   Primary SATs in England in 2004 (Adapted from Whetton, 2004)

When presented in this way the amount of testing looks daunting. It has been pointed out that 'the total amount of compulsory testing is in fact only 17 hours spread over nine years – an average of not even 2 hours per year' (Whetton 2004: 15). However, this statement does not reflect the impact that such assessments have on pupils or on practice within schools.

THE IMPACT OF 'HIGH STAKES' ASSESSMENT ON PUPILS

Many researchers on assessment, including ourselves, have written about the impact on pupils of different assessment purposes and practices (Harlen and Deakin Crick 2002). The research shows that schools feel under pressure to get more of their pupils achieving at higher levels in national tests. This pushes some teachers, especially those who have classes about to take national tests, to spend more time and energy on helping pupils to get good at doing those tests. This is often referred to as 'teaching to the test' and it means there is less time to actually develop pupils' skills and understanding in the various areas of the curriculum.

This is exactly what we found in a recent study of Year 6 pupils in urban areas of disadvantage (Hall *et al.* 2004). The external pencil-and-paper tests, which are designed to offer evidence to the government about how schools are raising standards got enormous attention in the daily life of pupils in the schools that were part of our study. Such is the perceived pressure in schools to do well in league tables that they sometimes feel unable to place sufficient emphasis on assessment designed to promote learning across the curriculum or on assessing learning through a variety of modes (see earlier section of this unit).

There are many potential consequences for pupils. 'High stakes' tests can lead teachers to adopt transmission styles of teaching and thus disadvantage students who prefer other, more creative ways, of learning. Practice tests, when repeatedly undertaken, can have a negative impact on the self-esteem of lower achieving pupils. Research from outside the UK suggests that pupils' expectations about the purpose of assessment reflects badly on summative approaches (Black 2003). For example, pupils believing that summative assessment was entirely for their schools and parents' benefit. Children who did less well in such assessments felt that their purpose was to make them work harder. It was a source of pressure that resulted in pupil anxiety and even fear.

Pupils used to a diet of summative assessments, based on written tests and based only on a few curriculum areas (often number and literacy) can take time in adapting to more formative approaches. The same can be true for teachers. For example, in response to calls for formative assessment many teachers produce formal summative tests that mimic the statutory tests. This again reflects the perceived importance of SATs. Weeden *et al.* (2002) make the point that the more important a quantitative measure becomes, 'the more it is likely to distort the processes it is suppose to monitor' (p. 34).

There is clearly an emotional/affective factor which is often overlooked in seeking the objective viewpoint that summative assessments are seen as presenting. Robert Reinecke (1998: 7) highlights this:

> Assessments, formal or informal, considered or casual, intentional or not, powerfully affect people, particularly students. The assessment climate that students experience is a crucial component of instruction and learning. Students' assessment experiences remain with them for a lifetime and substantially affect their capacity for future learning ... emotional charge is part of the character of assessment information.

For any assessment to have a positive impact on children's learning the way in which performance results are used and communicated is vitally important.

DIFFERENCES IN TESTING ACROSS THE UK

Pupils in England and in Northern Ireland are subjected to more testing than their peers in other parts of the UK. Teachers in Scotland, for instance, decide when their pupils are ready to take the external tests. Teachers at Key Stage 1 in Wales are no longer obliged to assess their pupils for the purpose of compiling league tables.

The following is a short extract from an important policy document in England, *Excellence and Enjoyment: A Strategy for Primary Schools* (DfES 2003: 2.29). It tells you what head teachers think is the best way of summarising a learner's achievements:

> At our headteacher conferences, headteachers argued that a teacher's overall, rounded assessment of a child's progress through the year (taking into account the regular tests and tasks that children do) was a more accurate guide to a child's progress at this age [Key Stage 1] than their performance in one particular set of tasks and tests.

Because head teachers in England are so concerned about testing at Key Stage 1, the government decided to commission research to see whether an approach which focuses more on teachers' judgements about pupils' progress throughout the year can result in accurate and rigorous assessments. Final reports of that work have yet to be published but early indications are that teachers' judgements can indeed offer accurate and sound assessments of pupil attainment.

Task 7.1.2
Assessing for accountability

What do you think about testing?

* Note down some advantages and disadvantages of testing all children at ages 7 and 11.
* Why do you think England, in particular, places such a strong emphasis on external testing for accountability purposes?

We are hopeful that in the near future England and Northern Ireland will revise its strong emphasis on external testing at Key Stages 1 and 2 in favour of more attention to teachers' own judgements based on a range of modes of assessment.

We would suggest that external testing in primary schools is part of a wider social preoccupation with measuring, league tables and auditing. If you consider other social services, for example, the health service and the police service you find a similar push towards accountability in the form of league tables. England has experienced all of this to a greater degree than in other parts of the UK. Education in England seems to be more politicised than other parts of the UK and politicians in England are less inclined to be influenced by professional groups like teachers and researchers. This means that in turn such groups have less power in educational decision-making in England than their counterparts have in Scotland, Wales and Northern Ireland.

A CRITIQUE OF CURRENT ASSESSMENT APPROACHES

Dylan Wiliam, a researcher on assessment over many years, has expressed concern about the narrowing effect on the curriculum of teachers teaching to the test – a point we noted earlier in this unit. Here are some key questions he poses:

- Why are students tested as individuals, when the world of work requires people who can work well in a team?
- Why do we test memory, when in the real world engineers and scientists never rely on memory? If they're stuck, they look things up?
- Why do we use timed tests, when it is usually far more important to get things done right than to get things done quickly?

He favours an approach that would support teachers' own judgements of pupil achievement, and the idea that this approach should replace all forms of testing, from the earliest stages through to GCSE and A-levels. He points out that this happens in Sweden. This is how he justifies his argument:

> In place of the current vicious spiral, in which only those aspects of learning that are easily measured are regarded as important, I propose developing a system of summative assessment based on moderated teacher assessment. A separate system, relying on 'light sampling' of the performance of schools, would provide stable and robust information for the purposes of accountability and policy-formation.

> (Wiliam 2002: 62)

He goes on to say that his preferred approach 'would also be likely to tackle boys' underachievement, because the current "all or nothing" test at the end of a key stage encourages boys to believe that they can make up lost ground at the last minute' (pp. 61–2). He envisages that there would be a large number of assessment tasks but not all students would undertake the same task. These good quality assessment tasks would cover the entire curriculum and they would be allocated randomly. This would guard against teaching to the test or as he puts it: 'the only way to teach to the test would be to teach the whole curriculum to every student' (p. 62).

Task 7.1.3
Replacing tests

- What do you think of Wiliam's ideas?
- Do you think his suggestions are more in line with what we know about learning and assessment, especially what we know about the impact of testing on pupils?
- Do you think his suggestions are feasible?
- How would these groups view his ideas: parents, students, teachers, politicians?

He suggests that schools that taught only a limited curriculum, or concentrated on, say, the most able students, would be shown up as ineffective.

SUMMARY

In this unit we have sought to define and describe summative assessment and ways of using it. We have also highlighted the (mostly negative) impact on learners of testing, especially high stakes testing. Whatever the national policy on external testing, as a class teacher, you will have a powerful influence over how you assess your pupils. In turn, how you assess your pupils will have considerable influence on how they perform, on how motivated they become as learners and on how they feel about themselves as learners. You are likely to influence the kind of lifelong learners they become.

To recap on the major points of the unit, we suggest that you re-visit the learning objectives we noted on the first page. As you do this, you might consider in what different ways you could demonstrate your understanding and knowledge of the topic.

ANNOTATED FURTHER READING

Information about National Assessments and examples of tasks, which are open to anyone to browse, can be found at www.aifl-na.net.

The following two articles provide evidence about the impact of 'high stakes' summative assessment on pupils, teachers, and teaching and learning:

Gipps, C. (1994) 'Developments in educational assessment: what makes a good test?', *Assessment in Education*, 1(3): 283–91. Although more than a decade old, this article provides an excellent account of what makes a good test.

Hall, K., Collins, J., Benjamin, S., Sheehy, K. and Nind, M. (2004) 'SATurated models of pupildom: assessment and inclusion/exclusion', *British Educational Research Journal*, 30(6): 801–17.

Reay, D. and Wiliam, D. (1999) '"I'll be a nothing": structure, agency and the construction of identity through assessment', *British Educational Research Journal*, 25(3): 343–54.

REFERENCES

Black, P. (2003) *Testing: Friend or Foe? Theory and Practice of Assessment and Testing*, London: RoutledgeFalmer.

Black, P. and William, D. (1998) *Inside the Black Box*, London: Kings College London.

Black, P., Harrison, C., Lee, C., Marshall, B. and Wiliam, D. (2003) *Assessment for Learning: Putting it into Practice*, Buckingham: Open University Press.

Department for Education and Skills (DfES) (2003) *Excellence and Enjoyment: A Strategy for Primary Schools*, London: DfES.

Drummond, M.J. (1999) 'Baseline assessment: a case for civil disobedience?', in C. Conner (ed.) *Assessment in Action in the Primary School*, London: Falmer Press.

Hall, K. and Burke, W. (2003) *Making Formative Assessment Work: Effective Practice in the Primary Classroom*, Buckingham: Open University Press.

Hall, K. and Harding, A. (2002) 'Level descriptions and teacher assessment: towards a community of assessment practice', *Educational Research*, 40(1): 1–16.

Hall, K., Collins, J., Benjamin, S., Sheehy, K. and Nind, M. (2004) 'SATurated models of pupildom: assessment and inclusion/exclusion', *British Educational Research Journal*, 30(6): 801–17.

Harlen, W. and Deakin Crick, R. (2002) 'A systematic review of the impact of summative assessment and tests on students' motivation for learning' (EPPI-Centre Review, version 1.1), *Research Evidence in Education Library*, London: EPPI-Centre, Social Science Research Unit, Institute of Education.

Nuttall, D. (1987) 'The validity of assessments', *European Journal of the Psychology of Education*, 11(2): 109–18.

Reinecke, R.A. (1998) *Challenging the Mind, Touching the Heart: Best Assessment Practice*, Thousand Oaks, CA: Corwin Oaks.

Threlfall, J. (2005) 'The formative use of assessment information in planning – the notion of contingent planning', *British Journal of Educational Studies*, 53(1): 54–65.

Weeden, P., Winter, J. and Broadfoot, P. (2002) *Assessment: What's In It for Schools?* London: Routledge Falmer.

Whetton, C. (2004) 'Reflections on Fifteen Years of National Assessment: Lessons, Successes and Mistakes', Paper presented at the 30th International Association for Educational Assessment Conference, 13–18 June 2004, Philadelphia, PA.

Wiliam, D. (2001) 'What is wrong with our educational assessment and what can be done about it?', *Education Review*, 15(1): 57–62.

Unit 7.2

Assessment for Learning: Formative Approaches

Caroline Gipps and Alison Pickering

INTRODUCTION

Assessment for learning (AFL) is a particular approach to assessment developed for teachers in classrooms. It is not the same as standardised tests or SATs you may have to give, but rather is a way of using informal assessment during ordinary classroom activities to improve learning. Here, assessment is seen as an integral part of the learning and teaching process rather than being 'added on' for summative purposes. This approach brings with it a rather different relationship between teacher and learner than in traditional models of assessment, since the pupil needs to become involved in discussions about the tasks (learning objectives), the assessment criteria (success criteria), their performance and what they need to do to improve: the relationship is more of a partnership with both pupil and teacher playing a role. We know that with appropriate guidance children as young as six or seven can do this.

Therefore, building on the previous unit on assessment (Unit 7.1), there are two key elements to assessment for learning which the unit will go on to unpack: the nature of the feedback given to the learner to help her/him understand the quality of their work and next steps, and the active engagement of the learner.

The early work of the Assessment Reform Group (1999) and of Black and William (1998b) showed that:

> Improving learning through assessment depends on five, deceptively simple, key factors:
> * the provision of effective feedback to pupils;
> * the active involvement of pupils in their own learning;

- adjusting teaching to take account of the results of assessment;
- a recognition of the profound influence assessment has on the motivation and self-esteem of pupils, both of which are crucial influences on learning;
- the need for pupils to be able to assess themselves and understand how to improve.

Since the publication of the Assessment Reform Group's (2002) summary of research-based principles of AFL there has been a considerable impact on classroom practice. The ten principles of effective teaching and learning identified by the ARG are now posted on the QCA website and form the basis of current approaches to learning and teaching in many classrooms. The ARG identifies ten principles to guide teachers in implementing Assessment for Learning in their classrooms. Some of these are addressed in this unit and suggestions are made for putting them into practice.

OBJECTIVES

By the end of the unit you should:

- understand the key factors which contribute to assessment for learning;
- have developed a range of strategies which will facilitate improved learning/teaching;
- have recognised that effective assessment is a powerful tool in raising achievement in the classroom.

ASSESSMENT FOR LEARNING: FROM THEORY TO PRACTICE

Of the ten principles of AFL these are the most relevant to you at this stage:

- *Assessment for learning should be recognised as central to classroom practice.* Much of what teachers and learners do in classrooms can be described as assessment. That is, tasks and questions prompt learners to demonstrate their knowledge, understanding and skills. What learners say and do is then observed and interpreted, and judgements are made about how learning can be improved. These assessment processes are an essential part of everyday classroom practice and involve both teachers and learners in reflection, dialogue and decision making.
- *Assessment for learning should promote commitment to learning goals and a shared understanding of the criteria by which they are assessed.* For effective learning to take place learners need to understand what it is they are trying to achieve – and want to achieve it. Understanding and commitment follow when learners have some part in deciding goals and identifying criteria for assessing progress. Communicating assessment criteria involves discussing them with learners using terms that they can understand, providing examples of how the criteria can be met in practice and engaging learners in peer – and self – assessment.
- *Learners should receive constructive guidance about how to improve.* Learners need information and guidance in order to plan the next steps in their learning. Teachers should: pinpoint the learner's strengths and advise on how to develop them; be clear and constructive about any weaknesses and how they might be addressed; provide opportunities for learners to improve upon their work.
- *Assessment for learning develops learners' capacity for self-assessment so that they can become reflective and self-managing.* Independent learners have the ability to seek out and gain new skills, new knowledge and new understandings. They are able to engage in self-reflection and

to identify the next steps in their leaning. Teachers should equip learners with the desire and the capacity to take charge of their learning through developing the skills of self-assessment.

(ARG 2002)

PLANNING FOR ASSESSMENT FOR LEARNING

Effective planning enables you to provide learning opportunities which match the needs of all the children. It should include the following:

- objectives which focus on learning rather than task-oriented objectives. The task then becomes the vehicle for the learning;
- strategies for finding out what the children already know so that you can pitch the learning/teaching at the appropriate level;
- an element of pupil choice;
- ways in which you can share the 'bigger picture' with the children so that they know what they are aiming for;
- mini-plenaries so that the children can regularly reflect back on the bigger picture;
- opportunities for peer and self assessment with and without teacher support.

Sharing the bigger picture

From the start, share the success criteria with your pupils. Articulate exactly what it is you will be assessing. In writing, for example, the success criteria might be 'a descriptive piece of writing using adjectives' but an assessment focus might include accurate presentation. This must be made clear to the children.

Teachers and pupils can create the success criteria together. Figure 7.2.1 on p. 359 shows a pupil self-assessment sheet for a history topic. You can display a large version on the wall and have an individual copy for each child. There are three levels of attainment here which can either be used for pupil self assessment or peer assessment.

Task 7.2.1
Student assessment sheet

Choose another area of the curriculum and construct a similar sheet to that in Figure 7.2.1

Discussion during the sessions and mini-plenaries

Discussions take place before, during and after each lesson so that the teacher can check the children's understanding and judge their progress. It also provides a vehicle for a continued sharing of the learning objectives. Here are some strategies for doing this:

What was it like to live here in the past?

Must
- understand that St. Paul's School was different in the past;
- make comparisons between the school in the past and as it is today.

Should

- recognise features of the school building and know how it has changed over time;
- enquire about some of the people who have worked at the school (both pupils and staff) and understand differences in working conditions at different times;
- be able to use a range of historical sources in a variety of ways.

Could

- describe and compare features of the school and identify changes on a time line;
- select and combine information from different sources.

Figure 7.2.1 Pupil self-assessment sheet

- Before the lesson, have discussions with the children to ascertain what they already know about the subject in order that you can plan the work effectively to include different levels of understanding. Identify in your planning the children you wish to support in that lesson.
- Once you have identified children's misconceptions or unexpected responses you can follow up with individual discussion during the session to clarify these.
- Monitor the children's progress throughout the lesson by asking them questions about the task and then sharing with them targets for the next steps in their learning.
- At intervals during the session remind the children of the lesson objectives, then ask children to feed back to the class what they have found out so far and what they still have to do to complete the task.
- Ask the children to evaluate their own progress against the success criteria given.

QUESTIONING

Effective questioning is the key to good teacher assessment; make sure you know which questions to use and when you will use them.

Teachers are always asking questions but in order to develop higher order thinking skills it is important to ask open-ended, child-centred questions (see Table 7.2.1). The use of open questioning is critical in encouraging children to offer their own opinions. The teacher then acknowledges that these opinions are a valid response. This approach to questioning is much more productive than a closed questioning technique where only one response is deemed 'correct' by the teacher, leaving the children guessing what the teacher wants to hear rather than basing their response on their own ideas. Ask follow-up questions to make the children think more deeply. For details of types of questioning in assessment observed in the classes of 'expert' primary teachers, see Gipps *et al*. 2000.

Table 7.2.1   How open-ended questions encourage thinking skills (from de Boo, 1999)

Type of question	Responses
What do you notice about …?	Descriptive observations
What can you tell me about …?	Inviting recalled information but content chosen by the children
What does it remind you of?	Seeing patterns/analogies
Which things do you think belong together? Why do you think that?	Seeing patterns/classifying and creative explanations
What do you think will happen next?	Creative predictions
What happened after you did that?	Descriptive reasoning/cause and effect/conclusions
Why do you think that happened? I wonder why it did that?	Creative hypotheses/explanations
Do you think you could do it differently?	Evaluation/reflective analysis
I wonder what made you think that?	Reflective self-awareness/metacognition
Anything else? Or?	Neutral/inviting more of the responses listed above

Thinking time

To encourage this process children must be given time to think more deeply before responding to questions.

Once you have asked a question allow the children 'thinking time' before listening to their responses. This has a twofold effect. First it encourages the more able to think more deeply and fosters higher order thinking skills but it also builds the confidence of those pupils who take longer to respond. Teacher expectation is important here, expecting a response from every child. A useful technique for encouraging this is the use of 'discussion partners'. The child first shares their ideas with a partner before sharing their response with the teacher or the class. In this way the children can test their ideas with their peers and perhaps adjust their thinking before offering a response which in turn helps them feel more confident about voicing a response.

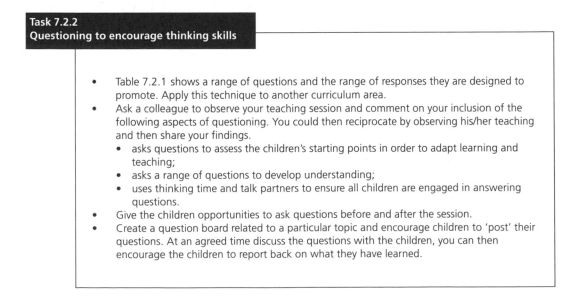

Task 7.2.2
Questioning to encourage thinking skills

- Table 7.2.1 shows a range of questions and the range of responses they are designed to promote. Apply this technique to another curriculum area.
- Ask a colleague to observe your teaching session and comment on your inclusion of the following aspects of questioning. You could then reciprocate by observing his/her teaching and then share your findings.
  - asks questions to assess the children's starting points in order to adapt learning and teaching;
  - asks a range of questions to develop understanding;
  - uses thinking time and talk partners to ensure all children are engaged in answering questions.
- Give the children opportunities to ask questions before and after the session.
- Create a question board related to a particular topic and encourage children to 'post' their questions. At an agreed time discuss the questions with the children, you can then encourage the children to report back on what they have learned.

PEER AND SELF ASSESSMENT

Pupils can assess themselves and can learn from their own and others' assessments. This will lead them to reflect on how they learn.

Children should be involved not only in their own but also in peer assessment. This gives children a central role in their own learning and is a really important shift from the teacher having all the responsibility for assessment to a position of sharing goals, self evaluation and them setting their own targets (Black and William 1998a).

This approach can be highly motivating but must be endorsed by a supportive classroom ethos which includes clear guidelines for the children in terms of supporting and guiding each other's learning. First there must be a clear focus and structure for the lesson. Children need a set of success and assessment criteria (see Planning for AFL above) by which to judge the success of their learning. These can be negotiated by yourself and the children. Try some of the following methods of engaging your children in their own assessment.

You can use 'Thumbs Up' to establish pupil understanding. Thumb up means that they have understood well, whereas thumb down indicates no understanding, and thumb sideways indicates a need for more help or time. This technique offers the teacher a quick indication of how the class has received the lesson.

'Traffic Lights' is another way for pupils to evaluate their learning against the learning objectives. They put a red, green or yellow dot against the learning objectives in a similar way to 'Thumbs Up' once again giving clear indications for target setting. After the children in the red, yellow, thumbs down or sideways categories have received additional adult input they can reassess themselves against the objective and revise their response. These techniques also help you to decide when particular objectives need to be revisited.

'Pinks and Greens' again allows the pupils to assess themselves. In this example the child highlights two aspects of their work in green which they feel fulfil the success criteria and identify one target for improvement which they underline in pink. This approach can also be used by pupils to assess the work of their peers.

Task 7.2.3
Self assessment

Using the pupil self-assessment sheet created in Task 7.2.1 ask your pupils to assess themselves using the 'Pinks and Greens' technique described above. Follow this up by asking them what they need to do to improve.

FEEDBACK

As Black and William argue: 'Feedback to any pupil should be about the particular qualities of his or her work, with advice on what he or she can do to improve, and should avoid comparisons with other pupils' (1998b: 9).

Effective feedback to children provides information to support self assessment and suggests steps which will lead to improvement. Feedback through written comments should refer back to the learning goals set at the beginning of the session and should be constructive. We know that many teachers focus

Evaluative feedback	• giving rewards and punishments;
	• expressing approval and disapproval.
Descriptive feedback	• telling children they are right or wrong;
	• describing why an answer is correct;
	• telling children what they have achieved and have not achieved;
	• specifying or implying a better way of doing something;
	• getting children to suggest ways they can improve.

Figure 7.2.2   Evaluative and descriptive feedback strategies

on spelling, punctuation, grammar or the structure of the piece of work often omitting or underplaying the objectives, so make sure that your comments relate directly to the learning and assessment objectives.

A useful way of thinking about/describing feedback is whether it is evaluative or descriptive (see Figure 7.2.2).

All too often, teachers provide evaluative feedback in the form of grades and short (usually non-specific) comments, praise or censure. This kind of feedback tells students whether they are doing okay or not, but it offers little direction for moving their learning forward. Regular critical evaluative feedback without guidance for how to improve can lower motivation and self-esteem.

Descriptive feedback, on the other hand, relates to the task at hand, the learner's performance, and what they might do to improve. For details of feedback observed in the classrooms of 'expert' primary teachers, see Gipps *et al*. 2000. For practical activities see Clarke (2003).

The ideal situation is when the teacher can discuss and annotate work with the child present so that targets can be set together, however this is not always possible so the teacher writes comments for the child to read. For these to be meaningful they must be linked clearly to the learning objectives and you must allow time on your plan for the child to read them. This can sometimes be forgotten and may therefore negate the value of the comments. Here is an example of written dialogue between teacher and pupil which leads to further reflection by the pupil:

Teacher comment   A really clear graph. I like the way it is set out. What do you think we should do with this information?

Pupil comment   See how much rubbish is in a bin, and see what thing is in there and how much of the things are in there. We should put up more recycle bins to keep the world safe. And we'll put them in the hall.

The teacher's comments have encouraged the child to interrogate the graph more fully.

RECOGNISING AND CELEBRATING CHILDREN'S WORK

You need to consider how a child's effort is recognised. Build in time for reflection at the end of the day or the week. In an Early Years setting good work may be celebrated in a discussion at the end of the session taking the opportunity to point out what makes it worthy of comment. Another method of highlighting good work is by taking photographs, providing a permanent reminder for both child and teacher. Teachers of younger children commonly write an accompanying explanation of the context of the piece and may include a record of any dialogue which has taken place. Some teachers simply display a chosen piece of work on the wall or on a bookstand so that everyone can share that pupil's success. The use of circle time is another opportunity to celebrate the products of sessions and is also an opportunity to assess pupil attitudes. These activities give the teacher an opportunity to focus on work which shows improvement and an understanding of subject progression. The activities are suitable for Key Stage 1 and 2 classrooms but with the children becoming increasingly involved in the selection of good work. It is important that you consider how these activities will be tracked. Will they be tracked by the teacher or the pupil? Will you keep student profiles?

Task 7.2.4
Questions to ask yourself in relation to your planning of AFL

- Does the assessment allow children multiple ways to demonstrate their learning across the range of curriculum activities?
- Does it assess the extent to which learning has taken place?
- How do you ensure that feedback from assessments allows the children opportunities to develop and progress in their learning by linking your comments to agreed success criteria and indicating the next steps to encourage further learning?
- How do assessment outcomes influence session planning and modifications to future curriculum planning?
- How will you/should you keep track of this?

Task 7.2.5
Peer reflection

You have had an opportunity to evaluate your practice in relation to pupil self assessment and questioning. Now ask one of your peers to observe another lesson and comment on another two of the principles of AFL identified by the ARG. You can then observe your peer's class and share your comments.

SUMMARY

Assessment for learning as opposed to assessment of learning is part of ongoing learning and teaching and is not a 'bolt on'. Its aim is to assess all areas of the curriculum as described in *Excellence and Enjoyment* (DfES 2003a). In order to achieve this it uses a wide range of strategies to secure a wider range of assessments. It is recognition of what a child can do and the identification of the next steps in their learning so that they can progress at a pace appropriate for them. This is done by a mixture of teacher-led assessment, negotiation and pupils sharing in the assessment process, so that they can eventually assess their own work and set appropriate targets.

An exciting and controversial aspect of assessment for learning is its use in summative assessment as outlined in the recent report of the Assessment Systems for the Future (ASF) project (2004) which highlights how the development of effective practice in formative assessment might impact on teachers' summative assessment.

The tasks in this unit address the following professional standards (DfES 2003b)

Planning

3.1.1 They set challenging teaching and learning objectives which are relevant to all pupils, they base these on knowledge of: the pupils; evidence of past and current achievement
3.1.2 They use teaching and learning objectives to plan lessons, and sequences of lesson, showing how they will assess pupils' learning

Teaching

3.3.3 They teach clearly structured lessons and sequences of work which interest and motivate pupils and which: make learning objectives clear to pupils; employ interactive teaching methods and collaborative work; promote independent learning that enables pupils to think for themselves, and plan and manage their own learning

Oral and written feedback

3.2.2 They monitor and assess as they teach, giving immediate and constructive feedback to support pupils as they learn. They involve pupils in reflecting on, evaluating, and improving their own performance

Evaluating

1.7 They are able to improve their own teaching by evaluating it
3.2.1 They make appropriate use of a range of monitoring and assessment strategies to evaluate pupils' progress towards planned learning objectives, and use this information to improve planning and teaching
3.2.4 They identify and support more able pupils, those who are working below age-related expectations, those who are failing to achieve their potential in learning

ANNOTATED FURTHER READING

Clarke, S. (2003) *Enriching Feedback in the Primary Classroom*, London: Hodder and Stoughton. Written by experienced practitioners, this book offers clear strategies for marking pupil work and effective feedback to the learner.

Gipps, C., McCallum, B. and Hargreaves, E. (2000) *What Makes a Good Primary School Teacher? Expert Classroom Strategies*, London: RoutledgeFalmer. This book describes, in non-academic language, the teaching, assessment and feedback strategies used by experienced primary teachers.

REFERENCES

Association for Achievement and Involvement the Assessment, www.aaia.org.uk.
Assessment Reform Group (1999) *Assessment for Learning, Beyond the Black Box*, Cambridge: University of Cambridge School of Education supported by The Nuffield Foundation.

Assessment Reform Group (2002) *Assessment For Learning: 10 Principles – Research-Based Principles to Guide Classroom Practice*, www.assessment-reform-group.org/ASF-report1.html.

Assessment Reform Group (2004) *Assessment Systems for the Future: ThePlace of Assessment by Teachers*, www.assessment-reform-group.org/ASF_report1.html.

Black, P.J. and William, D. (1998a) 'Assessment and classroom learning', *Assessment in Education*, 5(1): 7–74.

Black, P.J. and William, D. (1998b) *Inside the Black Box: Raising Standards Through Classroom Assessment*, London: School of Education, Kings College London.

Clarke, S. (2003) *Enriching Feedback in the Primary Classroom*, London: Hodder and Stoughton.

De Boo, M. (1999) *Using Science to Develop Thinking Skills at Key Stage 1*, London: National Association for Able Children in Education/David Fulton.

DfES (2003a) *Excellence and Enjoyment: A Strategy for Primary Schools*, London: DfES.

DfES (2003b) *Qualified to Teach: Professional Standards for QTS and Requirements for Initial Teacher Training*, London: DfES/TTA.

Gipps, C., McCallum, B., and Hargreaves, E. (2000) *What Makes a Good Primary School Teacher?: Expert Classroom Strategies*, London: RoutledgeFalmer.

Partnership in Practice

Unit 8.1

Managing Other Adults in the Classroom

Elizabeth Wood

As a new teacher coming into the profession, you will be expected to work collaboratively with a wide range of adults in your classroom, including teaching assistants, specialist teaching assistants for children with special educational needs, professionals from other agencies, students in training, parents and caregivers. In order to support effective teaching and learning, government policies have recognised the importance of using other adults to provide support for learning. As teachers are given more release time, teaching assistants will take on increased responsibility, under your direction: developing a partnership approach is essential to promoting high quality teaching and learning, and meeting the diverse interests, learning styles and needs of children. This unit focuses on three key themes of communication, collaboration and co-construction, which provide a framework for supporting learning. Being able to manage and work productively with other adults will make high demands on your interpersonal and managerial skills, and your professional knowledge. Practical tasks and vignettes provide guidance on developing these skills.

OBJECTIVES

By the end of this unit you should:

- understand the policy context regarding the role of teaching assistants, and parents in the Foundation Stage, and Key Stages 1 and 2;
- know about the findings of research studies, and understand their recommendations for professional practice;
- understand some practical skills and strategies which will help you develop a partnership approach based on communication, collaboration and co-construction;
- know how to deploy teaching assistants effectively to support children's learning.

THE POLICY PERSPECTIVE

National policy documents provide consistent support for a partnership approach with parents, adults and other professionals. There is a trend towards strengthening services for children and their families, and seeing children not just as pupils, but as members of different communities, all of which influence their learning journeys. Local Authorities regard Birth to 14 as a continuum, rather than a series of discrete phases. In the early years there is an established emphasis on working collaboratively across different sectors (education, health and social services) with children and their families. This 'joined up' approach is particularly significant for early intervention and support programmes, and is essential to high quality provision. These principles are equally important in Key Stages 1 and 2, because members of the whole school team, as well as other professionals, are integral to effective teaching and learning.

In the policy documents for the early years (birth to five) (DfEE/QCA 2000; DfES 2002), the term 'practitioner' is used for all adults who work in the setting, regardless of their roles and qualifications. A key principle of effective practice in the early years is that:

> Parents and practitioners should work together in an atmosphere of mutual respect within which children can have security and confidence.
>
> (QCA/DfEE 2000: 11)

The Foundation Stage highlights the importance of adult- and child-initiated activities (including play), to which all practitioners contribute, so that the curriculum reflects a continuum between work and play. There is consistent evidence from research (Wood and Attfield, 2005) that adults have an important role in helping children to plan their own activities, enriching and supporting play, extending children's agendas and interests, and acting as co-players. The following example shows how a teaching assistant inspired role play in 'Pepito's Pizza Place'.

The Reception children left the pizza café in a mess. The teaching assistant took this opportunity to develop and enrich the play theme, and planned collaboratively with the teacher. She closed down the café, and put up a notice from the 'Health, Hygiene and Safety Inspector', which listed all the reasons for the closure, with some imaginative touches: mouse droppings in the cupboard, and mould in the fridge. This intervention led to a wide range of activities; the children wrote a job specification for the cleaning and put it out to tender (this involved the school's cleaning staff). In science, they looked at different types of cleaning materials and ways of storing food safely. They planned to clean the café, then wrote to the inspector detailing their work, and arranging another inspection. The teaching assistant wrote back demanding to know who was responsible for keeping the café clean, and what jobs needed to be done. The children drew up a roster of activities, and also took on the role of the inspector. These activities provided many opportunities for curriculum-based learning, as well as stimulating creativity, imagination, playfulness and inclusion for all children. Because the teaching assistant was involved as a co-player she monitored the children's learning, collaborated with the class teacher on planning further activities, and contributed to the children's Foundation Stage assessment profiles.

THE NATIONAL LITERACY AND NUMERACY STRATEGIES

National Curriculum frameworks and strategies set out key pedagogical principles, curriculum content, and guidance on their implementation. However, it is essential that these frameworks are interpreted flexibly and that planning is responsive to the range of children's abilities. The notion that 'one size fits all' has given way to 'personalised learning', which demands effective deployment of support staff. Teaching assistants and additional adults should work in close partnership with teachers as they plan and teach literacy, both within the Literacy Hour and across the curriculum. Specialist teaching assistants may have responsibility for supporting children with special educational needs, or with English as an Additional Language (EAL). All teaching assistants can be involved in planning: they can help you select texts and other resources to ensure differentiation, and support children's literacy skills across the curriculum. They can also make notes about the children's progress and achievements in relation to the objectives for a lesson or scheme of work, and develop further plans with you. The National Literacy Strategy (DfEE, 1998) states that teachers can use their professional judgement in altering the balance between whole class, group and individual teaching. Therefore, developing your own 'designer' version is essential to creative planning, accurate differentiation, and ensuring that children are motivated, engaged and involved. For example, if you teach a mixed age class in Key Stage 1 or 2, you might consider a range of strategies to ensure differentiation:

- reducing whole class teaching time;
- planning more time for large groups (age/ability differentiation);
- deploying teaching assistants to a specific child or group of children, for specific tasks;
- using teaching assistants to lead small group, rather than whole class, plenaries.

The Numeracy Strategy (DfEE 1999) promotes flexibility in the timing, organisation and type of activities planned in each part of the lesson. You can provide a different mix of activities across the whole class, small groups, pairs and individual children. Teaching assistants can support this flexibility by working collaboratively on planning, monitoring, taking responsibility for activities, and making suggestions for extension, re-visiting, practice or consolidation.

By using policy frameworks as a guide rather than a straitjacket you can use your professional knowledge to decide where and how to deploy assistants to best effect. This will be influenced to some extent by their training and experience, and by the nature of the task. For example, teaching assistants or parents may be able to take a group reading session, but may not have the expertise to conduct a specific analysis and diagnosis of a child's reading difficulties. In contrast, a special needs support teacher or educational psychologist will be able to carry our more specialised diagnostic assessments to pinpoint a child's difficulties, or exceptional abilities.

Task 8.1.1
Sharing planning and assessment

Plan three activities in literacy and numeracy that will be managed by the teaching assistant, with a group of children. Ask the assistant to annotate samples of work from each activity, and each child. Make time to discuss the observations and feedback, and extend the discussion to include evidence of each child's achievement in related areas. Record your 'next steps', decide how these might be mapped into your planning cycle, and who will take responsibility for planning and implementing the activities. You can repeat this activity in any curriculum area.

Schools should have a policy and job description for the effective use of teaching assistants, along with guidance for involving parents in the classroom. You should become familiar with these policies, and check job descriptions so that you understand what can reasonably be expected of assistants. For example, their hours of work may be different, so you will need to organise time for planning, preparation of materials, discussion and feedback. As the next section shows, findings from research indicate that by working closely with teaching assistants you can co-construct knowledge and understanding of what pedagogical strategies and approaches are most effective with particular children. This aspiration is essential for supporting 'personalised learning', which involves recognising children's individual learning dispositions and supporting their learning journeys.

WHAT CAN RESEARCH TELL US ABOUT THE ROLE OF TEACHING ASSISTANTS AND PARENTS?

Research studies across the early years and primary phases have identified a number of problems with the effective use of classroom support, and have made recommendations for improving practice. Moyles and Suschitzky (1998) carried out a study of how differently trained adults worked together to support children's learning in Nursery and Key Stage 1 settings. They found that in both phases, teachers played a greater part in planning activities:

> Whereas much planning in the Nursery was said to be 'joint' or 'team', this often in reality meant that there was an overall discussion about the topic or areas to be covered, the teacher then developed the overall plan and individuals within the team were responsible for generating one or more activities to meet the curriculum intentions. At Key Stage 1 teachers did most of the planning, to the extent that classroom assistants had little idea of the learning intentions behind activities.
>
> (Moyles and Suschitzky 1998: 125)

On the basis of their findings, Moyles and Suschitzky identified the need for further opportunities for training, for teachers and assistants, in order to support the increasing complexity of their roles, and the demands of policy frameworks. Having a shared understanding of learning intentions, processes and outcomes is central to effective teaching and learning. A key issue for new teachers is being clear about whether the assistants are providing support for the teacher, general support for learning, or support for particular groups or individual learners.

In order to provide a differentiated curriculum for children with special educational needs, teachers and children need appropriate levels of support from Special Teaching Assistants and other professionals and agencies (Roffey 2001). John's case study shows how communication and collaboration worked successfully to support his inclusion in a mainstream school:

> John had cerebral palsy, and joined his Year 1 class at age 6, following additional time in the Foundation Stage. He had a statement of his special educational needs, and an Individual Education Plan. His Specialist Teaching Assistant made this transition with John, and was able to advise on the range of resources needed to support his learning and development. The teacher re-organised the classroom to enable him to move around more easily. They acquired Dycem mats, which create an adhesive surface for books, paper and other resources, and they transferred John's computer with its special programs and controls. The assistant supported John's transition, and provided continuity with John's parents. The teacher worked closely with his speech therapist, physiotherapist and educational psychologist. She liaised with the paediatrician and provided valuable information on John's progress and development. John's team worked collaboratively on removing barriers to his learning, supporting his progress and achievements, and ensuring consistency of approaches across home and school.

WHAT SUPPORT MIGHT BE AVAILABLE IN MY CLASS?

Teaching assistants may be temporary or permanent, full-time or part-time. They may be shared across classes or phases, attached to a specific class or to a specific child. As new funding for teacher release time comes on stream, schools are working towards employing assistants in every class. However, where this is not possible, such support may be targeted at a particular age group, a specific child or group of children, or a particular subject area. For those with special educational needs, the specialist teaching assistant is likely to stay with the child, and move to the next class in order to provide consistency and continuity. Specialist teachers and assistants may be peripatetic within the school, or within the LEA so that they provide occasional support for a child or group.

Teaching assistants have a wide range of training and backgrounds, and may include specialist teachers for children with English as an Additional Language and Special Educational Needs. Many assistants are qualified nursery nurses who have completed two years of training in child development, learning theory, knowledge about the policy and curriculum frameworks, and skills in planning, pedagogy, observation and assessment. A government aspiration is to ensure that all teaching assistants and pre-school practitioners have at least a Level 3 National Vocational Qualification, but many assistants have no formal training, and learn their skills 'on the job'. Therefore you have a significant role to play in ongoing training and professional development, by sharing your knowledge and modelling your skills.

Parents are also a valuable source of support for learning, but remember to check your school's policy on this, particularly regarding police checks. You need to clarify which parents or caregivers are available, and how much time they are willing to give. A couple of hours per week on a regular basis may be more manageable than whole or half days. Try to establish a clear pattern of who is available and when, so that you can plan accordingly. Most schools have a predominantly female workforce, so it is valuable to think about involving men because they can be positive role models for boys, as Peter found with his Year 2 class:

> Peter was concerned about the progress and achievements of a group of boys. They were de-motivated in literacy, had difficulties with handwriting, and were not interested in imaginative writing. He arranged for some men to come into the classroom over one term – all were parents and family members. They were involved in whole class and small group sessions, and talked about the different ways in which they use literacy and numeracy in their everyday lives, including the workplace. They read and played alongside the children. Most of the boys subsequently showed significantly improved interest and motivation in their writing: they saw real purposes for their writing, and became more imaginative in what they chose to write about. The challenge for Peter was to develop this 'one-off' initiative into a more sustained whole school policy.

Teaching assistants, and specialist teachers, may be involved in specific support programmes such as:

- additional literacy and numeracy support;
- Portage Programme (early intervention, home-school partnership for children under five);
- Reading Recovery;
- behaviour and social skills support (possibly with the support of a behaviour management team);
- counselling;
- extension programmes for gifted and talented children;
- specific support for children with SEN and EAL;
- speech/language therapy;
- homework programmes;
- peer tutoring, peer mediation, buddy systems.

Many of these support programmes require a partnership approach with parents and other professionals – a multi-disciplinary and multi-agency approach – as shown in John's case study. Roffey (2001) provides a detailed overview of all the different agencies and professionals that are available to provide support for children and their families, and who cross the borders between home, school and community. The support that is available covers all areas of children's lives – their behaviour, emotional and mental health and all aspects of their physical development. Children often experience short-term problems (such as an illness, accident or injury, family break-up, bereavement) that can impact on their learning and progress in school. It is important to take a holistic view of each child in your class: this will enable you to work creatively with support staff and parents to address problems as they arise, and to provide the consistency that children need in times of stress.

Task 8.1.2
Focusing on children with special educational needs

Identify the school's co-ordinator for special educational needs. Make time to talk to her/him, and to find out the range of support services that are available from other agencies, and the support that is available in school. Ask the co-ordinator to discuss strategies that she/he has found particularly effective in working collaboratively with teaching assistants.

HOW CAN I DEPLOY SUPPORT MOST EFFECTIVELY?

It is your responsibility to make decisions about how best to deploy teaching assistants, bearing in mind that providing high quality support for learning is the main aspiration. As teachers are given more release time, there will be more opportunities for developing shared responsibility. There are two complementary approaches:

- The teaching assistant provides support for the teacher, for example, by preparing materials, taking on some of the class administrative responsibilities, photocopying or researching websites.
- The teaching assistant provides support for individuals/groups, thus enabling the teacher to focus on other areas (for example, whole class teaching sessions, or specialist input with specific groups).

Support staff may work inside the classroom, or take groups or individuals to another space – perhaps somewhere quiet or with special resources. An assistant or other adult may be assigned to a child to support positive behaviour. In these instances, it is tempting to have the assistant shadow the child constantly, and to correct behaviour almost continuously. Whilst this strategy may make your life easier, it will not be productive in the longer term. Adults who work alongside children with challenging behaviour should be prepared to model appropriate behaviour, give praise and reinforcement, and talk through any difficulties. However, the main goal is to help children to take responsibility for changing their own behaviour, and acting independently of adults. Therefore a balance needs to be struck between constant surveillance, establishing realistic, and achievable, expectations and creating trust. It is also important to ensure that all adults in the classroom have a consistent approach to managing behaviour and routines. This does not rule out developing personal styles, but it is not helpful if you are a quiet, calm teacher and find that you have an assistant who shouts at the children.

DEVELOPING A PARTNERSHIP APPROACH: COMMUNICATION, COLLABORATION AND CO-CONSTRUCTION

All adults need to focus time and skills on managing support for learning and development, rather than managing behaviour and tasks. The 'three Cs' – communication, collaboration and co-construction – provide some guiding principles to underpin your practice.

Your first task is to establish good relationships with assistants and parent helpers, and open up channels of communication. Find out about their experience, training, personal interests and skills, what generic skills they might contribute, and their specialist skills and knowledge. If your teaching assistant is a qualified nursery nurse, make sure that you capitalise on her/his strengths and knowledge, for example by asking them to carry out observations, liaise with parents and caregivers, or plan a programme of work for a group or individual child.

Aim towards co-constructing your knowledge and understanding about how children learn. Co-constructing means building knowledge together, based on sharing values, expertise and ideas; clarifying roles and expectations; providing feedback; and engaging in reflective conversations about children's learning, the success (or failure) of planned activities, and the effectiveness of the curriculum offered. Schools should be seen as 'communities of learners' where adults are prepared to learn from each other, and from the children.

Sharing values and beliefs about children as learners will provide consistent principles and practices. Contemporary theories view children as strong, powerful and competent; learning is a joint endeavour, which involves co-construction of knowledge, skills and understanding, rather than a one-way transmission of a defined body of knowledge (Anning, *et al.* 2004). How adults view children profoundly influences how they behave and interact with them, what expectations they have, and how they assess children (Filer and Pollard 2000). For example, if you set up your classroom to encourage independence, decision-making, problem-solving, and giving children a sense of agency in their learning and behaviour, then teaching assistants should understand the underlying reasons for your decisions, and support these strategies.

Developing a strong collaboration with teaching assistants means involving them in the cycle of curriculum planning, carrying out activities and teaching tasks, and assessing children's learning. Following the recommendations from research, as well as policy guidance, ensure that you share the aims and intentions of learning activities, what learning outcomes you expect, and how the activity will be assessed. Remember that you are not just interested in whether a child has achieved the defined learning objectives. Encourage teaching assistants to identify children's interests, agendas, learning strategies, dispositions, misconceptions, and areas of struggle. Ensure that they are 'tuned in' to noticing how the child engaged with the activity, whether she persevered with difficulty, how she responded to a challenge, and what skills and strategies she used. You will need to model some of these skills yourself, so that you can co-construct a shared dialogue about children's progress and achievements.

If a specialist teaching assistant has been working in a previous class alongside a child with English as an additional language, or special educational needs, be prepared to listen and learn. Specialist teaching assistants build a valuable knowledge base about particular conditions or syndromes that can extend your own professional knowledge. Voluntary organisations (such as the National Autistic Society, Scope, the Down's Syndrome Association) provide valuable information that can be researched and shared within the teaching team.

Task 8.1.3
Developing Individual Education Plans

With the specialist teaching assistant, discuss a child's Individual Education Plan. Brainstorm a range of activities that will help the child to achieve the next goals, identify resources, and clarify areas of responsibility. Decide how you are going to record the child's progress, areas of difficulty and achievements. Discuss how you will communicate with the child's parents/caregivers, and how you will involve the child in assessment.

This 'feedback' assessment information can 'feedforward' into the next cycle of planning, which will develop further collaboration in reflecting on the effectiveness of your provision. Involving children in self-assessment is a highly effective strategy for supporting learning and thinking skills, so make sure that the teaching assistant gets feedback from the children. This can be verbal, written, or based on different forms of representation – drawings, paintings, maps, plans, models or constructions. Teaching assistants can lead plenary sessions, or circle time with small groups. Some children are reluctant to participate in whole class sessions; in contrast, small groups are less threatening, and provide a more intimate context in which children can achieve success. Again, sharing skills and expectations will help to make plenary or circle times more effective, for example by ensuring a mix of open-ended and closed questions to stimulate thinking and ideas.

Sharing assessment information is also integral to developing an effective partnership approach with parents and caregivers. However, this should not just be a one-way flow, from the school to the home. There is consistent evidence that schools undervalue the learning that goes on in the home and community, especially in different ethnic groups (Filer and Pollard, 2000; Brooker, 2002). For example, in a study of progression and continuity in the early years of school, Wood and Bennett (2001) found that teachers across Nursery, Reception and Year 1 classes all set targets for children's learning, and shared these with parents. The targets were related to different areas – behaviour, social skills, settling into a new class, literacy and numeracy. Parents were encouraged to help children achieve these targets, and many of the activities suggested were typical within the classroom. For example, schooled literacy practices such as learning phonics and key words, reading, and handwriting practice were typical school-home activities, which effectively colonised the home. Parents were also asked to provide support with social and behavioural skills, especially to help them make the transition across phases. One of the recommendations from recent research studies is that teachers should build on children's home experiences, and value the learning that goes on in the home and community. Teaching assistants can help to make these valuable links by taking time to talk with children and family members.

The following bullet points provide an aide-mémoire of skills and strategies:

- Find time to plan collaboratively, discuss the teaching assistant's assessments, and evaluate the activity.
- Clarify where the activity will be carried out.
- Clarify who is responsible for preparing materials and special resources, and make time for this before the lesson or activity.
- Where children have Individual Education Plans, ensure that these are shared with the assistants, and develop a programme of work that will achieve the targets set.
- Liaise with assistants to differentiate activities, based on feedback from their observations and interactions.
- Find time to evaluate existing resources, and identify new resources, particularly to support inclusion and cultural diversity (for example, books, games, toys, puzzles, computer games and programs).

USING TEACHING ASSISTANTS TO SUPPORT TRANSITION

In a report on the introduction of the Foundation Stage, OfSTED noted that teaching assistants can be used to support transitions across phases:

Teaching assistants frequently play an important role in the successful transition of pupils from Reception to Year 1. They contribute to assessment, support pupils with special educational needs, provide insights into the needs of individuals and maintain established routines where they change classes with pupils (OFSTED 2004: 2).

These principles apply equally to other transitions, from Key Stage 1 to 2, and on to Key Stage 3. Transition can be a stressful time for children: they worry about getting used to a new teacher or a new class, keeping up with the work, managing their books and equipment, finding their way around, losing touch with friends, and finding new friends. Teaching assistants can be involved in supporting children across transitions by:

- being a familiar face in a new context;
- taking small groups of children to visit their next class;
- getting to know children before they make the transition – visiting the class to work with groups, tell a story, or just be available to chat and answer questions;
- helping children to settle, and feel a sense of belonging.

Teaching assistants can also support teachers across the transition by being involved in:

- discussions about individual children;
- moderating judgements about children's work;
- contributing to the Foundation Stage Profile, and Records of Achievement;
- helping to run workshops for parents;
- sharing good practice, and supporting continuity in teaching approaches.

Task 8.1.4
For reflection and discussion

These questions will help you to reflect on what you have learnt from this unit and consider the practical implications:

- What skills and strengths can I draw on from the adults in my classroom?
- How can these be used to support children's learning?
- How can I make time to discuss planning with the teaching assistant?
- How can I involve teaching assistants in assessing children's learning, and encouraging children to participate in self-assessment?
- What information needs to be recorded, and how can we ensure that this feeds into planning for personalised learning?
- For children with English as an additional language, can a bilingual teaching assistant provide a more accurate indication of knowledge and understanding in their first language?

SUMMARY

The key themes of communication, collaboration and co-construction provide guiding principles for involving teaching assistants and other adults in the classroom. Sharing values and beliefs, clarifying aims and intentions, and sharing assessment information are all effective pedagogical strategies. Support staff can help children to become more involved in tasks and activities, and develop 'personalised learning'. Schools and classrooms should be places where everyone has a sense of agency, belonging and involvement, and can make a contribution to the community. Developing a partnership approach and working as part of a team will enable you to share your challenges, concerns, achievements and enjoyment of being a successful teacher.

ANNOTATED FURTHER READING

Campbell, A. and Fairbairn, G. (2005) *Working With Support in the Classroom*, Buckingham: Open University Press. This edited collection of chapters covers early years, primary and secondary education, and is a valuable resource for thinking critically and creatively about managing support for learning. The authors use stories to illustrate successful practice, and provide a range of ideas and strategies for supporting children's learning.

Wood, E. and Attfield, J. (2005) *Play, Learning and the Early Childhood Curriculum*, 2nd edition, London: Paul Chapman. This book is aimed at early years teachers, and focuses on creating unity between playing, learning and teaching. However, there is much valuable practical guidance on pedagogy, curriculum planning, assessment, and working collaboratively with other adults which is useful across the primary age range. There are many research-based practical examples of children learning through play, and detailed exploration of the role of adults.

REFERENCES

Anning, A., Cullen, J. and Fleer, M. (eds) (2004) *Early Childhood Education: Society and Culture*, London: Sage.
Brooker, L. (2002) *Starting School – Young Children Learning Cultures*, Buckingham: Open University Press.
DfEE (1998)*The National Literacy Strategy*, London: DfEE.
DfEE (1999) *The National Numeracy Strategy*, London: DfEE
DfEE/QCA (2000) *Curriculum Guidance for the Foundation Stage*, London: DfEE/QCA.
DfES (2002) *Birth to Three Matters: A Framework for Supporting Children in the Earliest Years*, London: DfES.
Filer, A. and Pollard, A. (2000) *The Social World of Pupil Assessment*, London: Continuum.
Moyles, J. and Suschitzky, W. (1998) 'Painting the cabbages red…! Differentially trained adults working together in early years settings to promote children's learning', in Abbott, L. and Pugh, G. (eds) *Training to Work in the Early Years. Developing the Climbing Frame*, Buckingham: Open University Press.
Ofsted (Office for Standards in Education) (2004) *Transition from the Reception Year to Year 1*, HMI 2221, www.ofsted.gov.uk.

Qualifications and Curriculum Authority/Department for Education and Employment (2000) *Curriculum Guidance for the Foundation Stage*, Sudbury: QCA Publications, QCA/00/587.

Roffey, S. (2001) *Special Needs in the Early Years: Collaboration, Communication and Coordination*, London: David Fulton.

Wood, E. and Attfield, J. (2005) *Play, Learning and the Early Childhood Curriculum*, 2nd edition, London: Paul Chapman.

Wood, E. and Bennett, N. (2001) 'Early childhood teachers' theories of progression and continuity', *International Journal of Early Years Education*, 9(3): 229–43.

Unit 8.2

Collaborating with Parents

Sue Beverton

INTRODUCTION

This unit concentrates mainly on helping you build strong and effective links with parents and using these to help the children in your class develop as learners. We will also take a look at building good relationships with governors and other community representatives and groups. A word about definitions: throughout the unit, the word 'parent' is taken to be the major care-giver(s), who may or may not be a mother and father living together, and may well be a person of a different generation than a parent, such as a grandparent or even an older sibling. The important aspect is that it is with the home circumstances and the major care-giver(s) within that context that we are trying to engage. The term 'collaborating' needs a little clarification too: it should be understood in its widest sense, and taken to mean trying to establish and promote ways of working with parents, as a body of people and as individuals, who have a major part to play in the education of the children in your class.

OBJECTIVES

By the end of this unit you should:

- have an understanding of the professional need to develop your relationships with parents of pupils in your class and school, both during school placement, and during your first and subsequent years of teaching;
- be aware of the range of partners and external agencies with which a primary school has to work;
- have an understanding of some ways in which parents can act to support their child's education;
- have an appreciation of the need for trust and understanding as the basis of a successful relationship between parents and school;
- have a set of constructive ideas with which you, as a beginning teacher, can begin to establish good home–school links.

PROFESSIONAL REQUIREMENTS FOR BEING ABLE TO WORK WELL WITH PARENTS

As a teacher in training in England you will know of the Teacher Training and Development Agency's standards for the award of Qualified Teacher Status. These ITT standards for QTS are divided into three sections and the first is concerned with 'Professional Values and Practice'. This section opens with the statement that 'Those awarded Qualified Teacher Status must understand and uphold the professional code of the General Teaching Council for England ...' (TTA website) S.1 and continues by setting down eight values. Running through them is a theme of being respectful towards all learners, considerate and committed to raising their achievement. Specifically, the fourth value is central to this unit: it requires trainee teachers to demonstrate that:

> They can communicate sensitively and effectively with parents and carers, recognising their roles in pupils' learning, and their rights, responsibilities and interests in this.
>
> (TDA, ITT Standards for QTS: S1.4)

This unit will show you why good relations with parents, carers and the wider community are beneficial and some ways in which you can work on developing them.

INTRODUCTION TO DEVELOPING RELATIONSHIPS WITH PARENTS, GOVERNORS AND PARTNERS IN THE COMMUNITY

A bit of history

The history of building successful home–school relationships has not always been a comfortable one. As far back as the Plowden Report (Central Advisory Council for Education 1967), there has been official recognition that parents can play an invaluable role in supporting their children's education. Plowden was in many respects a turning point for parental involvement – it showed how more could be done to encourage parents into school (with the introduction of Parent-Teacher Associations, for example) and it brought to light how important the home is as a learning environment. More recently, the European Commission (Desforges 2003) has stressed the importance of the educational capital provided by the home. Desforges' review suggests that the nature and degree of parents' involvement with their child's education may even be a greater influence on the child's educational outcomes than how good the school is!

> In the primary age range, the impact caused by different levels of parental involvement is much bigger than the differences associated with variations in the quality of schools. The scale of the impact is evident across all social classes and all ethnic groups.
>
> (Desforges 2003: 86)

So it may be no surprise to us that building strong home–school relationships is a growth area in current government strategy. We can see this policy theme emerging in the government White Paper *Excellence and Enjoyment* (DfES 2003). Either by strengthening existing arrangements or by introducing new ones, it proposed to:

*   enhance parent governor roles;
*   give parents more involvement in school inspection processes;
*   provide more information to parents in annual reports and prospectuses;
*   introduce home–school agreements;
*   increase information going to parents about the school's curriculum and performance.

Although the points in this list may seem rather daunting at first, in fact progress on all of them has been rapid. Certainly, it would be fair to say that we have moved on considerably from the Plowden stage of simply suggesting that the home is an important place of learning as well as the school. What you may notice about this list from *Excellence and Enjoyment* is that there is an underlying trend of parents having greater responsibilities as well as more rights.

Task 8.2.1
Exploring home–school links

Taking the list of bullet points above from *Excellence and Enjoyment* as a checklist, compare with a fellow student the practice in the schools you have recently been in or are preparing for your next teaching placement by visiting for planning purposes. There are three stages to this task:

1   Go to your respective class teachers for information about the school's current practice for each bullet point. If he/she cannot tell you, for example, how 'parent governor roles' exist and are supported, then you may need to ask a deputy or the head teacher. It is not advisable to pursue the head teacher on each point unless you are very sure they have the time to talk – he/she is a busy individual and won't thank you for chasing him/her around with a series of separate questions.
2   Confer with your fellow student.
3   Write a brief report, no more than one side of A4, on what you found and where there were points of different practice between the two schools.

Outcomes: this task may have shown up very similar or very different practices in the two schools. Either case, or a mixture of the two, tells us something about the state of 'formal' home–school relationships that may exist. Later in this unit we will return to this idea of formality, and look at the value of its counterpart, informal relationships (see p. 394).

Benefits of good relationships with parents

On one level, the fact that parents nowadays have rights that mean they can know quite a lot about their child's school and how it works means that schools have to make clear arrangements that allow these rights to be exercised. Open and positive relationships between school and home help a great deal in smoothing the lines of communication and dialogue between the two parties. On another level, with these parental rights come certain parental responsibilities. By exercising these responsibilities, parents can bring great benefits to their child's education. One area of responsibility parents have is to provide suitable learning role models on which their children can base their learning and behaviour. There is a strong line of research evidence, going back to Bruner (1983, 1986) and Tizard and Hughes (1984) and then re-emerging and acknowledged in policy texts around the time of the appearance of *Excellence and Enjoyment*, that a culture supports important intellectual growth in its young through dialogue between the more experienced adults and the less experienced children.

By providing an enquiring, interested and curious *attitude* to knowledge and information, and demonstrating this through *talking with* (not at) their children, parents can give their children fundamental learning skills that teachers will find valuable in school. In particular, children's language becomes developed in ways especially useful for learning.

Another way in which parents can be important role models is in their *social behaviour*: respect for others, honesty, kindness and friendliness will all help a child settle into school quickly and develop good relationships with their peers.

The benefits for a child's education from having acquired from an early age the habits of a *positive attitude to knowledge*, *good communication skills* and *positive behaviours towards others* are enormous. It is these qualities that are the bedrock of what a school is trying to achieve in building a good relationship with parents.

Task 8.2.2
Looking at pupils

- Taking each of the three italicised topics in the paragraph above in turn, identify instances when it was important for pupils to possess them in the classroom environment by referring to examples from lessons you have recently observed or taught yourself. Keep a note of your examples.
- For each example, comment briefly upon what learning was helped by the child possessing that particular skill or habit, and why it proved useful.

Governors

From a class teacher's perspective, governors are often an overlooked group of people. Perhaps head teachers are more aware of governors and their roles, because in many ways the head acts as chief executive to the governing body, which is more like a board of directors. Governors actually have enormous responsibility for their schools, as well as quite a lot of power. They answer for the financial state of the school and are accountable for the effectiveness of the education it provides. They make the staffing appointments and approve the school's various policies. In short, they have to oversee the general running of the school so that it provides a good education for pupils.

Some governors, individually or as a body, do not get very involved in the day-to-day side of school life. This may be desirable as teachers may already have plenty on their hands without having more demands for their attention. Alternatively, some governors, especially those who are parent governors, may see themselves as an integral part of school life. Also, schools have staff governors, who may or may not be teachers. The number of staff governors a school has depends upon its size. Whatever kind of relationship exists between school and governors, it is worth a school having a clear approach towards managing that relationship.

Other partners in the community

Traditionally, schools have been fairly isolated places, with well-marked boundaries to the social systems they contain. This has often been especially true of primary schools, which arguably have had in the past less reason than, say, large secondary schools to reach out into the local community. Secondary schools need contacts with local employers and careers services, or may find themselves making more use of support services and outside agencies such as the probation service, the police and so on. But the tradition of the isolated, self-contained primary school has been rapidly disappearing over recent years. Perhaps the development of the government strategy of inclusion has helped speed up this process. Inclusion is a major issue for schools now and you will no doubt be covering it as a theme in your training course. In brief, it means the school takes a social justice approach to education. The school's role is to provide education for all children, not just those it feels it can educate. It can mean rather than separating children by type of special educational need, and educating them in special schools, mainstream schools provide education for all children, in the case of full inclusion. This is not the place for a developed overview of the importance of inclusive education – you will find that in Unit 6.1 of this book. What is relevant here is that as a consequence largely of inclusive developments, many schools are changing and expanding their roles and remits.

Government-funded initiatives such as Extended Schools and Full Service Schools are examples. Extended and Full Service Schools offer the local community packages of services beyond simply the education of their child. They can include drop-in centres for single parents, places where information can be found out about family health and so on: essentially they are on-site community centres. You can look at the DfES website to find out more about them: www.dfes.gov.uk. The relationship between these new functions of school and the more traditional school roles can be a little tense, as everyone is adjusting to the new requirements they bring. If your school is such a school, then you can expect that there will be staff development and support to help you and your colleagues make these adaptations. On the DFES Teachernet page you can link to Case Studies that describe how schools have coped with these changes.

ESTABLISHING RELATIONSHIPS TO AID CHILDREN'S LEARNING

What you are aiming at – mutual respect with parents

Edwards and Warin (1999) looked into reasons why schools and teachers should invest in parental involvement activities. You may feel this is not something about which there could be much controversy, and that surely having parents involved with their child's education is a 'good thing'. In fact, Edwards and Warin raise a few questions about quite such a quick assumption. They found that many schools tried to enlist parents as 'long arms' of their own educational purposes. In doing this, schools were trying to make parents see things from their own (i.e. the schools') perspectives. Take the example of homework: many schools in the project evaluated by Edwards and Warin took the approach of trying to make parents see homework as important and carrying esteem, so that parents themselves would place more importance upon their children doing homework, thereby helping schools meet their academic goals. The evaluation concluded that such ways of developing parental involvement are rather one-sided. They are more likely to result in schools using homes for their own purposes, than in mutual trust and genuine understanding developing between two sets of partners.

So what you are trying to aim at fundamentally is a relationship of balanced and mutual respect. You are not trying to get parents to continue your own teaching into home, but rather to develop ways of building trust and understanding between home and school. From that basis, joint goals can be set between school and homes. This is not something that will be achieved overnight, not something that you can build single-handedly. It needs time and patience, and, if you're lucky, a school ethos already pointing in the right direction for this to develop. This may sound a tall order, and it probably is, but the hopeful and positive message is that if mutual trust and understanding can be developed, there is a far greater likelihood of future success in moving children forward, with schools and parents both making their own unique contributions in supporting children's learning.

Is there a right approach?

Most research suggests (e.g. Sanders and Epstein 2000; Raffaele and Knoff 1999) that many good home–school links result from starting modestly, for example, with a small scale parental involvement project within a school that in time moves on to becoming an action research project that the whole school adopts. Perhaps this would suit you? In such cases of success, it is all-important that the process aims at developing a relationship where parents share responsibility for planning, implementing and evaluating partnership practices.

There have been many projects and initiatives aimed at developing home–school links, but few have given the kind of evidence that other interested parties can take and apply as 'recipes'. Most studies have not been clear, for example, on whether improvements in students' learning have been caused by parental involvement, or whether such improvements would have happened anyway. One of the most thorough reviews of the whole area of growing parental involvement was that referred to above, undertaken by Raffaele and Knoff (1999). They considered 41 studies undertaken in the US, and their conclusions may be helpful in showing ways forward for UK primary schools and teachers. Consider the following checklist:

> *Guidelines for Building a Foundation of Core Beliefs for Home–School Collaboration Work*
> 1. Collaboration should be pro-active rather than reactive – *i.e. schools need to be prepared to put in effort to get parents to collaborate.*
> 2. Collaboration involves sensitivity to the wide-ranging circumstances of all students and families – *i.e. there's no one template that all parents will fit.*
> 3. Collaboration recognises and values the contributions parents have to make to the educational process – *i.e. parents have potentially different contributions to make from schools.*
> 4. Collaboration must engender parental empowerment – *i.e. all parents must be given a voice and that voice must be heard.*
>
> (adapted from Raffaele and Knoff 1999: 452)

Task 8.2.3
Evaluating parental collaboration

Reflect upon the four guidelines above. Then, taking a school with which you are familiar, try to think through how far that school has achieved each guideline.

This is asking you to make a simple, informal evaluation of that school's approach to parental collaboration. You might like to use a rough scale of, say, 0 to 10, where 0 = not attempting and 10 = fully achieving that guideline.

How well did the school do in your estimation? What does this (very rough and ready) score indicate to you about what changes it needs to make in its outlook towards parental collaboration? Write a brief commentary summarising your answers to these two questions.

Getting started

In this section I will give you some ideas to try out when you are in post. Do note, however, that it is impossible to give you a sure-fire recipe that will produce instant or guaranteed success. Basically, getting started on the road to good home–school links is to make a conscious decision to adopt the attitudes embodied in the guidelines above, and make small inroads into the task of realising them. Below are some ideas. They are a mix of some that you, an individual teacher, may wish to try and others that are more suitable as school-wide steps.

• Is there a parents' room at school? This would be a place where teachers do not go unless invited.
• Do you see parents informally at the school gate before, and especially after, school?
• Are parents welcomed into school to talk about their children? Does this happen often? Informally or by appointment?
• Do you have a means of communicating with parents such as a log book that travels regularly between home and school which parents and you can use to maintain a written dialogue with each other about helping their child's learning?
• Are there regular events in school about the pupils' curriculum and learning that invite parents' opinions?

The above ideas are possible ways of supplementing, not replacing, the means of home–school contact that most schools already have. Those existing measures, such as annual reports, Christmas plays and parties, celebrations of other festivals, sports days, outings to which parents may be invited, range across the spectrum from very formal to very informal: the difference about these latter forms of contact and those in the list of five points above is that the list is trying to build a common platform of shared understanding about children's learning. They are *not* instances where the school is presenting a particular 'showcase' to parents, or which try to inform (or, rather, teach) parents a particular set of ideas.

Underlying the last paragraph is the notion of trying to augment home–school relations by building approaches to home that treat parents as equals and valued partners – not another audience for teachers to perform before. This may not always be an easy step to take, because it can mean making deep-rooted changes to one's image of oneself as a teacher. It will, therefore, take time and is not to be rushed. The key thing to remember is that even if changes you try to make happen seem slow and progress is small, the result will be worthwhile in terms of longer-term relations with parents.

Listening to parents is an important skill to develop. You will find that allowing parents the time and space to talk to you about their child's learning from their point of view will help you see where and how you can support your pupils' learning with more sensitivity.

Task 8.2.4
Listening to teachers

During the next opportunity you have in your training, ask the class teacher with whom you are working, or your school mentor, to spend 15 minutes or so talking to you about the professional practice of communicating sensitively and effectively with parents. Here are some useful questions to ask:

- A pupil is misbehaving in class. What advice do they have about how to approach this with the parent? Do they have any 'dos and don'ts'? How would they hope to resolve the problem?
- A pupil is clearly not making progress. What would the teacher recommend as a way of broaching this with the parents and how would they try to work with the parent to best support the child's learning?

For each question, keep careful notes of the teacher's answers. These are two typical situations in which teachers often find themselves dealing with parents and you will find their experience invaluable

CONTINUING WORKING WITH PARENTS AND THE COMMUNITY

Who knows what?

One of the enduring problems at all levels and ages of education is getting learners to transfer what they have learned in one context and apply it in another. This can be a challenge within school, between school and home and from school to the community at large. For example, within school it can be very difficult for teachers to enable pupils to apply their understanding of particular concepts acquired in science, such as how and why some substances float and others sink in water, and use it to make sense of phenomena such as why a big, heavy iron boat stays afloat. Another example of learning transfer being hard to achieve can often be seen in pupils' literacy learning: during lessons on how to write in sentences, and use simple punctuation rules such as capital letters and full stops, pupils can apply these conventions appropriately. Then, maybe only later in the same day, they abandon these conventions when writing about, say, an event they have learned about in history. Of course, the challenge of promoting within-school learning transfer is something that primary teachers are well aware of: examples of when it does and does not happen are relatively easy to spot and opportunities for supporting learning transfer are reasonably under teachers' own control.

Transfer of learning in either direction between school and home or the wider community is, clearly, less under a teacher's immediate control. Indeed, following the line of argument set out above in this unit, it is not advocated here as a matter for teachers to control. Rather, it is an aspect of education that you may wish to focus on as a worthwhile vehicle for development of collaboration. The value of this focus is that you can build up children's knowledge and understanding with input from both inside and outside school, so to speak.

A simple starting point for learning transfer between home and school would be to set open homework tasks, to which there are no 'right' or 'wrong' answers, but which require children to find out information from their outside-school lives. Care must be taken not to set tasks that are intrusive upon family privacy, of course. Also, children's sensitivities must be protected – they may not wish to find out about something they feel would show them in a bad light if made public knowledge. Examples of reasonably safe, neutral tasks might be to set questions that require some finding out to be done about distances from home to shops, prices of certain goods, perhaps first names of previous generations of family members.

Responding and learning

A second step might be to bring home and school a little closer together. You could invite parents to come and talk to your class, or small groups of children if a whole class is a little daunting at first. The topic should be something about which the parents are the 'expert'. Nothing ambitious, just something that means they are more likely to be confident and comfortable. Places of interest that a parent has visited, a hobby or living in a different country are the sorts of topics that can work well. Try aiming for a programme, again not ambitious, of perhaps one or two such talks each term. Base some coursework around each talk, so that your pupils are prepared and have some understanding of what the topic is and can ask some questions. Have follow-up work planned, which does not have to be written, which expresses their engagement with the topic.

Once parents can see you value and respect them, and your pupils see that too, you can move towards the kind of reciprocal, balanced and two-way relationship that is most beneficial. You can invite ideas from parents, consulting them about their children's learning.

In the longer term, once you have moved on from your first year of teaching and gained further teaching experience, you may even wish to suggest to your school's senior management team that collaboration with parents is an area of school policy that you would like to offer as a target for your own continuing professional development.

SUMMARY

In this unit I have tried to give you an understanding of the need to develop your relationships with parents of pupils in your class and school, both during school placement, and during your first and subsequent years of teaching. There are numerous ways in which parents can support the education of their children and also in which you can build a successful and productive relationship with the most important partners you will work with. I have also tried to suggest a set of ways in which you, as a beginning teacher, can begin to establish good home–school links.

ANNOTATED FURTHER READING

Desforges, C. and Abouchaar, A. (2003) *The Impact of Parental Involvement, Parental Support and Family Education on Pupil Achievement and Adjustment: A Literature Review*, DfES Research Report RR433, London: DfES. If you wish to read a rounded and comprehensive review of the literature relating to the whole topic of parental involvement in schooling, then this report by Desforges should be helpful. It is written in a clear and accessible style and should help you gain a deeper understanding of many of the issues I have introduced you to in this unit.

Edwards, A. and Warin, J. (1999) 'Parental involvement in raising the achievement of primary school pupils: why bother?', *Oxford Review of Education*, 25(3): 325–41. This article by Edwards and Warin is useful if you want to read a research-based critique of policy in this area. It sets out why schools are thought to benefit from investing time and effort in parental involvement. The authors point out that, although aimed at improving children's performance, involving parents in classroom processes generates rather more complex matters. The article suggests that what tends to happen is primary schools turn to parents as classroom supports for their own teaching rather than enabling parents to contribute according to their strengths.

REFERENCES

Bruner, J. (1983) *Child's Talk: Learning to Use Language*, New York: Norton.

Bruner, J. (1986) *Actual Minds, Possible Worlds*, Cambridge, MA: Harvard University Press.

Central Advisory Council for Education (1967) *Children and Their Primary Schools* (The Plowden Report), London: HMSO.

Desforges, C. and Abouchaar, A. (2003) *The Impact of Parental Involvement, Parental Support and Family Education on Pupil Achievement and Adjustment: A Literature Review*, DfES Research Report RR433, London: DfES.

DfES (2003) *Excellence and Enjoyment – A Strategy for Primary Schools*, London: DfES.

Edwards, A. and Warin, J. (1999) 'Parental involvement in raising the achievement of primary school pupils: why bother?', *Oxford Review of Education*, 25(3): 325–41.

Fan, X. and Chen, M. (2001) 'Parental involvement and students' academic achievement: a meta-analysis', *Educational Psychological Review*, 13(1): 1–22.

Raffaele, L.M. and Knoff, H.M. (1999) 'Improving home–school collaboration with disadvantaged families: organisational principles, perspectives and approaches', *School Psychology Review*, 28(3): 448–66.

Sanders, M.G. and Epstein, J.L. (2000) 'The national network of partnership schools: how research influences practice', *Journal of Education for Children Placed At Risk*, 5(1–2): 61–76.

Tizard, B. and Hughes, M. (1984) *Young Children Learning: Talking and Thinking at Home and at School*, London: Fontana.

WEBSITES

Teacher Training and Development Agency – www.tda.gov.uk: follow links 'In training Teachers' to 'Qualifying to Teach' to Professional Standards for the Award of QTS.

General Teaching Council – www.gtce.org.uk: for 'Statement of Professional Values' follow links to 'standards/regulations/CodeofConductandPractice'.

Unit 8.3

Working Together: The Changing Role of the Teacher

Helen Moylett

INTRODUCTION

> Co-locating different services, in children's centres and extended schools, and the development of healthy schools, will mean more professionals working closely together, increasing the likelihood of identifying risk factors earlier and providing easier access to targeted and specialist support for children with additional needs within universal settings such as schools. Schools will benefit from hosting these multi-agency teams. Teachers will be freed up to concentrate on teaching, and barriers to learning will be more easily overcome – helping to raise standards.
>
> (DfES 2004a)

The days when you qualified as a teacher and looked forward to being able to work with your class on your own are gone. Yes, teachers are still autonomous professionals expected to be decision makers and leaders of learning for a class of children, but they can no longer shut the classroom door on the rest of the world. Any primary teacher is part of a wider team of professionals and other adults who work for, and with, children as they progress into, through and beyond the primary school.

Good relationships with other professionals has always been a feature of the best schools who perceive themselves as a part of a range of community services. However this way of relating to other agencies is no longer voluntary, and no longer entirely dependent on the goodwill, understanding and co-operation of those involved. The Children Act 2004 establishes a *duty* on local authorities to ensure co-operation between agencies and a *duty* on key partners, including education, to co-operate. This unit explores some of the issues relating to this Change for Children agenda and the ways in which the re-structuring and rethinking of services across local authorities is affecting the practice of primary education in schools. The unit will help you understand a national political agenda which is shaping services for children and families across education, health and social services and the ways in which teachers will increasingly work as part of multi-disciplinary teams.

OBJECTIVES

By the end of this unit you should:

- understand the main requirements of the Children Act 2004 as they relate to primary school practice;
- understand how the five *Every Child Matters: Change for Children* (DfES 2004a) outcomes – Being Healthy, Staying Safe, Enjoying and Achieving, Making a Positive Contribution and Achieving Economic Wellbeing – relate to primary teaching;
- understand more about how working with professionals from other agencies can support the learning and development of the whole child in meeting these outcomes.

BACKGROUND TO *EVERY CHILD MATTERS: CHANGE FOR CHILDREN*

The Laming Report and 'Every Child Matters'

In 2003 the government published a green paper called 'Every Child Matters'. This was released at the same time as the Laming Report on the inquiry into the death of Victoria Climbié (HM Government 2003). The report exposed huge failings in the system designed to protect our most vulnerable children. In this, and in other previous cases, intervention did not happen early enough because of poor co-ordination and failure to share information as well as inadequate management and training for frontline workers.

Every Child Matters: The Next Steps

'Every Child Matters' formed the basis of a wide-ranging consultation with parents, children and young people and those working in the full range of children's services. Following this consultation *Every Child Matters: The Next Steps* (DfES 204b) was published. It set out the five outcomes which are now shaping the *Change for Children* agenda and which will be explored in more detail further on in this unit.

The Five Outcomes

- Be healthy;
- stay safe;
- enjoy and achieve;
- make a positive contribution;
- achieve economic wellbeing.

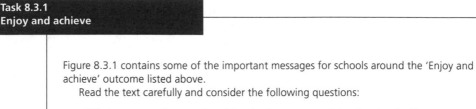

Task 8.3.1
Enjoy and achieve

Figure 8.3.1 contains some of the important messages for schools around the 'Enjoy and achieve' outcome listed above.

Read the text carefully and consider the following questions:

• What concerns does reading this raise for you as an intending teacher?
• Have you worked, or been on a placement, in a school that is working hard on raising achievement for *all* children? How did you know that was the case? What did you see and hear in classrooms, in the playground, in dining areas, in the staffroom?
• How did the staff's assessment of children's learning across the curriculum feed into individualised planning for specific groups or individuals?
• Have you ever been in a school where the children's assessment records included information from health, social services or from parents – what form did this take?

4.6 Schools are critical to ensuring every child has the opportunity to fulfil their potential. Our ambitions have to be bolder than merely protecting children from falling through the net: we must have high ambitions for all children. Raising standards in schools and inclusion must go hand in hand. In particular, schools have a critical role in raising the educational achievement of children in care and other groups that have consistently underachieved, for example some minority ethnic groups.

4.7 Our reforms support efforts to raise standards by personalising learning to suit the individual aspirations, circumstances and talents of each child. Instead of a deficit model that provides consistent but uniform services for most children, and only provides tailored support when children have more complex needs identified by the SEN or child protection process, our aim is to ensure that every child gets personalised learning, care and support. This aims to ensure all children have the opportunity to fulfil their potential and those with complex needs receive responsive services, quickly and accessibly on a graduated basis.

4.8 This vision requires new ways of working and collaboration between schools, and closer working between schools, communities and specialist services. Our understanding that high standards and social inclusion are interlinked ambitions is at the heart of our desire nationally and locally to integrate closely education, social care and health services. The leadership given locally by the Director of Children's Services should play a key role in facilitating such arrangements.

4.9 Many schools are already offering a range of extended services including parental and family learning opportunities, study support, after school activities, childcare, adult learning, health and social care as well as opening up their facilities for the wider community. Schools offering extended services report that the parental involvement and community links have had a direct impact on raising pupil attainment.

The presence of other professionals in the school has also ensured that the needs of children and young people are assessed in the round and any wider barriers to learning identified and needs addressed.

Figure 8.3.1   'Enjoy and achieve' outcome (Source: DfES 2004b: 38)

Every Child Matters: Change for Children

Every Child Matters: Change for Children explains how the Children Act (referred to in the introduction to this unit) forms the basis of a long-term programme of change. It helps the 150 local authorities in England to plan how they will deliver the improved outcomes for children required in the Act.

Figure 8.3.2 from *Every Child Matters: Change for Children* represents those five outcomes at the centre of all national and local authority work. As a classroom teacher you are involved in 'frontline delivery' and your major focus will be on the children and working with others to provide integrated services to make the outcomes happen. You will be supported by integrated processes, the planning or strategy which sets their direction and the governance arrangements which sustain them.

Inter-agency governance and integrated strategy

These are the responsibility of the local authority under the leadership of the Director of Children's Services.

Integrated processes

This is the stage where the integration at local authority level probably begins to have the most direct effect in schools and on the everyday working lives of teachers. Clearly strategy needs to be translated into practice through processes which help professionals work across agencies in an integrated way. One of the most significant developments is the Common Assessment Framework (CAF). This is a

Figure 8.3.2   Implementing the five outcomes for children (Source: DfES 2004a: 6)

national common process for initial assessment to identify more accurately and efficiently the additional needs of children and young people at risk of poor outcomes. The idea is to reduce the duplication of assessment, produce a shared language across agencies and improve referrals between agencies. The CAF will be implemented in all areas by 2008.

The benefits of early intervention and the crucial role that teachers can play is highlighted in this case study from Telford and Wrekin in *Every Child Matters: Change for Children* (p. 19):

> *Before co-ordinated early intervention*
>
> M had been receiving help at nursery school from the Behaviour Support Service due to his aggressive behaviour. However over the summer his behaviour worsened and his mother was concerned that the transition to reception class meant he would not get the same level of support. She contacted the Information Sharing and Assessment co-ordinator, who agreed to liaise with other agencies. A check on the data held for M revealed incomplete records, particularly of mental health issues; M's health visitor confirmed concerns about his sleep routines and an outstanding referral for speech therapy, while the school revealed concerns about M and his mother's difficulties.

> *After co-ordinated early intervention*
>
> The school undertook a Common Assessment with M's mother and from that planned how services would come together to form a 'team around the child' including an education welfare assistant, a health visitor and a teacher. As a result, the education welfare assistant worked with M at home and at school; a referral for speech therapy was made; and the health visitor continued to offer support to his mother, suggesting strategies for dealing with his behaviour. M's class teacher acted as the first point of contact for the family and information was shared on request with the other specialists about M's vulnerabilities and his behavioural difficulties. Due to this integrated approach to identifying and addressing the causes of M's behaviour, M's family now feel they are receiving co-ordinated support that meets his needs. His re-referral for speech therapy was prioritized due to his needs being set within a broader context of his educational and social development, and the team continues to work with M and his family to achieve more improvement.
>
> (DfES 2004a: 19)

Task 8.3.2
The team around the child

Read the Telford and Wrekin case study and reflect on the following questions:

- How do you think M's nursery school might have been more pro-active in easing the transition to primary school for him and his family?
- M's class teacher acting as the first point of contact for the family meant that s/he would have to make time to talk with them and other parents. How do schools you have worked in enable face to face communication with parents?
- M's class teacher would have to liaise with other professionals in order to deliver accurate information and to share it appropriately. What skills might you need to develop in order to do this effectively?

Integrated frontline delivery

As we have seen in the case study from Telford and Wrekin above, more integrated processes lead to professionals working better together. This in turn leads to children getting better support earlier. You will probably be wondering what the implications of all this might be for you as a newly qualified or intending teacher. In order to help you understand how the role of the teacher might develop as the *Change for Children* agenda develops you need to understand a little about the roles of other professionals you might work with, as well as something about children's centres and the changing role of schools as they become extended schools.

OTHER PROFESSIONALS

This section gives you a brief overview of the roles of the people from other agencies with whom you may well work. (It does not include teaching assistants and nursery nurses as their role is covered elsewhere in this book.)

Specialist teachers

Most local authorities employ specialist teachers of deaf and visually impaired children. Some also employ teachers who are experts in teaching children with autistic spectrum disorders. They have completed postgraduate qualifications in their area of expertise and will be able to give you and parents advice on the most appropriate ways to enable the children with these diagnoses to access the primary curriculum. If systems are working well they should know about any child who needs this support before they arrive at school.

Educational psychologists

Educational psychologists are often known as EPs and are all teachers who have taught for some years before completing Masters degrees in educational psychology. They will often have a very limited time available to advise colleagues in school. However, the school (via the SENCo and/or head teacher) can refer a child (with the consent of parents) to their service if there are significant concerns about the child's cognitive, social or emotional development. The EP will observe the child at school and at home and her/his report will often be crucial in determining future provision for the child (see other units for more detail re the SEN Code of Practice).

Health professionals

Paediatricians – the local child health development team will probably be led by a community paediatrician. Paediatricians are doctors specialising in child health. Children entering reception class may well have records which contain reports from local paediatricians – probably because they have ongoing health problems. The paediatrician will be able to give advice to teachers and parents but is unlikely to visit you in the classroom.

Speech and language therapists, health visitors, occupational therapists, physiotherapists – These are the people who are more likely to be regular visitors to a school or centre.

Speech and language therapists (SLTs or SALTs) will be able to give you advice on how to help all children who have any form of speech and language delay or difficulty – this is particularly helpful in the early years. Speech and language problems are very common and some schools and centres buy in sessions from an SLT to work with staff to equip them with strategies to help children. However there is a national shortage of SLTs and they have very little time to work in schools. If your school does not work with a local SLT and you know there are children receiving speech therapy outside school, ask parents to share the activities they have been asked to do at home with you. Schools can also refer children to the service.

Health visitors (HVs) – all children have a health visitor in the early years before they start school. They have practised as nurses before undertaking further training to become health visitors. They visit homes very early after the birth of a baby and advise parents on the full range of child health issues. Many schools and centres employ HVs to give informal advice and support to parents. HVs may alert the school if there are concerns about a child and/or family.

Occupational therapists (OTs) work with children to ensure that whatever their physical disabilities or needs they can access the curriculum. For instance they will be able to give you advice abut the type of chair the school might need to supply for a child with particular physical needs.

Physiotherapists (Physios) have a similar role to OTs but they concentrate on the children's physical condition. For instance the child with the chair in the example above might need particular exercises to increase lower limb mobility. The physio will be able to give advice to you and the parents about appropriate ways to manage this at home and school.

Social workers

Children you teach may be looked-after children (LAC). This may mean that they live with foster carers or in other residential accommodation. In this case they will be part of a social worker's caseload. The educational achievement of looked-after children is a national cause for concern. Social workers may ask for reports on these children's progress and you may be asked to meet them and other interested parties for review meetings. Other children may be deemed to be 'at risk' (see Unit 8.4 on child protection for more details on your role if this is the case).

Private and voluntary childcare providers

Before and after school care may be provided by a number of private and voluntary providers such as childminders, local pre-schools or day nurseries working on school premises or locally. Their staff may be play workers, nursery nurses, teachers and will have a range of professional backgrounds, experiences and qualifications. They will get to know children and parents informally and it is crucial to work with them in order to provide coherence and continuity of experience for children. If you are a reception class teacher you may be receiving children from a variety of settings and, again, working together is very important.

CHILDREN'S CENTRES

The children's centre programme is a main plank of the government's ten year strategy for early years and childcare, *Choice for Parents, The Best Start for Children* (HM Treasury, 2004). The strategy aims for greater choice for parents in how they balance their work commitments and family life through enhanced parental leave and easy access to Sure Start children's centres. The core offer of a children's centre includes integrated early learning, care, family support, health services, outreach services to children and families not attending the centre and access to training and employment advice. Children's centres are intended to be models of multi-agency and partnership working. At the heart of a centre will be high quality learning and full day care for children from birth to school age.

Many children's centres are based on existing early excellence centres, nursery schools, day nurseries and/or Sure Start local programmes. The aim is that there will be one in every community by 2010.

Teachers trained in early years have a crucial role in children's centres. *The Effective Provision of Pre-school Education (EPPE) Project* (1997–2003) (Sylva *et al.* 2004) clearly demonstrated that settings which employ staff with teaching qualifications show higher quality and their children make more progress. The centres will be, for many families and their children, their first experience of childcare and education. You could play an important part in ensuring that you establish a lifelong love of learning for children and increased educational achievement for parents as well. It is extremely unlikely that you would be employed as a newly qualified teacher in a children's centre where there is only one teacher, but in larger ones where there may be a team of teachers, this could be an interesting job, particularly if you have experienced multi-agency working before your teaching degree studies or have a degree in early childhood studies.

EXTENDED SCHOOLS

Like children's centres, extended schools are good bases for the delivery of services within local *Change for Children* programmes. Another strategy, the *Five Year Strategy for Children and Learners (DfES 2004d)*, sets out the government's expectation that all primary and secondary schools provide extended childcare services to parents and many will provide very similar services to children's centres. The core offer for an extended school will include a varied menu of activities such as homework clubs, sport, dance and drama, parenting support, widespread community use of the school's facilities and swift referral from schools to a wider range of specialised support services for pupils. Some extended schools will be on the same site as a children's centre and will have health services for example available on site.

By 2010 all primary schools will be providing childcare between 8am and 6pm all year round – either on site or in partnership with other schools, local providers or childminders, with half of all schools providing it before then. There is an expectation that all schools will contribute to the whole wellbeing of all the children and young people living in the locality by building an awareness of the five outcomes and reflecting them in their core activities. These five outcomes were first mentioned on p. 391. The next section unpacks what they mean in a bit more detail and focuses on a case study of one school's work across all five outcomes.

Be healthy	Physically healthy
	Mentally and emotionally healthy
	Sexually healthy
	Healthy lifestyles
	Parents, carers and families promote healthy choices
Stay safe	Safe from maltreatment, neglect, violence and sexual exploitation
	Safe from accidental injury and death
	Safe from bullying and discrimination
	Safe from crime and anti-social behaivour in and out of school
	Have security, stability and are cared for
	Parents, carers and families provide safe homes and stability
Enjoy and achieve	Ready for schoool
	Attend and enjoy school
	Achieve stretching national educational standards at primary school
	Achieve personal and social development and enjoy recreation
	Achieve stretching national educational standards at secondary school
	Parents, carers and families support learning
Make a positive contribution	Engage in decision-making and support the community and environment
	Engage in law-abiding and positive behaivour in and out of school
	Develop positive relationships and choose not to bully and discriminate
	Develop self-confidence and successfully deal with significant life changes and challenges
	Develop enterprising behaviour
	Parents, carers and families promote positive behaviour
Achieve economic well-being	Engage in further education, employment or training on leaving schoool
	Ready for employment
	Live in decent homes and sustainable communities
	Access to transport and material goods
	Live in households free from low income
	Parents, carers and families are supported to be economically active

Figure 8.3.3 The five outcomes (Source: DfES 2004a: 9)

THE FIVE OUTCOMES

All inspections, including Ofsted inspections of schools, will be looking for evidence of working towards these for all children. Figure 8.3.3 above provides a description of the five outcomes.

Task 8.3.3
Healthy eating at Unity Primary School

Read the case study on p. 399 and note how many of the outcomes are being met. Although this is an account of a healthy eating project, you will need to look at all five.

One school helping children meet the five outcomes

Case Study

Unity Primary School borders a leafy suburb and a run-down council estate. It has 150 children on roll. The school is open for breakfast club from 8.00 to 8.50am when school starts. It also has an after school club from 3.30 to 6.00pm. The school is working towards the Healthy School Standard. This year they are focusing particularly on healthy eating. This has involved all year groups.

The staff have planned a progressive curriculum and targets for children from the nursery class through to Year 6. Healthy eating activities have been linked to physical development and the importance of exercise and looking after your body. The nursery class has been working with the health visitor from the local Sure Start programme. The school council has been centrally involved in liaising between each class and the head and senior management team. They have also taken part in the negotiating with the cook and kitchen staff about the provision of healthier lunches. The termly newsletter has informed parents about the Healthy School Standard and the work being undertaken.

Last week the Year 6 class had a debate in front of the rest of KS2 around the motion 'This school should ban crisps and other high fat, high salt snacks at break times'. Despite a good defence of such snacks from the most able debater in the class, the motion was overwhelmingly carried with a large majority of children voting for it.

At the staff meeting to discuss this, these ideas for follow-up were suggested:

- immediately introduce a whole school ban on crisps etc. at break;
- get Y6 to repeat their debate for KS1 and see what the vote was like there;
- investigate funding free fruit for KS2 as KS1 already get it and nursery supply it too;
- get breakfast club and after school club staff involved – they have been left out so far;
- get the school council to discuss the outcome of the debate and make a decision about whether to go ahead with a ban;
- involve parents in discussion somehow as they send in the snacks with their children;
- involve the health visitor already working with the nursery class.

Task 8.3.4
If you worked at Unity Primary ...

What do you think you would have suggested?

This is what actually happened.

Each class discussed the outcome of the debate with their teacher and other staff. This took place at circle time, in small groups and as a whole class depending on the age and stage of the children. The staff suggested various ways forward such as writing to parents, having a healthy eating day for everyone, letting the school council decide etc. One of the Year 1 children suggested 'Let's have a feast!'. The rest of the class thought this was a great idea. So did other classes. Every child in the school took home an individually designed invite to their parents and carers inviting them to a 'Feast Day'.

On the Feast Day parents and/or other carers could come in for breakfast club, lunch or after school club or stay for the whole day if they wished. At these three meal times a large range of healthy food from different cultures was served. After parents had sampled the food they could stay for a making session with one of the staff – all the kitchen staff were involved in working with the parents as well as teaching assistants, nursery nurses and the head.

The Sure Start programme health visitor spent all day in the entrance hall welcoming people, encouraging them to try a range of dips made by the children with vegetables and fresh fruit and giving out information about cheap menu options for growing families. Her colleague from the health centre was helping and they were both giving parents the chance to talk informally with them about child health issues and the benefits of the Sure Start local programme for babies and young children. Many parents in the area find it hard to keep appointments and therefore they, and their children, often miss out on healthcare.

Staff from the local health club (two of whom were parents) were outside running short exercise classes and advising on safe exercise for all age groups. Staff from the local FE college had a stall advertising catering and health and beauty courses as well as return to learning and basic skills. They chatted to anyone interested and had leaflets available in a range of community languages.

All the classrooms and hall were open for parents to wander in and out of and the children and staff were all engaged in healthy eating and exercise activities all day. For the working parents who could only come for the end of after school club, there was not only food but also a chance to take part in a relaxation session in the hall.

Parents were asked to fill a simple form on their way out either by writing it themselves or talking it through with a member of staff or Y6 child. The form asked them if they had enjoyed the day, if they would like more opportunities to get involved and if they would be prepared to pay £1 per week in order that free fruit could be available for all the children. One hundred and three forms were returned. All were very positive about the day and all said they would be prepared to pay £1 per week. Two fathers volunteered to install two raised beds in the playground so that children could plant and grow their own herbs and vegetables. They wanted to make them raised beds so that they would be accessible to children in wheelchairs.

Three months on and the children no longer bring crisps to school; every child has a piece of fruit as a snack. The menus at breakfast club, lunch and after school club are healthier. Lynette, one of the after school helpers, who has four children who are all now at secondary school, has revealed great talent in Caribbean cooking and is now running a class on a Wednesday afternoon for anyone who wants to drop in. There are about ten regulars and up to six others. Lynette buys the ingredients, the school reimburses her and the participants pay what they can. Some weeks the class is in profit, some weeks it makes a loss. Lynette has gained in confidence as the weeks have gone by and has enrolled at the college to gain some formal qualifications. She is now trying to persuade a couple of other parents to teach the group some Greek and Pakistani dishes. Lynette has also been asked to go and talk to some of the parents with very young babies in the Sure Start programme about cooking on a budget.

The two health visitors take it in turns to drop in once a week before school, so any parent or carer who wants to have an informal chat can do so. In this way they have picked up some serious problems that needed to be referred to a GP and have been able to talk through and demystify some other ailments. The speech and language therapist employed by the Sure Start local programme has been in to meet the Foundation Stage staff and observe the way they work with children. She has taught staff some basic skills to improve children's speech and language in group situations. She has also taught the staff some basic Makaton signs which all the children in nursery and reception are using with pride.

Task 8.3.5
If you worked at Unity Primary …

Answer the following questions:

- How many of the outcomes were covered by the school in this initiative?
- Refer to the quotation from *Every Child Matters* (DfES 2004a) right at the beginning of this unit. Do you think Unity Primary School 'freed up' teachers 'to concentrate on teaching'?
- Have you ever heard teachers complaining about having to be social workers and substitute parents as well as educators?
- If what they are really saying is that they have to care for the children as well as educate them, why does this seem to be an issue?
- How might working with the health professionals involved support all children's learning and development?
- For instance learning Makaton is often done for the benefit of children who are deaf or have learning or language processing difficulties – why might it in fact benefit all children's learning?
- If you were a teacher at Unity Primary School what would you be interested in doing next?
- How might the school build on the two dads' interest in gardening to involve other male carers?

TRAINING AND THE COMMON CORE

The *Change for Children* agenda will gradually make all schools and early years settings more open, multi-professional places. You should now understand more about the opportunities this will offer you as a new teacher. You might at this stage have some concerns about training. Training in future will have to address what is known as the Common Core of Skills and Knowledge for the Children's Workforce; this will be embedded into school staff qualifications and training.

The skills and knowledge are set out in the Common Core Prospectus (2005) (see DfES website www.dfes.gov.uk/commoncore) under six main headings:

- effective communication and engagement with children, young people and families;
- child and young person development;
- safeguarding and promoting the welfare of the child;
- supporting transitions;
- multi-agency working;
- sharing information.

At the time of writing, the Children's Workforce Strategy is out for consultation and includes proposals for a review of the *Qualifying to Teach* standards (TTA 2003) in the light of the Common Core and to ensure that teachers are able to qualify to teach babies and young children from birth to three.

SUMMARY

This is an exciting time to be entering a career in children's services. The *Change for Children* agenda ensures that we will all be working much more closely with other professionals and the wider community. Teachers continue to have a major role in helping children to enjoy school and to achieve as much as they can, but they are also working on a broader remit around the development of the whole child and ensuring that children are kept safe and healthy as they become citizens who contribute to society and who are able to earn a living and support both themselves and future generations.

ANNOTATED FURTHER READING

Anning, A. (2005) 'Investigating the impact of working in multi-agency service delivery settings in the UK on early years practitioners' beliefs and practices', *Journal of Early Childhood Research*, 3(1): 19–50. This is a detailed report of research carried out into the values underpinning the actions of staff working in multi-agency teams in two early years centres. It will be of equal interest to those working in schools as the controversial issues and critical incident explored could also happen in primary schools and will be familiar.

Atkinson, M., Doherty, P. and Kinder, K. (2005) 'Multi-agency working: models, challenges and key factors for success', *Journal of Early Childhood Research*, 3(1): 7–17. This article is a report of the findings of a National Foundation for Educational Research (NFER) study sponsored by the Local Government Association. It is brief and explains models simply with diagrams. It identifies the need for a new, what it calls 'hybrid', professional who has experience and knowledge of other agencies. The link can be made here to the 'social pedagogue' mentioned in the Children's Workforce Strategy.

USEFUL WEBSITES

www.everychildmatters.gov.uk On this website you will find all the Every Child Matters documents and many helpful supplementary texts. They can be downloaded or ordered from DfES publications on dfes@prolog.uk.com or 0845 60 222 60. Some key texts available here are:

Every Child Matters: The Next Steps
Every Child Matters: Change for Children
Every Child Matters: Change for Children in Schools
Choice for Parents, the Best Start for Children: A Ten Year Strategy for Childcare
Children's Workforce Strategy
Common Assessment Framework.

www.dfes.gov.uk/commoncore This website gives you access to the Common Core Prospectus (2005). One to watch if you are interested in following the progress of reform to the children's workforce including how the Teacher Training Agency (TTA) (soon to be the Training and Development Agency (TDA)) is involved in the process.

www.teachernet.gov.uk/wholeschool/extendedschools/practicalknowhow/. As the title implies this site gives practical advice on becoming an extended school.

www.surestart.gov.uk. Everything you need to know about early years and childcare initiatives. Useful information on:

Sure Start local programmes

Children's centres

Early Excellence centres.

Research page includes downloadable versions of the EPPE longitudinal study reports. Useful quick links to DfES, Department of Work and Pensions, Department of Health, Parents Centre and Every Child Matters.

REFERENCES

Department for Education and Skills (DfES) (2004a) *Every Child Matters: Change for Children*, Nottingham: DfES Publications (DfES/1080/2004 ISBN 1 8447 83553).

Department for Education and Skills (DfES) (2004b) *Every Child Matters: The Next Steps*, Nottingham: DfES Publications (DfES/0240/2004 ISBN 1 84478 198).

Department for Education and Skills (DfES) (2004c) *Every Child Matters: Change for Children in Schools*, Nottingham: DfES Publications (DfES/1089/2004 ISBN 1 8447 83561).

Department for Education and Skills (DfES) (2004d) *Five Year Strategy for Children and Learners*, Norwich: The Stationery Office (TSO) (ISBN 0 10 162722 X).

Department for Education and Skills DfES (2004e) *Healthy Living Blueprint for Schools*, Nottingham: DfES Publications (DfES/0781/2004) ISBN 1 84478 305 7).

Department for Education and Skills (DfES) (2005) *Extended Schools: Access to Opportunities and Services For All, A Prospectus*, Nottingham: DfES Publications (1408–2005DOC-EN ISBN 1 84478 451 7).

HM Government (2003) *The Victoria Climbié Inquiry* (The Laming Report), Norwich: Her Majesty's Stationery Office (HMSO) (CM5730).

HM Government (2004) *Children Act*, London: The Stationery Office (TSO).

HM Treasury (2004) *Choice For Parents, The Best Start For Children: A Ten Year Strategy for Childcare*, Norwich: Her Majesty's Stationery Office (HMSO).

Sylva, K., Melhuish, E., Sammons, P., Siraj-Blatchford, I. and Taggart, B. (2004) *The Effective Provision of Pre-school Education (EPPE) Project: Findings from Pre-school to end of Key Stage1*, Nottingham: DfES Publications (SSU/FR/2004/01).

Teacher Training Agency (TTA) (2003) *Qualifying to Teach*, London: TTA (TPU 1064/1P/20K/FMP/JUL03).

Unit 8.4

Working Together: Understanding the Teacher's Pastoral Role

Ben Whitney

INTRODUCTION

One of the key characteristics of the British system of education is that it is based on a holistic understanding of children. Despite continuous testing and using examination outcomes as the preferred way of monitoring schools' effectiveness, there are clearly many factors that will influence a child's ability to learn at school, not only their intellectual capacity or the quality of their teaching. Many other pressures will also impact on learning and their eventual effect is often dependent on whether these issues were dealt with at the time or left unaddressed. Outcomes for socially disadvantaged children in particular are often poor.

Recent government thinking (in, for example, *Every Child Matters: Change for Children*, (DfES 2004) and *Change for Children in Schools* (DfES 2004)) has moved education professionals to the centre of the arrangements for meeting children's needs as part of a local Children's Services Authority. (This unit uses 'Local Authority' (LA) to include education services as it is no longer appropriate to talk about a 'Local Education Authority' (LEA) in isolation from social care and health.) All of the five key outcomes, especially 'Being Healthy', 'Staying Safe' and 'Enjoying and Achieving', impact directly on education and it is expected that the Children Act 2004 will lead to a radical repositioning of all schools to the heart of multi-agency family support.

Key responsibilities:

- monitoring pupils' school attendance and reasons given for their absence;
- determining whether absences are authorised or unauthorised according to school policy;
- recording concerns about children at risk of 'significant harm' under the school's procedures
- helping parents to access services for 'children in need';
- working with key professionals outside the school under agreed inter-agency safeguarding procedures.

While some of these responsibilities will also be addressed by non-teaching colleagues, you cannot teach a child you never see or if they are constantly preoccupied with the effects of their experiences at home. Making sure that children actually attend school as the law requires and that education staff play an appropriate part in carrying out the legal duties placed on all children's agencies to protect them from harm and abuse are crucial. This unit explores the relevant legal frameworks involved in these tasks and gives practical guidance about both managing attendance and dealing with concerns related to child protection.

OBJECTIVES

By the end of this unit you should:

- be familiar with the legal framework within which the wider pastoral responsibilities of schools are carried out;
- appreciate and be able to manage the appropriate duties of a class teacher for monitoring attendance and working with both parents and non-teaching colleagues to ensure that absences are followed-up and school or individual targets are met;
- have become more aware of the in-school procedures that should be in place to safeguard children and protect them from the risk of 'significant harm';
- understand the role of the teacher when working with colleagues from outside the school, such as education welfare officers and social workers.

SCHOOL ATTENDANCE

Legal framework

Since at least the Education Act 1870, there has been a sense that education is compulsory. In the early days, this was a gradual process of prising children away from the other activities that might occupy them as an alternative and holding parents in some way legally accountable for ensuring they received at least an elementary level of instruction. It is an open question whether there has ever been a total acceptance that education should come first in the lives of all children. (The rules were, for example, set aside during both wars when many older children returned to the workplace and many children still end up out of school for a variety of reasons.)

Provision is certainly more universal with younger children but the ever-greater numbers of children in pre-school education may give a misleading impression. It is only a generation or two since large numbers went through the system and into unskilled, if generally available work, with little or no formal qualifications to show for the previous ten years. Judging by the extent of poor literacy and numeracy in the current adult population, many must have been simply going through the motions. The importance to every child's future prospects of what you do at school, and from age 3 or 4, is a relatively recent idea.

Despite all the current concerns about 'truancy', unauthorised absence (the correct term) has risen only very slightly since the current recording system was introduced over ten years ago. Attendance has certainly risen more. Children are having less time off than they used to (NAO 2005). But somehow the absence seems to matter more now. Even if a commitment to regular attendance cannot be assumed, it has certainly become the majority view, with an ever-increasing period of time over which the child is required to participate, with an expectation that either training or further education should be the norm even beyond that.

Critics might suggest that if our education system was good enough, everyone would want their children to go anyway! But some element of legal encouragement has always been retained, and, along with it, the existence of the 'School Board Man' (sic) and their contemporary equivalent in the Education Welfare Service, in order to encourage the reluctant. Parents and children have a daily choice. Even the most stimulating and well-organised school needs to be aware of what may need to be done to ensure their pupils attend as they should. Early intervention at Key Stages 1 and 2 may reduce the risk of greater problems later. The signals you send then can make a real difference.

Absence is not necessarily an indicator of major family problems or evidence of an antisocial attitude in either child or parent. Some children just skip school occasionally, perhaps showing an entirely natural avoidance of something difficult or less than exciting, without necessarily repeating the behaviour over again. Parents sometimes have other more urgent priorities to deal with and school just has to wait till tomorrow. Much use of attendance and absence procedures is just a routine response and many situations are capable of relatively easy resolution through prompt action by school staff.

However, some cases of non-attendance, perhaps an increasing number, are but the tip of an iceberg in which not being at school is only the presenting problem betraying something much greater underneath. There are many vulnerable groups of children who cannot be expected to attend school while all else crumbles in chaos around them. These include those whose families are in crisis; those experimenting with drugs, alcohol or other substances; those with major mental health needs; many children in the public care system; the victims of abuse and of discrimination; child carers; and those grappling with the implications of homelessness, acute poverty, and domestic violence and bullying. These children in particular will need 'joined-up' solutions to their problems.

The law seeks to be realistic in recognising that 100 per cent attendance is not necessarily required, allowing for 'sickness and other unavoidable cause' (Education Act 1996 s.444). There is considerable discretion, given primarily to head teachers but also, to a limited extent, to parents, that enables situations that are less than perfect to be regarded as nonetheless satisfactory. Education can take place away from the actual building in other settings or, increasingly, by means of IT and distance learning, as well as by traditional methods. It is often more appropriate to adopt a 'welfare' approach where children have complex needs or there is major disruption to their family life. But there has been some pressure on LAs from the DfES to use their statutory powers more extensively. This cannot be done without teachers so it is important that you know what these powers are and the context in which they operate.

Registration regulations

Registration should be a significant part of the school day. Attendance registers are legal documents, which is why they must be kept strictly in accordance with the regulations (Education Act 1996 s.434(6)). Should a parent be prosecuted for failing to ensure their child attends, head teachers will be required to account to the court for any discrepancies or mistakes in the register. Any dispute between the parent and the LA about whether, for example, a given absence should have been authorised, will require the personal evidence of the head teacher in explaining the criteria used.

As almost every classroom teacher at Key Stages 1 and 2 will be involved in actually marking the register, whether manually or by computer, schools *must* have written and consistently-applied attendance policies that enable parents to know what the rules are and which ensure good practice by all staff. The decision about whether or not to authorise an absence determines whether or not the parent is committing an offence. Many schools authorise too generously or may never have established clear policies and procedures that are consistently applied. It should be clear whose responsibility it is to make a decision and what procedures are in place for clarifying any uncertainties or challenging parents' explanations for absence.

Traditionally, registers always had to be marked at the beginning of each half-day session. This is still the requirement for the morning, but from 1998 the DFES gave schools some flexibility about when they can mark afternoon registers. This was intended to catch those who go missing during the afternoon, but also raises a number of problems and few schools have seen the need for change, although some schools have systems for lesson-by-lesson monitoring in addition to the sessional mark.

There are four registration categories, one of which must be used for every half-day session for every child of compulsory school age:

- present;
- authorised absent;
- unauthorised absent;
- approved educational activity.

This last category enables schools to count those who are away from the premises for a legitimate reason such as an educational visit as 'present' for statistical purposes. The previous regulations classed all those not on the premises as 'authorised absent', even if the child was where they were supposed to be. This was plainly unreasonable and this change has given schools a welcome flexibility.

Education Act 1996

This outlines the basic legal obligations on parents and replaced the relevant sections of the Education Act 1944 and the Education Act 1993 from 1 November 1996:

- duty on parents
  S.7 of the Education Act 1996 says, 'the parent of every child of compulsory school age shall cause him to receive efficient full-time education suitable –
  (a) to his age, ability and aptitude and
  (b) to any special educational needs he may have, either by regular attendance at school or otherwise'.
- prosecution of parents
  Parents (not children) commit an offence if a registered pupil does not attend 'regularly' (s.444(1)). This duty includes any adult looking after the child, even if they are not actually related (though not staff from public agencies). Technically, any absence is an offence, unless authorised by the school. Enforcement is the responsibility of the LA where the school is (not now the LA in which the child lives).
- Antisocial Behaviour Act 2003 and Education (Penalty Notices) (England) Regulations 2004
  New powers came into force during 2004 (in England only) that have given LAs the option of formalising their responses to non-attendance but without the need for a court appearance. A Penalty Notice, along similar lines to a speeding fine, enables a parent to discharge their liability for unauthorised absences by paying a penalty. Penalties are currently £50 if paid within 28

days or £100 if paid within 42 days. Payment must be made in full, not by instalments. A written warning must be issued first so most LAs are not using them 'on the spot' but as part of a procedure where the parent is deemed primarily responsible for the absence. This might be particularly in relation to younger children or the response might be targeted at a particular school with the support of the head teacher.

There is also the capacity for parents to be summonsed for the 'enhanced offence under s.444(1A) of 'parentally condoned unauthorised absence'. Some LAs may now use these more serious proceedings rather than s.444(1), where an actual court appearance is considered appropriate. Convictions at this level carry a maximum fine of £2,500 and up to three months in prison, though this is very rare. The effectiveness of prosecution has always been a matter of some debate. Research suggests that prosecution is effective in about two-fifths of cases in that the children concerned subsequently improved their attendance (NFER 2003). But many LA officers also report that the proceedings often make little difference, that fines may be unpaid or that the threat of court action is often more effective than actually going ahead with it.

Every school needs to establish a good working relationship with their Education Welfare Officer, especially about referral criteria and to clarify the relative responsibilities of school and LA staff. A Parenting Contract may often be suggested as the first formal step where parents are proving less than co-operative. Legal enforcement will be at the end of a long process, but should always be considered if problems are not being resolved. It is essential for everyone to maintain a focus on raising attendance and challenging absence as part of the everyday life of the school. Attendance should never be assumed; it always has to be promoted, encouraged and rewarded, just like any other achievement.

Task 8.4.1
Attendance 1

Analyse attendance and absence figures in your school. There should be plenty of data available from computerised records and DFES returns. Does the data identify any patterns or trends? Is attendance rising? Are some groups of pupils more likely to be absent? What might be the reasons for this? How much of the absence is authorised by the school, and for what reasons, e.g. family holidays? What is the balance between authorised and unauthorised absences? What does your analysis suggest about which children should be the focus for the school's attendance-raising strategy?

Task 8.4.2
Attendance 2

Devise an incentive scheme to raise attendance in a class or year group. What kinds of prizes might be appropriate and how would they be awarded? Will they go to the children with the best attendance or those who show most improvement? How will it work? Is it the children, or the parents, who need the encouragement? What difference might this make to the kinds of rewards available? How might peer pressure best be used to encourage those who find regular attendance difficult? If your scheme is used, make sure it's included in the school's attendance policy and all parents are made aware of it.

CHILD PROTECTION

Inter-agency procedures

Teachers are not required to be experts at recognising child abuse. That is not their responsibility any more than a doctor can assess a child's special educational needs or reading performance. Child protection is an inter-agency process from start to finish but all professionals involved must be clear about their own role, not act some other person's role. Despite a sometimes negative public perception, considerable progress has been made in recent years in child protection, but significant changes are also underway (CSCI 2005).

A very large percentage of child protection concerns arise at school (DoH 1995). This is not surprising. Children spend more time there than almost anywhere else; relationships with the adults there are important, especially to younger children. S.175, Education Act 2002, in force from 1 June 2004, requires staff in every school, whatever its management status (including the independent sector), to co-operate with the agreed local inter-agency procedures for safeguarding and protecting children. In ensuring that this legal duty is carried out, the governors or proprietors must have regard to the guidance issued by the DFES in September 2004 (see Further Reading). Other LA officers may also be involved, but all school staff should expect to take individual responsibility for child protection in their own right.

The task of teaching (and non-teaching) staff is:

- to be sufficiently confident to recognise those situations that give most cause for concern;
- to refer them appropriately within the school's own and inter-agency procedures and support the child's need for longer-term protection if required.

Categories of abuse

Concerns about possible child abuse must be identified under four standard categories as outlined in government guidance *Working Together to Safeguard Children*, The Stationery Office (new edition expected 2006):

- *physical abuse* non-accidental cuts, bruises, fractures, wounds, burns, bites, poisoning etc.;
- *emotional abuse* extreme denial of love, care, attention and security;
- *sexual abuse* not only sexual activity but may involve video, photography or 'grooming' (preparation for abuse) and the internet;
- *neglect* failure to meet a child's basic need for food, warmth, protection, safety etc.

Other welfare concerns are more appropriately seen as 'children in need' under s.17 of the Children Act 1989. With parental agreement, referral may be made to other agencies for support on a voluntary basis. This process should be made easier in the near future with the introduction of a Common Assessment Framework that will enable all professionals involved with the family to work together more effectively in meeting the child's needs according to agreed thresholds of concern. Schools will be central to this process. If your concern suggests the child may be at risk of 'significant harm' under s.47 of the Children Act 1989 as in the four categories outlined above, parental consent is not required to make a referral in the child's best interests. Parents should be informed of the referral, unless this would put the child at increased risk of harm. But prevention of abuse is always preferable to waiting for a more serious incident.

The curriculum

A child protection concern may arise indirectly rather than by direct disclosure or because a member of staff sees an injury. Almost any subject area contains the potential for the child to choose that moment to share what is on their mind. Children generally trust their teachers and do not always see the significance of what they are saying. They may write about their experiences at home in a poem; or give an indication in a practical lesson that the nutrition standards are unacceptable. They may talk about how their parents punish them or use language that is attempting to describe sexual activity when faced with a conventional topic such as what they did in the holidays or the worst day of their life. Children choose to disclose when they are ready; so the teacher must always be ready too, even if 'child abuse' was nowhere near their expectations for that particular lesson.

Making referrals

Referrals to a social worker or the police would normally be made by the school's senior designated teacher on receipt of information from the child, a parent, a colleague or other source, though action may still be required even if they are not available. If you have concerns about a child, you should discuss them with the designated teacher to clarify whether referral under child protection procedures is appropriate. Always pass on disclosures of abuse under the four categories above and any related allegations, together with information about children with significant or suspicious injuries.

You do not have to establish first whether or not it is abuse; that is the job of the investigating agencies, not the school. Evidence of possible physical abuse makes a referral particularly urgent, partly as the child may need medical attention but also because any injury needs to be seen and assessed by a qualified medical practitioner as quickly as possible. These cases should be raised as early as possible in the school day to give maximum time for a response while the child is safe at school.

Children should not be promised confidentiality, or if you do promise it, be prepared to break it if the child then makes a disclosure of alleged abuse or you have other information that requires you to use the school's child protection procedures. You cannot protect such a child by yourself. Written records should be kept carefully within the school. When the child changes school, records should be passed to the new designated teacher as far as is possible. The ideal place for the child's whole protection history is in their current school.

Investigation and assessment

Following referral from any source, the social worker (jointly with the police if potential criminal charges are involved) will carry out an assessment of risk to the child. This will usually involve them contacting other relevant agencies that know the family, including other schools, and may include a strategy discussion/meeting with key professionals. The social worker will decide when to contact the family (it is always helpful if they advise the school accordingly and the referrer should receive a notification of the outcome of this initial assessment, even if no further action is being taken). If necessary they will make home visits, involve the child's parents, arrange to have the child medically examined, etc. Where the child is old enough, they may be interviewed on video about what has happened. This tape can then be used as evidence in any subsequent court proceedings.

Many cases are resolved quickly with practical advice and support to the parents, or programmes to deal, for example, with alcohol abuse or domestic violence. Other cases will require much longer involvement where sex offences or severe family breakdown and neglect are involved. Court proceedings may be taken or arrangements made for the child to be cared for by other members of the family or foster carers. Where children continue to live in situations of risk, a child protection conference may be called.

Initial Child Protection Conferences and Child Protection Plans

Conferences are often required at short notice. It is essential that a representative of the school attends the conference for any school-aged child, even if other education officers have also been invited. A written report may be required. The conference is an opportunity for all professionals involved with the family to consult about how they may best be protected and, in particular, to decide whether the child needs an on-going Child Protection Plan. If so, a Keyworker (social worker) and a Core Group will be appointed – someone from the child's school should always be a member of the Core Group. An outline Plan will be drawn up immediately and the Core Group will all be responsible for meeting regularly and for undertaking a more extensive assessment.

When a child has a Child Protection Plan, the senior designated teacher must decide who needs to be told. This should be on a 'need to know' basis and should certainly include the person with day-to-day responsibility for marking their attendance record. Procedures should be agreed about what to do if the child is absent or if further concerns are identified at school. The child's status should be reviewed every six months, after the first three months.

Policy issues

There must be a written policy for child protection within the school, which should be made known to all staff and parents. This will set out general principles, the duty to make referrals etc., including wider issues such as staff and volunteer appointments, the prohibition of corporal punishment, the use of restraint, curriculum issues and complaints procedures. Staff should have access to clear procedures within the school covering required documentation and defined responsibilities.

Ensuring such policy and procedures are in place is the responsibility of the Senior Management Team, the governing body and the designated senior teacher who must all work together to ensure a co-ordinated approach. Training should be available, especially to newly-appointed staff, both teaching and non-teaching, as part of the induction process. This will normally be part of the role of the designated teacher but additional training from LA and other agency specialists may also be available.

Allegations against teachers or other staff

Some child abuse cases raise additional issues because the abuse is complex, involves a number of adults or children, or because the person who is the subject of the allegation is a professional or volunteer in a position of trust rather than a parent. This is the context in which any concern about an adult within a school will be investigated. There is always the possibility that someone may seek to exploit their position as a consequence of relationships established at a school. Especially since Soham, it is essential that a school's child protection policy and procedures include an awareness of such a risk.

There is understandable concern among many teachers that careers may be irreparably damaged on the basis of flimsy or malicious allegations by children. This is actually extremely rare; most allegations have their roots in an incident of some kind, though some do end up only as 'unproven' one way or the other which is generally unsatisfactory. It is always better for a school to anticipate possible risks and to seek to prevent all reasonable risk of misunderstandings and false allegations. Proper policy and procedures are also likely to deter any individual seeking to use the school as a basis for inappropriate relationships with pupils. Agreed procedures should be applied to both teaching staff and to any volunteers and non-teaching staff who have direct contact with children, especially if they will be unsupervised or involved in high-risk activities such as supervising children dressing and undressing or being alone with children in cars, etc.

It is important to draw a distinction between complaints and allegations that involve misconduct or unprofessionalism, and those which specifically raise child protection concerns. Any concern which involves the possibility of physical abuse, emotional abuse or sexual abuse should always be discussed by the head teacher with senior LA officers and advice taken from outside the school. If child protection procedures are needed, investigations are carried out by social workers and the police as with any other referral. Head teachers, governors and LA officers must not carry out investigations themselves in these circumstances. If inter-agency action is required, there will be a strategy meeting at an early stage to agree a corporate approach. The views of the head teacher on any incident will be listened to carefully at this stage.

Corporal punishment, restraint and staff conduct

Teachers may occasionally need reminding that they are prohibited by law from using any form of punishment intended to inflict pain, including 'hitting, slapping or shaking' a child. Neither may they 'intimidate or humiliate' a child or make them carry out any kind of 'degrading punishment' (ss.548–50 Education Act 1996). This is a higher standard than that applied to parents. Teachers are permitted to use 'reasonable restraint' to protect a child or other children, in ways which are defined by clear, written procedures within the school.

Parents must be informed of the legitimate use of restraint where the head teacher is satisfied that the member of staff has acted appropriately. If parents are not satisfied, they may still choose to initiate an investigation under child protection procedures. These issues are considered in DfEE Circular 10/98 *Section 550A of the Education Act 1996: The Use of Force to Control or Restrain Pupils*, which every teacher should have read. It may also help to agree a staff code of conduct to avoid the risk of any misunderstanding about, for example, sharing private mobile phone numbers or meeting up with pupils outside school.

Task 8.4.3
Child protection 1

Carry out an evaluation of child protection procedures in a school where you are working. What information was made available to you as part of your induction? Is there a written policy and who knows about it? Are there children with a Child Protection Plan and, if so, what does this mean for their class teacher? Does the school, in your judgement, meet all the requirements of Circular 0027/2004 (see Further Reading) and what strengths and weaknesses have you identified?

<table>
<tr><td>Task 8.4.4
Child protection 2</td></tr>
</table>

You have been asked to provide a report on a child for a child protection conference. Ask to see a report that has been produced by another member of the school staff and consider what it includes. What do you see as the most important information for a school report to contain? Talk to the teacher or other representative who submitted the report and attended the conference and ask them what it felt like. If possible, attend a conference yourself, if only as an observer. Remember the need for careful confidentiality in all these discussions.

SUMMARY

These may not be the issues that initially attracted you to the idea of being a teacher. Perhaps you thought that other people would be responsible for these sensitive areas. It is true that teachers are primarily employed to teach and that schools may now contain a variety of other professionals in a supportive role, but the wider pastoral care of pupils still cannot happen without you. It will only enhance your effectiveness in the classroom if you can show the child that you understand them as a person. It may just have to be you who is needed to respond to a serious concern for their welfare. That is an immense privilege but one for which it pays to be well prepared.

ANNOTATED FURTHER READING

DfES Circular, *Safeguarding Children in Education*, 0027/2004, issued in September 2004 in conjunction with s.175 Education Act 2002. Available at: www.teachernet.gov.uk/childprotection. This Circular provides comprehensive guidance to schools on safeguarding and should be the basis of all local policy and procedures.

DfES, *Every Child Matters: Change for Children* (2004) and *Change for Children in Schools* (2004). The original report and subsequent additions are available at www.everychildmatters.gov.uk. These documents form part of the government's detailed response to the Laming Report into the death of Victoria Climbie, alongside the Children Act 2004.

DoH booklet, *What To Do if You're Worried a Child is Being Abused*. Free copies can be ordered by email: doh@prolog.uk.com or tel: 08701 555 455 quoting reference 31815. The designated teacher should ensure that copies are available in every school. This booklet explains the inter-agency child protection system and the role of the various professionals involved.

NSPCC (2003) *Learning to Protect: A Child Protection Resource Pack for Teacher Training*. Provides a range of activities and resources to support teaching and learning on child protection in Initial Teacher Training.

Reid, K. (2002) *Truancy: Working with Teachers, Pupils and Schools*, RoutledgeFalmer. A comprehensive and practical guide to strategies for raising school attendance.

Whitney, B. (2004) *Protecting Children: A Handbook For Teachers and School Managers*, RoutledgeFalmer. A comprehensive guide to the responsibilities of schools across the Safeguarding agenda.

REFERENCES

CSCI (Commission for Social Care Inspection) (2005) *Safeguarding Children: The Second Joint Chief Inspectors, Report on Arrangements to Safeguard Children*, London: CSCI.

DoH (Department of Health) (1995) *Child Protection: Messages from Research*, London: HMSO.

NAO (National Audit Office) (2005) *Improving School Attendance in England*, Norwich: TSO.

NFER (National Foundation of Educational Research) (2003) *School Attendance and the Prosecution of Parents: Effects and Effectiveness*, Slough: NFER.

Your Professional Development

Unit 9.1

Applying for Jobs and Preparing for Your Induction Year

Jane Medwell

INTRODUCTION

Your initial teacher training is only the first step in your career. Completing it is rather like completing your driving licence – you will be safe to teach a class but will still have plenty to learn about teaching and very limited experience to draw upon. The next step in your training comes during your year as a Newly Qualified Teacher (NQT). Towards the end of your training you will devote considerable energy to finding the right job for you. This is a job that you feel happy in and one that offers you the professional development you need to become a better teacher. By preparing your Career Entry and Development Profile thoughtfully, you can ensure you get the support you need in your NQT year. This unit should help you.

OBJECTIVES

By the end of this unit you should:

- understand the role of the NQT year;
- know how to look for a teaching post;
- be able to begin to write job applications;
- be able to start work on your CEDP;
- have considered the priorities for your NQT year.

APPLYING FOR A TEACHING JOB

During your training you may start to apply for jobs. This will necessitate some personal decisions about what area you aim to work in, in what sort of school you would like to work, how far your domestic commitments allow you to commute each day and whether you want a full-time post. This is the time to be realistic because your first teaching post is so important. It is no use finding the perfect post if you have to leave for work at 6am every day to get there, or doing your NQT year in a school that does not suit you and your educational beliefs. Deciding where to apply and what sort of schools to apply to is the first step.

Jobs suited to NQTs (starting in September) are advertised at any time from the previous October to the June or July before you start. If you have a target area you must not miss the job advertisement for that area or job. Teaching posts are usually advertised by individual schools or by NQT 'pools', whereby a group of schools recruit together. You must make sure you check the systems in place in your target areas – it is not uncommon for schools to advertise individually *and* be part of an education authority pool. Look first at the websites for the borough or LEA you are interested in. This will tell you where they advertise teaching posts – usually the Times Educational Supplement (Friday), a local newspaper and online. You may be able to arrange to have regular bulletins sent to you directly from the LEA.

When you respond to an advertisement the school or education authority will send you an information pack and details of how to apply for a job. Your ITT provider will give you further information about how to apply for a job and you should also look at all the information offered by your union.

Applying for jobs will take time and raises a number of issues for you:

- you will want to use your training experience positively in writing your application;
- you will need time out from your course for preparation, visits and interviews;
- you will want to ask for references and ensure your referees are clear about what is required.

USING YOUR EXPERIENCE POSITIVELY IN YOUR APPLICATION FOR A TEACHING POST

You will be given support in applying for a teaching post in your initial Teacher Training programme but it is important that your application includes insights from your ITT course and placements because this shows that you can learn from your experiences. When you write in response to an advertisement for a teaching post or for details of an NQT pool you will receive a person specification for the job. This may be general, simply listing a number of attributes sought in a successful applicant, such as appropriate teaching practice experience, ability to plan, deliver, monitor and evaluate children's learning, and so on. Alternatively, there may be very specific requirements associated with a school. As an NQT, you cannot become a curriculum co-ordinator in your NQT year but the school may well be seeking staff with particular areas of expertise.

There are two main types of written application for primary and early years teaching posts: the LEA or school application form, which usually includes a personal statement or letter of application, or your own CV and letter of application. The information pack you receive from the school or LEA will tell you what is required.

Complete application forms neatly and accurately and in a way that demonstrates enthusiasm. The usual rules for form filling apply: read the instructions carefully and follow them; write a draft first (and keep it for future reference); do not leave gaps but write N/A (Not Applicable); check all your dates and have all your information to hand; make sure your writing is neat and correctly spelled and make sure your personal statement (or letter) is effective. Plan plenty of time to fill in your application and make sure you have done a thorough review of your record of professional development or training plan.

Task 9.1.1
Reviewing your progress towards the standards

You review your progress throughout your training, but just as you apply for jobs is a key review point, so we suggest you conduct a thorough review just before you complete an application. Doing this helps you to:

- remember and revisit all the training tasks you have done – assignments, school tasks and even visits, some of which may have taken place a while ago;
- bring to mind all the training opportunities you took up on placement;
- identify progress you have made towards demonstrating the standards for the award of QTS;
- decide what constitutes evidence of your progress towards the standards for the award of QTS and to store this appropriately;
- prepare a portfolio of work in preparation for a job interview (see below);
- begin to formulate your areas of interest, strength and weakness in your NQT year (see below).

Go through your record of professional development (or training plan), reviewing your placement reports and academic work against the Professional Standards. Identify four areas where you have made progress and four areas in which you would like to improve.

You will be required to write either a supporting statement or a letter of application as part of an application form. The first thing you should do to prepare this is to examine thoroughly the person specification and/or job description to work out what the school or LEA is looking for. Then read the instructions for completing the form or letter very carefully. Filling out this form is a chore but it is your chance to market your skills. Do not be too modest or make impossible, exaggerated claims. The completed form will be slightly embarrassing, because it spells out your achievements and qualities, but it should not be untruthful. Mentors, personal tutors and teachers will help you to prepare your application and you should discuss a draft of your letter of application, supporting statement or CV (whichever is requested) with your tutor or mentor. Arrange a time in advance, as you cannot expect staff necessarily to be available at short notice.

There are many ways of writing your letter of application or supporting statement and there is no perfect template, but there are some key points you should bear in mind. Give a brief overview of your training (but do not repeat everything you have put in the application form) and mention your degree and any relevant projects, experiences or previous work. It is important to identify why you would suit the post, so say why you are applying for this post in particular. Include any local links, faith issues or visits to the school.

Your teaching placements during training are very important, so reference to your formal school placements should include when you did the placement, what years you have taught and the level of responsibility you took, but do not use up all your letter space by repeating what you have put on the form. Refer to special features of the placement such as open plan schools or team teaching. You could also refer to your placements to illustrate an aspect of your learning or an enthusiasm you have developed during your training. Such references could be to examples of how you plan, teach, monitor and evaluate learning outcomes, behaviour management strategies, work with parents, etc.

Write a little about your vision or beliefs for early years or primary education and the principles that underpin your practice. This might include beliefs about how children learn, classroom management, teaching styles, etc. If you can illustrate with an example of how you have learnt this on your course or school placement this can be very effective. This sort of information gives the school a flavour of you as a teacher.

Another part of your letter will include details of your personal experiences: leisure activities, interests or involvement with children. Make these relevant to your work as a teacher and be explicit about what skills you have.

One of the easier ways to organise this information is to identify a number of subheadings taken from the person specification or job description such as:

- teaching experiences (placements);
- commitment to teaching;
- knowledge, skills and aptitudes;
- planning and organisation;
- strengths and interests;
- personal qualities.

Organise your information under these headings. You can then remove your subheadings and have a well organised letter to discuss with your mentor, tutor or careers adviser. Write in the first person, check your grammar and use interesting adverbs and adjectives to lift the text. If in doubt, ask a friend to proof read your letter before you talk to your mentor or tutor.

Task 9.1.2
Writing a letter of application

Use the person specification from a job ad you have been looking at to review your experience, qualifications and knowledge skills and aptitudes. Go through each point asking yourself:

- What evidence do I have that I meet this criterion?
- What have I learnt about this on my placements and in my course of study?
- What else do I need to be able to do to achieve this?
- Finally, ask yourself what you want to focus on in your continuing professional development during the induction year.

Use the headings below to organise your information:

- teaching experiences (placements);
- commitment to teaching;
- knowledge, skills and aptitudes;
- planning and organisation;
- strengths and interests;
- personal qualities.

Write a letter of application, of not more than two sides of A4, setting out your experience, knowledge, skills and aptitudes and views about education. Discuss this general draft with your mentor, tutor or teacher and ask them to tell you about the impact and impression it makes. This letter can then form the basis of other letters that are tailored to suit a particular post.

In applying for your first teaching post, you may find yourself writing a curriculum vitae (CV) for the first time. Your CV sets out the important information about you on two sides of A4. Preparing for this is similar to preparing to fill in a form but you will need to print it out on good quality, white paper. As with the letter, prepare a general CV well in advance, but adapt it for each application so that it matches the person specification.

There are some things you can omit from a CV, such as your date of birth, age, marital status or ethnic origin. Photographs of yourself are not necessary for CVs for teaching posts and can trigger subconscious prejudice. Do not include failures on your CV – aim to keep it focused on what you have achieved. You should also leave out previous salary information or reasons for changing jobs, which are irrelevant.

The following things should be included on your CV:

- Contact details. Make sure that these are guaranteed routes to reach you, so if you have an email address that you rarely check, do not include it. Ideally, include your postal address, any telephone numbers you have (landline and mobile) and your email address if you will check it frequently.
- Your gender, if it is not obvious from your name.
- A short skills summary or supporting statement (see below).
- Your education. This is best organised as follows: primary, secondary, further, higher.
- Your qualifications, listed with the most recent first, including results.
- Your work experience and placement experiences – most recent first (any positions you held more than about ten years ago can be left out).
- Interests – only real and genuine ones, e.g. any sports in which you actively participate. If these hobbies and interests can convey a sense of your personality, all the better. Include any non-teaching qualifications that may have arisen from your hobbies or interests here too.
- Membership of professional associations (not including unions).
- Nationality, National Insurance Number and referee details can be included at the end of your CV.

A skills summary need only be around 200 words, but you can still cover a lot of ground. It should be written in the first person. Every word must have a use and grammar should be immaculate. Do not just repeat what experience you have had – your achievements, accountability and competence are more important and this is where you can really bring these out. Aim to give a sense of your creativity, personal management and integrity: the reader will want to see that you have strong communication skills and are perhaps even leadership potential. When writing a skills summary some people prefer to include a short bulleted list of around six key skills.

With only two sides of A4 the layout of a CV is important and you need to be economical with space. While the page should not look cluttered, excess space will look messy and ill thought-through.

- Present your contact details across the top of the first page (like a letterhead) to preserve space.
- Use a clear, standard font such as Times New Roman or Arial.
- Avoid abbreviations unless they are universally understood.

If you really cannot fit everything onto two sides of A4, try reducing the font size slightly. This will mean the print is still large enough to read, but will give you a little more room to play with. There really is not too much difference between 12 and 11 point in terms of readability.

When you have designed your CV on screen, print off a draft version and try to view it through fresh eyes. Is it likely to grab the attention of a reader within a few seconds? Is it visually pleasing? Are there any errors? It is a good idea to ask someone else to cast an eye over it as it is easy to miss typos on documents you have been working on yourself.

Writing a CV is not a one-off task. Once you have completed your CV, you will need to keep it up to date.

REFERENCES

You will usually be asked to supply the names, positions and contact details of two referees. The first should be a senior member of staff in your ITT provider. Check carefully who this should be. It is common for universities to use the name of the head of department, even though your tutor will probably actually write the reference. It is essential to get this name right for two reasons. If you do not get a first reference from your ITT provider the job advertiser will usually assume you have something to hide. Second, the reference system in a large ITT provider will be geared up for a swift response but it will only work if you get the right name. The wrong name will slow down your reference and may put you at a disadvantage.

Your second referee should usually be from your placement school – your mentor, class teacher or head teacher. Ask if the mentor or head teacher is prepared to offer you a reference. In most cases a reference is offered gladly. Professionals will not write a bad reference for anyone, but would decline to offer a reference if they could not truthfully recommend you. Mentors and head teachers will never decline to offer a reference simply because they do not want the effort.

Be quite clear who you intend to name as a referee. You might want to discuss this with your mentor or head so that you get the best reference. Will you name the mentor him or herself or the head teacher? Check that you know the full name, title and professional position of your referee and make sure that the mentor or head has your contact details and that you have theirs. You should contact them to let them know when you use their name as a referee in any application. Be clear about anything you would like your referee to mention (such as participation in out of school events) or avoid mentioning, such as a disability or illness. Say when you expect to be applying for jobs and whether these will be exclusively teaching jobs or will include things like vacation jobs or voluntary work. It is a good idea to give your referee a copy of your CV and a summary of your strengths as part of the process of asking for a reference. Schools that you have applied to may ring your second referee for an informal reference, particularly if you are applying for a job locally. You want your referee to be prepared for this and speak warmly about you, rather than be surprised and feel caught out.

VISITS AND INTERVIEWS DURING YOUR TRAINING

When you are considering applying for a job you may be invited to look around the school or you may ask to look around the school. Some schools schedule specific times and take a large number of applicants around the school together. This sort of tour is a very good way to find out about a school and whether it will suit you. However, it can present problems because of the time it takes out of your placement or taught course, especially if you are applying for posts at some distance. You must consider the impact of absence from school or university on your training and the cumulative impact of multiple visits, particularly as this is often a time when you are on school placement. You have to complete a certain amount of placement time in school and take sustained responsibility for the class on final placement and a large number of visits could affect the outcome of your placement. It may be better to try to visit schools after the end of the school day, or to explain to schools that your placement commitments prevent you from visiting informally.

Paula Grey

Eastleigh Cottage, 35 Thornton Hill, Cardiff CF21 9DE

Telephone: 0128 213 3567, mobile: 07337 632077, email: Paulie@yahoo.com

I am a newly qualified teacher trained to teach across the curriculum with the 5–11 age group. My previous work experience as an accountant has enabled me to develop an understanding of management in a large multi-national corporation as well as demonstrable communication skills. Part of my role was the delivery of internal training for new staff. During my initial teacher training I taught in an inner-city KS1 class and in two KS2 classes in a school with a large multi-racial population. In addition to my teaching I ran a successful 'Get Into Reading' after-school workshop for parents which crossed age and cultural boundaries and was recognised by the head and governors as a constructive addition to the wider school culture.

Education

Primary:	1982–1988 Abby Primary School, Cardiff
Secondary:	1988–1993 Newport High School for Girls, Newport
Further:	1993–1995 Newport Sixth Form College, Newport
Higher:	1995–1998 University of Reading BA
	1998–2004 Membership of the Society of Chartered Accountants
	2004–2005 Institute of Education, University of London PGCE

Qualifications

PGCE: Primary

Degree: Archaeology and Statistics 2.1

A levels: Mathematics A, Statistics A, Physics B, General studies B

GCSEs: Mathematics A, English literature A, English language B, Physics B, History A, ICT A, Art B, Geography B, French A, Biology B

Professional development

During my initial teacher training I completed an LEA-run 'Levelling Mathematics' course and attended a 'Developing Storysacks' training day.

Work Experience

2002–2003:	ITT placements: High Five School, Camden and Nelson Mandela Primary School, Westminster
1998–2002:	British International Bank, London, Accountant
1995–1998:	Vacation positions with Marks and Spencer and Dillons, Cwmbran

Interests

I have run a local Brownies group for some years. I also run to keep fit and have completed the London marathon.

Additional qualifications

Full, clean driving licence

South Glamorgan County Junior Football Coaching

Nationality British

National Insurance Number TY123456B

Referees available on request

Figure 9.1.1 A sample CV

You will almost always be given a tour of the school prior to interview and you would have the opportunity to withdraw from the interview after this if you did not think the school would suit you. If you apply for a job through a teaching pool you will usually go for an interview for the pool first and may then be invited to look around schools that have jobs available. This is a different sort of school visit from the informal pre-interview visit mentioned above because you will be looking at a school to see whether you would take a job there. You should go on these visits but be aware of the time consideration mentioned above.

When you have applied for a post and are invited to interview during course time, you should ask your tutor or mentor for permission to attend, thus missing the taught sessions or school placement that day. In practice this is a courtesy and you will always be given permission to attend interviews. It is a good idea to ask your mentor, tutor or class teacher to help you to prepare for interview and such preparation might take a number of forms:

- Discuss 'hot' topics in the educational press or recent initiatives in school. Identify and discuss issues in the Times Educational Supplement or another publication with a colleague, tutor or teacher. This will help you to explore the issues from another perspective. Consider what the effects of new ideas are for teachers, schools and children.
- Role-play a 'mock' interview with the tutor, mentor, teacher or another trainee. This can help you to conquer nerves and prepare your interview manner. Practise framing your replies at interview – a pause to think, for example, rather than rushing in and babbling. What sort of body language do you want to exhibit – or avoid? Consider how you will conclude the interview and what your final impression is to be.
- Ask a tutor or teacher to help you plan any teaching you are asked to do as part of your interview, but make sure you go to them with plenty of ideas and suggestions. It is not uncommon to be asked to teach something to a class. You will not be able to prepare a perfect lesson because you do not know the children, but you can still use a lesson plan to show that you know the relevant curricula, have good ideas, know a range of teaching strategies, are aware of a range of resources and have a good manner with children. Your tutor or mentor may be able to spot obvious faux pas or overambitious plans if you ask to discuss them.

INTERVIEW PORTFOLIOS

As a trainee you will be maintaining a training plan or record of professional development that contains evidence to demonstrate your achievement of the standards. This will contain placement assessment reports, observation notes, written assignments, mentor meeting notes and other evidence.

You may be asked to take this training plan or record with you to interview or to bring a portfolio. Even if you are not asked to bring a portfolio you may want to do so. You can offer this to your interviewers – they do not have to spend much time looking at it but it does indicate you are well prepared and professional.

An interview portfolio can be a substantial document but, more usually, is a slim document containing some of the following:

- Title and content page, preferably with a photo of you in a teaching situation.
- Concise CV.
- Placement assessment reports (one or more).
- A really good lesson plan or two, some examples of the work associated with the lesson and the lesson evaluation.

- A mentor, tutor or class teacher observation of a lesson that picks out a strength.
- A sample mentor meeting summary (to show you are focused and organised).
- An example of a written piece of work (and the marking sheet) if relevant.
- A few photos of you teaching. Choose these carefully as you really want to present a particular image. Generally you might choose one photo of you 'at the front' teaching a large group or class, one of you looking sensitive with a group and, ideally, one of you teaching elsewhere – perhaps on a school visit or outside! Remember, choose photos to suit that job. If the school is very ICT conscious, make sure there is a picture with you using ICT. If the school is keen to improve its physical education, a photo of your gym session would not go amiss! Make sure you follow your placement school policy on photo use and that the school, teachers and children are not identifiable.
- One or two photos of displays, school visits you have been on, after school clubs or assemblies you have done.
- Any evidence of your special interests – coaching certificates, first-aid, cookery, etc.

In practice, interview panels do not spend much time on interview portfolios and usually just flick through the content, so consider how you can create the best impression to someone who does this (the flick factor). For example, anything on the back of facing pages is unlikely to be seen, so either put less important pages here, or have a single sided portfolio with all pages facing the reader. Make sure your photos are well displayed, as they have a disproportionate impact. Although your portfolio may not command much time or attention, by preparing it you are not only demonstrating professionalism but also getting the chance to present a tailored image of your achievements to the panel, in addition to your written application.

INDUCTION FOR NEWLY QUALIFIED TEACHERS

Induction for newly qualified teachers (NQTs) is compulsory, follows initial teacher training and is the foundation for continuing professional development throughout your career. The induction period must be undertaken by NQTs who wish to work in maintained schools and non-maintained special schools. The induction period may also be done while working in independent schools but not all of them offer this. You can usually complete induction part-time, but it will take longer than the usual year. Check when you apply for a job, as failure to do a recognised induction will mean you do not gain QTS. You do not have to complete your induction period immediately after your initial teacher training, but time limits apply and you should check these on the Training and Development Agency for Schools (TDA) website (www.tda.gov.uk/induction). In the same way, not all types of supply work count towards NQT induction, so you must check this.

During the induction period you have to demonstrate you have continued to meet the standards of QTS, and met all the induction standards. You will have an individualised programme of support during the induction year from a designated induction tutor. This includes observations of your teaching by school staff and induction tutors, you observing more experienced teachers in different settings, and a professional review of progress at least every half term. You will also have the opportunity to attend school-centred in-service training provision and, often, external courses. During your induction year you will not teach more than 90 per cent of a normal timetable, to allow your induction to take place.

The head is responsible with appropriate bodies (for maintained schools and non-maintained special schools this is the LEA, and for independent schools it is either any LEA in England or a special body, the Independent Schools Council Teacher Induction Panel) and will make a final recommendation as to whether you have passed or failed your induction period. The appropriate body makes the final decision, and there is a right of appeal to the General Teaching Council for England (GTCE). The revised DfES guidance on induction, The Induction Support Programme for Newly Qualified Teachers (Reference: DfES/0458/2003), is now available online at www.tda.gov.uk/induction. You should ensure you check it.

THE CAREER ENTRY AND DEVELOPMENT PROFILE

The Career Entry and Development Profile is your key induction tool. It is the document you use to guide the process of reflection and review as you complete your initial teacher training and go through your induction year. You will notice that the headings of the standards for the award of QTS apply not only to your initial teacher training but also to your induction year, which is guided by the induction standards. The CEDP document suggests prompt questions that can be asked at the three key transition points:

- the end of Initial Teacher Training (Transition Point 1);
- the beginning of your NQT year (Transition Point 2);
- the end of your NQT year (or longer for part-time teachers) (Transition Point 3).

The personal development profile or record of professional development you have maintained throughout your initial teacher training will help you to summarise your achievements and identify areas for further work. These can be turned into targets for Transition Point 1 in the Career Entry and Development Profile.

The CEDP is prepared annually by the TDA and a hard copy will be given to you by your ITT provider near to the end of your training. It is also available as a package of online materials that you can access in advance. The webpages at www.tda.gov.uk provide information on the CEDP and induction in general. Here you can find descriptions of the processes that you will be undertaking at each of the three transition points. The online materials have interactive elements and sample formats for recording your responses, setting objectives, and writing action plans.

As you come to the end of your initial teacher training programme, you will want to think about how far you have come in your professional development. This process is likely to be a natural part of your initial teacher training programme. Your ITT provider will also help you to understand your own role in your induction. The Transition Point 1 section of the CEDP will help you to think about your experience from before, during and outside your formal training programme, including your placements, and to identify your key achievements and aspirations in relation to teaching.

You should aim to use the CEDP to set targets that:

- reflect and build on the strengths in your practice;
- develop aspects of the teacher's role in which you are particularly interested;
- provide more experience, or build up your expertise, in areas where you have developed to a more limited extent so far.

At Transition Point 1, the CEDP poses focus questions that you should reflect on. You are not expected to write lengthy answers to each question. It is the processes of reflection and professional discussion with your course tutor or mentor that are important and these will be reflected in the notes you make. The main questions for Transition Point 1 are:

- At this stage, which aspect(s) of teaching do you find most interesting and rewarding? What has led to your interest in these areas? How would you like to develop these interests?
- As you approach the award of QTS, what do you consider to be your main strengths and achievements as a teacher? Why do you think this? What examples do you have of your achievements in these areas?
- In which aspects of teaching would you value further experience in the future? For example: aspects of teaching about which you feel less confident, or where you have had limited opportunities to gain experience; areas of particular strength or interest on which you want to build further. At the moment, which of these areas do you particularly hope to develop during your induction period?
- As you look ahead to your career in teaching, you may be thinking about your longer-term professional aspirations and goals. Do you have any thoughts at this stage about how you would like to see your career develop?

You will record your responses to these questions in one of the formats offered for the CEDP Transition Point 1. You do not have to use all the sample formats – you choose the one that suits you best. Each format helps you to focus your thoughts about your experience so far and is a place for you to collate conclusions based on the evidence from your record of professional development or training plan. As a rough guide, three to five points for each of the main questions is about right in terms of offering a good range of material at the start of your induction year (Transition Point 2). Although the presentation of the CEDP is not its most important aspect, it is the document you will be taking to show your induction tutor, so you may want to word process your answers and include evidence. This shows your induction tutor not only your IT skills, but your professional approach.

Task 9.1.3
Using your record of professional development to prepare your CEDP

Note down your response to the questions above, where you might find evidence to support your thinking, and/or the reasoning that led you to this response. You will want to draw on evidence that is already available in your record of professional development or training plan, for example:

- reports on your teaching during your placements;
- observation reports written by your mentor, class teacher or course tutor;
- examples of your planning for placement;
- records of targets and objectives set during your ITT programme;
- your own audits of your progress towards the QTS standards;
- course assignments or subject audits.

Task 9.1.4
Framing your answers professionally

Consider an excerpt from the answers to some of the CEDP questions noted by Sophie and Alex, below:

- As you approach the award of QTS, what do you consider to be your main strengths and achievements as a teacher?

Sophie: I think I am a caring person and relate well to the children. I have really got on well with teachers but I have not had a chance to work with a TA. I want to work with a TA.

Alex: My placement reports identify my relationships with the children and teachers as one of my strengths. My final report suggested that good relationships with the children was part of my success at managing the class and my second placement report noted that I had worked particularly closely with other teachers in planning and assessment. I now want to develop my experience of planning for a TA in the classroom, as I have not experienced this.

- In which aspects of teaching would you value further experience in the future?

Sophie: I have not really had the chance to teach children with EAL during my placement and I would like to do much more of this and really cater for the EAL children in my class.

Alex: Although I have had training sessions and done an assignment about teaching children with EAL, my practical experience has been limited. In my induction year I would like to develop my experience of planning for and teaching children with EAL with the support of a more experienced teacher. I want to develop a reasonable repertoire of practical strategies.

Which answers:

- Use evidence well?
- Emphasise experience?
- Balance strengths and weaknesses?
- Offer the best indication of what action might be required?

The main point of Transition Point 1 is for you to review your achievements, needs and direction with a tutor or senior professional. Your ITT tutor should sign to confirm that your Transition Point 1 discussion took place and you cannot commence induction if you have not completed this meeting. A form for them to sign is included in the CEDP at Transition Point 1.

The CEDP is a mandatory part of ITT. It enables the school which employs you to:

- understand your strengths and experiences by the end of ITT;
- support your professional development through your NQT year;
- support constructive dialogue between NQTs and induction tutors;
- make links between induction, continuing professional development and performance management.

At Transition Point 2 (your meeting with your induction tutor) you will identify your targets and actions for the beginning of your induction, based on what is already in your CEDP.

If you have maintained a record of professional development or training plan as part of your ITT training, you will not find the CEDP totally unfamiliar. It simply continues the target setting, action, review cycle that you will be used to. Using your CEDP well will help you to make the most of your first job and your induction year.

SUMMARY

This unit gives you a broad overview of the whole topic of moving on in your professional development and training. You will need to allocate a substantial amount of time and attention to securing the right first teaching post, but when you have, you have real opportunities to develop as a professional. To do this you must take a clear eyed and realistic review of your achievements and further professional development needs and put these into your CEDP.

- When applying for jobs enlist the support of your mentor or tutor. They can look at applications and offer you mock interviews.
- Start considering applications early and allow plenty of time.
- Prepare each job application carefully, making sure you use the application format they want and that you set out your abilities and skills appropriately.
- Ensure you name the appropriate referees and that you have asked them if you may use them as referees.
- Use evidence from your training plan (or record of professional development) to prepare an interview portfolio. Make sure it presents the image you want for each job!
- The induction year has its own standards for induction and setting targets for these is a final placement task.
- Ensure you know about the CEDP before you meet your course tutor or mentor. You are responsible for preparing your CEDP. Use the website and your records to do this so that you go to the meeting with your ITT provider well organised and prepared.

ANNOTATED FURTHER READING

The Career Entry and Development Profile and support materials are available at:

www.tda.gov.uk/teachers/induction/cedp.

The Induction Support Programme for Newly Qualified Teachers (Reference: DfES/0458/2003) is now available at www.tda.gov.uk/induction. This site also provides detailed guidance about induction.

Detailed information about applying for a teaching post is available from the Association of Graduate Careers Advisory Services in the publication: AGCAS (2005) *Getting a Teaching Job In Schools: A Guide To Finding Your First Appointment.*

Most school vacancies are advertised in the *Times Educational Supplement* (Fridays) www.tesjobs.co.uk; *The Guardian* (Tuesdays) www.jobsunlimited.co.uk; *The Daily Telegraph* (Independent Schools) www.telegraph.co.uk; *The Independent* (Thursdays) www.independent.co.uk. Some of these operate an electronic job alert system.

For general information about teaching in the private sector:

Independent Schools Council Information Service (ISCIS) at www.iscis.uk.net.

Incorporated Association of Preparatory Schools (IAPS) at www.iaps.co.uk.

Your union is an excellent source of help, advice and support in applying for a teaching post:

www.teachersunion.org.uk (NASUWT); www.data.teachers.org.uk (NUT); www.askatl.org.uk (ATL).

Other useful online resources for finding a teaching post are available at:

www.eteach.com; www.teachernet.gov.uk; www.prospects.ac.uk.

Unit 9.2

Your Legal and Ethical Responsibilities

James Arthur

INTRODUCTION

What are the general legal and ethical challenges that will face you in your future teaching career? How can you as a new teacher be ethical and legal when you may not know with any certainty what it really means to be ethical and legal? These are questions that you need to address, but at the same time recognise that ethical dilemmas, by their very nature are not clear-cut. They can present themselves in schools as shapeless and difficult to grasp conundrums in response to which your immediate reaction is to ask a practical question – what should I do? You will need to consider and take note of the Teaching Standards, the General Teaching Council for England's Code of Professional Values and Practices and other education documents, such as the aims of the National Curriculum and the Statement of Values of the National Forum on Education and the Community. You will also need to understand that there is a value and legal framework against which ethical judgements are made in education. Teachers are not and neither should they be value neutral in their conduct. When you tell a pupil to stop shouting you are showing that you value the right over the wrong, the good over the bad. Teaching the difference between right and wrong is what teachers do much of the time despite the fact that society often blames teachers for failing to do exactly this. It is expected that you will be trustworthy in the sense that you will not misuse sensitive information provided to you about children and parents, that you will keep confidences and will respect all you have dealings with. Teaching is an ethical profession, it presupposes that something of value is to be taught and it is concerned with improving people – in other words personal formation.

This would appear to suggest that the teacher must require a 'good character' if they are to shape the character of the young. Indeed, on this view it is possible to argue that they should have better motives than ordinary people. Teachers share the moral obligations of any ordinary person, but ordinary people, however decent, do not have any specific moral or legal obligations of public service. This obligation to educate the young is not only morally good, but a morally better motive than simply teaching in order to earn a wage. However, this does not make a teacher a better person and a teacher may fail to live up to these ethical obligations. It is of course possible that many teachers do not enter teaching primarily from a motive of service to others. Carr (1993: 195) makes a very interesting point when he compares a doctor with a teacher. He suggests that a doctor may be dishonest and spiteful as a person, but that none of this may matter to a parent seeking his expertise to treat their child successfully. In contrast, a teacher who is competent and has the best teaching skills available in the subject they teach but is known to be privately a liar may well cause the parent to have grave reservations about placing their child in his care.

OBJECTIVES

At the end of this unit you should:

- understand the content of the General Teaching Council for England's Code of Professional Values and Practices;
- understand some of your legal and ethical responsibilities as a teacher;
- understand the difference and importance between statutory and non-statutory frameworks for teachers;
- understand the implications of being *in loco parentis*;
- have an understanding of the complexity of ethical decision-making in education.

ETHICS AND MORALITY IN THE CONTEXT OF TEACHING

Morality is about rules, principles and ideals which have the potential to guide the choices of our actions and which provide a basis for justifying or evaluating what we do. Ethics refers to the moral standards which apply to teaching as a profession. The term ethics therefore refers to the characteristic values of teachers. It attempts to describe the way in which their values are expressed through the practice of their role. In this sense the study and practice of professional ethics deals with practical questions about teaching and learning. The value of professional ethics is in the fact that teachers study the ethical principles and practices of the teaching profession in order to discover how belonging to that profession entails discovering what are the proper ways to act. The range of issues in teaching with ethical implications is immense. Ethics, for the teacher, involves both attitude and action. The former relates to the teacher's inner character or attitude as an ethical person: what one ought to become. Ethics for teachers will seek to motivate and guide them to become the best they can be as human beings. It should challenge teachers to be responsible and accountable for achieving certain attitudes and behaviours so as to achieve this ideal. The latter aspect of ethics for teachers is characterised by behaviour based on professional values and principles that enable teachers to evaluate and to amend their actions when they fall short of these values. How the teacher acts calls for choices to be made and this means being aware of the ethical dimensions of teaching and learning.

As you will discover, the teacher is not simply one whose contribution is limited to the teaching of a series of subjects and topics in the classroom. The demonstration of ethical conduct goes beyond the demonstration of your classroom competence. By concentrating on practical teaching skills and methods – the mechanics of teaching – it is possible to produce a teacher who is able to manage a class and instruct pupils. However, ethical teachers are aware of the larger social setting, have the flexibility to anticipate change, to adapt their methods to new demands, and when necessary to challenge the requirements laid upon them. Good teachers sense the importance of acquiring a wider perspective on human values. You need to be encouraged to develop a commitment to professional values that you are able to demonstrate through your personal example.

To gain qualified teacher status (QTS) you first need to demonstrate that you have met the Standards published by the government. The new Standards have an opening section on professional values and Denis Hayes has already addressed these standards in Unit 1.2. I will only comment here that Halstead and Taylor (2000: 177) recognise that two assumptions lie behind the Standards in professional values for teachers. First, that teachers see it as their role to influence the development of their pupils' values. Second, that pupils' values are 'influenced, consciously or otherwise by the example set by their teachers in their relationships, attitudes and teaching styles'. The very purpose of schools is to make a difference to the lives of pupils and so the moral and ethical dimensions of teaching provide the core value context in which teachers are located. You will be a role model, and it follows that when, in the classroom, you exhibit values or personal characteristics which are held to be at variance with what it is educationally desirable for pupils to acquire, then there will be cause for concern.

Teachers are still a major influence on pupils and the values they form. These values are reflected in what teachers choose to permit or encourage in the classroom – the way a teacher insists on accuracy in the work of pupils, or responds to their interests, conveys values which are clearly being introduced to those pupils. Teachers also represent the school's philosophy to the pupil and the larger public. A teacher cannot be entirely *neutral*, for pupils need the example of those who are not indifferent. They need teachers who are full of enthusiasms and commitments in their teaching. All the time teachers are teaching they are under examination by their pupils. Their characters are analysed; their fairness is examined; their inconsistencies are probed. Teaching is clearly a test of character for a student teacher. The teacher is a model of what it is to be a human being for pupils and no amount of competence in the class will compensate if the teacher is not an appropriate model.

Much has been written in the area of values in teaching and Wilson (1993: 113) speaks of moral dispositions when he says:

> Moral qualities are directly relevant to any kind of classroom practice: care for the pupil, enthusiasm for the subject, conscientiousness, determination, willingness to co-operate with colleagues and a host of others. Nobody, at least on reflection, really believes that effective teaching – let alone effective education – can be reduced to a set of skills; it requires certain dispositions of character. The attempt to avoid the question of what these dispositions are by emphasising pseudo-practical terms like 'competences' or 'professional' must fail.

The argument here is that teachers must provide support for classroom learning which goes beyond the mere mechanics of teaching. Elsewhere, Eraut (1994) argues that teachers have a moral commitment to serve the interests of their pupils by reflecting on their wellbeing and their progress and deciding how best these can be fostered. By doing this they contribute to the moral shaping of their pupils. As Sockett (1993: 14) observes: 'many teachers have a moral vision, a moral sense, and a moral motive however mixed up they may be in any individual'. Goodlad (1990) goes further, commenting that we need to address a fundamental void in the preparation of teachers:

> Teaching is fundamentally a moral enterprise in which adults ask and require children to change in directions chosen by the adults. Understanding teaching in this light confronts a teacher with potentially unsettling questions: By what authority do I push for change in the lives of these children? At what costs to their freedom and autonomy? Where does my responsibility for these young lives begin and end? How should I deal with true moral

dilemmas in which it is simply not possible to realise two goals or avoid two evils? How much pain and discomfort am I willing to endure on behalf of my student teachers? How are my own character flaws affecting the lives of others?

ETHICAL PRINCIPLES

Task 9.2.1
Ethical principles

Read the following principles and write down an example of how you might demonstrate these principles in the classroom or in school in any one week. You do not need to cover all of them, simply the ones that appear to you as relevant and appear in the week.

Teachers 'must':

- have intellectual integrity;
- have vocational integrity;
- show moral courage;
- exercise altruism;
- exercise impartiality;
- exercise human insight;
- assume the responsibility of influence;
- exercise humility;
- exercise collegiality;
- exercise partnership;
- exercise vigilance with regard to professional responsibilities and aspirations.

This list clearly demonstrates the ethical nature and obligations of teaching. Ethical issues are at the heart of teaching and are concerned with the way teaching is practised, organised, managed and planned. It is also inherently political because of the contested nature of teaching within the context of a state-sponsored education system.

THE CODE OF PROFESSIONAL VALUES AND PRACTICES

The introduction of the General Teaching Council for England's (GTC(E)) new *Code of Professional Values and Practices* (2002) makes clear that the role of the teacher is 'vital, unique and far reaching'. It states that: 'This Code sets out the beliefs, values, and attitudes that make up teacher professionalism'. It is recognised that many who are attracted to the profession have a 'strong sense of vocation'. The introduction concludes by stating that the teaching profession works within the framework of the law and within the framework of equal opportunities for all 'respecting individuals regardless of gender, marital status, religion, colour, race, ethnicity, class, sexual orientation, disability and age'. Unlike the teaching Standards, the GTC(E) Code does not as yet have notes of guidance in the areas covered in the Code, but the GTC(E) are developing such notes and student teachers need to make themselves aware of them. The actual Code consists of six sections and describe the professional values that underpin the practice of teaching in English schools. The Code encourages productive partnerships with parents, governors, professionals and between teachers themselves. In relation to pupils the Code seeks high expectations on the part of teachers and expects them to demonstrate the characteristics they are trying to inspire in pupils, such as tolerance, honesty, fairness, patience, and concern for others. The Code makes reference to helping to raise standards of achievement of pupils and in many respects is exactly like the Standards for teaching issued by the government.

The GTC(E) says they are produced as a source of encouragement for teachers and we have reprinted them below:

General Teaching Council for England
Code of Professional Values and Practices

Young People as Pupils

Teachers have insight into the learning needs of young people. They use professional judgement to meet those needs and to choose the best ways of motivating pupils to achieve success. They use assessment to inform and guide their work.

Teachers have high expectations for all pupils, helping them progress regardless of their personal circumstances and different needs and backgrounds. They work to make sure that pupils develop intellectually and personally, and to safeguard pupils' general health, safety and well-being. Teachers demonstrate the characteristics they are trying to inspire in pupils, including a spirit of intellectual enquiry, tolerance, honesty, fairness, patience, a genuine concern for other people and an appreciation of different backgrounds.

Teaching Colleagues

Teachers support their colleagues in achieving the highest professional standards. They are fully committed to sharing their own expertise and insights in the interests of the people they teach and are always open to learning from the effective practice of their colleagues. Teachers respect the rights of other people to equal opportunities and to dignity at work. They respect confidentiality where appropriate.

Other Professionals, Governors and Interested People

Teachers recognise that the well-being and development of pupils often depend on working in partnership with different professionals, the school governing body, support staff and other interested people within and beyond the school. They respect the skills, expertise and contributions of these colleagues and partners and are concerned to build productive working relationships with them in the interests of pupils.

Parents and Carers

Teachers respond sensitively to the differences in pupils' home backgrounds and circumstances and recognise the importance of working in partnership with parents and carers to understand and support their children's learning. They endeavour to communicate effectively and promote co-operation between the home and the school for the benefit of young people.

The School in Context

Teachers support the place of the school in the community and appreciate the importance of their own professional status in society. They recognise that professionalism involves using judgement over appropriate standards of personal behaviour.

Learning and Development

Teachers entering the teaching profession in England have been trained to a professional standard that has prepared them for the rigours and realities of the classroom. They understand that maintaining and developing their skills, knowledge and expertise is vital to achieving success. They take responsibility for their own continuing professional development, through the opportunities available to them, to make sure that pupils receive the best and most relevant education. Teachers continually reflect on their own practice, improve their skills and deepen their knowledge. They want to adapt their teaching appropriately to take account of new findings, ideas and technologies.

The Code is primarily a discussion document and the GTC(E) hope that it will have practical uses within schools. It is not a Code of Conduct and the GTC(E) make clear that 'This Code of Professional Values and Practice is therefore not a set of Standards against which teachers will be judged under the GTC(E)'s disciplinary powers nor is it appropriate for employers to use this Code in their own disciplinary procedures'. In order to analyse the Code it is useful to use the methodology of Friedman and Phillips (2003) since they developed five levels to reflect the degree of compulsion or coercion attached to a particular statement in a code as follows:

- *Level 1* signifies the highest degree of compulsion. It is the base level with an additional time perspective, e.g. shall at all times, must always.
- *Level 2* is the base level, e.g. shall, must, duty of care requires.
- *Level 3* is a mid-point between Levels 2 and 4, or Level 4 with an additional time perspective, e.g. should, ought, endeavour at all times.
- *Level 4* is language that implies advice rather than compulsion and stresses the use of professional judgement as the advised action is clearly not applicable to every circumstance, e.g. strive, it is preferable, shall endeavour.
- *Level 5* applies to those statements that are presented as almost a statement of fact with minimal compulsion, e.g. asked, a member recognises.

By examining the GTC(E)'s Code in terms of this structure it can be seen that it is written in language that requires the minimum of compulsion with the statements presented almost as fact: 'They are', 'Teachers recognise', 'They understand', 'Teachers support', 'Teachers demonstrate' and so on. There are no base level descriptions such as 'shall', 'must', or even 'should' or 'ought' in the Code. The Code has clearly been written as advice and encouragement to teachers, but how useful is it to you seeking concrete answers to what you should do? How can you put the Code into practice? The professional Standards use the same language as the Code and are very similar in content. The Code is not prioritised and is intended more as an aspirational document for teaching. As a result it is open to more than one interpretation. If the Code were written in a more exacting way then it would need to describe the context in which the words were used because of the complexity of the many situations in which teachers find themselves. The Code is not a set of rules – rather, it offers you the opportunity to reflect on what it means to be ethical in teaching. The Code does, however, speak about some obligations – the obligations that you owe to pupils, parents, local community, to your colleagues and to society.

Task 9.2.2
Mapping the ethical dimensions

Use the GTC(E)'s Code to map out how the values and practices relate to a week in your school teaching. Create a teaching diary and record how you address or encounter each of these statements in school. Which features most in your diary? Which features least? Why is this?

TEACHERS *IN LOCO PARENTIS*

The principle of *in loco parentis* was first outlined in the case of *Fitzgerald v Northcote* in 1865. It states that when a parent places his child with a teacher he delegates to him all his own authority, so far as it is necessary for the welfare of the child. More recently *in loco parentis* has developed to mean the teacher acting as a prudent parent. Teachers have therefore been judged in the courts on the standard of the prudent parent. Section 2(9) of The Children Act 1989 states that: 'A person who has parental responsibility for a child may not surrender or transfer any part of that responsibility to another but may arrange for some or all of it to be met by one or more persons acting on his behalf'. In light of this, schools need to establish before a child is admitted to a school the answer to the question: 'who has parental responsibility for this child?'. This is essential due to the increasing prevalence of less traditional parenting structures in society and the use of the term 'parents' in this unit refers to home carers and guardians as well as natural parents.

In regard to the position of the teacher Section 3(5) of the Act states:

A person who –
(a)   does not have parental responsibility for a particular child, but
(b)   has care of the child – may (subject to the provisions of the Act) do what is reasonable in all the circumstances of the care for the purpose of safeguarding or promoting the child's welfare.

Clearly the teacher owes a statutory duty of care towards the child in his or her class but some have questioned the usefulness of the principle of *in loco parentis*, especially as a teacher may well be responsible for over thirty children at one time. Teachers who deliver a National Curriculum and are judged fit for teaching according to national standards of competence may also be seen as servants of the State as opposed to being viewed as standing in for the parent.

The teacher of infant-aged children, for example, will be expected to demonstrate the way they utilise their teaching abilities and skills to create a sense of security in the class. They will protect the children in their care and promote qualities of self-esteem and confidence. They will show the children that they are valued and loved. In this situation, they inevitably share in parental responsibility and might be said to be truly acting *in loco parentis*. Home visiting by infant teachers is also common and leads to greater contact with parents and the sharing of information. Every teacher has a duty of care to their pupils and must supervise the pupils and care for their health and safety. In summary, the Children Act defines parents as all those who have 'parental responsibility' for a child whether or not they are a natural parent. You as a new teacher will need to remember that you will be expected to 'do what is reasonable in all the circumstances of the care for the purpose of safeguarding or promoting the child's welfare' – you have a duty of care. Consequently, you need to take reasonable steps to avoid exposing the child to any dangers that are reasonably foreseeable. This is your main legal responsibility. Because you hold a position of trust and confidence with respect to children, high standards of conduct are expected of you at all times

The Sexual Offences Act (2000) makes it a criminal offence if a teacher begins a relationship of a sexual nature with a child under the age of 18. The offence can carry a custodial sentence and will inevitably place the teacher on List 99 of the DfES which holds the names of all those people who have been prohibited from working with children and young people. New teachers should be aware of any child protection policies the school has but in particular new teachers should be aware of Circular 10/95 of the DfES on Protecting Children from Abuse which provides detailed guidance about physical contact with children and students. There are two paragraphs from this Circular that are worth quoting in full here:

> It is unnecessary and unrealistic to suggest that teachers should touch pupils only in emergencies. Particularly with younger pupils, touching them is inevitable and can give welcome reassurance to the child. However, teachers must bear in mind that even perfectly innocent actions can sometimes be misconstrued. Children may find being touched uncomfortable or distressing for a variety of reasons. It is important for teachers to be sensitive to a child's reaction to physical contact and to act appropriately. It is also important not to touch pupils, however casually, in ways or in parts of the body that might be considered indecent.
>
> Employers and senior staff have a responsibility to ensure that professional behaviour applies to relationships between staff and pupils or students, that all staff are clear about what constitutes appropriate behaviour and professional boundaries, and that those boundaries are maintained with the sensitive support and supervision required. That is important in all schools, but residential institutions need to be particularly mindful of this responsibility as do individuals in circumstances where there is one to one contact with pupils, for example, in the teaching of music or extra curricular activities.

All teachers therefore have a duty to treat children appropriately in this regard and to ensure that when they are unsure of any aspect of their own teaching conditions with children, they seek advice from an appropriate colleague.

THE 'STATUTORY' AND THE 'NON-STATUTORY'

'Statutory' means: of or pertaining to statute, that is, 'a written law passed by a properly constituted authority, e.g. an Act of Parliament' (Nelson Contemporary English Dictionary). The strictly statutory frameworks are:

- Legislation: Acts of Parliament;
- 'Orders' issued by the Secretary of State for Education under powers granted by legislation;
- GTC(E) Professional Code of Practice, backed by legislation;
- Contracts of Employment: subject to the general law of such contracts.

Legislation passed by Parliament includes Acts which are not exclusively confined to education. Very importantly, it includes general legislation such as the Disability Discrimination Act 1995 and the 1976 Race Relations Act and its Amendment in 2000. The latter imposed a new general duty on public authorities 'to make the promotion of race equality central to all their functions' . Both the 'Orders' issued by the Secretary of State for Education and the General Teaching Council for England's (GTC(E)) *Code of Professional Values and Practice for Teachers* (2002), have statutory status with the force of 'enabling'

Acts of Parliament behind them. The GTC(E) has powers conferred by legislation which include granting and removing an individual teacher's licence to teach in maintained schools in England. 'Orders' are issued which cover many detailed aspects of education policy. The most important set of principles governing teachers' statutory responsibilities and working time is contained in the School Teachers' Pay and Conditions Act, which is supported by an annual *Teachers' Pay and Conditions of Service* document. Teachers' individual contracts of employment set out, usually in detailed job specifications, the particular responsibilities attached to their appointments, and are subject to general contract and employment law. As a result of government policy, a wide range of day-to-day routine responsibilities formerly carried out by teachers is being passed to support staff. Some of the most important are: chasing absences, producing standard letters, collating pupil reports, administering and invigilating examinations, ordering supplies and equipment, minuting meetings and collecting money.

Teachers' professional responsibilities are framed by all of these statutory instruments, but they are also framed by other factors which have varying kinds of status, including *no* statutory status. Among the most important non-statutory frameworks are:

- Head teachers' discretionary authority;
- 'Guidance' issued by various statutory bodies;
- School policies;
- Professional custom and practice.

The status of head teachers' authority is an interesting case. Head teachers of maintained schools are bound by the national Pay and Conditions regulations, but the discretionary authority which they have is considerable, and can be instrumental in determining teachers' specific responsibilities. Teachers' job descriptions, for example, typically include clauses like, 'and such other duties and responsibilities as the head teacher may require'. Insofar as a job description is usually an adjunct to a contract of employment, this kind of clause has statutory status supported by employment law.

Moving to the domain of what is more clearly non-statutory, the most important is 'Guidance' issued by the Department for Education and Skills, OfSTED, or other agencies such as the Teacher Training Agency. But even the status of this can be somewhat uncertain. DfES guidance documents are usually marked, 'Status: Recommended', but at least one document on inclusive schooling is called, somewhat oddly, 'Statutory Guidance'. In practice, 'Guidance' contains recommendations which can often have substantial influence on schools, and on individual teachers' work. Most of the National Strategy policy, for example, is driven by non-statutory 'Guidance', and the operational detail of school inspections also resides in handbooks of guidance issued by OfSTED. Few schools, however, ever regard OfSTED guidance as in any sense 'optional'!

Another class of instruments which have a significant bearing on your professional responsibilities are school policies. Schools are statutorily required to have formal institutional policies on many aspects of their governance and internal arrangements. Formally speaking, these are *written*; and they are 'passed'

Task 9.2.3
Statutory and non-statutory guidance

Both statutory and non-statutory frameworks inform teachers' professional responsibilities. Collect all the school policies into a folder and decide which elements of them are statutory and which are non-statutory guidance. Which ones or elements will guide your conduct in the classroom, school and local community?

by a *properly constituted body* – the Governing Body of a school – which itself has formal legal standing supported by parliamentary Acts. By virtue of this, and the fact that most policy statements are responses to statutory regulations, they have considerable 'legal' force. However, such formal policy statements are entirely dependent on how the policies they describe or define are actually put into practice, which leaves considerable scope for marked variations both between schools and even within an individual school for 'operational slippage'. In secondary schools, for example, responsibility for certain things is devolved to subject departments or year divisions. An example might be a school's policy for marking pupils' work. Much depends on the consistency with which that kind of policy is managed in different departments. Finally, there is the whole issue of professional expectations which derive from custom and practice: unwritten, not normally the product of systematic formulation, but, nevertheless, powerful determinants of professional responsibilities, protocols, and conduct generally.

SUMMARY

The above simply introduces you to some of the main ethical and legal responsibilities you have as a teacher. It will be important for you to follow some of these up in detail or at least be able to identify the source of information if you need to follow them up in specific situations. The further reading below will help you in this.

ANNOTATED FURTHER READING

Arthur, J., Davison, J. and Lewis, M. (2005) *Professional Values and Practice*, Routledge: London. This textbook provides an introduction to a teacher's ethical and general legal responsibilities and part of which has been the basis for this unit.

University of Bristol Graduate School of Education *Guide to the Law* (up-dated annually). This document is available from Bristol University and contains a comprehensive and excellent survey of the law pertaining to teachers.

REFERENCES

Campbell, E. (2000) 'Professional ethics in teaching: towards the development of a code of practice', *Cambridge Journal of Education*, 30(2): 203–21.

Carr, D. (1993) 'Moral values and the teacher: beyond the pastoral and the permissive', *Journal of Philosophy of Education* 27(2): 193–227.

Eraut, M. (1994) *Developing Knowledge and Competence*, London: Falmer Press.

Friedman, A. and Phillips, M. (2003) *Codes of Conduct in the Professions: Do They Meet the Challenge?* Real World, Real People Conference Proceedings, 2–4 September 2003, University of Surrey, Roehampton, London.

Goodlad, J. (1990) *Teachers for Our Nations Schools*, San Francisco, CA: Jossey-Bass.

Halstead, M. and Taylor, M. (2000) 'Learning and teaching about values: a review of recent research', *Cambridge Journal of Education*, 3(2): 169–202.

Sockett, H. (1993) *The Moral Base for the Teaching Profession*, New York: Teachers College Press.

Wilson, J. (1993) *Reflection and Practice*, University of Western Ontario: Althouse Press.

Unit 9.3

Continuing Your Professional Development

Kit Field

INTRODUCTION

With workforce re-modelling, the development of extended schools, out of school learning and increased needs to access technology, the teaching profession is on the cusp of massive change. Education in the future will require that teachers lead and manage learning rather than simply deliver lessons. Continuing Professional Development (CPD) is more necessary than ever before, in order to give teaching professional status and teachers the confidence to work in a more autonomous way, thereby providing young people with the wherewithal to live productive lives in the future.

OBJECTIVES

By the end of this unit you should:

- appreciate the need for ongoing professional learning and development;
- understand the role of the many professional agencies associated with CPD;
- acknowledge the need to be pro-active in organising one's own professional development;
- appreciate what constitutes effective CPD from the perspectives of the individual, the school and the profession.

WHAT IS CPD?

There are three aspects to CPD: *continuing, professional* and *development.*

Continuing

Society is ever changing. If one goal of education is to prepare young people today for the world of tomorrow, no teacher can rely on lessons learned yesterday. Teachers must engage in learning for practical reasons. The CPD strategy (DfEE 2001) mentions the need for pupils to develop an enthusiasm for lifelong learning, as it is seen to be a key to success in adult life. Such an enthusiasm is more likely to develop if young people see their teachers modelling such practices.

O'Brien and MacBeath (1999: 70) comment:

> Teacher life-long learning in the form of continuing professional development (CPD) is increasingly regarded as an important means of contributing to the creation of more effective schools, and as integral to learning organisations.

To follow this argument through to its logical conclusion, lifelong learning leads to the development of a learning organisation, which continuously and collectively re-evaluates its purposes and seeks ways to develop the most effective and efficient ways of reaching its goals. Improvement is continuous if learning is ongoing.

Continuous and continuing learning is not problematic. The core 'business' of a school is teaching and learning. All teachers therefore have access to teaching and learning situations all day, prompting one Secretary of State for Education to assert that teachers learn best from and with other teachers (Morris 2001). This does suggest the need for contact, communication and regular access to other teachers. Putnam and Borko (2000) condemn the traditional view that teachers should 'find their own style' (p. 19) in that it encourages a paradigm of privacy. For them, the development of a community of learners leads to the establishment of a common theory and language, and opportunities to challenge assumptions. 'Continuing' Professional Development relies on regular interaction with colleagues.

Task 9.3.1
Learning alone/learning together

Which types of professional development activities are best conducted individually, and which in collaboration with others? What tools can be used to maximise the benefits of:

- joint planning;
- observation;
- team teaching;
- assessment levelling?

Professional

The word 'professional' is problematic. Certainly Morris (2001) uses the term to draw approval for the strategy from teachers, '... [CPD] ... is part of the re-professionalisation of what teachers should do, shout as loudly as we possibly can that, yes, we demand a lot of teachers'.

Professionalising teachers for some (e.g. Whitty 2000) means providing independence and self governance. Within the current government's CPD strategy, some allowance is made, in that teachers are encouraged to take responsibility for professional development, as, it is claimed, it is increasingly a requirement in other professions. This does not go as far as Whitty would want – to have, as a profession, a mandate to act on behalf of the state. Education is, and will continue to be subjected to and regulated by market forces and supervision by the government.

To a degree, some features of a profession are in place:

- teacher skills are based on theoretical knowledge;
- education in the skills is certified by examination;
- there is a code of conduct (DfEE 2001) oriented towards the public good;
- a new professional organisation (GTC) enjoys some power and influence.

(after Whitty 2000: 281)

The impact of the above are difficult to measure. Puttnam (2001) argues that the existence of the General Teaching Council (GTC) provides some self-regulation, and that the implementation of the CPD strategy will lead to 'thought leadership'.

Day's (1999) analysis, drawing on Hoyle's (1980) definitions of professionalism and professionality, is less positive. Characteristics of the 'restricted professional' are applicable. Action is intuitive, and learning is derived from the work base. Experience rather than theory is used to justify action. Teachers are not encouraged by the CPD strategy to become 'extended professionals', that is to locate practice in a broader political and social context. The extent to which teaching is 'value led' is also questionable. The 'values' are imposed; present in the latest official set of standards for QTS. The values have not emerged from the profession itself.

The CPD strategy is a move towards the professionalisation of teachers. It is contributing towards the professionality of teacher behaviour and practice, but, as yet stops short of providing the decision and policy making powers traditionally associated with professions.

Task 9.3.2
Accountability and responsibility for professional development

In which ways are you responsible and accountable to:

- yourself;
- your school;
- the community;
- the government?

Does this sense of responsibility oblige you to do anything?

Development

Field and Philpott (2000) comment on the modes of engaging with teaching and learning in the context of Initial Teacher Education (ITE). They identify activities which provide trainee teachers with learning opportunities, and the mentoring and coaching activities which shape actual practice. In the context of CPD, this involves learning, and changing (rather than shaping) practice. Development, or improvement of practice is then further enhanced by evaluation. Development, then, consists of two distinct phases:

- learning activities and processes;
- application and evaluation.

There is no option to withdraw from development. All teachers do model learning for their pupils, whether they choose to do so or not. Pupils experience teacher development at first-hand. With pupil learning as the core business of schools, Williams *et al.* (2001) are right to assert 'All teachers must model lifelong learning' (p. 198).

For motivational purposes, teachers, as learners, must recognise the fruits of their labour. Evaluation enhances learning and development. OfSTED inspections of CPD provision, and bids to government agencies for funding such provision both demand the demonstration of measurable impact on pupil learning. As Rhodes and Houghton-Hill (2000) confirm, the requirement to demonstrate linkage between professional learning of teachers and classroom improvement is firmly established. It is this linkage which served to convert professional learning into professional development.

Task 9.3.3
The purposes of self-auditing

What is the relationship between each of the following?

Needs, Wants, Learning, Development

How can you build on what has been learnt and developed as a student teacher, an NQT and a teacher in the early years of professional development?

CPD AND CAREER DEVELOPMENT

During the last two decades in England CPD has all too often been little more than an eclectic and unrelated assortment of in-service training events, narrowly focused on frequently changing policy initiatives and externally imposed agendas, pieced together reactively by individual teachers in response to extrinsic priorities rather than sought out pro-actively according to intrinsic training needs.

The notion of *training* as opposed to *learning and development* has prevailed, which has tended to be informed by the need to seek information about how to comply with changes in legislation or demands made by school development plans. This links in closely to the sets of National Standards for Teachers.

The standards are for:

- Trainee Teachers;
- Newly Qualified Teachers;
- Teachers approaching the 'Threshold';
- Advanced Skills Teachers;
- SENCOs;
- Subject Leaders;
- School Improvers;
- Head Teachers.

There are plans to revise these standards and to add to the raft those for 'Excellent Teachers'.

Built into the standards is the need for teachers and leaders to generate evidence of compliance with these standards. The Department for Education and Skills (DfES) website (http://www.teachernet.gov.uk/professionaldevelopment/standardsframework/) provides very straightforward guidance. Teachers may select an area of competence, click on their current status and also on the level to which they aspire. This leads to the two definitions of levels of competence. The teacher is then able to identify the gap between his/her current level and the higher level with some accuracy.

Task 9.3.4
Using national standards

- Use the DfES based website to articulate your current level of performance in relation to National Standards.
- Select the set of standards to which you aspire.
- Can you identify the gap between where you are now and where you want to be in the future?

KEY PLAYERS IN CPD IN ENGLAND

The DfES clearly occupies a powerful position in CPD. CPD is, though, a very cluttered playing field, and to assure maximum gain from the opportunities available teachers do need to understand the functions and roles of a range of institutions.

DfES

The Department for Education and Skills is the Government Ministry which provides guidance and support for Continuing Professional Development (CPD). Its position in relation to CPD is summarised as follows:

> Continuing professional development (CPD) includes any activity that increases teachers'
> knowledge or understanding, and their effectiveness in schools. It can help raise teaching
> and learning standards and improve job satisfaction. CPD is for all teachers, at any stage of
> their career.

> (http://www.teachernet.gov.uk/professionaldevelopment/)

Training and Development Agency for Schools (TDA) – formerly Teacher Training Agency (TTA)

The TDA is a government sponsored independent body. Its purpose is to raise standards by attracting able and committed people to teaching and by improving the quality of training for teachers and the wider school workforce. Government representatives have requested that the TDA extends its remit to take responsibility centrally for CPD in England.

The General Teaching Council (for England) (GTC(E))

The GTC(E) (2003) has also developed a framework which spells out what constitutes CPD. Teachers can use the framework to plan their CPD in relation to personal professional development needs, and evaluate the learning and development which occurs. The GTC intends that the framework resonates with the professional standards framework as well as the qualifications framework offered by higher education institutions.

National College for School Leadership (NCSL)

The College's Leadership Development Framework (LDF) is centred on the belief that schools should be supported in developing leaders at all levels (distributed leadership). Five stages of school leadership form part of a non-linear model within which the majority of NCSL's leadership development provision can be found. The five stages are:

- emergent leadership;
- established leadership;
- entry to headship;
- advanced leadership;
- consultant leadership.

A portfolio approach to recording development and the impact of actions on educational leadership are essential components of development in this area.

Higher Education qualifications framework

Many teachers follow Masters degree courses and programmes in education-related topics. The link between professional development and academic qualifications is becoming stronger as professional bodies such as the NCSL and GTC are seeking academic accreditation for teachers' engagement with their own 'frameworks'. In this way it is possible to use day-to-day professional experiences as a basis for study.

Local Education Authorities (LEAs)

Local Education Authorities (LEAs), as the employers of teachers within a local government authority, have a responsibility for teachers' conditions of service and are also accountable for the levels of performance of the pupils in the local schools. The requirement to produce an Education Development Plan demands that account is made of CPD and its impact in schools.

Private companies

Throughout the 1990s and early 2000s, private companies have entered the CPD market. Such companies are able to tender for national and regional projects as consultants and deliverers of CPD.

Task 9.3.5
Linking to the school development plan

Look at your school's Development Plan.

- Work out the extent to which each priority is driven by external forces.
- Now match up from which agency support for the achievement for each priority can be sought.
- Are there fixed development programmes for each priority?

WHY HAVE NATIONAL SYSTEMS FOR CPD?

There are three main reasons why teachers should maintain their own professional learning throughout their career. These are:

- to contribute to one's own level of competence, understanding, job satisfaction and career development;
- to make a positive contribution to improving the quality of learning for learners, and consequently the work of the institution as a whole;
- to help the education service keep pace with societal change, and to create an education service which is attractive, and of benefit, to all stakeholders.

Since the 1988 Education Reform Act there has been a preoccupation in CPD with making government initiatives such as national assessment, literacy and numeracy strategies, the NOF-funded ICT scheme, Excellence in Cities, Education Action Zones, Beacon or Specialist schools work (see also NFER 2000: 3). In other words, teachers were often either only able or required to attend events which focused on the implementation of such schemes. These initiatives have forced teachers to adapt practices in order to achieve identifiable and quantifiable improvements in pupil learning in relation to externally set benchmarks. There has, therefore, been the tendency to prioritise the types of CPD deemed to achieve the highest level of impact against these measures. Throughout a teaching career, teachers can expect to be required to learn new skills and ways of working.

By extending the remit of the TDA to oversee all CPD from a national perspective, it is clear that there is a recognition that it is necessary to ground a new approach in a richer understanding of current CPD provision and to ensure that an analysis of the challenges facing it are informed by the views and experience of all stakeholders. The extension of the remit acknowledges the TDA's achievements and is regarded as an expression of confidence in its effectiveness as a custodian of quality and standards.

However, taken as a whole, there remains as yet a problem for CPD, in that there is no *national system of CPD*. Such a national system would need to have the following characteristics:

- the provision of CPD being overseen by regional strategic partnerships;
- a single national framework of CPD standards marking progressively more demanding levels of professional achievement;
- a single national framework of awards, tied to the national framework of standards;
- a national unit of currency for CPD to facilitate credit accumulation and transfer (possibly based on M Level credits);
- a national framework for the Accreditation of Prior (Experiential) Learning (AP(E)L);
- funding for credit/award-based as well as non credit/award provision;

- a suitable balance in the allocation of funds between school and other agencies (recognising the limitations of the school as a planning unit for a national system);
- universal access by teachers to CPD, using all the resources of flexible learning;
- assessments and demonstrations of professional achievement consisting of the analysis of action in a field setting;
- national criteria for the measurement of impact;
- national criteria for the effectiveness of CPD strategic partnerships.

WHY SHOULD TEACHERS DO CPD?

> Our ambition is that all teachers should benefit from and contribute to professional development throughout their careers, and that professional development should be planned, appropriate to the individual concerned, and assessed for its impact on teaching and learning.
>
> (Kelly 2005)

Engagement with CPD is to be linked to pay. Headteachers and teacher bodies have been asked to strengthen the obligation (which was previously only moral) to engage with CPD. There are likely to be good reasons, in terms of teachers' conditions of work and salary, to undertake CPD.

In a busy professional life, there are several factors which facilitate CPD and indeed motivate teachers to undertake continuing learning and development. The GTC(E) professional learning framework for teachers delineates the following aspects of teachers' entitlement to professional learning (2003: 6). Teachers are entitled to, the framework suggests:

- have time to engage in sustained reflection and structured learning;
- create learning opportunities from everyday practice such as planning and assessing for learning;
- develop their ability to identify their own learning and development needs and those of others;
- develop an individual learning plan;
- have school-based learning, as well as course participation, recognised for accreditation;
- develop self-evaluation, observation and peer review skills;
- develop mentoring and coaching skills and their ability to offer professional dialogue and feedback;
- plan their longer-term career aspirations.

The argument is that CPD is necessary, and under certain conditions can be stimulating and motivating.

One purpose underpinning teaching must surely be to help to prepare pupils for future adult life. Proponents of lifelong learning rightly recognise that reaching adulthood does not signal the end of learning. As Wenger (1999: 38) succinctly puts it: 'Learners will inherit the earth. Knowers will find that they inhabit a world that no longer exists.'

CPD and professional learning surely should not only equip us to interpret and respond to the changing demands of practice and exercise our professional judgement in informed and creative ways; it should also be seen as a means for us to rejuvenate our practice to expand our professional repertoire, to increase our self-esteem, self-confidence and enthusiasm for teaching or, for example, our level of criticality and, thereby, achieve enhanced job satisfaction.

In this respect, CPD is about capacity building. Moon (2001) also notes the benefits of CPD in terms of the enhancement of performance through improved self-esteem. A sense of professional control and personal wellbeing can be seen to be essential ingredients in job satisfaction.

On the other hand, leaving CPD entirely in the hands of the individual teacher is counter-productive. Pachler *et al.* (2003) point out

> … it is hopeless for those with responsibility for leading professional development simply to urge practitioners to reflect, reflect again, reflect more and reflect deeper.

This 'caricature' serves to illustrate how empty a position can be that denies a body of learned knowledge that could inform and refine professional thinking (see also Lawes 2003). Exposure to, and engagement with relevant background literature can, therefore, be seen to be one very important continuing professional development activity for us to engage in throughout our careers.

Working across different types of schools through networking and collaboration, to engage in research and enquiry into teaching and learning processes and to begin to develop leadership capacity are informative, enjoyable, and become of greater interest if findings are relatable to existing bodies of knowledge and understanding. Learning and development through engagement demands, in simple terms, an integration of theoretical and practical perspectives

---

Task 9.3.6
Predicting the future

- Why did you choose to come into teaching?
- What do you think young people will need to know, understand and be able to do in the next 10, 20, 30 years?
- In what ways will you need to act differently in the future without compromising the values which underpinned your decision to become a teacher?

PLANNING YOUR CPD

Schools and teachers should 'continue to have the freedom and ultimately the responsibility to decide what specific development activity is most appropriate to them given their circumstances and school priorities' (Kelly 2005). However, planning CPD demands a full understanding of how different agencies influence CPD. Figure 9.3.1 on p. 450 is illustrative of the complexity.

It is important, therefore, to take care that CPD activities which we undertake do relate not only to our needs and wants in relation, for example, to developing aspects of our subject knowledge, but also in relation to the set of standards to which we aspire such as, for example, subject leadership. Teachers must be aware of the impact of their own learning and development, the opportunities offered by different institutions, and the extent to which they are also accountable to them. These bureaucratic demands suggest that it makes good sense to record one's CPD at all stages of the process. In a positive sense this becomes one means by which the teacher can get greater professional fulfilment and prepare him/herself for the future and for future promotion.

The National Professional Standards Framework represents a means by which to plan a career path within the education profession. No longer are higher salaries only available to those who relinquish teaching in favour of management and administrative tasks. 'Threshold' payments, and 'Advanced

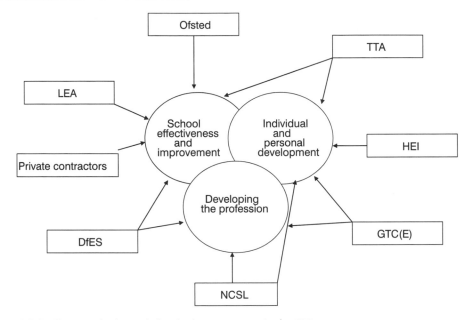

Figure 9.3.1 The complex interrelationsips between agencies for CPD

Skills Teacher' status, and in the future Excellent Teacher status are dependent in part on the provision of evidence of attainment in relation to national benchmarks and individually negotiated performance targets. Performance management procedures facilitate self auditing in relation to the national standards, target setting and the provision of evidence of professional learning and development. CPD must be linked to performance management.

The chief measure of accountability will be 'impact' (Kelly 2005). In planning one's CPD there is a need to consider intended outcomes. By auditing one's own performance, having an eye on future ambitions and aspirations, and giving due consideration to how engagement will lead to better pupil learning, the teacher can establish a starting point for a personal CPD plan.

Field's (2002) *Portfolio of Professional Development* is designed to assist teachers in the planning of their own CPD. The nine step process recommends a clear 'starting point', consideration of preferred professional learning styles, negotiation with the school in which the teacher works, the presentation of evidence of completion and finally an examination of the impact of the process. Figure 9.3.2 on p. 451 provides more detail.

A justification for the process can be found in the DfEE (2001) Code of Practice which accompanied the 2001 National Strategy for CPD. Modern and effective CPD is to be based upon nine key principles:

- teacher ownership, and a shared commitment to, and responsibility for (by teachers and schools) development;
- professional development should be centred on raising standards;
- development opportunities should match different needs;
- there should be equality of opportunity for professional development;
- new and innovative ways of using time and resources for CPD should be sought
- ICT should be central to CPD;
- high quality CPD depends upon schools being discerning customers;
- planning and evaluation are essential components of CPD;
- good practice should be shared and disseminated, using ICT.

(Adapted from DfEE 2001: 24)

Step	Purpose
1) Self-audit	To identify strengths and weaknesses, for example, in relation to the relevant set of standards, can act as a starting point for professional development and learning.
2) Initial statement	To articulate and make known to senior staff career aspirations and ambitions facilitates the planning of appropriate development activities.
3) Identifying professional development targets	The purpose of this step is to link need and aspirations to identifiable and demonstrable intended outcomes.
4) Planning professional learning and development opportunities	Planning learning involves the identification of learning and development activities. To maximise the learning outcomes you are encouraged to identify your own preferred learning style.
5) Writing a personal Professional Development Plan	The personal professional development plan enables the marrying of perceived need and preferred ways of attaining higher standards; and also provides the means for demonstrating and sharing aspects of good practice.
6) Chronicling professional development activities	This step suggests a way of logging participation in planned development activities, and provides a means of gathering evidence of participation.
7) Implementing changes and improvement plans	Professional learning is worthless unless it leads to a change and/or development in practice.
8) Evaluating change and/or improvement plans	This step involves reflecting upon personal professional learning experiences over an extended period of time.
9) Measuring the 'impact' of change and/or improvement projects	All professional development activities should – directly and/or indirectly – lead to a positive impact on learners. This step involves showing how personal professional learning has enabled the achievement of pre-stated targets which may include improved pupil performance.

Figure 9.3.2 The nine step process (adapted from Field, 2002)

This set of ten bullet points can serve as a professional and conceptual framework when teachers plan their own CPD. CPD must be seen as a process, and not a series of unlinked events.

DOING CPD

According to the DfEE (2001), successful professional development involves:

- a focus upon specific teaching and learning problems;
- opportunities for teachers to reflect on what they know and do already;
- opportunities for teachers to understand the rationale behind new ideas and approaches; to see theory demonstrated in practice; to be exposed to new expertise;
- sustained opportunities to experiment with new ideas and approaches, so that teachers can work out their implications for their own subject, pupils, school and community;
- opportunities for teachers to put their own interpretation on new strategies and ideas at work, building on their existing knowledge and skills;
- coaching and feedback on their professional practice over a period of weeks and months. This is a particularly important element, and can be decisive in determining whether changes in practice survive.

Clearly CPD is more than just attending courses and taking part in school 'INSET Days'.

Professional development needs to involve a considerable amount of practical application and evaluation of new methods and approaches. Arguably, a strong practice-orientation is essential in order for CPD to be 'effective', i.e. to bring about personal and professional learning.

New methodologies and knowledge are regularly published in academic journals and specialist literature and form the backbone of most higher education advanced courses, and the opportunity to develop and draw on practitioners' interpretations of theory is available, for example, through reading professional journals. Again, reading is not enough.

The draft GTC(E)professional learning framework (2002) proposes that teachers can expect to learn from and with colleagues in a range of ways; these might include:

- working within a learning or study team, perhaps with advice and guidance from a tutor;
- team teaching and planning;
- being mentored;
- observing demonstration lessons;
- attending 'Masterclasses';
- close study and evaluation of lessons with colleagues;
- being coached by a peer or more experienced colleague for specific areas of development;
- participating in whole school or team collaborative inquiry and problem-solving;
- planning and assessing with others;
- developing resources and ideas with colleagues.

By completing a Career Entry and Development Profile (CEDP) too, teachers should be comfortable using evidence to identify personal strengths and aspects of teaching that require further attention. This reflects an approach to identifying need, planning personal professional development and providing the evidence of successful completion of learning and development, which is suggested in Field's (2002) *Portfolio of Professional Development*. Portfolios should be more than a collection of artefacts and evidence. Importantly, it needs to include critical reflection clarifying why individual pieces were chosen and what learning they evidence.

The DfES (http://www.teachernet.gov.uk/development/) also provides support in the form of an electronic portfolio. Linking into national standards, personal ambitions and aspirations and indeed case studies of teachers in similar circumstances provide the stimuli for reflection. Valuable reflection requires the teacher to read theoretical and professional texts to enhance understanding and to gain the confidence to apply what has been learnt in real working situations.

EVALUATING CPD

Nationally

The Government and the teachers' representative body (GTC) are essentially in agreement about the purposes of CPD. These are to:

- develop a shared understanding in the profession about what professional development and learning should include;
- influence national policy and funding;
- raise teachers' expectations both on entry to the profession and of professional learning communities;
- enable teachers to reflect on how they can and do contribute to the professional, collective knowledge about teaching and learning;
- provide the basis for widening opportunities for accreditation and recruitment;
- provide support for school leaders in making time and support available.

(GTCE 2002: 11)

The professional context means that CPD is tied into performance management procedures, and also that it is linked to school improvement as expressed in the school development plan (Pollard 2002). This triangular relationship, in essence, provides the tension between the individual's needs and wants, and those of the school as an institution. Striking the balance is, of course, dependent upon the situation.

Individually

Frost *et al.* (2000) argue positively that real improvement and development are dependent upon teacher agency and a positive and supportive school culture. There is, as Moon (2001) notes, a direct relationship between teachers' morale and self-esteem and school improvement. Indeed, the National CPD Strategy does place 'professional development at the heart of school improvement' (DfEE 2001: para. 1).

Accounting for the impact CPD has on the individual, and linking this to the initial intended outcomes is motivating for the individual. CPD focused on the individual can have a 'multiplier effect'. This positive, added value, is, however, dependent upon accurate, thorough and rigorous self evaluation.

For the individual, CPD must address the outcomes of self evaluation in the form of an audit. This is not to insist that development is only related to weaknesses, but also to ambitions and aspirations. Part of being a professional is self-direction. Moon (2001) notes the influence of self-esteem and morale on performance, and that CPD provides the opportunity to enhance self-perception as a professional – through planning for, and evaluating the effect of, CPD on the individual teacher.

Institutionally

The relationship between teacher performance and development and school improvement is reciprocal (Day, 1999). CPD must therefore be in the context of institutional development. Indeed, it is worth reiterating that the National CPD strategy, does place 'professional development at the heart of school improvement' (DfEE 2001: para. 1).

The publication of performance tables, the development of 'value added measures' and the resultant culture of target setting are all embedding school effectiveness in the day-to-day practice of education professionals. Indeed, the ability to understand and use assessment data is contained within the National Standards for teachers at all stages of their career.

The concept of 'impact'

For some, 'impact funding' is perceived as a means of imposing a way of working, and less as a means of offering personal and professional development opportunities. Whitty (2000) sees the measures as a means of specifying outputs, and a way of defining the content of what teachers should do. This can lead to a feeling of de-professionalisation, and a restriction of autonomy and self-direction.

The development and changing of practice remains personal and fails to add to a community's collective body of knowledge if it is not externalised. Moon (2001) argues that dissemination of personal professional development is essential, if such developments are to add to teachers' repertoires and understanding of theory. Deep learning must stand the test of professional scrutiny and evaluation. Working in collaboration through Networked Learning Communities, Leadership Incentive Grant Groups and Excellence Clusters, for example, supports *externalisation*. Dissemination through the publication of academic journal articles has been seen to be inaccessible to teachers. The GTC(E) 'Teacher Research of the Month' and NCSL web-based Research Associate reports represent deliberate attempts to make good and best practice available to a wide range of interested professionals.

Accountability serves as a check for autonomy. A broader view of 'impact' as a measure of success is recommended by Holden (2002). Impact is more than improved assessment outcomes. He argues it is evidenced by changes in attitudes and behaviour. Professional learning therefore involves adaptations of practice, and Holden acknowledges that learning is an outcome of participation in new practices. This cyclical representation of professional development is justifiable, when coupled with evidence and research-based approaches.

Graham *et al.* (2000) expand upon the assessment of impact. An appreciation of what constitutes measures of success, at least in part, determines the nature and form of CPD. It is clear from Graham *et al.* that the focus for CPD is dual – in that it should be intended to benefit the individual and the school as shown in Table 9.3.1.

Table 9.3.1 Aspects of impact (adapted from Graham *et al.*, 2000: 29)

Aspects of impact	
Individual	*School*
Promotion	Recruitment
Motivation	Retention
Morale and job satisfaction	Participation in innovation
Sense of correctness	Development plans
Personal growth	Pupil assessment scores
Qualifications (professional)	

SUMMARY

Arguments presented in this unit suggest a third dimension for CPD – a 'profession led' approach. This approach is more about developing the profession, its capacity to change, and a sense of professional responsibility in place of accountability. This 'system' has in common with an 'individual led approach' a devolvement of power from the employer. It has in common with the 'systems led approach' a sense of collective responsibility to a governing body – the profession itself in a newly regulated form. The introduction of a 'middle way', shown in diagrammatic form in Figure 9.3.3, (which can lean towards the existing extreme forms in a way that addresses immediate needs) begins to form a complementary model as opposed to the competing models identified in the past. As a single framework it enables analysis of policy and practice in a way that does not exclude forms of CPD which may be necessary in certain circumstances.

It is, perhaps, therefore, Evidence Based Practice, and the engagement of education professionals in the uncovering and generation of evidence and data, as well as the requirement to respond to relevant

Complementary models for CPD

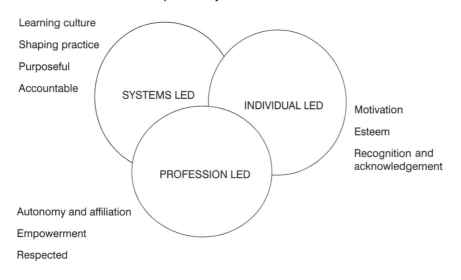

Figure 9.3.3 A third way for CPD

data that leads to the empowerment of the profession as a whole. Stenhouse's (1975) dream of the teacher as a researcher, yet within a clear framework of accountability, is perhaps an answer. As HEIs encourage action research as a way of effecting change, and a critical narrative/journal as the means of recording and disseminating real experiences, teachers do begin to establish an evidence base. Through collaboration with other agencies (TTA, DfES, GTC(E), NCSL), the profession will enjoy the opportunity of sharing and disseminating the process and outcomes of effective CPD.

ANNOTATED FURTHER READING

Day, C. (1999) *Developing Teachers: The Challenges of Lifelong Learning*, London: Falmer Press. *Developing Teachers* focuses upon the nature of teacher professionalism, the continuing professional development of teachers and the contexts in which this occurs. Using a range of international research and development work, Chris Day discusses the ways in which personal and professional contexts promote and inhibit improvement in teaching. He examines the effects of school leadership and culture; the place of appraisal and personal development records in teacher and school development; in-service as intervention, reflective practice, partnerships between schools and universities; and networks for improvement. Finally, he highlights the complexities of becoming and remaining an effective teacher in changing circumstances, arguing that without a focus on lifelong learning, teachers cannot provide the best learning opportunities for their students.

Field, K. (2002) *Portfolio of Professional Development: Structuring And Recording Teachers' Career Development*, London: Optimus Publishing. The *Portfolio of Professional Development* provides concise guidance to CPD coordinators, performance managers and individual teachers on the whole process of building individual professional development portfolios. Supported by a comprehensive range of templates, the *Portfolio* guides teachers through the whole process of planning and recording professional development activities. *The Portfolio* is a complete toolkit for individual teachers to record, reflect on, analyse, and set targets relating to professional development.

Moon, B., Butcher, J. and Bird, E. (eds) *Leading Professional Development in Education*, London: Routledge Falmer and Open University. This book provides a rich range of case studies and perspectives on the practical leadership tasks that underpin educational change. *Section 1* focuses on the nature of professional learning and the policy context in which educational reform takes place. *Section 2* explores the forms of leadership relevant to the differing contexts of professional development. *Section 3* explores mentoring, peer coaching, team and group work. *Section 4* analyses the experience of evidence-based work in medicine and the health service and the potential of applying this to education. *Section 5* looks at the potential role that interactive technologies can play in professional development.

REFERENCES

Day, C. (1999) *Developing Teachers: The Challenges Of Lifelong Learning*, London: Falmer Press.

DfEE (2001) *Learning And Teaching: A Strategy For Professional Development*, London. Available at http://www.teachernet.gov.uk/_doc/1289/CPD_Strategy.pdf.

Field, K. (2002) *Portfolio of Professional Development: Structuring and Recording Teachers Career Development*, London: Optimus Publishing.

Field, K. and Philpott, C. (2000) 'The impact of hosting student teachers on school effectiveness and school improvement', *Journal of In-Service Education*, 26(1): 115–38.

Frost, D., Durrant, J., Head, M. and Holden, G. (2000) *Teacher-led School Improvement*, London: RoutledgeFalmer.

Graham, J., Gough, B. and Beardsworth, R. (2000) *Partnerships in Continuing Professional Development*, A Joint Research Project by The Standing Committee for the Education and Training of Teachers and The University of East London.

GTCE (2002) *Professional Learning Framework: A Draft for Discussion And Development*, London: GTCE. Available at www.gtce.org.uk/pdfs/tplf/draft.pdf.

GTCE (2003) *The Teachers' Professional Learning Framework*, London: GTCE. Available at www.gtce.org.uk/pdfs/tplf.pdf.

Hammersley, M. (1997) 'Educational research and teaching: a response to David Hargreaves' TTA lecture', in Moon, B., Butcher, J. and Bird, E. (eds) *Leading Professional Development in Education*, London: RoutledgeFalmer and Open University Press.

Hargreaves, D.H. (1996) 'Teaching as a research-based profession: possibilities and prospects. Teacher Training Agency Annual Lecture 1996', in Moon, B., Butcher, J. and Bird, E. (eds) *Leading Professional Development in Education*, London: Routledge Falmer and Open University Press.

Holden, G. (2002) 'Towards a learning community: the role of mentoring in teacher-led school improvement', *Journal of In-Service Education*, 28(1): 9–22.

Hoyle, E. (1975) 'Professionality, professionalism and control in teaching', in Houghton, V. *et al.* (eds) *Management in Education: The Management of Organisations and Individuals*, London: Ward Lock Educational/Open University Press.

Hoyle E. (1980) 'Professionalization and deprofessionalization in education', in Hoyle, E. and Megarny, J. (eds) *World Yearbook of Education 1980: The Professional Development of Teachers*, London: Kogan Page.

Jones, C. (2001) *The Use of a Professional Development Portfolio Within a Masters Framework. Report on an Escalate Thematic Initiative*, Department of Education, University of Liverpool. Available at http://www.escalate.ac.uk/initiatives/CliffJones.php3.

Kelly, R. (2005) *Letter to the TTA Expanding upon the TTA's Extended Remit for CPD*, March 2005.

Lawes, S. (2003) 'What, when, how, and why?', *Theory and Foreign Language*, Winter: 28–39.

Moon, B. (2001) 'The changing agenda for professional development in education', in Moon, B., Butcher, J. and Bird, E. (eds) *Leading Professional Development in Education*, London: RoutledgeFalmer and Open University Press.

Morris, E. (2001) Keynote speech at the DfEE launch of *The National Strategy for CPD*, 1 March 2001.

NFER (2000) *Continuing Professional Development: Teachers' Perspectives – A Summary*, Slough: National Foundation for Educational Research.

O'Brien, J. and MacBeath, J. (1999) 'Co-ordinating staff development: the training and development of staff development coordinators', *Journal of In-Service Education*, 25(1): 69–84.

Pachler, N., Daly, C. and Lambert, D. (2003) 'Teacher learning: reconceptualising the relationship between theory and practical teaching in masters level course development', in *Proceedings Forum Quality Assurance in Distance-Learning and E-learning: International Quality Benchmarks in Postgraduate Education*, Krems, Austria, May 2002.

Pollard, A. (2002) *Reflective Teaching: Effective and Evidence-informed Professional Practice*, London: Continuum.

Putnam, R.T. and Borko, H. (2000) 'What do new views of knowledge and thinking have to say about research on teacher learning', in Moon, B., Butcher, J. and Bird, E. (eds) *Leading Professional Development in Education*, London: RoutledgeFalmer and Open University Press.

Puttnam, D. (2001) Closing address at the DfEE launch of the *National Strategy for CPD*, 1 March 2001.

Rhodes, C. and Houghton-Hill, S. (2000) 'The linkage of continuing professional development and the classroom experience of pupils: barriers perceived by senior managers in some secondary schools', *Journal of In-Service Education* 26(3): 423–36.

Stenhouse, L. (1975) *An Introduction to Curriculum Research and Development*, London: Heinemann.

Wenger, E. (1999) *Communities of Practice: Learning, Meaning and Identity*, Cambridge: Cambridge University Press.

Whitty, G. (2000) 'Teacher professionalism,' *New Times Journal of In-Service Education*, 26(2): 281–96.

Williams, S., MacAlpine, A. and McCall, C. (2001) *Leading and Managing Staff Through Challenging Times*, London: Stationery Office.

Index

eBooks – at www.eBookstore.tandf.co.uk

A library at your fingertips!

eBooks are electronic versions of printed books. You can store them on your PC/laptop or browse them online.

They have advantages for anyone needing rapid access to a wide variety of published, copyright information.

eBooks can help your research by enabling you to bookmark chapters, annotate text and use instant searches to find specific words or phrases. Several eBook files would fit on even a small laptop or PDA.

NEW: Save money by eSubscribing: cheap, online access to any eBook for as long as you need it.

Annual subscription packages

We now offer special low-cost bulk subscriptions to packages of eBooks in certain subject areas. These are available to libraries or to individuals.

For more information please contact webmaster.ebooks@tandf.co.uk

We're continually developing the eBook concept, so keep up to date by visiting the website.

www.eBookstore.tandf.co.uk